THE BEST OF

— AMERICA'S — TEST KITCHEN

BEST RECIPES, EQUIPMENT REVIEWS, AND TASTINGS

2021

AMERICA'S TEST KITCHEN

AMERICA'S TEST KITCHEN
21 Drydock Avenue, Boston, MA 02210

THE BEST OF AMERICA'S TEST KITCHEN 2021
Best Recipes, Equipment Reviews, and Tastings

ISBN: 978-1-948703-40-6
ISSN: 1940-3925

Manufactured in the United States of America
10 9 8 7 6 5 4 3 2 1

Distributed by Penguin Random House Publisher Services
Tel: 800-733-3000

EDITORIAL DIRECTOR, BOOKS: Adam Kowit
EXECUTIVE MANAGING EDITORS: Debra Hudak and Todd Meier
DEPUTY EDITOR: Megan Ginsberg
ASSISTANT EDITORS: Tess Berger and Sara Zatopek
DESIGN DIRECTOR: Lindsey Timko Chandler
DEPUTY ART DIRECTOR: Janet Taylor
PHOTOGRAPHY DIRECTOR: Julie Bozzo Cote
PHOTOGRAPHY PRODUCER: Meredith Mulcahy
SENIOR STAFF PHOTOGRAPHERS: Steve Klise and Daniel J. van Ackere
PHOTOGRAPHER: Kevin White
ADDITIONAL PHOTOGRAPHY: Keller + Keller and Carl Tremblay
FOOD STYLING: Tara Busa, Catrine Kelty, Chantal Lambeth, Kendra McKnight, Jessica Rudolph, Elle Simone Scott, and Kendra Smith
PHOTOSHOOT KITCHEN TEAM
    PHOTO TEAM MANAGER: Alli Berkey
    LEAD TEST COOK: Eric Haessler
    TEST COOKS: Hannah Fenton and Jacqueline Gochenouer
    ASSISTANT TEST COOKS: Gina McCreadie and Christa West
ILLUSTRATION: John Burgoyne
SENIOR MANAGER, PUBLISHING OPERATIONS: Taylor Argenzio
IMAGING MANAGER: Lauren Robbins
PRODUCTION AND IMAGING SPECIALISTS: Tricia Neumyer, Dennis Noble, and Amanda Yong
COPY EDITORS: Christine Campbell, April Poole, and Rachel Schowalter
PROOFREADER: Vicki Rowland
INDEXER: Elizabeth Parson

CHIEF CREATIVE OFFICER: Jack Bishop
EXECUTIVE EDITORIAL DIRECTORS: Julia Collin Davison and Bridget Lancaster

PICTURED ON FRONT COVER: Chocolate Pavlova with Berries and Whipped Cream (page 225)

CONTENTS

WELCOME TO AMERICA'S TEST KITCHEN

This book has been tested, written, and edited by the folks at America's Test Kitchen, where curious cooks become confident cooks. Located in Boston's Seaport District in the historic Innovation and Design Building, it features 15,000 square feet of kitchen space, including multiple photography and video studios. It is the home of *Cook's Illustrated* magazine and *Cook's Country* magazine and is the workday destination for more than 60 test cooks, editors, and cookware specialists. Our mission is to empower and inspire confidence, community, and creativity in the kitchen.

We start the process of testing a recipe with a complete lack of preconceptions, which means that we accept no claim, no technique, and no recipe at face value. We simply assemble as many variations as possible, test a half-dozen of the most promising, and taste the results blind. We then construct our own recipe and continue to test it, varying ingredients, techniques, and cooking times until we reach a consensus. As we like to say in the test kitchen, "We make the mistakes so you don't have to." The result, we hope, is the best version of a particular recipe, but we realize that only you can be the final judge of our success (or failure). We use the same rigorous approach when we test equipment and taste ingredients.

All of this would not be possible without a belief that good cooking, much like good music, is based on a foundation of objective technique. Some people like spicy foods and others don't, but there is a right way to sauté, there is a best way to cook a pot roast, and there are measurable scientific principles involved in producing perfectly beaten, stable egg whites. Our ultimate goal is to investigate the fundamental principles of cooking to give you the techniques, tools, and ingredients you need to become a better cook. It is as simple as that.

To see what goes on behind the scenes at America's Test Kitchen, check out our social media channels for kitchen snapshots, exclusive content, video tips, and much more. You can watch us work (in our actual test kitchen) by tuning in to *America's Test Kitchen* or *Cook's Country* on public television or on our websites. Download our award-winning podcast *Proof*, which goes beyond recipes to solve food mysteries (AmericasTestKitchen.com/proof), or listen in to test kitchen experts on public radio (SplendidTable.org) to hear insights that illuminate the truth about real home cooking. Want to hone your cooking skills or finally learn how to bake—with an America's Test Kitchen test cook? Enroll in one of our online cooking classes. And you can engage the next generation of home cooks with kid-tested recipes from America's Test Kitchen Kids.

Our community of home recipe testers provides valuable feedback on recipes under development by ensuring that they are foolproof. You can help us investigate the how and why behind successful recipes from your home kitchen. (Sign up at AmericasTestKitchen.com/recipe_testing.)

However you choose to visit us, we welcome you into our kitchen, where you can stand by our side as we test our way to the best recipes in America.

facebook.com/AmericasTestKitchen

twitter.com/TestKitchen

youtube.com/AmericasTestKitchen

instagram.com/TestKitchen

pinterest.com/TestKitchen

AmericasTestKitchen.com
CooksIllustrated.com
CooksCountry.com
OnlineCookingSchool.com
AmericasTestKitchen.com/kids

SALADE LYONNAISE

CHAPTER 1

SOUPS, SALADS, AND STARTERS

CREAMY WHITE BEAN SOUP WITH HERB OIL AND CRISPY CAPERS

✓ **WHY THIS RECIPE WORKS** To make a creamy, smooth, and quick bean soup, we started by briefly simmering canned great Northern beans and their seasoned canning liquid with softened aromatic vegetables and herbs. Heating the beans caused their starches to hydrate, which made the soup especially creamy. Blending the beans with a small amount of liquid helped their skins break down so that the puree was completely smooth. Chicken broth plus a little Parmesan cheese and butter boosted the soup's flavor and richness. Herb oil and crispy capers were quick-to-make but impressive garnishes that complemented the neutral soup base with vibrant color, flavor, and texture.

Ordering pureed soup at a restaurant just feels fancy. That's not because it's made from pricey ingredients or enriched with loads of cream; in fact, some of the best soups I've had have been based on common vegetables or legumes blended with broth or water. What impresses is the thoughtful composition of the dish: There's the soup itself, which is perfectly smooth after being pureed in a high-powered blender and then passed through an ultrafine-mesh strainer. And then there are the bold, diverse garnishes that sharpen the soup into something attention-grabbing, artful, and deeply flavorful.

But I'm here to let you in on a little secret: There's no need to go to a restaurant to have this experience. You can pull off something equally sumptuous and interesting without special equipment and with ingredients you probably already have in your pantry. And it all starts with a humble can of white beans. Not only are these legumes inexpensive and filling, but they are naturally creamy when pureed and have a mild flavor that provides the perfect canvas for a range of garnishes. And the fact that they're already cooked means you can devote a little extra effort to making garnishes that really pop.

The soup itself comes together in about 20 minutes. I started by softening some aromatics (chopped onion and celery) in olive oil and then added thyme sprigs, sliced garlic, and a touch of cayenne pepper. Next came two cans of great Northern beans—a moderately starchy variety that made the soup velvety but not stodgy—along with their seasoned canning liquid, which added more bean flavor and viscous body. I covered the saucepan and simmered the beans until they started to soften and break down slightly, removed the thyme sprigs, pureed the mixture in the blender, and then thinned it with a few cups of water.

The soup was silky but tasted a little flat and lean, so I worked in a couple tablespoons each of grated Parmesan and butter and swapped in chicken broth for the water. I purposely waited until the soup was done cooking before seasoning it with salt and lemon juice and adjusting its consistency with hot water, since the salt content of the beans and their canning liquid varies from brand to brand.

Then came the fun part: coming up with garnishes that would add brightness and contrast to the creamy, lean soup. My first idea was to whip up an easy, vibrant herb oil—something like a minimalist salsa verde made from extra-virgin olive oil, chopped parsley and basil, and capers. But although the oil tasted bright and fresh, the capers made it chunky and hard to drizzle elegantly over the surface of my soup. So I reengineered things to yield two interrelated garnishes instead of just one: First, I microwave-fried the capers in the oil, as we often do with aromatics such as garlic and shallots. After 5 minutes, the capers were crispy and delicate and had infused the oil with their briny punch. I strained out the capers and set them aside to cool; tossed the chopped herbs into the infused oil, which I drizzled over the silky soup; and followed with a sprinkling of the capers.

The tandem effect of the crispy capers and bright herb oil elevated the soup much more than either garnish would have on its own, and it inspired a few more pairings that delivered equally impressive visual and textural contrast. Even better, they came together from (mostly) pantry staples and required deceptively little work: garlicky bread crumbs and fragrant, spicy oil from pieces of fried chorizo; a dollop of thick, lemony yogurt alongside crispy needle-thin leek; and olive oil and crunchy bits of quick-pickled celery. With each combination, the soup took on a different character— like eating at a new restaurant every night.

—ANNIE PETITO, *Cook's Illustrated*

CREAMY WHITE BEAN SOUP WITH HERB OIL AND CRISPY CAPERS

Creamy White Bean Soup with Herb Oil and Crispy Capers

SERVES 4 TO 6

Use a conventional blender here to produce a smooth soup. Do not drain or rinse the beans; their liquid contributes to the soup's flavor and body. Because the salt content of canned beans varies from brand to brand, season the soup to taste at the end of cooking.

HERB OIL AND CRISPY CAPERS

- ⅓ cup extra-virgin olive oil
- ¼ cup capers, rinsed and patted dry
- 2 tablespoons minced fresh parsley
- 1 tablespoon chopped fresh basil

SOUP

- 2 tablespoons extra-virgin olive oil
- ½ cup chopped onion
- 1 small celery rib, chopped fine
- 3 sprigs fresh thyme
- 2 garlic cloves, sliced
-   Pinch cayenne pepper
- 2 (15-ounce) cans great Northern beans
- 2 tablespoons grated Parmesan cheese
- 2 cups chicken broth, divided
- 2 tablespoons unsalted butter
- ½ teaspoon lemon juice, plus extra for seasoning

NOTES FROM THE TEST KITCHEN

TWO TECHNIQUES TO ENSURE A SUPERSMOOTH SOUP
This soup is so lush and silky you'd think it was pureed in a high-powered blender, passed through a fine-mesh sieve, and enriched with cream. But in actuality it's nothing but beans, broth, butter, seasonings, and two effective techniques.

COOK CANNED BEANS
Heating canned beans loosens their starch granules (which we perceive as gritty on the tongue) and allows water to dilute the starch so that it's imperceptible.

PUREE WITH MINIMAL LIQUID
Blending the beans with a small amount of liquid (more liquid is added later) allows for lots of friction that helps grind their skins into a smooth puree. The liquid creates just enough of a vortex to keep the blender running.

---

1. FOR THE HERB OIL AND CRISPY CAPERS: Combine oil and capers in medium bowl (capers should be mostly submerged). Microwave until capers are darkened in color and have shrunk, about 5 minutes, stirring halfway through microwaving. Using slotted spoon, transfer capers to paper towel–lined plate (they will continue to crisp as they cool); set aside. Reserve caper oil.

2. FOR THE SOUP: Heat oil in large saucepan over medium heat until shimmering. Add onion and celery and cook, stirring frequently, until softened but not browned, 6 to 8 minutes. Add thyme sprigs, garlic, and cayenne and cook, stirring constantly, until fragrant, about 1 minute. Add beans and their liquid and stir to combine. Reduce heat to medium-low, cover, and cook, stirring occasionally, until beans are heated through and just starting to break down, 6 to 8 minutes. Remove saucepan from heat and discard thyme sprigs.

3. Process bean mixture and Parmesan in blender on low speed until thick, smooth puree forms, about 2 minutes. With blender running, add 1 cup broth and butter. Increase speed to high and continue to process until butter is incorporated and mixture is pourable, about 1 minute longer.

4. Return soup to clean, dry saucepan and whisk in remaining 1 cup broth. Cover and bring to simmer over medium heat, adjusting consistency with up to 1 cup hot water as needed. Off heat, stir in lemon juice. Season with salt and extra lemon juice to taste.

5. Stir parsley and basil into reserved caper oil. Drizzle each portion of soup with herb oil, sprinkle with reserved capers, and serve.

VARIATIONS

Creamy White Bean Soup with Chorizo Oil and Garlicky Bread Crumbs

Heat 1 tablespoon extra-virgin olive oil and ¼ cup panko bread crumbs in 8-inch skillet over medium heat. Cook, stirring frequently, until golden brown, 3 to 5 minutes. Add 1 teaspoon minced garlic and cook until fragrant, about 30 seconds. Transfer to bowl and stir in pinch table salt. Heat ¼ cup extra-virgin olive oil and 2½ ounces finely chopped Spanish-style chorizo sausage in now-empty skillet over medium heat Cook, stirring frequently, until chorizo is crispy, about 2 minutes. Using slotted spoon, transfer chorizo to paper towel–lined plate. Drizzle each portion of soup with chorizo oil and sprinkle with chorizo and bread crumbs.

Creamy White Bean Soup with Lemony Yogurt and Crispy Leek

Halve white and light green part of 1 leek lengthwise, then slice into very thin 2-inch-long strips. Wash and dry thoroughly. Toss with 2 tablespoons all-purpose flour in medium bowl. Stir in ½ cup vegetable oil. Microwave for 5 minutes. Stir and microwave 2 minutes longer. Repeat stirring and microwaving in 2-minute increments until leek begins to brown (4 to 6 minutes total), then repeat stirring and microwaving in 30-second increments until leek is deeply golden brown (30 seconds to 2 minutes total). Using slotted spoon, transfer leek to paper towel–lined plate; discard oil. Let leek drain and turn crispy, about 5 minutes, then season with salt to taste. Meanwhile, whisk ½ cup plain Greek yogurt, 3 tablespoons water, and 1 teaspoon grated lemon zest and 2 teaspoons lemon juice in bowl until smooth. Season with salt to taste. Drizzle each portion of soup with yogurt and sprinkle with leek.

Creamy White Bean Soup with Quick-Pickled Celery

Microwave ½ cup unseasoned rice vinegar, 1 tablespoon sugar, and ½ teaspoon table salt in medium bowl until simmering, 1 to 2 minutes. Stir in 1 finely chopped celery rib and let sit for 15 minutes. Drain celery, discarding liquid. Drizzle each portion of soup with 1 teaspoon extra-virgin olive oil and sprinkle with celery.

TUSCAN TOMATO AND BREAD SOUP

✔ **WHY THIS RECIPE WORKS** The traditional preparation for this classic Tuscan soup—day-old bread stirred into tomato sauce and doused in olive oil—is delicious, but it's inconsistent. By using a grocery staple such as sandwich bread and building a savory tomato soup around it, we ensured the same results every time. Canned crushed tomatoes provided both a heavy tomato presence and consistent texture without needing hours of cooking on the stovetop. Blooming sliced garlic in a generous amount of extra-virgin olive oil infused the soup with traditional flavors, boosted its savoriness, and eliminated any canned tomato flavor.

What impresses me most about Italian cuisine is how a dish based on something as humble as stale bread can still be unbelievably delicious. So it goes with pappa al pomodoro, the fantastic Tuscan bread and tomato soup perfumed with garlic and olive oil: A few key ingredients come together to make a bright, silky, ultra-flavorful soup in less time than I thought possible. I challenged myself to make a streamlined version from supermarket staples.

I tried several varieties of fresh tomatoes—globe, vine-ripened, plum, and even cherry—in a basic tomato soup, but peeling them was a pain and their quality was inconsistent; some were red, juicy, and ripe, while others were hard, pink, and virtually flavorless. Canned tomatoes would make my recipe easy and consistent throughout the year. My two finalists were canned whole peeled tomatoes and canned crushed tomatoes; I went with crushed to save myself the effort of crushing them by hand.

Next up was the bread. Did it really have to be Italian? I tested ciabatta, baguette, sourdough, sandwich bread, and supermarket Italian loaves. My tasters were emphatic in their belief that the bread should be only a supporting player, so anything too strong in flavor was out. Dense and crusty loaves didn't soften enough in the soup, so they were out, too. Soft, mild, and slightly sweet was the ideal bread profile here, and white sandwich bread fit the bill. Its sweetness nicely balanced out the acidity of the tomatoes, and the bread broke down quickly. Fresh or stale, white sandwich bread worked perfectly.

With the two main ingredients nailed down, working through the rest of the process was easy. I lightly browned some garlic in olive oil (with a pinch of red pepper flakes for kick) and then added a can of crushed tomatoes, the cubed sandwich bread, broth, and a sprig of fresh basil. I brought the soup to a simmer and cooked it for 15 minutes, at which point the bread was mostly broken down. A minute of brisk whisking helped the bread fully dissolve and incorporate, and a finishing dusting of Parmesan cheese, a splash of nice olive oil, and a light sprinkling of chopped basil brought the dish home.

—ALLI BERKEY, *Cook's Country*

FRENCH ONION SOUP

Tuscan Tomato and Bread Soup

SERVES 4

Good-quality olive oil makes a difference here. Depending on the brand of sandwich bread that you buy, 4 ounces can range from two and a half to four slices. It's best to use weight as your guide; if you don't have a scale, defer to the volume measurement.

   ¼ cup extra-virgin olive oil, plus extra for drizzling
   3 garlic cloves, sliced thin
   ¼ teaspoon red pepper flakes
   1 (28-ounce) can crushed tomatoes
   4 ounces hearty white sandwich bread, cut into
      ½-inch cubes (3 cups)
   2 cups chicken broth
   1 sprig fresh basil, plus 2 tablespoons chopped
   ½ teaspoon table salt
   ¼ teaspoon pepper
      Grated Parmesan cheese

1. Combine oil, garlic, and pepper flakes in large saucepan and cook over medium heat until garlic is lightly browned, about 4 minutes.

2. Stir in tomatoes, bread, broth, basil sprig, salt, and pepper and bring to boil over high heat. Reduce heat to medium, cover, and simmer vigorously until bread has softened completely and soup has thickened slightly, about 15 minutes, stirring occasionally.

3. Off heat, discard basil sprig. Whisk soup until bread has fully broken down and soup has thickened further, about 1 minute. Sprinkle with Parmesan and chopped basil, drizzle with extra oil, and serve.

FRENCH ONION SOUP

◯ **WHY THIS RECIPE WORKS** The key to this bistro classic was a shortcut-free, hour-long caramelization of the onions. We started with a mountain of sliced onions in a Dutch oven with some melted butter, salt (to draw out moisture), and sugar (to jump-start caramelization). We cooked the onions covered at first to trap steam and soften them, and then we removed the lid to allow the released liquid to evaporate. We continued to cook the onions, scraping up and stirring in the browned bits that formed on the bottom of the pot, until the onions were soft and caramel-colored. Deglazing with wine (red for its robust flavor) ensured that all the flavorful browned bits ended up in the soup. We added rich, meaty beef broth, as well as thyme and bay leaves, and simmered it all together until the flavors melded. To make the soup easier to eat, we decided to forgo the traditional toasted slice of baguette in favor of more easily spoonable croutons. To assemble, we ladled the soup into individual crocks and then topped them with the croutons, shredded Gruyère, and shredded Parmesan (for extra nuttiness). A bit of Gruyère under the croutons protected the bread from getting too soggy.

A crock of savory-sweet onion soup topped with crunchy croutons and bubbly cheese is as comforting as my favorite slippers. But here in the test kitchen, we're never satisfied with the status quo, so I decided to take another look at this bistro favorite to see if I could create a recipe that reduced the time needed to caramelize the onions and still produced great soup.

I tried all manner of innovative ingredients to see if I could add different flavors that would allow me to shortcut slowly cooking the onions. And while most iterations were fine, I was left facing an unavoidable fact: This classic is classic for a reason, and there's no beating the understated simplicity of traditional French onion soup. Test after test, tasters favored slow-cooked onions simmered with just stock, wine, and herbs over any fancy curveball variations I threw at them. I'd stick with a (mostly) classic version of this classic soup, streamlined as much as possible for the home cook.

Unable to lean on the crutch of distracting nontraditional additions, I had to nail down a method for perfectly caramelized onions. After dozens of tests (and lots of onion tears), I landed on a method that takes about an hour but requires little more than patience and some stirring. The onions come out meltingly soft, golden brown, and full of flavor.

To pick up all the flavorful bits stuck to the bottom and sides of the pot, I deglazed with a hefty pour of red wine, which tasted more richly savory than white, before adding beef stock, fresh thyme sprigs, and bay leaves. After a little simmering to meld the flavors, I ladled the soup into crocks, topped it with croutons and cheese, and placed the crocks (on a rimmed baking sheet) in a preheated oven until the cheese was bubbling. The result? A rich, sweet, perfect onion soup topped with soft, melted cheese. C'est magnifique!

—JESSICA RUDOLPH, *Cook's Country*

French Onion Soup

SERVES 6

Be patient when caramelizing the onions; the entire process takes 55 to 70 minutes. If you don't have oven-safe soup crocks, form six individual piles of croutons on a baking sheet, cover them with the cheese, and broil them on the middle oven rack until the cheese is melted, 1 to 3 minutes. Then use a spatula to transfer the crouton portions to the individual filled soup bowls. We like Better than Bouillon Roasted Beef Base.

4	tablespoons unsalted butter
4	pounds onions, halved and sliced thin
1¾	teaspoons table salt, divided
1	teaspoon sugar
1	cup dry red wine
8	cups beef broth
4	sprigs fresh thyme
2	bay leaves
¾	teaspoon pepper, divided
6	ounces baguette, cut into 1-inch cubes
3	tablespoons extra-virgin olive oil
8	ounces Gruyère cheese, shredded (2 cups)
1½	ounces Parmesan cheese, shredded (½ cup)

1. Melt butter in Dutch oven over medium-high heat. Stir in onions, 1 teaspoon salt, and sugar. Cover and cook, stirring occasionally, until onions release their liquid and are uniformly translucent, about 20 minutes.

2. Uncover and cook until liquid has evaporated and browned bits start to form on bottom of pot, 5 to 10 minutes. Reduce heat to medium and continue to cook, uncovered, until onions are caramel-colored, 30 to 40 minutes longer, stirring and scraping with wooden spoon as browned bits form on bottom of pot and spreading onions into even layer after stirring. (If onions or browned bits begin to scorch, reduce heat to medium-low.)

3. Stir in wine, scraping up any browned bits, and cook until nearly evaporated, about 1 minute. Stir in broth, thyme sprigs, bay leaves, ½ teaspoon pepper, and ½ teaspoon salt. Increase heat to high and bring to boil. Reduce heat to medium-low and simmer, uncovered, for 30 minutes.

4. Meanwhile, adjust oven rack to middle position and heat oven to 350 degrees. Toss baguette, oil, remaining ¼ teaspoon salt, and remaining ¼ teaspoon pepper together in bowl. Transfer to rimmed baking sheet and bake until golden and crisp, 15 to 18 minutes. Remove sheet from oven and set aside. Increase oven temperature to 500 degrees.

5. Set six 12-ounce ovensafe crocks on second rimmed baking sheet. Discard thyme sprigs and bay leaves and season soup with salt and pepper to taste. Divide soup evenly among crocks (about 1½ cups each). Divide 1 cup Gruyère evenly among crocks, top with croutons, and sprinkle with remaining Gruyère, then Parmesan. Bake until cheeses are melted and soup is bubbly around edges, 5 to 7 minutes. Let cool for 5 minutes before serving.

NOTES FROM THE TEST KITCHEN

GETTING THE TOP RIGHT

1. Toss cubed baguette with olive oil, salt, and pepper in bowl.

2. Toast croutons in 350-degree oven until crisp and golden brown.

3. Top soup with Gruyère, croutons, more Gruyère, and shredded Parmesan.

4. Bake in 500-degree oven until cheese is fully melted.

MEXICAN STREET-CORN CHOWDER

✓ **WHY THIS RECIPE WORKS** Sweet corn, tangy lime, spicy chili powder, and fresh cilantro combine in this soup inspired by the popular Mexican street food. To make the soup even more interesting, we prepared two easy toppings, sautéing poblano chiles for vegetal depth and cooking up Mexican chorizo until it turned deliciously crispy. We then toasted our corn in the flavorful rendered fat. After adding chicken broth and aromatics to the corn, we pureed most of it until it was creamy, leaving some corn kernels whole for a pleasant chunky texture. A final sprinkling of cilantro added bright freshness.

Whether it's boiled and buttered or charred to perfection over the grill, there's nothing quite like an ear of fresh, in-season corn. Bursting with bright, summery flavor, the vegetable is a quintessential component on backyard barbecue plates across the United States. But when the summer months have passed, the abundant vegetable can be harder to find at farmers' markets, and tending to the grill loses a bit of its charm.

Looking to create a corn-forward dish that could be enjoyed all year long, I racked my brain for alternatives. Here in Boston, one dish that transcends seasonality is creamy New England–style clam chowder. Could corn chowder serve as another culinary chameleon? The versions I'd had in the past had been underwhelming, to say the least: lacking in flavor, gluey in texture, or thin and insubstantial. I'd need to solve those problems and bring something new to the mix for a corn chowder with staying power.

Inspiration struck when my mind wandered south of the border. Mexican street corn (also known as elote) is a popular street-food preparation. It features a complex balance of flavors and textures with a powerful punch. To make it, an ear of charcoal-grilled corn is slathered in a tangy, creamy ingredient (often mayonnaise, crème fraîche, or Mexican crema) and rolled in a rich layer of crumbly, salty cotija cheese. A dusting of smoky chili powder, a hit of bright lime juice, and a sprinkling of fresh cilantro top it all off for a bold, flavorful finish. The whole thing is then served on a skewer to be conveniently eaten on the go.

But its many flavorful toppings mean that Mexican street corn can be a bit messy to make (and eat!) indoors. Plus, the classic charcoal-grilled flavor can be difficult to achieve on a stovetop—and outdoor grilling was a no-go for my year-round recipe. Could I find a way to incorporate the flavors of Mexican street corn into a chowder that would be creamy, sweet, slightly smoky, and—most important—wholly satisfying?

I started by sautéing fresh corn kernels on the stovetop until they were lightly browned, simmering them in a bit of chicken broth, and then pureeing the entire mixture in a blender until it was smooth. Pureeing the corn gave the chowder a pleasingly thick and creamy consistency, mimicking the effects of heavy dairy used in other chowders. But I found the mixture too homogeneous, and I missed the occasional sweet pop of whole kernels. Plus, when I continued to simmer the blended chowder on the stovetop, I found that the sugars released by the pulverized kernels made the mixture much too susceptible to scorching. To make matters even worse, the starchy puree soon turned from creamy to gluey. Fortunately I found an easy fix: Blending just 2 cups of the mixture and leaving the rest unblended solved all these problems in one go. I now had a clean-tasting, creamy, and sweet chowder with a welcome crunch from the intact kernels.

With the base flavor and texture of my chowder right where I wanted them to be, I turned my focus to preparing a few substantial toppings to accompany the chowder. Spicy Mexican-style chorizo added richness and contributed a slight smokiness. (I doubled down on smoky flavor by incorporating chili powder into the chowder base as well.) Sautéed poblano chiles added a vegetal crunch and a hint of spice and char to the mix.

But preparing the toppings separately was beginning to crowd my stovetop, and I wanted to streamline the process. Working in a large saucepan that would hold the entire recipe, I first sautéed the poblanos in a bit of oil and then transferred them to a bowl before adding the chorizo. The rendered fat left behind by the chorizo was perfect for sautéing my corn kernels, and it added complex layers of flavor that united the chowder components. As a bonus, by the time the chowder was ready, my toppings were already on hand for serving.

I divided the chowder into bowls, piled on the poblanos and chorizo, and added the finishing touches: a shower of fresh cilantro, a dusting of chili powder, and a citrusy lime wedge on the side. And there I had it— Mexican street corn in a bowl, ready to be enjoyed any time of year.

—RUSSELL SELANDER, *America's Test Kitchen Books*

Mexican Street-Corn Chowder
SERVES 2

For a creamy topping and even more brightness, mix up a quick sauce of sour cream and lime juice. If fresh corn isn't in season, frozen corn can be used instead. If you can't find Mexican chorizo, use dried Spanish chorizo or andouille sausage, cut into pieces.

- 1 tablespoon vegetable oil, divided
- 2 poblano chiles, stemmed, seeded, and sliced thin
- 4 garlic cloves, minced, divided
- 1¼ teaspoons chili powder, divided
- 2 ounces Mexican-style chorizo sausage, casings removed
- 4 ears corn, kernels cut from cobs (3½ cups)
- ⅛ teaspoon table salt
- 1½ cups chicken broth
- ¼ cup chopped fresh cilantro
  Lime wedges

1. Heat 1 teaspoon oil in large saucepan over medium heat until shimmering. Add poblanos and cook until just tender, 3 to 5 minutes. Stir in one-fourth of garlic and ¼ teaspoon chili powder and cook until fragrant. Transfer poblano mixture to bowl, cover with aluminum foil, and set aside until ready to serve. In now-empty saucepan, heat remaining 2 teaspoons oil over medium heat until shimmering. Add chorizo and cook until browned, about 3 minutes, breaking up meat with wooden spoon. Using slotted spoon, transfer chorizo to second bowl, covering with foil to keep warm.

2. Pour off all but 1 teaspoon fat from saucepan. (If necessary, add oil to equal 1 teaspoon.) Add corn to fat left in saucepan and cook over medium heat, stirring occasionally and scraping up any browned bits, until corn is lightly browned, about 5 minutes. Stir in salt, ¾ teaspoon chili powder, and remaining garlic and cook until fragrant, about 30 seconds. Stir in broth, scraping up any browned bits, and bring to simmer. Cook until corn is tender, about 2 minutes.

3. Process 2 cups soup in blender until very smooth, about 1 minute. Stir pureed soup into remaining soup in saucepan, adjusting consistency with hot water as needed, and season with salt and pepper to taste. Divide soup among individual serving bowls, then top with cilantro, poblanos, chorizo, and remaining ¼ teaspoon chili powder. Serve with lime wedges.

SPRING PEA SALAD

✓ **WHY THIS RECIPE WORKS** Spring is when peas are in season and at their sweetest, snappiest best. We wanted to showcase the three main types—English, snow, and sugar snap—in a knockout spring salad. First we briefly blanched the sugar snap and shelled English peas. Peas start converting their sugars to starch from the moment they're picked; a quick dip in boiling water dissolves their remaining sugars and makes them more available to taste, and the moist heat can even out any toughness in their skins. The more delicate snow peas lost too much of their crunch when blanched, so we left them raw. To add visual variety to the salad, we cut the snap peas into bite-size pieces and the snow peas on the bias into thin strips. This also helped them tangle with the other components: bright-red radishes cut into half-moons, handfuls of baby arugula, and lots of fresh mint. We tossed the salad with a little lemon juice and olive oil and plated it on top of a creamy yogurt-based dressing, which we combined with the salad as we served it. That way, the salad kept its vibrant, celebratory appearance.

Stir-frying or sautéing fresh snow and sugar snap peas or even frozen English peas is fine most of the year. But in spring, when these legumes are actually in season (and the only time fresh English peas are available), cooking them beyond the briefest blanch feels like a shame. This year, I decided to showcase all three peas in a knockout spring salad. Each variety would bring something different to the mix: English peas would add pops of earthy-sweet flavor, snap peas would bring lots of crunch, and snow peas would provide a more delicate crispness and mineral-y notes.

Though I knew I didn't want to thoroughly cook the peas, a brief dip in boiling water can improve their flavor and texture (and also set their bright-green color). That's because these legumes start converting their sugars into starch from the moment they're picked, so they can taste less sweet when eaten raw. A quick dunk in boiling salted water softens the peas' starchy structure, making the remaining sugar more available to taste. The peas' skins can also toughen after a few days off the vine, and moist heat can counteract that. Just 60 to 90 seconds followed by shocking in ice water did the trick for sugar snap and English peas (shelled first), but snow peas, which are naturally more tender, lost too much of their crunch, so I left them raw.

SPRING PEA SALAD

Any standout salad needs ingredients in a variety of shapes to make it interesting, so I cut the snap peas into bite-size chunks, which maintained their crunch (and allowed a peek at the peas inside the pods). I thinly sliced the raw snow peas on the bias to help them tangle with the other components.

To break up the legumes with more flavors and textures, I gathered a few other spring ingredients: Bright-red radishes sliced into half-moons contributed color and crunch, peppery baby arugula provided fluff and bulk, and lots of fresh mint leaves left whole or torn acted as a secondary salad green.

As for the dressing, I wanted something creamy that would cling and add richness without being cloying. I whisked minced garlic that I'd soaked in lemon juice (to mellow its sharp edge) together with tangy Greek yogurt, Dijon mustard, extra-virgin olive oil, salt, and pepper. But when I dressed the salad with this mixture, the creamy coating dulled its appearance. The simple fix: I spread the dressing onto the bottom of a serving dish and then placed the salad—tossed with a little olive oil and lemon juice—on top. Constructed this way, the salad kept its arresting appearance, and I could toss it all together at the table just before serving it.

This showpiece salad is a striking way to capture ephemeral spring peas, if only for a moment: They'll be gone in a flash.

—ANNIE PETITO, *Cook's Illustrated*

NOTES FROM THE TEST KITCHEN

THREE PEAS, THREE TYPES OF PREP
To bring out the best in each pea (and for an easy-to-eat salad), we treat them in different ways.

ENGLISH PEAS
Blanched for more sweetness

SNOW PEAS
Left raw for crisp texture; sliced into fork-friendly slivers

SUGAR SNAP PEAS
Cut into bite-size pieces; blanched for tenderness and sweetness

---

Spring Pea Salad

SERVES 4 TO 6

If you can't find fresh English peas, you can substitute ¾ cup of thawed frozen peas (there is no need to blanch them).

- 1 garlic clove, peeled
- 2 tablespoons plus 1 teaspoon lemon juice, divided
- 4 ounces sugar snap peas, strings removed, cut on bias into ½-inch pieces
- ½ teaspoon plus pinch table salt, divided, plus salt for blanching
- 9 ounces shell-on English peas, shelled (about ¾ cup)
- 5 tablespoons extra-virgin olive oil, divided
- ¼ cup plain Greek yogurt
- 2 teaspoons Dijon mustard
- ¼ teaspoon pepper
- 2 ounces (2 cups) baby arugula
- 4 ounces snow peas, strings removed, sliced thin on bias
- 4 radishes, trimmed, halved, and sliced into thin half-moons
- ⅓ cup fresh mint leaves, torn if large

1. Mince garlic and immediately combine with 2 tablespoons lemon juice in medium bowl; set aside. Fill large bowl halfway with ice and water. Nestle colander into ice bath. Line large plate with double layer of paper towels.

2. Bring 1 quart water to boil in medium saucepan over high heat. Add snap peas and 1 tablespoon salt and cook until snap peas are bright green and crisp-tender, about 1 minute. Using spider skimmer or slotted spoon, transfer snap peas to colander set in ice bath. Add English peas to boiling water and cook until bright green and tender, about 1½ minutes. Transfer to colander with snap peas. Once peas are chilled, lift colander from ice bath and transfer peas to prepared plate.

3. Whisk ¼ cup oil, yogurt, mustard, pepper, and ½ teaspoon salt into garlic mixture until combined. Spread dressing evenly over bottom of large shallow bowl or serving platter.

4. In separate large bowl, toss arugula, snow peas, radishes, mint, chilled peas, remaining 1 teaspoon lemon juice, remaining pinch salt, and remaining 1 tablespoon oil until evenly coated. Pile salad on top of dressing. Serve immediately, combining salad with dressing as you serve.

SALADE LYONNAISE

✓ **WHY THIS RECIPE WORKS** Choosing a mix of bitter greens—frisée and chicory—gave this salad enough heft and flavor to stand up to the richer elements of bacon and egg. To keep the flavor true to the French original, we used pancetta rather than American bacon, as it is unsmoked, salt cured, and rolled just like ventreche (also known as French pancetta). Making a warm vinaigrette with the rendered fat in the skillet infused the salad with even richer bacon flavor, and the heat also allowed us to gently tenderize the frisée. Poached eggs delivered both runny yolks and tender whites that easily melded into the salad.

There's a reason salade lyonnaise has long been iconic not only in its namesake city of Lyon but also throughout France. Its mix of bitter greens, salty bacon, poached egg, and punchy vinaigrette is simply perfect. The pungent greens stand up to the tart vinaigrette and are sturdy enough to hold up under the weight of the egg. Thick batons of bacon, or lardons, retain meaty chew even when browned and crisped. The vinaigrette, whisked together in the pan used to brown the bacon, has just the requisite acidity to balance the richness of the pork and the eggs' flowing yolks and tender whites. For my own rendition of this French classic, I wanted to ensure that I hit that same spot-on balance of crispy and chewy, cool and warm, and rich and bitter.

The more traditional versions of salade lyonnaise feature just a single green—frisée, a member of the chicory family with a sharp taste and frilly, resilient leaves that soften only slightly under a warm vinaigrette. Though frisée's feathery looks brought a certain elegance to the dish, on its own, the green made the salad feel spartan. Its wiry spikes also allowed too much of the dressing to fall to the bottom of the bowl. In search of a second green, I experimented with dandelion greens and two of frisée's cousins, escarole and chicory. While each did a fine job of filling out the salad, tasters liked chicory best. It brought just the right additional pungency to the mix, along with leaves that were a little more supple and broad enough to capture the dressing.

Next I considered the lardons. In France, these are often sliced from ventreche, pork belly that's unsmoked, salt cured, and fashioned into a roll, making it more similar to Italian pancetta than to smoked American bacon. Because ventreche is not readily available in the United States, pancetta was the obvious best substitute.

But since presliced pancetta is often cut into rounds that aren't thick enough to make nicely plump lardons, I bought the pork from the deli counter, where I made sure to ask for a generous ½-inch-thick slab.

Back in the test kitchen, I cut the pancetta into lardons about ¼ inch across, which I then sautéed in a nonstick skillet in a tablespoon of extra-virgin olive oil to ensure even browning. These lardons had the perfect meaty, chewy texture, but they tasted too salty. The easy fix was to blanch them for about 5 minutes in a couple cups of water before browning them.

The vinaigrette can make or break this salad. Too little acid and the greens taste overwhelmingly bitter; too much and the salad tastes unpalatably tart. I began by standardizing the amount of fat for the dressing. Since some of the fat from the pancetta was lost to the water during blanching, my first move was to compensate for that loss by upping the oil I was using to brown the lardons to 2 tablespoons. To keep this amount consistent, I poured off any excess fat in the pan after crisping them. Leaving the lardons in the pan, I then added some minced shallot, which I sautéed for 30 seconds to soften its raw edge. I took the pan off the heat and thought about how much vinegar to add.

Our standard formula for vinaigrette is 3 parts fat to 1 part acid, but I decided that using a 1:1 ratio here would give the dressing the boldness it needed. I stirred 2 tablespoons of red wine vinegar along with 4 teaspoons of Dijon mustard into the hot fat in the pan. I then drizzled this warm mixture over the salad, plated it, and topped each serving with a poached egg. I was gratified to find that the vinaigrette brought the perfect acidic punch to the salad, especially after I broke the egg with the side of my fork and stirred the rich yolk gently into the greens. There was just one problem: While the warm dressing had tenderized the frisée nicely, leaving it softened but still crisp, the chicory had lost all its crunch.

I tried a two-stage approach to incorporating the dressing. First I placed the frisée in the mixing bowl and drizzled the warm dressing on top. After an initial toss with my tongs the dressing had cooled quite a bit, so when I added the chicory and tossed everything again, it kept its crisp bite.

With that, my salade lyonnaise had it all: a perfect balance of lightness and indulgence, coolness and warmth, and crispiness and chewiness.

—STEVE DUNN, *Cook's Illustrated*

HARVEST BOWL

Salade Lyonnaise

SERVES 4

Order a ½-inch-thick slice of pancetta at the deli counter; presliced or diced pancetta is likely to dry out or become tough. If you can't find chicory or escarole, dandelion greens make a good substitute. If using escarole, strip away the first four or five outer leaves and reserve them for another use.

- 1 (½-inch-thick) slice pancetta (about 5 ounces)
- 2 tablespoons extra-virgin olive oil
- 1 tablespoon minced shallot
- 2 tablespoons red wine vinegar
- 4 teaspoons Dijon mustard
- 1 head frisée (6 ounces), torn into bite-size pieces
- 5 ounces chicory or escarole, torn into bite-size pieces (5 cups)
- 1 recipe Perfect Poached Eggs (recipe follows)

1. Cut pancetta into thirds crosswise; then cut each piece crosswise into ¼-inch-wide slices. Combine pancetta and 2 cups water in 10-inch nonstick skillet and bring to boil over medium-high heat. Boil for 5 minutes, then drain in colander. Return pancetta to now-empty skillet. Add oil and cook over medium-low heat, stirring occasionally, until lightly browned but still chewy, 4 to 6 minutes.

2. Pour off all but 2 tablespoons fat from skillet, leaving pancetta in skillet. Add shallot and cook, stirring frequently, until slightly softened, about 30 seconds. Off heat, add vinegar and mustard and stir to combine.

3. Drizzle vinaigrette over frisée in large bowl and toss thoroughly to coat. Add chicory and toss again. Season with salt and pepper to taste. Divide salad evenly among 4 plates. Gently place 1 egg on top of each salad, and season with salt and pepper to taste. Serve immediately.

Perfect Poached Eggs

MAKES 4 EGGS

Use the freshest eggs possible for this recipe.

- 4 large eggs
- 1 tablespoon distilled white vinegar
  Table salt for poaching

1. Bring 6 cups water to boil in Dutch oven over high heat. Meanwhile, crack eggs, one at a time, into colander. Let stand until loose, watery whites drain away from eggs, 20 to 30 seconds. Gently transfer eggs to 2-cup liquid measuring cup.

2. Add vinegar and 1 teaspoon salt to boiling water. Remove pot from heat. With lip of measuring cup just above surface of water, gently tip eggs into water, one at a time, leaving space between them. Cover pot and let stand until whites closest to yolks are just set and opaque, about 3 minutes. If after 3 minutes whites are not set, let stand in water, checking every 30 seconds, until whites are set.

3. Using slotted spoon, carefully lift and drain each egg over Dutch oven. Season with salt and pepper to taste, and serve.

HARVEST BOWL

✓ **WHY THIS RECIPE WORKS** A celebration of autumnal ingredients, this harvest bowl is the perfect way to feature caramelized roasted root vegetables in a satisfying salad. We especially liked sweet potatoes for their light earthiness and sweet notes. To bring all the elements together, we whisked up a cider and caraway vinaigrette, toasting and cracking the seeds but leaving them whole for appealing texture. For toppings, feta cheese added briny contrast and dried cranberries added color and more tartness.

I'm a huge fan of bowls. They can be grain-based, greens-based, noodle-based, and more; feature any protein or vegetable under the sun; come dotted with fruit or cheese or topped with any number of crunchy add-ins; and be finished with whatever dressing or sauce suits your fancy. The only absolute requirement, seemingly, is the bowl itself. But the thing that makes bowls so special and customizable—all the individual elements that can be swapped around at will—is also their downfall. A great bowl features an array of colors, textures, and flavors that come from a harmonious combination of components that often have to be prepared separately before the bowl is assembled. Preparing such a large number of elements—making a sauce, cooking a protein, prepping vegetables, choosing a topping—can be daunting, especially for a dish that's usually eaten as a casual lunch or light dinner. To cut down on the intimidation factor of homemade bowls complete with all the fixings, I aimed to simplify the preparation process and offer as many make-ahead options as possible.

Inspired by the autumn-themed "harvest bowls" I'd seen popping up on numerous restaurant menus as the weather turned cooler, I decided to create my own more accessible take on a seasonal salad bowl full of warm fall flavors. My first task was to decide what would make up the base of my bowl. I chose baby kale for its delicate, not overly fibrous crunch and its assertive, slightly peppery flavor that would stand up well to other bold flavors. To contribute even more substance to my salad, I also tested adding a grain. Nutty farro and wheat berries both performed well in my tests, as did earthy, toasty, and mildly chewy wild rice. The addition of one of these grains really upped the heartiness of the bowl, but I decided to make it optional for those looking for a lighter salad.

Now to determine the add-ins that would give my bowl its identity. I wanted to keep the bowl vegetarian, so to bulk it up, I settled on roasted sweet potatoes. Since the potatoes would be just one part of my dish, I cut them into smaller, more fork-friendly pieces than I would for a side dish and seasoned them with just olive oil and a bit of salt before roasting. Once roasted, the sweet potatoes could be refrigerated for up to two days before use, meaning that I could cook them ahead of time and then simply add them to my bowl when I was ready, streamlining the process.

Looking to add more color and textural contrast, I turned to another ingredient emblematic of fall: apples. Granny Smith apples offered a vibrant pop of lime-green color as well as bursts of cool, crisp acidity. Dried cranberries added even more color, chew, and a balancing sweetness. In search of a creamy element, I tried adding goat cheese. I liked its tangy earthiness, but the soft cheese disintegrated when I stirred my salad, turning the contents of the bowl into a gloppy, unappealing mess. I had better luck with crumbled feta, which held its shape and added a salty tang that nicely complemented the sweet cranberries.

My bowl was coming together well with a good balance of salty, sweet, sour, and earthy flavors and crisp and chewy textures, but I craved a little crunch. A sprinkling of nuts or seeds might suffice, but for even more interest, what about topping the bowl with a savory make-ahead brittle?

I first tried a combination of quinoa with various nuts, but the resulting brittle was, if anything, a little too crunchy. I had a lighter, more crisp texture in mind, so I next turned to experimenting with seeds. To a foundation of mild pepitas and sunflower seeds, I added a splash of maple syrup, 1 tablespoon of caraway seeds, and a couple tablespoons each of sesame seeds and nigella seeds. While nigella seeds may take some searching to find, I thought that their uniquely aromatic, floral flavor made them worth seeking out. To help bind everything together, I added an egg white and ½ cup of rolled oats. A final secret ingredient of sorts, soy sauce, didn't make the brittle taste of soy but instead enhanced its savoriness and balanced the sweetness of the syrup. After being pressed flat, baked until golden brown, and crumbled into pieces, the brittle could be stored for up to a month.

My last step was to whip up a dressing that would tie all the elements together. I needed a dressing that would hold its own against all the strong flavors already in play, so I opted for a vinaigrette made of tart cider vinegar and spicy Dijon mustard. Adding a teaspoon of toasted caraway seeds echoed the flavor of the brittle and cemented the salad's autumnal vibes.

I now had a salad bowl that was colorful and flavorful enough to rival any restaurant bowl. And when all its major components were made ahead of time, it came together in minutes.

—LEAH COLINS, *America's Test Kitchen Books*

Harvest Bowl

SERVES 2

To crack caraway seeds, rock the bottom edge of a skillet over the toasted seeds on a cutting board until they crack. To make the bowl heartier, you can add wild rice, farro, or wheat berries. We love the convenience of prepackaged baby kale in this recipe, but feel free to substitute any mixture of dark tender greens. Top the bowl with our Savory Seed Brittle (recipe follows), spiced nuts, or plain toasted nuts, if desired.

- 4 teaspoons cider vinegar
- 1 tablespoon water
- 2 teaspoons Dijon mustard
- 1 teaspoon caraway seeds, toasted and cracked
- ⅛ teaspoon table salt
- ⅛ teaspoon pepper

2 tablespoons extra-virgin olive oil

4 ounces (4 cups) baby kale

1 cup Roasted Sweet Potatoes (recipe follows)

½ Granny Smith apple, cored and cut into ½-inch pieces

2 ounces feta cheese, crumbled (½ cup)

2 tablespoons dried cranberries

Whisk vinegar, water, mustard, caraway seeds, salt, and pepper together in bowl. While whisking constantly, slowly drizzle in oil until combined. In second bowl, toss kale with half of vinaigrette to coat, then season with salt and pepper to taste. Divide among individual serving bowls, then top with sweet potatoes and apple. Drizzle with remaining dressing and sprinkle with feta and cranberries. Serve.

Roasted Sweet Potatoes

MAKES 2 CUPS

Choose potatoes that are as even in width as possible; trimming the small ends prevents them from burning. We like the texture that unpeeled potatoes add to our bowls; just be sure to scrub them well before prepping. You can peel the potatoes if you prefer.

1 pound sweet potatoes, trimmed, halved lengthwise, and sliced crosswise ¼ inch thick

1 tablespoon extra-virgin olive oil or vegetable oil

¼ teaspoon table salt

Adjust oven rack to middle position and heat oven to 400 degrees. Toss potatoes, oil, and salt together in bowl, then spread into even layer on rimmed baking sheet. Roast until potatoes are beginning to brown, 15 to 20 minutes, flipping slices halfway through roasting. Let potatoes cool for 5 minutes, then season with salt and pepper to taste. (Potatoes can be refrigerated for up to 2 days.)

Savory Seed Brittle

MAKES 2 CUPS

Do not substitute quick or instant oats in this recipe.

2 tablespoons maple syrup

1 large egg white

1 tablespoon extra-virgin olive oil or vegetable oil

1 tablespoon soy sauce

1 tablespoon caraway seeds, cracked

½ teaspoon table salt

¼ teaspoon pepper

½ cup old-fashioned rolled oats

⅓ cup raw sunflower seeds

⅓ cup raw pepitas

2 tablespoons sesame seeds

2 tablespoons nigella seeds

1. Adjust oven rack to upper-middle position and heat oven to 300 degrees. Line 8-inch square baking pan with parchment paper and spray parchment with vegetable oil spray. Whisk maple syrup, egg white, oil, soy sauce, caraway seeds, salt, and pepper together in large bowl. Stir in oats, sunflower seeds, pepitas, sesame seeds, and nigella seeds until well combined.

2. Transfer oat mixture to prepared pan and spread into even layer. Using stiff metal spatula, press oat mixture until very compact. Bake until golden brown and fragrant, 45 to 55 minutes, rotating pan halfway through baking.

3. Transfer pan to wire rack and let brittle cool completely, about 1 hour. Remove brittle from pan and break into pieces of desired size; discard parchment. (Brittle can be stored in airtight container at room temperature for up to 1 month.)

GREEN BEAN SALAD WITH CHERRY TOMATOES AND FETA

✓ **WHY THIS RECIPE WORKS** To ensure that the beans in this salad were tender, bright green, and deeply flavored, we blanched them in highly concentrated salt water (¼ cup salt to 2 quarts water). This quickly softened the pectin in the beans' skins, so they became tender before losing their vibrant color; it also seasoned them inside and out. We then made these flavorful green beans the star ingredient in a summer-perfect salad.

I love the gorgeous bright color of briefly blanched green beans in salad, but I've never loved their starchy, still-raw taste or their so-called crisp-tender texture, which is usually not tender at all. But cooking hearty vegetables such as green beans until they're soft

GREEN BEAN SALAD WITH CHERRY TOMATOES AND FETA

enough to be speared with a fork generally means you've got to boil the living color out of them—not to mention all their fresh, grassy flavor.

Years ago, I stumbled across a tip in Harold McGee's indispensable tome *On Food and Cooking* (1984) that described how heavily salted water speeds the cooking of vegetables. According to McGee, the key is to cook vegetables in extremely salty water—so salty that it has the same 3 percent concentration as seawater. I'd never acted on it since it translates into 2 tablespoons of salt per quart of water—an extraordinary amount, given that I usually throw that much into 4 quarts of water when blanching vegetables. Now, with loads of boiled green beans on the horizon, I decided to finally give it a try.

I boiled 1½ pounds of green beans in a solution of ½ cup of salt and 4 quarts of water alongside another batch with just 2 tablespoons of salt in the same amount of water. Sure enough, the beans in the heavily salted water were tender a full 5 minutes before the beans in the lightly salted water. They had also retained their vibrant green color, while the other beans had faded to a drab olive.

This was a neat discovery, but the one I made when I took a bite of the "seawater" beans was even more important: They tasted incredible. The heavily salted water had given them a meaty, highly seasoned, and intensely green-beany flavor without making them overly salty. The beans that had cooked with just a little salt, on the other hand, barely tasted seasoned at all.

What's so magical about supersalty water? According to McGee, when vegetables are cooked in salted water, sodium ions displace some of the calcium ions in their cell walls. Calcium ions strengthen pectin—the glue that holds plant cell walls together—by allowing it to form cross-links, and the ions' displacement prevents that cross-linking and causes the vegetable to soften. (It is for precisely the same reason that we like to brine dried beans in salt water: The displacement of the calcium ions in their skins softens them and prevents them from bursting during cooking.)

But ½ cup of salt was a lot to use for one dish. I wondered if I could get the same effect with less, so I tried going down to ¼ cup of salt per 4 quarts of water. The beans took slightly longer to tenderize, lost a little of their color, and were no longer as well seasoned or as

flavorful; clearly you need a strong salt concentration to get enough sodium to infiltrate the beans' sturdy skins. The solution (pun intended)? Keep the concentration the same but decrease the volumes of water and salt. Just ¼ cup of salt in 2 quarts of water did the trick and felt like a reasonable amount for such tender, vibrantly colored, and deeply flavorful green beans.

I highlighted the beans in a Mediterranean salad using tomatoes, fresh mint, parsley, and feta cheese. Not only was this a great salad, but I also had a terrific new blanching technique that I could apply to other vegetables as well.

—ANDREW JANJIGIAN, *Cook's Illustrated*

Green Bean Salad with Cherry Tomatoes and Feta

SERVES 4 TO 6

If you don't own a salad spinner, lay the green beans on a clean dish towel to dry in step 2. The blanched, shocked, and dried green beans can be refrigerated in a zipper-lock bag for up to two days.

1½	pounds green beans, trimmed and cut into 1- to 2-inch lengths
¼	teaspoon table salt, plus salt for blanching green beans
12	ounces cherry tomatoes, halved
¼	cup extra-virgin olive oil
2	tablespoons chopped fresh mint
2	tablespoons chopped fresh parsley
1	tablespoon lemon juice
¼	teaspoon pepper
2	ounces feta cheese, crumbled (½ cup)

1. Bring 2 quarts water to boil in large saucepan over high heat. Add green beans and ¼ cup salt, return to boil, and cook until green beans are bright green and tender, 5 to 8 minutes.

2. While green beans cook, fill large bowl halfway with ice and water. Drain green beans in colander and immediately transfer to ice bath. When green beans are no longer warm to touch, drain in colander and dry thoroughly in salad spinner.

3. Place green beans, tomatoes, oil, mint, parsley, lemon juice, pepper, and salt in bowl and toss to combine. Transfer to platter, sprinkle with feta, and serve.

ULTRACREAMY HUMMUS

✔ **WHY THIS RECIPE WORKS** This hummus is creamy and velvety-smooth, with a satisfyingly rich, balanced flavor. To achieve a perfectly smooth texture, we simmered canned chickpeas with water and baking soda for 20 minutes and then quickly removed their grainy skins by gently swishing them under a few changes of water. Tahini is a major source of richness and flavor in hummus. To avoid the bitter flavors that can come from tahini made with heavily roasted sesame seeds, we chose a tahini that was light-colored, which indicated that the seeds were only gently roasted. For balanced garlic flavor, we steeped the garlic in lemon juice and salt to extract its flavor and deactivate alliinase, the enzyme responsible for this allium's harsh bite. Finally, we added ample fresh lemon juice to give the hummus a bright flavor.

In one of the last reviews he penned before his untimely death in 2018, *Los Angeles Times* restaurant critic Jonathan Gold wrote lyrically about the hummus at the city's beloved Middle Eastern restaurant Bavel:

"The seriousness of a Middle Eastern restaurant rests in its hummus. Grainy, vaguely sour hummus is OK to send off in your children's brown-bag lunches, and the mayonnaise-y over-garlicked stuff may be exactly what you want to see alongside a takeout roast chicken . . . But the great kitchens, the ones that inspire hour-long drives and dinnertime haiku, tend to labor over their fragrant goo as assiduously as a French baker might over her baguettes."

The hummus Gold spoke of is fundamental throughout the Middle East, where it's often the focal point of a meal. A great version is so silky that it can be poured off a spoon and exhibits vivid yet balanced tahini flavor, garlic presence that's prominent but never "garlicky," and a lemony backbone that's tart without being sour.

And here's the best part: Superlative hummus requires only a little more time and effort to make than that lunch box stuff. Here's my approach, taken one component at a time.

How you treat the chickpeas affects the consistency of hummus more than any other factor because they are firm (even when cooked) and covered in tough skins. My most effective tricks were overcooking them and removing their skins. It takes hours to soak and simmer dried chickpeas, but simmering canned beans took about 20 minutes. (There's no shame here: Dried and canned beans are equally good in this recipe.) I also added baking soda to the saucepan, which raised the water's pH and helped the skins break down and slip off. By the end of cooking, there was a "raft" of skins floating on the surface that was easy to remove by draining and rinsing the beans a few times.

Tahini is hummus's major source of richness and flavor and significantly affects its consistency. Brand and color matter here, since the tahini's shade indicates how much the sesame seeds have been roasted. Lighter tahini, made with lightly roasted sesame seeds, tastes distinct but mild, whereas darker tahini, made with heavily roasted sesame seeds, is unpleasantly bitter.

One thing I discovered: It's important to process the other hummus ingredients before adding the tahini. That's because its proteins readily absorb water and clump, resulting in overly thick hummus. Processing the other ingredients without the tahini allows the water to disperse throughout the mixture; then, when the tahini is eventually added, its proteins can't immediately absorb the water and clump, and the hummus doesn't become stiff.

Water is often added to enhance the spread's creaminess. I started with ¼ cup and, depending on the consistency of the tahini and the hummus itself (it thickens as it sits), added more water by the teaspoon.

Typically, all the fat in hummus comes from tahini, but 2 tablespoons of extra-virgin olive oil made my version especially silky. To avoid overprocessing the oil, which can release bitter-tasting compounds, I added it with the tahini.

Instead of incorporating garlic directly into the hummus as most recipes call for, I briefly steeped a few minced cloves in lemon juice, strained and discarded them, and added only the infused juice to the dip—a technique from chef Michael Solomonov's popular hummus recipe and one that we've used in the past for Caesar dressing. The juice's acid neutralizes alliinase, the enzyme that creates garlic's harsh flavor. That way, we capture some—but not too much—of the garlic's sharp, raw bite and strain out the pulpy bits.

—ANDREW JANJIGIAN, *Cook's Illustrated*

Ultracreamy Hummus

SERVES 8 TO 10 (MAKES ABOUT 3 CUPS)

We like the light color and mild flavor of Ziyad Tahini Sesame Paste. The hummus will thicken slightly over time; add warm water, 1 tablespoon at a time, as needed to restore its creamy consistency. If desired, you can omit the parsley, reserved chickpeas, and extra cumin in step 5 and top with our Baharat-Spiced Beef Topping for Hummus or Spiced Walnut Topping for Hummus (recipes follow).

    2 (15-ounce) cans chickpeas, rinsed
    ½ teaspoon baking soda
    4 garlic cloves, peeled
    ⅓ cup lemon juice (2 lemons), plus extra for seasoning
    1 teaspoon table salt
    ¼ teaspoon ground cumin, plus extra for garnish
    ½ cup tahini, stirred well
    2 tablespoons extra-virgin olive oil, plus extra for drizzling
    1 tablespoon minced fresh parsley

1. Combine chickpeas, baking soda, and 6 cups water in medium saucepan and bring to boil over high heat. Reduce heat and simmer, stirring occasionally, until chickpea skins begin to float to surface and chickpeas are creamy and very soft, 20 to 25 minutes.

2. While chickpeas cook, mince garlic using garlic press or rasp-style grater. Measure out 1 tablespoon garlic and set aside; discard remaining garlic. Whisk lemon juice, salt, and reserved garlic together in small bowl and let sit for 10 minutes. Strain garlic-lemon mixture through fine-mesh strainer set over bowl, pressing on solids to extract as much liquid as possible; discard solids.

3. Drain chickpeas in colander and return to saucepan. Fill saucepan with cold water and gently swish chickpeas with your fingers to release skins. Pour off most of water into colander to collect skins, leaving chickpeas behind in saucepan. Repeat filling, swishing, and draining 3 or 4 times until most skins have been removed (this should yield about ¾ cup skins); discard skins. Transfer chickpeas to colander to drain.

4. Set aside 2 tablespoons whole chickpeas for garnish. Process remaining chickpeas, cumin, garlic-lemon mixture, and ¼ cup water in food processor until smooth, about 1 minute, scraping down sides of bowl as needed. Add tahini and oil and process until hummus is smooth, creamy, and light, about 1 minute, scraping down sides of bowl as needed. (Hummus should have pourable consistency similar to yogurt. If too thick, loosen with water, adding 1 teaspoon at a time.) Season with salt and extra lemon juice to taste.

5. Transfer to serving bowl and sprinkle with parsley, reserved chickpeas, and extra cumin. Drizzle with extra oil and serve. (Hummus can be refrigerated in airtight container for up to 5 days. Let sit, covered, at room temperature for 30 minutes before serving.)

Baharat-Spiced Beef Topping for Hummus

MAKES ABOUT 2 CUPS

Baharat is a warm, savory Middle Eastern spice blend. Ground lamb can be used in place of the beef, if desired. Toast the pine nuts in a dry skillet over medium-high heat until fragrant, 3 to 5 minutes. Serve the topping over hummus, garnishing with additional pine nuts and chopped fresh parsley.

    2 teaspoons water
    ½ teaspoon table salt
    ¼ teaspoon baking soda
    8 ounces 85 percent lean ground beef
    1 tablespoon extra-virgin olive oil
    ¼ cup finely chopped onion
    2 garlic cloves, minced
    1 teaspoon smoked hot paprika
    1 teaspoon ground cumin
    ¼ teaspoon pepper
    ¼ teaspoon ground coriander
    ⅛ teaspoon ground cloves
    ⅛ teaspoon ground cinnamon
    ¼ cup pine nuts, toasted
    2 teaspoons lemon juice

1. Combine water, salt, and baking soda in large bowl. Add beef and toss to combine. Let sit for 5 minutes.

2. Heat oil in 12-inch nonstick skillet over medium heat until shimmering. Add onion and garlic and cook, stirring occasionally, until onion is softened, 3 to 4 minutes. Add paprika, cumin, pepper, coriander, cloves, and cinnamon and cook, stirring constantly, until fragrant, about 30 seconds. Add beef and cook, breaking up meat with wooden spoon, until beef is no longer pink, about 5 minutes. Add pine nuts and lemon juice and toss to combine.

Spiced Walnut Topping for Hummus

MAKES ABOUT ¾ CUP

Do not overprocess the topping; it should remain coarse-textured. Serve the topping over hummus.

- ¾ **cup extra-virgin olive oil**
- ⅓ **cup walnuts**
- ¼ **cup paprika**
- ¼ **cup tomato paste**
- 2 **garlic cloves, peeled**
- 1 **teaspoon ground turmeric**
- ½ **teaspoon ground cumin**
- ½ **teaspoon ground allspice**
- ½ **teaspoon table salt**
- ¼ **teaspoon cayenne pepper**

Process all ingredients in food processor until uniform coarse puree forms, about 30 seconds, scraping down sides of bowl halfway through processing. (Topping can be refrigerated for up to 5 days.)

SPINACH-ARTICHOKE DIP

✔ **WHY THIS RECIPE WORKS** To amplify the spinach and artichoke flavors in this homemade version of a restaurant staple, we swapped dull, fibrous frozen spinach for sautéed fresh baby spinach and left tinny canned artichokes behind in favor of bright, tender marinated artichokes. Gouda's sweet and nutty flavor perfectly accentuated the artichokes, and it gave our dip a creamy, melty texture without causing it to congeal and turn stringy after cooling. Our streamlined method called for stirring all the ingredients together in one skillet before transferring the dip to a baking dish. After about 20 minutes in the oven, the top was golden brown and the edges were bubbling.

Spinach-artichoke dip is a crowd-pleasing comfort food, making it an ideal party appetizer. But all too often, the spinach and artichokes get lost in the overly cheesy mix. I set out to create a more balanced version.

I started by researching existing recipes and preparing the seven that looked the most promising. The finished dips ran the gamut from thin to stodgy to grassy to overwhelmingly cheesy. To achieve what I sought—a smooth, creamy dip that showcased bright spinach and nutty artichokes—I'd have to make some adjustments.

I began with some common ingredients: frozen spinach, canned artichokes, Parmesan cheese, melty Monterey Jack, a cream cheese/sour cream/mayonnaise binder, and garlic. I mixed everything together and baked it. The resulting dip looked the part, but the flavor fell flat. The biggest problem was the muddy-tasting, fibrous frozen spinach. For my next batch, I coarsely chopped some fresh baby spinach and sautéed it until it wilted. The resulting dip had a cleaner spinach flavor, and the leaves kept a distinct but soft texture.

Canned artichokes had tough, squeaky leaves and an overpoweringly tangy and briny flavor. Frozen artichokes were dull, with mushy hearts and leathery leaves, but jarred marinated artichokes were tender and had a subtle nutty flavor accented by their bright marinade, which my tasters and I loved.

The hefty dose of Parmesan I was using supplied the salty, savory backbone the dip needed, so it stayed. And while Monterey Jack seemed like a good choice to provide supple, melty texture, it seized and became stringy as it sat. The cheese turned my dip so stiff that the chips I dipped in it felt as if they were in danger of breaking. After exploring several options, I settled on an unlikely choice: gouda. This cheese melted even more smoothly, stayed creamy after it cooled, and had a toasty sweetness that accentuated the artichokes' nuttiness.

Sour cream proved unnecessary; using equal parts cream cheese and mayonnaise provided the perfect balance of tart and creamy. The garlic added a welcome punch. Lastly, black pepper and cayenne added a kick to offset the heavy richness.

My resulting dip was irresistibly creamy and cheesy, with a prominent spinach and artichoke presence. I knew that the dip would soon be gracing many of my appetizer spreads, but I worried about pulling it together in the midst of hectic party planning. I tried mixing the dip together and refrigerating it overnight; thankfully, it still tasted great when heated the next day. Now the only worry I'll have in regard to this dip is whether my guests will leave any for me.

—JESSICA RUDOLPH, *Cook's Country*

SPINACH-ARTICHOKE DIP

Spinach-Artichoke Dip

SERVES 10 TO 12

You will need one 12-ounce jar of marinated artichoke hearts to yield the 1⅓ cups called for here. You can substitute canned artichoke hearts if you can't find marinated. If you can find only 5-ounce packages of baby spinach, there's no need to buy a third package to make up the extra ounce; just make the dip with 10 ounces. Use the large holes of a box grater to shred the gouda and a rasp-style grater to grate the Parmesan. Serve with tortilla chips, crusty bread, pita chips, or your choice of vegetables.

- 1 tablespoon extra-virgin olive oil
- 3 garlic cloves, minced
- 11 ounces (11 cups) baby spinach, chopped coarse
- 8 ounces cream cheese, softened
- 6 ounces gouda cheese, shredded (1½ cups)
- 3 ounces Parmesan cheese, grated (1½ cups)
- 1⅓ cups marinated artichoke hearts, chopped
- 1 cup mayonnaise
- ¼ teaspoon pepper
- ⅛ teaspoon cayenne pepper

1. Adjust oven rack to middle position and heat oven to 400 degrees. Heat oil in 12-inch skillet over medium-high heat until shimmering. Add garlic and cook until fragrant, about 30 seconds. Add spinach, 1 handful at a time, allowing each to wilt slightly before adding next; cook until wilted and liquid has evaporated, about 4 minutes.

2. Off heat, add cream cheese and stir until melted and combined, about 1 minute. Stir in gouda, Parmesan, artichokes, mayonnaise, pepper, and cayenne until combined. Transfer to 2-quart baking dish and smooth top using rubber spatula.

3. Bake until spotty golden brown and bubbling around edges, about 22 minutes. Let cool for 10 minutes. Serve.

TO MAKE AHEAD: At end of step 2, let dip cool completely, wrap in plastic wrap, and refrigerate for up to 2 days. When ready to serve, continue with step 3, increasing baking time by 10 minutes.

MEDITERRANEAN WHIPPED ALMOND DIP

✓ WHY THIS RECIPE WORKS We wanted to create a foolproof recipe for a keto-friendly hummus-like dip that everyone could enjoy, not just keto dieters. Instead of relatively high-carb chickpeas, we turned to that great keto lifesaver—the nut. First, we experimented with a test kitchen recipe for cashew dip, but cashews were too carb heavy for keto. Would almonds work? When soaked until softened and then pureed with water, almonds took on a creaminess not unlike that of chickpeas. The blades of the blender whipped the mixture, giving it a surprisingly light texture. And because of almonds' neutral flavor, the addition of tahini and garlic steered the puree in the flavor direction of hummus. Lemon juice and extra-virgin olive oil boosted the taste and thinned the dip to a scoopable consistency. With an almond "hummus" to rival the chickpea original, we decided to create a fresh, herby variation using parsley, basil, chives, and dill along with lemon juice and zest.

These days it seems as though hummus is at the center of every appetizer platter, and rightfully so: This versatile chickpea dip can be dressed up in any number of ways with add-ins, seasonings, and toppings, and the dipping possibilities are just about endless. Even the chickpeas that make up the foundation of most hummuses can be swapped out for other beans or even a vegetable such as sweet potato. So I felt confident when I took it upon myself to create a hummus-like dip for *Easy Everyday Keto.* Even though chickpeas were out (too many carbs), I had a hunch that I could use nuts to create a similarly rich base to which I could add the signature flavors of hummus.

I had previously developed a cashew-based dip for another book, so I started my testing there. Cashews easily blended into a neutral-tasting base for a variety of flavors, but when I ran the numbers, I learned that cashews are relatively high in carbohydrates compared with other nuts, making them a poor choice for a nut-based keto-friendly recipe. Looking for a lower-carb option, I found a winner in blanched almonds. Almonds are relatively low in carbs, and with their fibrous skins removed they achieved a creamy consistency after being soaked and blended. Processing the almonds with ⅔ cup of water helped them break down and gave the mixture a dippable consistency. What's more, the vigorous blending action effectively whipped the dip, making it surprisingly light and airy.

With the texture down, I began playing with flavor profiles. Adding extra-virgin olive oil, tahini, a squeeze of lemon juice, and a clove of garlic to the blender along with the almonds gave the dip classic hummus flavor. Doubling the amount of lemon juice and adding fresh herbs made for a bright-tasting variation.

I was more than happy with the dip at this point, but there was one thing missing: a worthy accompaniment with which to scoop it up. I wanted a crisp, crunchy cracker that would complement the light, creamy dip.

Because keeping the carb count low is an essential consideration for a keto-friendly recipe, using wheat flour for the crackers was out of the question. My first thought was to attempt to make a cracker entirely out of cheese. While this may sound odd, it's not without precedent: When shredded, spread into a thin layer, and then heated, some cheeses set up into a crisp wafer known as frico. Pure cheese frico is too delicate to withstand dipping, but perhaps I could bolster its structure with other ingredients.

I first tried combining grated Parmesan and mozzarella with eggs and a small amount of almond flour. I poured the crepe batter–like mixture into a rimmed baking sheet and put the sheet in the oven to bake. The "cracker" that emerged was rubbery, with no snap to it at all. Back to the drawing board.

Thinking that the gooey, stretchy mozzarella was to blame for the lack of crisping, in my next tests I left it out and experimented with different ratios of Parmesan, eggs, and flour (I tried almond and coconut flour, both alone and in combination). These attempts were closer, but none had the crisp, crunchy texture I was after.

My breakthrough came thanks to a colleague who was working on a keto pizza recipe. When tasting the pizza crust he had developed—just Parmesan, almond flour, and a little egg mixed to a dough-like consistency, rolled out, and baked—another coworker remarked that it was almost cracker-like: crisp on the outside, with just a little chew on the inside. If I used the same ingredient ratios and simply rolled my dough out thinner before baking it, maybe I could achieve the all-over crispness I wanted from my crackers.

Several rounds of testing later, I had a method. I rolled the dough ⅛ inch thick before parbaking it in a 425-degree oven. At this point I cut the dough into individual crackers before baking them a few minutes longer at a lower temperature to fully brown and crisp them. Brushing the dough with an egg white mixture before baking enhanced the finished crackers' snap and shine. Finally, I tried adding mix-ins to take the crackers to the next level. A combination of sesame seeds, poppy seeds, and caraway seeds added extra crunch and even more structure to the crackers, ensuring that they were strong enough to stand up to any dip.

After months of testing, at last I had a pair of recipes that not only complemented one another perfectly but also could serve as the stars of any appetizer platter. Hummus, move aside.

—LAWMAN JOHNSON, *America's Test Kitchen Books*

Mediterranean Whipped Almond Dip
MAKES ABOUT 1¼ CUPS

Serve with crudités or Seeded Crackers (recipe follows). This dip is great for a crowd: Spread it evenly in a wide, shallow bowl; drizzle with an extra tablespoon of oil; and sprinkle with 1 tablespoon of your favorite minced fresh herb before serving.

5	**ounces blanched whole, slivered, or sliced almonds**
6	**tablespoons extra-virgin olive oil**
¼	**cup tahini**
1	**tablespoon lemon juice**
1	**garlic clove, minced**
½	**teaspoon table salt**
⅛	**teaspoon pepper**

1. Place almonds in bowl and add water to cover by 1 inch. Soak almonds at room temperature for at least 8 hours or up to 24 hours. Drain and rinse well.

2. Process almonds, ⅔ cup water, oil, tahini, lemon juice, garlic, salt, and pepper in blender until smooth, about 2 minutes, scraping down sides of blender jar as needed. Adjust consistency with extra water as needed. Season with salt and pepper to taste. Serve.

CRUNCHY KETTLE POTATO CHIPS

VARIATION

Mediterranean Whipped Almond Dip with Lemon and Fresh Herbs

We prefer a combination of herbs here, but you can use a single herb, if desired.

Increase lemon juice to 2 tablespoons and add ½ cup chopped fresh basil, chives, dill and/or parsley and 1 teaspoon grated lemon zest to blender with almonds.

Seeded Crackers

MAKES 36 CRACKERS

Make sure to roll the dough between two greased sheets of parchment to make shaping easier.

- 1½ ounces Parmesan cheese, grated (¾ cup)
- ½ cup (2 ounces) blanched, finely ground almond flour
- 1 large egg, plus 1 large egg white lightly beaten with 1 tablespoon water
- 2 tablespoons extra-virgin olive oil
- 1 teaspoon sesame seeds, toasted
- 1 teaspoon poppy seeds
- 1 teaspoon caraway seeds
- ¼ teaspoon table salt
- ½ teaspoon coarse sea salt (optional)

1. Adjust oven rack to middle position and heat oven to 425 degrees. Stir Parmesan, almond flour, whole egg, oil, sesame seeds, poppy seeds, caraway seeds, and table salt together in bowl. Press and roll dough between 2 sheets of greased parchment paper into 11 by 9-inch rectangle, about ⅛ inch thick. Remove top sheet of parchment and trim edges of dough to remove any tapering. Slide dough, still on parchment, onto baking sheet. Brush with egg white mixture, then poke at 2-inch intervals using fork. Sprinkle with sea salt, if using. Bake until dough is set and edges are beginning to brown, about 7 minutes, rotating sheet halfway through baking. Slide cracker, still on parchment, onto cutting board. Reduce oven temperature to 350 degrees.

2. Cut cracker lengthwise into four even strips, then cut crosswise into 1-inch-wide crackers. Carefully arrange crackers evenly on now-empty sheet, discarding parchment. Bake until golden brown and crisp, 4 to 6 minutes, rotating sheet halfway through baking. Transfer crackers to wire rack and let cool completely, about 30 minutes. Serve. (Crackers can be stored in airtight container for up to 1 week.)

CRUNCHY KETTLE POTATO CHIPS

✔ **WHY THIS RECIPE WORKS** To produce deeply crunchy kettle-style chips, we started by cutting russet potatoes into substantial ⅟₁₆-inch-thick slices. Frying them in moderately hot oil ensured that they cooked up crunchy—not hard or delicate. Initially heating the oil to a relatively hot 375 degrees quickly dried out the potatoes' exterior starches so that they were less sticky; stirring them frequently also prevented them from fusing together. Grinding the spice mixtures to a fine powder and tossing them with the still-hot chips ensured that the spices stuck.

My love for junk food is no secret in the test kitchen. In fact, I am the self-appointed unofficial keeper of the *Cook's Illustrated* team snack corner, which typically includes everything from chocolate bars and pretzels to popcorn and chips.

So I was excited when I was tasked with developing a recipe for thick and crunchy kettle chips. The prep work is a cinch—you don't even have to peel the potatoes—and the frying method is actually tailor-made for home cooks. Plus, if you've ever had freshly fried, still-warm chips, you know that they're a treat (especially homemade versions of flavors such as barbecue, sour cream and onion, and salt and vinegar). There's also a certain satisfaction that comes from producing snack food that could pass for store-bought.

Before I dive into the distinctive feature of kettle chips—deep, satisfying crunch—it helps to know the basic differences between this style of chip and the thin and crispy kind (think Lay's Classic). Crispy chips are cut thin and cooked relatively hot and fast, while kettle chips are cut roughly 50 percent thicker and fried at a lower temperature for longer.

Potato slice thickness certainly influences a chip's texture, but it's the frying time and temperature that make the most profound difference in the final product. In fact, when I dug through a stack of research papers to see how the two styles of chips are made commercially, it became clear that manufacturers have these details down to a science.

First, let's look at the kettle kind. They're batch-fried in vats of oil, the temperature of which follows a U-curve that is key to creating their characteristic crunch. The process goes like this: The potato slices are dropped into moderately hot (about 300-degree) oil, which plunges to about 250 degrees. As the oil slowly heats back up, the starches inside the potatoes absorb water, forming a sticky gel that glues the potato cell walls together, like mortar strengthening a rock wall. Finally, the water is driven off, leaving behind a rigid net of crisscrossed starch molecules with an open, crunchy structure. (All the while, the chips are stirred, which prevents sticking.)

Meanwhile, crispy chips are made by propelling the potato slices quickly and continuously through hot (about 350-degree) oil along a conveyor belt—a process called continuous frying—which ensures that the oil temperature holds steady at a high enough temperature for the starches to desiccate before they can absorb water and create much sticky gel. As a result, the chips are delicate and crispy.

Generally speaking, it's easy to follow a U-curve when frying at home because that drop in temperature happens naturally when you add cold food to hot oil, and it takes time to bring the oil back up to its starting temperature. But after making a few batches of kettle chips, I realized that you have to control both how steeply the temperature drops and how quickly it recovers. I also came to understand that frying in a regular pot on a regular stove—as opposed to using a commercial setup—has its limitations.

When making chips at home, there is only one variety of potato to choose: russet. Good chips come from high-starch, low-sugar potatoes. Commercial producers actually use special varieties that are extremely low in sugar to prevent overbrowning; common russets (more accurately known as Russet Burbanks) are the closest available alternative.

I sliced a pound of russets into ¹⁄₁₆-inch-thick rounds using a mandoline and then heated 2 quarts of oil in a 7-quart Dutch oven to 300 degrees, mimicking the commercial method. But when I added all the potatoes, the limitations of my ordinary pot quickly became obvious. The slices, which were covered in sticky surface starches, were crowded in the pot, and they stuck together even with constant stirring. So I took a cue from another test kitchen recipe for fried potatoes and heated the oil for my next batch to 375 degrees, knowing that the higher temperature would help immediately dry out the potatoes' surface starches and mitigate sticking (I'd still stir them as they fried).

Now the question was how much to turn down the heat, since that would determine how quickly the oil recovered to the 300-degree range and how much time the starches in the chips had to give up their water. I added the potatoes and played it safe by turning the stove dial to low. In total, that batch took more than

NOTES FROM THE TEST KITCHEN

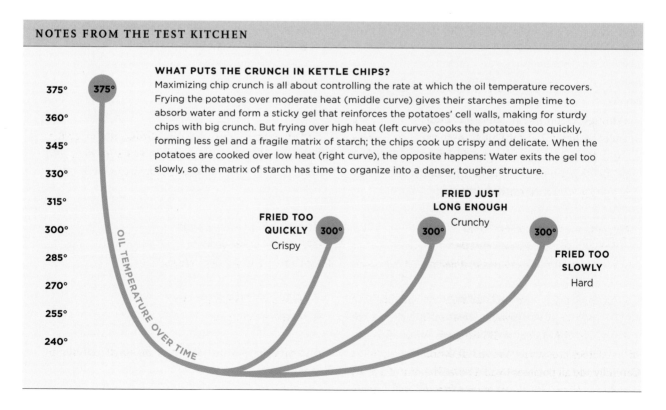

WHAT PUTS THE CRUNCH IN KETTLE CHIPS?

Maximizing chip crunch is all about controlling the rate at which the oil temperature recovers. Frying the potatoes over moderate heat (middle curve) gives their starches ample time to absorb water and form a sticky gel that reinforces the potatoes' cell walls, making for sturdy chips with big crunch. But frying over high heat (left curve) cooks the potatoes too quickly, forming less gel and a fragile matrix of starch; the chips cook up crispy and delicate. When the potatoes are cooked over low heat (right curve), the opposite happens: Water exits the gel too slowly, so the matrix of starch has time to organize into a denser, tougher structure.

375°
360°
345°
330°
315°
300°
285°
270°
255°
240°

375°

OIL TEMPERATURE OVER TIME

FRIED TOO QUICKLY
300°
Crispy

FRIED JUST LONG ENOUGH
300°
Crunchy

300°

FRIED TOO SLOWLY
Hard

20 minutes to fry, and the chips were unpleasantly hard. That's because with the longer cooking time, the water exited the gel so slowly that the starches had more time to organize into a denser, tougher structure.

Cranking the heat to high after adding the potatoes was also a mistake. First and foremost, the chips overbrowned. Second, a weaker gel formed and left behind a disorderly and brittle matrix of starch; as a result, the chips were more crispy than crunchy. Frying over medium heat was the answer: It allowed the oil to hover in that 250-degree "gel zone" for about 5 minutes so that the chips began to stiffen. After another 6 to 8 minutes—just 13 minutes total frying time—the oil temperature had rebounded to around 300 degrees, the rest of the water in the chips had evaporated, and they'd turned completely rigid and golden.

Now for those aforementioned seasonings. I imitated two classic flavors—sour cream and onion and salt and vinegar—with buttermilk powder and vinegar powder, respectively. A smoky spice mix for barbecue chips was easy to make with pantry staples such as smoked paprika, sugar, and garlic powder. Processing the seasonings in a spice grinder produced a fine powder that clung nicely when tossed with the hot chips.

If you're on the fence about DIY snack food, take it from this aficionado: You'll be wowed by these chips, and making them is easier than you'd think.

—ANNIE PETITO, *Cook's Illustrated*

Crunchy Kettle Potato Chips

SERVES 6

We strongly recommend using a mandoline to slice the potatoes. A heavy 7-quart Dutch oven safely accommodates the full batch of chips and helps the oil retain heat; do not use a smaller, lighter pot. Stirring the potatoes during frying minimizes sticking.

- 2 quarts vegetable oil for frying
- 1 pound russet potatoes, unpeeled
- ½ teaspoon table salt or 1 recipe topping (recipes follow)

1. Set wire rack in rimmed baking sheet and line with double layer of paper towels. Heat oil in large Dutch oven over medium heat to 375 degrees. While oil heats, slice potatoes crosswise ¹⁄₁₆ inch (1½ millimeters) thick. Carefully add all potatoes to oil, 1 small handful at a time, separating slices as much as possible (oil will bubble vigorously). Cook, stirring constantly with wooden spoon, until bubbling has calmed (it will not completely stop) and slices begin to stiffen, 2 to 4 minutes.

2. Continue to cook, stirring frequently, until shape of chips is set and slices are rigid at edges (chips will make rustling sound when stirred), about 5 minutes longer, adjusting heat as needed to maintain oil temperature between 240 and 250 degrees.

3. Continue to cook, stirring and flipping potatoes frequently with spider skimmer or slotted spoon, until all bubbling ceases and chips are crunchy and lightly browned, 6 to 8 minutes longer, adjusting heat as needed during final minutes of cooking to maintain oil temperature between 280 and 300 degrees. Using spider skimmer or slotted spoon, transfer chips to prepared rack. Sprinkle with salt or, if using topping, let chips cool for 30 seconds, then transfer chips to large bowl with topping and toss until evenly coated. Serve. (Chips can be stored in zipper-lock bag at room temperature for up to 5 days.)

Buttermilk and Chive Topping

MAKES ABOUT 2 TABLESPOONS

Look for buttermilk powder in the baking aisle.

- 4 teaspoons buttermilk powder
- 1 teaspoon garlic powder
- ½ teaspoon onion powder
- ½ teaspoon table salt
- ¼ teaspoon pepper
- 1 teaspoon dried chives

Grind buttermilk powder, garlic powder, onion powder, salt, and pepper in spice grinder to fine powder. Add chives and pulse until finely chopped, about 3 pulses.

Salt and Vinegar Topping

MAKES ABOUT 1 TABLESPOON

Look for vinegar powder online.

- 1 tablespoon vinegar powder
- ½ teaspoon table salt

Grind vinegar powder and salt in spice grinder to fine powder.

Smoky Barbecue Topping

MAKES ABOUT 2 TABLESPOONS

We recommend Simply Organic Smoked Paprika.

- 1 tablespoon smoked paprika
- 2 teaspoons sugar
- 1 teaspoon garlic powder
- ½ teaspoon onion powder
- ½ teaspoon table salt
  Pinch cayenne pepper

Grind all ingredients in spice grinder to fine powder.

VIETNAMESE SUMMER ROLLS (GOI CUON)

✓ **WHY THIS RECIPE WORKS** Springy noodles, crisp lettuce, an abundance of fresh herbs, and a bit of protein for heft make traditional Vietnamese summer rolls a pleasure to eat, but with all those components, building them yourself can be a bit daunting. Our goal was to streamline the process without sacrificing any flavor or texture. We put our own spin on the traditional practice of cooking the shrimp in the same water used to cook the pork: We used indirect rather than direct heat to ensure that the shrimp stayed tender and juicy. Though some recipes recommend soaking the rice paper wrappers until they're fully softened, we found that briefly dunking them in cold water and transferring them to the counter while they were still stiff left them with just enough surface moisture to hydrate them perfectly. This made the wrappers easier to work with and elastic enough to contain a generous amount of filling. Combining three different herbs and adding them to the rolls in a measured amount saved time. A spicy yet approachable peanut sauce and a traditional fish sauce and lime juice mixture called nuoc cham added moisture and complemented the delicate flavors of the rolls.

A Vietnamese summer roll is the epitome of cool elegance: an exquisitely balanced salad of fragrant herbs, crisp lettuce, springy noodles, and a modest amount of protein neatly bundled into a stretchy, translucent rice paper wrapper. The eating experience, on the other hand, is gloriously unrefined. You grab a roll and dunk one end into a creamy peanut-hoisin sauce or a mixture of fish sauce and lime juice or vinegar. Then you take a bite, and the flavors and textures burst across your palate. Dunk, bite, dunk, bite . . . Summer rolls are so light and refreshing that I can contentedly carry on this way for quite a while. But a word of caution: A summer roll is best eaten within moments of being made, before the wrapper dries out and becomes chewy or the moist fillings weaken it and cause the roll to rupture.

You can roll almost anything in a rice paper wrapper, but the fillings of a traditional Vietnamese summer roll are quite specific: rice vermicelli, boiled and rinsed to bouncy perfection; crisp lettuce; lots of fresh, leafy herbs; shrimp; and pork. I wanted my summer rolls to be as authentic as possible, so for the protein component, I knew I would need to use both shrimp and pork and cook them just right.

Pork belly is the preferred cut for use in summer rolls, so I started there. Following tradition, I simmered the meat in salted water until it was tender and then sliced it thin. The simplicity of the cooking method makes sense here: Summer rolls are all about balance, and though I love both grilled and roasted pork belly, their strong flavors would overwhelm those of the more delicate fillings in the roll.

But it took a good 40 minutes of simmering for the pork belly to become tender, so I was relieved to learn that pork shoulder is also sometimes used. It would require less cooking time, and like pork belly, it is a meaty-tasting cut that retains good flavor after simmering. I opted for boneless country-style ribs, which are cut from the shoulder and sold in the shape of a stick of butter—perfect for slicing evenly and placing into summer rolls. Two 5-ounce ribs took only about 10 minutes of simmering to cook through and turn tender. Once they were cooked, I pulled them out of the water to cool and then sliced them thin.

Traditionally, the shrimp are poached in the water that's left over from cooking the pork. I appreciate that kind of efficiency; after all, the water's already hot, and it's been seasoned by the pork and with salt, so why not take advantage? I brought the water to a boil, added some medium-large shrimp, covered the pot, and removed it from the heat. Using residual rather than direct heat reduced the risk of overcooking and produced plump and juicy shrimp. After just 3 minutes in the water, the shrimp were opaque, so I rinsed them in cold water to cool them down quickly and prevent overcooking, sliced them lengthwise, and placed them on a plate. On to the noodles.

VIETNAMESE SUMMER ROLLS (GOI CUON)

The frugal side of me was tempted to use the cooking water a third time to boil the noodles. But because the noodles are meant to provide a neutral background for the other ingredients, I decided against it. I boiled some fresh water and added a block of dried rice vermicelli. Three minutes later, I drained the noodles, rinsed them with cool water to halt the cooking and remove the sticky surface starch, and spread them on a plate to dry.

Summer rolls are sometimes called "salad rolls," and rightly so. The lettuce and herbs contribute appealing crunch, moisture, and freshness. I quickly learned that lettuces such as stiff-leafed iceberg and wide-ribbed romaine were not very cooperative when it came to rolling, so I opted for green (or red) leaf lettuce, which was more pliable.

Here's the most important thing to know about the herbs: You're going to use loads of them. In Vietnam, most meals are accompanied by a large plate of leafy herbs and lettuce that diners are encouraged to add liberally to their plates or bowls. Some herbs that are popular in Vietnamese cuisine aren't widely available in the United States, but mint, cilantro, and Thai basil are. I went with 1 cup of each. Rather than add each herb to the rolls individually, I tore them all into 1-inch pieces and combined them in a bowl. When the time came, I'd simply add a handful of the mix to each roll. I also sliced some scallions thin so I could sprinkle them in. They're not as charming as the Chinese chives that poke out of the summer rolls you see in Vietnam or in the homes of cooks with access to great Asian markets, but they'd add comparable freshness.

Now I was ready for the wrappers themselves. In their dried state, the thin rice flour disks are opaque and brittle, with one smooth side and one side patterned by the bamboo mat the wrapper is dried on. After a dip in water, however, the wrappers become soft, pliable, and translucent.

But how long was I supposed to dip them, and in what temperature water? The information I found in recipes was all over the place. After much testing, I landed on dunking the wrapper briefly in cold water before transferring it—still stiff—to the counter, where it continued to soften as I piled on the fillings.

Constructing the perfect summer roll is an acquired skill. First, fold a lettuce leaf (remove the rib if it's large) and place it on the lower third of the moistened wrapper. Spread some noodles over the lettuce (I like to use ⅓ cup per roll), and then top them with sliced scallions. Place two slices of pork over the scallions and ¼ cup of herb mix on top of that.

NOTES FROM THE TEST KITCHEN

ANATOMY OF A GREAT SUMMER ROLL

Each component of a summer roll offers subtle yet important flavors and textures that are complemented by bold dipping sauces.

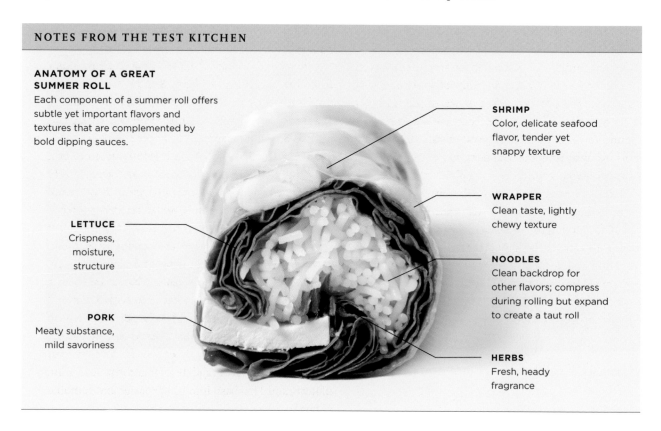

SHRIMP
Color, delicate seafood flavor, tender yet snappy texture

WRAPPER
Clean taste, lightly chewy texture

NOODLES
Clean backdrop for other flavors; compress during rolling but expand to create a taut roll

HERBS
Fresh, heady fragrance

LETTUCE
Crispness, moisture, structure

PORK
Meaty substance, mild savoriness

At this point, the wrapper will be fully hydrated and flexible and should feel tacky (which will help it stick to itself when rolled). Lift the bottom edge of the wrapper up and over the herbs and roll snugly but gently to enclose the filling in a tube. Then fold each side in to enclose the ends. Lastly, place three shrimp halves, pink side down for maximum visual appeal, on the remaining section of the wrapper and roll the wrapper up the rest of the way to form a neat cylinder.

To prevent the rolls from drying out and preserve their texture, transfer them to a platter, not touching each other, and cover them with plastic wrap. The rolls can also be constructed family-style; place all the fixings and a few bowls of water in the middle of the table and let each diner roll their own. But either way, you'll need a sauce or two.

Just as you would never eat a salad without dressing, a summer roll without a dipping sauce is unthinkable: A peanut-based hoisin sauce and tangy, savory nuoc cham are both perfect accompaniments to cool, mild summer rolls. I like to alternate between the two as I eat, switching after every bite. After all, summer rolls may be elegant, but eating them doesn't have to be.

—ANDREA GEARY, *Cook's Illustrated*

Vietnamese Summer Rolls (Goi Cuon)

SERVES 4

If desired, omit the pork, double the amount of shrimp (use the same timing and amounts of water and salt), and place three shrimp halves on top of the scallions. If Thai basil is unavailable, increase the mint and cilantro to 1½ cups each. A wooden surface will draw moisture away from the wrappers, so assemble the rolls directly on your counter or on a plastic cutting board. If part of the wrapper starts to dry out while you are forming the rolls, moisten it with your dampened fingers. One serving (three rolls) makes a light meal, but these rolls can also be halved crosswise using a sharp, wet knife and served as an appetizer. These rolls are best served immediately. If you like, serve Vietnamese Dipping Sauce (Nuoc Cham) (recipe follows) along with the Peanut-Hoisin Sauce.

PEANUT-HOISIN SAUCE

- 1 Thai chile, stemmed and sliced thin
- 1 garlic clove, minced
- 1 teaspoon kosher salt
- ⅔ cup water
- ⅓ cup creamy peanut butter
- 3 tablespoons hoisin sauce
- 2 tablespoons tomato paste
- 1 tablespoon distilled white vinegar

SUMMER ROLLS

- 6 ounces rice vermicelli
- 10 ounces boneless country-style pork ribs, trimmed
- 2 teaspoons kosher salt
- 18 medium-large shrimp (31 to 40 per pound), peeled, deveined, and tails removed
- 1 cup fresh mint leaves
- 1 cup fresh cilantro leaves and thin stems
- 1 cup Thai basil leaves
- 12 (8½-inch) round rice paper wrappers
- 12 leaves red or green leaf lettuce, thick ribs removed
- 2 scallions, sliced thin on bias

1. FOR THE PEANUT-HOISIN SAUCE: Using mortar and pestle (or on cutting board using flat side of chef's knife), mash Thai chile, garlic, and salt to fine paste. Transfer to medium bowl. Add water, peanut butter, hoisin, tomato paste, and vinegar and whisk until smooth.

2. FOR THE SUMMER ROLLS: Bring 2 quarts water to boil in medium saucepan. Stir in noodles. Cook until noodles are tender but not mushy, 3 to 4 minutes. Drain noodles and rinse with cold water until cool. Drain noodles again, then spread on large plate to dry.

3. Bring 2 quarts water to boil in now-empty saucepan. Add pork and salt. Reduce heat, cover, and simmer until thickest part of pork registers 150 degrees, 8 to 12 minutes. Transfer pork to cutting board, reserving water.

4. Return water to boil. Add shrimp and cover. Let stand off heat until shrimp are opaque throughout, about 3 minutes. Drain shrimp and rinse with cold water until cool. Transfer to cutting board. Pat shrimp dry and halve lengthwise. Transfer to second plate.

5. When pork is cool enough to handle, cut each rib crosswise into 2-inch lengths. Slice each 2-inch piece lengthwise ⅛ inch thick (you should have at least 24 slices) and transfer to plate with shrimp. Tear mint, cilantro, and Thai basil into 1-inch pieces and combine in bowl.

FRIED CALAMARI

6. Fill large bowl with cold water. Submerge 1 wrapper in water until wet on both sides, no longer than 2 seconds. Shake gently over bowl to remove excess water, then lay wrapper flat on counter (wrapper will be fairly stiff but will continue to soften as you assemble roll). Repeat with second wrapper and place next to first wrapper. Fold 1 lettuce leaf and place on lower third of first wrapper, leaving about ½-inch border on each side. Spread ⅓ cup noodles on top of lettuce, then sprinkle with 1 teaspoon scallions. Top scallions with 2 slices pork. Spread ¼ cup herb mixture over pork.

7. Bring lower edge of wrapper up and over herbs. Roll snugly but gently until long sides of greens and noodles are enclosed. Fold in sides to enclose ends. Arrange 3 shrimp halves, cut side up, on remaining section of wrapper. Continue to roll until filling is completely enclosed in neat cylinder. Transfer roll to serving platter, shrimp side up, and cover with plastic wrap. Repeat with second moistened wrapper. Repeat with remaining wrappers and filling, keeping completed rolls covered with plastic. Uncover and serve with sauce. (Leftovers can be wrapped tightly and refrigerated for up to 24 hours, but wrappers will become chewier and may break in places.)

Vietnamese Dipping Sauce (Nuoc Cham)
SERVES 4 (MAKES 1 CUP)

Hot water helps the sugar dissolve into the sauce. We recommend Red Boat 40°N Fish Sauce.

   3   tablespoons sugar, divided
   1   small Thai chile, stemmed and minced
   1   garlic clove, minced
   ⅔   cup hot water
   5   tablespoons fish sauce
   ¼   cup lime juice (2 limes)

Using mortar and pestle (or on cutting board using flat side of chef's knife), mash 1 tablespoon sugar, Thai chile, and garlic to fine paste. Transfer to medium bowl and add hot water and remaining 2 tablespoons sugar. Stir until sugar is dissolved. Stir in fish sauce and lime juice.

FRIED CALAMARI

WHY THIS RECIPE WORKS   Our fried calamari features tender, lightly springy squid encased in a crispy, lacy, golden-brown crust. We sliced the squid bodies into sizable ¾-inch-thick rings to keep them tender after frying. Dipping the squid in milk helped just enough of the dredge cling; proteins in the milk also encouraged browning when the milk soaked into the flour. We found that salting the milk bath, not the dredge or the fried pieces, seasoned the squid evenly. Dredging the squid in all-purpose flour (which contains proteins that brown) ensured that the coating turned deep golden brown before the squid had a chance to overcook and toughen. We added baking powder to the dredge to lighten the texture of the coating, and we shook off excess dredge to prevent the coating from clumping. Letting the coated pieces rest while the oil heated gave the coating time to hydrate, preventing a dusty film from forming on the exterior. Frying in two batches prevented the oil temperature from dropping too much, so the pieces browned and crisped quickly.

Fried calamari is an iconic restaurant appetizer across the United States, but that hasn't always been the case. In the 1970s and '80s, a handful of cephalopod supporters had to fight to move the needle on Americans' squid squeamishness. Among these vocal supporters were Massachusetts Institute of Technology student Paul Kalikstein, who outlined "The Marketability of Squid" in his graduate thesis, and reporter Florence Fabricant, whose 1978 appeal in the *New York Times* detailed the many practical perks of the "neglected seafood." Several state and federal marine programs also bolstered squid's popularity by encouraging restaurant chefs to replace overfished stocks with squid—and to call it by its more enticing Italian name, calamari—in an effort to buoy a struggling seafood industry.

These campaigns certainly made their mark: By the mid '90s you could find a plate of crispy rings and tentacles at any reliable sports bar or red-sauce joint in the country. Squid's bait-to-plate ascent was so impressive, in fact, that the *New York Times* used a "Fried Calamari Index" to compare the trajectories of other trendy foods over time.

However, home cooks rarely buy and prepare squid themselves, so I've decided to join the campaign and bait readers with a fried calamari recipe of my own. One of squid's best features is that it cooks in minutes, but since it can quickly go from tender to rubbery—the most recognizable flaw of subpar restaurant versions—I needed to nail down the frying time. And I needed a formula for the perfect coating: golden brown, crispy, and delicate.

Frying squid is superfast. All you do is dredge the pieces in a starchy coating that helps them crisp and brown quickly, drop them into a pot of hot oil, and then fish them out a few minutes later when they've turned golden brown. Next, just season the pieces with salt, pair them with a dipping sauce (or lemon wedges), and serve immediately.

But there's an inherent challenge to frying something that cooks so quickly: There's barely enough time for the exterior to brown and crisp before the interior overcooks. Squid is packed with collagen, which is why there's such a narrow window of doneness when it's pleasantly springy-tender. As the old adage goes, you can cook squid either hot and fast or low and slow, but avoid anything in between. So I focused on ways to keep the squid tender and to encourage the coating (for now, I used all-purpose flour) to brown rapidly.

Plenty of recipes call for soaking the squid in buttermilk or milk, because theoretically the lactic acid (though milk has only a small amount) tenderizes the squid and extends the cooking time before it toughens. But the soaking tests that I ran on squid with both types of dairy and for varying lengths of time showed that dairy did not affect tenderness. However, I did learn that dunking squid in milk—not buttermilk—before dredging it helps ensure that just enough of the starchy coating will cling. The thicker buttermilk grabbed too much dredge, and thinner water didn't grab enough, resulting in coatings that fried up either thick and tough or insubstantial. Plus, proteins and sugar in the milk encourage browning.

The one trick that enhanced tenderness was cutting thicker rings. Presliced squid rings tend to measure about ½ inch wide. By the time the coating was browned, these slim rings, which cooked very quickly, threatened to turn tough. It was better to buy whole cleaned squid and slice the bodies (also called "tubes") crosswise myself into ¾-inch-thick rings. (I cut any long tentacles to match the size of the shorter ones.)

I knew that the dredge I chose would impact the coating's texture and how quickly the calamari browned, so I decided to test all the starches I saw in recipes: rice flour, all-purpose flour, cornstarch, fine cornmeal, and semolina. I tossed 1 pound of squid in each dredge, making sure to shake off any excess; dropped half the pieces into 350-degree oil (frying in two batches ensured that the oil temperature didn't drop too much and prolong cooking); retrieved them as soon as they were tender (exactly 3 minutes later); and repeated the process with the second batch.

The coarse semolina fried up hard and the cornmeal gritty, while the rice flour was crunchy (not crispy) and the cornstarch was pale. But the all-purpose flour batch boasted deep golden color since the flour contains proteins that brown. Although it was dusty and not as delicate as I wanted, I moved forward with it and added baking powder to lighten up the texture. To rid the surface of that dusty film—I recognized this as unhydrated flour—I dredged the squid before heating the oil and spread the pieces out on a wire rack to hydrate while the oil came up to temperature.

Though the tweaks I'd made seemed subtle, they added up to exceptionally good fried calamari: lightly springy pieces encased in a delicate, lacy shell. I sprinkled salt onto the squid right when it came out of the oil, just as I would with any fried food, and dug in to what I thought was the perfect batch—but I quickly realized that the seasoning was off. Some bites were salt bombs, others bland. I tried again and seasoned the dredge instead. But the seasoning was still uneven, and this time the problem was obvious: The willowy tentacles picked up considerably more dredge—and thus considerably more salt—than the rings. The best approach turned out to be seasoning the milk so that the salt was evenly distributed.

All I needed were the fixings: a quick marinara sauce for the traditional red-sauce-joint style, and an even-quicker sriracha-spiked mayonnaise for a creamy version with a hit of heat. Equally successful as a crowd-pleasing party platter or a quick dinner, this was the stuff that food fads are made of.

—STEVE DUNN, *Cook's Illustrated*

Fried Calamari

SERVES 4

If desired, omit the lemon wedges and serve with Quick Marinara Sauce or Spicy Mayonnaise (recipes follow); make the sauce before preparing the squid. Use a Dutch oven that holds 6 quarts or more for this recipe. Precut squid will not be as tender as whole bodies that you cut yourself. You can double this recipe and fry the calamari in four batches; the amount of oil remains the same. We tested this recipe with King Arthur Gluten-Free Multi-Purpose Flour, and the results were acceptable.

½ cup milk

1 teaspoon table salt

1½ cups all-purpose flour

1 tablespoon baking powder

½ teaspoon pepper

1 pound squid, bodies sliced crosswise ¾ inch thick, extra-long tentacles trimmed to match length of shorter ones

2 quarts vegetable oil for frying

Lemon wedges

1. Set wire rack in rimmed baking sheet. Set second rack in second sheet and line with triple layer of paper towels. Heat oven to 200 degrees.

2. Whisk milk and salt together in medium bowl. Combine flour, baking powder, and pepper in second medium bowl. Add squid to milk mixture and toss to coat. Using your hands or slotted spoon, remove half of squid, allowing excess milk mixture to drip back into bowl, and add to bowl with flour mixture. Using your hands, toss squid to coat evenly. Gently shake off excess flour mixture and place coated squid in single layer on unlined rack. Repeat with remaining squid. Let sit for 10 minutes.

3. While squid rests, heat oil in Dutch oven over high heat to 350 degrees. Carefully add half of squid and fry for exactly 3 minutes (squid will be golden brown). Using slotted spoon or spider skimmer, transfer calamari to paper towel–lined rack and transfer to oven to keep warm. Return oil to 350 degrees and repeat with remaining squid. Transfer calamari to platter and serve immediately with lemon wedges.

Quick Marinara Sauce

SERVES 4 (MAKES 1½ CUPS)

Our favorite crushed tomatoes are made by SMT.

2 tablespoons extra-virgin olive oil

1 garlic clove, minced

1 (14.5-ounce) can crushed tomatoes

1 tablespoon chopped fresh basil

⅛ teaspoon sugar

Cook oil and garlic in 10-inch skillet over medium heat, stirring frequently, until fragrant but not browned, about 2 minutes. Stir in tomatoes and simmer until slightly thickened, about 5 minutes. Stir in basil and sugar and season with salt to taste.

Spicy Mayonnaise

SERVES 4 (MAKES 1¼ CUPS)

Our favorite mayonnaise is Blue Plate Real Mayonnaise; because this product can be hard to find in some parts of the United States, we also recommend Hellman's Real Mayonnaise.

1 cup mayonnaise

2 tablespoons sriracha

2 teaspoons grated lime zest plus 2 tablespoons juice

½ teaspoon smoked paprika

Whisk all ingredients together in bowl.

NOTES FROM THE TEST KITCHEN

SQUID 101

CLEANED SQUID IS SOLD IN TWO PARTS
Most fishmongers sell both squid bodies and squid tentacles. The bodies tend to be smooth and tender, while the tentacles offer pleasant chew and more surface area.

BUY WHOLE BODIES WHEN POSSIBLE
Though we've found the quality of precut rings to be just fine, buying whole bodies allows you to cut them to your own size specification.

GOOD SQUID LOOKS PRISTINE
Squid should look moist, shiny, and ivory-colored.

MOST SQUID HAS BEEN FROZEN
Unless you have access to squid direct from the boat, anything you buy has been previously frozen and treated with additives to inhibit spoilage. But that's fine: We found the quality of frozen squid to be good, and we didn't detect any off-flavors.

MEXICAN SHRIMP COCKTAIL (CÓCTEL DE CAMARÓN)

✔ **WHY THIS RECIPE WORKS** This popular Mexican dish consists of cooked shrimp tossed with chopped vegetables in a bright tomato sauce. For shrimp that were tender, not rubbery, we cooked them using residual heat. Bringing the cooking water to a full boil before adding the shrimp ensured that there was enough heat in the saucepan to cook them through. For a sauce that wasn't too sweet, we used a combination of savory V8 and ketchup plus lime juice and hot sauce. Cucumber and red onion added crunch, avocado added creaminess, and cilantro added freshness.

American shrimp cocktail will always be a classic, but I'm here to tell you that the Mexican take on the dish has a whole lot more personality. Cóctel de camarón offers plump, tender poached shrimp; crisp bites of raw onion and cucumber; and cool, creamy avocado all coated in a tangy, spicy-sweet tomato sauce. Eaten ice-cold with a spoon and saltines, it's like a festive, shrimp-packed Bloody Mary or gazpacho.

The success of cóctel de camarón lies in nailing the cooking of the shrimp and the sweetness and consistency of the sauce, which always contains ketchup. There are several ways to poach delicate proteins such as shrimp: Start cold and bring everything to a simmer; add the food to 160-degree water and fiddle with the stove to maintain a consistent temperature; or use carryover cooking. Using carryover cooking gave me the most consistent results: Adding 1¼ pounds of cold, raw shrimp to 3 cups of boiling water instantly dropped the water temperature to 155 degrees, ideal for poaching the delicate seafood. After 5 minutes off the heat, the shrimp were tender and opaque. For easy eating, I cut each one crosswise into three bite-size pieces.

With the shrimp all set, I tackled the sauce. Along with ketchup, the sauce for cóctel de camarón typically includes some variety of tomato juice (frequently Clamato) as well as hot sauce and fresh lime juice. Stirring together 1 cup of Clamato, ½ cup of ketchup, lime juice, and hot sauce yielded a sauce with a good clingy consistency, but tasters found it overly sweet. Since ketchup was the sole source of body, I hesitated to use less. Instead, I made three more batches: one with Clamato, one with tomato juice, and one with V8. The V8 version struck the right balance: equally sweet and savory, with a touch of tartness.

To round out the dish, I cut an avocado and half an English cucumber into bite-size chunks and finely chopped a red onion. Chopped cilantro contributed freshness. With my work complete, I set out saltines, lime wedges, and a bottle of hot sauce—essential accompaniments to a stellar cóctel de camarón.

—ANNIE PETITO, *Cook's Illustrated*

Mexican Shrimp Cocktail (Cóctel de Camarón)
SERVES 4 TO 6

We prefer untreated shrimp, but if your shrimp are treated with salt or additives such as sodium tripolyphosphate, do not add the salt in step 1. The balanced flavor of Valentina, Cholula, or Tapatío hot sauce works best here. If using a spicier, vinegary hot sauce such as Tabasco, start with half the amount called for and adjust to your taste after mixing. Saltines are a traditional accompaniment, but tortilla chips or thick-cut potato chips are also good.

1¼ pounds large shrimp (26 to 30 per pound), peeled, deveined, and tails removed
¼ teaspoon table salt, plus salt for cooking shrimp
1 cup V8 juice, chilled
½ cup ketchup
3 tablespoons lime juice (2 limes), plus lime wedges for serving
2 teaspoons hot sauce, plus extra for serving
½ English cucumber, cut into ½-inch pieces
1 cup finely chopped red onion
1 avocado, halved, pitted, and cut into ½-inch pieces
¼ cup chopped fresh cilantro
Saltines

1. Bring 3 cups water to boil in large saucepan over high heat. Stir in shrimp and 1 tablespoon salt. Cover and let stand off heat until shrimp are opaque, about 5 minutes, shaking saucepan halfway through standing time. Fill large bowl halfway with ice and water. Transfer shrimp to ice bath and let cool for 3 to 5 minutes. Once cool, cut each shrimp crosswise into 3 pieces.

2. Combine V8 juice, ketchup, lime juice, hot sauce, and salt in medium bowl. Add cucumber, onion, and shrimp and stir until evenly coated. Stir in avocado and cilantro. Portion cocktail into individual bowls or glasses and serve immediately, passing saltines, lime wedges, and extra hot sauce separately.

MEXICAN SHRIMP COCKTAIL (CÓCTEL DE CAMARÓN)

ASPARAGUS BAKED IN FOIL WITH CAPERS AND DILL

SIDE DISHES

SKILLET-ROASTED BROCCOLI

✓ **WHY THIS RECIPE WORKS** Deeply browned broccoli has a nutty flavor and a hint of crisp texture. To make it quickly on the stovetop, we cut broccoli crowns into wedges to create plenty of flat sides that sat flush with the surface of the skillet, and we steamed the broccoli initially to soften it. When the water evaporated, oil filled any gaps between broccoli and skillet for optimal browning.

Broccoli has always been there for us: It is reasonably priced, available year-round, and boasts stellar nutritional stats. How do we show our appreciation? We toss it haphazardly into stir-fries, steam it to a flavorless jade green, or—perhaps most insultingly—dip squeaky, raw florets into bottled ranch dressing. Doesn't broccoli deserve better?

I wanted a stovetop recipe that would come together quickly and achieve rich caramelization to enhance the meaty stems and delicate florets. It made sense to turn to the same general approach that we use for other skillet-roasted vegetables: steam first, brown second.

I cut about a pound of broccoli crowns into wedges to create flat sides for browning and carefully arranged them so as many as possible were flush with the pan surface. Next, I drizzled the wedges with oil and water, added salt, covered the pan, and cranked up the heat. After about 4 minutes, the broccoli was bright green and starting to soften, so I pressed the wedges against the skillet with my spatula for maximum contact with the pan and then replaced the lid. Once the stems were crisp-tender and the undersides had colored, I flipped the wedges to brown the second side. I then left the lid off so that any remaining water would evaporate.

This worked pretty well, but the broccoli wasn't as browned as I had envisioned. Increasing the oil from 2 tablespoons to 5 helped fill the gaps between broccoli and skillet for deep browning. Now to gild the lily.

Since sauces sogged out the beautifully crisped tips of the florets, I made three dry toppings. The first was a Parmesan, lemon zest, and black pepper topping with broad appeal. The other two call for umami-rich, crunchy, well-toasted seeds: One combines sesame seeds with orange zest and salt—my take on the Japanese dry condiment gomasio—and the other features sunflower seeds supported by nutritional yeast and smoked paprika.

—ANDREA GEARY, *Cook's Illustrated*

Skillet-Roasted Broccoli
SERVES 4

Make one topping recipe before cooking the broccoli, if desired (recipes follow).

- 1 recipe topping (recipes follow) (optional)
- 1¼ pounds broccoli crowns
- 5 tablespoons vegetable oil
- ¾ teaspoon kosher salt
- 2 tablespoons water

1. Sprinkle one-third of topping onto platter, if using. Cut broccoli crowns into 4 wedges if 3 to 4 inches in diameter or 6 wedges if 4 to 5 inches in diameter.

2. Add oil to 12-inch nonstick skillet and tilt skillet until oil covers surface. Add broccoli, cut side down (pieces will fit snugly; if a few pieces don't fit in bottom layer, place on top). Sprinkle evenly with salt and drizzle with water. Cover and cook over high heat, without moving broccoli, until broccoli is bright green, about 4 minutes.

3. Uncover and press gently on broccoli with back of spatula. Cover and cook until undersides of broccoli are deeply browned and stems are crisp-tender, 4 to 6 minutes. Off heat, uncover and turn broccoli so that second cut side is touching skillet. Move any pieces that were on top so they are flush with skillet surface. Continue to cook, uncovered, pressing gently on broccoli with back of spatula, until second cut side is charred, 3 to 5 minutes longer. Transfer to platter, sprinkle with remaining topping, if using, and serve.

Parmesan and Black Pepper Topping
MAKES ABOUT ½ CUP

Our favorite supermarket Parmesan cheese is Boar's Head Parmigiano-Reggiano.

- ½ teaspoon pepper
- ½ teaspoon lemon zest
- 1 ounce Parmesan cheese, grated (½ cup)

Using your fingers, mix pepper and lemon zest in small bowl until evenly mixed. Add Parmesan and toss with your fingers or fork until lemon zest and pepper are evenly distributed.

SKILLET-ROASTED BROCCOLI

Sesame and Orange Topping

MAKES ABOUT 2 TABLESPOONS

Toast the sesame seeds in a dry skillet set over medium heat, shaking pan occasionally.

- **2 tablespoons toasted sesame seeds, divided**
- **½ teaspoon orange zest**
- **¼ teaspoon kosher salt**

Using spice grinder or mortar and pestle, grind 1 tablespoon sesame seeds, orange zest, and salt to powder. Transfer to small bowl. Add remaining 1 tablespoon sesame seeds and toss with your fingers until orange zest is evenly distributed.

Smoky Sunflower Seed Topping

MAKES ABOUT 3 TABLESPOONS

Nutritional yeast is a nonleavening form of yeast with a nutty flavor; look for it in natural food stores.

- **2 tablespoons sunflower seeds, toasted**
- **1 tablespoon nutritional yeast**
- **½ teaspoon lemon zest**
- **¼ teaspoon smoked paprika**
- **¼ teaspoon kosher salt**

Using spice grinder or mortar and pestle, grind all ingredients until reduced to coarse powder.

NOTES FROM THE TEST KITCHEN

HOW TO CUT BROCCOLI CROWNS

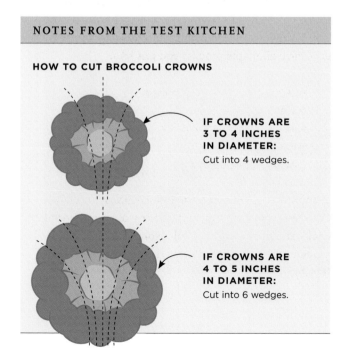

IF CROWNS ARE
3 TO 4 INCHES
IN DIAMETER:
Cut into 4 wedges.

IF CROWNS ARE
4 TO 5 INCHES
IN DIAMETER:
Cut into 6 wedges.

SKILLET-ROASTED CARROTS

✓ **WHY THIS RECIPE WORKS** Carrots take at least 40 minutes to roast in the oven. For roasted carrots in less than half the time, we moved the process to a covered skillet on the stovetop, where we steamed the carrots for about 8 minutes. This softened the carrots, which is important for two reasons: it released the sugars, making them available for browning, and it gave the carrots a bit of flex so they could be pressed flush against the work surface for optimal color. Once the lid was removed, the carrots needed only 5 to 7 minutes to develop oven-worthy roasty browning.

Roasting deepens carrots' earthy sweetness like no other cooking method, but the process monopolizes your oven for at least 45 minutes. I wanted great roasted carrots—with streaks of char, a tender bite, and a concentrated flavor—in less time and on the stove.

To soften them quickly, I needed to steam the carrots first. I selected 1½ pounds of large carrots from the bulk bin, since their thickness would translate into more cut surfaces for browning than skinnier bagged carrots. I cut them crosswise and then lengthwise into even pieces. When I placed the carrots in a skillet with water, salt, and oil, they didn't fit in a single layer, but steaming fixed that: After about 8 minutes of covered cooking, the carrots had shrunk enough that, with a shake of the skillet, they settled into an even layer.

Most of the water evaporated during that time, too, but to cook off more moisture and create as much deep browning and char as I could, I kept the heat on medium-high and let the carrots cook undisturbed for about 3 minutes. I then flipped the pieces so their pale sides were on the bottom and cooked them for a couple minutes more. This method was speedy—less than 15 minutes—but while the carrots were browned, no one would mistake them for oven-roasted.

I had two fixes: First, I increased the oil from 1 tablespoon to 2, since fat facilitates energy transfer and would allow the sugars in the carrots to caramelize fully. Second, while the first side of the carrots seared, I pressed them against the skillet with my spatula for maximum contact with the pan.

The finished carrots were richly browned, with concentrated sweet-savory flavor. If I hadn't made them myself, I would have sworn these carrots had been roasted in the oven.

—ANDREA GEARY, *Cook's Illustrated*

Skillet-Roasted Carrots

SERVES 4

We prefer large carrots from the bulk bin for this recipe. After cutting the carrots crosswise, quarter lengthwise any pieces that are larger than 1½ inches in diameter and halve lengthwise any pieces that are ¾ to 1½ inches in diameter. Leave whole any carrots that are narrower than ¾ inch. If desired, top the carrots with Mustard Bread Crumbs and Chives, Smoky Spiced Almonds and Parsley, or Spicy Maple Bread Crumbs (recipes follow) before serving; make the topping before cooking the carrots.

- ½ **cup water**
- ½ **teaspoon table salt**
- 1½ **pounds large carrots, peeled, cut crosswise into 3- to 4-inch lengths, and cut lengthwise into even pieces**
- 2 **tablespoons vegetable oil**

1. Mix water and salt in 12-inch nonstick skillet until salt is dissolved. Place carrots in skillet, arranging as many carrots flat side down as possible (carrots will not fit in single layer). Drizzle oil over carrots. Bring to boil over medium-high heat. Cover and cook, without moving carrots, until carrots are crisp-tender and water has almost evaporated, 8 to 10 minutes.

2. Uncover and gently shake skillet until carrots settle into even layer. Continue to cook, not moving carrots but occasionally pressing them gently against skillet with spatula, until water has completely evaporated and undersides of carrots are deeply browned, 3 to 5 minutes longer. Stir carrots and flip pale side down. Cook until second side is lightly browned, about 2 minutes. Transfer to serving dish and serve.

Mustard Bread Crumbs and Chives

MAKES ¼ CUP

The test kitchen's favorite Dijon mustard is Trois Petits Cochons Moutarde de Dijon. Our preferred black peppercorns are Tone's Whole Black Peppercorns.

- ¼ **cup panko bread crumbs**
- 1 **tablespoon Dijon mustard**
- 2 **teaspoons vegetable oil**
- 1 **tablespoon minced fresh chives**
- ⅛ **teaspoon pepper**

Combine panko, mustard, and oil in 12-inch nonstick skillet. Cook over medium-high heat, stirring constantly, until panko is crisp, dry, and golden brown, about 5 minutes. Transfer to small bowl and let cool completely, about 10 minutes. Stir in chives and pepper.

Smoky Spiced Almonds and Parsley

MAKES ¼ CUP

The test kitchen's favorite vegetable oil is Crisco Blends. Our preferred smoked paprika is Simply Organic Smoked Paprika.

- ¼ **cup sliced almonds, chopped fine**
- 1 **teaspoon vegetable oil**
- ½ **teaspoon smoked paprika**
- ⅛ **teaspoon table salt**
  Pinch cayenne pepper
- 1 **tablespoon chopped fresh parsley**

Combine almonds, oil, paprika, salt, and cayenne in 12-inch nonstick skillet. Cook over medium heat, stirring frequently, until almonds are fragrant and crisp, 3 to 4 minutes. Transfer to small bowl and let cool completely, about 10 minutes. Stir in parsley.

Spicy Maple Bread Crumbs

MAKES ¼ CUP

The test kitchen's favorite panko bread crumbs are Kikkoman Panko Japanese Style Bread Crumbs. We've found Grade A Dark Amber pure maple syrups to be very similar, so we recommend choosing the least expensive all-maple product you can find.

- 3 **tablespoons panko bread crumbs**
- 2 **teaspoons maple syrup**
- 2 **teaspoons vegetable oil**
- ⅛ **teaspoon table salt**
- ⅛ **teaspoon cayenne pepper**

Combine all ingredients in 12-inch nonstick skillet. Cook over medium-high heat, stirring constantly, until panko is crunchy and caramel-colored, 3 to 5 minutes. Transfer to small bowl and let cool completely, about 10 minutes.

BRAISED EGGPLANT WITH SOY, GARLIC, AND GINGER

BRAISED EGGPLANT

✓ **WHY THIS RECIPE WORKS** Our braised eggplant boasts a meltingly tender, creamy texture. We cut the eggplant into slim wedges, making sure that each piece had some skin attached to keep it from falling apart during cooking. Instead of treating the dish as a stir-fry, we braised the eggplant in a single batch. Once the eggplant was tender, we reduced the flavorful braising liquid to create a sauce.

As a professional cook, I have loads of vegetable preparation methods filed in my brain, which makes it easy to shop for and throw together weeknight meals. Are carrots looking good at the market? Roast them with a touch of butter and flavor according to whatever else is on the menu. Spinach? Sauté with aromatics. Asparagus? Pan-steam until crisp-tender. And so it goes: I have equally straightforward one-pan techniques for almost every vegetable out there. Except eggplant. Faced with a pile of these dark, glossy specimens, I'm stumped. Sure, I can make a great eggplant Parmesan or fire up the grill for baba ghanoush, but that's project cooking. If I just want a simple side dish, I'm out of ideas.

The result is that I often bypass eggplant, and that's a shame, because it is such a lovely vegetable (actually, botanically speaking, it's a berry). Eggplant is easy to prep and mild in flavor (modern varieties are bred to be less bitter than they once were), with extremely porous flesh that soaks up seasonings.

If I could come up with a one-pan side dish, my eggplant hang-ups might just be resolved forever. I had a hunch that braising might be the best cooking method to audition: Braised eggplant shows up in a diverse set of cuisines, from Thai to Japanese to Chinese to Mediterranean. Methods vary widely, but the result—pieces of eggplant that are supertender and almost custardy but remain intact—is always meaty, comforting, and deeply satisfying.

In the test kitchen, we often use a Dutch oven for braising, but here I reached for a 12-inch nonstick skillet. Its shallow, flared sides would allow for quick evaporation so I could simmer the eggplant in a sufficient volume of liquid and then quickly reduce it to a flavorful sauce that clung to the eggplant. But before I considered the seasonings, I'd work out the cooking method using just water.

I knew that the eggplant would shrink during braising, so I loaded roughly 1 pound of eggplant pieces into the skillet, added some water, put the lid on, and simmered for 15 minutes until the pulp was soft. At this point, I removed the lid and let the water bubble for another 15 minutes or so until it reduced to about ¼ cup. This dead-simple approach worked quite well.

Well, perhaps that's an overstatement: I was pleased with the texture of the eggplant, with its supple skin and creamy flesh, but when I stirred, the delicate pieces tended to break apart. So instead of using a spoon, I simply swirled the skillet.

That helped, but the size and shape of the pieces, as well as the eggplant variety, also had an impact on whether the chunks stayed intact. I knew that each piece needed to have some skin attached, since skinless flesh fell apart and muddied the sauce. Also, I wanted the recipe to work with the most commonly available types of eggplant, each with a different size and shape: long, slender Chinese or Japanese eggplant; larger, bulbous globe eggplant; and smaller Italian eggplant. Coin-shaped slices worked well for the Asian varieties but were too large for the others. Conversely, slicing into rounds and then into pie-shaped wedges was well suited to larger eggplant but not the smaller ones. The only method that worked across the board was cutting the eggplant in half crosswise and then lengthwise into slim, even wedges. This way, each piece was guaranteed to have a uniform ratio of skin to flesh no matter the dimensions of the eggplant. (It was also important to choose moderately sized Italian or globe eggplants: Cut into wedges, the big swaths of flesh that were created with large eggplants were more liable to break away from the skin.)

Now that I had nailed an accessible, adaptable technique that produced gorgeously creamy eggplant, the flavor possibilities were infinite.

One of my favorite ways to enjoy eggplant is in the rich, complex Sichuan dish yu xiang qie zi ("fish-fragrant eggplant," since the sauce is also used for fish). In that dish, the pieces are coated in a potent soy-garlic sauce, so I decided to simmer my eggplant in a braising liquid inspired by those flavors. I diluted a mixture of Shaoxing wine, soy sauce, sugar, and broad bean chili paste with water and bolstered it with a bit of cornstarch for body. As the eggplant simmered, its spongy flesh absorbed the delightfully salty, sweet, and spicy ingredients. I crowned the glistening dish with a couple of sliced scallions and a drizzle of toasted sesame oil. This was everything I wanted my eggplant to be: impossibly tender, intensely flavorful, and easy to put together.

And so I continued, next preparing a variation with warm Mediterranean spices and gussied up with fresh cilantro and a drizzle of yogurt. Both are a snap to prepare, leaving plenty of time to make a main course. That said, the recipes are so satisfying that I also like to offer them with rice as a vegetarian main course.

Can an eggplant inspire confidence? With these recipes in your back pocket, the answer is a resounding yes.

—STEVE DUNN, *Cook's Illustrated*

Braised Eggplant with Soy, Garlic, and Ginger
SERVES 4 TO 6

Large globe and Italian eggplants disintegrate when braised, so do not substitute a single 1- to 1¼-pound eggplant here. You can substitute 1 to 1¼ pounds of long, slim Chinese or Japanese eggplants if they are available; cut them as directed. Asian broad bean chili paste or sauce is also known as doubanjiang or, as the common brand Lee Kum Kee spells it, toban djan. This dish pairs nicely with rice and simply cooked chicken or pork, but you can omit the protein and serve it in larger portions as a vegetarian or vegan main course.

1½ cups water
¼ cup Shaoxing wine or dry sherry
2 tablespoons soy sauce
4 teaspoons sugar
2 teaspoons Asian broad bean chili paste
1 teaspoon cornstarch
2 (8- to 10-ounce) globe or Italian eggplants
1 tablespoon vegetable oil
1 garlic clove, minced
1 teaspoon grated fresh ginger
½ teaspoon toasted sesame oil
2 scallions, sliced thin on bias

1. Whisk water, Shaoxing wine, soy sauce, sugar, chili paste, and cornstarch in medium bowl until sugar is dissolved. Trim ½ inch from top and bottom of 1 eggplant. Halve eggplant crosswise. Cut each half lengthwise into 2 pieces. Cut each piece into ¾-inch-thick wedges. Repeat with remaining eggplant.

2. Heat vegetable oil in 12-inch nonstick skillet over medium heat until shimmering. Add garlic and ginger and cook, stirring constantly, until fragrant, about 30 seconds. Spread eggplant evenly in skillet (pieces will not form single layer). Pour Shaoxing wine mixture over eggplant. Increase heat to high and bring to boil. Reduce heat to maintain gentle boil. Cover and cook

NOTES FROM THE TEST KITCHEN

HOW TO PREP EGGPLANT FOR BRAISING
Peeled pieces of eggplant, as well as pieces that are too large, will disintegrate as they simmer. For intact pieces, it's important to choose a medium-size eggplant (if using a globe or Italian variety) and cut it so that each piece has some skin attached.

1. Cut eggplant in half crosswise.

2. Cut each half lengthwise to form two pieces.

3. Cut each piece into ¾-inch-thick wedges.

until eggplant is soft and has decreased in volume enough to form single layer on bottom of skillet, about 15 minutes, gently shaking skillet to settle eggplant halfway through cooking (some pieces will remain opaque).

3. Uncover and continue to cook, swirling skillet occasionally, until liquid is thickened and reduced to just a few tablespoons, 12 to 14 minutes longer. Transfer to platter, drizzle with sesame oil, sprinkle with scallions, and serve.

VARIATION

Braised Eggplant with Paprika, Coriander, and Yogurt
SERVES 4 TO 6

Large globe and Italian eggplants disintegrate when braised, so do not substitute a single 1- to 1¼-pound eggplant here. You can substitute 1 to 1¼ pounds of long, slim Chinese or Japanese eggplants if they are available; cut them as directed.

- 2 (8- to 10-ounce) globe or Italian eggplants
- 3 tablespoons vegetable oil
- 2 garlic cloves, minced
- 1 tablespoon tomato paste
- 2 teaspoons paprika
- 1 teaspoon table salt
- 1 teaspoon ground coriander
- ½ teaspoon sugar
- ½ teaspoon ground cumin
- ½ teaspoon ground cinnamon
- ½ teaspoon ground nutmeg
- ½ teaspoon ground ginger
- 2¾ cups water
- ⅓ cup plain whole-milk yogurt
- 2 tablespoons minced fresh cilantro

1. Trim ½ inch from top and bottom of 1 eggplant. Halve eggplant crosswise. Cut each half lengthwise into 2 pieces. Cut each piece into ¾-inch-thick wedges. Repeat with remaining eggplant.

2. Heat oil in 12-inch nonstick skillet over medium heat until shimmering. Add garlic and cook, stirring constantly, until fragrant, about 30 seconds. Add tomato paste, paprika, salt, coriander, sugar, cumin, cinnamon, nutmeg, and ginger and cook, stirring constantly, until mixture starts to darken, 1 to 2 minutes. Spread eggplant evenly in skillet (pieces will not form single layer).

Pour water over eggplant. Increase heat to high and bring to boil. Reduce heat to maintain gentle boil. Cover and cook until eggplant is soft and has decreased in volume enough to form single layer on bottom of skillet, about 15 minutes, gently shaking skillet to settle eggplant halfway through cooking (some pieces will remain opaque).

3. Uncover and continue to cook, swirling skillet occasionally, until liquid is thickened and reduced to just a few tablespoons, 12 to 14 minutes longer. Off heat, season with salt and pepper to taste. Transfer to platter, drizzle with yogurt, sprinkle with cilantro, and serve.

SKILLET-BRAISED FENNEL

☑ WHY THIS RECIPE WORKS To bring out the complex flavors of deeply browned and caramelized fennel, we used our favorite simple skillet-braising method. By simmering the fennel wedges in a covered nonstick skillet with just 1 cup of well-seasoned water, we jump-started the cooking of the fennel's interior so that it cooked in just 8 minutes, rendering it tender and juicy. Another round of cooking, this time uncovered, helped drive off any unwanted moisture and used the vegetable's natural sugars to achieve well-browned wedges. A quick stir-together vinaigrette of fresh thyme and lemon poured over the browned fennel added freshness and the right amount of bright acidity.

When fennel bulbs are roasted in a hot oven, they develop a sweet, almost nutty flavor, with an enchanting licorice undertone. But roasting them in the oven can take upwards of an hour. I wanted a speedy way to make deliciously sweet, tender, nicely browned fennel on the stovetop.

I started by chopping fennel bulbs into different-size wedges and sautéing them in olive oil. Small wedges fell apart, and those that were too big were a challenge to cook through evenly. One-inch wedges were just right for serving, and I found that they cooked most evenly when I added some water to help them steam through.

Through testing, I landed on placing the wedges in a skillet; adding a cup of water, a few tablespoons of oil, and some fresh thyme; and bringing the mixture to a boil. Then I reduced the heat, covered the skillet, and let the fennel steam until tender, about 8 minutes.

I uncovered the pan to let the water evaporate so that the wedges could pick up flavorful browning. Finally, I stirred together a simple dressing of lemon juice, honey, oil, and some minced fresh thyme to drizzle over the fennel.

—ALLI BERKEY, *Cook's Country*

Skillet-Braised Fennel

SERVES 4

Be sure to buy fennel with the stalks still attached. If you can find only stalkless bulbs, then look for those that weigh from 10 to 12 ounces each; they will weigh between 6 and 8 ounces when fully trimmed. The test kitchen prefers Bertolli Extra Virgin Olive Oil, Original, Rich Taste and California Olive Ranch Destination Series Everyday Extra Virgin Olive Oil.

  4 **(1-pound) fennel bulbs, stalks discarded**
  1 **cup water**
  ¼ **cup extra-virgin olive oil, divided**
  2 **sprigs fresh thyme, plus ½ teaspoon minced**
  ¾ **teaspoon plus ⅛ teaspoon table salt, divided**
  ¼ **teaspoon pepper**
  2 **teaspoons lemon juice**
  1 **teaspoon honey**

1. Halve fennel bulbs through core. Trim away and discard tough outer leaves. Cut halves into 1-inch-thick wedges through core, leaving core intact.

2. Arrange fennel, cut side down when possible, in 12-inch nonstick skillet. Add water, 2 tablespoons oil, thyme sprigs, ¾ teaspoon salt, and pepper to skillet and bring to boil over medium-high heat. Reduce heat to medium, cover, and cook until fennel is just tender and can be easily pierced with tip of paring knife, about 8 minutes.

3. Uncover, and continue to cook until water has evaporated, 6 to 10 minutes. Increase heat to medium-high and cook, turning fennel as needed, until browned on all sides, about 6 minutes. Transfer fennel to serving platter.

4. Whisk lemon juice, honey, minced thyme, remaining 2 tablespoons oil, and remaining ⅛ teaspoon salt together in bowl. Pour vinaigrette over fennel. Serve.

ROASTED BUTTERNUT SQUASH WITH APPLE

✔ **WHY THIS RECIPE WORKS** In order to highlight one of our favorite fall vegetables, we used the oven for most of the up-front work. We began by peeling the tough exterior of the squash until there was no yellow skin left. Instead of meticulously dicing the hard squash, we cut the squash in half lengthwise and then crosswise into 1-inch-thick pieces. The large pieces of squash caramelized beautifully, while their interiors remained ultracreamy. For a contrast of flavors, we added an apple during the last 8 minutes of cooking. After removing the squash and apple from the oven, we topped them with a zippy vinaigrette of minced shallot, red wine vinegar, and parsley.

Let's be honest: Does anyone get excited to see butternut squash in the grocery store? I think the reason for the lukewarm reception is that most recipes don't do the squash's earthy flavor justice. Instead of covering it up with creamy sauces or too many spices, I wanted to highlight its inherent sweetness by deeply caramelizing the squash in a hot oven.

After peeling the squash, I tested roasting cubes, chunks, and even halves. I settled on cutting a halved squash crosswise into 1-inch pieces; this gave me largeish pieces that were easy to manage on the plate and had the perfect ratio of flavorful browned exterior to creamy, soft interior. For intense caramelization, I set the oven to 450 degrees and adjusted the oven rack to the lowest position, nearest to the heat source.

To enhance the squash's mild sweetness, I wanted to make a simple vinaigrette to spoon over the roasted squash. I combined minced shallot for its gentle flavor, red wine vinegar for fruity tang, sugar for balance, red pepper flakes for kick, and parsley for freshness.

But the dish needed one more element to make it truly shine. The answer was right next to the squash in the supermarket: apples. Their mix of sweet and tart flavors accented the squash's sweetness without overpowering the dish. I cut one Gala apple (Fuji and Braeburn work great, too) into wedges and added them to the rimmed baking sheet with the squash, but they came out mushy. It was better, I found, to add the apples partway through the squash's cooking time. This way, they stayed relatively firm and provided plenty of complementary flavor. Now I'm excited for squash season.

—NATALIE ESTRADA, *Cook's Country*

ROASTED BUTTERNUT SQUASH WITH APPLE

Roasted Butternut Squash with Apple

SERVES 4 TO 6

When peeling the squash, be sure to also remove the fibrous yellow flesh just beneath the skin. The test kitchen's favorite red wine vinegar is Laurent du Clos Red Wine Vinegar; if you can't find it, we also recommend Pompeian Gourmet Red Wine Vinegar.

VINAIGRETTE

- 3 tablespoons red wine vinegar
- 1 tablespoon sugar
- ⅛ teaspoon table salt
- 3 tablespoons minced shallot
- 2 tablespoons chopped fresh parsley
- 2 tablespoons extra-virgin olive oil
- ¼ teaspoon red pepper flakes

SQUASH AND APPLE

- 1 (2¼- to 2¾-pound) butternut squash
- 3 tablespoons extra-virgin olive oil, divided
- 1 teaspoon table salt
- 1 Gala, Fuji, or Braeburn apple, unpeeled, cored, halved, and cut into ½-inch-thick wedges

1. FOR THE VINAIGRETTE: Stir vinegar, sugar, and salt in small bowl until sugar is dissolved. Stir in shallot, parsley, oil, and pepper flakes; set aside.

2. FOR THE SQUASH AND APPLE: Adjust oven rack to lowest position and heat oven to 450 degrees. Trim ends from squash and peel squash. Halve squash lengthwise and scrape out seeds. Place squash cut side down on cutting board and slice crosswise 1 inch thick.

3. Toss squash, 2 tablespoons oil, and salt together in bowl. Spread squash in even layer on rimmed baking sheet, cut side down. Roast until squash is tender and bottoms are beginning to brown, 14 to 16 minutes.

4. Toss apple and remaining 1 tablespoon oil together in now-empty bowl. Remove sheet from oven. Place apple between squash pieces on sheet, cut side down. (Do not flip squash.) Return sheet to oven and continue to roast until apple is tender and squash is fully browned on bottoms (tops of squash will not be browned), about 8 minutes longer.

5. Using spatula, transfer squash and apple to shallow platter and spread into even layer. Drizzle vinaigrette over top. Serve warm or at room temperature.

VARIATION

Roasted Butternut Squash with Pear and Pancetta
Reduce salt for squash to ½ teaspoon. Substitute 1 teaspoon minced fresh thyme for parsley and 1 Bosc pear for apple. Add 3 ounces pancetta, cut into ½-inch pieces, to sheet with pears in step 4.

ASPARAGUS BAKED IN FOIL

✓ WHY THIS RECIPE WORKS Asparagus roasted in an aluminum foil pouch gently cooks in steam created by its own juices and emerges from the packet tasting purely of itself. What's more, this method makes cleanup a breeze. We found that baking the packet in a 400-degree oven for 18 minutes was ideal for getting snappy yet tender, bright green stalks. Letting the packet rest undisturbed for 5 minutes out of the oven provided a gentle finish that ensured that all the spears were cooked through. Some briny capers, fresh dill, and grated lemon zest made this side dish extra-vibrant.

At my French technique–based culinary school, we learned the benefits of cooking delicate foods such as vegetables, fish fillets, and chicken breasts en papillote, which means enclosed in parchment-paper packets. The food cooks in steam created by its own juices and emerges from the packets tasting clean and deeply of itself—this is a good thing.

An even better thing—an intensely flavored sauce—is made by adding butter and aromatics to the packets. There's some theater at the table, too, as the bundles release a fragrant plume of steam when you cut into them. I fondly remember that the cleanup for these dishes was as simple as throwing away the remnants of the packets—a real boon for an overworked, overtired culinary student.

I wanted to develop a recipe to cook this abundant vegetable using this tried-and-true technique. To start, I washed and trimmed 2 pounds of medium-width asparagus. I started to assemble a packet made with parchment, but folding the paper's edges to hold a crimp was finicky. So I switched to easy-to-fold aluminum foil.

After a few rounds of asparagus that was either too crunchy or too mushy, I landed on baking the packet in a 400-degree oven for 18 minutes. While the timing seemed a little too precise, it was ideal for getting snappy yet tender, bright green stalks. Letting the packet rest undisturbed for 5 minutes out of the oven provided a gentle finish that ensured that all the spears were cooked through. To make this side extra-vibrant, I tossed the asparagus with some briny capers, dill, and lemon juice right before serving it. Perfect.

—MORGAN BOLLING, *Cook's Country*

Asparagus Baked in Foil with Capers and Dill

SERVES 4 TO 6

Look for asparagus spears that are about ½ inch thick at the base.

- 2 **pounds (½-inch-thick) asparagus, trimmed**
- 4 **tablespoons unsalted butter, cut into ½-inch pieces**
- 1 **shallot, minced**
- 2 **garlic cloves, minced**
- 1½ **teaspoons table salt**
- ½ **teaspoon pepper**
- 1 **tablespoon capers, rinsed**
- 1 **tablespoon chopped fresh dill**
- 1 **teaspoon lemon juice**

1. Adjust oven rack to middle position and heat oven to 400 degrees. Line baking sheet with 16 by 12-inch sheet of aluminum foil.

2. Arrange asparagus in center of foil with spears running parallel to short side of sheet, leaving 1½-inch border between bottom of spears and edge of foil. Sprinkle butter, shallot, garlic, salt, and pepper evenly over asparagus.

3. Place second 16 by 12-inch sheet of foil over asparagus. Starting with 1 edge, pinch sheets together and fold foil in toward center by ½ inch. Repeat folding 1 or 2 times to create tight seal. Continue folding remaining 3 edges of foil to create tightly sealed packet.

4. Transfer sheet to oven and cook for 18 minutes. Remove sheet from oven and let asparagus continue to steam in unopened packet 5 minutes longer (if using slightly thicker or thinner asparagus, increase or decrease this resting time by 2 minutes).

5. Using scissors or paring knife, carefully cut open top of packet, allowing steam to escape away from you. Sprinkle asparagus with capers, dill, and lemon juice.

Toss gently with tongs to combine. Using tongs, transfer asparagus to serving platter, then pour sauce from packet over top and serve. (Alternatively, serve directly from packet.)

EXTRA-CRUNCHY ONION RINGS

✔ **WHY THIS RECIPE WORKS** For onion rings with the crunchiest, craggiest crust and fully tender, sweet onions, we double-breaded ½-inch-thick rings in a mixture of buttermilk, seasoned flour, and cornstarch. To streamline the double-breading process and avoid having to bread the onion rings in several batches, we tossed all the buttermilk-soaked onions with the flour mixture in a large paper bag. (A double-bag setup ensured no blowouts or leaking.) To fry our ultracrunchy onion rings in as few batches as possible, we used plenty of oil and stirred gently during frying for even cooking. With the generous amounts of breading, the rings could stay in the hot oil longer, ensuring that the onions themselves were fully cooked and tender. These rings fried up supercrunchy and tasted even better dipped in a tangy, stir-together horseradish sauce.

Sweet, tender onions encased in a beautifully browned, crunchy coating—why would you ever choose fries when onion rings are in play? But onion rings can be a challenge to make at home—the recipes I tried used a ridiculous number of dishes and called for jumping through a lot of hoops, all for mediocre (or worse) results.

The most promising recipe called for dipping sliced onions into rich and tangy buttermilk and then dredging them in seasoned flour; the resulting rings had a coating reminiscent of great fried chicken. But I had to bread them twice (dunk in buttermilk, dredge in flour, re-dunk, and re-dredge) before frying the rings in a single layer in a Dutch oven, which meant frying almost 10 batches! Double-breading was clearly the key to great rings, but I was determined to find an easier way to do it. I sliced a mountain of onions, wiped away the tears, and got cooking.

Two things I discovered early in my testing were that adding both cornstarch and a little baking powder to the flour gave the fried rings extra lightness and crunch.

ULTIMATE EXTRA-CRUNCHY ONION RINGS

And for the frying, I found that with the right amount of oil (3 quarts), I could fry 2 pounds of sliced onions in just three batches. But what about simplifying the breading process?

A colleague gave me a great idea: He wondered if I could use the "shake and bake" paper bag method, which is how some people bread chicken pieces for frying. Eager to try it out, I grabbed a large mixing bowl and poured in a quart of buttermilk, and then doubled up two large paper grocery bags to make sure there was no risk of a bag blowout. I dumped in my flour mix, gave my rings a quick dip in the buttermilk, plopped them all into the bag, and gave the whole thing a vigorous shake. I returned the rings to the buttermilk and then to the bag again to build a thick coating. These rings fried up incredibly crunchy. They're great plain, but they're even better dipped in a flavorful, stir-together horseradish sauce.

—MATTHEW FAIRMAN, *Cook's Country*

Ultimate Extra-Crunchy Onion Rings

SERVES 6 TO 8

Look for large onions (about 1 pound each) for this recipe. Be sure to use a double-bagged large paper shopping bag in step 2. Note that the onions are double-breaded, so don't discard the flour bag after the first shake. Our favorite prepared horseradishes are Woeber's Pure Horseradish and Inglehoffer Cream Style Horseradish (also sold as Beaver Brand Grandma Rose's Hot Cream Horseradish). Our preferred Dijon mustard is Trois Petits Cochons Moutarde de Dijon.

SAUCE

- ½ cup mayonnaise
- 2 tablespoons prepared horseradish
- 2 tablespoons Dijon mustard
- ¼ teaspoon cayenne pepper
- ¼ teaspoon pepper

ONION RINGS

- 4 cups buttermilk
- 4 cups all-purpose flour
- ½ cup cornstarch
- 2 tablespoons Lawry's Seasoned Salt
- 2 tablespoons baking powder
- 2 teaspoons pepper
- ½ teaspoon table salt
- 2 large onions (1 pound each), peeled
- 3 quarts peanut or vegetable oil for frying

1. FOR THE SAUCE: Whisk all ingredients together in bowl; set aside.

2. FOR THE ONION RINGS: Adjust oven rack to middle position and heat oven to 200 degrees. Add buttermilk to large bowl. Combine flour, cornstarch, seasoned salt, baking powder, pepper, and salt in second large bowl. Transfer flour mixture to double-bagged large paper shopping bag. Slice onions crosswise into ½-inch-thick rounds. Reserve onion slices smaller than 2 inches in diameter for another use.

3. Separate remaining onion rounds into rings. Toss one-third of onion rings in buttermilk to thoroughly coat. Shake off excess buttermilk and transfer onion rings to flour mixture in bag. Repeat with remaining onion rings in 2 batches. Roll top of bag to seal and shake vigorously to coat onion rings in flour mixture. Remove onion rings from bag, shaking off excess flour mixture, and transfer to rimmed baking sheet.

4. Transfer one-third of onion rings back to buttermilk and toss to thoroughly coat. Shake off excess buttermilk and transfer onion rings back to flour mixture in bag. Repeat with remaining onion rings in 2 batches. Roll top of bag to seal and shake vigorously to coat onion rings in flour mixture. Pour contents of bag onto sheet. Separate any onion rings that stick together.

5. Line second rimmed baking sheet with triple layer of paper towels. Add oil to large Dutch oven until it measures about 2 inches deep and heat over medium-high heat to 375 degrees.

6. Add one-third of onion rings to hot oil and fry, without stirring, until breading is just set, 30 to 60 seconds. Stir gently with tongs or spider skimmer and continue to fry until dark golden brown, 3 to 5 minutes longer, flipping onion rings occasionally and separating any that stick together. Adjust burner, if necessary, to maintain oil temperature between 325 and 375 degrees. Transfer fried onion rings to paper towel–lined sheet and place in oven to keep warm.

7. Return oil to 375 degrees and repeat with remaining onion rings in 2 batches. Serve onion rings with sauce.

SWEET POTATO CRUNCH

✓ WHY THIS RECIPE WORKS Inspired by a family recipe, we were after a creamy sweet potato casserole topped with a crunchy, salty-sweet topping. Roasting the sweet potatoes rather than boiling or steaming them concentrated their sweet potato flavor. A splash of orange liqueur and a little brown sugar made them holiday-worthy. A simple stir-together streusel made with flour, brown sugar, salt, and melted butter tasted great and provided a contrasting crunch on top of the creamy sweet potatoes. A pinch of cayenne added to the topping carried a hint of heat.

I'm always thankful for my mom's sweet potatoes. She roasts the orange spuds in their jackets until they wrinkle and start to ooze a sort of natural sweet potato caramel, and then she removes the peels and whips the soft flesh in a stand mixer with a splash of orange liqueur for a citrusy kick. There is no marshmallow topping here; instead, my mother crowns the whipped potatoes with a mixture of crushed oatmeal cookies and melted butter. It may sound a little odd—and it is—but the result is a full-flavored, salty-sweet dish that is always in high demand at our holiday table.

My mom, who got the recipe from her mom, has tweaked the recipe to fit her tastes over the years, and I think it's nearly perfect as is. But just because there's one great version doesn't mean there can't be another. In the spirit of my mom's creativity, I wanted to create a recipe inspired by her version but with my own personal twist.

I started with 4 pounds of sweet potatoes (enough for a Thanksgiving crowd) and a package of oatmeal cookies. For the sake of due diligence, I tried boiling and steaming the sweet potatoes, but roasting was by far the best method; it produced concentrated—not diluted—sweet potato flavor. I also loved how the roasting sweet potatoes made the whole test kitchen smell like Thanksgiving.

As for the whipping, did I really need to haul out the stand mixer? In a word, no: A good romp with a potato masher gave the potatoes a silky texture without the need for a mixer. My tasters loved the orange liqueur, especially when I added grated orange zest and a little brown sugar to enhance it. The cookie topping was great, but when I tested it with different brands of oatmeal cookies, the results were wildly different—and inconsistency just won't do in the test kitchen.

Baking my own cookies to crumble was an option but seemed like too much work here. Instead, I pivoted to another sweet, crunchy topping: an easy stir-together streusel made with flour, brown sugar, and melted butter. The streusel tasted great and provided a proper contrasting crunch on top of the creamy sweet potatoes. A pinch of cayenne added to this topping carried a hint of heat and a reminder that this sweet dish had savory roots, too.

Since my mom reads *Cook's Country*, it's important for me to come out and say I know that no sweet potatoes will ever be as good as the ones she makes for me. So to differentiate our two recipes, I decided to give my version another name: Sweet Potato Crunch. I'm thankful for the many things I've learned from my mom—including how to make some truly amazing sweet potatoes.

—MORGAN BOLLING, *Cook's Country*

NOTES FROM THE TEST KITCHEN

SWEET POTATOES VERSUS YAMS
In the United States, sweet potatoes are often confused with yams. Although they are similar in shape, these two tubers are not closely related botanically. Yams, which are a staple food in parts of Asia, Africa, Central America, South America, and the West Indies, belong to the genus *Dioscorea* and typically have white flesh and sometimes a rough, shaggy exterior. Sweet potatoes, more popular in the United States, belong to the genus *Ipomoea* and usually have smoother skins and orange flesh.

SWEET
POTATO

YAM

Sweet Potato Crunch

SERVES 8

Buy potatoes of similar size and shape, no more than 1 pound each, so they cook at the same rate. Orange juice can be substituted for the Grand Marnier, if you prefer.

SWEET POTATOES

- 4 pounds sweet potatoes, unpeeled
- 4 tablespoons unsalted butter, melted
- 2 tablespoons Grand Marnier
- 1 tablespoon packed light brown sugar
- 1¼ teaspoons table salt
- 1 teaspoon grated orange zest

TOPPING

- ⅔ cup all-purpose flour
- ⅓ cup packed light brown sugar
- ¼ teaspoon table salt
- ⅛ teaspoon cayenne pepper
- 4 tablespoons unsalted butter, melted

1. FOR THE SWEET POTATOES: Adjust oven rack to upper-middle position and heat oven to 400 degrees. Line rimmed baking sheet with aluminum foil. Poke potatoes several times with paring knife and space evenly on prepared sheet. Bake until potatoes are very tender and can be easily squeezed with tongs, 1¼ to 1½ hours. Let potatoes sit until cool enough to handle, at least 20 minutes.

2. Remove and discard potato peels. Transfer potato flesh to large bowl and mash with potato masher until smooth. Stir in melted butter, Grand Marnier, sugar, salt, and orange zest. Transfer potato mixture to 8-inch square baking dish and spread into even layer with rubber spatula.

3. FOR THE TOPPING: Whisk flour, brown sugar, salt, and cayenne in bowl until fully combined. Stir in melted butter until mixture forms clumps. Break into pea-size pieces and distribute evenly over sweet potato mixture.

4. Bake until topping is fragrant and darkened slightly in color and potatoes are hot, 25 to 30 minutes. Let cool for 25 minutes before serving.

TO MAKE AHEAD: At end of step 2, let sweet potato mixture cool completely. Cover dish with aluminum foil and refrigerate for up to 24 hours. When ready to serve, bake, covered, for 15 minutes. Remove from oven, uncover, and continue with step 3.

SPANISH POTATOES WITH OLIVE OIL

✔ WHY THIS RECIPE WORKS Patatas panaderas, a simple yet luxurious dish of thinly sliced potatoes accented with onions and garlic and baked in white wine and plenty of olive oil, is little known outside of Spain, but it deserves a place among the iconic potato dishes of Europe. In our version, we covered the potatoes with a tight foil lid so that the potatoes could soften. We withheld the wine for the first 40 minutes of cooking to prevent its acid from interfering with the softening of the potatoes. Loosening the foil for the last 20 minutes allowed excess moisture to evaporate while keeping the potatoes moist, blond, and tender throughout.

It's widely accepted culinary arithmetic: Potatoes plus oil plus heat equals browned crispness. Think hash browns, french fries, and roasted potatoes. But Spanish cooks make a potato dish that defies standard mathematics; their patatas panaderas (translation: "bakers' potatoes") add up to meltingly tender potatoes with nary a hint of browning. (That's a good thing—I'll explain.)

It comes together easily: Thin slices of peeled potato are scattered with onions and garlic, bathed in high-quality extra-virgin olive oil and sometimes white wine, and then piled into a pan and baked. The oil adds richness without making the dish, well, oily, and the lack of browning means that the earthiness of the potatoes comes through loud and clear.

I peeled and thinly sliced 2½ pounds of Yukon Gold potatoes—their moderately waxy, buttery flesh makes them the closest thing we have to the yellow Monalisa and Álava varieties commonly used for this dish in Spain—and then coated the slices in ¼ cup of good extra-virgin olive oil. I stirred in plenty of salt and pepper, a thinly sliced onion, and some minced garlic and then transferred the mixture to a 13 by 9-inch baking dish that I covered tightly with aluminum foil and slid into a 400-degree oven. After an hour, the potatoes were beautifully tender but a touch dry. Bumping up the oil to ⅓ cup made the dish luxuriously rich and moist.

I was eager to see if a bit of wine would complement the simple seasonings, so I stirred ½ cup of a dry white wine into the next batch. But when I lifted the foil after an hour, the potatoes were too firm. As I looked over the recipes I found in my research, I noticed a correlation: Those with wine called for parcooking the potatoes before adding the wine. After reading some scientific literature on the topic, it all made sense: The problem was the wine—or, more specifically, the acid in the wine, which can hinder the softening of potatoes.

I really wanted to keep the wine, and happily, parcooking wouldn't necessarily mean pulling out a saucepan. Some recipes simply withheld the wine until the potatoes had softened under their foil cover, so I tried that. After 40 minutes, I poured the wine over the tender potatoes and left the dish uncovered for the remaining 20 minutes of cooking so that the alcohol could evaporate a bit, leaving the wine's faint sweet-tart flavor behind.

Unfortunately, these potatoes had a leathery brown top that interfered with the lush-and-tender-throughout effect I was going for. To allow the excess moisture to evaporate while discouraging browning, I loosely covered the dish but left the sides open so that the vapor could escape. I also lowered the oven temperature to a more moderate 350 degrees. These changes summed up to a winning version of patatas panaderas: blond all over, velvety, and full of flavor.

—ANDREA GEARY, *Cook's Illustrated*

Spanish Potatoes with Olive Oil and Wine (Patatas Panaderas)

SERVES 6

For the best results, be sure to use a fresh, high-quality extra-virgin olive oil here. Our favorite supermarket products are Bertolli Extra Virgin Olive Oil, Original, Rich Taste and California Olive Ranch Destination Series Everyday Extra Virgin Olive Oil. We developed this recipe using Diamond Crystal kosher salt; if using Morton kosher salt, decrease the amount to 2⅝ teaspoons. To make peeling and slicing easier, choose larger potatoes. These potatoes make an excellent accompaniment to roasted fish or pork.

- 2½ **pounds Yukon Gold potatoes, peeled and sliced crosswise ¼ inch thick**
- ⅓ **cup extra-virgin olive oil**
- 3½ **teaspoons kosher salt**
- ¼ **teaspoon pepper**
- 1 **onion, halved and sliced thin**
- 2 **garlic cloves, minced**
- ½ **cup dry white wine**

1. Adjust oven rack to middle position and heat oven to 400 degrees. Stir potatoes and oil in large bowl until potatoes are evenly coated. Stir in salt and pepper until well distributed. Stir in onion and garlic. Transfer potato mixture to 13 by 9-inch baking dish and spread into even layer. Cover tightly with aluminum foil and bake until potatoes can be easily pierced with tip of paring knife, about 40 minutes. Reduce oven temperature to 350 degrees.

2. Carefully remove foil and set aside. Pour wine evenly over potatoes. Lightly place reserved foil on top of dish, leaving sides open so moisture can escape, and return dish to oven. Bake until wine has evaporated or been absorbed (there will still be some oil bubbling around edges of dish), about 20 minutes. Carefully remove foil. Let cool for 10 minutes and serve.

ROASTED FINGERLING POTATOES

✔ **WHY THIS RECIPE WORKS** For creamy and tender roasted fingerling potatoes, we tossed the potatoes with oil and arranged them in a 13 by 9-inch metal baking pan, where they fit snugly in a single layer. Covering the pan with foil to start helped the potatoes steam instead of drying out in the hot oven. Removing the foil and letting the potatoes finish roasting uncovered allowed them to brown for more flavor. Shaking the pan halfway through roasting ensured that the browning was even. Chopping the thyme and sage with salt and then tossing the hot potatoes with the mixture helped us disperse all three ingredients more evenly over the potatoes.

Fingerling potatoes are often confused with new potatoes due to their small size and thin, tender skin. However, fingerlings are fully mature potatoes with an earthy nuttiness. Roasting is a great way to enhance their flavor with browning, and their diminutive size means they can be cooked whole. The only problem is that they can vary widely in shape (from crescent-like to knobby) and length (from 1 inch to nearly 5 inches). I wanted to see if I could get assorted sizes to cook at the same rate.

SPANISH POTATOES WITH OLIVE OIL AND WINE (PATATAS PANADERAS)

I started by tossing 2 pounds of fingerlings with salt and a few tablespoons of vegetable oil, spreading them on a rimmed baking sheet, and placing the sheet in a 450-degree oven. Thirty minutes later, the potatoes had deep patches of browning and the smaller ones were cooked through, but in general the skins were tough, and some of the larger spuds were still firm in the center. At such high heat, the exteriors were drying out before the larger potatoes had a chance to cook through. In addition, the potatoes weren't covering the entire baking sheet, allowing the residual oil on the sheet's exposed surface to polymerize in the hot oven—and polymerized oil is very difficult to clean. Instead, I moved the fingerlings to a 13 by 9-inch metal baking pan, where they fit snugly in a single layer.

I knew that crowding the potatoes would cause them to steam a bit, but that would be a good thing, helping them cook through without turning leathery. In fact, I covered the pan with aluminum foil to trap the steam. After 15 minutes, the tip of a knife easily pierced the largest potato, so I removed the foil and continued to roast the fingerlings so the skins could take on some color, shaking the pan a few times to ensure that they browned evenly.

About 20 minutes later, I could see that this approach worked: Both the large and small spuds were tender and creamy. Most varieties of fingerlings are waxy, and waxy potatoes hold their moisture better than, say, floury russets, so it's hard to dry them out. The extra steam from the larger potatoes also helped the smaller ones cook through.

To dress up my perfectly roasted fingerlings, I coated them with seasonings that would stick to their skins. For a simple yet classic combination, I tossed chopped thyme and sage leaves with the roasted potatoes in a bowl, where their heady fragrances wafted up as they hit the hot spuds.

But it was tricky to evenly disperse the small amount of herbs. For the next batch, I held off on adding salt prior to roasting the potatoes and instead added it to the herbs before I minced them. The increased volume made the ingredients easier to distribute evenly.

Two more potent toppings for my sophisticated, slender spuds included a zippy mix of lemon zest, garlic, and parsley and a salty-sharp take on cacio e pepe with Pecorino Romano and black pepper.

—ANNIE PETITO, *Cook's Illustrated*

Roasted Fingerling Potatoes with Mixed Herbs

SERVES 4

If using a glass or ceramic baking dish, increase the roasting time in step 1 by 5 minutes. This recipe can easily be doubled; roast the potatoes in two 13 by 9-inch baking pans on the same oven rack.

- 2 **pounds fingerling potatoes, unpeeled**
- 3 **tablespoons vegetable oil**
- 2 **teaspoons chopped fresh thyme**
- 2 **teaspoons chopped fresh sage**
- ½ **teaspoon table salt**

1. Adjust oven rack to middle position and heat oven to 450 degrees. In 13 by 9-inch baking pan, toss potatoes with oil until evenly coated. Arrange potatoes in even layer. Cover pan tightly with aluminum foil. Transfer pan to oven and roast for 15 minutes.

2. Carefully remove foil (steam will escape). Shake pan and continue to roast, uncovered, until potatoes are spotty brown and tender and largest potato can be pierced easily with tip of paring knife, about 20 minutes longer, shaking pan halfway through roasting.

3. While potatoes roast, chop thyme, sage, and salt until finely minced and well combined. Transfer potatoes and any oil to bowl and toss with herb mixture until evenly coated. Transfer potatoes to platter. Let cool for 5 minutes before serving.

NOTES FROM THE TEST KITCHEN

HOW TO ACHIEVE EVEN SEASONING

Instead of adding salt to the fingerlings prior to roasting, we combine it with herbs and then mince the mixture to create an herb-salt blend, which we toss the potatoes in after roasting. The increased volume makes it easier to evenly coat the roasted potatoes with the herbs.

**Roasted Fingerling Potatoes with
Parsley, Lemon, and Garlic**

Substitute 2 tablespoons chopped fresh parsley, 2 teaspoons grated lemon zest, and 1 minced garlic clove for thyme and sage.

**Roasted Fingerling Potatoes with
Pecorino and Black Pepper**

Omit thyme and sage. Once cooked potatoes have been transferred to bowl in step 3, toss with 2 tablespoons grated Pecorino Romano, 2 teaspoons pepper, and salt. Sprinkle potatoes with another 2 tablespoons grated Pecorino before serving.

POTATO TART

✔ **WHY THIS RECIPE WORKS** To prevent the potatoes from sliding around, we sliced them extra-thin and folded them into a mixture of softened cream cheese, Dijon mustard, thinly sliced shallot, and Parmesan cheese. A bit of rosemary served as the perfect savory pairing for the Parmesan. A light brush of egg white on the pastry dough before baking gave us a golden crust and acted as glue for holding a bit more cheese, making the crust just as savory as the filling.

A rustic tart can serve as an eye-catching dessert, but with the right filling, a tart can also be a handsomely nontraditional savory side dish. I wanted to create a recipe for a tart packed with potatoes and nutty Parmesan cheese.

The good news was that the test kitchen has a fantastic recipe for a buttery, crisp, easy-to-work-with tart dough that I could use as a reliable starting point. So I began my testing by filling batches of that dough with different kinds of potatoes (russet, Yukon Gold, and red) in different cuts (chunks, wedges, and thin rounds). I tossed the spuds with grated Parmesan and baked the tarts for a taste test.

My tasters liked the texture of russets sliced into thin rounds the best. When stacked up inside the dough, the sliced russets compacted into a pleasantly cohesive layer that cooked through evenly with no dry or underdone spots (problems that plagued the potatoes cut into chunks and wedges).

But something was missing. The Parmesan provided nice background flavor, but the tart needed a creamy element for richness and cohesion. I tried adding a little cream to the raw potatoes, but the filling became too liquid-y and made the dough soggy.

If I wanted something creamy and cheesy, why not try cream cheese? Plain cream cheese was a little, well, plain. I tried gussying it up and landed on a combination of an egg yolk for stability and richness, Parmesan cheese for nuttiness, Dijon mustard for its sharp tang, rosemary for its piney punch, and sliced shallot for a savory-sweet base flavor. By tossing the sliced potatoes with this potent, creamy mixture, I ensured that every bite was packed with flavor. A sprinkling of more Parmesan around the pastry's edge was the final flourish that took this rustic tart over the top.

—ALLI BERKEY, *Cook's Country*

Potato and Parmesan Tart

SERVES 6 TO 8

A mandoline makes quick work of evenly slicing the potatoes. We use russet potatoes for their starchiness here, but you can substitute Yukon Gold potatoes.

- 1½ cups (7½ ounces) all-purpose flour
- 1 teaspoon table salt, divided
- 10 tablespoons unsalted butter, cut into ½-inch pieces and chilled
- 6–7 tablespoons ice water
- 4 ounces cream cheese
- 2 ounces Parmesan cheese, grated (1 cup), divided
- 2 tablespoons extra-virgin olive oil
- 2 teaspoons Dijon mustard
- 1½ teaspoons minced fresh rosemary, divided
- ¼ teaspoon pepper
- 1 large egg, separated
- 1 pound russet potatoes, peeled and sliced ⅛ inch thick
- 1 shallot, sliced thin

1. Process flour and ½ teaspoon salt in food processor until combined, about 3 seconds. Scatter butter over top and pulse until mixture resembles coarse crumbs, about 10 pulses. Add 6 tablespoons ice water and process until almost no dry flour remains, about 10 seconds, scraping down sides of bowl after 5 seconds. Add up to 1 additional tablespoon ice water if dough doesn't come together.

CAST IRON POTATO KUGEL

2. Turn out dough onto lightly floured counter, form into 4-inch square, wrap tightly in plastic wrap, and refrigerate for 1 hour. (Wrapped dough can be refrigerated for up to 2 days or frozen for up to 1 month.)

3. Adjust oven rack to lower-middle position and heat oven to 375 degrees. Line rimmed baking sheet with parchment paper. Let chilled dough sit on counter to soften slightly before rolling, about 10 minutes. Roll dough into 14 by 11-inch rectangle on lightly floured counter, then transfer to prepared sheet.

4. Microwave cream cheese in large bowl until softened, 20 to 30 seconds. Whisk in ½ cup Parmesan, oil, mustard, 1 teaspoon rosemary, pepper, and remaining ½ teaspoon salt until combined, about 20 seconds. Whisk in egg yolk. Add potatoes and shallot to cream cheese mixture and stir to thoroughly coat potatoes.

5. Transfer filling to center of dough. Press filling into even layer, leaving 2-inch border on all sides. Sprinkle 6 tablespoons Parmesan and remaining ½ teaspoon rosemary over filling.

6. Grasp 1 long side of dough and fold about 1½ inches over filling. Repeat with opposing long side. Fold in short sides of dough, overlapping corners of dough to secure. Lightly beat egg white and brush over folded crust (you won't need it all). Sprinkle remaining 2 tablespoons Parmesan over crust.

7. Bake until crust and filling are golden brown and potatoes meet little resistance when poked with fork, about 45 minutes. Transfer sheet to wire rack and let tart cool for 10 minutes. Using metal spatula, loosen tart from parchment and carefully slide onto wire rack; let cool until just warm, about 20 minutes. Cut into slices and serve warm.

VARIATION

Potato and Blue Cheese Tart

Reduce Parmesan to ½ cup. Use ¼ cup in cream cheese mixture in step 4, 2 tablespoons to sprinkle over potatoes in step 5, and 2 tablespoons to sprinkle over folded crust in step 6. Add ¼ cup crumbled blue cheese to cream cheese mixture in step 4. Sprinkle additional ¼ cup crumbled blue cheese over potato mixture in step 5.

CAST IRON POTATO KUGEL

✔ **WHY THIS RECIPE WORKS** We were after an easy yet supersavory potato dish that was crisp on the outside but had a tender, fluffy interior. We used shredded russet potatoes for their starchiness and treated them with a saltwater solution to keep them from oxidizing to an unappetizing gray tinge. We flavored the spuds with sautéed onions and a generous amount of rendered chicken fat (schmaltz) and added eggs to bind it all together. Using a preheated cast-iron skillet gave us an extra-crispy edge.

Potato kugel, savory cousin to the Jewish home-style favorite noodle kugel, sounds so promising: shredded potatoes mixed with onion, eggs, and fat (often schmaltz, rendered chicken fat) and baked until crisp on the outside and fluffy on the inside. It's like one giant, sliceable latke.

But the recipes I tried were disappointing. Some kugels were eggy and rubbery, some were slimy, and all were overpowered by the sour tang of raw onion. I learned some things right off the bat: We preferred cooked onion to raw, savory schmaltz was our fat of choice, and squeezing the shredded potatoes dry reduced slipperiness.

Armed with this knowledge, I took a stab at an improved kugel. I softened 2 cups of finely chopped onions with a sizable dollop of schmaltz and used the food processor to quickly shred 3 pounds of peeled potatoes (starchy russets since a fluffy interior was the goal). I wrung the potatoes dry with a clean dish towel and mixed them together with the onions, beaten eggs, and generous amounts of salt and pepper. I spread this mixture in a casserole dish I had brushed with additional schmaltz and baked it until tender.

The resulting kugel had great flavor, and the interior texture was improved as well: fluffy yet still creamy. But the exterior was a tad too soft, and the potatoes had an unattractive gray cast.

To encourage more flavorful crusty browning at the edges, I made the next batch in a preheated cast-iron skillet. This worked beautifully. As for potato oxidation, I tried a technique we've used before in the test kitchen and tossed the shreds in a saltwater solution (since salt inhibits the enzyme responsible for discoloration). This made a marked difference, giving my next kugel a creamy white hue throughout.

Topped with a shower of minced chives, this kugel is as welcome on your springtime holiday table as it is next to your weeknight roast chicken.

—JESSICA RUDOLPH, *Cook's Country*

Cast Iron Potato Kugel

SERVES 8

You can find rendered chicken fat (schmaltz) in the frozen foods section of larger supermarkets. If you can't find it, you can substitute extra-virgin olive oil. We prefer using the shredding disk of a food processor to shred the potatoes, but you can also use the large holes of a box grater. Making the kugel in a seasoned cast-iron skillet ensures that it will have a crispy crust, but if you don't have one, you can use an ovensafe 10-inch nonstick skillet. Serve with sour cream, if desired.

- 6 tablespoons rendered chicken fat (schmaltz), divided
- 2 cups finely chopped onions
- ¾ teaspoon table salt, plus salt for tossing potatoes
- 3 pounds russet potatoes, unpeeled
- 4 large eggs
- 1¼ teaspoons pepper
- 1 tablespoon minced fresh chives

1. Adjust oven rack to upper-middle position and heat oven to 425 degrees. Heat 2 tablespoons chicken fat in 10-inch cast iron skillet over medium-high heat until shimmering. Add onions and cook, stirring occasionally, until softened, about 3 minutes. Transfer to bowl and set aside.

2. Whisk 2 cups water and 2 tablespoons salt in large bowl until salt is dissolved. Fit food processor with shredding disk. Peel potatoes and halve or quarter lengthwise as needed to fit through processor feed tube. Shred potatoes. Transfer potatoes to salt water and toss briefly to coat.

3. Drain potatoes in colander. Place one-quarter of shredded potatoes in center of clean dish towel. Gather ends of towel and twist tightly to wring out excess moisture from potatoes. Transfer dried potatoes to now-empty

bowl. Repeat 3 more times with remaining potatoes. Stir eggs, pepper, onions, and remaining ¾ teaspoon salt into potatoes until thoroughly combined.

4. Heat remaining ¼ cup chicken fat in now-empty skillet over medium-high heat until just smoking. Add potato mixture to skillet and distribute into even layer but do not press down or smooth top. Cook for 1 minute to set bottom.

5. Transfer to oven and bake until kugel is lightly browned on top, about 45 minutes. Let cool for 5 minutes. Cut into wedges in skillet. Sprinkle with chives and serve.

LOUISIANA-STYLE CORNBREAD DRESSING

✓ **WHY THIS RECIPE WORKS** For a bold Cajun take on one of our favorite Thanksgiving sides, we looked to wed classic Louisiana flavors with a simple, Southern-style cornbread dressing, known for its buttery top and almost creamy interior. We began by making a simple cornbread using equal parts cornmeal and flour, a touch of sugar, melted butter, eggs, and milk. While the cornbread baked, we sautéed a mix of chopped onions, green bell peppers, and celery along with smoky, spicy andouille sausage and bacon. After finishing the flavorful sauté with a tablespoon of Tony Chachere's Original Creole Seasoning and a couple cloves of minced garlic, we mixed it with our crumbled, warm cornbread and added just enough eggs and savory chicken broth to achieve a cohesive, set dressing. A final brush of melted butter before baking gave the dressing a rich, crisp, golden top.

Southern cornbread dressing has a crisp, buttery top and a moist, almost creamy interior. My wife's family in Louisiana makes one studded with smoky andouille sausage and bacon; it balances a Cajun-style spicy kick with sweet corn flavor. I set out to test my way to a no-fuss recipe for this flavorful side.

To start, I knew that store-bought cornbread was out—the quality is too inconsistent. Instead, I made my own, combining equal parts cornmeal and flour, a touch of sugar, melted butter, eggs, and milk. While some Southerners might scoff at the inclusion of flour, it adds a needed sturdiness to cornbread dressing. Some dressing recipes call for letting the cornbread go stale for the best results, but side-by-side tests showed that staling wasn't necessary.

To build a rich Louisiana flavor profile, I diced up a big link of bold andouille sausage and four slices of bacon. I added the meat to a skillet, along with an ample amount of onion, celery, and green bell pepper. Once the vegetables had softened, I bloomed a tablespoon of Creole seasoning in the rendered pork fat.

As soon as my cornbread was ready, I turned it out onto a baking sheet and broke it up with two forks. I then tossed it with the sausage and vegetables, fresh parsley, 3 cups of savory chicken broth, 1 cup of milk, and three beaten eggs. This ratio of milk and eggs to broth was just right to ensure a cohesive, set dressing that didn't become soggy. I put everything back into the casserole dish I used to bake my cornbread and, just before baking, I brushed the top with melted butter and used a spatula to create ridges on the surface. This resulted in a buttery, craggy top that added toasty flavor and crunchy texture. Delicious.

—MATTHEW FAIRMAN, *Cook's Country*

Louisiana-Style Cornbread Dressing
SERVES 10 TO 12

We developed this recipe with Quaker Yellow Cornmeal.

CORNBREAD

- 1½ cups (7½ ounces) all-purpose flour
- 1½ cups (7½ ounces) cornmeal
- 3 tablespoons sugar
- 1 tablespoon baking powder
- 1 teaspoon table salt
- 1¾ cups whole milk
- 3 large eggs
- 6 tablespoons unsalted butter, melted

DRESSING

- 2 tablespoons unsalted butter, plus 4 tablespoons unsalted butter, melted
- 12 ounces andouille sausage, cut into ¼-inch pieces
- 2 onions, chopped
- 2 green bell peppers, stemmed, seeded, and chopped
- 2 celery ribs, chopped
- 4 slices bacon, cut into ¼-inch pieces

- 1 tablespoon Tony Chachere's Original Creole Seasoning
- 2 garlic cloves, minced
- 3 cups chicken broth
- 1 cup whole milk
- 3 large eggs, lightly beaten
- ¾ cup chopped fresh parsley
- ½ teaspoon pepper

1. FOR THE CORNBREAD: Adjust oven rack to middle position and heat oven to 425 degrees. Spray 13 by 9-inch baking dish with vegetable oil spray.

2. Whisk flour, cornmeal, sugar, baking powder, and salt together in large bowl. Whisk milk, eggs, and melted butter together in second bowl. Whisk milk mixture into flour mixture until just combined. Transfer batter to prepared dish. Bake until cornbread is golden brown and toothpick inserted in center comes out clean, about 20 minutes.

3. FOR THE DRESSING: While cornbread bakes, melt 2 tablespoons butter in 12-inch nonstick skillet over medium-high heat. Add andouille, onions, bell peppers, celery, and bacon to skillet and cook until vegetables are softened, about 8 minutes. Add Creole seasoning and garlic and cook until fragrant, about 1 minute. Transfer sausage mixture to large bowl.

4. Turn out hot cornbread onto rimmed baking sheet and break into small pieces with two forks. (Cooled, crumbled cornbread can be transferred to zipper-lock bag and stored at room temperature for up to 24 hours.)

5. Transfer crumbled cornbread to bowl with sausage mixture. Add broth, milk, eggs, parsley, and pepper and stir to combine. Transfer dressing to now-empty dish and spread into even layer (do not pack down). Using side of rubber spatula or wooden spoon, create ridges about ½ inch apart on top of dressing.

6. Brush top of dressing with melted butter. Bake until browned and crisped on top and heated through, about 35 minutes. Let cool for 10 minutes and serve.

TO MAKE AHEAD: At end of step 5, let dressing cool completely (if using hot cornbread). Cover baking dish with plastic wrap and refrigerate for up to 24 hours or wrap in additional layer of aluminum foil and freeze for up to 1 month. To serve, thaw overnight in refrigerator if frozen. Proceed with step 6, extending baking time by 15 minutes and covering with foil for final 10 minutes of cooking if top begins to get too dark.

HOT BUTTERED LOBSTER ROLLS

PASTA, PIZZA, SANDWICHES, AND MORE

PASTITSIO

✔ **WHY THIS RECIPE WORKS** Our more efficient approach to pastitsio started with treating the ground beef with baking soda before cooking, which altered its chemistry and made it better able to hold on to moisture. We also skipped the usual browning steps to avoid toughening the meat's exterior. Cinnamon, oregano, dried mint, and paprika made the flavor profile distinctly Greek. A minimal amount of red wine plus lots of tomato paste (thinned with water) added brightness and savoriness. We further streamlined the method by parcooking the ziti (the closest substitute for authentic Greek "number 2" macaroni) in the hot béchamel; doing so hydrated the pasta just enough to ensure that it would be fully cooked after baking, and the pasta's starches helped thicken the béchamel. We then thickened the rest of the béchamel by whisking in cheese and an egg until it was spreadable. Sprinkling more cheese over the top encouraged the surface to brown.

Pastitsio is culinary pastiche in the most literal sense. It's a Greek meat and macaroni casserole inspired by similar Italian compositions such as baked ziti and lasagna ("pasticcio," the root of both "pastitsio" and "pastiche," is an old Italian term for a pie containing meat and pasta); the seasonings are Hellenic; and it's lavished with French béchamel. The dish is an alloy of language and cuisine.

What makes pastitsio stand out from its Italian analogues is most obvious when you look at a slice of it: Instead of being jumbled together or loosely stacked, the casserole's components are impressively stratified. The base layer typically features rows of wide-bore tubular pasta held together with a thin mortar of cheese and béchamel. Above that sits a band of tightly bound, robustly spiced ground meat and tomato sauce. Topping it all off is a plush blanket of cheesy, browned béchamel. A well-constructed version holds together so that in each forkful, the layers remain separate but are experienced together.

It's classic comfort fare and one of my favorite things to order at a Greek diner—the type of dish you find at the center of many Greek family meals. But since there's no hiding gluey or mushy noodles, dull or dry meat sauce, or grainy béchamel, the best versions take time and care to make. Streamlining the whole package without sacrificing its character was my goal, so I took on the challenge layer by layer.

A layer of neatly aligned tubular pasta bound by creamy, cheesy béchamel sauce is a hallmark of pastitsio; each slice should look like it contains rows of stacked pipes. Traditional recipes call for "number 2" macaroni: long tubes that look like wide bucatini (in prominent Greek brands, the "2" refers to this shape of noodle). I found that ziti, the most widely available match in terms of diameter, was actually easier to work with; the stubby Italian tubes fell into parallel orientation with almost no effort.

When it came to getting the texture of the pasta right, parcooking the pasta to just shy of al dente before assembling and baking was key. Cooked any less, the pasta tasted raw, while fully soft pasta collapsed and ruined the "stacked pipes" visual.

In many cuisines, béchamel—the classic white sauce made by thickening milk with a roux—is a background component with a subtle presence. It holds together the layers in lasagna, anchors the ham and Gruyère in a croque monsieur, and binds up the elbows in macaroni and cheese. But in pastitsio, béchamel gets its chance in the spotlight. The basic sauce is typically thickened with cheese and sometimes egg and then spread over the casserole into a distinct layer that bakes up custardy and browns deeply. (A portion of it also binds up the pasta layer.)

I thickened the béchamel in two stages: First, I used it to parcook the pasta, which leached starch that tightened up the sauce just enough to hold the ziti together. Then I strained out the pasta and thickened the sauce further by whisking in cheese and an egg. Now the sauce was spreadable. A sprinkling of more cheese over the top encouraged the surface to brown.

The most obvious difference between the meat sauce in pastitsio and a version you might find in an Italian pasta dish is the seasoning. Cinnamon and oregano are traditional flavors, and dried mint and paprika further distance it from anything in the Italian canon.

The sauce should be tight and concentrated and the ground beef tender—both reasons that most recipes call for a long, slow simmer. But I found a faster way to achieve both goals. Briefly treating 93 percent lean ground beef (which has enough fat to stay supple without making the sauce greasy) with baking soda before cooking altered the meat's chemistry so that it was better able to hold on to moisture, and skipping the usual browning step avoided toughening its exterior. I had tender meat in about half the original time.

PASTITSIO

Minimizing the amount of liquid also expedited cooking. One-quarter cup of red wine added brightness, and instead of reducing tomato sauce, I thinned out ultraconcentrated tomato paste with just enough water to make the finished sauce appropriately fluid.

—ANDREW JANJIGIAN, *Cook's Illustrated*

Pastitsio

SERVES 6

Don't use ground beef that's less than 93 percent lean or the dish will be greasy. We like the richness of whole milk for this dish, but you can substitute 2 percent low-fat milk, if desired. Do not use skim milk. Kasseri is a semifirm sheep's-milk cheese from Greece. If it's unavailable, substitute a mixture of 1½ ounces (¾ cup) grated Pecorino Romano and 3 ounces (¾ cup) shredded Provolone, adding ½ cup to the ziti in step 4, ½ cup to the béchamel, and the remaining ½ cup to the top of the béchamel. We strongly recommend using a spider skimmer to transfer the pasta to the baking dish, but a slotted spoon will work. To accommodate all the components, use a baking dish that is at least 2¼ inches tall.

MEAT SAUCE

- ¾ teaspoon table salt
- ¼ teaspoon baking soda
- 1 tablespoon plus ½ cup water, divided
- 8 ounces 93 percent lean ground beef
- 1 tablespoon vegetable oil
- ½ cup finely chopped onion
- 3 garlic cloves, minced
- 1¼ teaspoons ground cinnamon
- 1 teaspoon dried oregano
- 1 teaspoon dried mint
- 1 teaspoon paprika
- ⅛ teaspoon red pepper flakes
- ⅛ teaspoon pepper
- ¼ cup red wine
- ⅓ cup tomato paste

BÉCHAMEL AND PASTA

- 2 tablespoons unsalted butter
- 2 tablespoons all-purpose flour
- 1 garlic clove, minced
- ½ teaspoon table salt
- ¼ teaspoon grated nutmeg
- ⅛ teaspoon pepper

- 4 cups whole milk
- 8 ounces (2½ cups) ziti
- 4 ounces kasseri cheese, shredded (1 cup), divided
- 1 large egg, lightly beaten

1. FOR THE MEAT SAUCE: Mix salt, baking soda, and 1 tablespoon water in bowl. Add beef and toss until thoroughly combined. Set aside.

2. Heat oil in medium saucepan over medium heat until shimmering. Add onion and cook, stirring frequently, until softened, about 3 minutes. Stir in garlic, cinnamon, oregano, mint, paprika, pepper flakes, and pepper and cook until fragrant, 1 to 2 minutes. Add wine and cook, stirring occasionally, until mixture is thickened, 2 to 3 minutes. Add tomato paste, beef mixture, and remaining ½ cup water and cook, breaking up meat into pieces no larger than ¼ inch using wooden spoon, until beef has just lost its pink color, 3 to 5 minutes. Bring to simmer; cover, reduce heat to low, and simmer for 30 minutes, stirring occasionally. Off heat, season with salt to taste. (Meat sauce can be refrigerated in airtight container for up to 3 days. Heat through before proceeding with step 3.)

NOTES FROM THE TEST KITCHEN

THE SAUCE COOKS THE PASTA; THE PASTA COOKS THE SAUCE
Most pastitsio recipes call for parcooking the pasta, tossing it with a portion of the béchamel, and thickening the remaining béchamel with enough roux to make it spreadable, not runny. But when we realized that the pasta could cook in the béchamel, and that its starch could thicken the sauce, we combined these steps to make the process more efficient.

HOT BÉCHAMEL HYDRATES PASTA Briefly simmering and then steeping the ziti in the béchamel hydrates its starch just enough to ensure that it will be fully cooked after the pastitsio is baked.

PASTA STARCH THICKENS BÉCHAMEL
As the pasta softens, it leaches starch that thickens the béchamel (without it, the béchamel would require twice as much roux to thicken up appropriately).

3. FOR THE BÉCHAMEL AND PASTA: Adjust oven rack to middle position and heat oven to 375 degrees. Spray 8-inch square baking dish with vegetable oil spray and place on rimmed baking sheet. Melt butter in large saucepan over medium heat. Add flour, garlic, salt, nutmeg, and pepper and cook, stirring constantly, until golden and fragrant, about 1 minute. Slowly whisk in milk and bring to boil. Add pasta and return to simmer, stirring frequently to prevent sticking. When mixture reaches simmer, cover and let stand off heat, stirring occasionally, for 15 minutes (pasta will not be fully cooked).

4. Using spider skimmer, transfer pasta to prepared dish, leaving excess béchamel in saucepan. Sprinkle ⅓ cup kasseri over pasta and stir to combine. Using spatula, gently press pasta into even layer. Add ⅓ cup kasseri to béchamel and whisk to combine. Whisk egg into béchamel. Spread meat sauce over pasta and, using spatula, spread into even layer. Top with béchamel. Sprinkle remaining ⅓ cup kasseri over béchamel. Bake until top of pastitsio is puffed and spotty brown, 40 to 50 minutes. Let cool for 20 minutes. Serve.

CREAMY SPRING VEGETABLE LINGUINE

✓ **WHY THIS RECIPE WORKS** This deceptively simple pasta dish was a revelation to us: perfectly cooked al dente noodles in a silky sauce with a vibrant mix of vegetables and flavors—but without multiple pots, boiling water, or draining. Linguine was our favored shape—the thicker strands retained their bite in the ultrahigh heat of the Instant Pot. After cooking the pasta, we stirred in convenient jarred baby artichokes and frozen peas. By using exactly the right amount of water, we didn't need to drain the pasta; instead, we could capture all the starch that it released. This made it a cinch to emulsify grated Pecorino Romano and the residual cooking liquid into a luscious sauce. Lemon zest and fresh tarragon brightened the dish.

The Instant Pot multicooker promises to make home cooking easier and more accessible than ever by making it possible to create flavorful dishes in a fraction of the time it would take using conventional cooking methods. Tasked with developing recipes for the *Mediterranean Instant Pot* cookbook, I instantly knew that I wanted to use this versatile multicooker to its full potential to produce a hearty, full-flavored one-pot meal.

Prior experimentation with the Instant Pot had shown that it works great for cooking pasta; carefully timing the high-pressure cooking ensured that a variety of pasta shapes reached perfect doneness in minutes. Encouraged by this success, I set my sights on creating a dish using the classic Roman pasta dish cacio e pepe (literally "cheese and pepper") as my inspiration. This simple yet supersatisfying dish traditionally consists of tonnarelli pasta coated in a creamy sauce of Pecorino Romano or Parmesan cheese with a hefty dose of ground black pepper stirred in to give it a kick.

My first choice was to substitute the tonnarelli for similarly shaped but much easier to find spaghetti. But I quickly discovered a problem with using spaghetti: It was nearly impossible to settle on a cooking time that would reliably produce well-cooked pasta. The sweet spot between al dente strands and overcooked mush was too narrow to account for the variability among different multicookers; some machines cooked the pasta perfectly in 2 minutes, while others took only 1 minute, making this dish anything but foolproof.

What I needed was a thicker, more substantial pasta that would be better able to stand up to high-pressure cooking, so I tried swapping the spaghetti for heftier linguine. The linguine cooked perfectly in just 4 minutes, and I liked its pleasantly chewy texture, so it stayed.

Next, I experimented with the amount of water to use. Pasta is often cooked in an abundance of water and then drained to rid it of some of its sticky starch, but in this case I wanted to hold on to that starch to help emulsify the cheese for a beautifully creamy sauce that would cling to the noodles. The key was to cook the pasta in just enough water to allow me to forgo draining, keeping all the starch in the pot with the pasta. After several tests, I found that 5 cups of water plus a tablespoon of oil for richness was just the right amount to emulsify the cheese without turning the dish soupy. As for the cheese, I tested both Pecorino Romano and Parmesan before settling on the former, which I preferred for its distinctive, sharper flavor. Finely grating the cheese meant that it took just a few minutes of stirring to melt and meld with the starchy pasta water to create a luscious, pasta-coating sauce.

Now it was time to consider add-ins. Adding black pepper was a no-brainer; I stirred in ½ teaspoon along with the cheese to give a bit of a kick to my savory,

CHILLED SOBA NOODLES WITH CUCUMBER, SNOW PEAS, AND RADISHES

creamy emulsion. Traditional cacio e pepe stops there, but I wanted to make my dish a true one-pot meal full of fresh springtime flavors and contrasting textures. I've always loved the combination of bright lemon and tender green peas, so I added a couple teaspoons of grated lemon zest and a full cup of peas to the cooked pasta; the peas took only a few minutes to heat through and added appealing pops of color to the finished dish. Jarred baby artichokes, another low-prep spring vegetable, likewise needed only to be quartered, stirred into the warm pasta, and allowed to heat through. To round things out, I decided to add a couple tablespoons of aromatic chopped fresh tarragon, which nicely complemented the lemon.

This was a pasta dinner that had it all: Satisfying heft thanks to the linguine and cheese, a creamy sauce accented by the bite of pepper and the brightness of the lemon and tarragon, and the pop of color and textural contrast provided by the vegetables. All that was left to do was grab a fork and dig in.

—JOSEPH GITTER, *America's Test Kitchen Books*

Creamy Spring Vegetable Linguine

SERVES 4 TO 6

Do not substitute other pasta shapes in this dish, as they require different liquid amounts and will not work in this recipe.

1	pound linguine
5	cups water, plus extra as needed
1	tablespoon extra-virgin olive oil
1	teaspoon table salt
1	cup jarred whole baby artichokes packed in water, quartered
1	cup frozen peas, thawed
4	ounces finely grated Pecorino Romano (2 cups), plus extra for serving
½	teaspoon pepper
2	tablespoons chopped fresh tarragon
2	teaspoons grated lemon zest

1. Loosely wrap half of pasta in dish towel, then press bundle against corner of counter to break noodles into 6-inch lengths; repeat with remaining pasta.

2. Add pasta, water, oil, and salt to Instant Pot, making sure pasta is completely submerged. Lock lid in place and close pressure release valve. Select high pressure cook function and cook for 4 minutes. Turn off Instant Pot and quick-release pressure. Carefully remove lid, allowing steam to escape away from you.

3. Stir artichokes and peas into pasta, cover, and let sit until heated through, about 3 minutes. Gently stir in Pecorino and pepper until cheese is melted and fully combined, 1 to 2 minutes. Adjust consistency with extra hot water as needed. Stir in tarragon and lemon zest, and season with salt and pepper to taste. Serve, passing extra Pecorino separately.

CHILLED SOBA NOODLES WITH CUCUMBER, SNOW PEAS, AND RADISHES

✓ **WHY THIS RECIPE WORKS** Soba noodles, made from buckwheat flour or a blend of buckwheat and wheat flours, have a chewy texture and nutty flavor and are often enjoyed chilled. For a refreshing cold noodle salad, we cooked soba noodles in unsalted boiling water until they were tender but still resilient and rinsed them under cold running water to remove excess starch and prevent sticking. We then tossed the soba with a miso-based dressing, which clung to and flavored the noodles without overpowering their distinct flavor. We also cut a mix of vegetables into varying sizes so that they'd incorporate nicely into the noodles while adding crunch and color. Sprinkling strips of toasted nori over the top added more texture and a subtle briny taste.

Hearty, flavorful soba noodles are a staple of Japanese cooking. Made from buckwheat, the seed of a flowering plant closely related to rhubarb and sorrel, these noodles boast an earthy taste and a slightly chewy texture.

Soba noodles can be slurped up along with hot broth, but they also are often enjoyed in a spare bamboo-tray presentation featuring twists of chilled noodles; a dipping sauce made with soy sauce, mirin, and rice vinegar; a dab of wasabi on the side; and shredded toasted nori (dried seaweed). The simple dish, called zaru soba, is a beautiful way to showcase the noodles' earthy, nutty-sweet flavor and resilient chew.

There are also nontraditional recipes that take the concept and turn it into a more casual one-bowl noodle salad fleshed out with crisp vegetables and a flavorful dressing in place of the dipping sauce. The dish would be just right to tote to work for lunch or pair with salmon or tofu (and perhaps a glass of sake) as a light, refreshing dinner.

There are a couple of types of soba noodles that are easy to find in the United States. Pure buckwheat soba has a deep chestnut color, a pronounced (but pleasant) bitterness, and a coarse texture. Because buckwheat lacks gluten, an elastic protein that forms in the presence of water, these noodles can be quite fragile when dry and are less springy when boiled. The other commonly available type replaces some of the buckwheat flour with wheat flour. In taste tests, we preferred this type for its milder taste and, because of the gluten contributed by the wheat, its more resilient texture.

To cook the soba, I brought a large pot of unsalted water to a boil. Salt is typically not added to the cooking water for soba because manufacturers sometimes add salt to the noodles and because the soba is usually paired with a highly seasoned dressing or sauce.

Once the water was boiling, I added 8 ounces of soba noodles and gave them a quick stir to prevent sticking and ensure that they were submerged. Because soba varies so much from brand to brand, recommended boiling times range from 3 to 10 minutes. Ultimately, I found that it was best to follow the timing on the individual packages. Because soba noodles are more delicate than the typical wheat pasta, it was important to check them early and often during cooking.

Once they were tender but still retained their chew, I drained the noodles in a colander and promptly ran them under cold water until they felt slick. Rinsing is essential to stop further cooking and cool the noodles; it also removes sticky surface starch, helping the noodles remain distinct and separate.

With my soba ready to go, I whisked together a quick dressing inspired by the zaru soba dipping sauce. To soy sauce and salty-sweet mirin, I added nutty toasted sesame oil, sesame seeds, grated fresh ginger for zing, and red pepper flakes for a bit of heat.

When I tossed this mixture with the chilled soba, the soy dominated, and the thin dressing slid right off the noodles. So for my next batch, I reached for white miso thinned with a little water in place of the soy sauce. The thick, mildly sweet, umami-rich miso made for a velvety dressing that clung lightly to the soba and didn't obscure its subtleties. Next, I sliced up a medley of raw vegetables: clean, cool cucumber; snow peas; peppery red radishes; and scallions.

To help keep the vegetables from collecting at the bottom of the bowl, I cut them into shapes and sizes that would get entwined in the noodles. I noticed that the cucumbers shed a bit of water when I tossed them with the dressed noodles, so I decreased the water in the dressing by 1 tablespoon.

Finally, in a nod to how cold soba noodles are traditionally enjoyed, I added strips of toasted nori to my salad. Their understated briny taste was the perfect finishing touch.

—ANNIE PETITO, *Cook's Illustrated*

NOTES FROM THE TEST KITCHEN

VEGETABLE PREP SCHOOL

Here's how to strategically cut the vegetables into shapes that will get tangled in the noodles instead of dropping to the bottom of the bowl.

CUCUMBER
Quarter lengthwise, seed, and slice thin on bias.

SCALLIONS
Slice white and green parts thin on bias.

RADISHES
Trim ends, halve, and slice into thin half-moons.

SNOW PEAS
Remove strings and cut lengthwise into matchsticks.

Chilled Soba Noodles with Cucumber, Snow Peas, and Radishes

SERVES 4 TO 6

Sheets of nori, a dried seaweed that adds a subtle briny umami flavor and crisp texture to this salad, can be found in packets at Asian markets or in the Asian section of the supermarket. Plain pretoasted seaweed snacks can be substituted for the toasted nori, and yellow, red, or brown miso can be substituted for the white miso, if desired. This dish isn't meant to be overtly spicy, but if you prefer more heat, use the full ½ teaspoon of red pepper flakes. These chilled noodles pair nicely with salmon, shrimp, tofu, or chicken for lunch or a light dinner. Our favorite soba noodles are Shirakiku Soba Japanese Style Buck Wheat Noodle, and our favorite white miso is Hikari Organic White Miso.

8	ounces dried soba noodles
1	(8-inch square) sheet nori (optional)
3	tablespoons white miso
3	tablespoons mirin
2	tablespoons toasted sesame oil
1	tablespoon sesame seeds
1	teaspoon grated fresh ginger
¼–½	teaspoon red pepper flakes
⅓	English cucumber, quartered lengthwise, seeded, and sliced thin on bias
4	ounces snow peas, strings removed, cut lengthwise into matchsticks
4	radishes, trimmed, halved, and sliced into thin half-moons
3	scallions, sliced thin on bias

1. Bring 4 quarts water to boil in large pot. Stir in noodles and cook according to package directions, stirring occasionally, until noodles are cooked through but still retain some chew. Drain noodles and rinse under cold water until chilled. Drain well and transfer to large bowl.

2. Grip nori sheet, if using, with tongs and hold about 2 inches above low flame on gas burner. Toast nori, flipping every 3 to 5 seconds, until nori is aromatic and shrinks slightly, about 20 seconds. If you do not have a gas stove, toast nori on rimmed baking sheet in 275-degree oven until it is aromatic and shrinks slightly, 20 to 25 minutes, flipping nori halfway through toasting. Using scissors, cut nori into four 2-inch strips. Stack strips and cut crosswise into thin strips.

3. Combine miso, mirin, oil, 1 tablespoon water, sesame seeds, ginger, and pepper flakes in small bowl and whisk until smooth. Add dressing to noodles and toss to combine. Add cucumber, snow peas, radishes, scallions, and nori, if using, and toss well to evenly distribute. Season with salt to taste, and serve.

CAST IRON PAN PIZZA

✔ **WHY THIS RECIPE WORKS** We started with a simple stir-together pizza dough of bread flour, salt, yeast, and warm water; the warm water jump-started yeast activity so that the crumb was open and light. Instead of kneading the dough, we let it rest overnight in the refrigerator. During this rest, the dough's gluten strengthened enough for the crust to support the toppings but still have a tender crumb. Baking the pie in a generously oiled cast-iron skillet "fried" the outside of the crust. We also moved the skillet to the stove for the last few minutes of cooking to crisp up the underside of the crust. For the crispy cheese edge known as frico, we pressed shredded Monterey Jack cheese around the edge of the dough and up the sides of the skillet. For the sauce, we crushed canned whole tomatoes (which are less processed and therefore fresher-tasting than commercial crushed tomatoes) by hand, which allowed some of their juice to drain and ensured that the sauce would be thick enough to stay put on the pie. We then pureed the tomatoes in the food processor with classic seasonings—no cooking required.

It wasn't long ago that pan pizzas were dowdy pies associated with chain restaurants, but I like to think that those of us who grew up savoring these thick-crusted pizzas always knew they had more potential. And now they're getting their due: Respected pizzaiolas are finally giving these pies the same attention they've always lavished on thinner, more austere styles, and Americans are (re)acquiring a taste for them. Even Pizza Hut wants a better slice: The iconic chain recently revamped its signature pan pizza for the first time in decades.

If you ask me, the appeal of pan pizza is obvious. The crumb is thick, plush, and encased in a golden, crispy crust. The red sauce is thick and has a bright taste. And there's plenty of gooey, stretchy cheese. My favorite versions include a rim of fused-to-the-crust fried cheese called frico, a bonus feature that's borrowed from Detroit-style pies. It's also the most home cook–friendly pie you can make. In my recipe, there's literally 1 minute of kneading and no rolling or stretching. And because it's baked in a pan, there's no dicey transfer of the topped dough to a hot baking stone. In fact, it doesn't require any pizza-specific equipment at all. Here's how it works.

What makes a good pan pizza crust so different from other styles is the distinct textural contrast between its crispy, golden, rich-tasting edge and its tender, plush, airy interior. One good way to achieve that soft, light interior structure is to make a high-hydration dough: The more water that's in the mix, the bigger the bubbles and the airier the crumb. I found that a ratio of 8 ounces of water to 11 ounces of bread flour (the best choice of flour for building structure in dough, since it contains more gluten-forming proteins than all-purpose flour) produced a dough that was supple but not soupy.

All that water came with a few other perks, too. First, it helped the dough come together really easily; all I had to do was mix it into the dry ingredients with a wooden spoon or spatula. Second, it allowed me to almost entirely skip kneading as long as I let the dough rest overnight in the refrigerator. When given enough time, water can facilitate gluten development by helping the proteins in the flour find each other, enabling them to align and form the cross-links necessary for good structure. Third, the long fermentation in the refrigerator produced a dough with great flavor, since the cold temperature slowed the remaining yeast activity and allowed for the development of more complex-tasting acid by-products. (I did, however, need to start with warm water so that there was an initial burst of yeast activity to create lots of bubbles in the dough.) The upshot: As long as I kneaded the dough for just 1 minute after mixing, the water and the overnight rest did the rest of the work for me.

On to that crispy, golden edge, which forms as the pie bakes—or more truthfully, fries—in a well-oiled pan. Some recipes call for baking the pie in a round cake pan, but I opted for a 12-inch cast-iron skillet. I slicked the pan with 3 tablespoons of extra-virgin olive oil before baking the pie on the lowest rack so that the crust was as close as possible to the heat source. Using a cast-iron skillet allowed me to move the baked pie from the hot oven to the stovetop for the last few minutes of cooking; that way, I was able to give the underside of the crust a direct blast of heat without overbaking the interior or the toppings. (I did find that a greased round cake pan or pie plate was ideal for preshaping the dough before it rested; by the time the rest was over, all I had to do was press the dough gently into the skillet—no rolling or stretching required.)

"It's all about the crust" is an old pizza adage, but with pan pies, it's about the cheese, too. There's the usual top layer of gooey, stretchy mozzarella that you find on most pizza, and on the best versions there's also the frico: the lacy, crispy rim of fried cheese that forms where the cheese meets the side of the pan.

Shredded mozzarella was great for the top of the pie, but I found it too wet for frico; not enough moisture evaporated by the time the cheese browned, so the result was tough and bendy, not crispy. I experimented with drier options and landed on Monterey Jack. Not as dry (nor as salty) as Parmesan and more neutral than cheddar, it crisped up into a rich, savory ring. The trick was applying the cheese just right: I sprinkled the shreds over the ½-inch border of dough I had deliberately left unsauced and pressed them up the side of the pan so that they formed a mini cheese "wall." By the time the pizza finished baking 30 minutes later, it had deeply browned, crispy frico.

To offset the richness of the oil-fried crust and the abundant cheese, pan pizza sauce should be bright and fresh-tasting but also thick enough to stay put. I started with canned whole tomatoes and crushed them by hand in a fine-mesh strainer so that most of their juice drained away. (This would produce a thicker mixture than using commercial crushed tomatoes.) Then I turned them into a no-cook sauce by pureeing them in a food processor with extra-virgin olive oil, minced garlic, dried oregano, a pinch of red pepper flakes, and some sugar and salt for balance. The sauce came together in a flash and was packed with flavor.

—LAN LAM, *Cook's Illustrated*

Cast Iron Pan Pizza

SERVES 4

This pizza bakes in a 12-inch cast-iron skillet. Weigh the flour and water for the best results. Use a block cheese, not fresh mozzarella, for this recipe. Avoid preshredded cheese; it contains added starch, which gives the melted cheese a drier, chewier texture.

CAST IRON PAN PIZZA

DOUGH

- 2 cups (11 ounces) bread flour
- 1 teaspoon table salt
- 1 teaspoon instant or rapid-rise yeast
- 1 cup (8 ounces) warm water (105 to 110 degrees)
  Vegetable oil spray

SAUCE

- 1 (14.5-ounce) can whole peeled tomatoes
- 1 teaspoon extra-virgin olive oil
- 1 garlic clove, minced
- ¼ teaspoon sugar
- ¼ teaspoon table salt
- ¼ teaspoon dried oregano
  Pinch red pepper flakes

PIZZA

- 3 tablespoons extra-virgin olive oil
- 4 ounces Monterey Jack cheese, shredded (1 cup)
- 7 ounces whole-milk mozzarella cheese, shredded (1¼ cups)

1. FOR THE DOUGH: Using wooden spoon or spatula, stir flour, salt, and yeast together in bowl. Add warm water and mix until most of flour is moistened. Using your hands, knead dough in bowl until dough forms sticky ball, about 1 minute. Spray 9-inch pie plate or cake pan with oil spray. Transfer dough to prepared plate and press into 7- to 8-inch disk. Spray top of dough with oil spray. Cover tightly with plastic wrap and refrigerate for 12 to 24 hours.

2. FOR THE SAUCE: Place tomatoes in fine-mesh strainer and crush with your hands. Drain well, then transfer to food processor. Add oil, garlic, sugar, salt, oregano, and pepper flakes and process until smooth, about 30 seconds. (Sauce can be refrigerated for up to 3 days.)

3. FOR THE PIZZA: Two hours before baking, remove dough from refrigerator and let sit at room temperature for 30 minutes.

4. Coat bottom of 12-inch cast-iron skillet with oil. Transfer dough to prepared skillet and use your fingertips to flatten dough until it is ⅛ inch from edge of skillet. Cover tightly with plastic and let rest until slightly puffy, about 1½ hours.

5. Thirty minutes before baking, adjust oven rack to lowest position and heat oven to 400 degrees. Spread ½ cup sauce evenly over top of dough, leaving ½-inch border (save remaining sauce for another use). Sprinkle Monterey Jack evenly over border. Press Monterey Jack into side of skillet, forming ½- to ¾-inch-tall wall. (Not all cheese will stick to side of skillet.) Evenly sprinkle mozzarella over sauce. Bake until cheese at edge of skillet is well browned, 25 to 30 minutes.

6. Transfer skillet to stovetop and let sit until sizzling stops, about 3 minutes. Run butter knife around rim of skillet to loosen pizza. Using thin metal spatula, gently lift edge of pizza and peek at underside to assess browning. Cook pizza over medium heat until bottom crust is well browned, 2 to 5 minutes (skillet handle will be hot). Using 2 spatulas, transfer pizza to wire rack and let cool for 10 minutes. Slice and serve.

SKILLET TURKEY BURGERS

✓ **WHY THIS RECIPE WORKS** For juicy turkey burgers, we started by adding baking soda and gelatin to ground turkey to help keep it moist as it cooked. A few tablespoons of panko bread crumbs kept the meat from binding together too firmly. Gently tossing the ingredients together and lightly shaping the patties also helped create a pleasantly tender texture. Melted butter added richness, while soy sauce and Parmesan contributed savoriness. We also devised an unusual cooking method: Starting the patties in a cold skillet meant the exteriors could slowly start to brown while the interiors reached the 160-degree serving temperature. Covering the skillet enveloped the burgers in steam, so they cooked evenly from top to bottom.

Confession time: I genuinely enjoy turkey burgers. If you've encountered a truly bad version (plenty exist) or consider it a punishment to eat a burger made from anything but beef, hear me out: There's a lot to like about a well-made turkey burger. Think a light, juicy texture; savory meat; and a tender, well-browned crust.

For turkey burger success, you must first make peace with the obvious: Ground turkey isn't ground beef. It's very wet, which makes it hard to work with, yet it can easily cook up dry. That's because ground turkey must be cooked to 160 degrees. At that temperature, nearly all the turkey's abundant moisture will have been squeezed out by contracting proteins. Thorough mixing also causes the myosin (a sticky protein) in the ground turkey to link up tightly, so the burger turns dense.

Many recipes mitigate dry, compact patties by adding mix-ins such as vegetables, beans, and grains that either contribute or trap moisture or break up the texture of the patty. Unfortunately, with too many additions, the result often resembles a veggie burger, perpetuating the idea that ground turkey makes a laughable meal for a meat lover. It's true that to make an extraordinary burger, ground turkey needs a little help. The key is to choose the right mix-ins and use as little of them as you can get away with.

Pulsing a whole cut of turkey in the food processor would have allowed me to produce a coarse grind for a loose-textured patty, but that was too much trouble for an everyday recipe, so I set my sights on improving the preground stuff. Just like packaged ground beef, packaged ground turkey is blended to have a range of fat contents. I knew that the 99 percent lean type was a nonstarter; the greater amount of fat in 93 percent lean turkey (more widely available than 85 percent lean) would provide more flavor and moisture.

To address the dense consistency that the sticky myosin produces, I added panko bread crumbs to the patties, which physically disrupted the proteins and made the meat feel coarse and light (rather than tough and dense) on the tongue. For 1 pound of turkey, 3 tablespoons of panko did the job without making the burgers taste bready.

But panko wasn't a panacea. Kneading and squeezing the turkey to evenly incorporate the bread crumbs created too sturdy a myosin gel, resulting in a springy, sausage-like consistency. To get around this, I broke the slab of ground turkey into ½-inch pieces prior to adding the panko. This exposed more surface area for even dispersal of the crumbs, reduced the amount of mixing required, and kept the meat loose.

Now the turkey had a pleasant texture, but after reaching 160 degrees, it still wasn't juicy. A couple of test kitchen tricks took care of that. First, I bathed the meat in a solution of baking soda dissolved in a teaspoon of water. The baking soda solution raised the pH, changing the protein structure and enabling the meat to better retain moisture. (It also sped up the Maillard reaction, providing better browning.) Second, I added a bit of unflavored gelatin to hold moisture, creating a juicy mouthfeel.

A satisfying burger needs some richness, so next I added a bit of melted butter. A single tablespoon solidified when it hit the cold meat, creating tiny particles of fat throughout the patties that remelted during cooking to produce a rich taste and texture.

To augment the meat's savoriness, I experimented with adding glutamate-rich soy sauce, Parmesan, and ground shiitake mushrooms. The mushrooms overwhelmed the meat, but 1½ tablespoons of soy sauce

NOTES FROM THE TEST KITCHEN

TURKEY NEEDS HELP
Ground turkey is full of moisture—more so than ground beef—but since you have to cook it to 160 degrees, it's virtually impossible to keep the juices in the meat unless you give it some help. Here's how we deliver all the qualities that make a turkey burger taste good—really good.

JUICINESS
Baking soda helps the meat retain moisture; gelatin adds juicy richness.

SAVORY FLAVOR
Glutamate-rich soy sauce and Parmesan cheese contribute savoriness.

LIGHT, LOOSE CONSISTENCY
Panko bread crumbs prevent proteins from bonding too tightly.

RICH TASTE AND TEXTURE
Just 1 tablespoon of melted butter adds fat and richness to lean turkey.

SKILLET TURKEY BURGERS

together with 3 tablespoons of grated Parmesan packed a solid umami punch without being overpowering. When shaping the patties, I used a gentle hand to keep the burger mix coarse and loose.

We often cook burgers by searing the patties in a sizzling-hot skillet. But the interior of a turkey burger needs to be cooked thoroughly, and in a hot skillet the exterior is likely to overcook and turn leathery by the time the interior is done. Unless I wanted to negate all the advances I had already made, I needed to come up with a new method.

I made a couple of bold decisions. First, I would start the patties in a cold oiled skillet. Once they were in place, I turned the heat to medium, and then, when I started to hear sizzling, I covered the pan. The lid trapped the moisture that escaped from the turkey, enveloping the burgers in steam, so they cooked quickly and evenly. After about 2½ minutes, I flipped the patties (which were nicely browned on the bottom), covered them, and continued to cook them until they reached 160 degrees and the second side was golden brown. These burgers hit all the right notes: deep browning; a tender, browned crust; a pleasantly coarse and juicy texture; and rich, savory flavor.

I melted cheese onto the burgers and then sandwiched them between soft buns with the works: lettuce, tomato, ketchup, and mayonnaise. And for those times when I wanted to go all out, I created a recipe for my new favorite burger topping: quick-pickled avocado slices. Almost any fruit or vegetable can be pickled, including fatty avocados. The result is both creamy and tangy—the ideal crown for a turkey burger worth bragging about.

—ANNIE PETITO, *Cook's Illustrated*

Skillet Turkey Burgers

SERVES 4

A pair of fish spatulas works well for flipping the burgers. Serve with your favorite burger toppings and Pickled Avocado (recipe follows), if desired.

- 2 teaspoons vegetable oil
- 1 teaspoon water
- ¼ teaspoon baking soda
- 1 pound 93 percent lean ground turkey
- 1½ tablespoons soy sauce
- 1 tablespoon unsalted butter, melted
- 3 tablespoons panko bread crumbs
- 3 tablespoons grated Parmesan cheese
- ½ teaspoon unflavored gelatin
- ¼ teaspoon pepper
- ⅛ teaspoon table salt
- 4 slices American cheese (optional)
- 4 hamburger buns

1. Place oil in 12-inch nonstick skillet and set aside. Combine water and baking soda in small bowl. Place turkey in large bowl. Using your hands, break up turkey into rough ½-inch pieces. Drizzle baking soda mixture evenly over turkey, followed by soy sauce and melted butter. Evenly sprinkle panko, Parmesan, gelatin, pepper, and salt over turkey mixture. Using your hands, gently toss to combine.

2. Divide turkey into 4 lightly packed portions, about 4 ounces each. Gently flatten 1 portion into patty about ½ inch thick and about 4 inches in diameter. Transfer patty directly to prepared skillet and repeat with remaining portions.

3. Heat skillet over medium heat. When patties start to sizzle, cover skillet and cook until patties are well-browned on bottom, about 2½ minutes (if patties are not browned after 2½ minutes, increase heat). Carefully flip patties, cover, and continue to cook until second side is well browned and burgers register 160 degrees, 2½ to 3 minutes longer. Place 1 slice of cheese, if using, on each burger about 1 minute before burgers finish cooking. Transfer burgers to plate and let rest for 5 minutes, then transfer to buns and serve.

Pickled Avocado

SERVES 4

Use a relatively firm avocado for this recipe.

- ½ cup distilled white vinegar
- ½ cup water
- 1 tablespoon sugar
- 2 teaspoons table salt
- 1 ripe but firm avocado, halved,
  pitted, and sliced ¼ inch thick

Combine vinegar, water, sugar, and salt in medium bowl and whisk until sugar and salt are dissolved, about 30 seconds. Add avocado (avocado should be submerged) and refrigerate for at least 30 minutes or up to 2 hours. Drain and pat dry before using.

DOUBLE-DECKER DRIVE-THRU BURGERS

✓ **WHY THIS RECIPE WORKS** The double-decker—two all-beef patties, special sauce, lettuce, cheese, pickles, and onions on a sesame seed bun—has solidified its place in American pop culture. For our take on this iconic burger, we started with the classic triple bun setup, which we achieved by simply adding another bun bottom to each burger. We knew that a large 12-inch skillet would be essential to cook the eight patties for our double stacks, but we still needed to cook the burgers in two batches to avoid overcrowding the pan, which would cause our patties to steam rather than fry. To keep the thin patties from shrinking too much, we weighted them with a foil-lined pot as they cooked. Once the first set of patties had cooked, we topped each with a slice of cheese and placed them in a warm oven; in the time it took the cheese to melt, the second batch of quick-cooking patties was ready. For this burger's hallmark flavor, we topped them with our Classic Burger Sauce (page 83), along with some shredded lettuce, pickles, and finely chopped onion to re-create this delicious drive-thru classic at home.

From a bucket of fried chicken to the secret menu sandwich, each fast-food chain restaurant has its signature dish. When I pull up to a certain drive-thru window and hear the words "May I take your order?" I know exactly what I'm asking for. Yes, it's that iconic burger that manages to stuff two beef patties separated by an extra bun in between layers of iceberg lettuce, American cheese, beef patty, pickles, and onion. Smeared with a heavenly dose of "special sauce," this burger can possess you to circle back through the drive-thru lane again and again. I wanted to ditch the drive-thru and make my own double-decker burger that would pay homage to this fast-food classic.

Having two beef patties and three bun layers was nonnegotiable—after all, it's not the lettuce that makes this sandwich such a heavy hitter. The tangy-sweet secret sauce had to stay, too—no fancy aiolis on this burger. The rest was up to me. I would put this burger through its paces to craft the perfect rendition.

Hopeful that some top-secret tidbits may be hidden on the internet, I started there. I embarked upon my research with the patties and found that the fast-food chain uses two 1.6-ounce patties. To keep things simple, I rounded up to two 2-ounce patties, which meant 1 pound of meat for four burgers. Opting for 85 percent lean ground beef ensured that my burgers were bursting with juiciness.

Unlike a hefty bistro-style burger patty carefully cooked to medium-rare, fast-food patties are generally thin and cooked to medium-well or well-done. To achieve the ideal thickness, I fashioned a DIY burger press with a zipper-lock bag and a clear pie plate. I cut the sides off the bag, enclosed a 2-ounce portion of beef inside of it, and pressed it with the pie plate to a 3½-inch diameter.

As I cooked through batches upon batches of patties, one issue kept coming up: They were shrinking too much. When meat is cooked, heat forces water out, causing shrinkage. But if I pressed the patties into the hot pan, the crust would quickly "set" and prevent the burgers from shrinking. I tried smashing the beef with a metal spatula, but I couldn't get consistent results. I needed a tool that would apply even pressure to the patties. What about a Dutch oven? It fit into the skillet perfectly, and its heft ensured that the burgers would be uniformly smashed. The thin burgers cooked in just about 2 minutes.

When it comes to burger construction, the bun is usually an afterthought. But throwing an extra bun in the middle of my burger threw a wrench in my recipe. More research revealed that the fast-food chain in question uses a custom flat bun in the middle of their double-decker burger. I tried to mimic that by cutting whole buns into thirds, but it was a challenge to slice them evenly every time. I ended up calling for four buns and three bun bottoms—the bottoms' flatter shape would better mimic the center bun.

On to that supercharged sauce made from familiar condiments—ketchup, mayonnaise, and relish. I mixed this trio together along with a bit of sugar, white vinegar, and some black pepper to round out the flavors.

Finally, I had to determine how to embellish my burger. Supermelty American cheese was a no-brainer here—a fancy Gruyère or even a humble cheddar were just wrong. I kept the remaining toppings as traditional as possible—shredded iceberg lettuce, dill pickle chips for crunch and acidity, and chopped white onion for pungency (I rinsed the onion first to temper its bite).

Simply put, these double-decker drive-thru burgers are unapologetically over-the-top. Just one more thing: Can I get fries with that?

—LAWMAN JOHNSON, *America's Test Kitchen Books*

Double-Decker Drive-Thru Burgers

SERVES 4

Be careful not to overwork the beef in step 2 or the burgers may be tough once cooked. Our favorite hamburger buns are Martin's Sandwich Potato Rolls. Boar's Head makes our favorite American cheese.

- 1 pound 85 percent lean ground beef
- ½ teaspoon table salt
- ¼ teaspoon pepper
- 1 teaspoon vegetable oil
- 4 hamburger buns, plus 4 bun bottoms, divided
- 4 slices American cheese (4 ounces)
- ½ cup Classic Burger Sauce (recipe follows), divided, plus extra for serving
- 2 cups shredded iceberg lettuce, divided
- ¼ cup finely chopped onion, rinsed
- ¼ cup dill pickle chips

1. Adjust oven rack to middle position and heat oven to 250 degrees. Wrap bottom of Dutch oven with aluminum foil. Cut sides off 1-quart zipper-lock bag, leaving bottom seam intact.

2. Divide ground beef into eight 2-ounce portions, then roll each portion into ball. Working with 1 ball at a time, enclose in split bag. Using clear pie plate (so you can see size of patty), press ball into even 3½-inch patty. Remove patty from bag and transfer to platter. Sprinkle patties with salt and pepper.

3. Heat oil in 12-inch skillet over high heat until just smoking. Place 4 patties in skillet and weight with prepared pot. Cook until well browned on first side, 60 to 90 seconds. Flip patties, return pot, and continue to cook until browned on second side, about 60 seconds longer. Transfer burgers to rimmed baking sheet, top with American cheese, and keep warm in oven. Pour off all but 1 teaspoon fat from skillet and repeat with remaining 4 patties (do not top with cheese); transfer to sheet.

4. Spread ¼ cup burger sauce over 4 bun bottoms, then top with 1 cup lettuce and cheeseburgers. Spread remaining ¼ cup sauce over remaining 4 bun bottoms, then top with remaining 1 cup lettuce, remaining burgers, onion, and pickle chips. Place second set of burger stacks on top of first and top with bun tops. Serve, passing extra sauce separately.

Classic Burger Sauce

MAKES ABOUT 1 CUP

The test kitchen's favorite mayonnaise is Blue Plate Real Mayonnaise; since this product can be hard to find in some parts of the United States, we also recommend Hellmann's Real Mayonnaise (sold as Best Foods west of the Rockies).

- ½ cup mayonnaise
- ¼ cup ketchup
- 2 teaspoons sweet pickle relish
- 2 teaspoons sugar
- 2 teaspoons distilled white vinegar
- 1 teaspoon pepper

Whisk all ingredients together in bowl. (Sauce can be refrigerated in airtight container for up to 4 days; bring to room temperature before serving.)

VARIATION

Malt Vinegar–Mustard Burger Sauce
Omit relish. Substitute whole-grain mustard for ketchup and 1 tablespoon malt vinegar for white vinegar.

LAMB BURGERS WITH HALLOUMI AND BEET TZATZIKI

WHY THIS RECIPE WORKS The rich flavor of lamb makes for an exceptional burger experience. We decided to pair delicately spiced ground lamb patties with a colorful beet tzatziki, pan-seared halloumi cheese, and a drizzle of honey for a truly unique burger that could transport us to the Greek islands any night of the week. To give the ground lamb a flavor boost, we made a warm spice blend of coriander, oregano, and cinnamon. Slabs of firm, salty halloumi cheese developed a beautiful nutty brown crust when seared and nicely offset the richness of the lamb. For a creamy tang, we topped our burgers with a generous dollop of tzatziki, which we spiked with earthy beets to turn it a vivid pink. A drizzle of honey helped pull all the flavors together.

In my opinion, meze boards are the ultimate eating experience. Whether they're served up as an appetizer or as a light dinner for two, these massive Mediterranean spreads feature every taste and texture imaginable: briny feta cheese and olives, hearty lamb meatballs and stuffed grape leaves, creamy tzatziki and hummus swiped up with fluffy pita bread—the list goes on. While I could pick at these delicious finger foods one by one all night long, sometimes I crave all those bold flavors in one unforgettable bite. So when I was tasked with crafting a few playful burgers for *The Ultimate Burger* cookbook, I knew that one of them had to be meze board–inspired.

The patty is the heart of any burger, so I started there. And since lamb is the quintessential Mediterranean meat, I knew I'd be using it from the get-go. Inspired by Greek lamb meatballs, also known as keftedes arni, I flavored 1½ pounds of ground lamb with ground coriander for citrusy brightness; dried oregano for pungent, slightly minty notes; and cinnamon for a hint of warmth. Although these spices are assertive, I knew that I'd have to add more than usual for their flavors to stand up to the gaminess of the lamb. In total, I had to add more than a tablespoon of herbs and spices—1½ teaspoons each of coriander and oregano and ⅛ teaspoon of cinnamon—to detect their flavors with the strongly flavored lamb in the mix. I mixed the herbs, spices, and some pepper into the ground lamb, being careful not to overwork the meat.

When forming the patties, I found that ¾-inch-thick patties were ideal—neither too thick nor too thin. And to prevent the burgers from puffing up while they cooked, I made a slight indentation in the center of each raw patty. Sprinkled with a bit of salt, these patties were ready to take the heat.

Although in the test kitchen we usually sear burgers in neutral-tasting vegetable oil, I decided to sear my patties in extra-virgin olive oil to further boost their Mediterranean flavor. I heated a teaspoon of olive oil in a 12-inch skillet until the oil just started smoking and cooked the patties on both sides (indentation side up first) until they were cooked through but still had rosy centers. I then set them aside to rest so that they'd retain their juices.

With the burgers set, I had to decide which meze elements to include in topping form. I thought a creamy dip would be a nice complement to the hard-seared burger. I started off with a dollop of hummus, but it just didn't work here—its texture was too similar to that of the burger and the bun. I needed a bit of crunch to add some textural intrigue.

What about tzatziki, the yogurt-based dip that's the star of many a meze platter? Its cooling creaminess and slight crunch from the cucumbers would balance the gamy, fatty burger (similar to how tzatziki balances a rich, bready gyro). Tzatziki was definitely a step in the right direction, but I wanted even more crunch. Flipping through our Mediterranean cookbook for inspiration, I stumbled upon a test kitchen recipe for beet tzatziki, in which a shredded beet is added to the mix. Not only did this give the tzatziki a more crisp, slaw-like texture, but it added earthiness that cut through the rich lamb flavor and gave the sauce a vibrant hot pink color.

What's a burger—or a meze board—without cheese? When I think of Mediterranean cheeses, two spring instantly to mind: briny, crumbly feta and tangy, gooey halloumi. Since feta is resistant to melting and thus wouldn't create a cohesive burger, I chose to go with halloumi. Because it is poached in water or whey before packaging, halloumi has a high melting point, which makes it a great candidate for recipes that involve grilling and frying. When prepared this way, the cheese becomes crispy on the outside and melty on the inside—kind of like a savory marshmallow.

I pan-seared the halloumi slabs while the burgers rested, cooking the cheese in the same skillet I'd used for the burgers. Searing the cheese for about 3 minutes per side over medium heat gave me golden, crispy exteriors and tangy, chewy centers.

For the green element, I knew that plain old iceberg just wouldn't fly—what I needed was a boldly flavored salad green that could stand up to all the assertively flavored components at play. Baby arugula immediately came to mind; its peppery punch would add yet another layer of flavor to the burger.

I finally piled each element on the burger buns—first the burger, followed by the briny halloumi, tangy tzatziki, and spicy arugula. A drizzle of honey added a hit of sweetness that pulled everything together and balanced out the other bold flavors.

I know meze boards are meant to be shared, but I was happy to finally have a mini meze all to myself.

—JOSEPH GITTER, *America's Test Kitchen Books*

LAMB BURGERS WITH HALLOUMI AND BEET TZATZIKI

Lamb Burgers with Halloumi and Beet Tzatziki

SERVES 4

The test kitchen's favorite whole-milk Greek yogurt is Fage Total Classic Greek Yogurt.

1	beet, peeled and shredded (¾ cup)
¼	English cucumber, shredded
1	teaspoon table salt, divided
½	cup whole-milk Greek yogurt
3	tablespoons plus 1 teaspoon extra-virgin olive oil, divided
1	tablespoon minced fresh mint or dill
1	small garlic clove, minced
1½	pounds ground lamb
1½	teaspoons ground coriander
1½	teaspoons dried oregano
½	teaspoon pepper
⅛	teaspoon ground cinnamon
1	(8-ounce) block halloumi cheese, sliced crosswise into ½-inch-thick slabs
4	hamburger buns, toasted if desired
1½	ounces (1½ cups) baby arugula
1	tablespoon honey

1. Toss beet and cucumber with ½ teaspoon salt in colander set over medium bowl and let sit for 15 minutes. Discard any drained juices and wipe bowl clean with paper towels. Whisk yogurt, 2 tablespoons oil, mint, and garlic together in now-empty bowl, then stir in beet mixture. Cover and refrigerate for at least 1 hour or up to 2 days. Season with salt and pepper to taste.

2. Break ground lamb into small pieces in large bowl. Add coriander, oregano, pepper, and cinnamon and gently knead with your hands until well combined. Divide lamb mixture into 4 equal portions, then gently shape each portion into ¾-inch-thick patty. Using your fingertips, press center of each patty down until about ½ inch thick, creating slight indentation.

3. Season patties with remaining ½ teaspoon salt. Heat 1 teaspoon oil in 12-inch skillet over medium heat until just smoking. Transfer patties to skillet, indentation side up, and cook until well browned on first side, 2 to 4 minutes. Flip patties and continue to cook until browned on second side and meat registers 120 to 125 degrees (for medium-rare) or 130 to 135 (for medium), 3 to 5 minutes longer. Transfer burgers to platter and let rest for 5 minutes. Wipe skillet clean with paper towels.

4. Pat halloumi dry with paper towels. Heat remaining 1 tablespoon oil in now-empty skillet over medium heat until shimmering. Arrange halloumi in single layer in skillet and cook until golden brown, 2 to 4 minutes per side. Serve burgers on buns, topped with halloumi, tzatziki, and arugula, and drizzled with honey.

PAN BAGNAT (PROVENÇAL TUNA SANDWICH)

✓ WHY THIS RECIPE WORKS Our version of pan bagnat, a classic Provençal sandwich that shares many of the same ingredients as salade niçoise, features a crusty baguette packed with high-quality oil-packed tuna, olives, capers, tomatoes, hard-cooked eggs, fresh herbs, and a mustardy vinaigrette. We used a large baguette, which offered enough surface area to accommodate the filling, and removed the inner crumb from the bottom half of the loaf to create a trough that provided even more space. Processing the olives, capers, anchovies, and herbs into a coarse salad helped those components hold together, and applying the salad in two layers in the sandwich distributed its assertive flavors. To control the bread's moisture absorption, we toasted the halved baguette to dry out the crumb and then brushed the cut surfaces with olive oil, which helped waterproof it. Stirring the vinaigrette into the olive salad thickened the dressing so that it didn't oversaturate the crumb, and we also thoroughly drained the tuna and tomato slices to remove much of their liquid. Tightly wrapping the sandwich halves with plastic wrap and pressing them for at least an hour under a heavy Dutch oven tamped down the filling so that the whole package was compact enough to bite through.

The first thing to know about pan bagnat: It's not your everyday tuna sandwich.

To me, that means a mayonnaise-y deli salad that's sandwiched between slices of toasted wheat or rye bread. Pan bagnat, the iconic Provençal tuna sandwich, is something entirely different—and, dare I say, far more grand. It's essentially a niçoise salad served between two halves of a loaf of crusty bread: Chunks of high-quality canned tuna; sliced hard-cooked eggs, tomatoes, and red onion; briny niçoise olives and (sometimes) capers; anchovies; garlic; and fragrant herbs are carefully layered and dressed in a mustardy vinaigrette. And here's the brilliant part: The sandwich gets wrapped tightly with plastic wrap and pressed under a weight, which tamps down the piled-high filling. This step ensures that the whole package is compact enough to bite through and the filling slightly saturates the crumb without softening the crisp crust. ("Pan bagnat" means "bathed bread" in Niçard, the local variant of the Provençal dialect, referring to how cooks once "refreshed" the stale bread by softening it under a stream of water.)

This sandwich makes for perfect picnic fare because it's portable, and it's equally great for parties because it can be made up to a day ahead. But it's tricky to make well. Besides balancing all those assertive flavors, you have to carefully assemble the loosely packed ingredients so that they don't come tumbling out when you slice or bite into the sandwich. Not many cooks put so much thought into making sandwiches—but I was about to.

Great tuna and great bread are the core components of pan bagnat. I began by draining a couple of jars of the test kitchen's favorite oil-packed tuna; I found that using quality oil-packed tuna ensured that the fish had a moist, silky texture and rich, meaty flavor. As for the bread, the most traditional versions of pan bagnat feature a single-serving round roll, but a baguette, ciabatta, or bâtard that French bakers slice and sell by the portion is also common. I settled on a baguette because fewer slices would be necessary to portion the long loaf, which would, I hoped, allow more of the filling to stay intact. I hollowed out the bottom half—a typical step that makes space for the abundant filling and increases the ratio of filling to bread—and nestled the tuna in the trough. It was easy to shingle thin slices of tomato and eggs over the fish, but things started falling apart when I piled on the onion slices, olives, capers, anchovies, parsley, and marjoram (sweeter and more delicate than oregano or thyme, and distinctly Provençal) and doused the filling in vinaigrette.

I did my best to bundle the precariously full loaf in plastic wrap before halving it crosswise and weighting the halves beneath a Dutch oven for about an hour. But that didn't stop the olives, capers, and onions from tumbling out when I unwrapped the halves and cut the sandwiches into portions. I needed to make the looser ingredients more cohesive.

First, I borrowed red wine vinegar from the dressing to soak the sliced onion and garlic with a little salt, which mellowed the sharp bite of both alliums and had the bonus effect of wilting the onion and making it more compact. While that mixture sat, I finely chopped the olives, capers, anchovies, and herbs in the food processor and then tossed them with the onion mixture. I divvied it up by packing most of it into the trough beneath the tuna and spreading the rest across the top of the egg slices. These ingredients now stayed mostly contained, and with their briny, salty flavors sandwiching the rest of the filling, each bite tasted balanced.

There was just one problem: Placing the wet olive mixture directly against the bread meant that the crumb, which had been pleasantly moist, was now bordering on sodden.

I looked for ways to curb the amount of free liquid in the filling. One easy fix was to drain the juicy tomatoes on paper towels before placing them in the sandwich. I also combined some olive oil and mustard with the olive mixture so that the mustard could bind up the water from the vinegar and onions. In addition, I made the crumb water-resistant by brushing the cut surfaces of the baguette with more olive oil. I also decided to toast the baguette before building the sandwich, which would make the exterior more crisp.

When I capped this sandwich with the top of the baguette and sliced it crosswise, the filling stayed put and it was easy to wrap each half into a tidy torpedo. I assembled another Dutch oven "press," this time with a rimmed baking sheet between the pot and the bread to make the setup steadier and flipped the sandwiches after 30 minutes so that gravity could help evenly distribute the moisture.

The results? Each component of the filling was thoughtful, and the balance of flavors was pitch-perfect. Brushing oil on the bread kept enough liquid from the filling at bay so that the crumb was moistened but not sodden. And the make-ahead convenience meant that this would be just the thing to serve at backyard parties—yes, a tuna sandwich fit for company—as well as to have on hand for busy nights.

—ANDREW JANJIGIAN, *Cook's Illustrated*

Pan Bagnat (Provençal Tuna Sandwich)

SERVES 4 TO 6

We developed this recipe with Tonnino Tuna Fillets in Olive Oil, but you can substitute three 5-ounce cans of another oil-packed tuna. To accommodate the filling, the baguette should be approximately 18 inches long,

PAN BAGNAT (PROVENÇAL TUNA SANDWICH)

3 inches wide, and at least 2 inches tall. A ciabatta of similar size will work, as will individual ciabatta rolls. You can substitute 1 tablespoon of oregano for the marjoram and kalamata olives for the niçoise, if desired. Our favorite capers are Reese Non Pareil Capers, and our favorite anchovies are King Oscar Anchovies Flat Fillets in Olive Oil.

1 vine-ripened tomato, cored and sliced thin

1 small red onion, sliced thin

1 garlic clove, minced

¼ teaspoon table salt

3 tablespoons red wine vinegar

1 large baguette, halved horizontally

¾ cup niçoise olives, pitted

3 tablespoons capers, rinsed

3 anchovies, rinsed and patted dry

½ cup fresh parsley leaves and tender stems

2 tablespoons fresh marjoram leaves

½ cup extra-virgin olive oil, divided

2 tablespoons Dijon mustard

¼ teaspoon pepper

2 (6½-ounce) jars oil-packed tuna, drained

3 hard-cooked eggs, sliced thin

1. Adjust oven rack to middle position and heat oven to 350 degrees. Lay tomato slices on paper towel–lined plate and set aside. Place onion, garlic, salt, and vinegar in bowl and toss to combine. Using your hands or metal spoon, remove inner crumb from baguette bottom to create trough with ¼-inch border on sides and bottom. Place baguette halves cut side up on baking sheet and bake until very lightly toasted, 5 minutes.

2. Place olives, capers, anchovies, parsley, and marjoram in bowl of food processor and pulse until coarsely but evenly chopped, 10 to 12 pulses. Transfer olive mixture to bowl with onion mixture. Add ¼ cup oil, mustard, and pepper and toss to combine.

3. Brush inside of each baguette half with 1 tablespoon oil. Place two-thirds of olive mixture in hollow of baguette bottom and spread evenly. Distribute tuna evenly over olive mixture and drizzle with remaining 2 tablespoons oil. Shingle tomato slices over tuna. Shingle egg slices over tomato. Top eggs with remaining olive mixture and cap with baguette top (sandwich will be very full).

4. Press gently on sandwich and slice in half crosswise on bias. Wrap each half tightly in plastic wrap. Place rimmed baking sheet on top of sandwiches and weight with heavy Dutch oven or two 5-pound bags of flour or sugar for 1 hour, flipping sandwiches halfway through weighting. (Wrapped sandwiches can be refrigerated for up to 24 hours. Let come to room temperature before serving.)

5. Unwrap sandwiches, slice each sandwich in half (or in thirds to serve 6) on bias, and serve.

HOT BUTTERED LOBSTER ROLLS

✔ WHY THIS RECIPE WORKS For the perfect hot buttered lobster rolls, we started by simmering the lobsters whole in a large pot of heavily seasoned water until they were tender but still slightly undercooked. Once the lobster meat was removed and cut into bite-size pieces, we finished cooking it in a skillet along with butter and a bit of shallot for added sweetness and then spooned the buttered lobster into perfectly toasted rolls.

There are many ways to make a lobster roll—and I love them all. Where I live, near Boston, the cold mayonnaise and celery version is the most popular. But since butter and lobster make such a great match, I wanted to take a deep dive into the style of lobster roll that uses melted butter in place of the mayonnaise and celery. I set out to make the best version of the buttered style, one that would be easy to achieve for the home cook.

My first consideration was, of course, the lobster. Fresh, live lobster is plentiful (and often relatively inexpensive) where I live; the New England coast is the epicenter of the United States' lobster industry. But for the sake of cooks in other parts of the country, I knew I needed to look into other options. So in addition to using the meat from live local lobsters that I boiled and shelled myself, I made hot buttered lobster rolls using the meat from frozen lobster tails (which are sold raw and in the shells), canned chunk lobster meat, and a canister of preshelled meat from my fishmonger.

The canned chunk meat was mushy and lacking in flavor, and the preshelled meat was too chewy (likely as a result of overcooking). The lesson: Whether you buy live lobsters (our first choice) or frozen tails (our second choice), it's important to cook them yourself for the best-tasting, most tender meat.

Since neither chewy, stringy meat nor raw lobster would do, I knew that developing a foolproof cooking method would be key to this recipe's success. Knowing that I'd use the meat from the tails and claws of fresh lobsters (there are lots of tasty morsels in the body, too, but they are smaller and take a bit of work to get to), I determined that I'd need three 1½-pound lobsters to make four rolls. Using three lobsters meant that I couldn't cook them all at once in a standard Dutch oven; I'd need a larger stockpot to fit them. I tried poaching, boiling, simmering, and steaming the lobsters. Poaching took too long, and steaming resulted in uneven cooking. Simmering the lobsters in plenty of salted water (to ensure that they were well seasoned) was the way to go; in about 12 minutes, the lobster meat was perfectly cooked and—after a 10-minute rest—easy to remove from the shells.

As for how to incorporate the butter, my plan was to follow the advice of other recipes and toss the chopped shelled meat in melted butter in the same skillet I'd use to toast the hot dog buns. After a bit of testing, I found that it was most efficient to toast the buns first, remove them from the skillet, and then add 6 tablespoons of unsalted butter. Once the butter had melted, I tossed in the lobster meat and heated it through for a few minutes before scooping the sweet, glistening morsels into the buns. A minced shallot added to the butter provided another layer of sweet, savory flavor without overcomplicating things or overshadowing the lobster's sweetness.

But I ran into a problem. Since lobster meat is very delicate and prone to overcooking (and becoming rubbery and chewy), fully cooking the lobsters before warming the meat through in the skillet was causing the meat to overcook. To avoid this pitfall, I found that it was best to slightly undercook the lobsters during their initial simmer; after 10 minutes the meat was cooked almost all the way through and still came out of the shell easily. To finish, I again kept things simple: a sprinkling of minced chives along with lemon wedges on the side added just enough brightness to bring these lobster rolls over the top.

My colleagues were smitten with these buttery lobster rolls, so much so that a few claimed they were swearing off the cold, mayonnaise-based version forever. While I'm not ready to make that leap, these hot buttered lobster rolls are definitely going into my summer cooking rotation.

—ALLI BERKEY, *Cook's Country*

Hot Buttered Lobster Rolls

SERVES 4

For the best results, use live lobsters. If you cannot find live lobsters, eight 4- to 5-ounce frozen lobster tails can be substituted; reduce the cooking time in step 1 to 4 minutes, or cook until the meat registers 135 degrees. If New England–style hot dog buns, also known as "split-top" buns, are unavailable, you can substitute regular hot dog buns or, in a pinch, hamburger buns.

- 3 (1½-pound) live lobsters
- ¼ teaspoon table salt, plus salt for cooking lobsters
- 2 tablespoons unsalted butter, softened, plus 6 tablespoons cut into 6 pieces
- 4 New England–style hot dog buns
- 1 small shallot, minced (optional)
- 2 teaspoons minced fresh chives
  Lemon wedges

NOTES FROM THE TEST KITCHEN

HOW TO REMOVE MEAT FROM A COOKED LOBSTER
This is wet, messy work: Hold the lobster using clean dish towels to ensure a secure grip and protect yourself from cuts since the shells are sharp.

CLAWS
1. Twist to remove.
2. Separate claw pieces and knuckles.
3. Crack shells and dig out meat.

BODY
There are tasty morsels within the lobster's body, but they take a bit of work to get to. The small side legs are great for snacking on—some say their fine shreds of meat are the sweetest.

TAIL
1. Twist to separate from body.
2. Pull off small flippers.
3. Use shears to cut through underside of shell, or use your fingers to push meat out through larger (body side) opening.

TOOLS
Lobster crackers and forks are nice if you have them, but you can get by with kitchen shears, a chef's knife, and a butter knife for digging out the meat.

Illustration: Traci Daberko

1. Bring 6 quarts water to boil in large stockpot over high heat. Add lobsters and 3 tablespoons salt, making sure lobsters are completely submerged. Reduce heat to medium-low, cover, and cook for 10 minutes. Transfer lobsters to rimmed baking sheet and let cool for 10 minutes.

2. Remove lobster meat from claws and tails. Cut meat into rough ¾-inch pieces; set aside. Spread softened butter evenly on outer cut sides of buns. Toast outsides of buns in 12-inch skillet over medium heat. Transfer buns to serving platter.

3. Melt remaining 6 tablespoons butter in now-empty skillet over medium-low heat. Stir in shallot, if using; lobster; and salt and cook until lobster is heated through, about 2 minutes.

4. Using slotted spoon, divide lobster mixture among buns. Sprinkle lobster rolls with chives and drizzle with any remaining butter from skillet, if desired. Serve with lemon wedges.

CUBAN SANDWICHES

❤ **WHY THIS RECIPE WORKS** To make Cuban sandwiches at home that rival the prizewinners at the Cuban Sandwich Festival, we found it essential to make the traditional Cuban bread ourselves. Our recipe for Cuban bread yielded golden loaves so cottony on the inside and crisp on the outside that you'd think you were in the Sunshine State. For the filling, we built the sandwich in the traditional order: deli ham, Cuban roast pork, Genoa salami (a signature Tampa-only addition), Swiss cheese, and finally, pickles. Our recipe for Cuban Roast Pork with Mojo yielded deeply seasoned pork that was silky and moist with a mojo-inspired citrus punch. We chilled the cooked roast to make it easier to slice paper-thin, an important step in getting a clean, evenly pressed sandwich. We included a swipe of flavorful mojo sauce (from our Cuban roast pork recipe) on the bottom slice of bread for extra complexity and brightness. Adding the less traditional swipe of mayonnaise kept the sandwich moist. We put yellow mustard on only the top piece of bread so as not to overwhelm the sandwich. For perfect pressing, we used a heavy Dutch oven to weigh down the sandwiches and yield a faint crispy edge that gives this sandwich a real wow factor.

After my colleague Bryan Roof returned from the Cuban Sandwich Festival in Tampa, he set a goal for me: Create a home recipe for Cuban sandwiches that would stand up to the prizewinners he'd tasted. The sandwich is familiar on a basic level: Roasted spiced pork, ham, Swiss cheese, dill pickles, and yellow mustard on soft bread that's pressed and toasted until golden brown. In Tampa, the sandwich also includes Genoa salami.

That's a fantastic combination any way you look at it, so it's no surprise that there are as many variations of the sandwich as there are fans of it. I wanted to take it back to its Tampa roots: Yes, there'd be salami on it; yes, I'd follow the traditional, particular order of components and amounts of each; yes, I'd even make the bread; yes, all this for a sandwich. And yes (!), it would be worth it.

Let's start with the bread. A Cuban sandwich must be made on golden Cuban bread that's fluffy on the inside and crisp on the outside, which is not easy to find outside Florida. It's traditionally enriched with lard for a savory flavor (not sweet or yeasty like a typical sandwich loaf). When the fully assembled sandwich is toasted on the griddle, the bread is just sturdy enough to hold the many layers together as the flavors fuse.

I found it essential to slice the roast pork very thin. Thick slices interfered with a clean, even press, and shredded pork was harder to distribute evenly on the bread. Cooling the roast so it firmed up a bit before slicing meant that I could achieve the perfect thinness with a good sharp knife.

Taking inspiration from some creative cooks at the Tampa festival, I included a swipe of flavorful mojo sauce on each bottom slice of bread for extra complexity and brightness.

After 35 pork butts, 80 loaves of bread, and piles of ham, cheese, pickles, and more, I pressed and toasted my final batch of sandwiches. I cut them into their characteristic triangle shape, and coworkers began to swarm. The work is worth it. Just make sure you eat it point side up.

—CECILIA JENKINS, *Cook's Country*

Cuban Sandwiches

SERVES 4

We strongly prefer to use our Cuban Bread (page 94) for this recipe, but you can use four 7- to 8-inch soft white Italian-style sub rolls or two 15-inch loaves of soft supermarket Italian or French bread. To make slicing the Cuban roast pork easier, chill it thoroughly beforehand. Mojo and mayonnaise aren't typical ingredients in Tampa-style Cuban sandwiches, but they make nice additions. Serve with plantain chips, if desired.

1 recipe Cuban Bread (page 94)

¼ cup mojo from Cuban Roast Pork with Mojo (recipe follows) (optional)

¼ cup mayonnaise (optional)

12 ounces thinly sliced deli ham

10 ounces thinly sliced Cuban roast pork from Cuban Roast Pork with Mojo (2 cups) (recipe follows)

3 ounces thinly sliced deli Genoa salami with peppercorns

6 ounces thinly sliced deli Swiss cheese

16 dill pickle chips

¼ cup yellow mustard

4 tablespoons unsalted butter, cut into 4 pieces, divided

1. Adjust oven rack to middle position and heat oven to 200 degrees. Set wire rack in rimmed baking sheet. Cut each loaf of bread in half crosswise, then cut each piece in half horizontally.

2. Brush bread bottoms with mojo, if using, and spread with mayonnaise, if using. Layer on ham, followed by pork, salami, Swiss cheese, and pickles, overlapping and/or folding meats as needed to keep them from overhanging sides of bread. Spread mustard on bread tops. Cap sandwiches with bread tops.

3. Melt 1 tablespoon butter in 12-inch nonstick skillet over medium-low heat. Place 2 sandwiches in skillet, right side up, in alternating directions, and spread far apart. Place heavy Dutch oven on top and cook until bottoms of sandwiches are uniformly golden brown and feel firm when tapped, 5 to 7 minutes, rotating sandwiches in skillet as needed. (You will need to flip sandwiches to tap them.)

4. Transfer sandwiches to cutting board. Melt 1 tablespoon butter in now-empty skillet. Return sandwiches to skillet toasted side up. Place Dutch oven on top and continue to cook until second side is uniformly golden brown and feels firm when tapped, 3 to 5 minutes longer.

5. Transfer toasted sandwiches to prepared wire rack and place in oven to keep warm. Wipe skillet clean with paper towels. Repeat with remaining 2 tablespoons butter and remaining 2 sandwiches. Cut sandwiches in half on steep diagonal and serve.

Cuban Roast Pork with Mojo
SERVES 6 TO 8

Avoid buying a pork butt wrapped in netting; it will contain smaller, separate lobes of meat rather than one whole roast. The pork will take longer to cook in a stainless-steel pot than in an enameled cast-iron Dutch oven, the pot we used while developing the recipe. If using a stainless-steel pot, place a sheet of aluminum foil over the pot before affixing the lid. If you plan to make Cuban sandwiches with the leftovers, it is best to slice only what you want to serve and then slice the chilled leftover pork for the sandwiches. You will need about 10 ounces, or 2 cups, of pork and ¼ cup of mojo for the sandwiches. If using table salt, cut the amounts of salt in half.

PORK

⅓ cup kosher salt

⅓ cup packed light brown sugar

1 tablespoon grated lime zest (2 limes)

1 tablespoon grated orange zest

3 garlic cloves, minced

2 teaspoons ground cumin

2 teaspoons dried oregano

½ teaspoon red pepper flakes

1 (5-pound) boneless pork butt roast with fat cap

MOJO

⅓ cup extra-virgin olive oil

6 garlic cloves, minced

⅓ cup pineapple juice

⅓ cup orange juice

⅓ cup lime juice (3 limes)

1 tablespoon yellow mustard

1¼ teaspoons ground cumin

1 teaspoon kosher salt

¾ teaspoon pepper

¾ teaspoon dried oregano

¼ teaspoon red pepper flakes

Thinly sliced onion rounds

1. FOR THE PORK: Combine salt, sugar, lime zest, orange zest, garlic, cumin, oregano, and pepper flakes in bowl. Using sharp knife, trim fat cap on pork to ¼ inch. Cut 1-inch crosshatch pattern in fat cap.

2. Place pork on large double layer of plastic wrap. Sprinkle pork all over with salt mixture. Wrap pork tightly in plastic, place on plate, and refrigerate for at least 12 hours or up to 24 hours.

CUBAN SANDWICHES

3. Adjust oven rack to middle position and heat oven to 325 degrees. Unwrap pork; transfer to Dutch oven, fat side up; and pour 2 cups water around pork. Cover, transfer to oven, and cook until meat registers 175 degrees in center, 2½ to 3 hours.

4. Uncover pork and continue to cook until meat registers 195 degrees in center and fork slips easily in and out of meat, 45 minutes to 1¾ hours longer. Transfer pork to carving board, tent with aluminum foil, and let rest for 45 minutes.

5. FOR THE MOJO: While pork rests, heat oil and garlic in small saucepan over low heat, stirring often, until tiny bubbles appear and garlic is fragrant and straw-colored, 3 to 5 minutes. Let cool for at least 5 minutes. Whisk pineapple juice, orange juice, lime juice, mustard, cumin, salt, pepper, oregano, and pepper flakes into cooled garlic oil.

6. Slice pork as thin as possible (some meat may shred; this is OK) and transfer to serving platter. Serve with onion and mojo.

Cuban Bread

MAKES TWO 15-INCH LOAVES

You can substitute shortening for the lard, if desired. If you're strapped for time, you can ferment the sponge for at least 1 hour or up to 4 hours at room temperature instead of overnight. Be gentle when slashing the shaped loaves or they will bake up wide and squat.

SPONGE

¼ **cup water**

¼ **cup (1¼ ounces) all-purpose flour**

½ **teaspoon instant or rapid-rise yeast**

DOUGH

3 **cups (15 ounces) all-purpose flour**

2 **teaspoons instant or rapid-rise yeast**

1½ **teaspoons table salt**

1 **cup warm water (110 degrees)**

¼ **cup lard**

1 **(16 by 12-inch) rectangular disposable aluminum roasting pan**

1. FOR THE SPONGE: Whisk water, flour, and yeast with fork in liquid measuring cup until consistency of thin pancake batter. Cover with plastic wrap and refrigerate overnight (sponge will rise and collapse).

2. FOR THE DOUGH: Whisk flour, yeast, and salt together in bowl of stand mixer. Add warm water, lard, and sponge. Fit mixer with dough hook and mix on low speed until no dry flour remains, about 2 minutes, scraping down bowl as needed. Increase speed to medium and knead for 8 minutes. (Dough will be sticky and clear sides of bowl but still stick to bottom.)

3. Turn out dough onto lightly floured counter, sprinkle top with flour, and knead briefly to form smooth ball, about 30 seconds. Transfer dough to greased large bowl and turn to coat. Cover with plastic and let dough rise at room temperature until doubled in size, about 45 minutes.

4. Line rimless baking sheet with parchment paper. Turn out dough onto floured counter and cut into 2 equal pieces, about 14 ounces each.

5. Working with 1 piece of dough at a time, flatten into 10 by 6-inch rectangle with long side parallel to counter's edge. Fold top edge of rectangle down to midline, pressing to seal. Fold bottom edge of rectangle up to midline, pressing to seal. Fold dough in half so top and bottom edges meet; pinch seam and ends to seal. Flip dough seam side down and gently roll into 15-inch loaf with tapered ends.

6. Transfer loaf, seam side down, to 1 side of prepared sheet. Repeat shaping with second piece of dough and place about 3 inches from first loaf on other side of sheet. Cover loosely with plastic and let rise at room temperature until puffy, about 30 minutes. Adjust oven rack to middle position and heat oven to 450 degrees.

7. Using sharp paring knife in swift, fluid motion, make ⅛-inch-deep lengthwise slash along top of each loaf, starting and stopping about 1½ inches from ends. Cover loaves with inverted disposable pan. Bake for 20 minutes. Using tongs, remove disposable pan and continue to bake until loaves are light golden brown and centers register 210 degrees, 10 to 12 minutes longer.

8. Transfer loaves to wire rack and let cool for 30 minutes. Serve warm.

BACON, LETTUCE, AND FRIED GREEN TOMATO SANDWICHES

✓ **WHY THIS RECIPE WORKS** Fried green tomatoes sound good in theory, but in practice, the tomatoes themselves are often a letdown. But like all good Southern-style fried food, they ought to be full-flavored, well-seasoned, crunchy, and crispy. To that end, we began by sprinkling salt and sugar on the sliced tomatoes, drawing out their moisture and intensifying their flavor. We ditched the all-too-often gritty cornmeal in favor of unfailingly crunchy panko bread crumbs, and dredged the tomatoes twice in a boldly seasoned breading enhanced with Old Bay seasoning. Shallow frying the tomatoes reduced the amount of wasted oil and made easy work of getting them golden and crispy. To complete our sandwich, we mixed together a tangy, spicy mayonnaise, slathered it on a soft brioche roll, and piled on the bacon, shredded lettuce, and crispy fried tomatoes.

I'm a food-loving Southerner from one of America's great eating cities: Charleston, South Carolina. As such, there are dishes I'm expected to know and love, most of them quite rightly so. For instance, shrimp and grits—delicious!

Fried green tomatoes are on that list, too. And until a couple of months ago, I'd have been on board with the most avid fan of those tart, cornmeal-crusted tomatoes. But when I got into testing for my recipe for fried green tomato BLTs, I uncovered something downright dishonorable: My professed love for this southern favorite was a lie.

Let me explain. I researched dozens of recipes, picking the most delicious sounding ones to fry up in the test kitchen. I took pains to keep the fried tomatoes hot and crispy for each tasting. My colleagues and I dug in, and as it turned out, the only thing I like about (most) fried green tomatoes is the creamy, tangy dipping sauce, which can cover up a multitude of sins. I'm talking major culinary transgressions: soggy, grainy, chewy breading and bland, steamy tomatoes. These attempts were not fried green tomatoes at their best. They ought to have been crunchy, crispy, sweet-tart little jewels, well seasoned with a kick of spice.

I let my disappointment inspire me and set about making fried green tomatoes so good that they could stand alone—only then would I put them on a BLT. The recipe here is what emerged from that sad, soggy

valley, and it's one I'm proud of. To eradicate sogginess and erase the memory of those steamy, bland tomatoes, I sprinkled healthy amounts of salt and sugar on the sliced tomatoes, drawing out their moisture and intensifying their flavor before breading them. Instead of sometimes-gritty cornmeal, I used always-crunchy panko bread crumbs as the base of my breading, enhancing their flavor with Old Bay seasoning. And I doubled down on crunch by dredging the tomatoes in the breading not once, but twice.

After an easy shallow fry, the slices came out golden and crispy. A quick bite confirmed that they were ready for the BLT treatment. I mixed together a quick and tangy spicy mayonnaise, slathered it on a big, soft brioche roll, and then piled on the bacon, shredded lettuce, and crispy fried tomatoes. I hope you'll do the same, but do treat yourself to a bite of one of the fried tomatoes by itself; it's worth it.

—MATTHEW FAIRMAN, *Cook's Country*

Bacon, Lettuce, and Fried Green Tomato Sandwiches

SERVES 4

Look for green tomatoes that are about 3 inches in diameter. If possible, it's best to slice the tomatoes closer to ⅛ inch thick, but as long as they're less than ¼ inch thick, they will work well in this sandwich.

NOTES FROM THE TEST KITCHEN

SINGULAR SANDWICH SEASONINGS
Our recipe for Bacon, Lettuce, and Fried Green Tomato Sandwiches relies on two of our—and America's—favorite seasonings.

First up is Old Bay seasoning, a celery salt- and paprika-heavy mix that is a staple of seafood boils. We use it to give our coating a deep, complex seasoning.

Tabasco sauce needs no introduction, but it's worth noting that it's not the test kitchen's taste test winner for an all-around hot sauce. However, we found its vinegary, peppery bite to be perfect for putting a little kick in the mayonnaise that dresses the buns of these sandwiches.

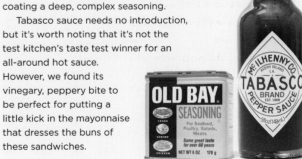

BACON, LETTUCE, AND FRIED GREEN TOMATO SANDWICHES

3 green tomatoes

1 tablespoon sugar

1½ teaspoons table salt, divided

½ cup mayonnaise

2 teaspoons Tabasco sauce

1½ cups all-purpose flour

1½ cups panko bread crumbs

1 tablespoon Old Bay seasoning

4 large eggs

1½ cups vegetable oil for frying

4 large brioche sandwich rolls, split and toasted

12 slices cooked bacon, halved

2 cups shredded iceberg lettuce

1. Core tomatoes and cut off rounded tops and bottoms. Slice tomatoes into twelve ⅛- to ¼-inch-thick slices (you may have some left over). Line rimmed baking sheet with triple layer of paper towels. Place tomato slices on prepared sheet and sprinkle on both sides with sugar and 1 teaspoon salt. Top tomatoes with triple layer of paper towels and let sit for 1 hour.

2. Meanwhile, whisk mayonnaise and Tabasco together in bowl; set aside.

3. Whisk flour, panko, Old Bay, and remaining ½ teaspoon salt together in large bowl. Beat eggs together in shallow dish. Remove top layer of paper towels from tomatoes. Transfer tomatoes to flour mixture and toss to coat.

4. Remove remaining paper towels from sheet and wipe sheet dry. Return tomatoes to now-empty sheet. Working with 1 slice at a time, dip tomatoes in egg, allowing excess to drip off, and transfer back to flour mixture, pressing firmly so coating adheres. Return tomatoes to sheet.

5. Line large plate with triple layer of paper towels. Add oil to 12-inch nonstick skillet and heat over medium-high heat to 350 degrees. Fry half of tomatoes until golden and crispy, about 2 minutes per side, reducing heat as needed if oil gets too hot. Using tongs, transfer fried tomatoes to prepared plate. Return oil to 350 degrees and repeat with remaining tomatoes.

6. Spread 1 tablespoon mayonnaise mixture on each roll bottom, then follow with 6 half-slices bacon and 3 fried tomatoes, overlapping slightly in center. Toss lettuce with remaining ¼ cup mayonnaise mixture in bowl and divide evenly among sandwiches. Top with roll tops and serve.

PUPUSAS

WHY THIS RECIPE WORKS Hydrating the masa harina with boiling rather than room-temperature water allowed the starches in the flour to absorb the water more quickly and completely, resulting in a well-hydrated dough that was easy to work with and didn't dry out when cooked. The proper ratio of masa dough to filling ensured that each bite of pupusa included plenty of melted cheese filling. Pressing the stuffed pupusas into 4-inch disks between sheets of plastic ensured uniform thickness and allowed us to cook four pupusas at once in a 12-inch skillet. The crunch and acidic brightness of curtido and salsa perfectly complemented the tender, savory patties.

Pupusas have been sustaining Latin Americans since pre-Columbian times. And when a food has that kind of longevity, you know it has to be good. Though Salvadorans and Hondurans both lay claim to the recipe, in El Salvador it is considered the national dish. There, these enticing packages are made by stuffing cheese, beans, braised meat, or a combination thereof into a ball of corn flour dough called masa. The ball is flattened into a 4- or 5-inch disk and cooked on a comal (a dry cast-iron griddle) until the tender corn cake forms a spotty-brown, crisp shell. Garnished with curtido (a bright slaw) and a spicy salsa, the result is downright irresistible.

The Salvadoran cooks I've seen shape pupusas look like they could do it in their sleep: They work masa into a fist-size cup, spoon in the filling, and pinch the dough closed to form a ball before slapping it back and forth between their hands to create a disk. The first time I tried, it was obvious that I was a novice. Using a dough made with the usual ratio of 2 parts masa harina (corn flour) to 1 part water, I formed the cakes as best I could. But the masa was too dry, which caused the pupusas to crack and the filling to spill out.

Using hot tap water instead of cool, as some recipes suggest, worked better since heat causes the starch in corn to absorb more water (just as it does in wheat flour). But boiling water was even more effective, allowing me to superhydrate the 2 cups of masa harina with a full 2 cups of water. Now the dough was a dream to handle, and the cakes cooked up as moist as could be.

But although the dough was no longer sticky, my pupusas were still thick at the centers and thin at the edges—even after all my practice. The filling never spread to the edges, leaving all but the centermost bites tasting of plain dough. I was determined to find a method that would allow even a novice like me to consistently form perfect pupusas.

I decided to try a riff on our technique for making tortillas. I rolled portions of my superhydrated masa into a ball, placed it inside a zipper-lock bag that I'd cut open at the seams, and used a glass pie plate to press it into a disk. I turned the disk out into my palm, placed some filling (more on that next) in the center, and gathered the dough to form a ball, which I again pressed with the pie plate to form a perfectly round pupusa of even thickness. Even a newbie could pull this off.

As for the filling, basic pupusas are stuffed with a delicious but hard to find fresh Salvadoran cheese called quesillo. Some recipes suggest swapping in mozzarella, but I found it too bland. Instead, I landed on a mix of Monterey Jack for its meltability and cotija—a readily available Mexican cheese—for its salty tang.

These perfectly flat, round pupusas, stuffed from edge to edge with salty, supple cheese, would fool anyone into thinking I'd been making them all my life.

—STEVE DUNN, *Cook's Illustrated*

Pupusas

SERVES 4 (MAKES 8 PUPUSAS)

For an accurate measurement of boiling water, bring a full kettle of water to a boil and then measure out the desired amount. Properly hydrated masa dough should be tacky, requiring damp hands to keep it from sticking to your palms. If the dough feels the slightest bit dry at any time, knead in warm tap water, 2 teaspoons at a time, until the dough is tacky. An occasional leak while frying the pupusas is to be expected, and the browned cheese is delicious. Feta cheese can be substituted for the cotija; if you can find quesillo, use 10 ounces in place of the cotija and Monterey Jack.

2	cups (8 ounces) masa harina
½	teaspoon table salt
2	cups boiling water, plus warm tap water as needed
2	teaspoons vegetable oil, divided
2	ounces cotija cheese, cut into 2 pieces
8	ounces Monterey Jack cheese, cut into 8 pieces
1	recipe Quick Salsa (recipe follows)
1	recipe Curtido (recipe follows)

1. Using marker, draw 4-inch circle in center of 1 side of 1-quart or 1-gallon zipper-lock bag. Cut open seams along both sides of bag, but leave bottom seam intact so bag opens completely.

2. Mix masa harina and salt together in medium bowl. Add boiling water and 1 teaspoon oil and mix with rubber spatula until soft dough forms. Cover dough and let rest for 20 minutes.

3. While dough rests, line rimmed baking sheet with parchment paper. Process cotija in food processor until cotija is finely chopped and resembles wet sand, about 20 seconds. Add Monterey Jack and process until mixture resembles wet oatmeal, about 30 seconds (it will not form cohesive mass). Remove processor blade. Form cheese mixture into 8 balls, weighing about 1¼ ounces each, and place balls on 1 half of prepared sheet.

4. Knead dough in bowl for 15 to 20 seconds. Test dough's hydration by flattening golf ball–size piece. If cracks larger than ¼ inch form around edges, add warm tap water, 2 teaspoons at a time, until dough is soft and slightly tacky. Transfer dough to counter, shape into large ball, and divide into 8 equal pieces. Using your damp hands, roll 1 dough piece into ball and place on empty half of prepared sheet. Cover with damp dish towel. Repeat with remaining dough pieces.

5. Place open cut bag marked side down on counter. Place 1 dough ball in center of circle. Fold other side of bag over ball. Using glass pie plate or 8-inch square baking dish, gently press dough to 4-inch diameter, using circle drawn on bag as guide. Turn out disk into your palm and place 1 cheese ball in center. Bring sides of dough up around filling and pinch top to seal. Remoisten your hands and roll ball until smooth, smoothing any cracks with your damp fingertip. Return ball to bag and slowly press to 4-inch diameter. Pinch closed any small cracks that form at edges. Return pupusa to sheet and cover with damp dish towel. Repeat with remaining dough and filling.

6. Heat remaining 1 teaspoon oil in 12-inch nonstick skillet over medium-high heat until shimmering. Wipe skillet clean with paper towels. Carefully lay 4 pupusas in skillet and cook until spotty brown on both sides, 2 to 4 minutes per side. Transfer to platter and repeat with remaining 4 pupusas. Serve warm with salsa and curtido.

TO MAKE AHEAD: At end of step 5, wrap baking sheet in plastic wrap and freeze until pupusas are solid. Wrap pupusas individually in plastic, then transfer pupusas to zipper-lock bag. Freeze for up to 1 month. Cook directly from frozen, increasing cooking time by 1 minute per side.

Quick Salsa

SERVES 4

For a spicier salsa, reserve and add the jalapeño seeds as desired.

- ¼ small red onion
- 2 tablespoons minced fresh cilantro
- ½ small jalapeño chile, seeded and minced
- 1 (14.5-ounce) can diced tomatoes, drained
- 2 teaspoons lime juice, plus extra for seasoning
- 1 small garlic clove, minced
- ¼ teaspoon table salt
  Pinch pepper

Pulse onion, cilantro, and jalapeño in food processor until finely chopped, 5 pulses, scraping down sides of bowl as needed. Add tomatoes, lime juice, garlic, salt, and pepper and process until smooth, 20 to 30 seconds. Season with salt and extra lime juice to taste.

NOTES FROM THE TEST KITCHEN

DETERMINE HYDRATION USING THE CRACK TEST
Before forming the pupusas, test the dough's hydration by flattening a golf ball–size piece of dough. If cracks larger than ¼ inch form around the edges, add more water, 2 teaspoons at a time.

TOO DRY
Large cracks form in a test piece of dough.

Curtido

SERVES 4

For a spicier slaw, reserve and add the jalapeño seeds as desired.

- 1 cup cider vinegar
- ½ cup water
- 1 tablespoon sugar
- 1½ teaspoons table salt
- ½ head green cabbage, cored and sliced thin (6 cups)
- 1 onion, sliced thin
- 1 large carrot, peeled and shredded
- 1 jalapeño chile, stemmed, seeded, and minced
- 1 teaspoon dried oregano
- 1 cup chopped fresh cilantro

Whisk vinegar, water, sugar, and salt in large bowl until sugar is dissolved. Add cabbage, onion, carrot, jalapeño, and oregano and toss to combine. Cover and refrigerate for at least 1 hour or up to 24 hours. Toss slaw, then drain. Return slaw to bowl and stir in cilantro.

EGGPLANT PECORINO

✓ WHY THIS RECIPE WORKS For a more restrained take on eggplant Parmesan, we skipped the bread crumbs and instead fried the eggplant in a thin flour and egg coating to create a light, fluffy exterior around each eggplant slice. We built four stacks of eggplant slices in a 13 by 9-inch baking dish, with sauce and cheese in between each layer. To create a quick, bright sauce, we sautéed onion, garlic, anchovies, red pepper flakes, and oregano in butter and then briefly simmered them with a combination of canned crushed tomatoes and diced tomatoes and their juice. We replaced the traditional Parmesan with Pecorino Romano, which added a nutty, tangy flavor that paired beautifully with the eggplant. Topping our eggplant stacks with creamy shredded fontina and finishing them under the broiler gave them a melty, browned, bubbly top.

Read the words "eggplant Parmesan" on almost any restaurant menu and you know what you're in for: a mountain of mozzarella, a loaf's worth of bread crumbs, a swimming pool of sweet red sauce, and, buried deep beneath it all, a fat slab of mushy eggplant. It's usually a heavy dish that requires a nap afterward.

But at La Campagna, a small strip mall restaurant in Westlake, Ohio, I was served a version of eggplant Parm that turned the concept on its head. A lighter hand produced a dish that actually showcased the eggplant in all the right ways: savory, faintly bitter, buttery, and satisfying. The cheese and sauce added just enough context to amplify the eggplant.

At La Campagna they slice the eggplant superthin, which nixes the possibility of a big bite of mush. Following this approach, I chose eggplants of a certain size—1 pound or smaller—and carefully cut them lengthwise into ¼-inch-thick slices.

I also decided to skip the bread crumbs and instead focus on frying the eggplant in a thin flour and egg coating. It's a simple process (dredge each slice in flour, dip it in beaten egg, and then shallow-fry in a skillet), but it takes a bit of patience because you have to do it in batches. It's worth the effort: The process creates a light, fluffy shell around each eggplant slice rather than a thick, bready coating—a much more refined result.

At the restaurant, the dish is served as an individual stack of about five slices of eggplant layered with cheese and sauce. This is easy to do in a restaurant, where you can build the stacks to order with prefried eggplant and sauce kept warm on the back of the stove and then throw each serving into the oven to finish. But I wanted a one-and-done solution to serve six people. So I built four stacks of eggplant in a 13 by 9-inch baking dish, with sauce and cheese in between the layers.

Since this dish already requires a fair amount of work, I wanted a deeply flavored sauce that would come together quickly. I sautéed onion, garlic, anchovies, red pepper flakes, and oregano in a couple tablespoons of butter just long enough to extract their flavors, about 3 minutes, and then added a combination of canned crushed tomatoes and diced tomatoes with their juice. A quick 10-minute simmer concentrated the sauce beautifully. I finished it with a fistful of chopped basil for a fresh note and a tablespoon of extra-virgin olive oil for some Italian-style richness.

And about that cheese: I love Parmesan, but at La Campagna they instead pair nutty, tangy Pecorino Romano with the soft, mild eggplant. I chose to follow suit in my dish. A final flourish of creamy shredded fontina cheese, melted and browned under the broiler, made my eggplant Parmesan—I mean, eggplant Pecorino—extra-special.

—BRYAN ROOF, *Cook's Country*

Eggplant Pecorino

SERVES 4 TO 6

Do not use eggplants weighing more than 1 pound each or the slices won't fit in the baking dish. Use a rasp-style grater to grate the Pecorino Romano; shred the fontina on the large holes of a box grater. Depending on the size of your eggplants, you may not need to use all three to get the 20 slices needed to assemble the casserole.

SAUCE

- 2 tablespoons unsalted butter
- ¼ cup finely chopped onion
- 3 garlic cloves, minced
- 2 anchovy fillets, rinsed and minced
- ¾ teaspoon table salt
- ¼ teaspoon red pepper flakes
- ¼ teaspoon dried oregano
- 1 (28-ounce) can crushed tomatoes
- 1 (14.5-ounce) can diced tomatoes
- ½ teaspoon sugar
- ¼ cup chopped fresh basil
- 1 tablespoon extra-virgin olive oil

EGGPLANT

- 3 (10- to 16-ounce) eggplants
- ½ cup all-purpose flour
- 4 large eggs
- 1 cup extra-virgin olive oil for frying
- 4 ounces Pecorino Romano cheese, grated (2 cups)
- 4 ounces fontina cheese, shredded (1 cup)

1. FOR THE SAUCE: Melt butter in medium saucepan over medium-low heat. Add onion, garlic, anchovies, salt, pepper flakes, and oregano and cook until onion is softened, about 3 minutes. Stir in crushed tomatoes, diced tomatoes and their juice, and sugar; increase heat to medium-high; and bring to simmer. Reduce heat to medium-low and simmer until slightly thickened, about 10 minutes. Off heat, stir in basil and oil. Season with salt and pepper to taste. Set aside. (Sauce can be refrigerated for up to 2 days.)

2. FOR THE EGGPLANT: Cut stem end off eggplants and discard. Cut ¼-inch-thick slice from 1 long side of each eggplant and discard. Using mandoline or slicing knife and starting on cut side, slice eggplants lengthwise ¼ inch thick until you have 20 slices total (you may not need all 3 eggplants).

EGGPLANT PECORINO

3. Place flour in shallow dish. Beat eggs in second shallow dish. Line baking sheet with triple layer of paper towels. Heat oil in 12-inch skillet over medium heat to 350 degrees (to take temperature, tilt skillet so oil pools on 1 side). Working with 3 or 4 slices at a time (depending on size of eggplant), dredge eggplant in flour, shaking off excess; dip in egg, allowing excess to drip off; then place in hot oil. Fry until lightly browned on both sides, about 1½ minutes per side. Transfer to prepared sheet. (As eggplant slices cool, you can stack them to make room on sheet.)

4. Adjust oven rack 6 inches from broiler element and heat oven to 375 degrees. Spread 1 cup sauce in bottom of broiler-safe 13 by 9-inch baking dish. Starting with largest slices of eggplant, place 4 eggplant slices side by side over sauce in dish. Spread ½ cup sauce over eggplant, then sprinkle ½ cup Pecorino over top. Repeat layering 3 times to make 4 stacks of 4 slices. Place remaining eggplant slices on top. Spread remaining sauce over top layer of eggplant, then sprinkle with fontina.

5. Bake until bubbling around edges and center of casserole is hot, about 30 minutes. Broil until fontina is lightly browned, 1 to 3 minutes. Let cool for 20 minutes. Serve.

TO MAKE AHEAD: Casserole can be assembled through step 4, without fontina, and refrigerated for up to 24 hours. When ready to serve, cover with aluminum foil and bake for 20 minutes. Remove foil, sprinkle with fontina, and continue to bake as directed in step 5.

FRESH TOMATO GALETTE

✓ **WHY THIS RECIPE WORKS** The hard part about baking with tomatoes is dealing with their unpredictable juice. But it's that juicy summer sweetness that makes them the perfect star of a savory tart. To bring out not only the tomatoes' best flavor but also their juice, we salted the slices and let them sit in a colander before building the tart. Shaking the colander well after a 30-minute rest helped ensure that no extra liquid entered the crust, and lining the inside of the crust with a layer of mustard and shredded Gruyère cheese provided added protection to keep the crust crisp.

A rustic tomato tart—aka tomato galette—is perfect for lunch or as a light supper with a salad, and it's a fantastic way to showcase the sweetness and flavor of ripe tomatoes. But tomatoes contain a lot of water, the enemy of crisp pastry crust. The crusts of more than a few tomato galette recipes I made during my research phase were so soggy that I couldn't cut a clean slice. And some attempts were dull in flavor, too. I headed back to the kitchen determined to make the best possible version.

The test kitchen has a recipe for an easy, crisp crust, but I knew I'd have to do something to extract some liquid from the tomatoes before putting them into that crust. Slicing and salting the tomatoes and letting them drain in a colander took just 30 minutes and allowed the tomatoes to retain more of their fresh flavor.

Speaking of flavor, I decided to add some cheese to the mix. I tested cheddar, mozzarella, Parmesan, gouda, and Gruyère; my tasters couldn't decide between the Parmesan and the Gruyère, so I used them both. I sprinkled the meltable Gruyère right onto the dough before layering the tomato slices on top, and I saved the Parmesan for sprinkling over the assembled galette. The cheeses added richness and also preserved the dough's crisp texture; the Gruyère helped waterproof the dough on the bottom while the wisps of Parmesan soaked up any extra moisture on top.

The galette was really good, but I had a feeling it could be better. Lightning struck when a colleague mentioned that she loved fresh tomato sandwiches not with mayonnaise but with mustard. Mustard! After a bit of testing, I determined that 2 teaspoons spread onto the raw crust provided the perfect gentle kick and brightness to this showstopping galette. If you like tomatoes, please try this recipe. It's a game changer.

—ALLI BERKEY, *Cook's Country*

Fresh Tomato Galette

SERVES 4 TO 6

Sharp cheddar cheese can be used in place of the Gruyère, if desired.

- 1½ cups (7½ ounces) all-purpose flour
- 2 teaspoons table salt, divided
- 10 tablespoons unsalted butter, cut into ½-inch pieces and chilled
- 6–7 tablespoons ice water
- 1½ pounds mixed tomatoes, cored and sliced ¼ inch thick
- 1 shallot, sliced thin
- 2 tablespoons extra-virgin olive oil
- 1 teaspoon minced fresh thyme

1 garlic clove, minced

¼ teaspoon pepper

2 teaspoons Dijon mustard

3 ounces Gruyère cheese, shredded (¾ cup)

2 tablespoons grated Parmesan cheese

1 large egg, lightly beaten

1 tablespoon chopped fresh basil

1. Process flour and ½ teaspoon salt in food processor until combined, about 3 seconds. Scatter butter over top and pulse until mixture resembles coarse crumbs, about 10 pulses. Transfer to large bowl. Sprinkle 6 tablespoons ice water over flour mixture. Using rubber spatula, stir and press dough until it sticks together, adding up to 1 tablespoon more ice water if dough doesn't come together.

2. Turn out dough onto lightly floured counter, form into 4-inch disk, wrap tightly in plastic wrap, and refrigerate for 1 hour. (Wrapped dough can be refrigerated for up to 2 days or frozen for up to 1 month.)

3. Toss tomatoes and 1 teaspoon salt together in second large bowl. Transfer tomatoes to colander and set colander in sink. Let tomatoes drain for 30 minutes.

4. Adjust oven rack to lower-middle position and heat oven to 375 degrees. Line rimmed baking sheet with parchment paper. Let chilled dough sit on counter to soften slightly, about 10 minutes, before rolling. Roll dough into 12-inch circle on lightly floured counter, then transfer to prepared sheet (dough may run up lip of sheet slightly; this is OK).

5. Shake colander well to rid tomatoes of excess juice. Combine tomatoes, shallot, oil, thyme, garlic, pepper, and remaining ½ teaspoon salt in now-empty bowl. Spread mustard over dough, leaving 1½-inch border. Sprinkle Gruyère in even layer over mustard. Shingle tomatoes and shallot on top of Gruyère in concentric circles, keeping within 1½-inch border. Sprinkle Parmesan over tomato mixture.

6. Carefully grasp 1 edge of dough and fold up about 1 inch over filling. Repeat around circumference of tart, overlapping dough every 2 inches, gently pinching pleated dough to secure. Brush folded dough with egg (you won't need it all).

7. Bake until crust is golden brown and tomatoes are bubbling, 45 to 50 minutes. Transfer sheet to wire rack and let galette cool for 10 minutes. Using metal spatula, loosen galette from parchment and carefully slide onto wire rack; let cool until just warm, about 20 minutes. Sprinkle with basil. Cut into wedges and serve.

PALAK DAL (SPINACH-LENTIL DAL WITH CUMIN AND MUSTARD SEEDS)

✔ WHY THIS RECIPE WORKS Quick-cooking red lentils are the centerpiece of our weeknight dal. Once they had softened, a vigorous whisk transformed them into a rustic, porridge-like stew without requiring us to break out a blender or food processor. Seasoning the lentils with a tadka (whole spices sizzled in ghee with aromatics) right before serving gave the dish loads of complexity, a gorgeous appearance, and an enticing aroma.

"Dal" is the Hindi term for dried peas, beans, and legumes and—somewhat confusingly—also refers to the dishes made from them. Dal in some form is consumed daily in most Indian households. Not only is it a complete protein when paired with rice or bread, but dal can be utterly packed with flavor.

But there's more: Dal made from quick-cooking lentils comes together easily and takes hardly any time to prepare, and it's nourishing, satisfying, and cheap. One of the real joys of dal is that it can take a near-endless variety of forms, from celebratory dal makhani, rich with butter and cream, to workday dishes consisting of only lentils, onion, and spices.

I set my sights on palak dal, a simple dal finished with spinach ("palak" means "spinach" in Hindi) that would be a great weeknight main. Here's the usual routine: Start by simmering dal in water, sometimes with turmeric and/or asafetida, the dried resin scraped from the root of the *Ferula assa-foetida* plant, which is said to be a digestive aid. When the mixture is soft and creamy, stir in a few handfuls of fresh spinach.

Next comes the real genius: tadka, a seasoning technique central to Indian cuisine that takes mere minutes. Just bloom whole spices (and sometimes aromatics) in fat, and then use the highly fragrant, visually stunning mixture as a glistening garnish.

Indian cooks often use a pressure cooker to expedite dal's longer cooking time, but for mine I decided to go with red lentils, as they break down in just 20 minutes on the stovetop. I simmered the lentils and turmeric in a 1:3 ratio of lentils to water, leaving out the asafetida, which can be hard to track down (I approximated its allium-like flavor with garlic and onion in the tadka). Whisking the mixture broke down the lentils even more

PALAK DAL (SPINACH-LENTIL DAL WITH CUMIN AND MUSTARD SEEDS)

and gave them a porridge-like consistency thick enough to spoon over rice. Finally, I wilted baby spinach in the dal and brightened it with fresh lemon juice.

Tadka time. Vegetable oil and ghee are both often used here, and I decided to try the former first. I sizzled ingredients in stages in 1 tablespoon of oil: Whole cumin and brown mustard seeds went in first (mustard seeds are not typically added to the tadka for this dish, but I love their taste and texture), followed by chopped onion, sliced garlic, grated ginger, dried arbol chiles, and a fresh serrano chile to give the dish a bit of heat. When the onions were golden brown, I spooned the tadka onto the stewy lentils. The sweetness, spice, and moderate heat of the tadka gave the dish big personality, not to mention that it looked gorgeous atop the ocher lentils. What's more, the cumin and mustard seeds provided bits of crunch.

My only complaints were that the dal tasted a little lean and the ginger was too prominent. To give the dish more richness, I switched the fat in the tadka from oil to ghee and bumped it up to 3 tablespoons. The ghee added welcome nutty sweetness and depth. Since not all cooks keep ghee on hand, I also came up with a sort of faux ghee made by quickly browning butter and discarding the browned milk solids.

I also moved the ginger from the tadka to the saucepan with the lentils—more cooking would soften its flavor. Finally, many cooks include fresh curry leaves in tadka. I loved their distinctively smoky, citrusy taste in contrast with the creamy, earthy lentils. Fragrant, complex, and comforting, this dish is now a regular on my table.

—STEVE DUNN, *Cook's Illustrated*

Palak Dal (Spinach-Lentil Dal with Cumin and Mustard Seeds)

SERVES 4 TO 6

You can use browned butter in place of the ghee: Melt 6 tablespoons of butter in a 10-inch skillet over medium-high heat and cook, swirling the skillet and stirring constantly with a rubber spatula, until the butter is browned. Then slowly pour the butter into a small heatproof bowl, leaving as much of the browned milk solids behind as possible. For less heat, remove the ribs and seeds of the serrano as desired. Fresh curry leaves add a wonderful aroma to this dal, but if they're unavailable, you can omit them. Yellow mustard seeds can be

substituted for brown. Monitor the spices and aromatics carefully during frying, reducing the heat if necessary to prevent scorching. Serve the dal with warm naan and basmati or another long-grain white rice.

1½ cups (10½ ounces) dried red lentils, picked over and rinsed
1 tablespoon grated fresh ginger
¾ teaspoon ground turmeric
6 ounces (6 cups) baby spinach
1½ teaspoons table salt
3 tablespoons ghee
1½ teaspoons brown mustard seeds
1½ teaspoons cumin seeds
1 large onion, chopped
15 curry leaves, roughly torn (optional)
6 garlic cloves, sliced
4 whole dried arbol chiles
1 serrano chile, halved lengthwise
1½ teaspoons lemon juice, plus extra for seasoning
⅓ cup chopped fresh cilantro

1. Bring 4½ cups water, lentils, ginger, and turmeric to boil in large saucepan over medium-high heat. Reduce heat to maintain vigorous simmer. Cook, uncovered, stirring occasionally, until lentils are soft and starting to break down, 18 to 20 minutes.

2. Whisk lentils vigorously until coarsely pureed, about 30 seconds. Continue to cook until lentils have consistency of loose polenta or oatmeal, up to 5 minutes longer. Stir in spinach and salt and continue to cook until spinach is fully wilted, 30 to 60 seconds longer. Cover and set aside off heat.

3. Melt ghee in 10-inch skillet over medium-high heat. Add mustard seeds and cumin seeds and cook, stirring constantly, until seeds sizzle and pop, about 30 seconds. Add onion and cook, stirring frequently, until onion is just starting to brown, about 5 minutes. Add curry leaves, if using; garlic; arbols; and serrano. Cook, stirring frequently, until onion and garlic are golden brown, 3 to 4 minutes.

4. Add lemon juice to lentils and stir to incorporate. (Dal should have consistency of loose polenta. If too thick, loosen with hot water, adding 1 tablespoon at a time.) Season with salt and extra lemon juice to taste. Transfer dal to serving bowl and spoon onion mixture on top. Sprinkle with cilantro and serve.

GREEK MEATBALLS

MEAT

PAN-SEARED STRIP STEAKS

✓ **WHY THIS RECIPE WORKS** Pan-searing strip or rib-eye steaks usually leads to a smoky, grease-splattered kitchen—but it doesn't have to. To devise a fast, mess-free method for achieving deeply seared, rosy meat, we started the steaks in a "cold" (not preheated) nonstick skillet over high heat and flipped them every 2 minutes; that way, the meat's temperature increased gradually, allowing a crust to build up on the outside without overcooking the interior. Because we were cooking in a nonstick skillet, it wasn't necessary to lubricate the skillet with oil; plus, the well-marbled meat exuded enough fat to achieve a good sear, and adding more simply encouraged splatter. We started cooking over high heat to burn off moisture and prevent the steaks from steaming but quickly lowered the heat to medium; at this temperature, the meat kept sizzling, but there was no risk of the fat smoking. Before serving, we sliced the steaks and sprinkled them with coarse sea salt so that every bite was well seasoned.

Searing steak on the grill is a pleasure. Outdoors, the smoke serves as ambiance and enticement to my guests, and the grill acts as a giant drip pan, requiring little cleanup beyond a quick postmeal scrub with a stiff brush. But stovetop searing inevitably causes smoke to billow and grease to splatter, so I rarely make a go of it. When I do, I use the reverse-sear method to cook the meat most of the way through in a low oven before pan searing so that the stovetop cooking can be brief. Still, that approach takes the better part of an hour and doesn't entirely avoid the smoke and splatter.

I wanted a fast, mess-free stovetop method for pan-searing strip or rib-eye steaks (my favorite cuts) that would achieve the evenly rosy interior and deeply browned crust that any good steak should have.

Every approach to steak cookery faces the same fundamental challenge: how to ensure that the exterior develops a deeply browned crust just as the interior comes up to temperature. Pulling it off is tricky because the outside of the steak needs lots of heat to brown, while the inside can't take more than minimal heat before it overcooks.

That's why the classic approach to pan searing—blasting each side of the steak with heat in a well-oiled, ripping-hot pan—doesn't work well. While it's fast and produces a great crust, a wide band of gray, overcooked meat can form just below the crust. What's more, the combination of all that high heat and fat is exactly what causes smoke and splatter. The reverse-sear method cooks steak beautifully—the interior is medium-rare from edge to edge with only a thin gray band, and the crust is rich and dark—thanks to its combination of low and high heat, which allows the meat to heat up slowly and evenly in a low oven before it's seared on the stovetop. But this method isn't for busy weeknights. What I really wanted was the outcome of reverse searing, the speed of stovetop searing, and no mess.

As I started to rethink the stovetop method, I realized that I could minimize splatter by cutting back on the oil, since the well-marbled steaks exude plenty of their own fat during cooking. (Fat splatters when moisture being pushed out of the meat hits it and explosively evaporates, splashing the fat out of the skillet.) In fact, I had a hunch that I could get away with skipping the oil altogether.

To make it work, I moved the cooking out of a stainless-steel skillet and into a nonstick (or carbon-steel) one. That not only made sticking a nonissue but also produced a more substantial crust because the nonstick pan didn't bond much to the meat's surface proteins as they browned. That meant more of those proteins remained on the meat instead of getting stuck to the pan.

I also started cooking the steaks in a "cold" (not preheated) pan. This was a surefire way to avoid the safety hazard of overheating a nonstick skillet, since the food kept the pan cool enough, even when it was over high heat, and the slow buildup of heat mimicked the low-oven phase of the reverse-sear method, warming the steaks gently and encouraging their fat to render without smoking. But to quickly drive off moisture so that the meat would sear instead of steam, I had to immediately crank the heat to high—and by the time each side of the meat was browned over a high flame, the rendered fat had started to smoke and the dreaded gray band had developed.

Clearly I had to reduce the heat, but the steaks' crusts would suffer unless I figured out a different way to get a deep sear. That's when I introduced our "frequent flipping" technique, where you flip the meat every 2 minutes instead of browning one side at a time. We've used it to brown other proteins (pork chops, swordfish steaks) without overcooking their interiors, and it works by taking advantage of heat transfer: When a protein is flipped, its hottest side is turned faceup, allowing heat to dissipate into the air while the other side gets a turn to sear. And as long as the pan is hot enough, the protein

PAN-SEARED STRIP STEAKS

gradually develops a rich crust, like multiple coats of paint applied to a wall. (Note: This method works only with thicker cuts, which can spend more time in the pan building up a crust before their interiors overcook.) The flipping worked so well that I was able to reduce the heat to medium partway through cooking, which completely avoided the gray band and the risk of smoking without impacting the crust.

My gentler method delivered the deep crust and edge-to-edge rosiness of the reverse sear but got the job done faster and avoided the mess. Instead of scrubbing grease off the stovetop, I buzzed together a quick herb sauce that made this weeknight classic company-worthy.

—ANDREW JANJIGIAN, *Cook's Illustrated*

Pan-Seared Strip Steaks

SERVES 4

This recipe also works with boneless rib-eye steaks of a similar thickness. If you have time, salt the steaks for at least 45 minutes or up to 24 hours before cooking: Sprinkle each of the steaks with 1 teaspoon of kosher salt, refrigerate them, and pat them dry with paper towels before cooking. Serve with Sauce Verte (recipe follows), if desired.

> 2 (12- to 16-ounce) boneless strip steaks,
>   1½ inches thick, trimmed
> 1 teaspoon pepper

1. Pat steaks dry with paper towels and sprinkle both sides with pepper. Place steaks 1 inch apart in cold nonstick skillet. Place skillet over high heat and cook steaks for 2 minutes. Flip steaks and cook on second side for 2 minutes. (Neither side of steaks will be browned at this point.)

2. Flip steaks, reduce heat to medium, and continue to cook, flipping steaks every 2 minutes, until browned and meat registers 120 to 125 degrees (for medium-rare), 4 to 10 minutes longer. (Steaks should be sizzling gently; if not, increase heat slightly. Reduce heat if skillet starts to smoke.)

3. Transfer steaks to carving board and let rest for 5 minutes. Slice steaks, season with coarse or flake sea salt to taste, and serve.

Sauce Verte

SERVES 4 (MAKES ABOUT ½ CUP)

If you like, omit the tarragon and increase the amounts of parsley and mint to ¾ cup each.

> ½ cup fresh parsley leaves
> ½ cup fresh mint leaves
> ½ cup fresh tarragon leaves
> 1 small shallot, chopped
> 1 tablespoon capers, rinsed
> 1 garlic clove, peeled
> 1 anchovy fillet, rinsed and patted dry
> ½ teaspoon kosher salt
> ¼ cup extra-virgin olive oil
> 1 teaspoon finely grated lemon zest plus
>   1 tablespoon juice

Process parsley, mint, tarragon, shallot, capers, garlic, anchovy, garlic, and salt in food processor until coarsely chopped, about 5 seconds. Add oil and lemon zest and juice and process until sauce is uniform, about 5 seconds, scraping down sides of bowl as needed.

GARLIC STEAKS

✓ **WHY THIS RECIPE WORKS** For perfectly cooked steaks with over-the-top garlic flavor, we began by marinating boneless strip steaks in a pungent mix of minced garlic, salt, and olive oil. By briefly cooking smashed garlic cloves in extra-virgin olive oil on the stovetop, we created a subtle garlic oil to use for both searing the marinated steaks and whipping up an emulsified garlic-butter sauce. Adding a bit of raw garlic to the garlic-butter sauce contributed freshness and bite to the mellowed toasted garlic. Finally, we garnished the steaks with the toasted garlic cloves for textural contrast and yet another layer of garlic flavor.

What's the best way to infuse steak with garlic flavor? That was the question I asked myself—and my colleagues—when my editor gave me the assignment to develop a recipe for garlicky strip steaks. (Strip steak is a favorite cut in the test kitchen for its combination of tenderness and big flavor). Was a garlic rub the best path forward? A garlicky oil marinade? A garlic-laden finishing sauce? I headed into the test kitchen to try them all.

Early tests proved that while steaks rubbed with garlic powder and granulated garlic tasted OK, they lacked the sharp kick of fresh garlic. So next I tested oil-based marinades with fresh garlic prepped in three different ways: minced, sliced, and smashed whole cloves (we know that garlic's flavor compounds are oil-soluble, so the oil helps the garlic express its potential). Minced garlic provided the most garlic flavor by far, which makes sense because the more finely garlic is chopped, the more flavor compounds are exposed. After 4 hours, I rinsed off the marinade (and dried the steaks). Rinsing before cooking prevented the bits of garlic in the marinade from burning in the skillet and turning bitter. I was glad to find that this rinsing didn't diminish the garlic flavor that had penetrated the steaks.

The meat tasted great—but, well, I have a thing for garlic and I wanted more. I found that lightly browning whole cloves of garlic in the oil I then used to cook the steaks was a solid move for ramping up the garlic flavor. Serving those mellowed, browned cloves with the steak added yet another layer of garlic flavor. And finally, whisking some of the hot garlic-infused oil into a simple combination of softened butter and minced garlic gave me a potent condiment to serve alongside the steaks.

To minimize smoking and ensure perfectly cooked meat, I started the steaks over medium heat, flipping them every few minutes. Gradually, a dark, savory, seasoned crust developed on each side. The resulting steaks were incredible: deeply browned, perfectly cooked, and smelling and tasting of rich, bright garlic. Fellow garlic lovers, I think we have a new favorite dish.

—ALLI BERKEY, *Cook's Country*

Garlic Steaks

SERVES 4

We developed this recipe using a nonstick skillet, but a cast-iron skillet will also work well. If you're using table salt, use 1½ teaspoons for the steaks and ¼ teaspoon for the garlic sauce and toasted garlic.

STEAKS

- ¼ **cup extra-virgin olive oil**
- 6 **garlic cloves, minced**
- 1 **tablespoon kosher salt, divided**
- 1½ **teaspoons pepper, divided**
- 2 **(1-pound) boneless strip steaks, 1½ inches thick, trimmed**

GARLIC SAUCE AND TOASTED GARLIC

- 4 **tablespoons unsalted butter, softened**
- 1 **garlic clove, minced, plus 6 garlic cloves, smashed and peeled**
- ½ **teaspoon kosher salt**
- ¼ **teaspoon pepper**
- ¼ **cup extra-virgin olive oil**
- 2 **sprigs fresh thyme**

1. FOR THE STEAKS: In 1-gallon zipper-lock bag, combine oil, garlic, 2 teaspoons salt, and 1 teaspoon pepper. Place steaks in bag and seal. Turn bag to evenly coat steaks in marinade. Refrigerate for at least 4 hours or up to 24 hours.

2. Remove steaks from marinade and rinse under cold water to remove any pieces of garlic; discard marinade. Pat steaks dry with paper towels. Sprinkle steaks with remaining 1 teaspoon salt and ½ teaspoon pepper; set aside.

NOTES FROM THE TEST KITCHEN

USING HOMEMADE GARLIC OIL TO CREATE MULTILAYERED GARLIC FLAVOR

1. Brown smashed garlic cloves in oil with fresh thyme sprigs.

2. Add some garlic oil to butter and minced garlic to make serving sauce.

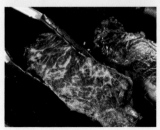

3. Cook steaks in remaining garlic oil; serve with sauce and toasted garlic cloves.

JAPANESE STEAKHOUSE DINNER

3. FOR THE GARLIC SAUCE AND TOASTED GARLIC: Combine butter, minced garlic, salt, and pepper in bowl. Heat oil, thyme sprigs, and smashed garlic in 12-inch nonstick skillet over medium heat until garlic has softened and turned light brown, about 5 minutes, flipping garlic as needed to ensure even browning.

4. Remove smashed garlic from skillet with slotted spoon and set aside; discard thyme sprigs. Add 2 tablespoons hot garlic oil from skillet to butter mixture and whisk to combine (mixture should be emulsified and creamy). Set aside.

5. Heat remaining 2 tablespoons garlic oil in skillet over medium heat until just smoking. Add steaks and cook, flipping every 2 minutes, until well browned and meat registers 115 degrees (for medium-rare), 12 to 16 minutes. Transfer steaks to carving board, tent with aluminum foil, and let rest for 10 minutes. Rewhisk sauce to make fluid again. Slice steaks thin and serve with sauce and reserved smashed garlic.

JAPANESE STEAKHOUSE DINNER

✔ **WHY THIS RECIPE WORKS** We wanted to deliver all the savory-sweet appeal of a hibachi steakhouse dinner at home. To mimic the powerful heat of the flattop, we used a large cast-iron skillet; we avoided crowding by cooking the steak and vegetables separately. To give the vegetables a savory start, we added them to the steak drippings in the still-hot skillet. We finished the sliced steaks and vegetables with a savory soy-garlic butter.

I'm turning 12 and I'm out for my birthday dinner. Across the counter from me is a wisecracking daredevil with a hip holster full of knives. He's juggling squeeze bottles and conjuring fireballs on a ripping-hot flat-top grill—and then he makes a flaming volcano out of a sliced onion. At some point, he hits my mom in the arm with a shrimp. I laugh until I cry, and then he serves me a plate of savory, buttery steak; caramelized stir-fried vegetables; zippy white sauce; and fried rice. Decades later, the taste of a "hibachi" dinner ("teppanyaki" would be a more accurate term) can still return me to that revelatory moment from my childhood.

Could I re-create the components of this dazzling meal at home? I made and tasted all the copycat recipes I could find, without much satisfaction. Undaunted, I talked my editor into joining me for lunch at the local Japanese steakhouse, where we tried to sleuth out just how the experts did it. The chef used a squeeze bottle filled with sake to conjure the famous fireballs, and then he picked up a bottle of seasoned soy sauce to squirt on pretty much everything. A mound of garlic butter also made its way into most dishes on the flattop. The flavors of garlic, soy sauce, butter, and sake permeated the meal.

With their knives and spatulas whirling, the pros use the broad cooking surface of the flattop to cook everything at once—steak, vegetables, and fried rice. But I knew I'd need to make some adjustments for my homemade version. To mimic the powerful heat of the flattop, I'd cook in a large cast-iron skillet. I'd also need to split the cooking into stages: steaks first and then the vegetables—this would also prevent the skillet from overcrowding and therefore encourage browning. As a bonus, this plan would allow the meat to rest while the vegetables cooked. At the restaurant we visited, they chop the steak right on the flattop and then add a good squirt of seasoned soy sauce and a knob of garlic butter on top, but I decided to make an all-in-one condiment by mixing together soy sauce, garlic, and melted butter. I cooked my steaks whole (tasters preferred rich, beefy rib eye to sirloin and filet), sliced them, and then drizzled on this magic condiment. Delicious.

For the vegetables, I chose the usual suspects: shiitake caps, onions, and zucchini, cut so that they would all be cooked through at the same time. For a superflavorful start, I added them to the drippings my rib eyes had left in the still-hot cast-iron skillet, and to ensure nice browning, I patted them into a single layer and resisted the urge to stir for a few minutes. After a stir and another pause for more browning, I added more soy-garlic butter and a splash of mirin—a sweetened rice wine—for the familiar finishing touch.

The results? Juicy slices of perfectly seared rib eye and beautifully browned and glazed vegetables that were just as good as those I'd had so many years ago. When served with the accompanying sauces and my recipe for simple fried rice, the meal was spot-on!

—MATTHEW FAIRMAN, *Cook's Country*

Japanese Steakhouse Steak and Vegetables

SERVES 4

Strip steaks can be substituted for the rib eyes, if desired. Mirin can be found in your supermarket's Asian foods section. We like to serve the steak and vegetables with Simple Hibachi-Style Fried Rice, Spicy Mayonnaise (Yum-Yum Sauce), Sweet Ginger Sauce, and White Mustard Sauce (recipes follow). If using a nonstick skillet, heat the oil in the skillet over medium-high heat until just smoking before adding the steaks in step 2. The test kitchen prefers Kikkoman Soy Sauce.

> 3 tablespoons unsalted butter, melted
>
> 2 tablespoons soy sauce
>
> 2 garlic cloves, minced
>
> 2 (1-pound) boneless rib-eye steaks, 1½ to 1¾ inches thick, trimmed
>
> 1¼ teaspoons white pepper, divided
>
> 1 teaspoon table salt, divided
>
> 1 tablespoon vegetable oil
>
> 2 zucchini (8 ounces each), halved lengthwise and sliced ¾ inch thick
>
> 2 onions, cut into ¾-inch pieces
>
> 6 ounces shiitake mushrooms, stemmed and halved if small or quartered if large
>
> 2 tablespoons mirin

1. Combine melted butter, soy sauce, and garlic in bowl; set aside. Pat steaks dry with paper towels and sprinkle with 1 teaspoon white pepper and ¾ teaspoon salt.

2. Heat 12-inch cast-iron skillet over medium-high heat for 5 minutes. Add oil to skillet and swirl to coat. Add steaks and cook, flipping steaks every 2 minutes, until well browned and meat registers 120 to 125 degrees (for medium-rare), 10 to 13 minutes. Transfer steaks to carving board, tent with aluminum foil, and let rest.

3. While steaks rest, add zucchini, onions, mushrooms, remaining ¼ teaspoon white pepper, and remaining ¼ teaspoon salt to fat left in skillet and stir to combine. Pat vegetables into even layer and cook over medium-high heat, without stirring, until beginning to brown, about 3 minutes. Stir and continue to cook 2 minutes longer. Add mirin and 2 tablespoons soy-garlic butter to skillet and continue to cook until liquid has evaporated and vegetables are well browned, about 2 minutes longer.

4. Transfer vegetables to serving platter. Slice steaks ¼ inch thick and transfer to platter with vegetables. Drizzle steaks with remaining soy-garlic butter. Serve.

Simple Hibachi-Style Fried Rice

SERVES 4

Mirin can be found in your supermarket's Asian foods section. Black pepper can be substituted for the white pepper, if desired.

> 1½ cups long-grain white rice
>
> 3 large eggs
>
> 1 teaspoon toasted sesame oil
>
> ¼ teaspoon table salt
>
> ¼ teaspoon white pepper
>
> 1 tablespoon unsalted butter, softened
>
> 1 garlic clove, minced
>
> 1 tablespoon vegetable oil
>
> 4 scallions, sliced ¼ inch thick
>
> 1½ tablespoons soy sauce
>
> 1½ tablespoons mirin

1. Bring 3 quarts water to boil in large saucepan over high heat. Add rice and cook, stirring occasionally, until just cooked through, about 12 minutes. Drain rice in

---

NOTES FROM THE TEST KITCHEN

TASTING SOY SAUCE

Packed with flavor-enhancing umami, soy sauce is one of the oldest food products in the world. It originated in China about 2,500 years ago and made the leap to Japan around the seventh century. Over time, it's been produced in a variety of styles and become a pantry staple worldwide.

We've learned over the years that not every bottle delivers the kind of nuance and balance that good soy sauce should, so we rounded up 10 top-selling nationally available products (three were tamari, a close relative of soy sauce that contains little to no wheat) and tasted them plain (with rice to cleanse the palate between samples) and cooked in a teriyaki sauce brushed over broiled chicken thighs. We liked soy sauces that were made the old-fashioned way and fermented for months to create complex flavor; our favorite of these was **Kikkoman Soy Sauce**.

fine-mesh strainer or colander. Whisk eggs, sesame oil, salt, and white pepper together in bowl; set aside. Combine butter and garlic in second bowl; set aside.

2. Heat vegetable oil in 12-inch nonstick skillet over medium-high heat until shimmering. Add egg mixture and stir with rubber spatula until set but still wet, about 15 seconds.

3. Add scallions and rice and cook until sizzling and popping loudly, about 3 minutes. Add soy sauce and mirin and cook, stirring constantly, until thoroughly combined, about 2 minutes. Stir in garlic butter until incorporated. Serve.

Spicy Mayonnaise (Yum-Yum Sauce)

SERVES 4 TO 6 (MAKES ABOUT ¾ CUP)

White miso can be substituted for the red miso, if desired. The test kitchen prefers Blue Plate Real Mayonnaise; if you can't find it, we also like Hellmann's Real Mayonnaise. Our favorite unsalted butter is Challenge Unsalted Butter.

- ½ cup mayonnaise
- 2 tablespoons water
- 1 tablespoon unsalted butter, melted
- 1 tablespoon red miso
- 1 teaspoon tomato paste
- ¼ teaspoon cayenne pepper
- ¼ teaspoon paprika
- ¼ teaspoon table salt

Whisk all ingredients together in bowl.

Sweet Ginger Sauce

SERVES 4 TO 6 (MAKES ABOUT ¾ CUP)

Be sure to use unseasoned rice vinegar here.

- ½ cup chopped onion
- 3 tablespoons sugar
- 3 tablespoons unseasoned rice vinegar
- 3 tablespoons soy sauce
- 1 (¾-inch) piece ginger, peeled and chopped

Process all ingredients in blender until smooth, about 15 seconds, scraping down sides of blender jar as needed.

White Mustard Sauce

SERVES 4 TO 6 (MAKES ABOUT ⅔ CUP)

Be sure to use toasted sesame oil here. If you prefer a spicier sauce, add more dry mustard.

- ½ cup heavy cream
- 2 tablespoons soy sauce
- 1½ teaspoons dry mustard
- 1½ teaspoons toasted sesame oil
- 1 teaspoon sugar

Vigorously whisk all ingredients in bowl until combined and slightly thickened.

ROASTED BEEF CHUCK ROAST WITH HORSERADISH-PARSLEY SAUCE

✔ **WHY THIS RECIPE WORKS** We chose chuck eye because it has a big, beefy flavor and is both easy to find and affordable. Pulling the roast apart at its natural line of fat and then cutting away and discarding the fat got rid of any chewy unrendered fat in the final roast. Tying the two pieces back together made for an evenly shaped, impressive-looking roast. Seasoning the meat overnight improved both the flavor and texture, and cooking the roast to a sweet spot between 145 and 150 degrees and slicing it paper-thin yielded ultratender meat. And to make this roast celebration-worthy, we stirred together a spicy horseradish-parsley sauce for serving.

Don't get me wrong; I love beef tenderloins and standing rib roasts as much as the next person. But sometimes you need a less expensive option. I wanted to see if I could create a celebration-worthy beef roast using one of my favorite affordable cuts: chuck-eye roast. Chuck eye has a big, beefy flavor and is easy to find—and it typically rings in at about a third of the cost of beef tenderloin.

Chuck-eye roast is cut from the shoulder of the cow—the chuck—so the muscles are hardworking and can be chewy when cooked too quickly. Cooking the meat low and slow helps it become tender. So to start my testing, I seasoned a 5-pound boneless beef chuck-eye roast with salt and pepper and cooked it in

ROASTED BEEF CHUCK ROAST WITH HORSERADISH-PARSLEY SAUCE

a 275-degree oven. I removed it when the center was medium-rare (120 degrees), as I would for tenderloin, and let it rest for 30 minutes before slicing. But this meat wasn't tender—it was chewy. Was my target temperature the problem?

To find out, I prepared half a dozen roasts, cooking each of them to a different final temperature. I landed on a sweet spot between 145 and 150 degrees in the center (which we usually call medium to medium-well). This meat was juicy and light rosy pink inside. As a bonus, since the roast took about 3½ hours to cook, the exterior developed nice color without a searing step. Letting the cooked meat rest a full 45 minutes before slicing allowed its internal juices to redistribute, resulting in the moistest meat (try saying that ten times fast). Plus, the resting time made it easier to slice the beef thin—an important step with this cut—so it was nice and tender.

Unfortunately, my tasters were put off by the strip of unrendered fat in the center of the chuck-eye roast. So for my next test, I took the raw roast and pulled it apart into two pieces right through this line of fat and then cut away (and discarded) the fat. I tried roasting these two small pieces, but the end results didn't look the part of a grand special-occasion roast. Instead, I seasoned each piece and tied them back together with twine to make one evenly shaped, impressive-looking hunk of meat. Allowing the salted-and-tied roast to sit overnight improved both the flavor and texture.

For a flavorful condiment, I auditioned both a creamy horseradish sauce and a fresh parsley sauce. My tasters couldn't decide between the two, so I combined them into one spicy, herby condiment to serve with the beef. I finally had a roast worthy of celebration, and I didn't have to break the bank to get there.

—MORGAN BOLLING, *Cook's Country*

Roasted Beef Chuck Roast with Horseradish-Parsley Sauce

SERVES 8 TO 10

Plan ahead: The roast must be seasoned at least 18 hours before cooking. If using table salt, cut the salt amounts in half. We recommend Woeber's Pure Horseradish and Inglehoffer Cream Style Horseradish (also sold as Beaver Brand Grandma Rose's Hot Cream Horseradish). The horseradish-parsley sauce can be refrigerated for up to two days; let it come to room temperature before serving.

BEEF

- 1 (5-pound) boneless beef chuck-eye roast, trimmed
- 2 tablespoons kosher salt
- 2 teaspoons pepper
- 2 tablespoons extra-virgin olive oil

SAUCE

- 1 cup fresh parsley leaves
- ¼ cup prepared horseradish
- 1 shallot, chopped
- 2 tablespoons capers, rinsed
- 1 tablespoon lemon juice
- 1 garlic clove, minced
- ½ teaspoon kosher salt
- ¾ cup extra-virgin olive oil

1. FOR THE BEEF: Pull roast into 2 pieces at major seam delineated by line of white fat, cutting with boning knife as needed. Using knife, remove large knobs of fat from each piece.

2. Sprinkle roasts all over with salt and pepper. Place roasts back together along major seam. Tie together with kitchen twine at 1-inch intervals to create 1 evenly shaped roast. Wrap tightly in plastic wrap and refrigerate for 18 to 24 hours.

3. Adjust oven rack to lower-middle position and heat oven to 275 degrees. Set wire rack in rimmed baking sheet. Unwrap roast and rub all over with oil. Place roast on prepared wire rack. Transfer sheet to oven and roast until meat registers 145 to 150 degrees, 3¼ to 3¾ hours. Transfer roast to carving board, tent with aluminum foil, and let rest for 45 minutes.

4. FOR THE SAUCE: Meanwhile, pulse parsley, horseradish, shallot, capers, lemon juice, garlic, and salt in food processor until parsley is finely chopped, 6 to 8 pulses, scraping down sides of bowl as needed. Transfer to bowl and stir in oil until combined. Season with salt to taste; set aside.

5. Slice roast thin, removing twine as you go so roast stays intact. Serve, passing sauce separately.

SHAKING BEEF

✔ **WHY THIS RECIPE WORKS** Shaking beef is a Vietnamese cross between a beef stir-fry and a watercress salad. We used sirloin steak tips for their beefy flavor and pleasant chewy texture. We first marinated the meat in a mixture of soy sauce, fish sauce, and molasses and then reserved the marinade to make the glaze. We coated the meat with oil (to prevent splattering) and then cooked it in two batches to give it ample room in the skillet. True to the dish's name, we shook and stirred the beef to develop good browning and to deglaze the skillet, which prevented the fond from burning. After setting aside the meat, we lightly softened a red onion in butter, added the reserved marinade (along with garlic, water, and cornstarch) to the skillet, and cooked it down to a glossy consistency. We coated the meat with the sauce and then placed it atop the watercress. A mixture of lime juice and pepper served as both a dressing for the salad and a dipping sauce for the meat. We served the beef with red rice (com do), a classic accompaniment to shaking beef.

Shaking beef, or bo luc lac, is a Vietnamese dish of stir-fried cubes of marinated beef and sliced onions served over a bed of watercress and accompanied by a dipping sauce of lime juice and pepper. The dish gets its name from the vigorous shaking and stirring required to achieve an even and thorough sear. The beef—well browned but still pink on the inside—is coated in a deeply savory glaze that also flavors and lightly wilts the watercress below it.

It's a study in contrasts: the warmth of the beef against the cool crunch of the watercress, its savory meatiness against the peppery bite of the cress and the tartness of the dipping sauce, not to mention the garlicky, tomato-rich "red rice" (com do) that is a common accompaniment.

The cut of beef varies from recipe to recipe. San Francisco's acclaimed Vietnamese eatery The Slanted Door started the trend of using filet mignon. But in Vietnamese households, the cut is likely to be chewier and less expensive. I decided to try the pricey filet as well as cheaper cuts such as flank steak, sirloin strip, and sirloin steak tips. My tasters preferred all these cuts to the filet, which they found bland. In the end, sirloin steak tips (also known as flap meat) won out for having the best beefy flavor, along with a pleasantly resilient texture.

The glaze for the beef packs a big umami punch. Besides garlic, sugar, and soy sauce, it often includes dark soy sauce (a more intensely flavored version of soy sauce), along with fish and oyster sauces and a flavor enhancer popular in many Vietnamese dishes called Maggi Seasoning. In a nod to French colonial influence, a knob of butter may also be added. I was happy to find that equal amounts of soy and fish sauces contributed plenty of umami richness. I also found that Maggi Seasoning could be swapped for the soy sauce. Dark soy sauce added molasses-like smoky sweetness to the mix, but it can be hard to find. To approximate its flavors, I simply replaced the sugar in the marinade with molasses.

Some recipes call for marinating the meat in one mixture and creating the glaze with another. For simplicity, I drained the marinade from the meat, added water and cornstarch, and then reduced it to a glaze once the meat was seared.

To cook the meat, I reached for my 12-inch nonstick skillet, which I knew would be essential for helping prevent the steak and the little bit of marinade left on its surface from sticking. To ensure good browning, cooking the meat in two batches and leaving the pieces well separated from one another was also a must. For my first go, I stirred the meat and shook the pan continually as many recipes directed. But I wanted the meat to get nice and dark on at least on one side, and

NOTES FROM THE TEST KITCHEN

GET THE RIGHT CRESS
In shaking beef, the watercress should provide peppery bite and crunch—elements that contrast with and balance the savory meat. That's why it's important to buy watercress, not its land-dwelling relative called upland cress. The latter's more delicate stems and smaller leaves don't deliver the same substantial crunch.

WATERCRESS
Use this

UPLAND CRESS
Not this

this approach proved too inconsistent. So next I tried leaving the pieces alone for the first few minutes before commencing with shaking and stirring. While this did create a good sear on the first side, now the fond was prone to burning.

That's when I realized something important: In addition to helping the meat cook evenly, shaking and stirring helps deglaze the pan—as the beef moves across the pan, it swipes up fond, coating the meat so that there is virtually no marinade left on the surface of the pan that could burn. With this in mind, I adjusted my technique. I placed the meat in the pan and swirled the pan occasionally as the first side cooked so that the meat moved around but didn't turn over. Only after the first side had browned sufficiently did I begin stirring and shaking the pan more vigorously to get the cubes to cook on all sides.

I found that about 3 to 4 minutes on the first side and 2 to 4 minutes on the remaining sides gave the meat a deep brown color on its exterior while still keeping it juicy and pink on the inside—a hallmark of shaking beef.

Another discovery: With all that open space in the pan, the oil had a tendency to splatter, especially once the meat began to shed moisture.

I sorted out a tidier work-around: Instead of adding the oil to the pan, I tossed the meat itself with the oil before placing it in the skillet, which prevented splattering almost entirely.

I opted to keep butter in the formula, since it added a little richness. To incorporate it, I used it to briefly soften the onion before adding the reserved marinade to the pan to reduce.

Now for the salad. While some recipes call for a variety of greens and herbs and sometimes tomatoes, I decided to keep things simple. The watercress itself was so punchy and vibrant, and its stems added such great crunch, that it seemed unnecessary to add anything else. While the glaze can serve double duty as a dressing for the salad, I also liked how the brightness of the lime-pepper dipping sauce helped balance out the flavors, so I used a small amount of it to drizzle over the salad, too.

The next time you want to make a steak dinner, consider shaking beef—a deeply savory steak dish and refreshing salad all in one.

—ANDREW JANJIGIAN, *Cook's Illustrated*

Shaking Beef (Bo Luc Lac)

SERVES 4

Sirloin steak tips are often sold as flap meat. They can be packaged as whole steaks, cubes, or strips. We prefer to buy whole steaks so we can cut our own steak tips. Maggi Seasoning can be used in place of the soy sauce, if desired. Serve with our Vietnamese Red Rice (Com Do) (page 120) or steamed white rice.

- 4 teaspoons fish sauce
- 4 teaspoons soy sauce
- 2 teaspoons molasses
- 1 pound sirloin steak tips, trimmed and cut into ¾-inch cubes
- 4 ounces (4 cups) watercress, torn into bite-size pieces
- ¼ cup lime juice (2 limes)
- 1 teaspoon pepper
- ¼ cup water
- 2 garlic cloves, minced
- ¾ teaspoon cornstarch
- 4 teaspoons vegetable oil, divided
- 1 tablespoon unsalted butter
- 1 small red onion, sliced thin

1. Whisk fish sauce, soy sauce, and molasses together in medium bowl. Add beef and toss to coat. Let sit at room temperature for 15 minutes. Spread watercress in shallow serving bowl. Combine lime juice and pepper in small bowl and set aside.

2. Using tongs, transfer beef to second medium bowl, letting as much marinade as possible drain back into first bowl. Add water, garlic, and cornstarch to marinade in first bowl and whisk to combine; set aside. Add 2 teaspoons oil to beef and toss to coat.

3. Heat 1 teaspoon oil in 12-inch nonstick skillet over medium-high heat until just smoking. Using tongs, wipe skillet clean with paper towels. Add half of beef to skillet, leaving space between pieces. Cook, swirling skillet gently and occasionally to capture any fond that collects on bottom of skillet, until beef is browned on first side, 3 to 4 minutes. Continue to cook, stirring and shaking skillet frequently, until beef is coated and browned and center is just pink (to check for doneness, remove larger piece and cut in half), 2 to 4 minutes longer. Transfer beef to clean bowl. Wipe skillet clean with wet paper towels and repeat with remaining 1 teaspoon oil and remaining beef.

4. Melt butter in now-empty skillet over medium heat. Add onion and cook, stirring occasionally, until just beginning to soften, about 1 minute. Add reserved marinade and bring to boil. Cook, stirring occasionally, until thickened and glossy, about 2 minutes. Add beef and any accumulated juices and toss to coat. Scatter beef mixture and sauce over watercress. Drizzle 2 teaspoons lime juice mixture over salad. Divide remaining lime juice mixture among small bowls for dipping and serve with salad.

Vietnamese Red Rice (Com Do)

SERVES 4 TO 6

We based this recipe on a version made by Vietnamese cooking authority Andrea Nguyen. If jasmine rice is unavailable, substitute another long-grain white rice. Maggi Seasoning can be used in place of the soy sauce, if desired. The test kitchen prefers Dynasty Jasmine Rice. Our favorite tubed tomato paste is Cento Double Concentrated Tomato Paste, and our favorite canned tomato paste is Cento Tomato Paste.

1½	cups jasmine rice
2	tablespoons unsalted butter
4	garlic cloves, minced
3	tablespoons tomato paste
1¾	cups water
2	teaspoons soy sauce
½	teaspoon table salt

1. Place rice in fine-mesh strainer and rinse under cold running water until water runs clear. Drain well. Melt butter in medium saucepan over medium-high heat. Add rice and cook, stirring constantly, until grains become chalky and opaque, 1 to 3 minutes. Add garlic and cook, stirring constantly, until fragrant, about 30 seconds. Add tomato paste and cook, stirring constantly, until tomato paste is evenly distributed, about 1 minute.

2. Add water, soy sauce, and salt and bring to boil. Cover, reduce heat to low, and cook until liquid is absorbed and rice is tender, about 20 minutes. Let stand off heat, covered, for 10 minutes. Fluff rice with fork and stir to combine. Serve.

PLOV

✓ **WHY THIS RECIPE WORKS** This classic, highly revered beef-and-carrot rice dish from Uzbekistan is worthy of being the centerpiece of the table. The most challenging part of making it is getting the meat to reach perfect tenderness at the same time that the rice finishes cooking and the moisture has evaporated or been absorbed into the rice. To eliminate tricky timing issues, we removed the beef from the saucepan when it was tender and added it back to the pilaf only when the rice was nearly done. Placing a layer of aluminum foil between the saucepan and the lid ensured a tight seal, so all of the flavorful cooking liquid was retained during the braising step and then absorbed into the rice on the stovetop. A grated carrot added at the beginning of cooking provided sweet, earthy flavor throughout, while larger carrot chunks added later became tender but remained intact. Traditional dried barberries supplied bracing pops of acidity. A whole head of garlic, simmered with the meat and then used to garnish the platter, distinguished this dish from other Silk Road rice dishes.

What do you eat when you're celebrating? Soup dumplings? Prime rib? A tower of cream puffs festooned with spun sugar? In Uzbekistan, the answer is rice pilaf, no question about it.

Known as plov (or osh), Uzbekistan's fragrant combination of savory spiced rice, tender meat, and velvety carrots studded with tangy, garnet-colored dried barberries is piled high on a platter and garnished with a head of spreadably soft garlic. The ultimate expression of generosity, community, and national identity, plov is prepared at every feast by a master of the art, known as an oshpaz, who cooks in a huge wok-shaped cauldron called a kazan and may serve hundreds of guests from a single batch.

Uzbekistani home cooks make plov, too, but on a smaller scale. The process starts with sautéing loads of onions and carrots in a large pot. Then some spices (cumin, coriander, and black pepper), salt, and barberries are tossed in. Chunks of beef or lamb are added and cooked for a bit before water is added to almost cover the meat. A head of garlic is plunked in the center, the pot is covered, and everything is cooked over moderate heat until the meat is almost tender. Then comes the rice.

RICE PILAF WITH BEEF AND CARROTS (PLOV)

Typically, cooks smooth the rice (a long-grain variety) into an even layer over the stew and then crank up the heat. The goal is to bring the flavorful liquid to a hard boil so that it is forced through the rice to flavor it without disturbing the dish's distinct layers. Cooks then lower the heat, cover the pot, and let the rice finish cooking.

And therein lies the challenge of plov: The meat must turn tender at the exact time the rice is cooked and the moisture has evaporated or been absorbed, leaving the pot neither scorched nor flooded.

Multiple tries left me with over- or undercooked beef (I used boneless short ribs), sodden or crunchy rice, and a crusted pot—not to mention mushy carrots and dull flavor. I'd have to find my own way.

My first changes were simple, starting with searing the beef. This created a rich fond that would flavor the rice, making the dish beefy from top to bottom. I did the searing in a saucepan, not a Dutch oven, knowing that the Dutch oven's broad surface would cause swifter evaporation, making it more difficult to cook the rice later. Then I transferred the meat to a plate and added the onions to the saucepan; their moisture handily loosened the fond from the bottom.

I followed with the carrots, but instead of cutting them into chunks and adding them all at once—which guarantees they'll turn pulpy—I grated the largest one and added it to the saucepan with garlic, cumin, and coriander. The grated carrot would meld into the dish over the course of cooking, distributing its sweetness throughout. I cut the remaining carrots into batons that I would add later, so they'd retain their shape.

I stirred in half the barberries with the aromatics and spices and reserved the rest for scattering over the finished dish. Then I returned the seared beef to the saucepan along with enough water to submerge it halfway, placed a head of garlic in the center (a traditional addition to the dish), covered the saucepan, and let everything simmer on the stovetop. A little over an hour later, I fished out the meat (to prevent it from overcooking) and the head of garlic, setting them aside while I added the carrot batons and rice, which I spread evenly over the top.

Per tradition, I turned up the heat to infuse the rice with meaty, savory goodness and then turned it down and covered the saucepan. While the rice cooked, I cut the short ribs into cubes and then folded them back into the mixture when the rice was about half cooked.

My plov was a success: The grated carrot had flavored the dish and then melded into the mixture, while the chunkier pieces were tender but intact. The minced garlic and barberries had depth and zing, and the meat and rice were perfectly cooked.

But here's a nugget of test kitchen insight: A recipe that works once doesn't necessarily work consistently. I couldn't reliably repeat my success. Sometimes the moisture evaporated too soon, leaving the rice hard and the saucepan scorched, and adding more water often made the pilaf soggy.

The funny thing about rice is that though it has a reputation for being finicky, it's actually predictable in that it always absorbs water in a 1:1 ratio by volume. What is finicky is how much water evaporates during cooking, since that can vary depending on the heat level, the diameter of your saucepan, and how tightly its lid fits. It seemed to me that the key to solving the plov challenge was controlling evaporation.

So I made three more changes. First, instead of cranking the heat to push the flavorful liquid up through the rice, I stirred the rice and carrots into the

NOTES FROM THE TEST KITCHEN

FOIL MAKES IT FAIL-SAFE

The rice in plov is cooked via the absorption method, which means there is just enough liquid in the pot to hydrate and gel the rice's starch. But a lid that doesn't provide a perfect seal can allow too much liquid to escape, leaving some of the grains dry and hard. Crimping a sheet of aluminum foil over the pot before topping it with the lid ensures that every bit of the flavorful cooking liquid is retained and absorbed into the rice.

stew and gently simmered the rice so that it would cook more slowly and evenly. Second, I crimped a piece of foil over the saucepan before adding the lid to ensure a tight seal. Last, I moved the braising step to the oven; its steady, even heat would be the best defense against erratic evaporation (and the fact that the plov could cook unattended was a happy bonus).

These changes enabled me to turn out batch after batch of perfect plov. I piled the last batch on a platter, sprinkled it with the reserved barberries, and finished it with sliced scallions. Finally, I added the garlic head that marked it as Uzbekistan's favorite feast food. I was in the mood to celebrate.

—ANDREA GEARY, *Cook's Illustrated*

Rice Pilaf with Beef and Carrots (Plov)

SERVES 4

Grate the largest carrot on the large holes of a box grater. You can substitute 1¼ pounds of blade steak, about 1 inch thick, for the boneless short ribs; halve the steak along the central line of connective tissue,

NOTES FROM THE TEST KITCHEN

CARROTS TWO WAYS

Carrots are as important to plov as the meat (the ratio of carrot to beef is almost 1:1). To give them even more prominence in our pilaf, we use them in two ways. First, we grate the largest carrot and add it with the aromatics so that its earthy sweetness flavors the dish. Then we cut the others into chunky batons that we add in the last phase of cooking so that they retain their shape and add pops of color.

SHREDS
Flavor cooking liquid

BATONS
Add bright color and texture

and then remove the tissue. Don't substitute bone-in short ribs. If barberries are unavailable, combine 2 tablespoons of dried currants and 1 tablespoon of lemon juice in a small bowl. Microwave, covered, until very steamy, about 1 minute. Add the currants (and any residual lemon juice) to the plov as directed. Diners can mix individual cloves of the cooked garlic into their pilaf.

> 5 **carrots, peeled**
> 1 **pound boneless beef short ribs, trimmed**
> 1½ **teaspoons table salt, divided**
> 1 **tablespoon vegetable oil**
> 2 **onions, quartered through root end and sliced ¼ inch thick**
> 2 **tablespoons dried barberries, divided**
> 3 **garlic cloves, minced, plus 1 head garlic, outer papery skin removed and top ½ inch cut off**
> 1 **tablespoon ground cumin**
> 2 **teaspoons ground coriander**
> ½ **teaspoon pepper**
> 1¾ **cups water**
> 1 **cup basmati rice, rinsed and drained**
> 2 **scallions, sliced thin**

1. Adjust oven rack to middle position and heat oven to 350 degrees. Grate largest carrot. Cut remaining 4 carrots into 2 by ½-inch pieces.

2. Pat beef dry with paper towels and sprinkle all over with ½ teaspoon salt. Heat oil in large saucepan over medium-high heat until shimmering. Add beef and cook until well browned on all sides, 10 to 12 minutes. Using tongs, transfer beef to bowl.

3. Add onions and remaining 1 teaspoon salt to saucepan. Cover and cook, stirring occasionally and scraping up any browned bits, until onions are soft, about 5 minutes. Add 1 tablespoon barberries, minced garlic, cumin, coriander, pepper, and grated carrot and cook, stirring constantly, until garlic and spices are fragrant, 1 to 2 minutes. Spread mixture into even layer. Return beef to saucepan, nestling it into vegetables. Add water and any accumulated beef juices. Place garlic head in center of saucepan. Increase heat to high and bring mixture to vigorous simmer. Remove saucepan from heat; place large sheet of aluminum foil over saucepan, crimp tightly to seal, and cover tightly with lid. Transfer saucepan to oven and cook until meat is fork tender, 1¼ to 1½ hours.

GREEN CHILI WITH PORK (CHILE VERDE CON CERDO)

4. Transfer beef and garlic head to cutting board. Stir rice and remaining carrots into cooking liquid (saucepan handle will be hot). Bring to simmer over medium heat. Adjust heat to maintain simmer; replace foil, cover, and cook until liquid level has dropped below rice and rice is half cooked, about 10 minutes.

5. While rice cooks, cut beef into ½-inch cubes. Gently fold beef into rice mixture, making sure to incorporate rice on bottom of saucepan. Replace foil, cover, and continue to cook until rice is tender and moisture is fully absorbed, 10 to 15 minutes longer. (Check rice every 5 minutes by sliding butter knife to bottom of center of saucepan and gently pushing rice aside; if bottom appears to be drying out, reduce heat slightly.)

6. Pile pilaf on platter. Sprinkle with scallions and remaining 1 tablespoon barberries. Garnish with garlic head and serve.

GREEN CHILI WITH PORK

✔ **WHY THIS RECIPE WORKS** To make a meaty, vibrant chile verde, we started by salting chunks of fat- and collagen-rich pork butt roast for an hour, which ensured that the meat cooked up well seasoned and juicy. Gently braising the pork in the oven allowed the meat's fat and collagen to thoroughly break down, making it supple. Browning the pork trimmings (chopped coarse to maximize their surface area) instead of the chunks built a savory fond without drying out the surface of the meat. Broiling the tomatillos, poblanos, jalapeño, and garlic concentrated their flavors and imbued them with a touch of smokiness. Seasoning the chili with warm spices and sugar softened its acidity and heat. Omitting broth and water minimized the amount of liquid in the pot, so that the salsa—the only source of liquid—reduced to a tight, flavorful sauce.

Before I delve into the specifics of my recipe for chile verde con cerdo, the classic Mexican stew of pork simmered in a tangy tomatillo and green chile sauce, I have a secret to share: When it comes to braising meat, all recipes work more or less the same way.

Of course, I'm not talking about specific ingredients. American pot roast, daube Provençal, and pork vindaloo are made with completely different seasonings and taste nothing alike. But if you look closely at how each dish is put together, the processes have the same

basic approach: Brown the meat to build a flavorful fond, add a modest amount of liquid, cover the pot, and simmer it all gently until the meat is tender and the liquid has reduced to a concentrated, deeply savory sauce.

The beauty of this universal framework is that once you know how it works, you can make countless variations. Tuscan peposo. Chinese red-cooked beef. Hungarian goulash. Even if you're not familiar with a particular braise, you have a road map for how to make it—a pretty powerful culinary tool.

That's where I started with my recipe for chile verde. When I applied the basic formula along with a handful of the test kitchen's best braising practices, I found my way to a dish of tender pork cloaked in a vibrant, meaty sauce—perfect for serving alongside rice or tucking into warm tortillas.

Fat-streaked, collagen-rich boneless pork butt roast is almost always the cut used in this chili; during cooking, the collagen breaks down into gelatin that turns the pork supple. I trimmed a roughly 4-pound roast, cut it into 1½-inch chunks (which would be as easy to eat wrapped in a tortilla as from a fork), and seasoned it with kosher salt to help it stay juicy. I didn't brown the pieces; we often forgo that step when meat sitting above the surface of the liquid will brown during braising (as it would here) and/or when a sauce has so much flavor that a lack of browning isn't noticeable. Skipping browning saves time and prevents the meat's exterior from drying out.

Charring the vegetables, a common step in preparing chile verde, concentrates their flavors and imbues them with a pleasant touch of bitterness. So while the salted pork rested, I loaded up a foil-lined rimmed baking sheet with tomatillos (husked, rinsed, and dried), moderately spicy poblano chiles (stemmed, halved, and seeded), a large onion (cut through the root end into wedges), and a handful of unpeeled garlic cloves. I drizzled the vegetables with oil and slid the sheet under the broiler for about 10 minutes.

When the vegetables were charred, I peeled the chiles and garlic, discarding the skins (there was no need to peel the thin-skinned tomatillos), and blitzed everything in a food processor until it formed a rough puree. Then I sautéed some oregano and cumin in a Dutch oven before adding the salsa, pork, and a few cups of chicken broth blended with water; bringing it all to a simmer; and braising the mixture gently in the oven.

The pork turned nicely tender after 90 minutes, but the liquid remained thin even after I cooked the chili for another hour. Plus, it tasted sharp and lacked the meaty backbone that any chili should have.

The savory flavor produced by browning would balance the acidity nicely, but I had a workaround that allowed me to leave the stew meat alone: browning the pork trimmings instead. We've used this trick when we want to build fond without subjecting the meat to a hard sear, so I thought it would work here.

I placed the trimmings (chopped coarse to maximize their surface area) in a Dutch oven with a cup of water and brought the mixture to a simmer. Strange as that sounds, we've found that you can produce a much richer fond by simmering the meat first, since the liquid extracts meat juices and fat much more thoroughly than searing does; when the liquid evaporates, the bottom of the pot is coated with a substantial layer of fond.

Built on that rich layer of fond, the chili tasted noticeably meatier. In fact, a good bit of browning had accumulated on the interior walls of the pot, too. Letting the pot sit covered after braising trapped steam that loosened that "side fond" so that I could scrape every last bit into the chili. But the chili's consistency was still so soupy that the pork pieces floated in it like little icebergs.

Clearly, there was too much liquid in the pot, so I incrementally decreased the amounts of broth and water I was adding—until I eliminated both altogether. The salsa alone made a fine braising liquid and reduced to a tight, concentrated sauce by the time the meat was tender. The pectin-rich tomatillos helped, too, thickening the sauce as it cooked.

I tweaked the flavors, adding a jalapeño for more distinct but measured heat; bay leaves for herbal depth; cinnamon, cloves, and sugar for subtle warmth and sweetness; and minced cilantro for freshness.

The contrast between the rich pork and the tangy, spicy sauce reminded me why chile verde is one of the world's greatest braises, and I was gratified to think that my new-school method had made it even more efficient. Whether you serve it over rice, swaddled in warm corn tortillas, or both, you won't regret adding chile verde to your braised-meat repertoire.

—STEVE DUNN, *Cook's Illustrated*

Green Chili with Pork (Chile Verde con Cerdo)
SERVES 6 TO 8

Pork butt roast is often labeled Boston butt in the supermarket. If your jalapeño is shorter than 3 inches long, you may wish to use two. If fresh tomatillos are unavailable, substitute three 11-ounce cans of tomatillos, drained, rinsed, and patted dry; broil as directed. Serve with white rice and/or warm corn tortillas.

1 (3½- to 4-pound) boneless pork butt roast, trimmed and cut into 1½-inch pieces, trimmings reserved

1 tablespoon plus 1 teaspoon kosher salt, divided

1 cup water

1½ pounds tomatillos, husks and stems removed, rinsed well and dried

5 poblano chiles, stemmed, halved, and seeded

1 large onion, cut into 8 wedges through root end

5 garlic cloves, unpeeled

1 jalapeño chile, stemmed and halved

1 tablespoon vegetable oil

1 teaspoon dried oregano

1 teaspoon ground cumin

⅛ teaspoon ground cinnamon

Pinch ground cloves

2 bay leaves

2 teaspoons sugar

1 teaspoon pepper

½ cup minced fresh cilantro, plus extra for serving

Lime wedges

1. Toss pork pieces with 1 tablespoon salt in large bowl. Cover and refrigerate for 1 hour. Meanwhile, chop pork trimmings coarse. Transfer to Dutch oven. Add water and bring to simmer over high heat. Cook, adjusting heat to maintain vigorous simmer and stirring occasionally, until all liquid evaporates and trimmings begin to sizzle, about 12 minutes. Continue to cook, stirring frequently, until dark fond forms on bottom of pot and trimmings have browned and crisped, about 6 minutes longer. Using slotted spoon, discard trimmings. Pour off all but 2 tablespoons fat; set aside pot.

2. Adjust 1 oven rack to lower-middle position and second rack 6 inches from broiler element and heat broiler. Line rimmed baking sheet with aluminum foil. Place tomatillos, poblanos, onion, garlic, and jalapeño on prepared sheet and drizzle with oil. Arrange chiles skin side up. Broil until chile skins are blackened and vegetables begin to soften, 10 to 13 minutes, rotating sheet halfway through broiling. Transfer poblanos, jalapeño, and garlic to cutting board.

3. Turn off broiler and heat oven to 325 degrees. Transfer tomatillos, onion, and any accumulated juices to food processor. When poblanos, jalapeño, and garlic are cool enough to handle, remove and discard skins (it's OK if some small bits of chile skin remain). Remove seeds from jalapeño and reserve. Add poblanos, jalapeño, and garlic to processor. Pulse until mixture is roughly pureed, about 10 pulses, scraping down sides of bowl as needed. If spicier chili is desired, add reserved jalapeño seeds and pulse 3 times.

4. Heat reserved fat in pot over medium heat until just shimmering. Add oregano, cumin, cinnamon, and cloves and cook, stirring constantly, until fragrant, about 30 seconds. Stir in tomatillo mixture, bay leaves, sugar, pepper, and remaining 1 teaspoon salt, scraping up any browned bits. Stir in pork and bring to simmer. Cover, transfer to oven, and cook until pork is tender, about 1½ hours, stirring halfway through cooking.

5. Remove pot from oven and let sit, covered, for 10 minutes. Discard bay leaves. Using heatproof rubber spatula, scrape browned bits from sides of pot. Stir in any fat that has risen to top of chili. Stir in cilantro; season with salt and pepper to taste. Serve, passing lime wedges and extra cilantro separately.

NOTES FROM THE TEST KITCHEN

WHAT MAKES THIS CHILI "VERDE"?
Hint: It's more than just green chiles. The braising liquid gets its vibrant flavor and color from four key components.

POBLANOS: Moderately spicy, herbal

TOMATILLOS: Tangy (their pectin also thickens the sauce)

JALAPEÑO: Spicy, grassy

CILANTRO: Fresh

SPANISH PORK KEBABS

✔ WHY THIS RECIPE WORKS Pinchos morunos is a dish normally served as part of a tapas spread, but it works equally well as an entrée. To develop our version of these Spanish pork kebabs, we used country-style ribs for both their convenience and their ability to remain juicy and tender when grilled. To increase juiciness, we brined the pork for 30 minutes before cutting it into cubes and coating it with a robust spice paste that included garlic, lemon, ginger, coriander, smoked paprika, and fresh oregano. And because country-style ribs contain a mix of lighter loin meat and darker shoulder meat, we kept the light meat and dark meat on separate skewers and cooked each to its ideal temperature (140 and 155 degrees, respectively) to ensure that the light meat didn't overcook and the dark meat wasn't chewy.

If you're not familiar with pinchos morunos, let me fill you in: The dish consists of chunks of pork that are heavily seasoned with a bright, heady spice paste (lemon, garlic, smoked paprika, cumin, and coriander are common components); skewered; charred over hot coals; and served as part of a tapas spread. "Pincho" ("spike" or "thorn") points to cooking the meat kebab-style; "morunos" implies a Moorish influence. I've become such a fan of the dish that I've taken to serving pinchos not just as a tapa but as the center of a meal.

Getting to a great recipe required overcoming the inherent challenge of pork kebabs: The cuts that are typically used—tenderloin and loin—are lean, which means they are unforgiving on a hot grill and can easily turn dry and mealy. But there is another choice that's easy to find and fashion into bite-size pieces: country-style ribs. In an early test, this cut showed promise, so I decided to move forward with it.

A salty marinade helped the pork retain some moisture, but the meat needed all the help it could get to stay juicy, so I opted for a brine, which would draw water into the meat. I would incorporate the seasonings from the marinade in the form of a spice paste applied just before grilling.

As I worked, I noticed that the pork behaved a lot like chicken: Even when I left it on the grill long enough to char, the darker meat stayed juicy, thanks to its more abundant fat and collagen, whereas the leaner, lighter bites were dry. We cook light- and dark-meat chicken to different temperatures, so why not do the same with pork? I placed two skewers of dark meat over the coals. Six minutes later, I added two skewers of light meat. At 155 degrees, the dark meat was well charred yet still tender and juicy; the light meat was lightly charred and beautifully moist at 140 degrees.

Finally, I perfected the spice paste. Lemon, garlic, and spices (such as cayenne and black pepper for heat) offered complexity. Ginger added zing, and fresh oregano—mixed into the paste and sprinkled onto the cooked kebabs—contributed herbal freshness.

—ANDREW JANJIGIAN, *Cook's Illustrated*

Spanish Grilled Pork Kebabs (Pinchos Morunos)

SERVES 4

You will need four or five 12-inch metal skewers for this recipe. Look for country-style ribs with an even distribution of light and dark meat. We prefer natural pork, but if your pork is enhanced (injected with a salt solution), do not brine it in step 1.

- 3 tablespoons table salt for brining
- 2 pounds boneless country-style pork ribs, trimmed
- ¼ cup vegetable oil
- 2 tablespoons lemon juice, plus lemon wedges for serving
- 6 garlic cloves, minced
- 1 tablespoon grated fresh ginger
- 2 teaspoons minced fresh oregano, divided
- 2 teaspoons smoked paprika
- 1 teaspoon ground coriander
- 1 teaspoon table salt
- ½ teaspoon ground cumin
- ½ teaspoon pepper
- ¼ teaspoon cayenne pepper

1. Dissolve 3 tablespoons salt in 1½ quarts cold water in large container. Submerge ribs in brine and let stand at room temperature for 30 minutes. Meanwhile, whisk oil, lemon juice, garlic, ginger, 1 teaspoon oregano, paprika, coriander, salt, cumin, pepper, and cayenne in small bowl until combined.

2. Remove pork from brine and pat dry with paper towels. Cut ribs into 1-inch chunks; place dark meat and light meat in separate bowls. Divide spice paste proportionately between bowls and toss to coat. Thread light

and dark meat onto separate skewers (do not crowd pieces). Place dark meat kebabs on left side of rimmed baking sheet and light meat kebabs on right side.

3A. FOR A CHARCOAL GRILL: Open bottom vent completely. Light large chimney starter filled with charcoal briquettes (6 quarts). When top coals are partially covered with ash, pour evenly over half of grill. Set cooking grate in place, cover, and open lid vent completely. Heat grill until hot, about 5 minutes.

3B. FOR A GAS GRILL: Turn all burners to high, cover, and heat grill until hot, about 15 minutes. Leave primary burner on high and turn off other burner(s).

4. Clean and oil cooking grate. Place dark meat on hotter side of grill and cook for 6 minutes. Flip dark meat and add light meat to hotter side of grill. Cook for 4 minutes, then flip all kebabs. Continue to cook, flipping kebabs every 4 minutes, until dark meat is well charred and registers 155 degrees and light meat is lightly charred and registers 140 degrees, 4 to 8 minutes longer. Transfer to serving platter, tent with aluminum foil, and let rest for 5 minutes. Remove pork from skewers, toss to combine, sprinkle with remaining 1 teaspoon oregano, and serve, passing lemon wedges separately.

SPIRAL-SLICED HAM GLAZED WITH CIDER-VINEGAR CARAMEL

✔ **WHY THIS RECIPE WORKS** We found that several existing recipes for spiral-sliced ham produced meat that was leathery on the exterior with a glaze that flavored only the outermost edge. For moist meat throughout, we placed our ham in an oven bag, which traps juices and creates a moist environment that cooks it in less time than the dry air of the oven would, and reheated it in a 250-degree oven. We then brushed it with a sweet-tart caramel glaze. Since the sugar in the mixture was already caramelized, the glaze needed only a few minutes in a hot oven to acquire a deep mahogany sheen. Finally, we thinned some of the remaining caramel with ham juices to create a sauce to accompany the smoky, salty ham.

Many recipes for spiral-sliced ham—which has been injected with or immersed in a brine of water, curing salt, and a sweetener; fully cooked; and smoked by the

SPIRAL-SLICED HAM GLAZED WITH CIDER-VINEGAR CARAMEL

manufacturer—call for heating the ham in a roasting pan covered in foil in a 325-degree oven. But I found this approach to be flawed: By the time the center of the meat is warm, the exterior is certain to be parched.

Then there is the sweet glaze that is traditionally painted onto the ham. It's a great contrast to the smoky, salty meat, but I'm always disappointed that it flavors only the very edge of the thin slices. What's more, many recipes call for returning the ham to a hot oven for 20 to 30 minutes to help the sugary glaze caramelize and set, a surefire way to further desiccate the exterior.

I had a better way: I slid the ham into an oven bag and placed it in an oven set to just 250 degrees. The gentle heat warmed the interior and exterior of the ham at a similar rate. Meanwhile, the bag trapped juices, creating a humid environment that transferred heat more efficiently than dry air. In fact, when we compared two hams heated at 250 degrees—one in an oven bag and one covered in foil—the bagged ham came to temperature 25 percent (or 1 hour) faster than the foil-covered one. (That's not just because an oven bag speeds cooking; since foil reflects heat, it actually slows down cooking.)

To fix the issues with the glaze, I started by making a generous amount of caramel on the stovetop; augmented it with cider vinegar, pepper, and five-spice powder; and brushed some of it onto the ham. With the caramelization step taken care of in advance, the ham needed only 5 minutes in a 450-degree oven for the glaze to develop a mahogany sheen. (I pulled the ham from the 250-degree oven when it registered 110 degrees, knowing that the final blast in a hot oven would cause the meat to climb to the desired 120 to 125 degrees for serving.) Next, I stirred some of the meaty ham juices that were trapped in the oven bag into the remaining caramel. This sweet, tart, savory sauce could be drizzled onto the slices so that every bite—not just the ones on the edge—would taste just right.

—STEVE DUNN, *Cook's Illustrated*

Spiral-Sliced Ham Glazed with Cider-Vinegar Caramel

SERVES 12 TO 14

We recommend a shank-end ham because the bone configuration makes it easier to carve; look for a half ham with a tapered, pointed end. We developed this recipe using Turkey Size Reynolds Kitchens Oven Bags.

1 (7- to 10-pound) spiral-sliced, bone-in half ham, preferably shank end

1 large oven bag

1¼ cups sugar

½ cup water

3 tablespoons light corn syrup

1¼ cups cider vinegar

½ teaspoon pepper

¼ teaspoon five-spice powder

1. Adjust oven rack to lower-middle position and heat oven to 250 degrees. Line rimmed baking sheet with aluminum foil and set wire rack in sheet. Unwrap ham and, if necessary, discard plastic disk covering bone. Place ham cut side down in oven bag. Insert temperature probe (if using) through top of ham into center. Tie bag shut and place ham cut side down on prepared wire rack. Bake until center registers 110 degrees, 3½ to 4½ hours.

2. Bring sugar, water, and corn syrup to boil in large heavy-bottomed saucepan over medium-high heat. Cook, without stirring, until mixture is straw-colored, 6 to 8 minutes. While sugar mixture cooks, microwave vinegar in bowl until steaming, about 90 seconds; set aside. Once sugar mixture is straw-colored, reduce heat to low and continue to cook, swirling saucepan occasionally, until mixture is dark amber–colored and just smoking and registers 360 to 370 degrees, 2 to 5 minutes longer. Off heat, add warm vinegar a little at a time, whisking after each addition (some caramel may harden but will melt as sauce continues to cook). When bubbling subsides, add pepper and five-spice powder. Cook over medium-high heat, stirring occasionally, until reduced to 1⅓ cups, 5 to 7 minutes.

3. Remove sheet from oven and increase oven temperature to 450 degrees. Once oven reaches temperature, remove ham from bag and transfer to carving board. Reserve ¼ cup juices from bag; discard bag and remaining juices. Remove wire rack, leaving foil in place, and return ham to sheet, cut side down. Brush ham evenly with ⅓ cup caramel. Transfer sheet to oven and cook until glaze is bubbling and starting to brown in places, 5 to 7 minutes. Add reserved juices to remaining 1 cup caramel and whisk to combine.

4. Slice ham and serve, passing caramel sauce separately.

LION'S HEAD MEATBALLS

✔ **WHY THIS RECIPE WORKS** These giant, savory, tender-yet-springy pork meatballs from eastern China are pure comfort food. For a streamlined approach, we started with commercial ground pork. We treated the meat with a baking soda solution before cooking, which helped it retain juices over the relatively long cooking time. We lightly seasoned the meat with soy sauce, sugar, Shaoxing wine, ginger, scallions, and white pepper for well-rounded savory flavor that still tasted distinctly porky. Beating the pork mixture in a stand mixer caused its sticky proteins to link up into a strong network that trapped fat and moisture, resulting in a texture that was resilient and unctuous. Braising the meatballs for 1½ hours in the oven broke down the pork's collagen so that the meatballs were tender. Adding the cabbage for the last 30 minutes of cooking allowed it to soften and absorb the flavor of the chicken broth without turning mushy. Soaking rice vermicelli in just-boiled water softened the noodles but didn't overcook them.

The meatballs I loved growing up were my grandmother's: a pleasingly coarse but tender mix of beef, pork, and veal that she seasoned boldly with Parmesan and herbs, browned, and then simmered in a bright-red sauce.

Chinese lion's head meatballs are very different. For one thing, they're made entirely from pork and seasoned only subtly with aromatics such as minced scallions, grated fresh ginger, and white pepper, as well as modest amounts of Shaoxing wine and usually soy sauce—choices that enhance (rather than detract from) their porky, umami-rich profile. But what really makes them stand apart from other meatballs is their size and texture: They're as big as tennis balls and boast a seemingly paradoxical combination of spoon-tenderness and sausage-like spring and juiciness. (Read on and I'll explain the two-part method for achieving their unique texture.)

To color the meatballs' exteriors and make them more savory, cooks often brown the meatballs before slowly braising them in clean-tasting chicken broth on a bed of napa cabbage leaves. The meatballs are typically served with the softened greens, rice noodles and/or steamed white rice, and a ladle's worth of the broth in which they cooked. The large spheres fringed with the leafy greens are said to look like a lion's mane, hence the name.

They taste milder than most meatballs I've had and also mild in comparison to the intense flavors common to foods in other regions of China. But according to food journalist and Chinese cookbook author Fuchsia Dunlop, this mildness reflects the dish's origins. Lion's head meatballs are emblematic of the cuisine of Jiangnan, which is known for its gentleness, or "qing dan"—a term meaning "light" to convey the food's simple, unadulterated quality. To me, the dish is the Chinese equivalent of matzo ball soup: simple, soothing, and deeply savory.

Cooks traditionally start by hand-mincing some form of fatty pork—most often belly, though some recipes call for shoulder or butt—with the aforementioned seasonings and maybe an egg. But many contemporary recipes streamline things by calling for ground pork, so I seasoned 2 pounds of ground pork with salt and a couple of tablespoons of soy sauce, which enhanced the pork's flavor without adding too much liquid. I also added a bit of sugar, Shaoxing wine, white pepper, minced scallion whites, and grated fresh ginger. I added an egg to give the meatballs some structure before moving on to the first unique element of the meatball-making process: the mixing method.

Many recipes, including Dunlop's, call for working the meat vigorously by stirring and/or slapping it against the side of the mixing bowl. The effect is similar to sausage making, where thoroughly kneading the meat causes its sticky myosin proteins to cross-link and bind together into a strong network that makes the meat cohesive, fine-textured, and springy. It also helps trap moisture and fat for juicy meatballs.

We've achieved that sausage-like spring in other recipes by beating ground meat in a stand mixer, so I made a batch of meatballs using the machine and another using the traditional approach to see how each affected the texture. As a point of comparison, I also mixed a batch gently by hand, as I would Italian meatballs. I formed each mixture into balls with my wet hands (to prevent the meat from sticking to me) and then set them aside (skipping browning) while I laid a single layer of napa cabbage leaves in a few Dutch ovens, added a quart of chicken broth to each pot, and brought the broth to a boil. I carefully arranged the meatballs on the leaves, covered the pots, and braised the meatballs in a 325-degree oven for 2 hours (the ambient heat would cook the meatballs gently with minimal attention).

LION'S HEAD MEATBALLS (SHIZI TOU)

As expected, the hand-mixed meatballs were tender, coarse, and a tad dry (because the myosin hadn't gelled as much, they hadn't trapped much moisture). Meanwhile, the meatballs made in the stand mixer were just as smooth, springy, and juicy as those made the traditional way, confirming that the mixer was a great option. But I took that sausage-y effect one step further by adding baking soda to the meat, knowing that the alkalinity would help the proteins dissolve and create a smoother, more cohesive mixture.

The baking soda treatment came with one other perk: It raised the pH of the meat so that the meat retained more moisture during cooking and cooked up more tender. In fact, the baking soda was so effective that I could cut the braising time down to 1½ hours and produce meatballs that were every bit as tender and juicy as the 2-hour batch. But I couldn't shorten the cooking time more than that: Ground pork typically comes from a tough cut such as shoulder or butt, so even though it's ground into tiny pieces, its collagen still requires a lengthy exposure to moist heat to properly break down and tenderize.

What wasn't great was the cabbage, which had turned to mush during braising. The whole leaves were also hard to eat, so I cut them into pieces and added them to the dish 30 minutes before the meatballs were done cooking. To do so, I transferred the parcooked meatballs from the broth to a plate, added the leaves, and then nestled the meatballs on top of them. When returning the meatballs to the pot, I took the opportunity to flip them so the side sitting above the broth could moisten and the other side could color—no separate browning step necessary.

While the pot was in the oven, I softened some rice vermicelli in just-boiled water off the heat until the noodles were fully tender. I drained them, rinsed them under cold water to remove excess starch, drained them again, and portioned them into soup bowls. Then came the meatballs, cabbage, broth, and a handful of thinly sliced scallion greens—as well as a clean, savory aroma and a feeling of comfort-food satisfaction that rivaled (well, almost rivaled) the way I felt about my grandmother's meatballs.

—ANNIE PETITO, *Cook's Illustrated*

Lion's Head Meatballs (Shizi Tou)

SERVES 4 TO 6

Fully cooked ground pork can retain a slightly pink hue. Don't be concerned if the meatballs crack while cooking. Shaoxing wine is a Chinese rice wine that can be found at Asian markets; if you can't find it, use dry sherry.

- ¾ teaspoon baking soda
- ½ teaspoon table salt
- 2 pounds ground pork
- 1 large egg, lightly beaten
- 2 scallions, white parts minced, green parts sliced thin
- 2 tablespoons soy sauce
- 2 tablespoons Shaoxing wine or dry sherry
- 4 teaspoons sugar
- 2 teaspoons grated fresh ginger
- ½ teaspoon white pepper
- 4 cups chicken broth
- 1 small head napa cabbage (1½ pounds), quartered lengthwise, cored, and cut crosswise into 2-inch pieces
- 4 ounces rice vermicelli

1. Adjust oven rack to lower-middle position and heat oven to 325 degrees. Whisk baking soda, salt, and 2 tablespoons water together in bowl of stand mixer. Add pork to baking soda mixture and toss to combine. Add egg, scallion whites, soy sauce, Shaoxing wine, sugar, ginger, and white pepper. Fit stand mixer with paddle and beat on medium speed until mixture is well combined and has stiffened and started to pull away from sides of bowl and pork has slightly lightened in color, 45 to 60 seconds. Using your wet hands, form about ½ cup (4½ ounces) pork mixture into 3-inch round meatball; repeat with remaining mixture to form 8 meatballs.

2. Bring broth to boil in large Dutch oven over high heat. Off heat, carefully arrange meatballs in pot (seven around perimeter and one in center; meatballs will not be totally submerged). Cover pot, transfer to oven, and cook for 1 hour.

3. Transfer meatballs to large plate. Add cabbage to pot in even layer and arrange meatballs over cabbage, paler side up. Cover, return pot to oven, and continue to cook until meatballs are lightly browned and cabbage is softened, about 30 minutes longer.

4. While meatballs and cabbage cook, bring 4 quarts water to boil in large pot. Off heat, add vermicelli and let sit, stirring occasionally, until vermicelli is fully tender, 10 to 15 minutes. Drain, rinse with cold water, drain again, and distribute evenly among 4 to 6 large soup bowls.

5. Ladle meatballs, cabbage, and broth into bowls of noodles. Sprinkle with scallion greens and serve.

GOAN PORK VINDALOO

✔ WHY THIS RECIPE WORKS The word "vindaloo" has evolved to indicate a searingly hot curry, but the traditional Goan dish is a brightly flavored but relatively mild pork braise made with dried Kashmiri chiles and plenty of spices such as cinnamon, cloves, and cardamom. We used a combination of guajillo chiles, paprika, and tea to provide the bright color, mild heat, earthy flavor, and hint of astringency typically imparted by the hard-to-find Kashmiri chiles. Vindaloo should have a pronounced vinegary tang, but we found that adding the vinegar at the beginning made the meat chalky. We withheld it until halfway through cooking so that we could use less but still enjoy the characteristic acidity. Moving the cooking from the stovetop to the oven made this dish hands-off and foolproof.

Food challenges such as belly-buster sundaes, six-alarm chili, and 32-ounce black-and-blue porterhouse steaks aren't my thing. That's why I had always sidestepped vindaloo, which I had thought must sit at the top of every culinary thrill-seeker's list of favorite fiery Indian dishes. I prefer mild to medium-hot curries in which the painstakingly calibrated flavors of ginger, garlic, and spices haven't been obliterated by searing heat. But it turns out that I had been mistaken about vindaloo, at least in its original form.

The scorching vindaloo served at many Indian restaurants in the United States and England is actually an offshoot of the original Goan version, which is composed of moist nuggets of pork braised to tenderness in their own juices and a fragrant paste of spices such as cinnamon and cardamom, mild dried Kashmiri chiles, and fresh ginger and garlic. Plenty of coconut vinegar (or sometimes tamarind) balances the rich pork,

but the dish has little to no other liquid, so the potent, bright-red sauce thickly coats the meat. Rice; naan; or Goan pao, which are nearly identical to America's soft, slightly sweet dinner rolls, are ideal companions. This sounded like a vindaloo I could get behind.

Before I could follow a traditional Goan recipe, I needed to source two of the key ingredients: coconut vinegar and Kashmiri chiles. I was able to locate coconut vinegar—an acidic but not coconutty product with a sweet aroma made from coconut tree sap—at my neighborhood Indian grocer, and I ordered whole dried Kashmiri chiles from an online source.

Following the Goan recipe, I used a blender to grind together a spice paste, sometimes called a wet masala. Along with ¾ cup of the coconut vinegar and 12 Kashmiri chiles, many other flavors typical of the cuisine were represented: cumin, black pepper, cinnamon, cardamom, nutmeg, cloves, fresh ginger, and garlic.

Given the option of pork belly or pork butt, I opted for the latter because it's easier to find and leaner, though still plenty rich. I trimmed the roast and cut it into 1-inch chunks. Recipes called for marinating the meat in the masala for anywhere from 4 to 48 hours; I was worried about the pork being damaged by all the acidity, so I opted for the shorter time.

I sautéed some onions in oil, added the marinated meat, and cooked the curry over low heat. I lingered nervously near the pot for the first 45 minutes, stirring occasionally, worried that the dry-ish mixture would scorch before the pork's juices loosened it up. After 90 minutes, when the paste had transformed into a thick and fragrant sauce, I took a bite.

With one taste I understood why the original vindaloo is so venerated. The coconut vinegar contributed a pleasing brightness tempered by a hint of sweetness, and the Kashmiri chiles gave the masala rich complexity and a touch of heat that complemented the spices. But just as I had feared, the 4-hour bath in the acidic masala had turned the meat dry.

I made the Goan recipe again, skipping the marinating time altogether in the hope that the meat would emerge juicier. I also moved the pot to a 325-degree oven once the mixture was bubbling on the stovetop so that I wouldn't have to worry about it scorching. After 90 minutes, I sampled the meat. It was still dry, even though I'd skipped marinating. That's because there was still plenty of vinegar in the pot. The acidic treatment lowered the pH of meat to a point where the proteins squeezed out moisture.

And thus my conundrum: I couldn't get rid of the vinegar because vindaloo needs a certain amount of tang. But vinegar doesn't just add an acidic taste, it also affects texture. What's more, when you add the vinegar matters because it is volatile—meaning that its flavor and acidity dissipate easily during cooking. Ultimately, the solution was to add less vinegar, late in the cooking process. Instead of adding ¾ cup of vinegar at the start of cooking, I poured in just ⅓ cup halfway through the cooking time. The lesser amount of acid wasn't enough to adversely affect the texture of the meat, but enough of the vinegar's tang remained for my dish to taste like vindaloo.

My final challenge was to find better substitutes for the coconut vinegar and the Kashmiri chiles so that in the future I could make vindaloo without sourcing specialty ingredients. The vinegar was easy: Its sweet aroma made the cider vinegar I always have on hand a good sub.

My dive into the world of dried Kashmiri chiles was not as straightforward. Most sources describe them as vibrantly red but mild in flavor, so some cookbook authors suggest substituting paprika. Confusingly, others recommend swapping in arbols—among the hottest of dried chiles—one for one. Vindaloo is known for its milder spiciness, so that swap didn't make much sense.

To zero in on the flavor of Kashmiri chiles, I softened some of my dwindling supply in water, blended them with a bit of salt to bring out the flavor, and tasted the bright red puree. It was only slightly hot, a little fruity, and it had a subtly astringent finish, reminiscent of well-steeped tea.

Guajillo chiles provided the slight fruitiness and mild heat, and just 1 tablespoon of paprika boosted the color of the masala. The Kashmiri chile profile was almost complete, but the notion of adding tea for astringency kept nagging at me: I considered making a strong tannic infusion and mixing it into the masala, but I knew it would make the sauce too soupy. Finally, I just emptied a couple of tea bags into the masala. It worked. These substitutions produced a vindaloo that tasted almost exactly like the one I'd made with Kashmiri chiles and coconut vinegar.

I'm content to leave modern versions of pork vindaloo to the culinary daredevils; this version, deliciously intense in its own right, is the one I'll return to again and again.

—ANDREA GEARY, *Cook's Illustrated*

NOTES FROM THE TEST KITCHEN

SEEKING A SUB FOR KASHMIRI CHILES?

Kashmiri chiles—valued for their vibrant color and mild heat—are a principal ingredient in vindaloo, but they usually require ordering online. Our substitution is a combination of dried guajillo chiles, which are similarly mild and fruity; paprika for a vivid red color boost; and black tea leaves for a slightly astringent finish.

THE REAL DEAL
Kashmiri chiles

SMART SUB
Guajillos + paprika + tea

Goan Pork Vindaloo
SERVES 8

Pork butt roast is often labeled Boston butt. If you don't have loose tea, open up two or three black tea bags and measure out 2 teaspoons of tea. Decaffeinated tea can be used if desired. Traditional Goan vindaloo is not very spicy, but if you prefer more heat, add up to ½ teaspoon of cayenne pepper. Serve with white rice, naan, or Goan pao.

- 4 large dried guajillo chiles, wiped clean, stemmed, seeded, and torn into 1-inch pieces (about 1 ounce)
- 1 cup water, divided
- 1 (1½-inch) piece fresh ginger, peeled and sliced crosswise ⅛ inch thick
- 6 garlic cloves, chopped coarse
- 1 tablespoon paprika
- 1 tablespoon ground cumin
- 2 teaspoons loose black tea
- 2 teaspoons table salt
- 1 teaspoon pepper
- ¼–½ teaspoon cayenne pepper (optional)
- ½ teaspoon ground cinnamon
- ½ teaspoon ground cardamom
- ¼ teaspoon ground cloves
- ¼ teaspoon ground nutmeg
- 1 (3- to 3½-pound) boneless pork butt roast, trimmed and cut into 1-inch pieces
- 1 tablespoon vegetable oil
- 1 large onion, chopped fine
- ⅓ cup apple cider vinegar

1. Combine guajillos and ½ cup water in bowl and microwave until steaming, about 1½ minutes. Let sit until guajillos are softened, about 10 minutes. While guajillos soften, adjust oven rack to middle position and heat oven to 325 degrees. Process guajillo mixture; ginger; garlic; paprika; cumin; tea; salt; pepper; cayenne, if using; cinnamon; cardamom; cloves; and nutmeg in blender on low speed until smooth paste forms, 1½ to 2 minutes. With blender running, add remaining ½ cup water. Increase speed to high for 1 minute. Add pork to large bowl; pour spice paste over pork and mix thoroughly.

2. Heat oil in Dutch oven over medium heat until shimmering. Add onion and cook, stirring frequently, until soft and golden, 7 to 9 minutes. Add pork mixture and stir to combine. Spread mixture into even layer.

Continue to cook until mixture begins to bubble, about 2 minutes longer. Cover pot, transfer to oven, and cook for 40 minutes. Stir in vinegar. Cover and return to oven. Continue to cook until fork inserted into pork meets little or no resistance, 40 to 50 minutes longer. Let stand, uncovered, for 10 minutes. Stir and serve.

PORK CORDON BLEU

✔ **WHY THIS RECIPE WORKS** For a contemporary take on chicken cordon bleu, we got rid of the chicken and used pork tenderloin instead. We began by making our own cutlets from a 1-pound tenderloin, pounding them to a ¼-inch thickness to ensure that they would cook quickly. After breading the cutlets, we lightly fried them in a nonstick skillet. To balance the rich flavors, we made a quick sauce with sour cream, Dijon mustard, and chives. We dolloped the sauce on the fried cutlets, topped them with Black Forest ham and Gruyère cheese, and broiled them.

Chicken cordon bleu, or "blue ribbon" chicken, features a boneless breast that's stuffed with (or rolled around) a ham and cheese filling, coated in bread crumbs, and baked or fried. It's a well-loved dish but, in my opinion, it's one that could use a bit of a refresh. What's more, I wanted to swap out chicken breast in favor of tender, mildly sweet pork tenderloin. And I wanted it to be fast and easy enough for a weeknight.

Classic cordon bleu calls for Black Forest ham, and it was the best option here too, for its consistently robust flavor and wide availability. After experimenting with several different cheeses, I settled on Gruyère for its nutty flavor and smooth meltability.

As for the construction, many cordon bleu recipes call for cutting a pocket into the side of a chicken or pork cutlet and then stuffing the pocket with cheese and ham, but I wanted an easier method. I tried pounding pieces of the tenderloin into cutlets, rolling them around the filling, and tying the bundles with twine, but it wasn't easy.

My next thought was to sandwich the ham and cheese between two cutlets, but the assembled mass was too thick to cook through before the bread crumbs on the exterior burned. In the end, the solution was to create a simple stack.

PORK CORDON BLEU

I started by cutting a pork tenderloin into four equal pieces, standing the pieces on end (cut side up), and pounding them out into cutlets. Covering the pork pieces with plastic wrap while pounding helped contain any mess. From there I breaded and pan-fried the cutlets and then topped each with ham and cheese and slid the stacks under the broiler to bubble and brown.

How about a sauce? I stirred together potent Dijon mustard, sour cream, chives, and a bit of salt and pepper for a creamy, tangy sauce that balanced the rich meat and cheese. Rather than using the sauce just as a garnish, I spread a tablespoon right on top of the fried cutlets before adding the ham and cheese and broiling them. This dish was definitely worthy of a blue ribbon.

—NATALIE ESTRADA, *Cook's Country*

Pork Cordon Bleu

SERVES 4

For the best results, be sure to purchase a tenderloin that weighs no more than 1 pound. We like to serve these cutlets with a green salad.

MUSTARD SAUCE

- ¾ cup sour cream
- ¼ cup Dijon mustard
- 2 tablespoons minced fresh chives
- ⅛ teaspoon table salt
- ⅛ teaspoon pepper

PORK

- ¼ cup all-purpose flour
- 2 large eggs
- 1 tablespoon Dijon mustard
- 1½ cups panko bread crumbs
- 1 (14- to 16-ounce) pork tenderloin, trimmed
- ¼ teaspoon table salt
- ¼ teaspoon pepper
- ½ cup vegetable oil for frying
- 8 thin slices deli Black Forest ham (8 ounces)
- 4 ounces Gruyère cheese, shredded (1 cup)

1. FOR THE MUSTARD SAUCE: Combine all ingredients in bowl; set aside.

2. FOR THE PORK: Adjust oven rack 6 inches from broiler element and heat broiler. Place flour in shallow dish. Lightly beat eggs and mustard together in second shallow dish. Place panko in third shallow dish.

3. Cut tenderloin crosswise into 4 equal pieces. Working with 1 piece at a time, arrange tenderloin pieces cut side up on cutting board. Cover with plastic wrap and pound to even ¼-inch thickness with meat pounder. Pat cutlets dry with paper towels and sprinkle with salt and pepper.

4. Dredge cutlets in flour, shaking off excess; dip in egg mixture, allowing excess to drip off; then coat with panko, pressing to adhere. Transfer cutlets to plate.

5. Set wire rack in rimmed baking sheet. Heat oil in 12-inch nonstick skillet over medium-high heat to 350 degrees. Place 2 cutlets in skillet and cook until golden brown on first side, about 3 minutes.

6. Using 2 spatulas, gently flip cutlets and continue to cook until golden brown on second side and just cooked through, about 3 minutes longer. Transfer to prepared rack. Return oil to 350 degrees and repeat with remaining 2 cutlets.

7. Spread 2 tablespoons mustard sauce over top of each cutlet, leaving ¼-inch border. Place 2 slices ham on each cutlet, folding ham as needed to keep from overhanging cutlet. Sprinkle ¼ cup Gruyère over ham on each cutlet.

8. Broil until Gruyère is melted and lightly browned in spots, 2 to 3 minutes. Serve cutlets with remaining mustard sauce.

PORK STROGANOFF

✓ WHY THIS RECIPE WORKS Pork tenderloin might not be the traditional choice for stroganoff, but with its faintly sweet flavor and relatively low price, we found that it made for an excellent riff on this supercomforting dish of creamy noodles and meat. To enhance the tenderloin's relatively mild flavor, we layered in salty, intense pork flavor by first crisping up a bit of diced pancetta. From there, we dredged thin slices of pork tenderloin in seasoned flour to ensure that the pork remained tender and to add body and creaminess to the sauce. After quickly browning the pork and creating flavorful fond in the pot, we added earthy cremini mushrooms, floral sage, and concentrated tomato paste for a savory underpinning. A bit of white wine added brightness, and cooking the noodles in the saucy mix of wine and chicken broth ensured that they soaked up lots of flavor.

During the bleak winter months here in the Northeast, nothing's quite as comforting as a bowl of warm stroganoff—soft noodles, strips of tender and flavorful meat, and a supercreamy sauce. But instead of using expensive beef tenderloin, the cut most frequently called for in recipes for this dish, I wanted to use pork tenderloin, a favorite in my kitchen for its subtle sweetness and reasonable price. Traditional? Nope, and that's perfectly OK.

I knew that I had to cook the pork relatively quickly so it wouldn't dry out. I began by cutting the tenderloin in half lengthwise and then sliced each half ¼ inch thick. Next, I dredged the pork in flour to promote browning. I seared the pieces for about 3 minutes and then removed them from the pot with a slotted spoon. The leftover fond served as a base to build a flavorful sauce.

I added mushrooms, onion, sage, garlic, and tomato paste for a savory underpinning. Once these ingredients started to brown, I added chicken broth and wine, scraped up the fond, and continued to cook the sauce until it was silky. I returned the pork to the mix, poured the saucy mixture over cooked egg noodles, and . . . well, let's just say this stroganoff was missing some punch. It was watery and weak without much pork flavor.

My first move was to introduce some pancetta up front. I cut it up and rendered its fat in the pot before cooking the tenderloin. This added deep, meaty, complex notes to enhance the tenderloin's more demure flavors.

Next, I decided to cook the noodles directly in the sauce, allowing them to soak up more flavor while also adding a bit of starchy body to the sauce. A quick 10-minute simmer and the noodles were al dente. Off the heat, I added tangy sour cream and a bit more sage and sprinkled some chives over the top. I finally achieved what I'd been searching for: a stroganoff that was satisfying, comforting, and rich—and easy enough (just one pot!) for a weeknight.

—NATALIE ESTRADA, *Cook's Country*

Pork Stroganoff

SERVES 4

Be sure to buy a ¼-inch-thick hunk of pancetta from the deli counter rather than presliced pancetta, as larger chunks are important here.

3 ounces pancetta, cut into ¼-inch pieces

1 tablespoon extra-virgin olive oil

1 (12-ounce) pork tenderloin, trimmed, halved lengthwise, and sliced crosswise ¼ inch thick

3 tablespoons all-purpose flour, divided

1 teaspoon table salt, divided

1 teaspoon pepper, divided

3 tablespoons unsalted butter, divided

12 ounces cremini mushrooms, trimmed and sliced thin

1 large onion, chopped fine

4 teaspoons chopped fresh sage, divided

3 garlic cloves, minced

2 teaspoons tomato paste

4 cups chicken broth

¼ cup dry white wine

8 ounces (4 cups) egg noodles

½ cup sour cream

2 tablespoons minced fresh chives

1. Cook pancetta and oil in Dutch oven over medium heat until pancetta is lightly browned and crispy, about 10 minutes. Using slotted spoon, transfer pancetta to large plate, leaving fat in pot.

2. Toss pork, 2 tablespoons flour, ½ teaspoon salt, and ½ teaspoon pepper together in bowl. Add 1 tablespoon butter to fat left in pot and melt over high heat. Add pork in single layer, breaking up any clumps, and cook, without stirring, until browned on bottom, about 2 minutes. Stir and continue to cook until pork is no longer pink, about 1 minute longer. Transfer to plate with pancetta.

3. Melt remaining 2 tablespoons butter in now-empty pot over medium heat. Add mushrooms, onion, remaining ½ teaspoon salt, and remaining ½ teaspoon pepper and cook until any liquid has evaporated and vegetables have just begun to brown, 7 to 9 minutes. Add 1 tablespoon sage, garlic, tomato paste, and remaining 1 tablespoon flour and cook until fragrant, about 30 seconds.

4. Stir in broth and wine and bring to simmer, scraping up any browned bits. Stir in noodles and cook, uncovered, stirring occasionally, until noodles are just tender, 9 to 11 minutes.

5. Add pork and pancetta and cook until warmed through, about 1 minute. Off heat, stir in sour cream and remaining 1 teaspoon sage until thoroughly combined. Season with salt and pepper to taste. Sprinkle with chives and serve.

NORTH CAROLINA BARBECUE PORK

NORTH CAROLINA BARBECUE PORK

✓ **WHY THIS RECIPE WORKS** To create North Carolina barbecue pork on a charcoal grill, we used a grill setup called a charcoal snake. This C-shaped array of smoldering briquettes provided low, slow, indirect heat to the center of the grill for upwards of 5 hours, so we needed to refuel only once during the long cooking time. Wrapping the bone-in pork butt in foil when it reached 170 degrees gave the meat plenty of time to absorb smoke flavor and get a crusty bark without its exterior getting too bitter.

When you're talking barbecue in North Carolina, you're talking pork. But that's just the beginning: Different parts of the state treat the dish differently. Pitmasters in the eastern part of the state traditionally cook whole hogs on open pits. But in the area in and around Lexington, closer to the middle of the state, they usually cook hulking bone-in pork shoulders in closed brick pits. Both styles use low, direct heat and plenty of smoke, ideally from smoldering hickory logs. There are distinctions in how the pork is served and sauced, but I'll get to those in a moment.

I set out to emulate each of these two styles using a single method, with a recipe built for a backyard grill.

I opted for a smoking technique we've used before in the test kitchen: a charcoal snake. With a water-filled pan directly below the pork to moderate the grill's temperature, I was able to cook the pork through with only one charcoal reload. The meat was mostly tender, but its exterior char was too dark and bitter-tasting.

The fix was pulling the pork off the grill and wrapping it in aluminum foil when it reached 170 degrees. This gave the meat 4 to 5 hours to absorb smoke and get nice and crusty before it was wrapped; the foil prevented further browning while allowing the pork to finish cooking to doneness. Pausing to wrap the pork also provided the perfect opportunity to refuel the snake. Once the pork registered 200 degrees, I pulled it off the grill, still wrapped, to rest for 1½ hours.

The pork was cooked perfectly, but I still had work to do. In eastern North Carolina you're more likely to get finely chopped whole hog 'cue, while in Lexington people can choose chopped, sliced, or chopped coarse with the option to request outside brown (aka extra-smoky bark). And while the sauces in both parts of the state are tangy, eastern North Carolina sauce should be simply salty, fiery, and vinegary. Lexington-style sauce contains a little ketchup, which makes it redder, sweeter, and a touch thicker.

—MORGAN BOLLING, *Cook's Country*

North Carolina Barbecue Pork
SERVES 8 TO 10

We developed this recipe using a 22-inch Weber kettle grill. Plan ahead: The pork butt must be seasoned at least 18 hours before it is cooked. We like to serve eastern North Carolina–style barbecue pork with collard greens, coleslaw, and cornbread, and Lexington-style barbecue pork with hush puppies, french fries, and red slaw.

- 3 tablespoons kosher salt
- 1½ tablespoons pepper
- 1 (6-pound) bone-in pork butt roast, with ¼-inch fat cap
- 1 (13 by 9-inch) disposable aluminum pan
- 4 (3-inch) wood chunks
- 1 recipe Eastern North Carolina–Style Barbecue Sauce or Lexington-Style Barbecue Sauce (page 142)

1. Combine salt and pepper in bowl. Place pork butt on large sheet of plastic wrap and season all over with salt mixture. Wrap tightly with plastic and refrigerate for 18 to 24 hours.

2. Open bottom grill vent completely. Set up charcoal snake: Arrange 60 briquettes, 2 briquettes wide, around perimeter of grill, overlapping slightly so briquettes are touching, leaving 6-inch gap between ends of snake. Place second layer of 60 briquettes, also 2 briquettes wide, on top of first. (Completed snake should be 2 briquettes wide by 2 briquettes high.)

3. Starting 4 inches from 1 end of snake, evenly space wood chunks on top of snake. Place disposable pan in center of grill so short end of pan runs parallel to gap in snake. Fill pan with 4 cups water.

4. Light chimney starter filled with 15 briquettes. When coals are partially covered with ash, pour over 1 end of snake. Make sure lit coals touch only 1 end of snake. Use tongs if necessary to move any coals that touch other end of snake.

5. Set cooking grate in place. Clean and oil cooking grate. Unwrap pork and position fat side down over water pan. Insert temperature probe into thickest part of pork. Cover grill, positioning lid vent over gap in snake. Cook, without opening grill, until pork registers 170 degrees, 4 to 5 hours.

6. Place 2 large sheets of aluminum foil on rimmed baking sheet. Remove probe from pork. Using oven mitts, lift pork and transfer to center of foil, fat side down. Wrap tightly with first sheet of foil, minimizing air pockets between foil and pork. Wrap with second sheet of foil. (Use additional foil, if necessary, to completely wrap pork.)Foil wrap should be airtight. Make small mark on foil with marker to keep track of fat side.

7. Remove cooking grate. Starting at still-unlit end of snake, pour 2 quarts unlit briquettes about one-third of way around perimeter of grill over gap in snake and spent coals. Replace cooking grate. Return wrapped pork to grill over water pan, fat side down. Re-insert probe into thickest part of pork. Cover grill and continue to cook until pork registers 200 degrees, 1 to 1½ hours longer.

8. Remove probe. Transfer pork to carving board, fat side up, and let rest in foil for 1½ hours. Remove bone from pork. For eastern North Carolina style, chop pork into ¼-inch pieces. For Lexington style, chop pork with cleaver into 1-inch pieces. Toss with ⅔ cup sauce. Serve, passing remaining sauce separately.

Eastern North Carolina–Style Barbecue Sauce
MAKES ABOUT 2½ CUPS

One 12-ounce bottle of Texas Pete Original Hot Sauce will yield more than enough for this recipe.

- 1½ cups cider vinegar
- 1 cup Texas Pete Original Hot Sauce
- ¼ cup packed light brown sugar
- 2 teaspoons kosher salt
- 1 teaspoon pepper
- 1 teaspoon red pepper flakes

Whisk all ingredients together in bowl.

Lexington-Style Barbecue Sauce
MAKES ABOUT 2½ CUPS

This sauce is meant to be tangy and salty to balance the rich smoked pork.

- 2 cups cider vinegar
- 1 cup ketchup
- 2 teaspoons granulated garlic

- 2 teaspoons pepper
- 1½ teaspoons kosher salt
- 1 teaspoon red pepper flakes

Combine all ingredients in small saucepan and bring to boil over medium-high heat. Reduce heat to medium-low and simmer for 5 minutes. Transfer sauce to bowl and let cool completely.

GREEK MEATBALLS

✔ **WHY THIS RECIPE WORKS** Inspired by the Greek meatballs at Johnny's Restaurant in Homewood, Alabama, we wanted to make our own version with tender, juicy ground lamb; lemony brightness; and bold yet balanced seasoning from garlic, spices, and herbs. We chose crushed saltine crackers and milk as a panade to keep the meatballs tender and juicy. Lemon zest and minced garlic added punch, and citrusy coriander and earthy cumin provided complexity. Aromatic mint and scallions, as well as dried oregano with its slight licorice undertones, provided the best herb mix. We roasted the meatballs instead of searing them in a skillet for hands-off browning and no splatter and then served them with a smooth tahini-yogurt dip.

At Johnny's Restaurant in Homewood, Alabama, you won't find the meatballs on top of spaghetti, all covered with cheese. At Johnny's, they're a reflection of owner Tim Hontzas's Greek heritage and Southern upbringing, made with lamb and full of bright herb flavor and warm spices. Inspired, I hit the kitchen to create my own version.

Existing recipes for Greek meatballs (aka keftedes) gave me mixed results. Some versions were perfect but required more work than I wanted to invest. Other versions were unbalanced: too heavy on the cinnamon, for example, or too light on the herbs. My goal was to create a tender, juicy meatball with a Greek twist that had bold yet balanced garlic and herb flavor and was perfumed with spices and lemony brightness.

I started with ground lamb, a core ingredient in Greek cuisine. Tasters agreed that fresh mint and scallions, as well as dried oregano with its licorice undertones, provided the best mix. Garlic and lemon zest added pungency and brightness, and citrusy coriander and earthy cumin provided fragrant complexity and depth.

A panade—a mixture of liquid and starch—can help keep meatballs tender and juicy. After experimenting with panko and regular dried bread crumbs (too gummy) and fresh bread crumbs (too sweet), I chose crushed saltines and milk. Just right.

I prefer roasting meatballs in the oven to searing them on the stovetop because it means hands-off browning and no splatter. For these party-size meatballs, I found that 450 degrees for about 20 minutes did the trick: The meatballs were cooked through, with flavorful browning on top. A quick tahini and yogurt dip was just perfect for these Greek-inspired snacks.

Now these were meatballs worth singing about.

—CECELIA JENKINS, *Cook's Country*

Greek Meatballs

SERVES 8 TO 10

You can substitute ground beef for the ground lamb.

MEATBALLS

20	square saltines
½	cup milk
½	cup chopped fresh mint, plus leaves for sprinkling
6	scallions, minced
2	tablespoons dried oregano
5	garlic cloves, minced
1	tablespoon grated lemon zest
2	teaspoons ground cumin
2	teaspoons ground coriander
1½	teaspoons pepper
1¼	teaspoons table salt
2	pounds ground lamb

SAUCE

1	cup plain whole-milk yogurt
½	cup tahini
¼	cup lemon juice (2 lemons)
1	teaspoon table salt
½	teaspoon pepper

1. FOR THE MEATBALLS: Adjust oven rack to upper-middle position and heat oven to 450 degrees. Set wire rack in aluminum foil–lined rimmed baking sheet.

2. Place saltines in large zipper-lock bag, seal bag, and crush fine with rolling pin (you should end up with 1 scant cup crushed saltines). Combine saltines and milk in large bowl, mashing with rubber spatula until paste forms, about 1 minute.

3. Add chopped mint, scallions, oregano, garlic, lemon zest, cumin, coriander, pepper, and salt to saltine mixture and mash until thoroughly combined. Add lamb and mix with your hands until thoroughly combined.

4. Divide mixture into 40 portions (1 heaping tablespoon each). Roll portions between your wet hands to form 1½-inch meatballs and evenly space on prepared wire rack. Roast until meatballs are lightly browned, about 20 minutes.

5. FOR THE SAUCE: While meatballs roast, whisk all ingredients together in bowl; set aside.

6. Using tongs, transfer meatballs to serving platter. Serve with sauce and sprinkle individual portions with mint leaves.

TO MAKE AHEAD: Uncooked meatballs can be frozen for up to 2 months. After shaping meatballs in step 4, transfer to greased plate and freeze until completely frozen, at least 2 hours. Transfer frozen meatballs to 1-gallon zipper-lock freezer bag. To serve, cook from frozen and increase roasting time to 25 minutes.

NOTES FROM THE TEST KITCHEN

E-Z FREEZE
To make the meatballs ahead, simply freeze the raw meatballs on a plate, transfer to a zipper-lock bag, and freeze them for up to two months. You can cook the frozen meatballs on a wire rack set in a rimmed baking sheet.

1. Freeze on plate

2. Bag and keep in freezer

3. Cook from frozen on wire rack

OVEN-STEAMED FISH WITH SCALLIONS AND GINGER

CHAPTER 5

POULTRY AND SEAFOOD

EASY GRILL-ROASTED WHOLE CHICKEN

✔ **WHY THIS RECIPE WORKS** Grilling the chicken over indirect heat for the majority of the cooking time allowed it to cook gently and evenly throughout. To ensure that it picked up distinct grill flavor, we moved the chicken over direct heat for the last few minutes of cooking and added a wood chip packet to the fire, which subtly infused the meat with smoke. Draining the bird's cavity midway through cooking prevented the fatty juices from dripping onto the fire and causing flare-ups. With no salt treatments or knife work, the chicken was ready for the grill in no time.

Like so many of our fans, I love a simple roast chicken that tastes of nothing but concentrated chicken-y goodness. The test kitchen's most popular chicken recipe, Weeknight Roast Chicken, accomplishes exactly that—and with a method that couldn't be easier. There's no brining, no salting, no knife work, and no dirtying of dishes required.

I wanted to create an equally simple method for the grill, and as with the Weeknight Roast Chicken recipe, pretreatments and extensive prep work were off the table. So were rubs, marinades, and sauces. But I did want the bird to taste of the grill—not so much as to overpower the clean chicken flavor, but enough that you could tell that it had been cooked on the grill.

There are two main ways to achieve grill flavor. You can cook the food over direct heat, which produces char—the dark browning that develops where food comes in contact with the hot cooking grate—as well as all the new flavor compounds that develop when meat juices and rendered fat drip onto the heat source, break down, vaporize, and condense on the surface of the food. You can also add a wood chip packet to the fire to produce smoke, which also rises up and condenses on the food.

For the moment, I put aside the notion of adding smoke flavor and thought about how to use direct heat. Trying to cook a whole chicken over direct heat on the grill would be as silly as trying to sear it in a skillet. The exterior would obviously overcook before the interior cooked through. And while some measure of fatty juices dripping onto the coals creates desirable grill flavor, too much triggers significant flare-ups that leave a layer of black carbon on the bird's exterior that overwhelms its mild flavor. That's why most recipes for grilling a whole bird call for indirect heat, which cooks the meat gently and evenly—but also produces results without much grill flavor.

My solution incorporated both indirect and direct heat. I built a fire with heat sources (charcoal or gas) on either side of the grill and a cooler zone down the middle and cooked the chicken, breast side up, over the cooler zone until the breast hit 130 degrees; at that point, a good amount of the bird's fat had been rendered, so I figured flare-ups wouldn't be an issue. Then I finished cooking the chicken over the hotter zone, flipping it breast side down after a few minutes so that both the top and bottom received direct heat.

What I hadn't accounted for was that the chicken's cavity became a receptacle for its fatty juices; when I turned the chicken over, that liquid sloshed onto the fire and flames shot up, scorching the bird's exterior. Plus, the breast meat was now a tad dry even though I had pulled the chicken off the grill as soon as it reached its target temperature of 160 degrees. My fix was to grab the bird by the cavity using tongs and drain the juices into a bowl before moving it to the hotter side of the grill.

As for the dry meat, I remembered that the hotter the cooking temperature, the higher the meat's temperature will climb after cooking. Finishing over direct heat caused the chicken's temperature to rise rapidly. To account for that carryover effect, I pulled the bird off the grill when it registered 155 degrees.

Now the chicken was moist, with evenly bronzed skin and a good measure of that unmistakable char. Time to add some smoke for another layer of grill flavor.

The trick would be calibrating the smoke's effect to keep it from overwhelming the clean chicken taste. I tried various amounts of wood chips using our standard method—wrapping them in aluminum foil and cutting a pair of slits in the packet to allow just enough airflow for the chips to smoke steadily—and I found that I needed just ¼ to ½ cup of chips (depending on whether I was using charcoal or gas, respectively) to generate the subtle smoke flavor I wanted. I also made sure to use dry wood chips, since they start smoking right away while the bird is still cold, and smoke condenses much more readily on cold surfaces.

After about an hour on the grill, my ideal grill-roasted chicken was ready: succulent, subtly smoky meat encased in deeply golden skin. Behold, your (and my) new go-to method for roasting chicken—alfresco.

—STEVE DUNN, *Cook's Illustrated*

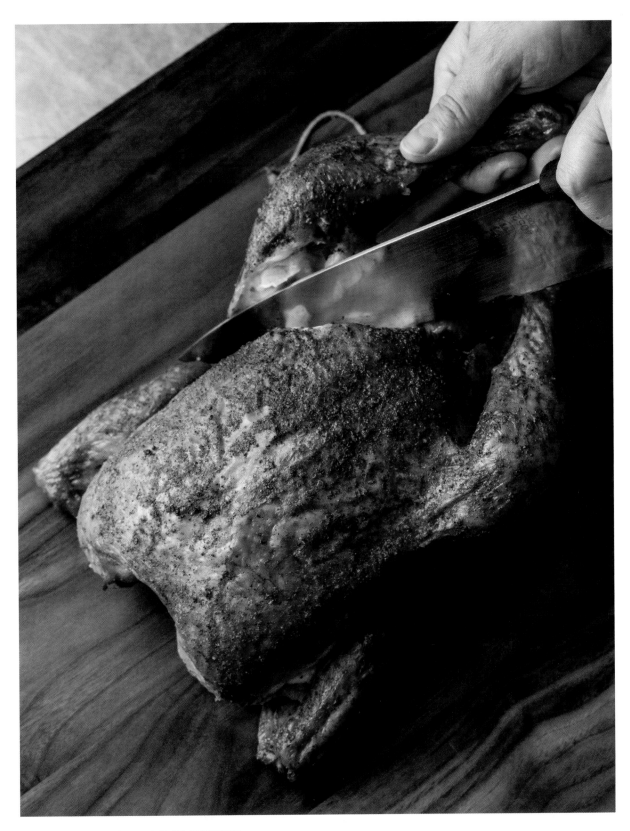

EASY GRILL-ROASTED WHOLE CHICKEN

Easy Grill-Roasted Whole Chicken

SERVES 4

We developed this recipe on a three-burner gas grill with burners that run from front to back. In this recipe, we refer to the two outside burners as the primary burners and the center burner as the secondary burner. If you're using a two-burner grill, use the side with the wood chips as the primary burner and the other side as the secondary burner. Adjust the primary burner to maintain a grill temperature between 375 and 400 degrees. Place the chicken 6 inches from the primary burner and rotate it after 25 minutes of cooking in step 4 so that it cooks evenly.

- 1 tablespoon kosher salt
- ½ teaspoon pepper
- 1 (3½- to 4½-pound) whole chicken, giblets discarded
- 1 tablespoon vegetable oil
- ¼–½ cup wood chips

1. Combine salt and pepper in bowl. Pat chicken dry with paper towels, then rub entire surface of chicken with oil. Sprinkle salt mixture all over chicken and rub in mixture with your hands to evenly coat. Tie legs together with kitchen twine and tuck wingtips behind back.

2. Using large piece of heavy-duty aluminum foil, wrap chips (¼ cup if using charcoal; ½ cup if using gas) in 8 by 4½-inch foil packet. (Make sure chips do not poke holes in sides or bottom of packet.) Cut 2 evenly spaced 2-inch slits in top of packet.

3A. FOR A CHARCOAL GRILL: Open bottom vent halfway. Light large chimney starter mounded with charcoal briquettes (7 quarts). When top coals are partially covered with ash, pour into 2 banked piles on either side of grill. Place wood chip packet on 1 pile of coals. Set cooking grate in place, cover, and open lid vent halfway. Heat grill until hot and wood chips are smoking, about 5 minutes. (Grill temperature will reach about 400 degrees and will fall to about 350 degrees by end of cooking.)

3B. FOR A GAS GRILL: Remove cooking grate and place wood chip packet directly on 1 primary burner. Set grate in place, turn all burners to high, cover, and heat grill until hot and wood chips are smoking, about 15 minutes. Turn primary burners (two outside burners) to medium-high and turn off secondary (center) burner. (Adjust primary burners as needed to maintain grill temperature between 400 and 425 degrees.)

4. Clean and oil cooking grate. Place chicken, breast side up with cavity facing toward you, in center of grill, making sure chicken is centered between hotter sides of grill. Cover (position lid vent over chicken if using charcoal) and cook until breast registers 130 degrees, 45 to 55 minutes.

5. Using long grill tongs, reach into cavity and carefully lift chicken by breast. Holding chicken over bowl or container, tilt chicken toward you to allow fat and juices to drain from cavity. Transfer chicken, breast side up, to hotter side of grill (without wood chip packet) and cook, covered, until back is deep golden brown, about 5 minutes. Using tongs, flip chicken breast side down; cover and continue to cook over hotter side of grill until breast is deep golden brown, about 5 minutes longer. Using tongs, flip chicken breast side up and return it to center of grill; take internal temperature of breast. If breast registers 155 degrees, transfer chicken to carving board. If breast registers less than 155 degrees, cover and continue to cook in center of grill, checking temperature every 2 minutes, until it registers 155 degrees, 2 to 10 minutes longer. Let chicken rest, uncovered, for 20 minutes. Carve chicken and serve.

NOTES FROM THE TEST KITCHEN

A GRILLER'S TOOLBOX
If you want to create the unmistakable flavors associated with the grill—earthy, savory char and nuanced smokiness—without overcooking the food, you have to use the tools that produce them.

DIRECT HEAT
How It Works: When food is placed directly over the heat, the searing-hot cooking grate creates char marks that impart a range of smoky, earthy, and even sweet flavors. In addition, meat juices and rendered fat can drip onto the coals, where they break down and vaporize (and sometimes create small flare-ups), and then condense on the food, adding more grill flavor.

INDIRECT HEAT
How It Works: Placing food over a cooler zone—not directly over the heat—cooks it gently so that the outside doesn't burn before the inside finishes cooking. Note that cooking only over indirect heat and without smoke will yield little grill flavor.

SMOKE
How It Works: Wood—either large chunks or chips wrapped in a foil packet—that's placed in the fire will not ignite due to limited airflow. Instead, it will smoke, flavoring the food's exterior. Cutting two slits in the foil packet allows enough airflow for the wood chips to smoke steadily.

CHICKEN SCHNITZEL

✓ **WHY THIS RECIPE WORKS** Chicken schnitzel is defined by thin, tender, juicy cutlets coated in a fine, wrinkly crust that puffs away from the meat during frying. Halving and pounding the chicken breasts ¼ inch thick ensured that the cutlets were tender and delicate. Fine store-bought bread crumbs held in place by an egg wash formed a compact crust, and adding oil to the eggs made the coating slightly elastic. Using a large Dutch oven filled with just 2 cups of oil meant there was plenty of head-space when agitating the pot, so the oil washed over the cutlets without spilling. Bathing the cutlets in oil quickly set the crust so that the breading trapped steam, which then caused the coating to puff away from the meat.

Loosely defined, schnitzel is a piece of meat that's been pounded thin, breaded, and fried—but frankly, that undersells it. There's an elegance to this Austrian classic's svelte profile, and even more so to its unique crust: The crumb is particularly fine and closely packed, and instead of hugging the meat the way most breadings do, it puffs away from the cutlet as it fries, forming an airy, wrinkly shell that's not at all greasy. Serving it with a squeeze of lemon and a bright-tasting salad accentuates its lightness. Done well, it manages to be both casual comfort food and dinner party fare.

Austrians typically prepare schnitzel with veal or pork, but plenty of recipes swap in other proteins that are comparably tender and mild, especially chicken breast. The switch sounded appealing to me—who doesn't need more ideas for preparing boneless, skinless breasts?—and I figured it would be as easy as slipping chicken into our existing recipe for pork schnitzel.

Making schnitzel is a lot like breading and frying any other cutlet: Pound the meat, dredge it in flour, dip it in egg wash, coat it in bread crumbs, and fry it. But in this case, you're making a few targeted changes. First, the bread crumbs are fine, not coarse, so they sit very close together and form a compact coating that can trap steam. Second, there is a little oil in the egg wash, which makes the crust slightly flexible and therefore capable of expanding. Third, the cutlets are fried in just a couple of cups of oil in a deep pot, which is gently agitated during cooking so that the hot oil washes over the meat and quickly sets the crust. When this happens, that compact, stretchable breading traps steam and inflates, puffing away from the meat.

I began to go through the motions, pounding four chicken breasts to the same ⅛-inch thickness that I would have with pork. But the amount of pounding required to flatten a plump chicken breast caused the meat to tear and become ragged. I tried halving the breasts horizontally, hoping that would minimize the number of strokes needed to thin them out, but the meat still tore. Eventually, I learned that chicken is actually more tender than pork, which meant I didn't need to pound the meat quite as thin to make delicate cutlets. Instead, I halved the breasts and pounded them to a more modest ¼-inch thickness.

I seasoned the cutlets with salt and pepper and coated them one at a time in flour, followed by egg wash and homemade bread crumbs. After each step, I made sure to shake off excess flour and allow some of the egg wash to drip back into the dish so that the coating would be sheer. Next, I heated 2 cups of oil to 350 degrees in a Dutch oven and laid two or three cutlets at a time in the oil, being careful not to overlap them. Then I continuously agitated the pot—which had just enough oil to wash over the cutlets but not enough to splatter over the sides—for the minute or so that it took the crust to turn puffy, wrinkly, and golden brown.

After fishing the cutlets out of the oil, I blotted them dry and took a quick taste before frying the second batch. They were great: tender, crispy, and delicate in a way that fried chicken never is. My only grievance was the homemade bread crumbs, which had taken longer to make than the schnitzel itself. Fine, even crumbs were a must, but was it really necessary to cube, dry, and process sandwich bread to make my own?

Coarse, crunchy panko bread crumbs were exactly what I didn't want for schnitzel, but since I always keep a container on hand, I tried blitzing them in the food processor to see if they would work as a coating. They were a disappointment, frying up hard and crunchy. But there was some good—and surprising—news: When I tried regular store-bought bread crumbs, they produced a coating that was even more delicate, puffy, and golden than one made from homemade crumbs.

With the time I saved, I put together two bright salads: a rémoulade of fennel, celery, and apple, and one with cucumbers and lots of dill, made creamy and tangy with Greek yogurt. Either one turns the schnitzel into a complete package that's easy and quick—and more refined than your everyday cutlet dinner.

—STEVE DUNN, *Cook's Illustrated*

CHICKEN SCHNITZEL

Chicken Schnitzel

SERVES 4 TO 6

Use fine, unseasoned store-bought bread crumbs for this recipe. We used Diamond Crystal Kosher Salt in this recipe; if using Morton Kosher Salt, sprinkle each cutlet with only ½ teaspoon. The ample space provided by a large Dutch oven is necessary here; do not attempt to use a smaller pot. Serve with Apple-Fennel Rémoulade or Cucumber-Dill Salad (recipes follow), if desired.

- ½ cup all-purpose flour
- 2 large eggs
- 1 tablespoon vegetable oil
- 2 cups plain dried bread crumbs
- 4 (6- to 8-ounce) boneless, skinless chicken breasts, trimmed
- 2 tablespoons kosher salt
- 1 teaspoon pepper
- 2 cups vegetable oil for frying
  Lemon wedges

1. Spread flour in shallow dish. Beat eggs and 1 tablespoon oil in second shallow dish. Place bread crumbs in third shallow dish. Set wire rack in rimmed baking sheet. Line second rimmed baking sheet with double layer of paper towels. Adjust oven rack to middle position and heat oven to 200 degrees.

2. Halve chicken breasts horizontally to form 8 cutlets of even thickness. Place 1 cutlet between 2 sheets of plastic wrap and pound to ¼-inch thickness. Repeat with remaining cutlets. Sprinkle each cutlet on both sides with ¾ teaspoon salt and ⅛ teaspoon pepper.

3. Working with 1 cutlet at a time, dredge cutlets thoroughly in flour, shaking off excess, then coat with egg mixture, allowing excess to drip back into dish to ensure very thin coating. Coat evenly with bread crumbs, pressing on crumbs to adhere. Place cutlets on prepared wire rack, taking care not to overlap cutlets. Let coating dry for 5 minutes.

4. Add 2 cups oil to large Dutch oven and heat over medium-high heat to 350 degrees. Lay 2 or 3 cutlets (depending on size) in oil, without overlapping them, and cook, shaking pot continuously and gently, until cutlets are wrinkled and light golden brown on both sides, 1 to 1½ minutes per side. Transfer cutlets to paper towel–lined sheet, flip to blot excess oil, and transfer sheet to oven to keep warm. Repeat with remaining cutlets. Serve immediately with lemon wedges.

Apple-Fennel Rémoulade

SERVES 6 TO 8

Any variety of apple can be used here, but we recommend using a crisp-sweet variety such as Fuji, Gala, or Honeycrisp. The test kitchen's favorite capers are Reese Non Pareil Capers.

- ¼ cup mayonnaise
- 2 tablespoons whole-grain mustard
- 2 tablespoons lemon juice
- 2 tablespoons capers, rinsed, plus 1 tablespoon brine
- 4 celery ribs, sliced thin on bias
- 1 fennel bulb, 1 tablespoon fronds minced, stalks discarded, bulb halved, cored, and sliced thin crosswise
- 1 apple, cored and cut into 2-inch-long matchsticks

Whisk mayonnaise, mustard, lemon juice, and caper brine together in large bowl. Add celery, fennel bulb, apple, and capers and toss to combine. Season with salt and pepper to taste. Top with fennel fronds and serve.

Cucumber-Dill Salad

SERVES 6 TO 8

The fat percentage of the Greek yogurt doesn't matter here; use what you prefer.

- 2 English cucumbers, halved lengthwise and sliced thin
- 2 teaspoons kosher salt
- ⅓ cup plain Greek yogurt
- 4 teaspoons cider vinegar
- 1 tablespoon extra-virgin olive oil
- 2 teaspoons Dijon mustard
- 1 large shallot, halved through root end and sliced thin
- ¼ cup chopped fresh dill

1. Place cucumbers in colander and toss with salt. Set colander in sink and let stand for 30 minutes. Whisk yogurt, vinegar, oil, and mustard together in large bowl and set aside.

2. Gently shake colander to drain excess liquid, then blot cucumbers dry with paper towels. Add cucumbers, shallot, and dill to bowl with dressing and toss gently to combine. Season with salt and pepper to taste, and serve.

JAPANESE FRIED CHICKEN THIGHS (KARAAGE)

✔ WHY THIS RECIPE WORKS Our version of this Japanese classic started with boneless, skinless chicken thighs, which eliminated the need to debone the meat at home. Cutting the chicken into narrow strips instead of small chunks created fewer pieces to handle. Briefly marinating the meat in a mixture of soy sauce, sake, ginger, and garlic (seasoned with a little salt and sugar) imbued the chicken with deeply savory, aromatic flavor. Dredging the chicken in cornstarch—instead of traditional potato starch—made for a less sticky coating. Shaking off the excess starch and letting the dredged pieces rest while the oil heated gave the starch time to hydrate. Dabbing any dry patches with reserved marinade prevented dustiness.

I've never met a bite of fried chicken that I didn't like, but my favorite is the first bite of a fried chicken thigh. The crunch is big because thighs are thin and tapered, so there's a high ratio of crispy crust to chicken. And when you bite through that crust, you're met with juicy, rich dark meat.

Happily for me, a Japanese style of fried chicken called karaage not only traditionally uses chicken thighs but is also very easy to prepare. To make it, you debone bone-in, skin-on chicken thighs; cut the meat into small chunks; marinate them in a soy-and-sake-based mixture that's seasoned with garlic, ginger, salt, and sugar; dredge them in potato starch; and fry them until they're brown and crispy. Because the pieces are small, you need only a few cups of oil to submerge them, and the frying time is fast. Plus, thanks to the thighs' abundant fat and collagen, there's no risk that the meat will dry out during frying. You don't even have to temp the pieces; once they're golden and crispy, they're done.

For all these reasons, karaage is my favorite style of fried chicken both to eat and to make. That said, I've always wanted to take a closer look at the potato starch: Though it fries up exceptionally crispy, it forms a sticky coating that can be difficult to manage as you cook; it can also be hard to find in conventional supermarkets.

Before I got started, I decided to streamline the already-efficient method by doing away with the knife work needed to debone skin-on thighs. Instead, I opted for 1½ pounds of boneless, skinless chicken thighs, which I trimmed and cut into strips instead of smaller chunks. That created about 20 pieces—half as many to

marinate, dredge, and fry, and each one with plenty of surface area to maintain the perfect ratio of crispy crust to juicy meat.

I marinated the chicken for 30 minutes before moving to a head-to-head starch test: potato (the traditional choice) versus corn. I dredged half the strips in potato starch and half in cornstarch and then fried each batch in a Dutch oven filled with 4 cups of 325-degree vegetable oil. I let the strips fry until they were crispy, which took no more than 5 minutes.

Both starch options came with challenges, starting with the aforementioned stickiness of the potato starch coating. Once it hit the hot oil, the potato starch formed a gluey gel that made the pieces stick to everything—the tongs, the pot, each other—and trying to separate them while they bubbled in the hot oil was dicey. The cornstarch batch didn't turn gluey, so it was a cinch to fry, but the cooked pieces were coated in a fine dusting of unhydrated starch that felt sandy on the tongue.

The key difference turned out to be how the two types of starch absorb water: Potato starch is more absorbent than cornstarch, and in this case it had soaked up so much liquid from the marinade that it turned sticky. The cornstarch hadn't absorbed enough of the marinade—hence the powdery residue.

Ultimately, I opted for cornstarch because it's readily available and because it would be easier to fix my dredging method than it would be to fuss with clumps of sticky chicken in hot oil. (A good rule of thumb from my restaurant days: Any time you can move the challenging parts of cooking to the prep stage as opposed to the cooking stage, you avoid a lot of headaches.)

The question was how to get the cornstarch to absorb more of the marinade. My first instinct was to mix some into a slurry with the marinade and microwave it, since heating cornstarch makes it more absorbent. But as I'd found with the potato starch, it was hard to keep the gel-coated chicken strips separate in the hot oil.

I dug a little deeper into my potato starch versus cornstarch research and realized I'd overlooked an important point: Cornstarch not only absorbs less water than potato starch does but also absorbs water more slowly, which made me wonder if simply letting the coated chicken rest before cooking would allow more of the cornstarch to hydrate.

For the next batch, I went back to dredging the marinated chicken in dry cornstarch but made sure to dredge before I heated the oil to allow time for the cornstarch to hydrate. I could see improvement as soon as I pulled the fried chicken from the oil: The coating was golden and crunchy with just a few spare dry patches. To fix that, I made sure to shake off any excess cornstarch after dredging the chicken. Then, just before frying, I checked the chicken pieces for dry patches and used the back of a spoon to dab them with reserved marinade. That moistened the starch just enough that it fried up into a crispy, cohesive crust.

While the chicken drained on a paper towel–lined rack, I cut up some lemon wedges for serving. Lemon is the traditional karaage accompaniment, and for good reason: The acid cuts through the richness of the fried dark meat, and the tangy fruit deftly underscores (without overpowering) the bright heat of the ginger in the marinade. There may be no better application for a squeeze of citrus. If you love fried chicken but don't love frying, this may be the recipe for you.

—LAN LAM, *Cook's Illustrated*

NOTES FROM THE TEST KITCHEN

KEYS TO A CRUNCHY, COHESIVE CRUST
These tricks are subtle, but they make all the difference when it comes to creating a crust with big crunch.

SHAKE Dredge marinated chicken pieces one at a time, making sure to shake off any excess cornstarch that would otherwise leave dusty residue on cooked crust.

LET REST While oil heats, let dredged chicken rest. This gives cornstarch time to absorb moisture and hydrate, ensuring cohesive crust.

DAB Before frying, use back of spoon to moisten any dry patches of coating with reserved marinade.

Japanese Fried Chicken Thighs (Karaage)
SERVES 4 TO 6

We recommend using a rasp-style grater to grate the ginger. Do not substitute chicken breasts for the thighs; they will dry out during frying. There's no need to take the temperature of the chicken; it will be cooked through by the time it is golden brown and crispy. Leftover frying oil can be cooled, strained, and saved for later use.

- 3 **tablespoons soy sauce**
- 2 **tablespoons sake**
- 1 **tablespoon grated fresh ginger**
- 2 **garlic cloves, minced**
- ¾ **teaspoon sugar**
- ⅛ **teaspoon table salt**
- 1½ **pounds boneless, skinless chicken thighs, trimmed and cut crosswise into 1- to 1½-inch-wide strips**
- 1¼ **cups cornstarch**
- 1 **quart vegetable oil for frying**
  Lemon wedges

1. Combine soy sauce, sake, ginger, garlic, sugar, and salt in medium bowl. Add chicken and toss to combine. Let sit at room temperature for 30 minutes. While chicken marinates, line rimmed baking sheet with parchment paper. Set wire rack in second rimmed baking sheet and line rack with triple layer of paper towels. Place cornstarch in wide bowl.

2. Lift chicken from marinade, 1 piece at a time, allowing excess marinade to drip back into bowl but leaving any garlic or ginger bits on chicken. Coat chicken with cornstarch, shake off excess, and place on parchment-lined sheet. Reserve marinade.

3. Heat oil in large Dutch oven over medium-high heat to 325 degrees. While oil heats, check chicken pieces for white patches of dry cornstarch. Dip back of spoon in reserved marinade and gently press onto dry spots to lightly moisten.

4. Using tongs, add half of chicken, 1 piece at a time, to oil in single layer. Cook, adjusting burner, if necessary, to maintain oil temperature between 300 and 325 degrees, until chicken is golden brown and crispy, 4 to 5 minutes. Using spider skimmer or slotted spoon, transfer chicken to paper towel–lined rack. Return oil to 325 degrees and repeat with remaining chicken. Serve with lemon wedges.

GRILLED BONELESS, SKINLESS CHICKEN BREASTS

WHY THIS RECIPE WORKS The perfect grilled boneless, skinless chicken breasts are juicy, savory, and well browned and can be served as is or added to salads or sandwiches. We first pounded the chicken ½ inch thick so that the breasts cooked through evenly. Soaking the chicken for 30 minutes in a potent "brinerade" seasoned it and added moisture that helped keep it juicy during cooking; we spiked the saltwater with just enough umami-rich fish sauce to add savory depth without any trace of fishiness, as well as honey to encourage browning and balance the salt. We coated the chicken in a little oil before grilling it to keep it from sticking to the grates, and cooking it over a hot fire ensured that it browned deeply.

Boneless, skinless chicken breasts are not the easiest cut to grill, but they might be the most practical. Without skin, bones, and fat, they lack the insulation and succulence of dark meat or bone-in, skin-on parts, but they cook much faster. Plus, neutral breast meat goes with anything—bold sauces, sandwiches, salads, taco fixings—and the grill gives it a savory character that roasting and sautéing can't match.

I started by pounding four breasts ½ inch thick so that they'd cook evenly. Then I thought carefully about how to treat them to ensure well-seasoned, juicy meat. Instead of brining them in plain saltwater, I spiked the solution with fish sauce. The soak would help the chicken retain its juices when cooked over the hot fire, and the glutamate-rich fish sauce (I added 3 tablespoons per ⅓ cup water) would add salinity and umami depth without imparting a distinct flavor (as soy sauce would) or making the chicken taste fishy.

The one drawback of brining was that the water would thwart browning, so I added a couple tablespoons of honey to the brinerade. The honey's reducing sugars would add complexity and encourage browning before the lean meat overcooked. After soaking the chicken breasts for 30 minutes (to ensure full contact between the chicken and the liquid, I brined them in a zipper-lock bag and pressed out as much air as possible), I let the excess liquid drip off and placed them over a hot fire. Deep, attractive grill marks developed within minutes. But then I tried flipping the breasts—and tore them ragged because they stuck to the grates.

Oiling the meat before cooking it helped ensure a clean release; once flipped, the breasts needed just a few more minutes to hit their 160-degree target.

The results were juicy, tender, deeply but neutrally savory, and so versatile that I found myself grilling double batches (you can easily fit eight breasts on the grill) just so that I could have chicken on hand for quick, easy meals all week long.

—ANNIE PETITO, *Cook's Illustrated*

Grilled Boneless, Skinless Chicken Breasts
SERVES 4

This recipe can easily be doubled. Serve the chicken with our Red Pepper–Almond Sauce (recipe follows), pair it with a vegetable or starch, use it in sandwiches or tacos, or slice it and add it to a salad. Red Boat makes our favorite fish sauce.

- 4 **(6- to 8-ounce) boneless, skinless chicken breasts, trimmed**
- ⅓ **cup water**
- 3 **tablespoons fish sauce**
- 2 **tablespoons honey**
- 1 **teaspoon table salt**
- ⅛ **teaspoon pepper**
- 1 **tablespoon vegetable oil**

1. Cover chicken breasts with plastic wrap and pound gently with meat pounder until ½ inch thick. Whisk water, fish sauce, honey, salt, and pepper together in bowl. Transfer mixture to 1-gallon zipper-lock bag. Add chicken, press out air, seal bag, and turn bag so that contents are evenly distributed. Refrigerate for 30 minutes.

2A. FOR A CHARCOAL GRILL: Open bottom vent completely. Light large chimney starter filled with charcoal briquettes (6 quarts). When top coals are partially covered with ash, pour evenly over grill. Set cooking grate in place, cover, and open lid vent completely. Heat grill until hot, about 5 minutes.

2B. FOR A GAS GRILL: Turn all burners to high, cover, and heat grill until hot, about 15 minutes. Leave all burners on high.

3. Remove chicken from brine, letting excess drip off (do not pat dry), then toss with oil in second bowl until evenly coated.

GRILLED BONELESS, SKINLESS CHICKEN BREASTS

4. Clean and oil cooking grate. Place chicken, skinned side down, on grill and cook (covered if using gas) until chicken develops dark grill marks, 3 to 5 minutes. Gently release chicken from cooking grate, flip, and continue to cook until chicken registers 160 degrees, 3 to 5 minutes longer. Transfer chicken to cutting board and tent with aluminum foil. Let rest for 5 minutes before serving.

Red Pepper–Almond Sauce

SERVES 4

The peppers in this recipe can be grilled over the same hot fire that you use to grill the chicken.

- 5 **teaspoons sherry vinegar**
- 1 **garlic clove, minced**
- ¾ **teaspoon table salt**
- 2 **red bell peppers, stemmed, seeded, and quartered**
- 1 **tablespoon vegetable oil**
- ¼ **cup almonds, toasted**
- 2 **teaspoons toasted sesame oil**
- ½ **teaspoon smoked paprika**
  Pinch cayenne pepper

1. Combine vinegar, garlic, and salt in bowl.

2. Toss bell peppers with vegetable oil. Grill bell peppers, skin side down, over hot fire (covered if using gas), until well charred, 5 to 7 minutes. Flip and cook until lightly charred on second side, about 2 minutes. Transfer bell peppers to bowl and cover tightly with aluminum foil.

3. Pulse almonds in food processor until finely chopped, 10 to 12 pulses. Add sesame oil, paprika, cayenne, vinegar mixture, and bell peppers (do not remove skins) and process until smooth, about 45 seconds, scraping down sides of bowl as needed. Loosen with water as needed and season with salt to taste.

GRILLED JERK CHICKEN

✔ **WHY THIS RECIPE WORKS** Our spicy-but-nuanced, bold grilled jerk chicken starts with the jerk paste. We blended fiery habaneros (more readily available and less intense than the traditionally used Scotch bonnet peppers), scallions, and garlic with 10 whole thyme sprigs for a big herby punch that didn't require time-consuming leaf-picking. Soy sauce added depth, cider vinegar contributed brightness, and warm spices (allspice, cinnamon, and ginger) provided the characteristic jerk flavor while brown sugar rounded out the spicy edge. After marinating bone-in chicken pieces in the paste, we first cooked the chicken on the cooler side of the grill, covered, which helped the marinade stick to the chicken and not slide off over direct heat and burn. Once the chicken was cooked through, we brushed it with a little reserved marinade for even more jerk flavor and seared it on the hotter side of the grill. Tasters preferred the chicken charred over the hotter side of the grill, not smoked per tradition. It picked up plenty of grill flavor and tasted cleaner, without any acrid or harsh smokiness.

Let me start by asking three questions: How spicy is too spicy? When does "smoky" cross the line into "campfire"? And finally, when is it considered a compliment to be called a "master of jerk"?

These were all things I needed to consider in my quest to develop a recipe for bold yet nuanced grilled jerk chicken. Jerk seasoning is Jamaican in origin; the spice paste is traditionally based on Scotch bonnet chiles, thyme, spices, garlic, and scallions. Variations abound, and most traditional versions are smoked over pimento wood (from the tree that gives us allspice berries).

I selected five promising recipes to try. I made the jerk pastes; slathered them on bone-in, skin-on chicken pieces; fired up the grills; and got cooking. The good: The smell of smoke, chicken, and spices was amazing. The bad: None of the recipes turned out great. Some were overpoweringly spicy, some were bitter and acrid from too much smoke, and some tasted awkwardly out of balance. What's more, the wet jerk pastes made it hard to render the chicken's fat, which resulted in flabby skin. I knew I could do better.

My first step was to perfect my version of jerk paste. Since Scotch bonnet peppers can be hard to find, I decided to use habaneros, their similarly fiery cousins, instead. To the blender I added a couple of habaneros, four scallions, a good handful of fresh thyme leaves, garlic, brown sugar for sweetness and depth, salt, and some vegetable oil and buzzed everything to a paste. This first stab was decent, but the paste definitely needed more seasoning and complexity.

I considered adding more salt until a colleague suggested soy sauce instead; just ¼ cup worked great, contributing salty, savory depth to the paste. A bit of ground allspice, ginger, and cinnamon brought the requisite warm spice profile, and a little vinegar helped balance the brown sugar. In subsequent tests, my tasters kept asking for more thyme, and as I increased the amount, I grew more and more frustrated with the laborious task of pulling the tiny leaves from the stems. On a whim, I tossed a whole bunch of fresh thyme—stems and all—into the blender; my tasters loved the big herby punch and had no idea there were stems in the paste. Win.

Determining the best grilling method took a bit of trial and error, but I finally landed on a foolproof method. After marinating the chicken in the jerk paste, I set up the grill with a cooler side and a hotter side. I grilled the chicken pieces on the cooler side until they were cooked through before brushing them with a little reserved marinade (for a fresh burst of jerk flavor) and searing them on the hotter side of the grill. As for the smoke, my tasters surprisingly preferred the chicken without it. The jerk flavor came through more clearly, and the chicken was picking up plenty of char and grill flavor anyway.

This chicken is bold, but it's balanced. And this recipe will help you, too, become a master of jerk.

—CECILIA JENKINS, *Cook's Country*

Grilled Jerk Chicken

SERVES 4

Plan ahead: The chicken needs to marinate for at least 1 hour before it's cooked. Use more or fewer habaneros depending on your desired level of spiciness. You can also remove the seeds and ribs from the habaneros or substitute jalapeños for less heat. We recommend wearing rubber gloves or plastic bags on your hands when handling the chiles. Use thyme sprigs with a generous amount of leaves; there's no need to separate the leaves from the stems. Keep a close eye on the chicken in step 5 since it can char quickly.

- 4 **scallions**
- ¼ **cup vegetable oil**
- ¼ **cup soy sauce**
- 2 **tablespoons cider vinegar**
- 2 **tablespoons packed brown sugar**
- 10 **sprigs fresh thyme**
- 5 **garlic cloves, peeled**
- 1–2 **habanero chiles, stemmed**
- 2½ **teaspoons ground allspice**
- 1½ **teaspoons table salt**
- ½ **teaspoon ground cinnamon**
- ½ **teaspoon ground ginger**
- 3 **pounds bone-in chicken pieces (split breasts cut in half crosswise, drumsticks, and/or thighs), trimmed**
  Lime wedges

1. Process scallions, oil, soy sauce, vinegar, sugar, thyme sprigs, garlic, habanero(s), allspice, salt, cinnamon, and ginger in blender until smooth, about 30 seconds, scraping down sides of blender jar as needed. Measure out ¼ cup marinade and refrigerate until ready to use.

2. Place chicken and remaining marinade in 1-gallon zipper-lock bag. Press out air, seal bag, and turn to coat chicken in marinade. Refrigerate for at least 1 hour or up to 24 hours, turning occasionally.

3A. FOR A CHARCOAL GRILL: Open bottom vent completely. Light large chimney starter mounded with charcoal briquettes (7 quarts). When top coals are partially covered with ash, pour evenly over half of grill. Set cooking grate in place, cover, and open lid vent completely. Heat grill until hot, about 5 minutes.

3B. FOR A GAS GRILL: Turn all burners to high, cover, and heat grill until hot, about 15 minutes. Leave primary burner on high and turn off other burner(s). (Adjust primary burner [or, if using 3-burner grill, primary burner and second burner] as needed to maintain grill temperature between 450 and 500 degrees.)

4. Clean and oil cooking grate. Place chicken skin side up on cooler side of grill, with breast pieces farthest away from heat. Cover and cook until breasts register 160 degrees and drumsticks/thighs register 175 degrees, 22 to 30 minutes, transferring pieces to plate, skin side up, as they come to temperature. (Re-cover grill after checking pieces for doneness.)

5. Brush skin side of chicken with half of reserved marinade. Place chicken skin side down on hotter side of grill. (Turn all burners to high if using gas.) Brush with remaining reserved marinade and cook until lightly charred, 1 to 3 minutes per side. Check browning often and move pieces as needed to avoid flare-ups.

6. Transfer chicken to platter, tent with aluminum foil, and let rest for 5 to 10 minutes. Serve with lime wedges.

CHICKEN PROVENÇAL

CHICKEN PROVENÇAL

✓ **WHY THIS RECIPE WORKS** We wanted to create a southern France–inspired chicken dinner with a bright, savory sauce that would be ready in about 30 minutes. Dredging the chicken in flour helped create a crispy exterior. We reserved a bit of the flour dredge to thicken the drippings in the pan and create a luscious sauce. After we seared the chicken, we sautéed a potent mix of shallots, garlic, thyme, and supersavory anchovies in the rendered fat to give our sauce a flavorful base. From there, we stirred in bright, sweet-savory cherry tomatoes; briny kalamata olives; and a splash of complex, mildly acidic vermouth to create a sauce with compelling character.

Chicken Provençal sounds fancy, doesn't it? But it's just chicken cooked with the signature flavors and ingredients of Provence, the region of southeast France that borders Italy and the Mediterranean Sea. We're talking herbs, wine, olives, tomatoes, and olive oil—ingredients that are just as common in the United States as they are in Europe. Having long seen recipes for this dish in cookbooks and cooking magazines, I set out to create a weeknight version that used common ingredients to elevate chicken to a new level of deliciousness.

For a dish with such a clear geographic origin, the recipes I found for it were surprisingly all over the map. I had quite a few choices ahead of me: Should I opt for a whole chicken or chicken parts? Red wine or white? Dried herbs or fresh? My first decision was to use bone-in, skin-on chicken thighs; their dark meat is moist and flavorful, and they cook in much less time than a whole chicken. I'd sear the thighs in olive oil, remove them from the skillet, and then build a base of aromatic vegetables and tomatoes that I could use to finish cooking the chicken—basic braising technique.

I started the sauce by sautéing sweet, thinly sliced shallots. Garlic and anchovies—minced so that they'd disappear into the sauce—were no-brainers as the next stir-ins, but now I had to figure out how to handle the tomato component. Canned tomato products tasted good but brought the dish too close to stew territory; my tasters preferred a version made with a heap of halved cherry tomatoes, which wrinkled and released their juice in the hot skillet. Red wine was a little too distinct (in flavor and color) here, and while white wine was good, we preferred the more complex flavor of dry vermouth in the sauce.

Many recipes with "Provençal" in the name call for herbes de Provence, the region's signature herb blend that typically includes rosemary, thyme, oregano, and savory. Most versions sold in the United States also contain lavender, which my tasters didn't care for in this dish: "Great for soap, but not for chicken." After a bit of experimenting, I found that fresh thyme sprigs provided plenty of heady herbal presence.

With the sauce built, I returned the browned, parcooked thighs to the skillet. I arranged the thighs skin side up so they peeked above the sauce; this would help keep the skin nice and crispy. Then I popped the skillet in a 400-degree oven so the chicken could cook through. This version was pretty good, but the tomatoes had released so much juice that the sauce was too thin. The solution? Dredging the raw thighs in flour before browning them and adding another teaspoon of flour to the sauce ingredients. The flour thickened the fragrant sauce just enough so that it was spoonable but not runny. This dish was now ready for the table—and to take a place in my weeknight rotation.

—ALLI BERKEY, *Cook's Country*

Chicken Provençal

SERVES 4 TO 6

You can substitute four 10- to 12-ounce bone-in split chicken breasts for the thighs, if desired. Simply extend the cooking time in step 4 to 30 minutes or until the chicken registers 160 degrees. You can substitute any dry white wine for the vermouth, if desired.

- 8 (5- to 7-ounce) bone-in chicken thighs, trimmed
- ½ teaspoon table salt, divided
- ½ teaspoon pepper, divided
- ½ cup all-purpose flour
- 3 tablespoons extra-virgin olive oil
- 2 shallots, halved and sliced thin
- 3 sprigs fresh thyme
- 3 garlic cloves, minced
- 2 anchovy fillets, rinsed and minced
- ¼ teaspoon red pepper flakes
- 12 ounces cherry tomatoes, halved
- ½ cup pitted kalamata olives, halved
- ½ cup dry vermouth
- ½ cup fresh parsley leaves

1. Adjust oven rack to middle position and heat oven to 400 degrees. Pat chicken dry with paper towels. Sprinkle chicken all over with ¼ teaspoon salt and ¼ teaspoon pepper. Place flour in shallow dish. Dredge chicken in flour, 1 piece at a time, turning to coat all sides. Shake to remove any excess flour, then transfer chicken to large plate. Reserve 1 teaspoon flour; discard remaining flour.

2. Heat oil in 12-inch ovensafe skillet over medium-high heat until just smoking. Add chicken and cook until golden brown on both sides, about 3 minutes per side. Return chicken to plate, skin side up. Carefully pour off all but 2 tablespoons fat from skillet.

3. Return skillet to medium heat. Add shallots to fat left in skillet and cook until softened, about 2 minutes. Stir in thyme sprigs, garlic, anchovies, pepper flakes, and reserved flour and cook until fragrant, about 30 seconds. Stir in tomatoes, olives, vermouth, remaining ¼ teaspoon salt, and remaining ¼ teaspoon pepper, scraping up any browned bits.

4. Return chicken to skillet, skin side up, and bring sauce to boil. Transfer skillet to oven and cook until chicken registers 175 degrees, about 25 minutes. Sprinkle with parsley and serve.

CHICKEN BIRYANI

✔ **WHY THIS RECIPE WORKS** In a classic chicken biryani, boldly spiced and perfectly fluffy basmati rice is lavished with rich butter and studded with dried fruit. The saffron-and-spice-infused rice is layered with marinated and sauced chicken, and the two are baked together before being topped with fried onions and chopped herbs. But the classic preparation takes a lot of time, effort, and dishes to make. For a streamlined version, we used chunks of boneless chicken thighs and skipped the lengthy marinating. We also found that we could sauté the onion in butter rather than deep-fry it and then brown the chicken in the same large skillet. Finally, rather than partially cooking the rice in spice-infused water—which often resulted in either under- or overcooked rice—we discovered that we could cook the rice through and then steam it briefly with the chicken. Garnished with fresh mint and cilantro, browned onions, and an easy, herby yogurt sauce, this streamlined biryani hit all the notes of the classic version, but with much less time and effort.

My ideal chicken biryani features fluffy, butter-infused basmati rice combined with dried fruit and nuts, spiced chicken, and a bright garnish. The rice—a confetti of vermillion saffron and white grains—is layered with sauced chicken pieces and topped with fried onions and a shower of fresh herbs. It is a celebration of the delicious complexity of Indian cooking and a staple of Indian American restaurants.

But making classic chicken biryani takes time and a fair amount of equipment, as I found when I prepared a few existing recipes. For each, I toasted and ground myriad whole spices. I cut up a chicken and marinated it for up to 48 hours before browning it. I soaked and rinsed rice and then parcooked it in spice-infused water, and I sliced and deep-fried a heap of onions. Finally, I layered the rice and chicken into a casserole dish, covered it tightly, and steamed everything in the oven. The biryanis were delicious, but I wondered if there was a faster path to a similarly tasty payoff.

I made some important timesaving discoveries in my early testing. First, I learned that I could still end up with flavorful, juicy chicken by using chunks of boneless chicken thighs and skipping the lengthy marinating in favor of cooking the chunks in the marinade ingredients. (Plus, the pieces of boneless thighs were easier to eat.) Second, I found that I could prepare the whole recipe on the stovetop, thankfully eliminating the need for the oven.

I also learned that I could save a pan by sautéing the onion in butter instead of deep-frying it and then browning the chicken in the same skillet. Finally, rather than partially cooking the rice up front and steaming it to doneness later—which made it hard to get perfectly cooked rice—I could cook the rice through (in spiced water) and then steam it just briefly with the chicken at the end. Now I just had to prune the ingredient list.

For the whole spices to season the rice, my tasters loved the simple combination of a cinnamon stick, cumin seeds, and heady, floral saffron. To season the chicken, garam masala delivered complexity without my having to buy, toast, and grind a litany of spices.

I simply browned the chicken chunks and then stirred in the garam masala, ginger, garlic, and chile, followed by some creamy, tangy whole-milk yogurt to add moisture to the chicken layer.

I stirred a fistful of dried currants into the cooked rice and, taking a cue from a recipe I found in my research, poured over the butter I'd used to sauté the onion.

I spooned the rice on top of the chicken in the pan, added the bright red-orange saffron (bloomed in a little warm water), and then covered and steamed it all for 5 minutes to bring the flavors together. With my tasters assembled, I lifted the lid off my biryani and invited them to lean closer and breathe in the incredible aroma. With garnishes of fried onion, fresh mint and cilantro, and an herby yogurt sauce, this streamlined biryani looked and tasted every bit as good as it smelled.

—MATTHEW FAIRMAN, *Cook's Country*

Chicken Biryani

SERVES 6

To make this dish spicier, reserve and add the jalapeño seeds to the biryani as desired. You can substitute long-grain white rice for the basmati, if you like; it will be less fluffy and will need to cook for about 12 minutes in step 3.

GARNISH AND SAUCE

- 3 tablespoons warm water
- ½ teaspoon saffron threads, crumbled
- 1 cup plain whole-milk yogurt
- 2 tablespoons chopped fresh cilantro
- 2 tablespoons chopped fresh mint
- 1 garlic clove, minced
- ¼ teaspoon table salt
- ¼ teaspoon pepper

BIRYANI

- 6 tablespoons unsalted butter
- 2 cups thinly sliced onion
- 1¼ teaspoons table salt, divided, plus salt for cooking rice
- 1 cinnamon stick
- 2 teaspoons cumin seeds
- 2 cups basmati rice
- ⅓ cup dried currants
- 2 pounds boneless, skinless chicken thighs, trimmed and cut into 1½-inch chunks
- ½ teaspoon pepper
- 1 jalapeño chile, stemmed, seeded, and minced
- 1 tablespoon grated fresh ginger
- 1 tablespoon garam masala
- 3 garlic cloves, minced
- ½ cup plain whole-milk yogurt
- 2 tablespoons chopped fresh mint
- 2 tablespoons chopped fresh cilantro

1. FOR THE GARNISH AND SAUCE: Combine water and saffron in bowl and set aside. Combine yogurt, cilantro, mint, garlic, salt, and pepper in second bowl and set aside.

2. FOR THE BIRYANI: Set fine-mesh strainer in medium bowl. Melt butter in 12-inch nonstick skillet over medium heat. Add onion and cook, stirring often, until dark brown, 11 to 14 minutes. Transfer onion to prepared strainer and press with spatula to squeeze out excess butter (reserve butter). Spread onion on small plate and sprinkle with ¼ teaspoon salt. Set aside onion and butter (do not wash skillet).

3. Meanwhile, bring 12 cups water, cinnamon stick, and cumin seeds to boil in large saucepan over high heat. Add rice and 1 tablespoon salt and cook, stirring occasionally, until tender, about 10 minutes. Drain rice in fine-mesh strainer. Return rice to saucepan and stir in currants, reserved butter, and ¼ teaspoon salt; cover and set aside.

4. Combine chicken, pepper, and remaining ¾ teaspoon salt in now-empty skillet and cook over medium-high heat until browned and cooked through, about 10 minutes. Stir in jalapeño, ginger, garam masala, and garlic and cook until fragrant, about 1 minute. Off heat, stir in yogurt until combined.

5. Spoon rice over chicken mixture and spread into even layer. Drizzle saffron mixture evenly over rice, spiraling in from edge of skillet to center. Cover skillet, return to medium heat, and cook until heated through and steam escapes from under lid, about 5 minutes. Off heat, sprinkle biryani with mint, cilantro, and reserved fried onion. Serve with yogurt sauce.

NOTES FROM THE TEST KITCHEN

GIVE THE ONIONS TIME TO BROWN
To get the sliced onion to express all its depth and sweetness, you need to cook it past the "golden brown" stage to fully dark brown (below). Be patient.

SOY SAUCE CHICKEN WINGS

✓ **WHY THIS RECIPE WORKS** For supersavory chicken wings, we marinated split wings in a simple combination of soy sauce, vegetable oil, brown sugar, garlic, and cayenne pepper. We cooked them for a little more than an hour in a moderate 350-degree oven to achieve meltingly tender meat—any less time and the fat didn't fully render, leaving the skin unpleasantly chewy.

When I was growing up, the best part of family birthday celebrations was my Nana's soy sauce chicken wings. They were so simple—whole wings marinated in soy sauce, vegetable oil, and garlic powder and baked in a dish—but they were intensely seasoned and almost impossibly tender, with a sticky, savory skin that always left us clamoring for more.

More than a decade has passed since the last time I tasted Nana's wings, but after stumbling across an old jotted-down recipe of hers, I have been itching to re-create them. Following the handwritten instructions, I made a batch, called over my coworkers, and awaited a verdict. They agreed that, with just a bit of work, these easy, tasty wings could be perfected. I brought my Nana's recipe into the test kitchen and got to work, hoping to improve it while staying true to its straightforward spirit.

My first tweak was obvious: Nana's whole wings were cumbersome to eat and stayed a bit flabby at the joint. Splitting the wings into flats and drumettes allowed more fat to render out and made them easier to handle.

Next I nixed the garlic powder, suspecting that I could get better garlic flavor by using fresh garlic in the marinade. Minced garlic stuck to the wings and burned and turned bitter in the oven, but whole smashed garlic cloves imbued the marinade with unmistakable garlic flavor. A bit of cayenne pepper brought extra verve. The wings were coming together, but my tasters were hoping for a little more depth and a more refined soy flavor. A quarter cup of brown sugar added caramel-like sweetness that brought everything into balance.

With the flavor now spot-on, I just had to nail down the texture. I had been crowding the wings in a baking dish, like Nana had, but when I spread them out on a rimmed baking sheet and gave them room to breathe, the fat in each wing was able to fully render, making the skin sticky-soft all over without any chewy fat pockets. A little more than an hour in a 350-degree oven was just enough time to render the fat while keeping the meat juicy and tender. A final flourish of sliced scallions added a welcome freshness plus visual appeal to boot—I think Nana would approve.

—JESSICA RUDOLPH, *Cook's Country*

Soy Sauce Chicken Wings
SERVES 4 TO 6

We prefer to buy whole chicken wings and butcher them ourselves because they tend to be larger than wings that come presplit. If you can find only presplit wings, opt for larger ones, if possible. Three pounds of chicken wings is about 12 whole chicken wings, which will yield about 24 pieces of chicken (12 drumettes and 12 flats) once broken down.

- ¾ **cup soy sauce**
- ¼ **cup vegetable oil**
- ¼ **cup packed brown sugar**
- 12 **garlic cloves, smashed and peeled**
- ½ **teaspoon cayenne pepper**
- 3 **pounds chicken wings, cut at joints, wingtips discarded**
- 2 **scallions, sliced thin on bias**

1. Combine soy sauce, oil, sugar, garlic, and cayenne in 1-gallon zipper-lock bag. Add wings to marinade, press out air, seal bag, and turn to distribute marinade. Refrigerate for at least 2 hours or up to 6 hours.

2. Adjust oven rack to middle position and heat oven to 350 degrees. Line rimmed baking sheet with aluminum foil and spray with vegetable oil spray. Remove wings from marinade and arrange in single layer, fatty side up, on prepared sheet; discard marinade. Bake until evenly well browned, about 1 hour 5 minutes. Transfer wings to platter, sprinkle with scallions, and serve.

SOY SAUCE CHICKEN WINGS

CHICKEN CROQUETTES WITH LEMON-SCALLION SAUCE

✓ **WHY THIS RECIPE WORKS** We developed a chicken croquette with a crunchy exterior to contrast its soft, rich chicken filling. Taking a nontraditional route, we bound shredded chicken with instant mashed potato flakes (just as tasty, more consistent, and easier than using home-made mashed potatoes) before shaping, breading, and frying it. A coating of fresh bread crumbs gave the croquettes the crunchiest exterior, and cayenne pepper, fresh scallions, and garlic added intrigue to the filling.

The word "croquette" comes from the French word "croquer," meaning "to crunch." When biting into a good chicken croquette, you should not just feel the crunch but hear it, too, as you crack through the exterior into the soft, rich chicken filling.

To get started with my recipe development, I made a few different styles of croquettes using existing recipes. Two promising lessons made my path forward clear: Shallow frying worked just as well as deep frying (and saved a ton of oil), and using shredded rotisserie chicken was a perfectly acceptable shortcut.

Most of these croquette recipes called for making an extra-thick white sauce of flour and dairy, stirring in shredded chicken before chilling the mixture (to help it set), and then scooping, shaping, breading, and frying the mixture in nugget-size portions. This yielded croquettes with nice creamy centers, but the time and mess it required did not feel worth it.

While it was less common, I loved a light, fluffy version of croquettes that combined shredded chicken with leftover mashed potatoes for a binder. However, calling for leftover mashed potatoes was a nonstarter. Cooks add different amounts of butter and cream to their spuds, so no two people would have the same mashed potatoes in their refrigerators. I tried making mashed potatoes from scratch, but this took nearly as long as preparing and chilling a cream sauce.

In a moment of inspiration, I made a batch of chicken croquettes using instant potato flakes. The flakes were a breeze to use, and my coworkers devoured the croquettes without ever knowing. Perfect.

I tested coating the croquettes with panko and dried bread crumbs, but I preferred fresh bread crumbs—which are as easy to make as dropping bread (and a little flour) in the food processor—for the best crunch. Dipping the shaped chicken mixture into beaten egg helped the bread crumbs adhere to the croquettes. Not as quick as prefab crumbs, but worth it.

For maximum flavor, I added fresh scallions, garlic, and spicy cayenne pepper to the chicken-potato mixture. And to make them even better, I stirred together a quick lemon-scallion sauce for dipping.

—MORGAN BOLLING, *Cook's Country*

Chicken Croquettes with Lemon-Scallion Sauce

SERVES 4 TO 6

An average-size rotisserie chicken should yield between 3 and 4 cups of shredded meat, which is more than enough for this recipe. The test kitchen's favorite white sandwich bread is Arnold Country White Bread.

LEMON-SCALLION SAUCE
- ½ cup mayonnaise
- 1 scallion, minced
- 1 teaspoon grated lemon zest plus 1 tablespoon juice
- 1 tablespoon water

CROQUETTES
- 3 slices hearty white sandwich bread, torn into 1-inch pieces
- 1 tablespoon all-purpose flour
- 2 large eggs
- 1½ cups finely shredded rotisserie chicken
- 1¼ cups plain instant mashed potato flakes
- 4 scallions, sliced thin
- 2 garlic cloves, minced
- 1¼ teaspoons table salt
- 1 teaspoon pepper
- ⅛ teaspoon cayenne pepper
- 1½ cups half-and-half
- 2 tablespoons unsalted butter
- 2 cups vegetable oil for frying

1. FOR THE LEMON-SCALLION SAUCE: Combine all ingredients in bowl. Cover with plastic wrap and refrigerate until ready to serve.

2. FOR THE CROQUETTES: Process bread and flour in food processor until finely ground, about 30 seconds; transfer to shallow dish and set aside. Beat eggs together in second shallow dish; set aside.

3. Combine chicken, potato flakes, scallions, garlic, salt, pepper, and cayenne in large bowl. Combine half-and-half and butter in 2-cup liquid measuring cup and microwave, covered, until butter is melted and mixture is hot, about 3 minutes. Add to chicken mixture and stir to combine (mixture will thicken as it sits).

4. Divide chicken mixture into 20 equal portions (about 2 tablespoons each). Using your moistened hands, shape each portion into 3-inch log with pointed ends. Working with 3 to 4 croquettes at a time, dip in eggs, turning to coat and allowing excess to drip off; then coat with bread-crumb mixture. Transfer to rimmed baking sheet. (Breaded croquettes can be covered with plastic wrap and refrigerated for up to 24 hours.)

5. Line second rimmed baking sheet with triple layer of paper towels. Heat oil in 12-inch nonstick skillet over medium heat to 350 degrees. Add 10 croquettes and cook until deep golden brown on first side, about 2 minutes. Using tongs, carefully flip croquettes and continue to cook until deep golden brown on second side, about 3 minutes longer. Adjust burner, if necessary, to maintain oil temperature between 300 and 350 degrees.

6. Transfer croquettes to paper towel–lined sheet. Return oil to 350 degrees and repeat with remaining croquettes. Serve with lemon-scallion sauce.

CASHEW CHICKEN

ⓥ **WHY THIS RECIPE WORKS**   To ensure that the chunks of stir-fried chicken in this dish were flavorful and remained tender and juicy, we gave them a quick soak in a mixture of soy sauce, dry sherry, toasted sesame oil, and cornstarch. The cornstarch not only coated the lean chicken and protected its exterior from becoming dry and tough but also thickened the stir-fry sauce. For cashew chicken that treated the cashews as more than just a garnish, we deeply toasted them in the same oil we later used for the stir-fry, so their flavor permeated the whole dish.

Crunchy, golden-brown, buttery cashews and tender morsels of juicy stir-fried chicken all awash in a salty-sweet, glossy brown sauce— what more could you ask from a recipe you can pull together in less time than it takes to steam some rice? My version hits all the right notes, and since it's made at home, it's hotter and fresher than takeout.

To ensure that this flavorful dish hit all the right notes, I briefly marinated chunks of chicken in a mixture of soy sauce, dry sherry, toasted sesame oil, and cornstarch. In addition to thickening the sauce and coating the lean chicken, preventing it from drying out, the cornstarch also gives the stir-fry sauce an attractive glossy sheen.

I prepared the other ingredients while the chicken marinated. For an easy, intensely flavored sauce, I started with a base of sweet-savory hoisin (a multi-layered ingredient that includes soybeans, vinegar, and chiles), stirred in a bit more soy sauce for balance, and thinned it with some water. A tablespoon of balsamic vinegar brightened the sauce and stood in for the more traditional (but less readily available) Chinese black vinegar, and a mix of scallions, garlic, ginger, and red pepper flakes added fresh, pungent bite. Sliced celery is a common addition, and I liked it for its crisp texture and mild vegetal flavor.

As for those cashews, most recipes call for quickly toasting cashew pieces and dropping them in at the end. And while the results of that method are OK, I wanted my recipe to treat the cashews as more than just a garnish. To that end, I added more cashews than most recipes call for, and I used whole nuts rather than pieces to make certain that they didn't get lost in the finished dish. More important, I deeply toasted the cashews in the same oil I later used for the stir-fry, so their flavor permeated the whole dish. Using moderate heat and stirring frequently turned them a beautiful golden brown, crisped them thoroughly, and deepened and concentrated their nutty flavor.

—MATTHEW FAIRMAN, *Cook's Country*

NOTES FROM THE TEST KITCHEN

WHY TOAST THE NUTS?
Toasting nuts intensifies and blooms their flavor, as well as makes them crunchier. Properly toasted nuts are lightly browned not just on the outside, but all the way through their interiors. Be sure to stir frequently when toasting nuts to prevent scorching.

WHOLE ROAST DUCKS WITH CHERRY SAUCE

Cashew Chicken

SERVES 4

Be sure to have all the ingredients prepared and close by so that you're equipped for fast cooking. The test kitchen's favorite toasted sesame oil is Ottogi Premium Roasted Sesame Oil. Kikkoman makes our favorite hoisin sauce. Serve with white rice.

1½	pounds boneless, skinless chicken breasts, trimmed and cut into ¾-inch pieces
5	tablespoons soy sauce, divided
2	tablespoons cornstarch
1	tablespoon dry sherry
1	teaspoon toasted sesame oil
⅓	cup hoisin sauce
⅓	cup water
1	tablespoon balsamic vinegar
3	tablespoons vegetable oil
1	cup raw cashews
2	celery ribs, sliced on bias ¼-inch thick
6	scallions, white parts sliced thin, green parts cut into 1-inch pieces
2	garlic cloves, minced
1	teaspoon grated fresh ginger
½	teaspoon red pepper flakes

1. Combine chicken, 2 tablespoons soy sauce, cornstarch, sherry, and sesame oil in bowl. Combine hoisin, water, vinegar, and remaining 3 tablespoons soy sauce in separate bowl.

2. Heat vegetable oil in 12-inch nonstick skillet over medium heat until shimmering. Add cashews and cook, stirring constantly, until golden brown, 4 to 6 minutes, reducing heat if cashews begin to darken too quickly. Using slotted spoon, transfer cashews to small bowl.

3. Heat oil left in skillet over medium-high heat until just smoking. Add chicken and cook, stirring frequently, until beginning to brown and no longer translucent, about 3 minutes. Add celery, scallion whites, garlic, ginger, and pepper flakes and cook until celery is just beginning to soften, about 2 minutes.

4. Add hoisin mixture, bring to boil, and cook until chicken is cooked through and sauce is thickened, 1 to 3 minutes. Off heat, stir in scallion greens and cashews. Serve.

WHOLE ROAST DUCKS WITH CHERRY SAUCE

WHY THIS RECIPE WORKS To ensure tender, evenly cooked meat and deeply browned skin, we crosshatched the skin and the fat to create escape routes for the rendered fat. Salting the meat for at least 6 hours ensured that it was well seasoned and helped it retain moisture during cooking. Braising the legs cooked them most of the way through before the entire bird finished roasting in the oven. Brushing a soy sauce–maple syrup glaze over the ducks encouraged deep browning. A bright, fruity sauce of cherries simmered with more soy sauce and maple syrup plus red wine vinegar, cornstarch, and thyme made for a vibrant accompaniment that balanced the rich meat.

To all the dark meat lovers out there: You've been roasting the wrong bird.

All due respect to succulent chicken and turkey leg quarters, but they make up only a fraction of the whole bird, which is why you should consider roasting duck. It's all dark meat, since both the breast and leg portions are well-exercised muscles with ample fat, and it's imbued with a sultry, bass-note richness that chicken and turkey just don't have. The duck's breast is also relatively flat, which enables its skin to brown remarkably evenly, and it's versatile for entertaining: Pair one bird with a bright sauce and you've got an intimate dinner party showpiece. Roast two—doable in one pan—and you can feed a crowd.

Here's the catch: The qualities that make duck special to eat also make it a challenge to cook well. But I've got an approachable method all figured out. Allow me to explain.

Think of duck as the "red meat" of poultry. Its dark crimson color and rich, assertive flavor—even in the breast meat—come from the myoglobin in its abundant red muscle fibers, which are necessary for endurance activities such as flying. (Turkeys and chickens have fewer muscle fibers because they perform only quick bursts of flight.) Duck is also much fattier than other poultry: Its edible portion (meat and skin) contains about 28 percent fat, while the edible portion of a chicken contains between 2.5 and 8 percent fat. Most of a duck's fat builds up as a thick layer of subcutaneous padding that adds to the bird's insulation and buoyancy in the water. Finally, duck breasts are thinner, flatter, and blockier than other poultry breasts, and their wings are longer. The breed you're most likely to find in supermarkets, Pekin, weighs a pound or so more than an average chicken.

Because duck is so fatty, it's important not only to trim it thoroughly of excess fat around the neck and cavity but also to treat its skin like the fat cap on a pork or beef roast and score it extensively. These channels, which I cut into the breast as well as the thighs, also allow the salt rubbed over the skin to penetrate more deeply over a 6-hour rest. Salting the duck helps keep it juicy and thoroughly seasons the rich meat to highlight its full flavor.

Cooking duck presents the same familiar challenge as cooking other types of whole poultry: getting the breasts and legs to cook at the same rate. But because duck breast is thinner than chicken or turkey breast, it cooks through even more quickly than they do, making it even more of a challenge to get the tougher legs and thighs to turn tender and succulent before the breast overcooks and dries out.

My solution: Give the leg portions a head start by braising them. I do this by submerging the bottom half of the ducks in water in a roasting pan and vigorously simmering them on the stove until the leg quarters register 145 to 160 degrees. Meanwhile, because the breasts don't have contact with the water, they cook more slowly and reach only 110 to 130 degrees. Once the leg quarters have reached the target temperature, I move the birds to a V-rack, glaze them, put them back in the roasting pan (emptied of braising liquid) and move them to the oven. The leg quarters are far enough along that they will turn tender by the time the breast meat reaches its doneness temperature of 160 degrees. The upshot: a superbly flavorful, perfectly cooked holiday centerpiece that your guests are sure to remember for a long time to come.

—LAN LAM, *Cook's Illustrated*

Whole Roast Ducks with Cherry Sauce

SERVES 8

Pekin ducks may also be labeled as Long Island ducks and are typically sold frozen. Thaw the ducks in the refrigerator for 24 hours. Use a roasting pan that measures at least 14 by 12 inches. This recipe was developed using Diamond Crystal kosher salt. If you use Morton kosher salt, use 3 tablespoons. Do not thaw the cherries before using. If desired, pulse the cherries in a food

processor until coarsely chopped. In step 4, the crumpled aluminum foil prevents the rendered fat from smoking. Even when the duck is fully cooked, its juices will have a reddish hue.

DUCKS

2 (5½- to 6-pound) Pekin ducks
¼ cup kosher salt, divided
2 tablespoons maple syrup
1 tablespoon soy sauce

CHERRY SAUCE

⅓ cup maple syrup
¼ cup red wine vinegar
4 teaspoons soy sauce
2 teaspoons cornstarch
½ teaspoon pepper
2 sprigs fresh thyme
18 ounces frozen sweet cherries, quartered

1. FOR THE DUCKS: Working with 1 duck at a time, use your hands to remove large fat deposits from bottom of cavity. Using kitchen shears, trim excess neck skin from top of breast; remove tail and first 2 segments from each wing, leaving only drumette. Arrange duck breast side up. With tip of sharp knife, cut slits spaced ¾ inch apart in crosshatch pattern in skin and fat of breast, being careful not to cut into meat. Flip duck breast side down. Cut parallel slits spaced ¾ inch apart in skin and fat of each thigh (do not crosshatch).

2. Rub 2 teaspoons salt into cavity of 1 duck. Rub 1 teaspoon salt into breast, taking care to rub salt into slits. Rub 1 tablespoon salt into skin of rest of duck. Align skin at bottom of cavity so 1 side overlaps other by at least ½ inch. Use sturdy toothpick to pin skin layers to each other to close cavity. Place duck on rimmed baking sheet. Repeat with second duck. Refrigerate uncovered for 6 to 24 hours.

3. Place ducks breast side up in roasting pan. Add water until at least half of thighs are submerged but most of breasts remain above water, about 14 cups. Bring to boil over high heat. Reduce heat to maintain vigorous simmer. Cook until thermometer inserted into thickest part of drumstick, all the way to bone, registers 145 to 160 degrees, 45 minutes to 1 hour 5 minutes. After 20 minutes of cooking, adjust oven rack to lower-middle position and heat oven to 425 degrees. Stir maple syrup and soy sauce together in bowl.

4. Set V-rack on rimmed baking sheet and spray with vegetable oil spray. Remove roasting pan from heat. Using tongs and spatula, lift ducks from pan one at a time, allow liquid to drain, and transfer to V-rack breast side up. Brush breasts and tops of drumsticks with one-third of maple syrup mixture. Flip ducks and brush remaining mixture over backs and sides. Transfer braising liquid to pot or large bowl to cool. (Once cool, defat liquid and reserve liquid and/or fat for another use, if desired.) Rinse roasting pan and wipe clean using wad of paper towels. Crumple 20-inch length of aluminum foil into loose ball. Uncrumple foil and place in roasting pan. Set V-rack on foil. Roast ducks until backs are golden brown and breasts register 140 to 150 degrees, about 20 minutes.

5. Remove roasting pan from oven. Using tongs and spatula, flip ducks breast side up. Continue to roast until breasts register 160 to 165 degrees, 15 to 25 minutes longer. Transfer ducks to carving board and let rest for 20 minutes.

6. FOR THE CHERRY SAUCE: Whisk maple syrup, vinegar, soy sauce, cornstarch, and pepper together in small saucepan. Add thyme sprigs and bring to simmer over medium-high heat, stirring constantly using rubber spatula. Continue to cook, stirring constantly, until mixture thickens, 2 to 3 minutes longer. Stir in cherries

and cook, stirring occasionally, until sauce has consistency of maple syrup, 5 to 8 minutes. Discard thyme sprigs and season with salt and pepper to taste. Transfer to serving bowl. Carve ducks and serve, passing sauce separately.

COD WITH WARM BEET AND ARUGULA SALAD

✓ WHY THIS RECIPE WORKS Since delicate fish fillets cook so quickly in the Instant Pot, we were pleased to discover that we could stagger the cooking times of different ingredients and still create a full meal in under an hour. We love the combination of sweet, earthy beets and light, buttery cod. We started by braising our beets for just 3 minutes under pressure—a process that can otherwise take up to an hour. What's more, the intense heat of the Instant Pot rendered the nutrient-packed skins of our unpeeled beets utterly undetectable. Next, we created a foil sling on which to suspend our cod atop the beets and cooked both for just 2 minutes. Arugula, a lemony dressing, and a sprinkling of dukkah—a crunchy, flavor-packed Egyptian condiment—brought it all together.

In recent years, the Mediterranean diet—a varied approach to eating that emphasizes vegetables and fruits, legumes, whole grains, lean proteins, nuts and seeds, and heart-healthy oils and fats—has surged in popularity. And one of the most popular kitchen appliances is the Instant Pot, so it was a win-win challenge for the test kitchen to put the two together to create our *Mediterranean Instant Pot* cookbook. Many Instant Pot recipes are red meat–centered dishes more fit for a New England snowstorm than for springtime on the Amalfi Coast, so I'd have to reconsider my Instant Pot cookery with the Mediterranean diet in mind.

Seafood is often the main source of protein in the Mediterranean diet. And while a multicooker isn't usually my cooking vessel of choice when it comes to delicate fish, I was determined to find just the right approach for yielding a one-pot meal of quick, easy, perfectly cooked fish and a hearty vegetable.

I started by considering the cut of the fish and determined that 1½-inch-thick cod fillets fit the bill— they become flaky and tender when properly cooked, yet they remain firm in the high-pressure conditions of

---

NOTES FROM THE TEST KITCHEN

TIPS FOR CROSSHATCHING

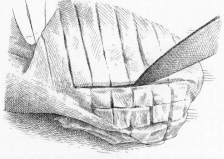

1. USE THE TIP OF YOUR KNIFE
This allows you to feel exactly where you're cutting.

2. MAKE MULTIPLE STROKES PER CUT
Because it's tricky to cut to exactly where the fat hits the meat, first slice through the skin and some fat, and then run the knife tip through the slit to get down to the meat.

3. TRY NOT TO NICK THE MEAT
If you do, dark juices can leak and stain the bird.

a multicooker. I found that the cod cooked to perfection in just 2 minutes using the high-pressure-cook function, and the moist environment of the Instant Pot gave the fish a surprisingly silky, buttery quality.

With the cod squared away, I turned to the vegetable side, which I hoped I could cook in tandem with the fish. Since cod has such a mild flavor, I wanted to pair it with a bold-flavored vegetable. How about beets? While it takes beets about an hour to become tender in the oven or on the stovetop, I was confident that the Instant Pot could cut back on their cooking time.

I scrubbed and trimmed 1½ pounds of beets, leaving their skins on, and then cut them into wedges. Using the multicooker's sauté function, I sweated a shallot and some garlic in olive oil before adding the beets, a bit of chicken broth, and the cod fillets. I locked the lid in place, cooked everything under high pressure for 5 minutes, and then quick-released the pressure. This was a partial success; the beets were tender, and their tough skins were rendered virtually unnoticeable, but the fish was dry, falling apart, and stained an unappealing pink hue. The dish also needed a flavor boost.

First, I'd address the texture and appearance of the cod by staggering the cooking of the beets and fish. (Since the beets and the cod each cooked so quickly, I wasn't concerned about losing time by going under pressure more than once; I could still have dinner on the table in less time than it would take to cook the beets using more traditional methods.) After sautéing the beets, I pressure-cooked them on their own for 3 minutes and quick-released the pressure. At this point the parcooked beets needed just a couple minutes more to reach perfection.

Time for the fish: Previous tests had shown that using a foil sling when cooking delicate foods such as fish made it easier to lift the food from the deep Instant Pot. The foil sling would have an additional benefit here: Elevating the fillets above the beets would prevent them from taking on the vegetable's pink color. I gently perched the sling holding the cod atop the parcooked beets and then cooked the whole lot on high pressure for another 2 minutes. The fish emerged perfectly cooked, and the beets were velvety and moist.

To kick up the flavors, I drizzled the cod with extra-virgin olive oil and sprinkled it with dukkah, a Mediterranean nut-based condiment, which added a bit of crunch and much-needed richness to the lean fish. And to perfect the beets, I mixed them with bright lemon juice and peppery arugula, creating a warm salad to serve alongside the cod. Now this was a dinner worth hauling out the Instant Pot for.

—NICOLE KONSTANTINAKOS, *America's Test Kitchen Books*

Cod with Warm Beet and Arugula Salad
SERVES 4

Look for beets measuring approximately 2 inches in diameter. Haddock and striped bass are good substitutes for the cod. Thin tail-end fillets can be folded to achieve proper thickness. The cod should register about 135 degrees after cooking; if it doesn't, partially cover the pot with the lid and continue to cook the fish using the highest sauté function until the desired temperature is achieved. Serve with lemon wedges.

¼	cup extra-virgin olive oil, divided, plus extra for drizzling
1	shallot, sliced thin
2	garlic cloves, minced
1½	pounds small beets, scrubbed, trimmed, and cut into ½-inch wedges
½	cup chicken or vegetable broth
1	tablespoon dukkah, plus extra for sprinkling
¼	teaspoon table salt
4	(6-ounce) skinless cod fillets, 1½ inches thick
1	tablespoon lemon juice
2	ounces (2 cups) baby arugula

1. Using highest sauté function, heat 1 tablespoon oil in Instant Pot until shimmering. Add shallot and cook until softened, about 2 minutes. Stir in garlic and cook until fragrant, about 30 seconds. Stir in beets and broth. Lock lid in place and close pressure release valve. Select high pressure cook function and cook for 3 minutes. Turn off Instant Pot and quick-release pressure. Carefully remove lid, allowing steam to escape away from you.

2. Fold sheet of aluminum foil into 16 by 6-inch sling. Combine dukkah, salt, and 2 tablespoons oil in bowl, then brush cod with dukkah mixture. Arrange cod skinned side down in center of sling. Using sling, lower cod into Instant Pot; allow narrow edges of sling to rest along sides of insert. Lock lid in place and close pressure release valve. Select high pressure cook function and cook for 2 minutes.

COD WITH WARM BEET AND ARUGULA SALAD

3. Turn off Instant Pot and quick-release pressure. Carefully remove lid, allowing steam to escape away from you. Using sling, transfer cod to large plate. Tent with foil and let rest while finishing beet salad.

4. Combine lemon juice and remaining 1 tablespoon oil in large bowl. Using slotted spoon, transfer beets to bowl with lemon juice mixture. Add arugula and gently toss to combine. Season with salt and pepper to taste. Serve cod with salad, sprinkling individual portions with extra dukkah and drizzling with extra oil.

OVEN-STEAMED FISH WITH SCALLIONS AND GINGER

✓ **WHY THIS RECIPE WORKS** Classic Chinese and French methods for steaming fish produce moist, flavorful results. We used the best of both approaches to come up with an entirely new method that's easy and equally impressive. We started by swapping the steamer (or the individual parchment envelopes) for a tightly covered baking pan and the stovetop for a hot oven. Placing the skinless fillets on a foil sling allowed the fish to flavor the cooking liquid and made it easy to transfer the fish to a serving platter without the fillets falling apart. Removing the fish from the oven before it was fully cooked prevented it from overcooking when finished with sizzling-hot ginger-infused oil.

If you're not steaming fish, you should be. It's a delicate method for cooking a delicate protein that leads to supremely moist, tender results. It's fast enough to do on a weeknight but delivers company-worthy elegance. And when it's done well, there's a real flavor benefit—if you know how to season and dress the fish.

Both Chinese and French cuisines have classic approaches to steaming. Cantonese cooks steam fish whole (typically sprinkled with aromatics such as garlic, ginger, and scallions) in a bamboo steamer set in a wok filled with a few inches of boiling water. Once cooked, the fish is transferred to a platter, doused with soy sauce and maybe a splash of Shaoxing wine, and garnished with fresh scallions. The final flourish is a drizzle of hot oil that sizzles as it hits the fish, releasing a cloud of delicate aromas into the air.

The French technique, called "en papillote" ("in paper"), calls for enclosing individual fillets in parchment or foil envelopes with vegetables, perhaps a bit of fat, and a splash of wine or broth and then baking the packets in the oven. Each diner then gets their own parcel of fish, vegetables, and steaming cooking liquid to open at the table.

There's a lot to love about both approaches, but I've long wanted a mash-up that offers what I consider to be the best of each: the bold, fresh flavors and hot oil drizzle of the Chinese method and the convenient oven cooking and flavorful fish jus of the French method. Drawing inspiration from both and using easy-to-find fillets would lead to my ideal steamed fish.

Though the steaming would take place in the oven, crimping the fillets in individual packets was a labor of love that I'd save for another time—not to mention the fact that opening the packets at the table would make it difficult to drizzle the cooked fillets with the hot oil.

Instead, I decided to steam all the fillets together in a single makeshift packet: a foil-covered metal baking pan. I arranged four skinless cod fillets in the pan and topped them with some sliced garlic and neatly julienned scallions and ginger. Next, I pondered the cooking liquid. Since the fillets would be sitting in the liquid rather than above it in a steamer, it made sense to follow the French method and use something more flavorful than plain water. As a starting point, I whisked together a few tablespoons of soy sauce, some Shaoxing wine, and a bit of nutty toasted sesame oil; poured it around the fillets; and then covered the pan tightly with foil. After about 15 minutes in a 450-degree oven, the fillets hit their target doneness temperature of 135 degrees.

I worked carefully to maneuver the tidy fillets onto the serving platter, but they flaked apart anyway. Then, when I finished them with sliced scallions and a splash of hot oil (which sent up an enticing aroma), the combined effect of carryover cooking and the oil caused them to overcook slightly. The presentation wasn't great either: The now-soggy aromatics clung to the top of the fish.

I had an idea for keeping the fillets intact: Treat them like bar cookies and cook them on top of a foil sling. That way, I could gently lift all the fillets out of the pan at once and deposit them onto the serving platter with minimal disturbance. I folded an 18 by 12-inch piece of foil in half lengthwise to create a sling, sprayed it lightly with vegetable oil spray to prevent sticking, laid the sling in the pan, and placed the fillets on top.

I covered the pan with foil and placed it in the oven, but this time I made sure to take the fish out earlier, when it had just reached 125 degrees, trusting that the hot oil and carryover cooking would help it reach its target temperature. I then grasped each end of the foil sling and transferred the delicate fillets to the platter, carefully sliding the foil out from under the fillets so that I didn't dislodge a single flake. I poured the juices from the pan over and around the fish, topped it with scallions, and drizzled it with the hot oil.

Now the fillets were perfectly cooked and moist, and the cooking-liquid-turned-sauce balanced the delicately clean flavors of the fish. Seasoning the cooking liquid with a little sugar, salt, and white pepper (more floral and delicate than black pepper) made those flavors pop even more, but it was a subtle tweak I made to the aromatics that really gave the sauce depth: Rather than place the garlic, ginger, and scallions on top of the fish, where they turned sadly limp, I laid them in the baking pan underneath the foil sling so that they could infuse the cooking liquid and wouldn't cling to the cooked fillets. Once the fillets were safely deposited on the serving platter, I strained the spent aromatics and drizzled the flavorful liquid over the fish.

I scattered the fresh scallions over the fillets and was about to pour the oil over the fish when I realized that I could add even more sweet-spicy fragrance and texture to the dish by adding slivers of ginger to the hot oil, where they would turn aromatic, golden, and crispy. Paired with the sauce, this would make a fragrant dressing for the steamed rice I planned to serve on the side. Scattering cilantro sprigs over the top made my quick, new-school interpretation of steamed fish feel as elegant as it was efficient.

—ANDREA GEARY, *Cook's Illustrated*

Oven-Steamed Fish with Scallions and Ginger
SERVES 4

Haddock, red snapper, halibut, and sea bass can be substituted for the cod as long as the fillets are about 1 inch thick. If the fillets are uneven, fold the thinner ends under when placing the fillets in the pan. If using a glass baking dish, add 5 minutes to the cooking time. To ensure that the fish doesn't overcook, remove it from the oven when it registers 125 to 130 degrees; it will continue to cook as it is plated. Serve with steamed rice and vegetables.

 8   scallions, trimmed, divided
 1   (3-inch) piece ginger, peeled, divided
 3   garlic cloves, sliced thin
 4   (6-ounce) skinless cod fillets, about 1 inch thick
 3   tablespoons soy sauce
 2   tablespoons Shaoxing wine or dry sherry
1½   teaspoons toasted sesame oil
1½   teaspoons sugar
 ¼   teaspoon table salt
 ¼   teaspoon white pepper
 2   tablespoons vegetable oil
 ⅓   cup fresh cilantro leaves and thin stems

1. Adjust oven rack to middle position and heat oven to 450 degrees. Chop 6 scallions coarse and spread evenly in 13 by 9-inch baking pan. Slice remaining 2 scallions thin on bias and set aside. Chop 2 inches ginger coarse and spread in pan with chopped scallions. Slice remaining 1 inch ginger into matchsticks and set aside. Sprinkle garlic over scallions and ginger in pan.

2. Fold 18 by 12-inch piece of aluminum foil lengthwise to create 18 by 6-inch sling and spray lightly with vegetable oil spray. Place sling in pan lengthwise, with extra foil hanging over ends of pan. Arrange cod on sling. If fillets vary in thickness, place thinner fillets in middle and thicker fillets at ends.

BUTTER-BASTED FISH FILLETS WITH GARLIC AND THYME

3. Whisk soy sauce, Shaoxing wine, sesame oil, sugar, salt, and white pepper in small bowl until combined. Pour around cod. Cover pan tightly with foil and bake until fish registers 125 to 130 degrees, 12 to 14 minutes.

4. Grasping sling at both ends, carefully transfer sling and cod to deep platter. Place spatula at 1 end of fillets to hold in place and carefully slide out sling from under cod. Strain cooking liquid through fine-mesh strainer set over bowl, pressing on solids to extract liquid; discard solids. Pour strained liquid over cod. Sprinkle reserved scallions over cod. Heat vegetable oil in small skillet over high heat until shimmering. Reduce heat to low, add reserved ginger, and cook, stirring, until ginger begins to brown and crisp, 20 to 30 seconds. Drizzle oil and ginger over cod (oil will crackle). Top with cilantro and serve.

BUTTER-BASTED FISH FILLETS WITH GARLIC AND THYME

✅ **WHY THIS RECIPE WORKS** Butter basting, a technique that involves repeatedly spooning sizzling butter over food as it cooks, is great for mild, lean, flaky fish such as cod, haddock, or snapper. The butter helps cook the top of the fillet as the skillet heats the bottom, allowing you to flip the fish only once and early in the cooking process—before the flesh has become too fragile—so it stays intact. The nutty, aromatic butter, which we enhanced with thyme sprigs and crushed garlic cloves, bathed the mild fish in savory flavor. We alternated basting with direct-heat cooking on the burner, taking the temperature of the fish so we knew exactly when the fillets were done.

Want to know a secret? Even as a professional cook, I used to get a little nervous when it came time to sauté fish. Fish is expensive, and it can go from juicy to dry in a blink. And when you're dealing with flaky types such as cod, there is a good chance that the fragile fillets will fall apart when flipped.

These days, however, I cook cod and similar fish with ease, and the results are outstanding. That's because I butter-baste—a technique that involves repeatedly spooning sizzling butter over food as it cooks. I'll explain the mechanics in a bit, but first, a rundown on why it's so effective.

Bathing fish in hot butter has multiple benefits. It encourages Maillard reactions that add complexity and help develop a golden crust. Maillard reactions also turn the milk solids in the butter nutty and sweet as it browns. Those flavors, along with aromatics added to the butter, enhance the lean, mild fish. Butter basting also cooks food from above and below—the hot fat cooks the top while the skillet cooks the bottom. This means you don't have to flip the fish later on, when it is especially delicate.

Butter basting can seem intimidating because things move quickly, and chefs often rely on touch and instinct alone to know when the fish is done. But I developed an approach that's easy to master, and it even involves a few breaks along the way.

Start by cooking two 1-inch-thick fillets in an oiled nonstick or carbon-steel skillet for 4 minutes. Turn the fillets over—this is the only flip in the process, and since it happens early on, the fillets will still be firm enough to stay intact—and cook them for a minute on the second side before adding cubed butter. Once the butter is melted, the real fun begins. Tilt the skillet toward you to pool the fat, and use a deep spoon to pour the butter over the fish for 15 seconds. There's no need to rush; just baste until the time is up. Now, take a break: Put the skillet flat on the burner and let the fish cook for 30 seconds. Baste again, and then take the temperature of the fish. This "on-off" method moderates the skillet's heat, and tracking the fish's temperature removes any guesswork about when it's done.

When the fish registers 130 degrees, add thyme and garlic to the far side of the skillet to keep any spattering away from your hands; the fillets will keep the aromatics out of the butter as you baste. Continue to alternate between cooking and basting until the fish registers 140 degrees. As you work, the perfume of browned butter and aromatics will waft from the skillet, and when you're done, the fish will be intact, golden, moist, and richly flavored. But that's not the only reward. The other one comes in the final moments of cooking, when you feel like a rock-star chef.

—STEVE DUNN, *Cook's Illustrated*

SERVES 2

You can substitute red snapper or haddock for the cod. The "skinned" side of a skinless fillet can be identified by its streaky, slightly darker appearance.

2 **(6-ounce) skinless cod fillets, about 1 inch thick**

½ **teaspoon kosher salt**

⅛ **teaspoon pepper**

1 **tablespoon vegetable oil**

3 **tablespoons unsalted butter, cut into ½-inch cubes**

2 **garlic cloves, crushed and peeled**

4 **sprigs fresh thyme**

Lemon wedges

1. Pat all sides of fillets dry with paper towels. Sprinkle on all sides with salt and pepper. Heat oil in 12-inch nonstick or carbon-steel skillet over medium-high heat until just smoking. Reduce heat to medium and place fillets skinned side down in skillet. Gently press on each fillet with spatula for 5 seconds to ensure good contact with skillet. Cook fillets, without moving them, until underside is light golden brown, 4 to 5 minutes.

2. Using 2 spatulas, gently flip fillets. Cook for 1 minute. Scatter butter around fillets. When butter is melted, tilt skillet slightly toward you so butter pools at front of skillet. Using large spoon, scoop up melted butter and pour over fillets repeatedly for 15 seconds. Place skillet flat on burner and continue to cook 30 seconds longer.

Tilt skillet and baste for 15 seconds. Place skillet flat on burner and take temperature of thickest part of each fillet. Continue to alternate basting and cooking until fillets register 130 degrees. Add garlic and thyme sprigs to skillet at 12 o'clock position (butter will spatter). When spattering has subsided, continue basting and cooking until fillets register 140 degrees at thickest point. (Total cooking time will range from 8 to 10 minutes.)

3. Transfer fillets to individual plates. Discard garlic. Top each fillet with thyme sprigs, pour butter over fillets, and serve with lemon wedges.

SLOW-ROASTED SALMON WITH CHIVES AND LEMON

✓ **WHY THIS RECIPE WORKS** Though slow roasting is an uncommon method for cooking fish, here it gave us ultratender, buttery salmon. First we sprinkled the fish with a mixture of brown sugar and salt to evoke the flavors of cured salmon. A very low 250-degree oven kept the fish from overcooking and minimized any carryover cooking once it was out of the oven. Finally, we poured a light, bright mixture of extra-virgin olive oil, lemon zest, lemon juice, and chives over the succulent fish.

Having worked in professional kitchens for many years, I offer this advice for cooking salmon: Slow down, and go big. Let me explain.

NOTES FROM THE TEST KITCHEN

BUTTER BASTING: EASY AS 1, 2, 3

1. BASTE Tilt skillet toward you and repeatedly spoon butter over fish for 15 seconds.

2. REST Place skillet flat on burner and cook fish for 30 seconds.

3. BASTE Repeat steps 1 and 2 until fish registers 140 degrees.

I've learned the hard way that it's easy to overcook a fillet of salmon—or any fish, for that matter—especially if you are trying to cook several pieces at once. Better to cook one big piece gently at a low temperature. The method is easy and foolproof: The window of optimal doneness is wider and the fish is harder to overcook. Plus, salmon flesh takes on a silky, buttery texture when cooked gently. And finally, there's less splattery mess and fishy smell when you slow-roast salmon in the oven. That's a lot of benefit for a little extra time.

Knowing I wanted to work with a 2½-pound piece of fish that would feed about six people, I tested roasting temperatures ranging from 170 to 350 degrees. Not surprisingly, I found that lower temperatures produced salmon that was moister, silkier, and more evenly cooked. That said, I didn't want to wait 2 hours (or longer) for the fish to cook at the lowest temperature. I found that the happy medium of temperature and time was 250 degrees for 1 hour.

The texture of the salmon was amazing, and I wanted to bump up the flavor to match it. Many of our recipes for grilled or smoked salmon call for rubbing the flesh with a mixture of salt and sugar and then letting it sit for an hour or more before cooking; as the salmon sits, the salt-sugar mixture lightly cures it, drawing out excess moisture and deeply seasoning the fish. But I didn't want to wait, so I tried sprinkling the salmon with sugar and salt and immediately popping it in the low oven. My tasters loved the sweetness the sugar provided, but they wanted a bit more complexity. A switch to brown sugar did the trick and, as a bonus, it gave the cooked salmon a lovely rusty hue.

For a final flourish, I decided to whisk together a simple lemony vinaigrette—just olive oil, lemon zest and juice, and sliced chives—to pour over the fish as soon as it came out of the oven. This dressing mingled with the juices in the baking dish to create a light, bright, savory sauce that perfectly accented the richness of the salmon. This method proved so successful that I made a variation with garlic, mustard, and dill, as well as a version with cayenne and parsley. A worthy mantra for cooking salmon, and for life: Slow down, and go big.

—ALLI BERKEY, *Cook's Country*

Slow-Roasted Salmon with Chives and Lemon
SERVES 6

You can substitute granulated sugar for the brown sugar, if desired. If a 2½-pound salmon fillet is unavailable, you can use six 6- to 8-ounce skinless salmon fillets instead. In step 1, sprinkle both sides of the fillets evenly with the sugar mixture and arrange them side by side in the baking dish so they are touching. The cooking time remains the same. We prefer farm-raised salmon here; if using wild salmon, reduce the cooking time to 45 to 50 minutes, or until the salmon registers 120 degrees. If you're using table salt, use ¾ teaspoon (½ teaspoon in step 1 and ¼ teaspoon in step 3).

- 1 tablespoon packed brown sugar
- 1½ teaspoons kosher salt, divided
- ½ teaspoon pepper
- 1 (2½-pound) skinless center-cut salmon fillet, about 1½ inches thick
- ¼ cup extra-virgin olive oil
- 2 tablespoons sliced fresh chives
- 2 teaspoons grated lemon zest plus 1½ tablespoons juice

1. Adjust oven rack to middle position and heat oven to 250 degrees. Combine sugar, 1 teaspoon salt, and pepper in small bowl. Sprinkle salmon all over with sugar mixture.

2. Place salmon, flesh side up, in 13 by 9-inch baking dish. Roast until center is still translucent when checked with tip of paring knife and registers 125 degrees (for medium-rare), 55 to 60 minutes.

3. Meanwhile, combine oil, chives, lemon zest and juice, and remaining ½ teaspoon salt in bowl.

4. Remove dish from oven and immediately pour oil mixture evenly over salmon. Let rest for 5 minutes. Using spatula and spoon, portion salmon and sauce onto serving platter. Stir together any juices left in dish and spoon over salmon. Serve.

VARIATIONS
Slow-Roasted Salmon with Dill and Garlic
Substitute 1 teaspoon dry mustard for pepper. Add 1 teaspoon garlic powder to sugar mixture. Substitute chopped fresh dill for chives.

Slow-Roasted Salmon with Parsley and Cayenne
Substitute cayenne pepper for pepper and chopped fresh parsley for chives.

BRIOCHE DINNER ROLLS

CHAPTER 6

BREAKFAST, BRUNCH, AND BREADS

CHOCOLATE BRIOCHE BUNS

✓ **WHY THIS RECIPE WORKS** While we love frosted, glazed, and molten creations, chocolate decadence doesn't have to come in an ooey-gooey package—especially at breakfast time. We wanted a breakfast bun with some restraint, one that would make a beautiful addition to Sunday brunch and would be buttery, rich, substantial, and tender. Our first thought was brioche: Enriched with eggs and butter, the bread is a perfectly rich pairing for our star ingredient. Sure, we could have just added chocolate chips to a standard roll, but that seemed like an afterthought. We wanted a bun with chocolate as a truly integral component, so we shaped spirals of plain and chocolate-flavored doughs. Using bread flour ensured that the dough would have enough structure to later fill and shape into scrolls. To make chocolate brioche dough, we added a generous ⅓ cup of cocoa powder to half the dough. Shaping our impressive buns was easier than we thought. We rolled the separate plain and chocolate doughs into squares and stacked them with a luxurious filling of bittersweet chocolate, cocoa powder, butter, and confectioners' sugar (made tacky with an egg white) in the middle. We refrigerated the layered doughs so that they would firm up before rolling, cutting, and coiling. We also refrigerated the shaped buns to proof overnight so that we wouldn't have to wake up with the sun to enjoy them.

Sometimes you just need to have chocolate for breakfast. Specifically, I craved a chocolate bun with a touch of refinement—something that would get my day off to a great start and not overwhelm my tastebuds with overly sweet, cloying flavors. Since breakfast buns often take a long time to make from start to finish—longer than many cooks are willing to spend in the kitchen before they've had breakfast—I also wanted a recipe that would allow me to complete most of the work the night before so that all I had left to do in the morning was bake the buns and dig in.

I liked the idea of using buttery, eggy brioche dough as the base of my buns, so my first step was to develop the perfect recipe for a brioche dough that would be tender and supple once baked but still sturdy enough to hold an appealing shape. Once I had that down, I would think about how best to add the chocolate.

I'm a big fan of the test kitchen's no-knead brioche method, which employs a series of folds, resting periods, and a long refrigeration time to build gluten in the dough instead of using a stand mixer. Unfortunately, using this method meant that after the refrigeration period I would still have to shape the buns and let them rise in the morning before baking. Since I wanted buns that I could shape, proof in the refrigerator overnight, and then just take out and bake when I was ready, the no-knead method was out. Instead, I borrowed a method from our recipe for Brioche Hamburger Buns (page 200). I started by mixing together flour, yeast, and salt in the bowl of a stand mixer and then slowly added a combination of water, eggs, and sugar until a dough formed. Next I beat in 12 tablespoons of unsalted butter (an amount that I found ideal for a rich but nongreasy dough), 1 tablespoon at a time, and then continued kneading until the dough was smooth and elastic, another 11 to 13 minutes. I tested both all-purpose and bread flour and found that higher-protein bread flour worked better here to give the enriched dough the structure it needed for shaping.

Now it was time for the fun part: incorporating the chocolate. To begin with, I tried stirring cocoa powder directly into the brioche dough. I found that ⅓ cup of cocoa powder gave the dough a nice color without interfering with its texture. Even better, I discovered that if I added the cocoa to only half the dough, setting the other half aside, the contrasting colors of the two doughs made for striking-looking buns once layered together and shaped. Twisting the buns into a sophisticated S shape took the elegance to the next level.

The chocolate flavor still wasn't as pronounced as I wanted it, so I decided to try adding a chocolaty filling. A combination of melted bittersweet chocolate and more cocoa powder delivered bold chocolate flavor. Stirring in some butter and ¼ cup of confectioners' sugar tempered the filling's bitterness without making it too sweet. I now had a filling that was smooth and spreadable—too much so, in fact. The filling was oozing out from between the layers of dough as I attempted to shape the buns. Some kind of binder was in order, and a single egg white fit the bill perfectly. Waiting for the chocolate mixture to cool before adding the egg white was essential to ensure that the hot mixture didn't accidentally cook the egg.

To simplify the shaping process, I started by pressing both my plain and chocolate doughs into 6 by 6-inch squares, which were easier to handle than larger sizes. I spread the filling over the square of plain dough, set the chocolate dough on top, and then placed the dough

CHOCOLATE BRIOCHE BUNS

in the refrigerator for 30 minutes to help the filling firm up for mess-free shaping. Once the dough was chilled, I rolled it into a 12 by 16-inch rectangle, cut it into strips, and coiled the ends of each strip in opposite directions to create my signature S-curl shape.

My buns now needed at least 2 hours to proof in the refrigerator, but I found that they could chill in the fridge at this stage for up to 24 hours. I loved the flexibility this gave to the recipe, since it meant I could prepare the buns the day before, refrigerate them overnight, and then simply bake them in the morning. About 18 minutes in a 350-degree oven produced enough oven spring for soft brioche buns without too much browning, ensuring the most dramatic contrast between the colors of the plain and chocolate doughs.

Whether I'm making them as an impressive brunch offering or as a soul-satisfying breakfast just for me, these buns are sure to get the day off to a great, stress-free start. Just as chocolate should.

—LEAH COLINS, *America's Test Kitchen Books*

Chocolate Brioche Buns

MAKES 12 BUNS

When kneading the dough on medium-low speed, the mixer can wobble and move on the counter. Place a dish towel or shelf liner underneath it to keep it in place, and watch it closely.

DOUGH

- 3⅔ cups (20⅛ ounces) bread flour
- 2¼ teaspoons instant or rapid-rise yeast
- 1½ teaspoons table salt
- 1 cup water, room temperature
- 2 large eggs plus 1 large yolk
- ½ cup (3½ ounces) granulated sugar
- 12 tablespoons unsalted butter, cut into 12 pieces and softened
- ⅓ cup (1 ounce) unsweetened cocoa powder

FILLING

- 2 ounces bittersweet chocolate, chopped
- 4 tablespoons unsalted butter
- 3 tablespoons unsweetened cocoa powder
- ¼ cup (1 ounce) confectioners' sugar
- 1 large egg white, plus 1 large egg, lightly beaten with 1 tablespoon water

SHAPING CHOCOLATE BRIOCHE BUNS

1. Press plain dough into 6 by 6-inch square.

2. Spread chocolate filling over dough, leaving ¼-inch border.

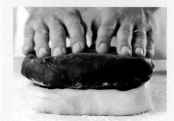

3. Press chocolate dough into 6 by 6-inch square. Place on top of filling and press gently to adhere. Cover loosely with greased plastic wrap and refrigerate for 30 minutes.

4. Press and roll dough into 12 by 16-inch rectangle with short side parallel to counter edge.

5. Starting at 1 short side, cut dough into twelve 16 by 1-inch strips.

6. Working with 1 dough strip at a time, tightly coil ends in opposite directions to form S shape.

1. **FOR THE DOUGH:** Whisk flour, yeast, and salt together in bowl of stand mixer. Whisk room-temperature water, eggs and yolk, and sugar together in 4-cup liquid measuring cup. Using dough hook on low speed, slowly add water mixture to flour mixture and mix until cohesive dough starts to form and no dry flour remains, about 2 minutes, scraping down bowl as needed.

2. Increase speed to medium-low; add butter, 1 piece at a time; and knead until butter is fully incorporated, about 4 minutes. Continue to knead until dough is smooth and elastic and clears sides of bowl, 11 to 13 minutes longer.

3. Transfer dough to lightly floured counter and divide in half. Knead half of dough by hand to form smooth, round ball, about 30 seconds. Place dough seam side down in lightly greased large bowl or container. Return remaining half of dough to mixer, add cocoa, and knead on medium-low speed until cocoa is evenly incorporated, about 2 minutes. Transfer dough to lightly floured counter and knead by hand to form smooth, round ball, about 30 seconds. Place second dough ball seam side down in second lightly greased large bowl or container. Cover bowls tightly with plastic wrap and let rise at room temperature until increased in size by half, 45 minutes to 1 hour.

4. **FOR THE FILLING:** Microwave chocolate, butter, and cocoa in bowl at 50 percent power, stirring occasionally, until melted and smooth, about 2 minutes. Stir in sugar until combined and let cool completely, about 30 minutes. Whisk in egg white until fully combined and mixture turns glossy.

5. Line baking sheet with parchment paper and lightly flour parchment. Transfer plain dough seam side down to prepared sheet and press into 6 by 6-inch square. Spread filling over dough, leaving ¼-inch border. Press chocolate dough into 6 by 6-inch square on lightly floured counter. Place on top of filling and press gently to adhere. Cover loosely with greased plastic and refrigerate for 30 minutes.

6. Line 2 rimmed baking sheets with parchment paper. Transfer chilled dough square to lightly floured counter. Press and roll dough into 12 by 16-inch rectangle with short side parallel to counter edge. Using sharp pizza wheel or knife, starting at 1 short side, cut dough into twelve 16 by 1-inch strips. Working with 1 dough strip at a time, tightly coil ends of strips in opposite directions to form S shape. Arrange buns on prepared sheets, six per sheet, spaced about 2½ inches apart. Cover loosely with greased plastic and refrigerate for at least 2 hours or up to 24 hours.

7. One hour before baking, remove buns from refrigerator and let sit at room temperature. Adjust oven racks to upper-middle and lower-middle positions and heat oven to 350 degrees. Gently brush buns with egg wash and bake until golden brown, 18 to 22 minutes, switching and rotating sheets halfway through baking. Transfer buns to wire rack and let cool completely, about 30 minutes. Serve.

STROUD'S CINNAMON ROLLS

✓ WHY THIS RECIPE WORKS Unlike their spiraled cousins, these soft and fluffy rolls are coated, not filled, with a crunchy, buttery cinnamon sugar mixture. They're modeled after the dinner rolls at Stroud's Oak Ridge Manor House in Kansas City, Missouri. For our version, we used a yeasted dough enriched with milk, butter, and eggs for a pillowy, tender roll. After bringing the dough together in a stand mixer and letting it rise, we shaped individual rolls and rolled them in melted butter and cinnamon sugar to ensure an even coating and then let them rise once more in a baking dish. After baking them, we brushed them thickly with a cinnamon sugar butter for richness and crunch.

They may not be the image you conjure when you think of cinnamon rolls, but the rolls served at Stroud's Oak Ridge Manor use a similar buttery cinnamon sugar mixture as well as just enough salt to be noticeable. Instead of being swirled up inside, however, the mixture just coats the outside of the rolls. And unlike traditional cinnamon rolls, these are not covered in frosting—they're served with lunch or dinner alongside fried chicken.

In the test kitchen, I started with a yeasted dough from our archives. It produces a pillowy and lightly sweet roll that's enriched with butter, milk, and eggs—perfect for this application. I mixed the dough in a stand mixer and let it rise for an hour before portioning and rolling it into smaller dough balls.

For the good stuff, I stirred together melted butter, sugar, cinnamon, and salt. I poured some of this goo into the bottom of a baking dish, like they do at Stroud's, and then tucked my dough balls into the dish to let

STROUD'S CINNAMON ROLLS

them rise again. Topped with more goo and baked, the golden rolls smelled heavenly, but they were stickier than I wanted.

Rethinking the goo, I tried rolling individual dough balls in melted butter and cinnamon sugar to avoid the sugar collecting in empty spaces between the rolls. This batch was more promising, cleanly releasing from the dish with an even, sugary coating, but it was missing butteriness. The solution was easy: I brushed a second, smaller batch of the sugar-butter mixture onto the baked rolls while they were still hot from the oven. As they rested, the rolls absorbed buttery richness, and the extra sugar made the coating even more crunchy.

I wanted to have cinnamon rolls any time of day, so I made a batch through the sugar-rolling step and refrigerated it overnight. I baked the rolls the next morning, and they were indistinguishable from a same-day batch. So go ahead and make these for breakfast, too.

—JESSICA RUDOLPH, *Cook's Country*

Stroud's Cinnamon Rolls

MAKES 15 ROLLS

We developed this recipe using a 4½-quart stand mixer. If using a larger mixer, you may need to increase the mixing time after adding the butter in step 2 to about 10 minutes. If the dough doesn't come together in the mixer, switch to a paddle attachment and mix just until the dough comes together. Then switch back to the dough hook and keep kneading. Use an instant-read thermometer to make sure that the milk is the correct temperature. We developed this recipe using a ceramic baking dish. If you choose to use a metal baking pan, reduce the baking time to 20 minutes. The slight tackiness of the dough aids in rolling it into smooth balls in step 4, so do not dust your counter with flour.

DOUGH

- ½ cup plus 2 tablespoons warm milk (110 degrees)
- 1 large egg
- 2 cups plus 2 tablespoons (10⅝ ounces) all-purpose flour
- 1½ teaspoons instant or rapid-rise yeast
- 2 tablespoons sugar
- 1 teaspoon table salt
- 4 tablespoons unsalted butter, softened

COATING

- 1¼ cups (8¾ ounces) sugar
- 4 teaspoons ground cinnamon
- ½ teaspoon table salt
- 12 tablespoons unsalted butter, melted, divided

1. FOR THE DOUGH: Whisk milk and egg together in bowl of stand mixer. Add flour and yeast. Fit mixer with dough hook and mix on low speed until all flour is moistened, about 2 minutes, scraping down dough hook and sides of bowl as needed. Let stand for 15 minutes.

2. Add sugar and salt and mix on medium-low speed for 5 minutes. With mixer running, add butter, 1 tablespoon at a time. Continue to mix on medium-low speed 5 minutes longer, scraping down dough hook and bowl occasionally (dough will stick to bottom of bowl). Transfer dough to greased large bowl. Cover tightly with plastic wrap and let rise at room temperature until doubled in size, about 1 hour.

3. FOR THE COATING: Combine sugar, cinnamon, and salt in bowl. Reserve ¾ cup sugar mixture. Place remaining sugar mixture in shallow dish. Place 6 tablespoons melted butter in second shallow dish.

4. Grease 13 by 9-inch baking dish. Turn out dough onto counter and divide into fifteen 1⅓-ounce portions; divide any remaining dough evenly among portions. Working with 1 portion at a time, cup dough with your palm and roll against counter into smooth, tight ball.

5. Working with 3 or 4 dough balls at a time, roll dough balls in melted butter in shallow dish, then roll in cinnamon sugar in shallow dish. Place dough balls in prepared dish in 3 rows of five. Cover loosely with plastic and let rise at room temperature until doubled in size, about 1 hour (cinnamon sugar coating may crack during rising; this is OK). Adjust oven rack to middle position and heat oven to 350 degrees.

6. Bake until rolls are puffed and golden brown and register at least 200 degrees in center, about 25 minutes. Whisk reserved cinnamon sugar and remaining 6 tablespoons melted butter in bowl until combined (mixture may look separated). Brush tops and sides of hot rolls with cinnamon sugar–butter mixture (use all of it) and let cool in dish for 10 minutes. Remove rolls from dish and serve warm.

TO MAKE AHEAD: Before letting dough balls rise for second time in step 5, cover baking dish with plastic wrap and refrigerate for up to 24 hours. Let dough balls sit at room temperature for 1 hour before baking.

CRUMPETS

✓ **WHY THIS RECIPE WORKS** Crumpets—thick, yeasted rounds with moist, slightly elastic, honeycombed interiors and holes that cover the surface—can be hard to find in the United States, and homemade versions rarely live up to commercial products. Most home cooks don't own special crumpet rings to corral the batter, so instead we made three large crumpets in a small nonstick skillet and cut them into wedges to share. Combining all-purpose flour with bleached cake flour lowered the overall gluten content of our crumpet batter and the temperature at which it set, allowing the crumpets to cook through rapidly. Trading the conventional low-and-slow cooking method (which results in dense crumpets with few holes) for an initial blast of high heat quickly converted the water in the batter to steam; this expanded air bubbles already in the batter and powered their upward expansion before the crumpet had a chance to firm up, producing the proper spongy texture and holey appearance. Lowering the heat allowed the crumpets to cook through without burning on the bottom, and lifting a small amount of raw batter off the top of the crumpets before flipping them ensured that the maximum number of holes was preserved.

Ten years. That's how long I've been trying to make crumpets at home. When I lived in Scotland, I routinely bought packages of the thick, yeasted rounds at the grocery store, toasted them, and then slathered them with butter and jam or creamed honey. They reminded me of the English muffins I'd eaten growing up, but with their own charming features: exteriors that crisp up when toasted and moist, slightly elastic interiors full of deep holes that capture anything spread across them.

Making my own crumpets seemed logical when I moved back to the United States and realized that they're not nearly as available. Plus, I figured homemade specimens would easily outclass the commercial ones. But even after trying no less than 15 recipes, I hadn't made a single crumpet as good as one from the supermarket. The biggest problem? Their holes didn't reach all the way to the top—and a crumpet without holes at the top is just a dense, yeasty, chewy pancake.

A holey honeycomb structure is a crumpet's defining feature, and I was determined to find a way to reproduce it. And while I was taking on that challenge, I decided I would also figure out a way to skip using crumpet rings so that everyone could make these treats at home.

I started by mixing flour, baking powder, yeast, and salt with warm water until I had a thick batter. The two leaveners work in tandem to create a crumpet's unique interior structure: Baking powder creates air bubbles when the batter is mixed, yeast causes the holes to expand when the batter rests, and both yeast and baking powder cause the holes to expand when the batter cooks.

I let the batter rest until it had doubled in volume, about 40 minutes. Following other recipes, I then added a little more water, though I didn't yet understand the purpose of this second addition except that it loosened up the now-thick batter. Then, instead of portioning the batter into 3- or 4-inch crumpet rings set in a skillet, I poured about a third of it into an 8-inch nonstick skillet that I'd lightly greased and heated over a low flame for about 5 minutes. I kept the heat down as the crumpets cooked; every recipe I'd read called for a low-and-slow approach. Subjecting the batter to at least 12 minutes of gentle heat allows it to cook all the way from bottom to top without burning the underside; plus, there is no need to flip the crumpet before the surface is dry, which would smear any uncooked batter into the holes.

This approach seemed promising: Bubbles rose to the top all over the crumpet and started to burst at the edges. But after about 10 minutes, the bubbles in the center stopped bursting and I found myself popping them with a toothpick. However, this extra effort was all for naught: The batter in the center was still quite loose, so the holes just filled in. Desperate to cook the batter on top, I flipped the crumpets, which just pushed batter into the few holes that had formed. I didn't know what was causing the failure, so I tweaked a whole host of variables. Nothing helped.

I'd dug deep when researching crumpet recipes, but I went back to look for anything that might explain why the center tunnels hadn't made it to the top. I even enlisted my colleagues for help. That's when *Cook's Illustrated* intern Claire Toliver handed me an obscure scientific paper she found online: D. L. Pyle's "Crumpet Structures: Experimental and Modelling Studies."

Contrary to everything I'd read, Pyle revealed that the biggest key to crumpets' unique structure is not low heat but actually very high heat. It causes the water in the batter to convert rapidly to steam, which quickly expands the carbon dioxide bubbles and powers their upward expansion before the batter has a chance to firm up. (Also, much of the carbon dioxide formed during the rising phase is dissolved in the liquid batter, and the heat forces that carbon dioxide out of solution.) Now I understood the purpose of that second addition of water: Because it doesn't have as much time to be absorbed by the flour, it provides "steam power" that facilitates the creation of the tunnels, giving the crumpets the appropriate light, spongy honeycomb structure. And according to the paper, crumpets should cook through in a mere 3 minutes, not 12.

With renewed hope, I mixed up the same formula, but this time I cranked the heat to high just after adding the batter. It was thrilling to watch bubbles rise to the surface and then break, leaving holes that remained open as the top dried out. But as soon as I smelled carbon and saw wisps of smoke emanating from the skillet—then lifted the crumpet to see its charred bottom—I knew I still had work to do.

Fortunately, I realized that the crumpets needed just a quick blast of heat to mostly establish the tunnels; Pyle's paper actually notes that roughly 75 percent of the structure is established within the first 30 seconds of cooking. So I reduced the heat to medium-low after the first 45 seconds of cooking to avoid burning. The only drawback: Without high heat continuing to dry out the batter, the surface of the crumpet remained raw and loose, obscuring the holes. But I came up with two clever fixes.

First, I replaced a portion of the all-purpose flour with cake flour. Because the latter is bleached, its starch granules are better able to absorb water, and they gel at a lower temperature and set sooner, so there was less raw batter left after cooking. Second, I removed the teaspoon or two of residual raw batter by lifting it off with the back of a flat spatula, revealing the holes beneath, and then flipped the crumpet to thoroughly dry out the surface. (I returned the excess batter to the bowl for the next crumpet.)

Once they'd cooled, I cut the crumpets into wedges, toasted them, and then spread them with butter and jam. After 10 years, I'd found a way to make proper spongy, honeycombed crumpets. My own personal holey grail.

—ANDREA GEARY, *Cook's Illustrated*

Crumpets

SERVES 6 (MAKES 3 LARGE CRUMPETS)

Because the heavily leavened batter will continue to rise as you cook, we call for dividing it into thirds rather than measuring by volume. (The cooked crumpets will all be about the same size.) We developed this recipe on a gas stovetop, which is very responsive. If you're using an electric stovetop, use two burners: Heat the skillet on one burner set to low for 5 minutes, and then increase the heat to medium for 1 minute before adding the batter and set the second burner to high. Move the skillet between the medium and high burners for the appropriate heat level. A digital timer is helpful for this recipe.

NOTES FROM THE TEST KITCHEN

WHAT EXACTLY IS A CRUMPET?
Crumpets and English muffins are often mistaken for one another, but they have distinct features.

ENGLISH MUFFIN
Smooth top and bottom; split before toasting to dry out and crisp interior nooks and crannies

CRUMPET
Holey top; smooth bottom; spongy and honeycombed interior; toasted whole to crisp up exterior

1 cup (5 ounces) all-purpose flour

1 cup (4 ounces) bleached cake flour

2 teaspoons instant or rapid-rise yeast

¾ teaspoon baking powder

½ teaspoon table salt

1½ cups warm water (105 to 110 degrees), divided

½ teaspoon vegetable oil

Salted butter and jam or creamed honey

1. Whisk all-purpose flour, cake flour, yeast, baking powder, and salt together in 8-cup liquid measuring cup. Add 1¼ cups warm water and whisk until smooth. Cover and let rise in warm place until doubled in volume, about 40 minutes.

2. Heat oil in 8-inch nonstick skillet over low heat for at least 5 minutes. While skillet heats, add remaining ¼ cup warm water to batter and whisk until smooth.

3. Increase heat to medium and heat skillet for 1 minute. Using paper towel, wipe out skillet, leaving thin film of oil on bottom and sides. Pour one-third of batter into skillet and increase heat to high. Cook for 45 seconds (bubbles will be visible just under surface of entire crumpet). Reduce heat to medium-low and continue to cook until edges are risen, set, and beginning to dry out, about 4 minutes longer. (Gently lift edge and peek at underside of crumpet occasionally; reduce heat if underside is getting too dark, and increase heat if underside doesn't appear to be browning.)

4. Slide skillet off heat. Place dry, flat spatula on top of crumpet and pull up sharply to remove excess batter and reveal holes. Scrape excess batter from spatula back into measuring cup. Repeat procedure until holes are exposed over entire surface. Flip crumpet, return skillet to burner, increase heat to high, and cook until edges of second side are lightly browned, 1 to 2 minutes. Invert crumpet onto wire rack. Immediately add half of remaining batter to skillet. Return skillet to high heat and repeat cooking process (omitting 5-minute preheat). Repeat with remaining batter. Let crumpets cool completely.

5. To serve, cut each crumpet into 4 wedges and toast until crumpets are heated through and exteriors are crisp. Spread crumpets generously with butter and jam and serve. (Untoasted crumpets can be transferred to zipper-lock bag and refrigerated for up to 1 week or frozen for up to 1 month.)

YEASTED DOUGHNUTS

✔ **WHY THIS RECIPE WORKS** Our yeasted doughnuts are moist but light, with a tender chew and restrained sweetness, thanks to a careful balance of fat, sugar, and moisture in the dough. We chilled the dough overnight—a step called cold fermentation—so that it was faster to make the doughnuts in the morning. The dough also developed more complex flavor and was easier to handle when cold. Shutting the cut doughnuts in the oven with a loaf pan of boiling water—a makeshift baker's proof box—encouraged them to rise quickly. We then briefly fried them on both sides in moderately hot oil until they turned golden brown. We dipped them in a fluid confectioners' sugar-based glaze, which set into a sheer, matte shell.

The best doughnuts are the freshest doughnuts, and the freshest doughnuts are the ones you make yourself.

That's true for all doughnuts but especially true for yeasted doughnuts. When you bite into one that's freshly fried, the soft, gently elastic dough yields in a way that feels satisfying and indulgent even before you taste just how buttery it is, and the glossy glaze dissolves in your mouth without a trace of graininess. Those ephemeral qualities won't just satiate your craving for sweets; they'll delight you—and ruin your taste for anything that's more than a few hours out of the oil.

That's what happened to me, and it's why I spent the better part of two months sweating over my formula for my ideal yeasted doughnuts. I rolled, cut, and fried my way through cloyingly rich doughs and leaner ones with bready chew; battled gas bubbles that made the doughnuts puff up—and deflate—like balloons; and learned that the pale ring that forms around the doughnut's midsection is a sign of a properly risen, light doughnut. The results—as iconic as what you'd get from the best doughnut shop, but fresher—were worth it. Plus, knowing that I can churn out pro-caliber sweets has been so empowering that I've since wondered, as Homer Simpson famously did, if there's anything doughnuts can't do.

Yeasted doughnuts are made from bread dough enriched with fat, sugar, and dairy. You stir together flour, sugar, and yeast in a stand mixer; moisten the dry ingredients with milk or water and eggs and mix to form

CRUMPETS

a cohesive mass; work in salt and softened butter (waiting to add the salt and fat allows plenty of gluten to develop); and knead until the mixture forms a satiny dough. Then you let it rise for as little as 1 hour or as long as overnight, roll it out to about ½ inch thick, cut out rings (or rounds, if you're filling them), let them rise again, and deep-fry them. Last comes the sweet part: glazing or frosting them and then filling them with jam or cream if desired.

The trick was calibrating how enriched the dough should be to produce moist doughnuts with light chew and restrained sweetness. Getting it right was largely a question of how much fat, sugar, and water I added in relation to the flour, so I started by making doughnuts from four classic doughs that span a range of richness and sweetness: brioche; challah; American sandwich bread; and the plush, feathery Japanese milk bread called shokupan, which contains more fat and gluten than ordinary sandwich bread.

Butter made up nearly half the brioche dough, which explained why its doughnuts fried up heavy. The leaner, lower-hydration challah and sandwich formulas were dry. The moderately rich, relatively wet milk bread dough yielded moist, airy doughnuts, but their crumb was too chewy. And when I fried them, the air bubbles left gaping holes between the crust and crumb.

Making more-tender doughnuts was simply a matter of minimizing gluten development: I switched from bread flour to all-purpose, which contains fewer gluten-forming proteins, and boosted the sweetness and fat in the dough (both of which interfere with gluten development) by adding a bit more granulated sugar and using all milk instead of a combination of milk and water. And I did away with the big gas bubbles by slightly lowering the dough's hydration: Less liquid made the crumb tighter, so the gas bubbles that formed during fermentation couldn't grow big and make the crumb coarse. Ultimately, I landed on a formula that made a drier dough but doughnuts that were still moist and tender.

Before glazing, frosting, and filling the doughnuts, I thought about how the timing of the first and second rises affected when the doughnuts would be ready to eat. If I wanted them for breakfast, I didn't want to spend the better part of the morning waiting for the dough to rise, so I mixed up more dough, let it rise at room temperature for an hour (to jump-start yeast activity, which would slow down in the fridge), and refrigerated it overnight. This cold fermentation step built more convenient timing into the recipe and allowed the dough to develop more complex flavor and its gluten to relax so that it was pliable. I easily rolled out the chilled dough into a 10 by 13-inch rectangle and then stamped out 12 rings with 3- and 1-inch cutters.

The drawback to working with chilled dough was that the doughnuts took 2 hours to rise at room temperature, so I sped up the process by setting up a loaf pan with boiling water on the bottom rack of my oven and the doughnuts and their holes (set on a baking sheet lined with parchment paper) on the middle rack. In the steamy environment, the doughnuts puffed up in about 45 minutes.

During that time, I heated 2 quarts of oil to 360 degrees in a roomy Dutch oven (a wok would also work well), where I could fry four doughnuts at a time. When I placed them in the oil, the rings floated calmly like inner tubes—no messy splatter—for about 60 to 90 seconds per side. I fished them out when they were golden brown, with pale rings around their midsections—a visual cue that the dough had risen properly and expanded evenly during frying—and transferred them to a rack to cool slightly while I mixed up the glaze.

Confectioners' sugar and hot water produced a thin, opaque fluid that dried sheer; those ingredients also made a satiny base for my chocolate frosting. As an homage to Homer Simpson himself, I made a vivid magenta raspberry frosting and topped it with rainbow sprinkles. I also made some jelly doughnuts because, well, why not?

The kitchen looked like a proper doughnut shop: pillowy rings, rounds, and holes embellished in sweet, colorful ways. Making and eating them made me feel like a pro—and so happy.

—ANNIE PETITO, *Cook's Illustrated*

Yeasted Doughnuts

MAKES 12 DOUGHNUTS

You'll need two large baking sheets and two wire racks for this recipe. You'll also need 3-inch and 1-inch round cutters. For the best results, weigh the flour for the doughnuts and the confectioners' sugar for the glaze. Heating the oil slowly will make it easier to control the temperature when frying. Use a Dutch oven that holds 6 quarts or more. You can omit the glaze and frost the doughnuts with our Chocolate Frosting or Raspberry Frosting (page 193).

DOUGHNUTS

4½ cups (22½ ounces) all-purpose flour

½ cup (3½ ounces) granulated sugar

1 teaspoon instant or rapid-rise yeast

1½ cups milk

1 large egg

1½ teaspoons table salt

8 tablespoons unsalted butter, cut into ½-inch pieces and softened

2 quarts vegetable oil for frying

GLAZE

3¼ cups (13 ounces) confectioners' sugar

½ cup hot water

Pinch table salt

1. FOR THE DOUGHNUTS: Stir flour, sugar, and yeast together in bowl of stand mixer. Add milk and egg and mix with rubber spatula until all ingredients are moistened. Fit mixer with dough hook and mix on medium-low speed until cohesive mass forms, about 2 minutes, scraping down bowl if necessary. Cover bowl with plastic wrap and let stand for 20 minutes.

2. Add salt and mix on medium-low speed until dough is smooth and elastic and clears sides of bowl, 5 to 7 minutes. With mixer running, add butter, few pieces at a time, and continue to mix until butter is fully incorporated and dough is smooth and elastic and clears sides of bowl, 7 to 13 minutes longer, scraping down bowl halfway through mixing. Transfer dough to lightly greased large bowl, flip dough, and form into ball. Cover bowl with plastic. Let sit at room temperature for 1 hour. Transfer to refrigerator and chill overnight (or up to 2 days).

3. Adjust oven racks to lowest and middle positions. Place loaf pan on lower rack. Line rimmed baking sheet with parchment paper and grease parchment. Transfer dough to lightly floured counter. Press into 8-inch square of even thickness, expelling as much air as possible. Roll dough into 10 by 13-inch rectangle, about ½ inch thick. Using 3-inch round cutter dipped in flour, cut 12 rounds. Using 1-inch round cutter dipped in flour, cut hole out of center of each round. Transfer doughnuts and holes to prepared sheet. (If desired, use 1-inch cutter to cut small rounds from remaining dough. Transfer to sheet with doughnuts.) Bring kettle or small saucepan of water to boil.

4. Pour 1 cup boiling water into loaf pan. Place sheet on upper rack, uncovered. Close oven and allow doughnuts to rise until dough increases in height by 50 percent and springs back very slowly when pressed with your knuckle, 45 minutes to 1 hour.

NOTES FROM THE TEST KITCHEN

HOW TO MAKE THE DOUGHNUTS
After letting the dough rise overnight, you can have fresh, pro-caliber doughnuts on the table in time for breakfast.

1. Roll dough into 10 by 13-inch, ½-inch-thick rectangle.

2. Cut 12 rounds and holes using 3- and 1-inch cutters.

3. Let rise until dough slowly springs back when pressed.

4. Fry in 360-degree oil until golden brown; flip and repeat.

5. Dip in glaze and let stand on wire rack until dry.

YEASTED DOUGHNUTS WITH CHOCOLATE FROSTING

5. FOR THE GLAZE: Whisk sugar, hot water, and salt in medium bowl until smooth.

6. About 20 minutes before end of rising time, add oil to large Dutch oven until it measures about 1½ inches deep and heat over medium-low heat to 360 degrees. Set wire rack in second rimmed baking sheet and line with triple layer of paper towels. Using both your hands, gently place 4 risen doughnuts in oil. Cook until golden brown on undersides, 1 to 1½ minutes, adjusting burner as necessary to maintain oil temperature between 350 and 365 degrees. Using spider skimmer, flip doughnuts and cook until second sides are browned, 1 to 1½ minutes. Transfer doughnuts to prepared rack. Return oil to 360 degrees and repeat twice with remaining doughnuts. For doughnut holes, transfer all to oil and stir gently and constantly until golden brown, about 2 minutes. Transfer to prepared rack to cool. Let doughnuts sit until cool enough to handle, at least 5 minutes.

7. Set clean wire rack in now-empty sheet. Working with 1 doughnut at a time, dip both sides of doughnut in glaze, allowing excess to drip back into bowl. Place on unlined rack. Repeat with doughnut holes. Let doughnuts and holes stand until glaze has become slightly matte and dry to touch, 15 to 30 minutes, before serving.

Chocolate Frosting

MAKES 1½ CUPS

If the frosting stiffens before you use it, microwave it at 50 percent power, stirring every 30 seconds, until smooth and fluid. This frosting can be made up to 2 days in advance. To frost the doughnuts, dip the top half of one cooled doughnut at a time into the frosting until it is evenly coated, allowing the excess to drip back into the bowl. Invert the doughnut and place it on a wire rack. Top the doughnuts with rainbow sprinkles, if desired; let them stand until the frosting has become slightly matte and is dry to the touch, 15 to 30 minutes, before serving.

- 4 ounces bittersweet chocolate, chopped fine
- ½ cup water
- 2 cups (8 ounces) confectioners' sugar
- 2 tablespoons unsweetened cocoa powder
   Pinch table salt

Microwave chocolate and water in medium bowl at 50 percent power until chocolate is melted, about 30 seconds. Whisk in sugar, cocoa, and salt until smooth and fluid. Let cool slightly before using.

Raspberry Frosting

MAKES 1 CUP

If the frosting stiffens before you use it, add hot water, 1 teaspoon at a time, until the frosting is thick but fluid. To frost the doughnuts, dip the top half of one cooled doughnut at a time into the frosting until it is evenly coated, allowing the excess to drip back into the bowl. Invert the doughnut and place it on a wire rack. Top the doughnuts with rainbow sprinkles, if desired; let them stand until the frosting has become slightly matte and is dry to the touch, 15 to 30 minutes, before serving.

- 8 ounces (1⅔ cups) frozen raspberries, thawed
- 2 cups (8 ounces) confectioners' sugar
   Pinch table salt

Process raspberries in blender until smooth. Strain puree through fine-mesh strainer into bowl or measuring cup. Measure out 6 tablespoons puree for frosting (reserve remaining puree for another use). In medium bowl, whisk sugar, salt, and puree until smooth.

Jelly Doughnuts

MAKES 12 DOUGHNUTS

You'll need two large baking sheets and one wire rack for this recipe. You'll also need a 3-inch round cutter and a ¼-inch round pastry tip. For the best results, weigh the flour for the doughnuts. Heating the oil slowly will make it easier to control the temperature when frying. Use a Dutch oven that holds 6 quarts or more.

DOUGHNUTS

- 4½ cups (22½ ounces) all-purpose flour
- ½ cup (3½ ounces) sugar
- 1 teaspoon instant or rapid-rise yeast
- 1½ cups milk
- 1 large egg
- 1½ teaspoons table salt
- 8 tablespoons unsalted butter, cut into ½-inch cubes and softened
- 2 quarts vegetable oil for frying

FILLING AND COATING

1 cup (7 ounces) sugar

1½ cups seedless raspberry jam

1. FOR THE DOUGHNUTS: Stir flour, sugar, and yeast together in bowl of stand mixer. Add milk and egg and mix with rubber spatula until all ingredients are moistened. Fit mixer with dough hook and mix on medium-low speed until cohesive mass forms, about 2 minutes, scraping down bowl if necessary. Cover bowl with plastic wrap and let stand for 20 minutes.

2. Add salt and mix on medium-low speed until dough is smooth and elastic and clears sides of bowl, 5 to 7 minutes. With mixer running, add butter, few pieces at a time, and continue to mix until butter is fully incorporated and dough is smooth and elastic and clears sides of bowl, 7 to 13 minutes longer, scraping down bowl halfway through mixing. Transfer dough to lightly greased large bowl, flip dough, and form into ball. Cover bowl with plastic. Let sit at room temperature for 1 hour. Transfer to refrigerator and chill overnight (or up to 2 days).

3. Adjust oven racks to lowest and middle position. Place loaf pan on lower rack. Line rimmed baking sheet with parchment paper and grease parchment. Transfer dough to lightly floured counter. Press into 8-inch square of even thickness, expelling as much air as possible. Roll dough into 10 by 13-inch rectangle, about ½ inch thick. Using 3-inch round cutter dipped in flour, cut 12 rounds. Transfer doughnuts to prepared sheet. Bring kettle or small saucepan of water to boil.

4. Pour 1 cup boiling water into loaf pan. Place sheet on upper rack, uncovered. Close oven and allow doughnuts to rise until dough increases in height by 50 percent and springs back very slowly when pressed with your knuckle, about 1 hour.

5. About 20 minutes before end of rising time, add oil to large Dutch oven until it measures about 1½ inches deep and heat over medium-low heat to 330 degrees. Set wire rack in second rimmed baking sheet and line with triple layer of paper towels. Using both your hands, gently place 4 risen doughnuts in oil. Cook until golden brown on undersides, 1½ to 2 minutes, adjusting burner as necessary to maintain oil temperature between 325 and 340 degrees. Using spider skimmer, flip doughnuts and cook until second sides are browned, 1½ to 2 minutes. Transfer doughnuts to prepared rack. Repeat with remaining doughnuts. Let cool completely, about 20 minutes.

6. FOR THE FILLING AND COATING: Place sugar in small bowl. Spoon jam into pastry bag or zipper-lock bag fitted with ¼-inch round pastry tip.

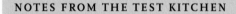

NOTES FROM THE TEST KITCHEN

HOW WE RAISED THE DOUGH(NUT)

Enriched, fried, and coated in sugar, yeasted doughnuts are fundamentally decadent. But thanks to ample—not excessive—richness and sweetness, plus proper rising, our dough fries up plush but light, with tender chew, and is just the right canvas for glazing, frosting, or filling.

1. SOFT, MOIST CRUMB
A careful balance of fat, sugar, and liquid produced tender doughnuts with delicate chew.

2. THIN, GOLDEN CRUST
Fried in moderately hot oil for about a minute per side, the dough's exterior sets and browns just enough.

3. "MIDRIFF"
The pale belt that forms around the dough's midsection during frying shows that the crumb is airy and expanded evenly.

7. Working with 1 doughnut at a time, coat all sides of doughnut in sugar and return to rack. Insert paring knife through side of 1 doughnut until tip almost reaches opposite edge. Swing knife through doughnut, creating large pocket. Repeat with remaining doughnuts. Stand doughnuts slit side up in 13 by 9-inch baking pan.

8. To fill doughnuts, insert pastry tip ¾ inch into opening and squeeze gently until jam just starts to appear around opening, about 2 tablespoons jam per doughnut. Let doughnuts stand in pan for 10 minutes to allow jam to settle. Serve.

APPLE CIDER DOUGHNUTS

✔ **WHY THIS RECIPE WORKS** These sweet treats are a must-have when visiting apple orchards in the fall. But far too often the apple flavor is lost. For our homemade version, we were able to cut out the time-consuming step of boiling cider by simply stirring tart, intensely flavorful apple juice concentrate right into the dough. A slightly higher ratio of flour to liquid ingredients helped us control the dough's wetness without refrigerating it for hours to tighten it up. Using acidic buttermilk activated the leaveners and gave the doughnuts extra lift and lightness. A bit of cinnamon and nutmeg provided the right fall flavors to complement the doughnuts' sweetness. After frying them, we gave our old-fashioned doughnuts a quick toss in cinnamon sugar seasoned with a touch of salt to add a final layer of flavor and a sugary crunch.

The air gets sweeter as you walk through the dirt lot toward the apple orchard in fall. It's the aroma of hot apple cider doughnuts straight from the fryer: warm and spicy. But these treats can be a bait and switch, promising apple flavor but rarely delivering it. I challenged myself to make a home version that packed in a ton of apple flavor. Believe it or not, it can be done!

After researching existing recipes, I gathered the basics: flour, sugar, eggs, butter, and milk. I needed a formula that would yield doughnuts with a rich flavor, tender interior, and lightly crunchy exterior. I settled on 2½ cups of flour, one egg, and ¾ cup of milk for richness and moisture. Four tablespoons of melted, cooled butter gave me plenty of butter flavor and a workable dough.

Leavening came next. I started with both baking powder and baking soda, a combination we've found makes for fluffy doughnuts in other recipes. However, without any acid to activate the baking soda, my doughnuts never puffed up while they cooked. Swapping acidic buttermilk for the milk unleashed the power of the baking soda while also adding a bit of tang.

I had light, tender doughnuts, but I still needed apple flavor. I tried adding store-bought apple cider, boiled cider (reduced for strong flavor), and even shredded apple, but my tasters were disappointed. I needed a new idea.

That was when a colleague mentioned apple juice concentrate. It provided intense apple flavor—no cooking required. I replaced some of the buttermilk with thawed apple juice concentrate to balance the wet and dry ratios and crossed my fingers.

A quick run through with my round cutters and my doughnuts were ready to fry. When the doughnuts were deep golden brown, I removed them from the oil and tossed them in cinnamon sugar. The sweet apple flavor came through in every bite.

—ALLI BERKEY, *Cook's Country*

Apple Cider Doughnuts

MAKES 12 DOUGHNUTS AND 12 DOUGHNUT HOLES

Use a Dutch oven that holds 6 quarts or more for this recipe. You will need 3-inch and 1-inch round cutters.

COATING

- ½ cup (3½ ounces) sugar
- ⅛ teaspoon ground cinnamon
-    Pinch table salt

DOUGHNUTS

- 2½ cups (12½ ounces) all-purpose flour
- 1 teaspoon baking powder
- ½ teaspoon baking soda
- ½ teaspoon ground cinnamon
- ¼ teaspoon ground nutmeg
- ¼ teaspoon table salt
- ½ cup thawed apple juice concentrate
- ⅓ cup (2⅓ ounces) sugar
- ¼ cup buttermilk
- 4 tablespoons unsalted butter, melted and cooled
- 1 large egg
- 2 quarts vegetable oil for frying

1. **FOR THE COATING:** Whisk sugar, cinnamon, and salt together in medium bowl; set aside.

2. **FOR THE DOUGHNUTS:** Whisk flour, baking powder, baking soda, cinnamon, nutmeg, and salt together in bowl. Whisk apple juice concentrate, sugar, buttermilk, melted butter, and egg together in large bowl. Whisk half of flour mixture into apple juice concentrate mixture until smooth. Add remaining flour mixture; using rubber spatula, use folding motion to mix and press dough until all flour is hydrated and no dry bits remain. (Dough can be covered with plastic wrap and refrigerated for up to 24 hours.)

3. Dust counter heavily with flour. Turn out dough onto floured counter, then dust top of dough with additional flour. Using your floured hands, gently pat dough into 1/3-inch-thick round, 10 to 11 inches in diameter. Using floured 3-inch round cutter, cut out 9 to 10 doughnut rounds. Using 1-inch round cutter, cut hole in center of each round.

4. Lightly dust rimmed baking sheet with flour. Transfer doughnut rounds and holes to prepared sheet. Combine dough scraps, then knead into cohesive ball and pat into 1/3-inch-thick round. Cut out 2 or 3 more doughnut rounds and holes (you should have 12 of each). Transfer to sheet and refrigerate while heating oil.

5. Set wire rack in second rimmed baking sheet and line half of rack with triple layer of paper towels. Add oil to large Dutch oven until it measures about 1½ inches deep and heat over medium-high heat to 350 degrees. Add 6 doughnut rounds and cook, flipping every 30 seconds, until deep golden brown, about 2 minutes. Adjust burner as needed to maintain oil temperature between 325 and 350 degrees.

6. Using spider skimmer or slotted spoon, transfer doughnuts to paper towel–lined side of prepared rack and let sit while frying remaining doughnut rounds. Return oil to 350 degrees and repeat with remaining doughnut rounds.

7. Return oil to 350 degrees and, using spider skimmer or slotted spoon, carefully add doughnut holes to hot oil. Cook, stirring often, until deep golden brown, about 2 minutes. Transfer to paper towel–lined side of wire rack. Lightly toss doughnuts and doughnut holes in coating and transfer to unlined side of wire rack. Serve.

ITALIAN FLATBREADS (PIADINE)

✔ **WHY THIS RECIPE WORKS** For chewy-tender flatbreads with an open crumb, we added baking powder to the dough, as well as ample amounts of fat and water that diluted the gluten strands, keeping the dough soft and pliable without making it too rich. Rolling the dough into 9-inch rounds made for substantial breads that fit perfectly in the cast-iron pan, which we preheated thoroughly so that they would brown quickly without drying out.

Making bread, whether it's crusty baguettes or plush, buttery brioche, is incredibly rewarding. But it almost always takes a long time—and, depending on the loaf, a lot of finesse.

That's why I love making flatbreads. With little to no yeast, these thin, rustic rounds come together fast and cook up even faster, sometimes right on the stovetop. And piadina, the centuries-old Italian flatbread, might be the easiest and fastest to make of all.

Originally from the northern region of Emilia-Romagna but now popular all over Italy, piadina ("little plate") delivers a moist, tender chew that falls somewhere between the texture of a flour tortilla and that of an unpuffed pita. Traditionally, the dough was made from flour, salt, lard (Emilia-Romagna is pig country), and water, and the breads were baked on earthenware disks over an open fire. Contemporary recipes often call for leavening the dough with baking powder and cooking the rounds in a cast-iron skillet on the stovetop, but the process is just as quick (about an hour) and straightforward: Mix the ingredients to form a smooth dough, let it rest briefly, roll it into disks, poke them with a fork to prevent puffing, cook them until spotty brown on both sides, and eat them warm—usually folded around sandwich fillings such as meats, cheeses, greens, or spreadable sweets such as Nutella or ricotta with honey.

A few ingredients, an hour's work, and endless versatility? No wonder this bread enjoys a cultlike following (it has even been the subject of poetic verse). I could feel myself joining in the fervor even before I started cooking.

ITALIAN FLATBREADS (PIADINE)

The first decision I wanted to make was whether to include baking powder, since that would significantly affect the texture of the bread.

I mixed two batches of dough in the food processor, adding ¾ teaspoon of baking powder to one batch along with the flour and salt. Then I worked ⅓ cup of lard into each, followed by a slow stream of water that transformed the mixture into a soft dough. I shaped each batch into four balls, covered them with plastic wrap, and let them sit for 30 minutes so that the gluten would relax and make rolling them out easier. I then rolled them into 10-inch disks (a common size), poked them, and cooked one from each batch in a preheated 12-inch cast-iron skillet.

Both breads were tender and a bit too rich thanks to all that fat in the dough. But the leavened crumb was softer and more open, preferred to that of the denser unleavened piadina. The baking powder was in, and going forward I also rolled each round to 9 inches in diameter, which helped the rounds sit flat in the skillet (the actual cooking surface of a 12-inch skillet can be less than 10 inches, so a 9-inch round just fits).

Before decreasing the amount of fat in the dough, I wanted to know if the lard was contributing something unique that other, more conventional fats didn't offer.

I set up a four-way test of doughs made with lard, butter, and vegetable and olive oils, and it was immediately clear that there was neither a flavor nor a texture benefit to the lard. (Meanwhile, the flavors of butter and olive oil were too distinct.) The fact that there was no textural benefit was surprising, since swapping a saturated fat (such as lard) for an unsaturated fat (such as vegetable oil) can lead to disastrous results in some applications (such as pie dough or flaky biscuits). But here, with a lower ratio of fat to flour in the dough, it didn't matter, so I opted for pantry-friendly vegetable oil.

From there, I made a batch of lean breads with just 2 tablespoons of vegetable oil, but they were dry and tough, so I went up to 3 tablespoons, figuring that would restore the crumb's tenderness. But even then the bread was dry, so I stuck with 3 tablespoons of oil and increased the water. Without making the bread too sticky to handle, the extra liquid hydrated the dough and made it less dense so that the piadine were softer and more flexible but retained just enough chew.

The piadine were great (especially when warm; their softness and pliability are ephemeral) and almost ready for fillings, except that they tended to char in spots instead of brown attractively. I'd been preheating my cast-iron skillet over a strong flame, so I ran a couple of lower-heat tests and found that moderate heat was the way to go; turning the burner to low caused the breads to dry out before they had a chance to brown.

I kept the breads folded in half under a clean dish towel so that they held their heat and their shape (think "training" a rolled cake), which made them easy to fill with thin slices of rich, salty cured meats; cheeses; or vegetables and tidy to eat as sandwiches. And, frankly, the filling possibilities were endless (see "Get Your Fill[ing]" for our favorites).

You don't have to fill them, though. Who doesn't love a swath of plush, fresh bread alongside a bowl of soup? Or a salad. Scrambled eggs. Soft cheese. Creamy dips. The list goes on. And since you can basically make piadine on a whim, you should.

—ANNIE PETITO, *Cook's Illustrated*

Italian Flatbreads (Piadine)

MAKES 4 FLATBREADS

We use pantry-friendly vegetable oil because the flatbreads it makes are similar in flavor and texture to those made with traditional lard. If you'd prefer to use lard, increase the amount to ¼ cup to account for its lower density. Do not substitute butter or olive oil; their flavors are obtrusive here. A nonstick skillet can be used in place of cast iron; increase the heat to medium-high and preheat the empty skillet with ½ teaspoon of oil until shimmering; wipe out the oil before proceeding with the recipe.

- 2 cups (10 ounces) all-purpose flour
- ¾ teaspoon baking powder
- ½ teaspoon table salt
- 3 tablespoons vegetable oil
- ¾ cup water

1. Process flour, baking powder, and salt in food processor until combined, about 5 seconds. Add oil and process until no visible bits of fat remain, about 10 seconds. With processor running, slowly add water; process until most of dough forms soft, slightly tacky ball that clears sides of workbowl, 30 to 60 seconds (there may be small bits of loose dough).

2. Transfer dough to counter and gently knead until smooth, about 15 seconds. Divide dough into 4 equal pieces and shape each into ball. Working with 1 dough ball at a time, place ball seam side down on clean counter and, using your cupped hand, drag in small circles until ball is taut and smooth. Cover dough balls loosely with plastic wrap. Let rest for 30 minutes.

3. Pat 1 dough ball into 5-inch disk on lightly floured counter (keep remaining dough balls covered). Roll disk into 9-inch round, flouring counter as needed to prevent sticking. Repeat with remaining dough balls.

4. Heat 12-inch cast-iron skillet over medium heat until drop of water dripped onto surface sizzles immediately, about 3 minutes. Prick 1 dough round all over with fork, then carefully place in skillet. Cook until underside is spotty brown, 1 to 2 minutes, using fork to pop any large bubbles that form. Flip round and cook until second side is spotty brown, 1 to 2 minutes (flatbread should still be pliable). Transfer piadina to plate, gently fold in half, and cover with clean dish towel to keep warm. Repeat with remaining dough rounds, stacking piadine and re-covering with towel as they finish. Serve warm. (Piadine can be stored in zipper-lock bag for up to 2 days. Reheat in cast-iron skillet over medium-high heat for 20 to 30 seconds per side, until warmed through.)

NOTES FROM THE TEST KITCHEN

GET YOUR FILL(ING)
The flatbreads are an excellent accompaniment to any dish that pairs well with fresh bread, but they're tailor-made for folding around a flavorful filling—sweet or savory. A few of our favorite combinations are salami, fontina, and artichoke hearts; roasted red peppers, balsamic vinegar, arugula, and ricotta; and tomato, mozzarella, basil, and olive oil. But use your imagination.

MEATS	Salami, mortadella, prosciutto, 'nduja (spreadable sausage), bresaola
GREENS	Arugula, basil, sautéed greens (broccoli rabe, spinach, chard)
CHEESES	Ricotta, mozzarella, stracchino or goat cheese, fontina, mascarpone
VEGETABLES	Artichoke hearts, roasted red peppers, tomatoes
SWEETS	Nutella (with mascarpone), honey (with ricotta)

BRIOCHE BUNS AND MORE

WHY THIS RECIPE WORKS We wanted glossy, amber-colored brioche with its signature paper-thin crust; buttery flavor; and impossibly soft, feathery interior. To build structure in this butter-laden dough (which can be difficult since fat shortens the sturdy gluten strands), we used bread flour, which contains more protein than all-purpose flour does and thus develops gluten more readily. We mixed together the flour, yeast, water, and eggs and let the dough rest before adding the sugar, salt, and butter; since sugar and salt slow hydration, withholding them helped the flour fully hydrate, a necessary step for maximum gluten formation. We then added softened butter 1 tablespoon at a time so that the gluten had time to develop between additions. Another 10 minutes of kneading finished building the dough's structure. Simply cupping and rolling portions of the risen dough against the counter pulled the dough into taut balls that, when pressed with the bottom of a measuring cup, baked into the perfect-size hamburger buns.

Brioche, the classic French bread enriched with plenty of butter and eggs, is perfect as a hamburger bun, dinner roll, or sandwich bread. Its paper-thin, amber crust; dairy-sweet flavor; impossibly soft interior; and buttery aroma make it the gold standard in bread, no matter the format. I wanted to achieve this standard by employing a straightforward method that even novice bakers could use to make brioche buns, rolls, or loaves.

I started with buns. Hamburger buns are usually made from a lean sandwich bread dough; I found a recipe for 12 buns that called for just one egg and a little butter. The buns get their structure from kneading in a stand mixer for about 5 minutes—the kneading realigns the strands of gluten in the dough, creating a strong framework that supports the buns as they rise and bake. This also develops the buns' chew.

Brioche is made a bit differently. Since brioche dough has more eggs and lots more butter than sandwich bread dough does, it has a significantly higher ratio of fat to flour. Fat shortens gluten strands, inhibiting their formation. Because of that, the butter is kneaded into the dough gradually (1 tablespoon at a time) while the mixer is running so the gluten has enough time to develop between additions. Once the butter is fully incorporated, the dough must be kneaded for a long time to sufficiently develop its structure.

Some brioche recipes call for a full 45 minutes of extra kneading in the stand mixer, but I had a few tricks up my sleeve that I hoped would help minimize the kneading time. The first trick was to use bread flour instead of all-purpose flour. Because bread flour has more protein than all-purpose flour does, it more readily develops gluten, which I needed here due to all the fat in the dough. The second trick was a power nap. Let me explain.

With 3⅔ cups of bread flour and a full tablespoon of yeast in the mixer bowl (this dough required more than one packet of yeast—usually 2¼ teaspoons—to help it rise under the weight of all that fat), I mixed in water and eggs until a dough formed. I then stopped the mixer and let the dough sit before adding the sugar, salt, and butter. This resting time, known as autolyse, allowed the flour to fully hydrate, a necessary step for gluten formation. Both sugar and salt slow hydration, so withholding them for a bit helped the flour better absorb the liquid and thus promoted gluten development.

Now for the butter. Softened butter incorporated into the dough more easily than cold butter did; I found that 13 tablespoons was just enough to give the brioche a rich, buttery flavor while still keeping the texture light and airy. After 10 minutes of kneading, the dough was silky, supple, and elastic. It was ready to rise.

After the dough had risen for an hour on the counter, it was time to shape it into buns. I found that simply cupping and rolling each portion of dough against the counter pulled it into a taut ball. I then flattened each ball with the bottom of a dry measuring cup so that it would bake up into the perfect bun shape.

The silky, fluffy, feather-light chew of these burger buns was sturdy enough to hold up to a meaty, juicy burger without crumbling or sogging out. What's more, the versatile dough proved easy to shape into a pair of loaves (great for morning toast) or a big batch of dinner rolls. Choose your own baking adventure!

—CECELIA JENKINS, *Cook's Country*

Brioche Hamburger Buns

MAKES 12 BUNS

All-purpose flour can be substituted for the bread flour, but the buns won't be as tall; use the same amount of all-purpose flour by weight, not by volume.

3⅔ cups (20⅛ ounces) bread flour

1 tablespoon instant or rapid-rise yeast

1¼ cups (10 ounces) water, room temperature

2 large eggs, plus 1 large egg, lightly beaten

¼ cup (1¾ ounces) sugar

2½ teaspoons table salt

13 tablespoons unsalted butter, cut into 13 pieces and softened

1½ teaspoons sesame seeds (optional)

1. Whisk flour and yeast together in bowl of stand mixer, then add room-temperature water and 2 eggs. Fit mixer with dough hook and mix on low speed until dough comes together and no dry flour remains, about 2 minutes, scraping down bowl and dough hook frequently. Turn off mixer, cover bowl with dish towel or plastic wrap, and let dough stand for 15 minutes.

2. Add sugar and salt to dough and knead on medium-low speed until incorporated, about 30 seconds. Increase speed to medium and, with mixer running, add butter 1 piece at a time, allowing each piece to incorporate before adding next, about 3 minutes total, scraping down bowl and dough hook as needed. Continue to knead on medium speed until dough is elastic and pulls away cleanly from sides of bowl, about 10 minutes longer. Transfer dough to greased large bowl. Cover tightly with plastic and let rise at room temperature until doubled in size, about 1 hour.

3. Line 2 rimmed baking sheets with parchment paper. Turn out dough onto counter and divide dough into twelve 3-ounce portions; divide any remaining dough evenly among portions. Working with 1 dough portion at a time, cup dough with your palm and roll against counter into smooth, tight ball. Evenly space 6 dough balls on each prepared sheet. Using greased bottom of dry measuring cup, press dough balls to 3-inch diameter, about ¾ inch thick. Poke any air bubbles in dough balls with tip of paring knife.

4. Cover loosely with plastic and let rise at room temperature until doubled in size, about 1 hour. Adjust oven racks to upper-middle and lower-middle positions and heat oven to 350 degrees.

5. Discard plastic and brush tops and sides of dough balls with beaten egg (you do not need to use all of it). Sprinkle tops of dough balls with sesame seeds, if using.

6. Bake until buns are deep golden brown and register 205 to 210 degrees in center, 18 to 20 minutes, switching and rotating sheets halfway through baking.

Transfer sheets to wire racks and let cool completely, about 30 minutes. Serve. (Buns can be stored in zipper-lock bags at room temperature for up to 2 days or frozen for up to 1 month.)

TO MAKE AHEAD (BUNS): At end of step 4, refrigerate dough balls, still covered in plastic wrap, for up to 24 hours. Let dough balls sit at room temperature for 1 hour before proceeding with recipe.

VARIATIONS

Brioche Dinner Rolls

Omit sesame seeds. After first rise, divide dough into twenty-four 1½-ounce portions, dividing any remaining dough evenly among portions. Cup each dough portion with your palm and roll against counter into smooth, tight ball. Place in greased 13 by 9-inch baking pan in 4 rows of six. Cover with plastic wrap and let rise until doubled in size, about 1 hour. Adjust oven rack to middle position and heat oven to 350 degrees. Brush dough balls with beaten egg. Increase baking time to 25 minutes. Let rolls cool in pan for 15 minutes, then transfer to wire rack and brush with 1 tablespoon softened unsalted butter.

Brioche Sandwich Loaves

Omit sesame seeds. After first rise, divide dough into 2 equal pieces. Press each piece of dough into 8 by 5-inch rectangle with long side parallel to counter edge. Working with 1 piece of dough at a time, fold top edge of rectangle down to midline, pressing to seal. Fold bottom edge of rectangle up to midline and pinch to seal. Flip dough seam side down and gently push on ends to shape into 7 by 3-inch rectangle. Transfer loaves, seam side down, to 2 greased 8½ by 4½-inch loaf pans and pat gently to fill pans. Cover with plastic wrap and let rise until doubled in size, about 1 hour. Adjust oven rack to middle position and heat oven to 350 degrees. Brush loaves with beaten egg. Increase baking time to 32 minutes, switching and rotating pans halfway through baking. Let loaves cool in pans for 15 minutes. Remove loaves from pans and let cool completely on wire rack, about 1 hour.

TO MAKE AHEAD (ROLLS AND LOAVES): Before second rise, cover with plastic wrap and refrigerate for up to 24 hours. Let dough sit at room temperature for 2 hours before baking. Increase baking time by 5 minutes.

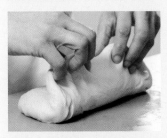

ADJARULI KHACHAPURI

✓ WHY THIS RECIPE WORKS Adjaruli khachapuri, a boat-shaped bread stuffed with melted cheese, hails from the country of Georgia in the Caucasus region of central Asia. When the bread is still hot from the oven, the molten cheese is topped with an egg and butter and stirred together tableside. Diners then tear off chunks of the crust to dunk into the gooey cheese. For our version, we used a simple pizza dough since it was easy to shape, provided structure to contain the oozy cheese, and had a satisfyingly chewy texture and mild flavor. We found that a mixture of mozzarella and feta approximated the briny, salty tang and stringy texture found in traditional Georgian cheeses such as sulguni and imeruli. Stirring in an egg yolk and a pat of butter right before serving kept the gooey cheese filling smooth and stretchy.

ADJARULI KHACHAPURI

Adjaruli khachapuri, originally from the country of Georgia, is more common stateside than ever. It's showing up in restaurants, on social media, and on trend lists. It's not hard to see why: Khachapuri—essentially bread filled with melty cheese—is like a cross between deep-dish pizza and cheese fondue. And then some.

There are several distinct styles; the shape I chose to work with is similar to a flattened football. When filled with a pool of molten cheese and topped with an egg and butter, which are stirred in before serving, the result is like a cheesy bread bowl. Diners tear off chunks of the crusty bread to dunk into the gooey cheese inside.

I started with a simple pizza dough, knowing that it would be easy to shape, provide structure to contain the oozy cheese, and have a satisfyingly chewy texture and mild flavor. I whipped together a batch in the food processor and let it rise for a couple of hours. I then shaped it by rolling it first into a circle, nudging the edges into a football shape, and pinching the ends closed.

Georgian cheeses such as sulguni and imeruli—both mozzarella-like cheeses—are most traditional, providing a sharp flavor and epic meltiness. I wanted to replicate their flavor and texture with supermarket cheeses. I found that a mixture of mozzarella and feta approximated the briny tang and stringy texture found in the Georgian cheeses. I piled my cheeses high in my dough boat, popped it into the oven, and watched as the dough baked while the cheeses bubbled.

As soon as the bread was out of the oven, I added a raw egg yolk and a pat of butter to the filling. Both additions are standard and necessary: The egg yolk helps make a cohesive filling, and the butter provides richness. I stirred everything together until the cheese was smooth and stretchy. The only task remaining was persuading my tasters to let it cool slightly before diving in—I failed every time.

—JESSICA RUDOLPH, *Cook's Country*

Adjaruli Khachapuri

SERVES 6

Using cold water to make the dough keeps it from overheating in the food processor. Use block mozzarella, not fresh, here.

- 1¾ cups (8¾ ounces) all-purpose flour
- 1½ teaspoons sugar
- 1 teaspoon instant or rapid-rise yeast
- ¾ teaspoon table salt
- ½ cup plus 2 tablespoons cold water
- 1 tablespoon extra-virgin olive oil
- 6 ounces whole-milk mozzarella cheese, shredded (1½ cups)
- 6 ounces feta cheese, crumbled (1½ cups)
- 1 large egg yolk
- 1 tablespoon unsalted butter

1. Process flour, sugar, yeast, and salt in food processor until combined, about 3 seconds. With processor running, slowly add cold water and oil and process until dough forms sticky ball that clears sides of bowl, 30 to 60 seconds.

2. Transfer dough to counter and knead until smooth, about 1 minute. Shape dough into tight ball and place in greased bowl. Cover bowl with plastic wrap and let dough rise at room temperature until almost doubled in size, 2 to 2½ hours. (Alternatively, dough can rise in refrigerator until doubled in size, about 24 hours. Let come to room temperature, about 2 hours, before proceeding.)

3. Turn out dough onto lightly floured 16 by 12-inch sheet of parchment paper and coat lightly with flour. Flatten into 8-inch disk using your hands. Using rolling pin, roll dough into 12-inch circle, dusting dough lightly with flour as needed.

4. Roll bottom edge of dough 2½ inches in toward center. Rotate parchment 180 degrees and roll bottom edge of dough (directly opposite first rolled side) 2½ inches in toward center. (Opposing edges of rolled sides should be 7 inches apart.)

5. Roll ends of rolled sides toward centerline and pinch firmly together to form football shape about 12 inches long and about 7 inches across at its widest point. Transfer parchment with dough to rimmed baking sheet. Cover loosely with plastic and let rise until puffy, 30 minutes to 1 hour. Adjust oven rack to middle position and heat oven to 450 degrees.

6. Combine mozzarella and feta in bowl. Fill dough with cheese mixture, lightly compacting and mounding in center (cheese will be piled higher than edge of dough). Bake until crust is well browned and cheese is bubbly and beginning to brown in spots, 15 to 17 minutes. Transfer sheet to wire rack. Add egg yolk and butter to cheese filling and stir with fork until fully incorporated and cheese is smooth and stretchy. Lift parchment off sheet and slide bread onto serving platter. Serve immediately.

SHEET-PAN HASH BROWNS

✔ **WHY THIS RECIPE WORKS** To make one batch of hash browns that could serve four to six people, we turned to the oven and a rimmed baking sheet. We found that shredded starchy potatoes made tough, chewy hash browns, so to keep them crispy and creamy, we used only moderately starchy Yukon Gold potatoes and quickly soaked the raw shreds in water to remove excess surface starch. We also wrung out the potatoes in a dish towel to eliminate excess moisture that would inhibit browning. Then, to avoid a stuck-on mess, we greased the baking sheet with vegetable oil spray. Packing the shreds down on the sheet flattened them together into a potato cake, not hash browns, so we lightly distributed them in an even layer on the sheet to keep the integrity of the shreds. A 450-degree oven was hot enough to crisp the top and bottom of the hash browns, but not so hot that the top and bottom browned before the middle cooked through. Instead of a complicated flipping procedure, we simply flipped sections of the hash browns with a metal spatula and returned the sheet to the oven for a crispy result.

Order up! Hash browns! Practiced short-order cooks keep a mound of these crispy shredded spuds cooking on their flat-top griddles all through the breakfast rush. But a home cook has two options: using frozen supermarket hash browns (convenient but not very good) or shredding potatoes and cooking them in a skillet. Skillet hash browns are great, but you need to cook multiple batches to serve more than two people—not ideal. Could I find a way to make enough hash browns to feed four to six people in a single batch at home?

In most home kitchens, a rimmed baking sheet is the closest thing in size to a flat-top griddle, so that's what I decided to use. This meant I'd bake my hash browns in the oven. But my first tests weren't very promising. They variously yielded starchy, clumpy tangles; anemic browning and a leathery texture; burnt edges; and undercooked interiors. I wanted hash browns that were deep golden brown on both sides, with a satisfying mix of crispy and creamy textures.

There's no getting around shredding potatoes for hash browns, but luckily the food processor makes it easier. But you still have to peel the potatoes—or do you? A side-by-side test showed that the skins aren't a problem here as long as you wash the potatoes prior to grating. My tasters preferred Yukon Gold potatoes to starchier

russets, and 3 pounds proved the right amount. I found that a little pretreatment of the potatoes was necessary for the best results; first you need to soak the shredded potatoes in water to remove some excess surface starch (so that the shreds don't fry up gummy), and then you need to wring out the raw shreds in a dish towel to remove excess moisture that would inhibit browning.

Tossing the potato shreds in a little fat kept them from drying out in the oven; I chose oil over butter because butter contains water, which I'd already worked to minimize. Greasing the baking sheet lightly with vegetable oil spray ensured that no stubborn bits of potato stuck to the sheet. And lightly distributing the mass of shreds into an even layer made for even cooking.

As for the oven temperature, my tests showed that I needed enough heat to crisp the hash browns, but too much heat caused deep browning on the top and bottom before the interior cooked through. It turned out that 450 degrees on the middle rack was perfect; after about 30 minutes, I removed the hot sheet and used a spatula to flip the hash browns in segments. Then I popped the sheet back into the oven for about 8 minutes to finish cooking the potatoes and to crisp the top. Order up!

—CECELIA JENKINS, *Cook's Country*

Sheet-Pan Hash Browns
SERVES 4 TO 6

We prefer to use the shredding disk of a food processor to shred the potatoes, but you can also use the large holes of a box grater. These hash browns are great topped with sliced American cheese, chopped ham, and sautéed onions and peppers.

- **3 pounds Yukon Gold potatoes, unpeeled**
- **6 tablespoons extra-virgin olive oil**
- **1 teaspoon table salt**
- **¼ teaspoon pepper**

1. Adjust oven rack to middle position and heat oven to 450 degrees. Fit food processor with shredding disk. Halve or quarter potatoes as needed to fit through processor hopper, then shred potatoes. Transfer potatoes to large bowl and cover with cold water. Let sit for 5 minutes.

2. One handful at a time, lift potatoes out of water and transfer to colander; discard water. Rinse and dry bowl.

SHEET-PAN HASH BROWNS

3. Place one-quarter of potatoes in center of clean dish towel. Gather ends of towel and twist tightly to wring out excess moisture from potatoes. Transfer dried potatoes to now-empty bowl. Repeat 3 more times with remaining potatoes.

4. Add oil, salt, and pepper to potatoes and toss to combine. Lightly spray 16 by 11-inch rimmed baking sheet with vegetable oil spray. Distribute potatoes in even layer on sheet, but do not pack down. Bake until top of potatoes is spotty brown, 32 to 35 minutes.

5. Remove sheet from oven. Flip hash browns in segments with metal spatula. Return sheet to oven and continue to bake until deep golden brown on top, 6 to 8 minutes longer. Season with salt and pepper to taste. Serve.

SAVORY CREPES

⚓ **WHY THIS RECIPE WORKS** In Brittany, France, crepes are made with buckwheat flour. Because buckwheat flour is gluten-free, the pancakes can easily turn out brittle and inflexible. Using a combination of buckwheat flour and gluten-forming all-purpose flour produced crepes that were pliable yet resilient. Increasing the salt and butter rounded out the bitter edge of the buckwheat, so the crepes were nutty, rich, and well seasoned. We also thought up a few variations in which we swapped rye and whole-wheat flours for the buckwheat and all-purpose flours and played around with savory fillings.

Brittany, France, is renowned for its crepes—but not only the lightly sweet, relatively neutral type that you sprinkle with sugar or smear with jam. Galettes bretonnes are dark and savory, with a distinctive earthiness that makes them an integral part of a dish, not just an understated wrapper. That's because they're made from rich, mineral-y buckwheat, which thrives in the cool Breton climate. A galette complète is the classic preparation; it consists of a crepe glossed with salted butter and folded around ham, Gruyère, and an oozy egg.

Crepes are simply thin, unleavened pancakes, and after a bit of practice—our recipes yield more crepes than are needed for the fillings—you'll be able to cook them with confidence. They also keep beautifully, and a stash of savory crepes can be a secret weapon for a stylish meal in a hurry.

I suspected that simply swapping buckwheat for all-purpose flour in our sweet crepe recipe wouldn't be exactly right, since buckwheat is unrelated to wheat and is gluten-free, but doing so would at least get the development process started. I whisked buckwheat flour together with salt (omitting the sugar), milk, eggs, and melted salted butter and then heated a nonstick skillet over low heat for 5 minutes. Thorough heating is imperative for even browning. I swirled ⅓ cup of batter around the pan to create a thin pancake, and when the surface was dry and the edges were browned, I loosened the sides with a rubber spatula and flipped the crepe with my fingertips to brown the second side.

Due to the lack of structure-forming gluten, these crepes had little flexibility and the dry fragility of burnt parchment. This explained why many recipes call for blending in some gluten-forming all-purpose flour. I followed suit, ultimately finding that a mixture with 75 percent buckwheat flour and 25 percent all-purpose flour yielded tender yet resilient crepes.

The all-purpose flour also helped balance the buckwheat's robust flavor. But for some, its mineral-y, bitter edge was still too strong, so I doubled the butter and salt, which made the crepes nutty and smooth.

Instead of building each galette complète individually in a skillet (the typical approach), I assembled four on a baking sheet and popped them into a hot oven.

With my galettes complètes complete, I saw an opportunity to experiment with other whole-grain flours. Rye and whole-wheat seemed ideal, since both have loads of character. And because these flours are gluten forming, I suspected that I might be able to use 100 percent rye flour or 100 percent whole-wheat flour in my recipe. A few tests proved that I was correct; after adjusting the hydration levels, I was churning out stacks of big-personality crepes—and fresh fillings to go with them.

The buckwheat, whole-wheat, and rye crepes each paired well with all the fillings I came up with, but I particularly like the rye crepes with a smoked salmon, pickled shallot, and caper-studded crème fraîche combo inspired by blini toppings. The earthy whole-wheat crepes are a lovely match for a rich mixture of cremini mushrooms and asparagus bound with cream and Pecorino Romano cheese.

—ANNIE PETITO, *Cook's Illustrated*

Buckwheat Crepes

MAKES 10 CREPES

If the skillet begins to smoke, remove it from the burner and turn down the heat. Unsalted butter can be substituted for the salted butter. If using unsalted butter, add an additional ¼ teaspoon of salt to the batter.

- ½ teaspoon vegetable oil
- ¾ cup (3⅜ ounces) buckwheat flour
- ¼ cup (1¼ ounces) all-purpose flour
- ½ teaspoon table salt
- 2 cups milk
- 3 large eggs
- 4 tablespoons salted butter, melted and cooled

1. Heat oil in 12-inch nonstick skillet over low heat for at least 5 minutes.

2. While skillet heats, whisk buckwheat flour, all-purpose flour, and salt together in medium bowl. In second bowl, whisk together milk and eggs. Add half of milk mixture to flour mixture and whisk until smooth. Add melted butter and whisk until incorporated. Whisk in remaining milk mixture until smooth.

3. Using paper towel, wipe out skillet, leaving thin film of oil on bottom and sides. Increase heat to medium and let skillet heat for 1 minute. Test heat of skillet by placing 1 teaspoon batter in center and

---

NOTES FROM THE TEST KITCHEN

MAKING CREPES (IT'S ALL IN THE WRIST)

LIFT AND TILT Lift skillet off heat and tilt slightly away from you. Pour ⅓ cup batter into far side of skillet.

SWIRL Turn your wrist to rotate skillet clockwise and spread batter over entire skillet bottom.

---

cooking for 20 seconds. If mini crepe is golden brown on bottom, skillet is properly heated; if it is too light or too dark, adjust heat accordingly and retest.

4. Lift skillet off heat and pour ⅓ cup batter into far side of skillet; swirl gently in clockwise direction until batter evenly covers bottom of skillet. Return skillet to heat and cook crepe, without moving it, until surface is dry and crepe starts to brown at edges, loosening crepe from sides of skillet with rubber spatula, about 35 seconds. Gently slide spatula underneath edge of crepe, grasp edge with your fingertips, and flip crepe. Cook until second side is lightly spotted, about 20 seconds. Transfer crepe to wire rack. Return skillet to heat for 10 seconds before repeating with remaining batter. As crepes are done, stack on rack. Serve.

TO MAKE AHEAD: Crepes can be wrapped tightly in plastic wrap and refrigerated for up to 3 days or stacked between sheets of parchment paper and frozen for up to 1 month. Allow frozen crepes to thaw completely in refrigerator before using.

VARIATIONS

Rye Crepes

Substitute 1 cup (5½ ounces) rye flour for buckwheat flour and omit all-purpose flour. Increase milk to 2½ cups. Substitute unsalted butter for salted butter.

Whole-Wheat Crepes

Substitute 1 cup (5½ ounces) whole-wheat flour for buckwheat flour and omit all-purpose flour. Substitute unsalted butter for salted butter.

Buckwheat Crepes with Ham, Egg, and Cheese (Galettes Complètes)

SERVES 4

Serve with salad for a light lunch or brunch.

- 4 Buckwheat Crepes
- 4 thin slices deli ham (2 ounces)
- 5½ ounces Gruyère cheese, shredded (1⅓ cups)
- 4 large eggs
- 1 tablespoon salted butter, melted
- 4 teaspoons chopped fresh chives

1. Adjust oven rack to middle position and heat oven to 450 degrees. Line rimmed baking sheet with parchment paper and spray with vegetable oil spray.

BUCKWHEAT CREPES WITH HAM, EGG, AND CHEESE (GALETTES COMPLÈTES)

2. Arrange crepes spotty side down on prepared sheet (they will hang over edge). Working with 1 crepe at a time, place 1 slice of ham in center of crepe, followed by ⅓ cup Gruyère, covering ham evenly. Make small well in center of Gruyère. Crack 1 egg into well. Fold in 4 sides, pressing to adhere.

3. Brush crepe edges with melted butter and transfer sheet to oven. Bake until egg whites are uniformly set and yolks have filmed over but are still runny, 8 to 10 minutes. Using thin metal spatula, transfer each crepe to plate and sprinkle with 1 teaspoon chives. Serve immediately.

Rye Crepes with Smoked Salmon, Crème Fraîche, and Pickled Shallots

SERVES 4

Our favorite smoked salmon is Spence & Co. Traditional Scottish Style Smoked Salmon.

⅓ cup distilled white vinegar
2 tablespoons sugar
2 shallots, sliced thin
¾ cup crème fraîche
3 tablespoons capers, rinsed and chopped
3 tablespoons finely chopped fresh chives
1½ teaspoons grated lemon zest plus 1½ tablespoons juice
¼ teaspoon table salt
¼ teaspoon pepper
8 Rye Crepes (page 207)
8 ounces smoked salmon

1. Combine vinegar and sugar in small bowl and microwave until sugar is dissolved and vinegar is steaming, about 30 seconds. Add shallots and stir to combine. Cover and let cool completely, about 30 minutes. Drain shallots and discard liquid.

2. Combine crème fraîche, capers, chives, lemon zest and juice, salt, and pepper in medium bowl.

3. Place crepes on large plate and invert second plate over crepes. Microwave until crepes are warm, 30 to 45 seconds (45 to 60 seconds if crepes have cooled completely). Working with 1 crepe at a time, spread 2 tablespoons crème fraîche mixture across bottom half of crepe, followed by 1 ounce smoked salmon and one-eighth of shallots. Fold crepes in half and then into quarters. Transfer to plate and serve.

Whole-Wheat Crepes with Creamy Sautéed Mushrooms and Asparagus

SERVES 4

You can substitute white mushrooms for the cremini, if desired. The test kitchen prefers Challenge Unsalted Butter and Boar's Head Pecorino Romano.

1½ pounds cremini mushrooms, trimmed and sliced ¼ inch thick
¼ cup water
½ teaspoon vegetable oil
1 tablespoon unsalted butter
1 shallot, minced
½ teaspoon table salt
¼ teaspoon pepper
8 ounces asparagus, trimmed and cut on bias ¼ inch thick
⅔ cup heavy cream
6 tablespoons grated Pecorino Romano cheese
½ teaspoon grated lemon zest
8 Whole-Wheat Crepes (page 207)

1. Combine mushrooms and water in 12-inch non-stick skillet and cook over high heat, stirring occasionally, until skillet is almost dry and mushrooms begin to sizzle, 4 to 8 minutes. Reduce heat to medium-high. Add oil and toss until mushrooms are evenly coated. Continue to cook, stirring occasionally, until mushrooms are well browned, 4 to 8 minutes longer. Reduce heat to medium.

2. Push mushrooms to sides of skillet. Add butter to center. Once butter has melted, add shallot, salt, and pepper to center and cook, stirring constantly, until fragrant, about 30 seconds. Add asparagus and cook, stirring occasionally, until just tender, about 1 minute. Reduce heat to medium-low, add cream, and cook, stirring occasionally, until reduced by half, about 1 minute. Off heat, add Pecorino and lemon zest, stirring until cheese is melted and mushroom mixture is creamy.

3. Place crepes on large plate and invert second plate over crepes. Microwave until crepes are warm, 30 to 45 seconds (45 to 60 seconds if crepes have cooled completely). Working with 1 crepe at a time, spread ⅓ cup mushroom mixture across bottom half of crepe. Fold crepes in half and then into quarters. Transfer to plate and serve.

SMOKED SALMON BRUNCH PLATES

✓ **WHY THIS RECIPE WORKS** There is no brunch dish more iconic than a New York–style smoked salmon bagel plate. But with a conventional bagel topping out at more than 50 grams of net carbs, this perennial favorite is off-limits for a keto diet. We could have swapped in keto bread for the bagel, but a test cook suggested portobello mushrooms. We roasted the portobellos on a preheated baking sheet in a moderate oven to achieve a crispy exterior. Scoring the caps was essential—it drove away excess moisture and prevented the mushrooms from turning chewy. We loved how substantial the just-crispy mushrooms were against the tangy cream cheese and fatty smoked salmon. What's more, a pair of trimmed portobellos contains less than 4 grams of net carbs. As for toppings, capers, parsley or dill, and minced shallot were essential for this classic dish, and a sliced egg made for an incredibly satisfying meal.

On a typical weekday morning, I might agree with the old adage that "breakfast is the most important meal of the day." On the weekend, however, when mornings are longer and friends can linger over a shared meal, that title belongs to brunch.

Unfortunately for those on the keto diet, many brunch standards (breads, bagels, waffles, pastries, etc.) are carb-laden nonstarters. So when I was tasked with creating a satisfying and brunch-worthy meal for our book *Easy Everyday Keto*, I knew I'd face some serious hurdles. Not afraid of a challenge, I decided to tackle a quintessential dish with a carb at its center: the smoked salmon bagel plate.

Luckily for me, many of the dish's elements are already great for keto. A generous smear of cream cheese, a layer of assertively flavored smoked salmon, a sprinkling of briny capers, and a squeeze of brightening lemon juice—along with minced herbs and shallots—were all a must. For richness and added protein, I'd also include some thin-sliced hard-cooked eggs. Easy. But without a good substitute for a hearty, chewy bagel still warm from the oven, my dish lacked a solid foundation.

When a coworker suggested portobello mushroom caps, I balked at the thought of sogged-out, leathery, muddy-tasting disks competing with the bright and carefully balanced layers of my brunch plate. But when

prepared according to the test kitchen's preferred method, which involves removing the gills, scoring the caps, and roasting the mushrooms until they begin to crisp, portobellos become something far more enticing than the waterlogged standard. In fact, these crispy-edged, warm, toasted rounds would fit the bagel bill perfectly. With the rest of my recipe components already decided, all that was left was to wait for the weekend.

—JOSEPH GITTER, *America's Test Kitchen Books*

Smoked Salmon Brunch Plates

SERVES 2

Use portobello mushroom caps measuring 4 to 5 inches in diameter. We find it best to use a spoon to scrape the gills off the underside of the portobellos.

- 4 portobello mushroom caps (3 ounces each), gills removed
- 3 tablespoons extra-virgin olive oil, divided
- ⅛ teaspoon table salt
- 2 ounces cream cheese, softened
- 4 ounces smoked salmon
- 1 recipe Easy-Peel Hard-Cooked Eggs (recipe follows), sliced thin
- 1 tablespoon capers, rinsed and minced
- 1 tablespoon minced shallot
- 1 tablespoon minced fresh parsley and/or dill
- ¼ teaspoon lemon juice

1. Adjust oven rack to upper-middle position, place rimmed baking sheet on rack, and heat oven to 400 degrees. Using sharp knife, cut ¼-inch slits, spaced ½ inch apart, in crosshatch pattern on surface (non gill side) of mushrooms.

2. Brush both sides of mushroom caps with 2 tablespoons oil and sprinkle with salt. Carefully place caps gill side up on preheated sheet and roast until mushrooms have released some of their juices and begun to brown around edges, 8 to 12 minutes. Flip caps and continue to roast until liquid has completely evaporated and caps are golden brown, 8 to 12 minutes longer. Transfer mushrooms to plate and let cool slightly.

3. Spread cream cheese over gill side of mushroom caps and arrange caps on 2 individual serving plates. Top with salmon, eggs, capers, shallot, and parsley. Season with pepper to taste and drizzle with lemon juice and remaining 1 tablespoon oil. Serve.

Easy-Peel Hard-Cooked Eggs

MAKES 2 EGGS

Be sure to use large eggs that have no cracks and are cold from the refrigerator. If you don't have a steamer basket, gently place the eggs in the water; they can rest above the water or be partially submerged. You can cook as many as 12 eggs without altering the timing, as long as you use a pot and steamer basket large enough to hold the eggs in a single layer. The cooked eggs can be refrigerated for up to five days and peeled when needed.

2 large eggs

1. Bring 1 inch water to rolling boil in medium saucepan over high heat. Place eggs in steamer basket. Transfer basket to saucepan. Cover, reduce heat to medium (small wisps of steam should escape from beneath lid), and cook eggs for 13 minutes.

2. When eggs are almost finished cooking, combine 2 cups ice cubes and 2 cups cold water in medium bowl. Using tongs or spoon, transfer eggs to ice bath; let sit for 15 minutes. Peel before using.

CHINESE RICE PORRIDGE

✔ **WHY THIS RECIPE WORKS** Great congee (Chinese rice porridge) features soft, barely intact grains gently bound by their silky, viscous cooking liquid; the result should be fluid but thick and creamy enough to suspend any toppings. Our formula started with a 13:1 ratio of liquid to long-grain white rice, which produced an appropriately loose porridge. Then we simmered the rice vigorously to encourage the grains to break down in about 45 minutes, partially covering the pot to help the contents cook quickly while minimizing evaporation. To prevent the congee from boiling over, we rinsed excess starch from the raw rice and wedged a wooden spoon between the lid and the side of the pot, giving the water bubbles a chance to escape. We also made a couple of toppings: microwave-fried shallots and a quick-cooking stir-fried pork topping.

Congee is one of the earliest and most enduring forms of culinary thrift. For centuries, maybe even millennia, Chinese cooks have stretched their rice by boiling it in plenty of water until it dissolves into something that hovers between starch and soup. The milky-white gruel is Dickensian in the best possible way: plain sustenance that's economical and appealing at any time of day.

That's particularly true at breakfast, when congee is consumed the way oatmeal is in Western diets. It is dead-simple and forgiving to make; without much thought, you can improvise a version that's good enough. But the variety of rice, the type and amount of liquid, and the cooking time all affect its flavor and consistency. I wanted a foolproof recipe.

Depending on the regional style, congee can be thick and glossy or comparatively thin. Since I found plenty of recipes that fall in between those distinct styles, I felt justified in making my own ideal hybrid: a thick but pourable porridge done up with an assortment of fun-to-cook, versatile toppings. With kitchen staples, it would be a simple snack; with substantial proteins, it would be the ultimate rice bowl.

Congee can be made with any kind of rice, but long-grain varieties are common. I chose conventional long-grain but also liked jasmine. To nail that perfect porridge consistency, I dug into the factors that affect it most: the ratio of water to rice and the cooking time.

According to recipes I found, ratios can vary from about 7 parts water to 1 part rice to more than double that. I tried a few, bringing 1 cup of rice and various amounts of water to a boil in Dutch ovens and gently simmering them uncovered for 1½ hours. It didn't take long to see that the results were better—thick and creamy yet fluid rather than stodgy—when there was more water in the mix. After a bit more tinkering, I settled on a ratio of 10 cups liquid to ¾ cup rice (about 13:1). At this point, I also opted to cut the water with 1 cup of chicken broth, which added just enough savory backbone without obscuring the congee's clean flavor.

Most congee recipes call for simmering the rice for a minimum of 45 minutes or as long as 1½ hours. This allows for the grains to thoroughly break down and release their starches into the cooking liquid, producing congee's signature texture and glossy, pearly sheen.

Using my newly calibrated liquid-to-rice ratio, I confirmed that 1½ hours of gentle but steady simmering produced the smoothest, creamiest congee. But could I expedite the process? I tried soaking the raw rice and even soaking and then freezing it before cooking. Neither helped much. What if I just turned up the heat?

As it turned out, vigorously simmering the rice produced porridge every bit as creamy as the low-and-slow method did in about half the time. But I had to partially cover the pot to speed cooking and minimize evaporation, which caused the starchy liquid to boil over. Fortunately, I could avoid the problem by rinsing the rice to remove any excess surface starch that would fuel the formation of starchy gel, and wedging a wooden spoon between the lid and the pot kept them well separated, giving the bubbles plenty of space to escape.

With my porridge clocking in at under an hour, I put together a few easy toppings. But I always keep "project" accompaniments in mind, too; rich braised meats or assertive condiments such as savory chili crisp can transform this dish into something so extraordinary that you might forget it comes from almost nothing.

—ANDREW JANJIGIAN, *Cook's Illustrated*

Congee (Chinese Rice Porridge)

SERVES 4 TO 6

For vegetarian congee, substitute water for the chicken broth. Jasmine rice can be substituted for conventional long-grain white rice; do not use basmati. Look for Chinese black vinegar in Asian supermarkets. Serve with soft-cooked eggs, Microwave-Fried Shallots, and/ or Stir-Fried Ground Pork Topping for Congee (recipes follow), if desired.

- ¾ cup long-grain white rice
- 1 cup chicken broth
- ¾ teaspoon table salt
  - Scallions, sliced thin on bias
  - Fresh cilantro leaves
  - Dry-roasted peanuts, chopped coarse
  - Chili oil
  - Soy sauce
  - Chinese black vinegar

1. Place rice in fine-mesh strainer and rinse under cold running water until water runs clear. Drain well and transfer to Dutch oven. Add broth, salt, and 9 cups water and bring to boil over high heat. Reduce heat to maintain vigorous simmer. Cover pot, tucking wooden spoon horizontally between pot and lid to hold lid ajar. Cook, stirring occasionally, until mixture is thickened, glossy, and reduced by half, 45 to 50 minutes.

2. Serve congee in bowls, passing scallions, cilantro, peanuts, oil, soy sauce, and vinegar separately.

Microwave-Fried Shallots

SERVES 4 TO 6

Our favorite vegetable oil is Crisco Blends.

- 3 shallots, sliced thin
- ½ cup vegetable oil

Combine shallots and oil in medium bowl. Microwave for 5 minutes. Stir and continue to microwave 2 minutes longer. Repeat stirring and microwaving in 2-minute increments until beginning to brown (4 to 6 minutes). Repeat stirring and microwaving in 30-second increments until deep golden brown (30 seconds to 2 minutes). Using slotted spoon, transfer shallots to paper towel–lined plate; season with salt to taste. Let drain and crisp, about 5 minutes.

Stir-Fried Ground Pork Topping for Congee

SERVES 4 TO 6

Spoon over congee to serve.

- 8 ounces ground pork
- 1 tablespoon water
- ¼ teaspoon table salt
- ⅛ teaspoon baking soda
- 1 garlic clove, minced
- 1 teaspoon minced fresh ginger
- 1 teaspoon soy sauce
- 1 teaspoon Shaoxing wine or dry sherry
- 1 teaspoon cornstarch
- ½ teaspoon sugar
- ¼ teaspoon white pepper
- 1 teaspoon vegetable oil

1. Toss pork, water, salt, and baking soda in bowl until thoroughly combined. Add garlic, ginger, soy sauce, Shaoxing wine, cornstarch, sugar, and white pepper and toss until thoroughly combined.

2. Heat oil in 12-inch nonstick skillet over medium-high heat until just smoking. Add pork mixture and cook, breaking meat into ¼-inch pieces with wooden spoon, until pork is no longer pink and just beginning to brown.

CONGEE (CHINESE RICE PORRIDGE)

PORTUGUESE EGG TARTS

DESSERTS AND DRINKS

CARAMEL-ESPRESSO YULE LOG

✓ **WHY THIS RECIPE WORKS** The first step in making a successful rolled cake is choosing the right cake. We picked chiffon for its whipped egg whites, which provided resilience; its oil, which provided moist tenderness; and its baking powder, which provided extra lift. While many recipes involve rolling the warm cake in a sugar-coated towel to "train" it into shape, we found that doing so dried out the surface, making it hard for the ganache to adhere, so we opted for a clean, damp towel instead. For the filling, we started with a classic caramel and added espresso powder, cream, and a stealth ingredient: cream cheese. Its tang was barely detectable but kept the sweetness in check, and it also gave the whipped filling enough body to stay put when the cake was rolled, resulting in a graceful spiral every time. A simple ganache made with bittersweet chocolate and cream (plus a bit of corn syrup for added flexibility and cling) made the perfect "bark."

When it comes to holiday celebrations, I'm a traditionalist. But somehow I'd managed never to make a Yule log. It's not only one of the oldest finales to a Christmas feast but also a dessert with a huge "wow" factor: a moist, tender cake rolled around a rich, creamy filling; coated in frosting; and adorned with playful woodsy garnishes. This year I decided I would finally take on the elaborate holiday project.

But as I started to review recipes, I found I was more likely to read about how suspenseful—even harrowing—the dessert can be to assemble than about how wonderful it can be to eat. Will the filling be squeezed out as you roll? Will the cake crack? After all that work and stress, will your creation look convincingly log-like? Or more like a pile of mulch?

Of course, my own recipe had to be delicious. But it also had to be a sure thing: a cake that rolled without fracturing and a filling that stayed put, all encased in a neat layer of frosting.

I familiarized myself with the basic method: Bake cake batter in a shallow rimmed baking sheet. Invert the hot cake onto a confectioners' sugar–dusted dish towel (the sugar prevents sticking) and roll it up so that the cake sets into a curled shape as it cools. Unroll the cake, spread the filling over the cake, and roll it up again—without the towel this time. Then cover the whole thing with buttercream or a rich ganache.

Though chocolate cake is more common, I decided on a vanilla cake. But as I started to bake, I noticed a problem: Sponge cake—the most common choice for rolled cakes—has a bouncy texture due to its large amount of whipped eggs and small amount of fat. But that bounce also means that sponge cake can be a tad chewy. It's also prone to cracking if it's overbaked.

I decided to try a chiffon cake, which is similar to sponge but has more fat that helps tenderize it and makes it more forgiving when baked. Our recipe calls for whisking egg yolks, water, vanilla, and vegetable oil into the dry ingredients and then whipping the egg whites and folding them into the batter. Even if you lose some volume while folding, the baking powder ensures a fluffy cake.

I baked a chiffon cake, rolled it in a dish towel, and then unfurled it once it had cooled. I then spread on a placeholder filling of sweetened whipped cream and rolled the cake back up. While the log chilled, I heated some cream, poured it over chopped bittersweet chocolate with a bit of corn syrup for shine, and stirred everything together to make a smooth ganache, my choice for the frosting "bark." When the ganache had cooled and thickened, I spread it over my cake.

Chiffon had been an excellent choice: It was fluffy but also tender, moist, and crack-free. But now I had new problems: Lots of the soft filling had squished out, and the ganache had a worrisome tendency to separate from the surface of the roll when I sliced the cake.

The ganache was peeling because the cake's exterior was dry. Thankfully, the fix was simple. An outlier approach by Julia Child ditched the confectioners' sugar and instead called for wrapping the cake in a damp dish towel. This worked like a charm, and the ganache now adhered nicely. The damp towel also left the surface so moist that the cake could be wrapped, filled, and chilled for two days with no ill effects.

Emboldened by Child's nonconformism, I decided to break from tradition yet again: Instead of rolling up the cake from the long side, which I found awkward and unwieldy, I rolled up mine from the short side, which made it much easier to control the center of the cake as I rolled. This technique produced a chubbier, more impressive log with a graceful spiral.

I next turned my attention to the filling. It needed some real personality to stand up to the bittersweet chocolate ganache. Espresso powder would amp up the cream, but so would caramel. Why not use both?

CARAMEL-ESPRESSO YULE LOG

The bitterness of the coffee would complement the sweet caramel. I brought a cup of heavy cream and some espresso powder to a simmer in one pot while melting some sugar in another. When the sugar had caramelized, I whisked in the warm cream. Then I added a cup of cold cream to cool the mixture and refrigerated it. This filling whipped up just like regular whipped cream, and its flavor was outstanding, if a little sweet.

Last task: Find an easy way to firm up the filling so that it would stay put. I tried adding mascarpone, the soft Italian cheese. It thickened the filling a bit, but not enough. How about cream cheese? I melted some into the warm caramel before chilling the mixture.

This new filling whipped to a promisingly thick buttercream-like consistency. A quick taste revealed that the cream cheese had tempered the sweetness of the filling without making it taste cheesy. Best of all, the filling didn't move when I rolled the springy yet cooperative cake. Suddenly, rolling a Yule log had gone from anxiety-inducing to exhilarating.

Trimming the ends of my Yule log revealed an elegant spiral within. I then cut off one end on the bias and attached it to the side of the log with some ganache before frosting the rest of the log. But I left the cut ends exposed to show off the perfect swirl.

As a finishing touch, I traced the tines of a fork over the surface of the ganache to create a bark-like effect, and my project was complete. Turns out, when you match the ideal cake to the ideal filling, making a log can be as easy as falling off one.

—ANDREA GEARY, *Cook's Illustrated*

Caramel-Espresso Yule Log

SERVES 10 TO 12

We developed this recipe using Philadelphia Cream Cheese Brick Original. The filling has to chill for at least 1½ hours before whipping, so make it before organizing the ingredients for the cake and the ganache. A smooth dish towel works best for rolling the cake. Some of the cake may cling to the towel, but it washes out easily. Use a high-quality chocolate for the ganache. We prefer to leave the cut surfaces of the log exposed, but there is enough ganache to cover them, if desired. For a more elaborate presentation, place the cake on a bed of Chocolate Crumbles (recipe follows) and decorate with Meringue Bracket-Style Mushrooms (page 220).

FILLING

- 2 cups heavy cream, divided
- 1 tablespoon instant espresso powder
- ¾ cup (5¼ ounces) granulated sugar
- ¼ cup water
- 1 tablespoon light corn syrup
- 4 ounces cream cheese, cut into 8 pieces and softened

CAKE

- 1⅓ cups (5⅓ ounces) cake flour
- ¾ cup (5¼ ounces) granulated sugar
- 1½ teaspoons baking powder
- ¼ teaspoon table salt
- 5 large eggs, separated
- ½ cup vegetable oil
- ¼ cup water
- 2 teaspoons vanilla extract
- ¼ teaspoon cream of tartar

GANACHE

- ¾ cup heavy cream
- 6 ounces bittersweet chocolate, chopped fine
- 2 teaspoons light corn syrup

Confectioners' sugar (optional)

1. FOR THE FILLING: Pour 1 cup cream into wide bowl. Whisk together espresso powder and remaining 1 cup cream in small saucepan and bring to simmer over medium heat. Remove from heat and cover to keep hot. Bring sugar, water, and corn syrup to boil in large heavy-bottomed saucepan over medium-high heat. Cook, without stirring, until mixture is straw-colored, 6 to 8 minutes. Reduce heat to medium-low and continue to cook, swirling saucepan occasionally, until mixture is deep coppery brown and just starting to smoke, 4 to 7 minutes longer. Off heat, carefully whisk in hot cream mixture a little at a time (caramel will bubble and steam). Add cream cheese. Cover and let sit for 5 minutes. Whisk until mostly smooth (some small flecks of cream cheese are OK). Transfer mixture to bowl with cream and stir to combine. Cover and refrigerate until mixture registers 50 degrees or below, at least 1½ hours or up to 4 days.

2. FOR THE CAKE: Adjust oven rack to middle position and heat oven to 350 degrees. Lightly grease 18 by 13-inch rimmed baking sheet, line with parchment paper, and lightly grease parchment. Whisk flour, sugar, baking powder, and salt together in large, wide bowl. Whisk egg yolks, oil, water, and vanilla into flour mixture until smooth batter forms.

3. Using stand mixer fitted with whisk attachment, whip egg whites and cream of tartar on medium-low speed until foamy, about 1 minute. Increase speed to medium-high and whip until stiff peaks form, 1½ to 2 minutes. Transfer one-third of whipped egg whites to batter and whisk gently until mixture is lightened. Using rubber spatula, gently fold remaining egg whites into batter. Pour batter into prepared sheet and spread evenly. Firmly tap sheet on counter 3 times to remove large air bubbles. Bake until cake springs back when pressed lightly in center, 12 to 14 minutes. While cake bakes, soak clean dish towel with water and wring out thoroughly.

4. Transfer sheet to wire rack. Immediately run knife around edge of sheet, then carefully invert cake onto second wire rack. Carefully remove parchment. Lay damp towel over cake and invert first wire rack over towel. Invert cake and remove rack. Starting from short side, gently roll cake and towel together into jelly roll shape. Let cake cool on rack, seam side down, for 1 hour.

5. FOR THE GANACHE: Bring cream to simmer in small saucepan over medium heat. Place chocolate and corn syrup in bowl, pour cream over top, and let stand for 1 minute. Whisk mixture until smooth. Let cool until mixture has consistency of pudding, about 1 hour.

6. Transfer chilled filling to bowl of stand mixer fitted with whisk attachment. Whip on high speed until mixture is thick and fluffy and resembles buttercream frosting, 1½ to 2 minutes. Gently unroll cake with short side parallel to counter edge (innermost edge of cake will remain slightly curled; do not flatten). Spread filling evenly over cake, leaving ½-inch margin on each short side. Reroll cake, leaving towel behind as you roll. Wrap in plastic wrap and refrigerate for at least 20 minutes or up to 2 days.

7. Arrange two 12 by 4-inch strips of parchment 1 inch apart on serving platter. Unwrap cake and place on cutting board. Using sharp chef's knife, trim ½-inch slice from each end of log, wiping knife clean between cuts; discard trimmings. To make branch stump, cut 1 end of cake at 45-degree angle, starting 1½ inches from end of log (shorter side of stump will be 1½ inches long). Transfer larger cake piece to platter, centering it lengthwise on parchment. To attach stump, rest straight side of smaller piece against side of log. Fill in top of space between pieces with about 1 tablespoon ganache. Using offset spatula, gently spread remaining ganache over log, leaving cut ends exposed. Use tines of fork to make wood-grain pattern on surface of ganache. Carefully slide parchment from beneath cake (hold stump in place with your fingertip while sliding out parchment). Refrigerate cake, uncovered, to slightly set ganache, about 20 minutes. (Cake can be covered loosely and refrigerated for up to 24 hours; let stand at room temperature for 30 minutes before serving.) Dust lightly with confectioners' sugar, if using. To slice, dip sharp knife in very hot water and wipe dry between cuts. Serve.

NOTES FROM THE TEST KITCHEN

YULE LOG DISASTERS

Our early experiments produced a variety of tragic results.

FILLING TSUNAMI
A bit of filling is displaced with each turn, so it builds in front of the log, finally overflowing at the last turn.

CAKE DROUGHT
Sponge cake—the typical choice—has lots of whipped eggs and little fat, so it's dry and prone to cracking if overbaked.

FROST(ING) HEAVE
When the crumb is too dry, the ganache has nothing to cling to and separates from the cake when it's sliced.

Chocolate Crumbles

MAKES 2 CUPS

We like to scatter these crumbles around the base of our Yule log to simulate the forest floor, but they also make a great topping for ice cream or cupcakes. If using with the Yule log, the optional ground pistachios make convincing "sawdust."

6 tablespoons unsalted butter, cut into ½-inch pieces

2 ounces bittersweet chocolate, chopped

1 cup (5 ounces) all-purpose flour

½ cup packed (3½ ounces) dark brown sugar

⅓ cup (1 ounce) unsweetened cocoa powder

¼ teaspoon table salt

¼ cup shelled pistachios, toasted and ground fine (optional)

1. Adjust oven rack to middle position and heat oven to 350 degrees. Line rimmed baking sheet with parchment paper. Combine butter and chocolate in medium bowl and microwave until melted, about 1 minute, stirring halfway through microwaving. Add flour, sugar, cocoa, and salt and mix until thoroughly combined and crumbly dough forms.

2. Crumble dough over prepared sheet. Bake until crumbles are dry, fragrant, and starting to crisp, about 15 minutes, stirring halfway through baking. Transfer sheet to wire rack and let crumbles cool completely (crumbles will continue to crisp as they cool). Crumbles can be stored in airtight container at room temperature for up to 2 weeks.

Meringue Bracket-Style Mushrooms

MAKES ABOUT 30 MERINGUES

You will need a pastry bag and a pastry tip with a ¼-inch round opening, available at craft stores, for this recipe. The meringues can be made up to two weeks in advance; store them in an airtight container directly after cooling. This recipe will make more mushrooms than you need, so you can select your favorites for decorating your Yule log. For the best results, attach them to the log no more than 10 minutes before serving.

3 large egg whites

¼ teaspoon cream of tartar

Pinch table salt

⅔ cup (4⅔ ounces) sugar

1. Adjust oven racks to upper-middle and lower-middle positions and heat oven to 200 degrees. Using pencil, draw 15 half-circles ranging from 1 to 2 inches wide on 1 sheet of parchment paper, leaving at least 1½ inches between half-circles. Repeat with second sheet of parchment. Place parchment pencil side down on 2 rimmed baking sheets.

2. Using stand mixer fitted with whisk attachment, whip egg whites on medium speed until foamy, about 1 minute. Add cream of tartar and salt; increase speed to medium-high; and whip until soft peaks form, about 1 minute. With mixer running, slowly add sugar. Increase speed to high and whip until very thick and stiff peaks form, 3 to 4 minutes.

3. Fit pastry bag with ¼-inch round pastry tip and fill with meringue. Using half-circle as guide, pipe concentric arcs of meringue, either smooth or frilly, until half-circle is filled. Repeat with remaining half-circles. Pipe a stem, about ½ inch wide and 1 inch long, onto straight side of each half-circle. Moisten your fingertip with water and smooth any unwanted peaks. Bake meringues for 2 hours, turn off oven, and leave meringues in oven until dry and crisp, about 30 minutes.

4. After Yule log has come to room temperature, and no more than 10 minutes before serving, use paring knife to make small incision in side of log. Gently insert mushroom stem into incision until straight side of mushroom rests against log. Repeat with desired number of mushrooms.

FINANCIERS (ALMOND–BROWNED BUTTER CAKES)

✓ **WHY THIS RECIPE WORKS** For financiers with complex almond flavor and contrasting textures, we started by spraying a mini-muffin tin with baking spray with flour. The flour in the spray helped the sides of the cakes rise along with the center, preventing doming. We then stirred together almond flour, sugar, all-purpose flour, and egg whites. We opted for granulated sugar, which doesn't totally dissolve in the egg whites, to ensure a pleasantly coarse texture. Once these ingredients were whisked together, it was just a matter of stirring in nutty browned butter and baking the cakes.

Mignardises are tiny treats offered to restaurant guests at the end of a meal. Because they are consumed in one or two bites and need to leave a lasting impression, the best versions feature intense flavors and contrasting textures. Early in my career, one of my tasks as a pastry prep cook was to prepare an assortment of these

FINANCIERS (ALMOND–BROWNED BUTTER CAKES)

delicacies, including indulgent truffles, jewel-toned fruit jellies, and glossy macarons. But nothing was as popular as the financiers.

The thin shells of these miniature cakes crunch satisfyingly when bitten, bringing forth the richness of nutty browned butter and toasted almonds. Inside, the crumb is moist, chewy, and cakey, with an aroma similar to that of almond extract.

For all their nuance and elegance, financiers are incredibly easy to make: Just whisk together almond flour, all-purpose flour, sugar, and salt; stir in egg whites and browned butter; and bake in generously buttered individual molds.

In this simple recipe, each ingredient plays a unique role. Let's start with the flours. Almond flour is primary; for a batch of two dozen financiers, ¾ cup of almond flour is enough to infuse the batter with a deep, nutty taste. A small amount of all-purpose flour keeps the cakes' interiors moist.

Next up is sugar. Sugar is responsible for the financiers' crackly exterior. Many recipes, including mine, contain more sugar by weight than flour. As the cakes bake, the sugar caramelizes, turning pliable. Then, as the cakes cool, the sugar becomes brittle, creating the crisp shell that is the mark of a good financier.

Sugar also affects the interior crumb of the cakes, which should offer repeated resistance as you chew. Specifically, the ratio of sugar to egg whites is important. I found the sweet—and chewy—spot with 3 ounces egg whites to 4 ounces sugar.

Finally, there's the browned butter, which adds flavor and richness. I browned 5 tablespoons of butter and stirred it into the batter.

Many recipes suggest baking financiers in mini-muffin tins instead of the traditional molds that few home cooks own, so I gave this technique a try. In any pan, a substantial barrier of fat is necessary to prevent the cakes from sticking. Individually coating 24 mini-muffin tin cups with softened butter was tedious, so I used vegetable oil spray instead.

In a 375-degree oven, my financiers baked evenly, and they emerged well browned. But their tops baked up with domes instead of the relatively flat tops that are their hallmark.

I happened upon the solution when I switched from vegetable oil spray to baking spray with flour. Baking spray helps baked goods release by providing a physical barrier between the pan and the food; the flour it contains also changes the rate at which a batter cooks. The flour particles in the spray form a tiny gap where the batter meets the metal—tiny, but important. Here's why: The flour provided some insulation so that the sides of the financiers could rise more before setting, resulting in sides that were mostly even with the top.

With my financiers finally looking the part, I customized them with a variety of add-ins, including fresh fruit, nuts, citrus zest, warm spices, and dark chocolate chunks. If you're looking for an easy way to wow your guests with just two bites, you've got to give this recipe a try.

—LAN LAM, *Cook's Illustrated*

Financiers (Almond–Browned Butter Cakes)
MAKES 24 CAKES

You'll need a 24-cup mini-muffin tin for this recipe. Because egg whites can vary in size, measuring the whites by weight or volume is essential. Baking spray with flour ensures that the cakes bake up with appropriately flat tops; we don't recommend substituting vegetable oil spray in this recipe. To enjoy the crisp edges of the cakes, eat them on the day they're baked; store leftovers in an airtight container at room temperature for up to three days.

- 5 tablespoons unsalted butter
- ¾ cup (3 ounces) finely ground almond flour
- ½ cup plus 1 tablespoon (4 ounces) sugar
- 2 tablespoons all-purpose flour
- ⅛ teaspoon table salt
- ⅓ cup (3 ounces) egg whites (3 to 4 large eggs)

1. Adjust oven rack to middle position and heat oven to 375 degrees. Generously spray 24-cup mini-muffin tin with baking spray with flour. Melt butter in 10-inch skillet over medium-high heat. Cook, stirring and scraping skillet constantly with rubber spatula, until milk solids are dark golden brown and butter has nutty aroma, 1 to 3 minutes. Immediately transfer butter to heatproof bowl.

2. Whisk almond flour, sugar, all-purpose flour, and salt together in second bowl. Add egg whites. Using rubber spatula, stir until combined, mashing any lumps against side of bowl until mixture is smooth. Stir in butter until incorporated. Distribute batter evenly among prepared muffin cups (cups will be about half full).

3. Bake until edges are well browned and tops are golden, about 14 minutes, rotating muffin tin halfway through baking. Remove tin from oven and immediately invert wire rack on top of tin. Invert rack and tin; carefully remove tin. Turn cakes right side up and let cool for at least 20 minutes before serving.

VARIATIONS

Chocolate Chunk Financiers

Place ½-inch chunk of dark chocolate on top of each cake before baking. Don't press chocolate into batter or it will sink and stick to muffin tin.

Citrus or Spice Financiers

Add ¾ teaspoon grated citrus zest or ¼ teaspoon ground cinnamon, ginger, or cardamom to batter.

Nut Financiers

Sprinkle lightly toasted sliced almonds on top of batter. Or, instead of using almond flour, grind 3 ounces untoasted pistachios, hazelnuts, pecans, or whole unblanched almonds with the all-purpose flour in food processor.

Raspberry Financiers

Place 1 small raspberry on its side on top of each cake before baking. Don't press raspberry into batter or it will sink and stick to muffin tin.

Stone Fruit Financiers

Choose tart, slightly underripe plums, peaches, apricots, or nectarines. Cut fruit into wedges, slice wedges thin, and shingle 2 pieces on top of each cake before baking.

CHOCOLATE PAVLOVA WITH BERRIES AND WHIPPED CREAM

WHY THIS RECIPE WORKS If you associate chocolate decadence only with the ultrafudgy and dense, this ethereal chocolate pavlova will expand your chocolate horizons—in a glamorous display. Pavlova is a large meringue base for billowy whipped cream and a topping. But unlike uniformly crunchy meringue cookies, pavlova offers a range of textures: a crisp outer shell; a tender, marshmallowy interior; and a pleasant chew where the two meet. Chocolate pavlova was particularly intriguing to us: The richness of bar chocolate would balance some of the sweetness of the meringue. Instead of Italian meringue, which calls for the unnerving task of drizzling hot sugar syrup into egg whites, our pavlova is made with a Swiss meringue: Sugar is dissolved in the whites as they're heated over simmering water and then whipped. Chopped chocolate weighed down the meringue, interrupting the delicate structure and texture. Instead we folded in finely grated bittersweet chocolate to flavor every bite. Lightly sweetened whipped cream and berries brought things further into balance and made for a beautiful presentation of colors and textures. The grated chocolate gave the meringue plenty of flavor, but we couldn't resist drizzling melted chocolate on top. The showstopping dessert was light in texture but not in chocolate flavor, making it the perfect ending to a rich meal.

There aren't many desserts much prettier than pavlova. Named after famed Russian prima ballerina Anna Pavlova (and bearing a striking resemblance to the dancer's tutu), the showstopping centerpiece starts with a base of crisp-chewy meringue. Though the exterior of this billowy round may resemble a traditional meringue cookie, which is uniformly dry, crunchy, and sweet, this scaled-up version has a world of complexity waiting inside. As you take a bite, the crisp, crackly surface yields to a pleasingly chewy interface, which, in turn, surrounds a soft and delectably marshmallowy center. To top this layered base, you pile on an airy mound of whipped cream and stud the whole thing with fresh fruit for a gorgeous finish. It's the dessert equivalent of the Sugar Plum Fairy.

So when I was tasked with developing a recipe for the "Dazzling Desserts" chapter of our book *Everything Chocolate*, I knew that pavlova would fit the bill perfectly. But just how I'd incorporate rich chocolate into this typically simple dessert—without weighing it down—remained to be determined. My colleague Annie Petito had recently developed a foolproof recipe for the traditional version, so I took my initial cues from her. Though the majority of pavlova recipes rely on a French meringue base, which requires careful timing and absolute precision when combining the sugar and egg whites, Annie's version calls for making a Swiss meringue. She'd discovered that this more forgiving style—which involves heating the sugar and egg whites over a double boiler before whipping them—yielded

CHOCOLATE PAVLOVA WITH BERRIES AND WHIPPED CREAM

the most consistent results and an ideal texture. With this road map I was surely on my way to success. But how would the carefully calibrated mixture fare when given the chocolate treatment?

Adding cocoa powder (I tried both natural and Dutch-processed varieties) to the meringue base seemed like an easy enough route, but my pavlovas baked up overly gooey and soft with an unusual, off-putting gray color and not enough chocolate flavor. Incorporating cacao nibs, which would retain their shape and preserve the color of the meringue, seemed like a sophisticated choice for a sophisticated dessert. But their one-note bitterness and distracting crunch disturbed the delicate balance of textures and flavors in the base. Milk chocolate, on the other hand, yielded a pavlova that was cloyingly sweet.

Bittersweet chocolate fared much better—it provided the perfect edge to cut the meringue's marshmallowy sweetness. But larger chopped pieces of bar chocolate sunk in the meringue and weighed down the airy mixture. To more evenly distribute the chocolate, I tried grating it. Success! The finely grated pieces stayed put while the meringue baked, and the base retained its signature pale color—now with attractive dark flecks of the bittersweet chocolate distributed evenly throughout. Leaving the meringue in the oven to cool after baking it ensured that the interior would set up to the appropriate consistency and allowed the exterior to become perfectly crisp and crackly. With the rich chocolate seamlessly incorporated into the light and airy meringue, flavor and texture were finally dancing in their own pas de deux.

With the base sorted, I moved on to the finishing touches. One of the best things about serving pavlova for company is that the baked meringue can be made up to a week ahead and the rest of the elements can be prepared just before serving. I wanted to minimize fuss on event night, so I opted to top my meringue with a simple, lightly sweetened whipped cream that came together in minutes. The tartness of fresh berries (I used a mixture of blackberries, blueberries, and raspberries—no slicing required) played well against the rich, chocolaty-sweet base, and a drizzle of melted bittersweet chocolate over the top brought the whole dish together for added richness and a showstopping presentation. My pavlova was finished—and ready for the spotlight.

—SAMANTHA BLOCK, *America's Test Kitchen Books*

Chocolate Pavlova with Berries and Whipped Cream

SERVES 10

Because eggs can vary in size, measuring the egg whites by weight or volume is essential to ensure that you are working with the correct ratio of egg whites to sugar. Open the oven door as infrequently as possible while the meringue is inside. Do not worry if the meringue cracks; it's part of the dessert's charm.

MERINGUE

1½ cups (10½ ounces) sugar

¾ cup (6 ounces) egg whites (5 to 7 large eggs)

1½ teaspoons distilled white vinegar

1½ teaspoons cornstarch

1 teaspoon vanilla extract

2 ounces bittersweet chocolate, grated

TOPPING

2 pounds (6 cups) blackberries, blueberries, and/or raspberries

3 tablespoons sugar, divided

Pinch table salt

2 ounces bittersweet chocolate, chopped fine

2 cups heavy cream, chilled

1. FOR THE MERINGUE: Adjust oven rack to middle position and heat oven to 250 degrees. Using pencil, draw 10-inch circle in center of 18 by 13-inch piece of parchment paper. Combine sugar and egg whites in bowl of stand mixer; place bowl over saucepan filled with 1 inch simmering water, making sure water does not touch bottom of bowl. Whisking gently but constantly, heat until sugar is dissolved and mixture registers 160 to 165 degrees, 5 to 8 minutes.

2. Fit mixer with whisk attachment and whip mixture on high speed until meringue forms stiff peaks, is smooth and creamy, and is bright white with sheen, about 4 minutes (bowl may still be slightly warm to touch). Stop mixer and scrape down bowl with spatula. Add vinegar, cornstarch, and vanilla and whip on high speed until combined, about 10 seconds. Remove bowl and, using rubber spatula, fold in chocolate.

3. Spoon about ¼ teaspoon meringue onto each corner of rimmed baking sheet. Press parchment, marked side down, onto sheet to secure. Pile meringue in center of circle on parchment. Using circle as guide, spread and smooth meringue with back of spoon or spatula from center outward, building 10-inch disk that is slightly higher around edges. Finished disk should measure about 1 inch high with ¼-inch depression in center.

4. Bake meringue until exterior is dry and crisp and meringue releases cleanly from parchment when gently lifted at edge with thin metal spatula, 1 to 1½ hours. Meringue should be quite pale (a hint of creamy color is OK). Turn off oven, prop door open with wooden

spoon, and let meringue cool in oven for 1½ hours. Remove sheet from oven and let meringue cool completely before topping, about 15 minutes. (Cooled meringue can be wrapped tightly in plastic wrap and stored at room temperature for up to 1 week.)

5. FOR THE TOPPING: Toss berries with 1 tablespoon sugar and salt in large bowl. Set aside for 30 minutes. Meanwhile, microwave chocolate in bowl at 50 percent power, stirring occasionally, until melted, about 1 minute. Set aside to cool slightly.

6. Before serving, whip cream and remaining 2 tablespoons sugar in clean, dry bowl of stand mixer fitted with whisk attachment on medium-low speed until foamy, about 1 minute. Increase speed to high and whip until soft peaks form, 1 to 3 minutes.

7. Carefully peel meringue away from parchment and place on large serving platter. Spoon whipped cream into center of meringue. Spoon berries in even layer over whipped cream, then drizzle with melted chocolate. Let sit for at least 5 minutes or up to 1 hour. Slice and serve.

NOTES FROM THE TEST KITCHEN

MAKING CHOCOLATE PAVLOVA WITH BERRIES AND WHIPPED CREAM

1. Whip hot egg white mixture on high speed until meringue forms stiff peaks, is smooth and creamy, and is bright white with sheen, about 4 minutes.

2. Scrape down bowl. Add vinegar, cornstarch, and vanilla and whip on high speed until combined, about 10 seconds. Fold in grated chocolate.

3. Pile meringue in center of circle on prepared parchment.

4. Spread and smooth meringue with back of spoon or spatula from center outward, building 10-inch disk that is slightly higher around edges.

5. Carefully peel baked meringue away from parchment and place on large serving platter. Spoon whipped cream into center of meringue.

6. Spoon berries in even layer over whipped cream. Drizzle with melted chocolate. Slice and serve.

BUTTERMILK-VANILLA PANNA COTTA WITH BERRIES AND HONEY

✓ **WHY THIS RECIPE WORKS** Our silky-smooth buttermilk panna cotta is an elegant dessert that requires some waiting but hardly any work. We made it even simpler by skipping the traditional step of sprinkling gelatin over cold water to bloom it before dissolving it in hot cream. Instead, we whisked together the gelatin, sugar, and salt and then whisked in cold heavy cream. Dispersed by the sugar and salt, the gelatin granules had plenty of space to absorb water from the cream, which readied the gelatin for heating. Bringing the mixture to 150 degrees ensured that the gelatin fully dissolved and the floral notes of the vanilla bean were infused into the cream. We let the mixture cool to 110 degrees before adding the buttermilk to prevent curdling. Finally, we portioned and chilled the panna cotta and refrigerated it until it was time to serve. Its tangy richness was the perfect foil for a variety of toppings.

I have a long history with panna cotta. I figure I've made at least 1,000 batches, because it has been on the dessert menu of every restaurant I've ever worked at. No wonder: Panna cotta is pure in flavor, endlessly adaptable, and ridiculously easy to make. It is also prepared in advance. Each of these perks makes it a recipe that all cooks should know.

Panna cotta (Italian for "cooked cream") is made by setting sugar-sweetened cream and often milk, yogurt, or buttermilk with gelatin to produce a luscious, wobbly, opaque dessert with a clean, milky taste. The usual procedure is to warm the dairy with sugar and then stir in bloomed gelatin (more about this later) until it dissolves. The mixture is then divided among ramekins, chilled for at least 6 hours, and unmolded (it's also lovely served straight from small glasses).

As easy as panna cotta is to make, you still need to use the right proportions of ingredients to achieve the perfect lush consistency. Also, the gelatin must be handled properly: Too much yields a firm, rubbery mass, and if there is too little or it is mishandled, you'll end up with dessert soup.

I've always preferred panna cotta made with equal parts buttermilk and heavy cream. The buttermilk's tangy edge adds depth and moderates the richness of the heavy cream, and the heavy cream plays an important practical role: It can be heated past 150 degrees—the temperature at which I have found that gelatin reliably dissolves and flavorings can be infused into it—without curdling. Curdling happens when a protein in dairy called casein clumps when heated. But heavy cream has enough fat to dilute the casein molecules, preventing clumps. Since lean buttermilk can curdle at temperatures as low as 110 degrees, I like to heat the cream, sugar, and bloomed gelatin and then wait for the mixture to cool before stirring in the buttermilk.

Now, about gelatin, the key—and somewhat temperamental—ingredient in panna cotta. I started by "blooming" it, meaning I hydrated it in cold water.

There are two methods for blooming powdered gelatin. The most common is to sprinkle it in an even layer on a dish of cold water, where it slowly hydrates. For my panna cotta, I found that the other approach, called "bulking," was even easier. It's done by whisking the gelatin together with sugar (or another dry ingredient) before mixing it into water—or, in this case, cream, which contains plenty of water. The sugar helps separate the gelatin granules so that they remain independent while they disperse throughout the watery liquid and can hydrate thoroughly and evenly.

Next, I heated the mixture to dissolve the gelatin. As the mixture cooled, it set into a solid gel.

To serve eight, I thickened 4 cups of dairy with 2 teaspoons of gelatin. This was just the right amount to produce a satiny-smooth, lush dessert that managed to be ethereally light and creamy at the same time. I whisked the gelatin together with sugar and a pinch of salt, added 2 cups of cold cream, and let the mixture sit for 5 minutes. Next, I heated the mixture until it reached 150 degrees and the gelatin had dissolved. Finally, I let the cream-sugar-gelatin combination cool to about 105 degrees before stirring in 2 cups of buttermilk. Now it was ready to be portioned and chilled.

With my basic recipe complete, I capitalized on one of the many advantages of panna cotta: It takes beautifully to flavorings. I made one version infused with an aromatic vanilla bean and then garnished with a drizzle of honey and fresh raspberries and blackberries—an elegant take on berries and cream. Then for something different yet still luxurious, I steeped grapefruit zest in the cream and garnished the panna cotta with crunchy caramel-coated almonds. But my hands-down favorite was Thai basil–infused panna cotta topped with strawberries that I had macerated with sugar and black pepper.

—LAN LAM, *Cook's Illustrated*

Buttermilk-Vanilla Panna Cotta with Berries and Honey

SERVES 8

Make sure to unmold the panna cotta onto cool plates. If you'd rather not unmold the panna cotta, substitute 5- to 6-ounce glasses for the ramekins.

> ½ cup (3½ ounces) sugar
> 2 teaspoons unflavored gelatin
>   Pinch table salt
> 2 cups heavy cream
> 1 vanilla bean
> 2 cups buttermilk
>   Honey
>   Raspberries and/or blackberries

1. Whisk sugar, gelatin, and salt in small saucepan until very well combined. Whisk in cream and let sit for 5 minutes. Cut vanilla bean in half lengthwise. Using tip of paring knife, scrape out seeds. Add bean and seeds to cream mixture. Cook over medium heat, stirring occasionally, until mixture registers 150 to

160 degrees, about 5 minutes. Remove from heat and let mixture cool to 105 to 110 degrees, about 15 minutes. Strain cream mixture through fine-mesh strainer into medium bowl, pressing on solids to extract as much liquid as possible. Gently whisk in buttermilk.

2. Set eight 5-ounce ramekins on rimmed baking sheet. Divide buttermilk mixture evenly among ramekins. Invert second rimmed baking sheet, cover ramekins with sheet, and carefully transfer to refrigerator. Chill for at least 6 hours or up to 3 days (if chilling for more than 6 hours, cover each ramekin with plastic wrap).

3. Working with 1 panna cotta at a time, insert paring knife between panna cotta and side of ramekin. Gently run knife around edge of ramekin to loosen panna cotta. Cover ramekin with serving plate and invert panna cotta onto plate. (You may need to gently jiggle ramekin.) Drizzle each panna cotta with honey, then top with 3 to 5 berries and serve.

VARIATIONS

Buttermilk-Grapefruit Panna Cotta with Caramel-Coated Almonds

Substitute 2 tablespoons grated grapefruit zest (2 grapefruits) for vanilla bean. Omit honey and berries. Sprinkle 1 recipe Caramel-Coated Almonds (recipe follows) on panna cotta before serving.

Buttermilk–Thai Basil Panna Cotta with Peppery Strawberries

Substitute 1 cup fresh Thai basil leaves for vanilla bean. Omit honey and berries. Divide 1 recipe Peppery Strawberries (recipe follows) evenly among panna cotta and garnish with extra basil before serving.

Caramel-Coated Almonds

MAKES ABOUT 1 CUP

The caramel will darken as it cools, so remove the almonds from the pot when the caramel is pale gold.

- ¾ **cup water**
- ¾ **cup vegetable oil**
- ½ **cup sliced almonds**
- ¼ **cup (1¾ ounces) sugar**
- ¼ **teaspoon table salt**

Set fine-mesh strainer over medium bowl. Line rimmed baking sheet with parchment paper. Combine all ingredients in medium saucepan and bring to vigorous simmer over medium-high heat. (Mixture will be very bubbly.) Cook, stirring frequently with rubber spatula, until oil and sugar syrup separate, about 10 minutes. Continue to cook, stirring constantly, until almonds are coated in pale gold caramel, 2 to 4 minutes longer (caramel will darken as it cools). Immediately transfer to prepared strainer. Working quickly, stir and press mixture to remove excess oil. Transfer to prepared sheet and, using spatula, press almonds into single layer. (If caramel sets up too much, briefly warm mixture in low oven.) Let cool for 15 minutes, then break into bite-size pieces. (Almonds can be stored in airtight container at room temperature for up to 3 days.)

Peppery Strawberries

MAKES ABOUT 1 CUP

Use a paring knife to hull the strawberries.

- 6 **ounces strawberries, hulled and quartered (about 1 cup)**
- 1 **teaspoon sugar**
- ⅛ **teaspoon pepper**
  Pinch table salt

Place strawberries in bowl. Sprinkle sugar, pepper, and salt over strawberries and toss to combine. Let mixture sit for at least 15 minutes or up to 2 hours before serving.

APPLE CRUMBLE

✔ **WHY THIS RECIPE WORKS** Making an apple crumble that tastes primarily of apples starts with plenty of fruit. We tossed 4 pounds of apples with some lemon juice to enhance their bright flavor. Adding just 2 tablespoons of brown sugar to the filling kept the apples from tasting too sweet. We baked the apples in a covered pan before applying the topping, which allowed them to collapse into a thick layer of filling. Adding nuts to the streusel loosened its consistency so that it didn't bake up dense. Applying the topping midway through baking minimized its exposure to the juicy fruit, preventing it from becoming soggy.

BUTTERMILK-VANILLA PANNA COTTA WITH BERRIES AND HONEY

A rustic apple crumble has always been my favorite way to highlight apples: It lets their bright, tart character shine. But even recipes that promise to put the apples first inevitably have you bury the fruit in sugar and then double down on that sweetness by blanketing it with a thick layer of streusel. By the time you add a scoop of ice cream, the whole ensemble tastes sweet from top to bottom and totally misses the point—it's like heating really good olive oil so that it loses its grassy bite or cooking a thick, well-marbled steak until the center goes gray.

Don't get me wrong: I love everything about apple crumble—the pragmatism of using up the fruit, the throw-together ease, and the satisfying contrast of tangy, tender fruit against a buttery, delicately crunchy topping. And I'm not antisugar; the fruit's acid needs a healthy dose of the sweet stuff to make a dessert that feels gratifying and balanced. But for the sake of apple lovers such as myself, it was time to bake a better crumble: one that celebrates the apples by dialing down the sweetness and packing in as much fruit as possible.

Using a tart apple might seem like the most logical starting point for a bright-tasting filling, but if you've done much baking with apples, you know that you can't base the choice on flavor alone. Bracingly tart Granny Smiths, for example, can collapse into mush when baked, so we often avoid them in the test kitchen when we want the cooked fruit to retain some shape. Instead, I opted for Golden Delicious, an apple variety that offers year-round and near-universal availability, balanced sweet-tart flavor (later, I'd work out a way to make it brighter), and structural integrity.

Most recipes call for piling a few pounds of apples into an 8-inch square baking dish, making sure to leave at least ¼ inch of headspace for the streusel. But this leads to a ratio problem: Apples shrink down as they cook, and by the time they're tender, you're left with a scant layer of filling (2 parts filling to 1 part topping is a common result). Plus, the moisture that the apples exude during baking saturates the part of the streusel where the filling and topping meet, producing a soggy, pasty interface.

To bulk up the ratio of filling to topping, I started with 4 pounds of apples, peeling, coring, and cutting them into small chunks so that they'd fit as compactly as possible into the baking dish and seasoning them with 2 tablespoons of sugar—less than half the amount that I've seen in other recipes—and a little cinnamon. But the fruit mounded over the edge of the dish, so

when I tried covering it with a simple streusel (flour, dark brown sugar, salt, and melted butter), the soft clumps tumbled off.

That explained why most recipes refrain from loading up on the apples, but I realized that there was a way to fit all 4 pounds of fruit by taking advantage of its tendency to shrink: I parcooked the apples before applying the topping, so they collapsed and created a substantial but compact layer of filling with just enough headspace for the streusel. The trick was baking the apples on the lower rack in a hot oven (the closer that food is to the oven floor, the closer it is to the heat source) with a sheet of aluminum foil crimped over the baking dish to trap steam, until they started to collapse. Then I uncovered the dish, smoothed the apples into an even layer that sat about ¼ inch below the lip of the baking dish, scattered the streusel over the top, and returned the dish to the oven for another half-hour to brown the topping.

Chockablock with apples and capped with just enough streusel, the crumble's proportions were in good shape—about a 5:1 ratio of filling to topping. But the texture and flavor of the fruit were not. The apples touching the edges of the dish had broken down into sauce by the time the topping browned, so going forward I moved the crumble to a higher oven rack after I applied the topping; that put some distance between the apple layer and the heat source so that it cooked more gently during the second phase and brought the streusel closer to the heat reflecting off the oven ceiling, helping it brown quickly. (Using a metal baking pan also helped prevent carryover cooking, since it retains less heat outside the oven than a glass dish.) To punch up the apples' acidity and overall flavor, I tossed the fruit with 2 tablespoons of lemon juice and a touch of salt before baking. (This also lowered the pH of the dish, helping the fruit maintain its shape during cooking.)

Waiting to apply the streusel until midway through baking had the added benefit of minimizing the time it spent soaking up liquid from the fruit, so now there was less of that soggy interface. But the dough touching the fruit was still a bit soft and damp, while the rest was actually loose and dry, like a too-short cookie. It was a textural schism, and to fix it, I needed two opposing solutions to work in tandem.

The first was water—an unusual addition to streusel dough that hydrated the dry flour, dissolved some of the sugar so that it was less gritty, and helped the dough form larger clumps. Two teaspoons of water plus

2 teaspoons of vanilla extract (which also added depth to the streusel's flavor) moistened the dough. The second was nuts. Plenty of crumble recipes call for mixing them into the topping, and when I worked in some chopped almonds, they added not just crunch but also fat that made the filling more resistant to the fruit's exuded moisture. What's more, the nuts loosened up the structure of the topping so that it didn't bake up compact and dense. I also made sure to scatter the streusel loosely over the apples to allow more of the fruit's moisture to escape during baking.

Scooping out the fruit-packed crumble was visual proof that the apples were finally getting their due. Tasting the clean, bright punch of the filling alongside the nutty, buttery, not-too-sweet streusel topping was even more convincing.

—ANDREW JANJIGIAN, *Cook's Illustrated*

Apple Crumble

SERVES 6 TO 8

We like Golden Delicious apples because of their ubiquity and consistent quality, but this recipe also works with Braeburn or Honeycrisp apples or a mix of all three. You should have 4 pounds of apples before peeling and coring. Dark brown sugar gives the topping a deeper color, but light brown sugar will also work. Do not use a glass baking dish here, since it retains heat after baking and may cause the apples to overcook. If you like, serve the crumble with ice cream or lightly whipped cream.

- 4 **pounds Golden Delicious apples, peeled, cored, and cut into ¾-inch pieces**
- 2 **tablespoons packed plus ½ cup packed (3½ ounces) dark brown sugar, divided**
- 2 **tablespoons lemon juice**
- 1 **teaspoon table salt, divided**
- ¾ **teaspoon ground cinnamon**
- 1 **cup (5 ounces) all-purpose flour**
- ½ **cup sliced almonds, chopped fine**
- 6 **tablespoons unsalted butter, melted**
- 2 **teaspoons vanilla extract**
- 2 **teaspoons water**

1. Adjust oven racks to upper-middle and lowest positions and heat oven to 400 degrees. Toss apples, 2 tablespoons sugar, lemon juice, ½ teaspoon salt, and cinnamon together in large bowl. Transfer to 8-inch square baking pan with at least 2-inch sides and press into even layer. Cover pan tightly with aluminum foil and place on rimmed baking sheet. Transfer sheet to oven and bake on lower rack for 35 minutes.

2. While apples bake, whisk flour, almonds, remaining ½ cup sugar, and remaining ½ teaspoon salt in medium bowl until combined. Add melted butter, vanilla, and water and stir with spatula until clumps form and no dry flour remains.

3. Remove sheet from oven and smooth top of apples with spatula. If apples have not collapsed enough to leave at least ¼ inch of space below rim of pan, replace foil, return sheet to oven, and continue to bake 5 to 15 minutes longer.

4. Scatter topping evenly over apples, breaking up any clumps larger than a marble. Transfer sheet to upper rack and bake until topping is evenly browned and filling is just bubbling at edges, 25 to 35 minutes. Transfer pan to wire rack and let cool for at least 45 minutes before serving.

PINEAPPLE UPSIDE-DOWN CAKE

✓ **WHY THIS RECIPE WORKS** For a showstopping update on this beautiful retro cake that doubled down on pineapple flavor, we started with fresh pineapple instead of canned and used round cutters to make our own rings for a classic look. To prevent the juicy fresh fruit from sogging out the top of the cake during baking, we simmered the rings in a mixture of pineapple juice and brown sugar to tenderize them and drive off some of their excess moisture. After transferring the softened rings to the cake pan with the requisite ruby-red maraschino cherries, we cooked down the juice-sugar mixture and added butter to make a luscious pineapple caramel sauce. By doubling the typical amount of caramel, we were able to ensure a beautifully glossy cake top and reserve some pineapple-flavored caramel to brush onto the other side of the cake while it rested, thus permeating the cake with pineapple flavor through and through. To loosen the remaining caramel so that it would soak into the cake bottom and add an intoxicating aromatic complexity, we stirred in a bit of dark rum and a touch more fresh pineapple juice.

PINEAPPLE UPSIDE-DOWN CAKE

With glistening rings of sweet-tart pineapple and ruby pops of maraschino cherries adorning a buttery, tender yellow cake, the pineapple upside-down cake is one of America's most iconic desserts. At its most basic, the dessert is a stir-together yellow cake baked atop butter, brown sugar, canned pineapple rings, and jarred cherries and then inverted once baked so that the fruit is on top.

My colleagues and I sampled five recipes for this cake, and we were surprised to find that while the cakes looked great, they simply weren't as delicious or as special as they should have been. To start, the cakes themselves didn't have pineapple flavor, and the toppings had metallic notes from the canned fruit. The versions we tried with chunks of fresh pineapple were better, but we all missed the retro beauty of the rings. Plus, all the cakes we tried looked a little dull and lacked a glossy caramel sheen.

We decided it was time for an update. I wanted my version to have loads of fresh pineapple flavor; a moist, buttery, simple-to-make yellow cake with pineapple flavor of its own; and a stunning, glossy look that amplified the iconic appeal of the rings.

I began by cutting a fresh pineapple into ½-inch-thick slices. Then I used round cutters to punch out clean circles and remove the tough core. I set the rings in a greased 9-inch round cake pan with melted butter and brown sugar. I then poured a simple yellow cake batter on top and popped the pan into the oven. Yes, the flavor of the pineapple rings was much fresher, but the fruit was still a little tough and the moisture it exuded made the cake soggy and mushy. And the cake still didn't look glossy or have its own pineapple flavor.

In my next test, I tried to solve the sogginess problem while also doubling down on pineapple flavor. I grabbed a 12-inch skillet and cooked the pineapple rings in a mixture of 1 cup of pineapple juice and an increased amount of brown sugar. This tenderized the fruit and cooked off some of its juice; I hoped it would also give me more caramel to leave the cake with a glossy shine.

Once I'd transferred the rings to the cake pan, I concentrated and caramelized the mixture of juice and sugar in the pan by simmering it until it was syrupy; I then added butter to create a pineapple-flavored caramel sauce. Half the sauce went into the cake pan with the pineapple. While the cake baked, I thinned out the remainder of the pineapple caramel with some dark rum—to cut the sweetness and add aromatic complexity—and a bit more fresh pineapple juice for

vibrancy. Then, while the cake cooled, I poked holes all over it with a toothpick and brushed most of my pineapple-rum caramel on top to let it soak in. I reserved a bit of the caramel sauce to brush on before serving.

As I turned out this new, juiced-up version of my cake, I was delighted to find that it looked positively stunning. There was just enough extra pineapple caramel to leave a few drips on the platter and create the right gooey consistency and glossy shine, but not so much as to make the cake soggy.

The real revelation came when we all dug in. The rings were tender, juicy, and vibrant. The cake was ultrabuttery and balanced by the complex, heady pineapple-rum caramel soak. The essence of sunshiny pineapple carried through the entire experience, from top to bottom. This was a pineapple upside-down cake fit for a special occasion.

—MATTHEW FAIRMAN, *Cook's Country*

Pineapple Upside-Down Cake
SERVES 8

You will need a 3¼-inch round cutter and a 1¼-inch round cutter or apple corer to make the pineapple rings. If you prefer, you can substitute 2 additional tablespoons of pineapple juice for the rum in step 5.

- 1 pineapple, peeled
- 1½ cups packed (10½ ounces) light brown sugar
- 1 cup plus 2 tablespoons pineapple juice, divided
- 7 maraschino cherries, stemmed and patted dry
- 12 tablespoons unsalted butter, cut into 12 pieces, plus 8 tablespoons melted
- 1 teaspoon table salt, divided
- 2 tablespoons dark rum
- 1½ cups (7½ ounces) all-purpose flour
- 1 teaspoon baking powder
- 1 cup (7 ounces) granulated sugar
- ½ cup whole milk
- 2 large eggs
- 1 teaspoon vanilla extract

1. Adjust oven rack to middle position and heat oven to 350 degrees. Grease 9-inch round cake pan, line with parchment paper, and grease parchment.

2. Cut seven ½-inch-thick crosswise slices from pineapple. (Reserve remaining pineapple for another use.) Using 3¼-inch round cutter, cut slices into neat rounds;

discard trimmings. Using 1¼-inch round cutter or apple corer, remove core from pineapple slices to create rings; discard core pieces.

3. Combine brown sugar and 1 cup pineapple juice in 12-inch skillet. Add pineapple rings to skillet in single layer. Bring to boil over medium-high heat and cook until rings have softened, about 10 minutes, flipping rings halfway through cooking. Transfer rings to prepared pan, placing 1 ring in center of pan and arranging remaining 6 rings around circumference of pan (rings will fit snugly in pan without overlapping). Place cherries in centers of rings.

NOTES FROM THE TEST KITCHEN

REINVENTING THE (PINEAPPLE) RINGS

USE FRESH FRUIT Top and tail fresh pineapple, then cut off rind.

CREATE RINGS Use round cutters to remove tough core from slices.

COOK RINGS IN SYRUP Simmer rings in pineapple juice and brown sugar.

REDUCE SYRUP Remove cooked rings and boil syrup down to rich caramel.

---

4. Return brown sugar mixture to boil over medium-high heat and cook, stirring frequently, until rubber spatula dragged across bottom of skillet leaves trail that fills in slowly, bubbles increase in size, and mixture registers 260 degrees, 3 to 6 minutes. Carefully stir in 12 tablespoons butter and ½ teaspoon salt until butter is melted (caramel may look separated at first). Return mixture to boil and cook until frothy and uniform in texture, about 1 minute. Let caramel cool off heat for 5 minutes.

5. Transfer caramel to 4-cup liquid measuring cup. Pour ¾ cup caramel evenly over pineapple rings, gently shaking pan to distribute. Whisk rum and remaining 2 tablespoons pineapple juice into remaining caramel; set aside.

6. Whisk flour, baking powder, and remaining ½ teaspoon salt together in bowl. Whisk granulated sugar, milk, eggs, and vanilla in large bowl until smooth, about 1 minute. Whisk 8 tablespoons melted butter into milk mixture until combined. Whisk flour mixture into milk mixture until no dry flour remains.

7. Transfer batter to prepared pan and smooth top with rubber spatula. Bake until light golden brown and toothpick inserted in center comes out clean, 50 minutes to 1 hour.

8. Transfer pan to wire rack. Immediately run paring knife between cake and sides of pan. Using toothpick, poke about 80 holes evenly over cake. Microwave reserved caramel mixture until warm, about 1 minute. Brush cake with ½ cup reserved caramel mixture. Let cake cool in pan for 25 minutes. Carefully invert cake onto serving plate. Brush top of cake with remaining reserved caramel mixture as desired. Serve warm or at room temperature, passing any remaining caramel mixture separately.

BACI DI DAMA (ITALIAN HAZELNUT COOKIES)

✓ **WHY THIS RECIPE WORKS** These miniature Italian hazelnut-chocolate sandwich cookies are typically made from a very rich, fragile dough that easily crumbles when you roll it. Reducing the amount of butter and nuts in the dough made it firmer but still plenty rich and tender. Leaving bits of skin on the nuts also helped firm up the dough and added complex flavor and attractive color. To avoid scooping and weighing dozens of portions of dough, we pressed the dough into a parchment paper–lined square baking pan, briefly froze it to firm it up, and cut a "portion grid" into the resulting dough block. Melting dark chocolate in the microwave and letting it cool and thicken slightly before spooning it onto the inverted cookies ensured that it didn't drip off the sides. We gently pressed the second cookie on top to spread the filling just to the edges, and then we let the cookies rest for 15 minutes before serving so that the chocolate could set.

If I had a dollar for every time someone came up to my workstation in the test kitchen and proclaimed, "Those cookies are so cute!" I could retire. But endearing as they are, baci di dama are also fussy, and a few batches into my recipe development, I wanted to retire.

Hailing from the Piedmont region of Italy, baci di dama are sandwich cookies that consist of two tiny hazelnut buttons held together by a slim chocolate filling. (Their name translates as "lady's kisses" because each sandwich is said to resemble a woman's pursed lips.) Sandwich cookies are laborious to make by nature, but these are made from a short, fragile dough that must be chilled for at least an hour lest it soften too much to be workable. And because the cookies are bite-size, the portioning step is a real bear: A single batch makes dozens of cookies, each of which must be measured (often weighed) precisely so that all the sandwich halves match up perfectly. Once the cookies have been baked and cooled, half of them are overturned and dolloped with melted chocolate (or sometimes Nutella or ganache), gently topped with the remaining cookies so that the filling spreads just to the edges, and left to sit briefly so that the chocolate sets.

All this I learned after being lured in by not just their visual charm but their flavor and consistency, too. A recipe from Italian cookbook author Domenica Marchetti was the best and simplest I'd made, and it yielded cookies that were rich with nuts and butter and that carefully balanced ample structure with the tenderness of great shortbread. The results looked and tasted so good (even days later) that I picked apart the process to see where it could be made faster and easier.

Marchetti's food-processor method for making the dough is easier than most classic recipes, which call for mixing the ingredients by hand. All you do is grind hazelnuts (toasted and skinned), butter, flour, sugar, and salt until the nuts are broken down and a dough comes together. It's the portioning and chilling

steps that really drag out the process, so I took a hard look at the ingredient list to see how I could make a firmer dough that would require less chilling.

The high ratio of fat to flour is what makes a short dough such as this one soft and fragile, so I tried making a leaner version. Marchetti's formula already called for slightly less butter (and considerably less sugar) than most classic Piedmontese recipes, and when I reduced the butter and sugar a bit further while also cutting back on the nuts, I ended up with a dough that still boasted plenty of richness and nutty flavor but was firm enough that I could get away with just a quick stint in the freezer before portioning it.

There was one more subtle but tedious task I streamlined before moving on to the portioning project: rubbing every bit of papery skin from the toasted hazelnuts. Since I was grinding the nuts very fine, I wondered if it was necessary to be quite so thorough—or necessary to skin them at all—so I baked batches of cookies made with skinned, partially skinned (rubbed briefly after toasting), and skin-on hazelnuts. The surprising news: Not only was it easier to partially skin the nuts, but leaving some of the papery bits attached resulted in a slightly drier yet more flavorful and resilient dough with attractive dark flecks. (Forgoing skinning altogether made the dough too dry and a tad savory, thanks to the tannins in the skins.)

Precisely portioning the dough is the most important step when making any sandwich cookie, and it's even more crucial here because the cookies' button-like charm relies on having two perfect halves. But scooping and weighing dozens of tiny dough pieces felt tedious, so I tried alternative methods, such as a "gnocchi" approach where you roll the dough into ropes and cut each rope into equal portions. It worked well enough but wasn't as efficient as the method we developed to portion chocolate truffles: Press the dough into a parchment paper–lined baking pan; freeze it for 10 minutes to firm it up; turn out the chilled block onto the counter; and cut a "portion grid" by halving the dough lengthwise, halving those halves lengthwise, cutting the rows in half again, rotating the dough 90 degrees, and making equally spaced perpendicular cuts. It took just minutes to make equal portions that I rolled into balls and baked.

While the cookies cooled, I mapped out the most efficient way to assemble the sandwiches and melted a couple of ounces of bittersweet chocolate in the microwave for the filling. (Neither ganache nor Nutella firmed up enough to lock the cookies together.) Piping the chocolate from a zipper-lock bag with the corner snipped off didn't work since the heat of my hands made the chocolate too runny. But I did find a trick for portioning the melted chocolate. I allowed it to cool and thicken a bit before spooning it onto the overturned cookies. Letting the sandwiches sit for about 15 minutes before serving allowed the chocolate to cool and set.

My no-fuss approach to skinning the nuts, mixing the dough in a food processor, and making a portion grid added up to a really approachable recipe. As for the cookies themselves, they were rich and complexly nutty, with a dark, bittersweet snap—and so cute.

—STEVE DUNN, *Cook's Illustrated*

Baci di Dama (Italian Hazelnut Cookies)
MAKES 32 SANDWICH COOKIES

Toast the hazelnuts on a rimmed baking sheet in a 325-degree oven until they're fragrant, 13 to 15 minutes, shaking the sheet halfway through toasting. To skin them, gather the warm hazelnuts in a dish towel and rub to remove some of the skins. A square-cornered metal baking pan works best for shaping the dough. If using a baking dish with rounded corners, be sure to square the corners of the dough before portioning it. We prefer Ghirardelli 60% Cacao Bittersweet Chocolate Premium Baking Bar for this recipe.

- ¾ cup hazelnuts, toasted and partially skinned
- ⅔ cup (3⅓ ounces) all-purpose flour
- ⅓ cup (2⅓ ounces) sugar
- ⅛ teaspoon table salt
- 6 tablespoons unsalted butter, cut into
  ½-inch pieces and chilled
- 2 ounces bittersweet chocolate, chopped

1. Adjust oven rack to middle position and heat oven to 325 degrees. Line 2 rimmed baking sheets with parchment paper. Line bottom of 8-inch square baking pan with parchment. Process hazelnuts, flour, sugar, and salt in food processor until hazelnuts are very finely ground, 20 to 25 seconds. Add butter and pulse until dough just comes together, 20 to 25 pulses.

2. Transfer dough to counter, knead briefly to form smooth ball, place in prepared pan, and press into even layer that covers bottom of pan. Freeze for 10 minutes. Run knife or bench scraper between dough and edge of pan to loosen. Turn out dough onto counter and

discard parchment. Cut dough into 64 squares (8 rows by 8 rows). Roll dough squares into balls and evenly space 32 dough balls on each prepared sheet. Bake, 1 sheet at a time, until cookies look dry and are fragrant (cookies will settle but not spread), about 20 minutes, rotating sheet halfway through baking. Transfer sheet to wire rack and let cookies cool completely, about 30 minutes.

3. Microwave chocolate in small bowl at 50 percent power, stirring every 20 seconds, until melted, 1 to 2 minutes. Let chocolate cool at room temperature until it is slightly thickened and registers 80 degrees, about 10 minutes. Invert half of cookies on each sheet. Using ¼-teaspoon measure, spoon chocolate onto flat surfaces of all inverted cookies. Top with remaining cookies, pressing lightly to adhere. Let chocolate set for at least 15 minutes before serving. (Cookies can be stored in airtight container at room temperature for up to 10 days.)

CHOCOLATE CHIP COOKIE ICE CREAM SANDWICHES

✓ **WHY THIS RECIPE WORKS** Our well-proportioned sandwiches feature relatively small, thin cookies and precise scoops of ice cream that give each bite the perfect combination of textures and flavors. We added water to the dough to prevent the cookies from turning rock-hard in the freezer, as well as plenty of browned butter, dark brown sugar, vanilla, and salt to compensate for the flavor-dulling effect of the freezer. Mini chocolate chips provided bursts of chocolate flavor and delicately crunchy texture.

Ten years ago, *Cook's Illustrated* published a recipe for chocolate chip cookies that we consider perfect: crisp, deeply caramelized edges; chewy centers; gooey pockets of dark chocolate; and complex, toffee-like flavor that's not too sweet. Trust me when I say that a glass of milk will never know a better companion.

So when I decided to make chocolate chip cookie ice cream sandwiches, I figured I had the cookie part all figured out. I baked off a batch, sandwiched two around a scoop of my favorite premium ice cream, and froze the sandwich until solid.

Then I tried to take a bite. The cookies were so hard my teeth couldn't get through them, and all that force caused the ice cream to squish out the sides. When

CHOCOLATE CHIP COOKIE ICE CREAM SANDWICHES

I finally did bite through the cookies, I found that the cold temperature had completely dulled their exceptional butterscotch flavor.

Obviously, these chocolate chip cookies weren't perfect for ice cream sandwiches, but I hoped they'd be a good jumping-off point for calibrating a great sandwich cookie. To compensate for the freezer's flavor-dulling effect, I wanted even more deep toffee flavor packed into a cookie that would be thin and tender enough to bite through when cold but still firm enough to house a generous layer of ice cream.

I figured out that 2 parts ice cream to 1 part cookies was the ideal ratio. The cookies I'd been using were each about ½ inch thick; once I'd added a 2-inch-thick layer of ice cream, it was all too much of a mouthful—the frozen-dessert equivalent of a New York deli sandwich. Quarter-inch-thick cookies surrounding a 1-inch-thick ice cream center would make for a more edible package.

Fortunately, it was easy to make thinner cookies: I again made the dough for our chocolate chip cookies, but instead of baking the cookies at 375 degrees, I dropped the temperature to 325 degrees so that the dough had more time to spread before it set.

These cookies were not only thinner but also flatter and more uniform in texture from edge to edge, since the lower baking temperature had allowed the edges and centers to bake at nearly the same rate. But once frozen, the cookies were still hard and brittle.

One small fix was to swap out the regular chocolate chips for mini morsels. The mini chips were easier to bite through; in fact, I enjoyed their delicate crunch so much that I pressed more into the ice cream around the rim of the sandwich for a dose of Chipwich nostalgia.

But then I made a fortuitous discovery. Until now, I'd been freezing the sandwiches for just a few hours. When I happened to leave a batch in the freezer for nearly 24 hours, I noticed that the cookies were much softer than before, clearly having absorbed more moisture from the ice cream over time. It made me wonder if I should be making a moister cookie from the start.

To find out, I went straight to the source, adding various amounts of water to the dough along with the egg and vanilla. Ultimately, I settled on 2 tablespoons, which, combined with a good 8 hours in the freezer, made for cookies sturdy enough to sandwich the ice cream but tender enough to bite through with just a hint of snap.

I also replaced the granulated sugar with more dark brown sugar, since the molasses in brown sugar is a source of simple sugars (glucose and fructose) that are hygroscopic—that is, very effective at attracting water.

Brown sugar also boosted that prized deep toffee flavor, though not quite enough, so I also browned all the butter, which coaxed out a round, nutty flavor. I also upped the amounts of vanilla and salt, all of which added up to cookies that boasted big toffee-like, hazelnutty richness even after spending hours in the freezer.

Now that the cookies were squared away, I focused on instituting some best practices for making tidy, professional-looking ice cream sandwiches. Making sure to center the scoops of ice cream on the cookies translated into neater results. Paying attention to the ice cream itself mattered, too: Premium products with lower overrun—the amount of air that gets added during churning to make ice cream light and fluffy rather than dense—were harder to scoop straight from the freezer, so when I used those, I briefly tempered, or softened, the ice cream in the refrigerator to make scooping easier.

If you love the deep toffee flavor and crisp-tender texture of our Perfect Chocolate Chip Cookies, you'll appreciate this ice cream sandwich version, too. And if you were raised on Chipwiches, consider this a nostalgic upgrade.

—LAN LAM, *Cook's Illustrated*

Chocolate Chip Cookie Ice Cream Sandwiches
MAKES 12 SANDWICHES

These sandwiches should be made at least 8 hours before serving. For the best results, weigh the flour and sugar for the cookies. We prefer the deeper flavor of dark brown sugar here, but light brown sugar will also work. Use your favorite ice cream. If using a premium ice cream such as Ben & Jerry's or Häagen-Dazs, which is likely to be harder than a less-premium brand when frozen, let the ice cream soften slightly in the refrigerator before scooping. If you have it, a #16 scoop works well for portioning the ice cream. Our favorite pure vanilla extract is Simply Organic Pure Vanilla Extract, and our favorite imitation extract is Baker's Imitation Vanilla Flavor. We like these sandwiches with chocolate chips pressed into the sides, but the garnish is optional.

10 tablespoons unsalted butter

¾ cup packed (5¼ ounces) dark brown sugar

¾ teaspoon table salt

1 cup plus 2 tablespoons (5⅔ ounces) all-purpose flour

¼ teaspoon baking soda

1 large egg

2 tablespoons water

2 teaspoons vanilla extract

½ cup (3 ounces) mini semisweet chocolate chips, plus 1 cup for optional garnish

3 pints ice cream

1. Adjust oven rack to middle position and heat oven to 325 degrees. Melt butter in 10-inch skillet over medium-high heat. Cook, stirring and scraping skillet constantly with rubber spatula, until milk solids are dark golden brown and butter has nutty aroma, 1 to 3 minutes. Immediately transfer to heatproof large bowl. Whisk in sugar and salt until fully incorporated and let mixture cool for 10 minutes. Meanwhile, line 2 rimmed baking sheets with parchment paper. Stir flour and baking soda together in second bowl; set aside.

2. Add egg, water, and vanilla to browned butter mixture and whisk until smooth, about 30 seconds. Using rubber spatula, stir in flour mixture until combined. Stir in ½ cup chocolate chips. (Dough will be very soft.)

3. Using #60 scoop or 1-tablespoon measure, evenly space 12 mounds of dough on each prepared sheet. Bake cookies, 1 sheet at a time, until puffed and golden brown, 9 to 12 minutes, rotating sheet halfway through baking. Let cookies cool on sheet for 5 minutes, then transfer to wire rack and let cool completely, about 45 minutes. Place 1 sheet, still lined with parchment, in freezer.

4. Place 4 cookies upside down on counter. Quickly deposit 2-inch-tall, 2-inch-wide scoop of ice cream in center of each cookie. Place 1 cookie from wire rack right side up on top of each scoop. Gently press and twist each sandwich between your hands until ice cream spreads to edges of cookies (this doesn't have to be perfect; ice cream can be neatened after chilling). Transfer sandwiches to sheet in freezer. Repeat with remaining cookies and remaining ice cream. Place 1 cup chocolate chips, if using, in shallow bowl or pie plate.

5. Remove first 4 sandwiches from freezer. Working with 1 sandwich at a time, hold sandwiches over bowl of chocolate chips and gently press chocolate chips into

sides of sandwiches with your other hand, neatening ice cream if necessary. Return garnished sandwiches to freezer and repeat with remaining 8 sandwiches in 2 batches. Freeze sandwiches for at least 8 hours before serving. (Sandwiches can be individually wrapped tightly in plastic wrap, transferred to zipper-lock bag, and frozen for up to 2 months.)

NANAIMO BARS

✓ **WHY THIS RECIPE WORKS** Canadian Nanaimo bars are no-bake bar cookies that feature three distinct layers: a coconutty cookie base, a custardy center, and a chocolate ganache top. For our version, we blitzed graham crackers and shredded coconut in the food processor and bound them with melted chocolate and corn syrup to create a chewy yet sturdy base. The soft middle layer is traditionally made using custard powder, an ingredient common in Canadian kitchens. But we found a work-around for U.S. cooks: Nonfat dry milk powder contributed a sweet-salty flavor and gave the filling its signature soft-yet-set texture. A quick ganache of melted chocolate chips, butter, and corn syrup slathered over the chilled filling helped these Nanaimo bars shine.

Nanaimo, a small city on Vancouver Island in the Canadian province of British Columbia, is just a few miles from Washington State, yet the city's namesake sweet is virtually unknown in the United States. But Nanaimo ("nuh-NIGH-moe") bars deserve a bigger stage. These three-layer bars, with their coconutty cookie bases, creamy centers, and chocolate ganache tops, have a spectrum of sweet flavors and satisfying textures worthy of international recognition.

To bring the bars stateside, I found five different recipes for Nanaimo bars, including a version from Nanaimo's city government. I spread them out for my tasters and we assessed, layer by layer.

While some recipes took a no-cook route for the base, my favorite from this initial lineup called for cooking butter, sugar, cocoa powder, and an egg in a double boiler and then stirring in graham cracker crumbs, coconut, and chopped nuts once the mixture had thickened. Tasters loved the fudgy and slightly chewy texture of this crust: sturdy enough to carry

NANAIMO BARS

around but soft enough to sink your teeth into without destroying the bar. But I wanted to see if I could achieve it in an easier way.

I first ditched the egg, which requires cooking to do its work as a binder and stabilizing agent. Instead, I turned to chocolate chips, which I melted in the microwave and stirred into the mixture. Once cooled, the crust was firm—but too firm, almost candy bar–like. In my next test, I added some corn syrup and achieved the slightly softer result I was after.

In most recipes, that soft middle layer is made by creaming butter, confectioners' sugar, vanilla, and custard powder, an ingredient common in Canadian kitchens. Though it's hard to find in the United States, we found a supplier and ordered some to see what it was all about. Much like instant pudding mix, it contains cornstarch, salt, vanilla, and coloring. It didn't taste like much on its own, but when used as the base for the custard layer in the bars, it contributed eggy richness and a golden color. I needed to find a work-around for U.S. cooks.

I considered making a homemade custard from scratch, but the ideal thickness and sturdiness (I wanted the filling to hold its shape once sliced) proved elusive. So I experimented with instant pudding mix, which made the bars too sweet. Next I tried cornstarch, which I mixed with butter, sugar, and heavy cream, but it lacked flavor. Nonfat dry milk powder turned out to be the solution. Combined with the other ingredients, it produced a rich, buttery, vanilla-y, salty-sweet filling with the perfect consistency.

Nearly all the recipes I'd found had included a matching top layer of ganache made by melting chocolate chips and butter. It's hard to improve on that. But adding a tablespoon of corn syrup made the ganache easier to slather over the chilled filling and gave the chocolate a winning shine once it was fully set.

Nanaimo bars, welcome to *Cook's Country*. We are so glad you're here.

—MORGAN BOLLING, *Cook's Country*

Nanaimo Bars

MAKES 18 BARS

For bars with tidy edges, be sure to wipe your knife clean with a dish towel after each cut. We developed this recipe with Ghirardelli 60% Premium Baking Chips.

CRUST

- ½ cup (3 ounces) bittersweet chocolate chips
- 6 whole graham crackers, broken into 1-inch pieces
- ⅔ cup (2 ounces) sweetened shredded coconut
- ½ cup pecans, toasted
- ¼ cup (¾ ounce) unsweetened cocoa powder
- ⅛ teaspoon table salt
- ⅓ cup light corn syrup

FILLING

- 1¼ cups (5 ounces) confectioners' sugar
- 8 tablespoons unsalted butter, softened
- ¼ cup (¾ ounce) nonfat dry milk powder
- ⅛ teaspoon table salt
- ¼ cup heavy cream
- 2 teaspoons vanilla extract

TOPPING

- ⅔ cup (4 ounces) bittersweet chocolate chips
- 2 tablespoons unsalted butter
- 1 tablespoon light corn syrup

1. FOR THE CRUST: Make foil sling for 8-inch square baking pan by folding 2 long sheets of aluminum foil so each is 8 inches wide. Lay sheets of foil in pan perpendicular to each other, with extra foil hanging over edges of pan. Push foil into corners and up sides of pan, smoothing foil flush to pan. Spray foil with vegetable oil spray.

2. Microwave chocolate chips in bowl at 50 percent power, stirring occasionally, until melted, 1 to 2 minutes. Process cracker pieces, coconut, pecans, cocoa, and salt in food processor until cracker pieces are finely ground, about 30 seconds. Add corn syrup and melted chocolate and pulse until combined, 8 to 10 pulses (mixture should hold together when pinched with your fingers). Transfer to prepared pan. Using bottom of greased measuring cup, press crumbs into even layer in bottom of pan. Refrigerate while making filling.

3. FOR THE FILLING: In clean, dry workbowl, process sugar, butter, milk powder, and salt until smooth, about 30 seconds, scraping down sides of bowl as needed. Add cream and vanilla and process until fully combined, about 15 seconds. Spread filling evenly over crust. Cover pan with plastic wrap and refrigerate until filling is set and firm, about 2 hours.

4. FOR THE TOPPING: Microwave chocolate chips, butter, and corn syrup in bowl at 50 percent power, stirring occasionally, until chocolate chips and butter are melted and mixture is smooth, 1 to 2 minutes. Using offset spatula, spread chocolate mixture evenly over set filling. Refrigerate until topping is set, about 30 minutes.

5. Using foil overhang, lift bars out of pan and transfer to cutting board; discard foil. Using chef's knife, trim outer ¼ inch of square to make neat edges (wipe knife clean with dish towel after each cut). Cut square into thirds to create 3 rectangles. Cut each rectangle crosswise into 6 equal pieces. Let bars sit at room temperature for 20 minutes before serving. (Bars can be refrigerated for up to 2 days.)

PORTUGUESE EGG TARTS

✔ **WHY THIS RECIPE WORKS** The sweet, supercreamy vanilla-and-lemon-scented custard filling and crisp pastry shell of petite Portuguese egg tarts leave many a tourist yearning for these iconic pastries upon returning home. Store-bought puff pastry, parbaked in muffin tin cups, gave us the most shattering crust beneath the custard filling. To get the classic swirled pastry layers, we rolled the puff pastry dough into logs, sliced it into rounds, and pressed it into the muffin tin cups. While many of our custard recipes use cornstarch as a thickener, we found that flour helped this custard withstand the high oven heat necessary to achieve the spotty brown surface found on traditional tarts.

When a friend says they're going to Portugal to "find themselves," I'm convinced that what they're actually hoping to find are Portuguese egg tarts, or pastéis de nata. These delectable mini pastries are made by filling a flaky pastry dough with a fragrant egg-based custard and caramelizing them to perfection. A favorite of sweet-toothed tourists around the world, their small size makes them a superb snack for strolling the streets of Lisbon. I wanted to enjoy pastéis de nata without having to leave the country—or even my kitchen.

Before attempting to re-create this iconic treat in the test kitchen, my team and I sampled some egg tarts from a local Portuguese bakery. We fell for the textural contrast between the impossibly creamy filling and shatteringly crisp crust. Now that I had a firm goal in mind, I worked my way through a handful of existing recipes to find the best qualities of each. Some recipes produced superdoughy crusts from pouring the hot custard filling over raw dough; others turned out grainy fillings caused by cooking the tarts in an excessively hot oven. A few called for fussy techniques or special equipment that I didn't want to bother with. My goal was to get as close as possible to the real pastéis de nata while uncovering some shortcuts for the everyday home baker.

I started with the crust. Of course, traditional bakeries make their own pastry from scratch, laminating butter with dough to create layers of flaky puff-pastry goodness. But making puff pastry from scratch is time-consuming and labor-intensive—after all, this isn't *The Great British Bake Off*. I resolved to use store-bought puff pastry, which we use in numerous test kitchen recipes.

While puff pastry becomes pretty crisp when baked, the pastéis de nata's crust is on another level of flakiness. Many recipes call for rolling a sheet of puff pastry into a log, slicing it into rounds, and pressing the slices into the mini tart pans. When I tested out this technique, my pastries had exponentially more flaky layers; plus, this step gave the bottom of my tarts their signature spiral look. Oh, and about those mini tart pans—a 12-cup muffin tin was a convenient swap.

Time to move on to the custard. Although recipes vary slightly across the board—the type of dairy used, the type of thickener used, how the sugar is incorporated—the technique is pretty standard: Bring the dairy and sugar to a simmer, carefully incorporate egg yolks and the thickener, and simmer the custard until it reaches the desired consistency. Sticking with this familiar method was tempting, but I was intrigued by egg tart recipes that called for streaming sugar syrup into the dairy mixture. While this approach produced a silky-smooth custard, it was no better than more traditional, less fussy methods. So I circled back to the classic custard: I simmered milk and heavy cream with sugar, whisked it into a bit of all-purpose flour, added eight egg yolks, and returned the whole mixture to the stove to simmer until it thickened. I poured it through a fine-mesh strainer to ensure that it was silky-smooth.

Most recipes I found infused the custard with lemon zest, cinnamon, vanilla, or all three. Some called for adding a whole cinnamon stick to the custard base, but my tasters found this overpowering; instead, I'd sprinkle each custard with ground cinnamon (and confectioners' sugar) before serving. For delicate lemon flavor, I let a few strips of zest steep in the milk mixture and added a splash of vanilla extract along with the egg yolks.

When I added the custard to the raw pastry shells and baked them, the pastry emerged from the oven pale and doughy. For crisp, well-browned crusts, some par-baking was in order. After pressing the dough slices into each muffin tin cup, I pricked them to prevent puffing, lined the tart shells with muffin tin liners, filled the liners with pie weights, and baked them at 350 degrees for about 10 minutes; then, I topped the muffin tin with foil and baked them 5 minutes longer.

After letting the empty tart shells cool for a bit, I poured in the custard filling. At this point, the tarts are typically baked at a high temperature so that they can achieve their characteristic splotchy browning. I cranked up the oven to 500 degrees and baked them on the upper-middle rack of the oven for about 10 minutes—enough time to develop those distinctive brown spots. This was Portuguese pastry perfection.

—CAMILA CHAPARRO, *America's Test Kitchen Books*

Portuguese Egg Tarts

SERVES 12

We serve these tarts with a sprinkle of cinnamon and confectioners' sugar as they do in Portugal. To thaw frozen puff pastry, let it sit either in the refrigerator for 24 hours or at room temperature for 30 minutes to 1 hour.

1½ (9½ by 9-inch) sheets puff pastry, thawed

1½ cups whole milk

1 cup (7 ounces) granulated sugar

¾ cup heavy cream

2 (3-inch) strips lemon zest

¼ cup (1¼ ounces) all-purpose flour

½ teaspoon table salt

8 large egg yolks

1½ teaspoons vanilla extract

Confectioners' sugar

Ground cinnamon

1. Unfold puff pastry sheets on clean counter. Brush tops lightly with water. Roll full pastry sheet into tight log and pinch seam to seal. Roll short side of half pastry sheet into tight log and pinch seam to seal. Transfer to rimmed baking sheet, cover loosely with plastic wrap, and refrigerate until firm, at least 30 minutes.

2. Spray 12-cup muffin tin with vegetable oil spray. Using serrated knife, trim off uneven ends of each pastry log and discard. Cut twelve 1-inch slices from pastry logs and place 1 slice in each muffin tin cup, cut side up. Using your moistened fingers, press pastry into bottom and up sides of muffin cups so pastry reaches top of cups (pastry should be very thin). Prick pastry shells all over with fork and refrigerate until pastry is firm, about 20 minutes.

3. Adjust oven racks to upper-middle and lower-middle positions and heat oven to 350 degrees. Line pastry shells with muffin tin liners and fill with pie weights. Place muffin tin on lower rack and bake until pastry is puffed but still pale, about 10 minutes. Cover muffin tin with aluminum foil and continue to bake until pastry is just blond at edges, about 5 minutes longer. Transfer muffin tin to wire rack, discard foil, and let pastry shells cool slightly, 10 to 15 minutes. Remove liners and weights. Increase oven temperature to 500 degrees.

4. Combine milk, granulated sugar, cream, and lemon zest in medium saucepan and cook over medium-low heat, stirring occasionally, until steaming, about 6 minutes. Off heat, let mixture steep for 15 minutes; discard zest. Whisk flour and salt together in bowl, then gradually whisk in milk mixture. Whisk in egg yolks and vanilla until smooth. Return egg mixture to saucepan and cook over medium-low heat, whisking constantly, until mixture begins to thicken, 6 to 8 minutes. Strain mixture through fine-mesh strainer into clean bowl.

5. Divide custard evenly among pastry shells. Bake on upper rack until shells are dark golden brown and crisp and custard is puffed and spotty brown, 8 to 11 minutes. Let tarts cool in muffin tin on wire rack for 10 minutes. Remove tarts from muffin tin and let cool on wire rack for 15 minutes. Dust with confectioners' sugar and cinnamon and serve warm or at room temperature.

FRESH PLUM-GINGER PIE WITH WHOLE-WHEAT LATTICE-TOP CRUST

✓ **WHY THIS RECIPE WORKS** For a new type of summer fruit pie, we piled ginger-scented fresh plums into a buttery whole-wheat crust. Leaving the skins on the plums kept the slices intact during baking, and we thickened the plum juice with cornstarch to make a translucent, sliceable gel. For a whole-wheat crust that was both flaky and tender, we waterproofed some of the flour with butter so that it couldn't form gluten and therefore remained tender. The remaining flour was hydrated with water, so it formed plenty of gluten and baked up flaky.

Baking a blueberry, peach, or cherry pie is a terrific way to celebrate the abundant fruits of summer. But I urge you to consider another, less common fruit filling for your next summer pie: plums. The sweetness of ripe plums is offset by their acidity level, which is higher than those of most other fruits; when baked, plums offer a unique sweet-tart fruitiness that will have you smitten from the first bite.

For my pie, I used red or blue-black round plums (2½ pounds for a 9-inch pie); they are the most common and have an appealing sweet yet bright flavor. If you've ever made a peach pie, you probably remember the tedious process of blanching and peeling the fruit so that the resilient skins don't ruin the tender, sliceable texture of the filling. Well, I'm happy to report that with plums, peeling is not only unnecessary but also detrimental. Plum skins are so thin and tender that they don't detract from the succulent flesh, and if you remove the crimson-violet skins, the pie is not nearly as attractive.

I cut the plums into slim wedges, added them to a bowl with ¾ cup of sugar, and let them macerate for 15 minutes. The juice that the sugar pulled out of the fruit could be used to dissolve a thickener.

I wanted my thickener to produce a clear filling to show off the plums. That meant that flour, which has a tendency to turn cloudy in fruit pie fillings, was out. In our recipe for fresh peach pie, we use both cornstarch and pectin to create a translucent gel. But plums have more pectin than peaches (one of the reasons they're popular for jams), so cornstarch alone was sufficient.

Adding citrus is a common way to enhance fruit pie fillings; here, I added floral lemon zest and tangy lemon juice to accentuate the tartness of the fruit. To perfume the plums with a sophisticated spiciness, I also added both ground and fresh ginger.

If my jammy, gingery filling has convinced you that plum pie is worth adding to your rotation, great. Now, allow me to push you even further outside the box with a pie dough that calls for whole-wheat flour.

If you're thinking that it would be wise to shy away from adding whole-grain flour to a pie crust since whole-grain flours are lower in gluten—and can therefore produce disappointingly dense or crumbly baked goods—you'd normally be right. But my colleague Andrea Geary came up with a unique method for adding whole-wheat flour to pie dough that produces wonderfully tender and flaky results.

The method calls for using the food processor to make a paste with 1½ cups of whole-wheat flour and two sticks of butter, effectively waterproofing the flour (no matter what kind of flour you use) and making it hard for the flour's proteins to hydrate and form gluten. The paste is then broken into chunks that are coated with 1 cup of all-purpose flour before being tossed with half a stick of grated butter. Finally, ½ cup of ice water is added, which hydrates the unprotected portion of flour and allows plenty of gluten to form. Each nugget of the whole-wheat flour dough is thus surrounded by a jacket of higher-gluten dough that provides plenty of structure.

I used this whole-wheat dough to create a pie with a lattice top—a must since it would allow some of the plums' moisture to evaporate during baking. Luckily, the lattice was easy to weave since the dough was relatively sturdy, and the pie baked up looking as great as it tasted. The crust was beautifully tender and flaky, with a tawny color and a nutty aroma that paired beautifully with the ginger-scented plum filling.

With this success under my belt, I also experimented with an earthy rye pie dough that Andrea developed, finding that it made a great match for another fruit that's underused in pie: apricots. I flavored the apricots with cardamom and vanilla to enhance their aromatic sweetness.

—LEAH COLINS, *America's Test Kitchen Books*

FRESH PLUM-GINGER PIE WITH WHOLE-WHEAT LATTICE-TOP CRUST

Fresh Plum-Ginger Pie with Whole-Wheat Lattice-Top Crust

SERVES 8

Be sure to weigh the flour. For the best flavor, use recently purchased whole-wheat flour or whole-wheat flour that has been stored in the freezer for less than a year. In the mixing stage, this dough will be moister than most pie doughs, but as it chills, it will become more workable. Roll the dough on a well-floured counter. If at any point the dough is too stiff to work with, let it sit at room temperature until it is slightly softened but still very cold. Conversely, if the dough becomes too soft to work with, refrigerate it for 30 minutes to let it firm up.

PIE DOUGH

- **20** tablespoons (2½ sticks) unsalted butter, chilled, divided
- **1½** cups (8¼ ounces) whole-wheat flour
- **2** tablespoons sugar
- **1** teaspoon table salt
- **1** cup (5 ounces) all-purpose flour
- **½** cup ice water, divided

FILLING

- **¾** cup (5¼ ounces) sugar
- **3** tablespoons cornstarch
- **2** teaspoons grated lemon zest plus 1 tablespoon juice
- **1** teaspoon grated fresh ginger
- **¼** teaspoon ground ginger
- **¼** teaspoon table salt
- **2½** pounds plums, halved, pitted, and cut into ¼-inch-thick wedges
- **1** large egg, lightly beaten with 1 tablespoon water

1. FOR THE PIE DOUGH: Grate 4 tablespoons butter on large holes of box grater. Transfer to freezer. Cut remaining 16 tablespoons butter into ½-inch cubes; set aside. Pulse whole-wheat flour, sugar, and salt in food processor until combined, 2 pulses. Add cubed butter and process until homogeneous paste forms, about 2 minutes. Using your hands, carefully break paste into 2-inch chunks and redistribute evenly around processor blade. Add all-purpose flour and pulse until mixture is broken into pieces no larger than 1 inch (most pieces will be much smaller), 4 to 5 pulses. Transfer mixture to medium bowl. Add grated butter and toss until butter pieces are separated and coated with flour.

2. Sprinkle ¼ cup ice water over mixture. Toss with rubber spatula until mixture is evenly moistened. Sprinkle remaining ¼ cup ice water over mixture and toss to combine. Press dough with spatula until dough sticks together. Use spatula to divide dough into 2 even pieces. Transfer each piece to separate sheet of plastic wrap. Working with 1 piece at a time, draw edges of plastic over dough and press firmly on sides and top to form compact, fissure-free mass. Press 1 piece into 5-inch disk. Press remaining piece into 5-inch square. Wrap separately in plastic and refrigerate dough for at least 2 hours or up to 2 days. Let chilled dough sit on counter to soften slightly, about 10 minutes, before rolling. (Wrapped dough can be frozen for up to 1 month. If frozen, let dough thaw completely on counter before rolling.)

3. Line rimmed baking sheet with parchment paper. Roll dough square into 10½ by 14-inch rectangle on well-floured counter. Transfer dough to prepared sheet and refrigerate for 10 minutes. Meanwhile, roll dough disk into 12-inch circle on well-floured counter. Roll dough loosely around rolling pin and gently unroll it onto 9-inch pie plate, leaving at least 1-inch overhang around edge. Ease dough into plate by gently lifting edge of dough with your hand while pressing into plate bottom with your other hand. Trim overhang to ½ inch beyond lip of plate. Wrap dough-lined plate loosely in plastic and refrigerate until dough is firm, about 30 minutes.

4. Transfer chilled dough rectangle, still on baking sheet, to counter. Using pizza wheel, fluted pastry wheel, or paring knife, trim ¼ inch of dough from long sides of rectangle, then cut rectangle lengthwise into eight 1¼-inch-wide strips. Refrigerate strips on sheet until firm, about 30 minutes.

5. FOR THE FILLING: Adjust oven rack to middle position and heat oven to 400 degrees. Whisk sugar, cornstarch, lemon zest, fresh ginger, ground ginger, and salt together in large bowl. Stir in plums and lemon juice and let sit for 15 minutes. Spread plum mixture into even layer in chilled dough-lined plate.

6. To make lattice, evenly space 4 dough strips across top of pie, parallel to counter edge. Fold back first and third strips almost completely. Lay 1 strip across pie, perpendicular to counter edge, keeping it snug against folded edges of dough strips. Unfold first and third strips over top of perpendicular strip. Fold back second and fourth strips and add second perpendicular strip. Repeat, alternating between folding back first and third strips and second and fourth strips and laying remaining strips evenly across pie to create lattice pattern. Shift strips as needed so they are evenly spaced over top of pie. Trim excess lattice ends, press edges of bottom crust and lattice strips together, and fold under;

folded edge should be flush with edge of plate. Crimp dough evenly around edge of plate using your fingers. Brush dough with egg wash.

7. Bake pie on aluminum foil–lined rimmed baking sheet until crust is golden, 20 to 25 minutes. Reduce oven temperature to 350 degrees and continue to bake until juices are bubbling and crust is deep golden brown, 35 to 50 minutes longer. Let cool on wire rack until filling has set, about 4 hours. Serve.

NOTES FROM THE TEST KITCHEN

WEAVING A LATTICE TOP

1. Evenly space 4 dough strips across top of pie, parallel to counter edge.

2. Fold back first and third strips almost completely. Lay 1 strip across pie, perpendicular to counter edge.

3. Unfold first and third strips over top of perpendicular strip.

4. Fold back second and fourth strips and add second perpendicular strip. Unfold second and fourth strips.

5. Repeat, alternating between folding back first and third strips and second and fourth strips and laying remaining strips evenly across pie.

6. Trim lattice ends, press edges of bottom crust and lattice strips together, and fold under. Crimp dough evenly around edge of plate.

Fresh Apricot, Vanilla, and Cardamom Pie with Rye Lattice-Top Crust

SERVES 8

If at any point the dough is too stiff to work with, let it sit at room temperature until it is slightly softened but still very cold. Conversely, if the dough becomes too soft to work with, refrigerate it to firm it up. The test kitchen prefers Challenge Unsalted Butter.

PIE DOUGH

20 tablespoons (2½ sticks) unsalted butter, chilled, divided

1½ cups (8¼ ounces) rye flour

2 tablespoons sugar

1 teaspoon table salt

1 cup (5 ounces) all-purpose flour

½ cup ice water, divided

FILLING

1 vanilla bean

1 cup (7 ounces) sugar

3 tablespoons cornstarch

1 teaspoon grated lemon zest plus 1 tablespoon juice

¼ teaspoon ground cardamom

¼ teaspoon table salt

2½ pounds apricots, halved, pitted, and cut into ½-inch-thick wedges

1 large egg, lightly beaten with 1 tablespoon water

1. FOR THE PIE DOUGH: Grate 4 tablespoons butter on large holes of box grater. Transfer to freezer. Cut remaining 16 tablespoons butter into ½-inch cubes; set aside. Pulse rye flour, sugar, and salt in food processor until combined, 2 pulses. Add cubed butter and process until homogeneous paste forms, about 2 minutes. Using your hands, carefully break paste into 2-inch chunks and redistribute evenly around processor blade.

CHOCOLATE PECAN PIE

Add all-purpose flour and pulse until mixture is broken into pieces no larger than 1 inch (most pieces will be much smaller), 4 to 5 pulses. Transfer mixture to medium bowl. Add grated butter and toss until butter pieces are separated and coated with flour.

2. Sprinkle ¼ cup ice water over mixture. Toss with rubber spatula until mixture is evenly moistened. Sprinkle remaining ¼ cup ice water over mixture and toss to combine. Press dough with spatula until dough sticks together. Use spatula to divide dough into 2 even pieces. Transfer each piece to separate sheet of plastic wrap. Working with 1 piece at a time, draw edges of plastic over dough and press firmly on sides and top to form compact, fissure-free mass. Press 1 piece into 5-inch disk. Press remaining piece into 5-inch square. Wrap separately in plastic and refrigerate dough for at least 2 hours or up to 2 days. Let chilled dough sit on counter to soften slightly, about 10 minutes, before rolling. (Wrapped dough can be frozen for up to 1 month. If frozen, let dough thaw completely on counter before rolling.)

3. Line rimmed baking sheet with parchment paper. Roll dough square into 10½ by 14-inch rectangle on well-floured counter. Transfer dough to prepared sheet and refrigerate for 10 minutes. Meanwhile, roll dough disk into 12-inch circle on well-floured counter. Roll dough loosely around rolling pin and gently unroll it onto 9-inch pie plate, leaving at least 1-inch overhang around edge. Ease dough into plate by gently lifting edge of dough with your hand while pressing into plate bottom with your other hand. Trim overhang to ½ inch beyond lip of plate. Wrap dough-lined plate loosely in plastic and refrigerate until dough is firm, about 30 minutes.

4. Transfer chilled dough rectangle, still on baking sheet, to counter. Using pizza wheel, fluted pastry wheel, or paring knife, trim ¼ inch of dough from long sides of rectangle, then cut rectangle lengthwise into eight 1¼-inch-wide strips. Refrigerate strips on sheet until firm, about 30 minutes.

5. FOR THE FILLING: Adjust oven rack to middle position and heat oven to 400 degrees. Cut vanilla bean in half lengthwise. Using tip of paring knife, scrape seeds into large bowl. Add sugar, cornstarch, lemon zest, cardamom, and salt and whisk to combine. Stir in apricots and lemon juice and let sit for 15 minutes. Spread apricot mixture into even layer in chilled dough-lined plate.

6. To make lattice, evenly space 4 dough strips across top of pie, parallel to counter edge. Fold back first and third strips almost completely. Lay 1 strip across pie, perpendicular to counter edge, keeping it snug against folded edges of dough strips. Unfold first and third strips over top of perpendicular strip. Fold back second and fourth strips and add second perpendicular strip. Repeat, alternating between folding back first and third strips and second and fourth strips and laying remaining strips evenly across pie to create lattice pattern. Shift strips as needed so they are evenly spaced over top of pie. Trim excess lattice ends, press edges of bottom crust and lattice strips together, and fold under; folded edge should be flush with edge of plate. Crimp dough evenly around edge of plate using your fingers. Brush dough with egg wash.

7. Bake pie on aluminum foil–lined rimmed baking sheet until crust is golden, 20 to 25 minutes. Reduce oven temperature to 350 degrees and continue to bake until juices are bubbling and crust is deep golden brown, 35 to 50 minutes longer. Let cool on wire rack until filling has set, about 4 hours. Serve.

CHOCOLATE PECAN PIE

✔ WHY THIS RECIPE WORKS Our goal for this pie was a creamy, smooth, and sliceable chocolate filling (not a brownie-like texture nor a pooling puddle of syrup). To keep the filling easy, we simply stirred all the ingredients together. So the pie was not overly sweet, we used just ¾ cup of brown sugar, ¾ cup of corn syrup, and unsweetened chocolate; just 2 ounces of unsweetened chocolate was enough to give the filling complexity and balanced chocolate flavor. For the crust, we turned to our all-butter pie dough since it comes together in a snap and bakes up with rich, buttery flavor. Used in its parbaked form, the crust didn't turn soggy under the wet filling. Parbaking also set the crust's shape, so it baked evenly once it was filled. (Baked from raw with the filling, the dough bubbled up under the lightweight filling, so the filling and crust baked unevenly.) We toasted the nuts to provide textural contrast and to prevent the nuts from turning spongy in the filling. To ensure that the filling was creamy but set, we baked the filled pie for 1 hour, until the custard registered 185 to 190 degrees and the top of the pie just began to crack.

Chocolate pecan pie is a welcome shake-up to your usual pecan pie—still traditional but with a fun twist. It's not a complicated idea: Put some chocolate and pecans into a pie crust (usually prebaked); pour in a filling of eggs, brown sugar, and corn syrup; and bake. The nuts float to the surface to create a crunchy top layer while the filling (a translucent custard) firms up into a silky, sliceable texture.

After making several recipes for this pie, the challenges were clear. Most fillings were much too sweet. Some contained only a sprinkling of nuts; others didn't fully lean into the chocolate and had just a few chips thrown into the filling. A few became disappointing puddles of syrup, while others were too fudgy, like a brownie pie with nuts. I wanted a creamy, balanced chocolate filling that held its shape plus a crisp and buttery crust and crunchy pecans for satisfying textural contrast.

Luckily for me, I had a great starting point: Our recipe for an easy all-butter pie crust is a cinch to work with and tastes amazing. A gentle parbaking ensured that the crust would stay crisp once filled.

For the filling, I knew I had to keep the sweetness level in check. To do so, I looked at the amounts of brown sugar and corn syrup in most pecan pies—often at least 1 cup of each—and dropped them down to ¾ cup of each. I also turned to unsweetened chocolate to showcase complex, slightly bitter, rich chocolate notes and balance the filling's flavor. Just 2 ounces of unsweetened chocolate melted with butter made a luxurious, cohesive chocolate filling when combined with the eggs and sugar. Chopping the pecans made it easier to cut nice slices, and toasting the nuts maximized their flavor and kept them from becoming spongy in the filling.

If you've ever made a cheesecake, regular pecan pie, or a custard pie, you know that these pies can be difficult to bake—just how jiggly is "jiggly in the center," anyway? After several days and dozens of pies, I found that the pie was perfectly done after just over an hour on the bottom rack of a 325-degree oven. At this point, the center is still a little jiggly, but there are more concrete cues to doneness: The top layer will crack a bit and the filling will register between 185 and 190 degrees on an instant-read thermometer. No more guesswork on when to pull the pie for a perfectly smooth and silky filling.

Could this pie be any more irresistible? Yes. A quick bourbon-infused whipped cream dolloped on each slice took it over the top.

—CECELIA JENKINS, *Cook's Country*

Chocolate Pecan Pie

SERVES 8

Chilling the pie dough for 2 hours is important; even if you plan to freeze the dough for later use, do not skip this step. Toast the pecans on a rimmed baking sheet in a 300-degree oven for 7 to 10 minutes, stirring occasionally. You can substitute other pie weights for the sugar, if desired. This pie needs to cool for at least 4 hours to set the filling.

CRUST

- 1½ cups (7½ ounces) all-purpose flour
- 1 tablespoon granulated sugar, plus sugar to use as pie weight
- ½ teaspoon table salt
- 12 tablespoons unsalted butter, cut into ½-inch pieces and chilled
- 6 tablespoons ice water

FILLING

- 6 tablespoons unsalted butter
- 2 ounces unsweetened chocolate, chopped fine
- ¾ cup light corn syrup
- ¾ cup packed (5¼ ounces) brown sugar
- 3 large eggs
- 1 tablespoon vanilla extract
- ½ teaspoon table salt
- 2 cups pecans, toasted and chopped coarse

WHIPPED CREAM

- 1 cup heavy cream, chilled
- 3 tablespoons packed brown sugar
- 1–2 tablespoons bourbon
- ½ teaspoon vanilla extract
    Pinch table salt

1. FOR THE CRUST: Process flour, sugar, and salt in food processor until combined, about 3 seconds. Scatter butter over top and pulse until irregular large chunks of butter form with some small pieces throughout, about 5 pulses. Add ice water and process until little balls of butter form and almost no dry flour remains, about 10 seconds, scraping down sides of bowl after 5 seconds.

2. Turn out dough onto clean counter and gather into ball. Sprinkle dough and counter generously with flour and shape dough into 6-inch disk, pressing any cracked edges back together. Roll dough into 13-inch circle, reflouring counter and dough as needed.

3. Roll dough loosely around rolling pin and gently unroll it onto 9-inch pie plate, leaving at least 1-inch overhang around edge. Ease dough into plate by gently lifting edge of dough with your hand while pressing into plate bottom with your other hand. Trim overhang to ½ inch beyond lip of plate.

4. Tuck overhang under itself; folded edge should be flush with edge of plate. Crimp dough evenly around edge of plate using your knuckles. Pierce bottom and sides of dough all over with fork, about 40 times. Wrap dough-lined plate loosely in plastic wrap and refrigerate until dough is very firm, at least 2 hours or up to 2 days. (After being refrigerated for 2 hours, dough-lined plate can be wrapped tightly in plastic and frozen for up to 1 month. Let dough thaw at room temperature for 25 minutes before using.)

5. Adjust oven rack to lowest position and heat oven to 375 degrees. Line chilled pie shell with aluminum foil and, while pressing into plate bottom with 1 hand to keep foil flush with bottom of plate, work foil around crimped edge with your other hand. Fill foil to lip of plate with sugar. Transfer plate to wire rack set in rimmed baking sheet. Bake until edges are dry and pale, about 45 minutes. Remove foil and sugar, rotate sheet, and continue to bake until center of crust is light golden brown, 20 to 25 minutes longer. Remove sheet from oven, keeping pie shell on wire rack in sheet. Lower oven temperature to 325 degrees. (Pie shell needn't cool completely before proceeding.)

6. FOR THE FILLING: Melt butter and chocolate in bowl at 50 percent power, stirring halfway through microwaving, until melted, about 2 minutes. Add corn syrup, sugar, eggs, vanilla, and salt to butter mixture and whisk until combined. Stir in pecans.

7. Place pie shell on rimmed baking sheet. Pour filling into shell and distribute evenly with rubber spatula. Bake until pecan layer that forms on top begins to crack and filling in center of pie registers 185 to 190 degrees (filling will jiggle slightly when pie is shaken), 1 hour to 1 hour 5 minutes, rotating sheet halfway through baking. Let pie cool on wire rack until set, at least 4 hours.

8. FOR THE WHIPPED CREAM: Using stand mixer fitted with whisk attachment, whip cream, sugar, 1 tablespoon bourbon, vanilla, and salt on medium-low speed until foamy, about 1 minute. Increase speed to high and whip

until soft peaks form, 1 to 3 minutes. Add remaining 1 tablespoon bourbon to taste. (Whipped cream can be refrigerated in airtight container for up to 24 hours.)

9. Serve pie with whipped cream.

TO MAKE AHEAD: At end of step 7, pie can be wrapped tightly in plastic wrap, then in aluminum foil, and frozen for up to 1 week. To serve, unwrap pie completely and let thaw at room temperature for 5 hours. Make whipped cream while pie thaws.

BUTTERNUT SQUASH PIE WITH BROWNED BUTTER AND SAGE

✓ WHY THIS RECIPE WORKS Pumpkin isn't the only winter squash that works in desserts—slightly earthier butternut is a lovely alternative to the pie norm. To distinguish this pie from its cousin, we incorporated browned butter for nutty richness. Mincing some sage and cooking it with the butter before adding it to the filling allowed this classic fall herb to subtly flavor the pie without being too prominent. A sage-flecked pie dough further enforced the slightly savory, fall-inspired flavors at play.

When I think "pie," the first thing to spring to mind, word-association-style, is pumpkin. This holiday table mainstay is so ubiquitous that, along with apple and pecan, it could very well be considered one of the pillars of pie-dom. I can devour a slice of pumpkin pie with the best of them, but when I was given a chance to develop recipes for *The Perfect Pie*, I jumped at the opportunity to do something a little different and shake up the fall pie landscape.

I knew right away that I wanted to ditch the pumpkin and go for a more sophisticated yet playful flavor profile. Squash, sage, and browned butter are classic autumn ingredients that are often featured together, but they're typically used only in savory preparations. I wasn't about to be limited by mere convention, though. I was confident that, by carefully balancing these elements with more typical pie flavors, I could bring them over to the sweet side.

I approached the pie as I would any other custard pie: by first setting out to get the filling just right. Out of the myriad types of squashes available to me, I chose to use bright orange butternut as my base. Its subtle sweetness would work to my advantage as I straddled the savory-sweet line, and its gorgeous color would give my pie an appealing presentation.

While choosing the squash was easy, deciding how to prepare it and how much to use took more deliberation. Butternut squashes vary in size, but even when I erred on the smaller side, using a whole squash almost unfailingly produced far too much filling for a single pie. After several trials, I determined that 30 ounces of squash (about 5 cups of 1-inch pieces) was just the right amount. As for how to soften the hard squash enough to incorporate it into a smooth filling, I took a page from a test kitchen recipe for squash-filled ravioli and used the microwave. Microwaving 1-inch chunks of the squash in a covered bowl took only about 15 minutes of hands-off time and yielded perfectly fork-tender pieces that I could then add to a food processor to combine with my other ingredients.

For nutty complexity, adding browned butter to my filling was a no-brainer. I simply melted butter in a small skillet over medium-high heat until it was dark golden brown and fragrant, taking care not to burn it. Adding granulated sugar amped up the squash's natural sweetness, but I found that I liked brown sugar even better; the caramel and toffee notes it contributed nicely complemented the browned butter. Warm freshly grated ginger and ground nutmeg added subtle spice notes that gently ushered the filling's flavor profile from savory to sweet, and a teaspoon of salt enhanced all the flavors. Just a minute in the food processor yielded a smooth, cohesive mixture. I still felt that it was lacking something, though. Up to now I'd been planning to add the sage just to the crust, but I decided to try a bit in the filling as well. A teaspoon of minced fresh sage, which I added to the butter as it browned, infused the filling with its distinctive flavor.

The moisture content of squash can be unpredictable, so to make my recipe foolproof, I next transferred the mixture to a saucepan and cooked it on the stovetop to evaporate excess moisture until it was reduced to 2½ cups. This meant that no matter how watery my squash was to begin with, I was guaranteed consistent results every time, with the bonus that my flavors became even more concentrated and intense.

The mixture went back into the food processor for a final addition of cream, milk, eggs, and vanilla. Overprocessing the mixture at this stage caused disaster, aerating the filling and causing it to soufflé in the oven and then settle and crack as it cooled. Carefully limiting the mixing time to no more than 15 seconds—just long enough to combine all the ingredients—helped ensure a smooth, crack-free custard filling, as did baking the filling at a low, steady 300 degrees.

Now for the crust. I followed the test kitchen's recipe for all-butter pie dough, adding 1½ tablespoons of fresh sage directly to the flour-sugar mixture before incorporating the butter and water. This amount was just enough to give the crust a subtle herbiness without making it taste overwhelmingly savory. I rolled it out, blind-baked it, and then added the filling while it was still warm before popping my pie into the oven for another 25 to 35 minutes. The result: a perfectly set, festive pie heady with the aromas of sage and browned butter.

But before I called it quits, I wanted to nail a wow-worthy presentation. Most custard pies are single-crust affairs, and that works just fine here, too, but I was after something extraordinary. I doubled my crust recipe to make enough for a double-crust pie and used the second half of the dough to create cutouts that I placed on top of the pie. Placing the raw cutouts atop the unbaked custard filling caused them to sink and get soggy, so instead I attached some of the cutouts to the crust and baked the remaining cutouts separately, delicately placing them around the perimeter once the pie was completely set and cooled. My truly memorable pie was now ready for any occasion.

—LEAH COLINS, *America's Test Kitchen Books*

Butternut Squash Pie with Browned Butter and Sage

SERVES 8

For even more sage flavor, we like to use our sage dough, but you can use any single-crust pie dough. If you want to top your pie with cutouts like in the photo, double the dough recipe, divide it into two equal portions, and use the extra dough for the cutouts.

DOUGH

- **10 tablespoons unsalted butter, chilled, divided**
- **1¼ cups (6¼ ounces) all-purpose flour, divided**
- **1½ tablespoons minced fresh sage**
- **1 tablespoon sugar**
- **½ teaspoon table salt**
- **¼ cup ice water, divided**

BUTTERNUT SQUASH PIE WITH BROWNED BUTTER AND SAGE

FILLING

    8   tablespoons unsalted butter, cut into 8 pieces
    1   teaspoon minced fresh sage
   30   ounces butternut squash, peeled, seeded,
        and cut into 1-inch pieces (5 cups)
    1   teaspoon table salt
    1   teaspoon grated fresh ginger
    ¼   teaspoon ground nutmeg
    ¾   cup packed (5¼ ounces) brown sugar
    ¾   cup heavy cream
    ⅔   cup whole milk
    2   large eggs plus 2 large yolks
    1   teaspoon vanilla extract

1. FOR THE DOUGH: Grate 2 tablespoons butter on large holes of box grater and place in freezer. Cut remaining 8 tablespoons butter into ½-inch cubes.

2. Pulse ¾ cup flour, sage, sugar, and salt in food processor until combined, 2 pulses. Add cubed butter and process until homogeneous paste forms, about 30 seconds. Using your hands, carefully break paste into 2-inch chunks and redistribute evenly around processor blade. Add remaining ½ cup flour and pulse until mixture is broken into pieces no larger than 1 inch (most pieces will be much smaller), 4 to 5 pulses. Transfer mixture to bowl. Add grated butter and toss until butter pieces are separated and coated with flour.

3. Sprinkle 2 tablespoons ice water over mixture. Toss with rubber spatula until mixture is evenly moistened. Sprinkle remaining 2 tablespoons ice water over mixture and toss to combine. Press dough with spatula until dough sticks together. Transfer dough to sheet of plastic wrap. Draw edges of plastic over dough and press firmly on sides and top to form compact, fissure-free mass. Wrap in plastic and form into 5-inch disk. Refrigerate dough for at least 2 hours or up to 2 days. Let chilled dough sit on counter to soften slightly, about 10 minutes, before rolling. (Wrapped dough can be frozen for up to 1 month. If frozen, let dough thaw completely on counter before rolling.)

4. Roll dough into 12-inch circle on floured counter. Roll dough loosely around rolling pin and gently unroll it onto 9-inch pie plate, letting excess dough hang over edge. Ease dough into plate by gently lifting edge of dough with your hand while pressing into plate bottom with your other hand.

5. Trim overhang to ½ inch beyond lip of plate. Tuck overhang under itself; folded edge should be flush with edge of plate. Crimp dough evenly around edge of plate. Wrap dough-lined plate loosely in plastic wrap and refrigerate until firm, about 30 minutes. Adjust oven rack to middle position and heat oven to 350 degrees.

6. FOR THE FILLING: Heat butter and sage in 8-inch skillet over medium-high heat until butter is melted. Continue to cook, swirling skillet occasionally, until butter is dark golden brown and has nutty aroma, about 2 minutes longer; set aside. Microwave squash in covered bowl until very soft and easily pierced with fork, 15 to 18 minutes, stirring halfway through microwaving. Carefully uncover, allowing steam to escape away from you, then drain squash; transfer to food processor. Add salt, ginger, nutmeg, and browned butter and process until smooth, about 1 minute, scraping down sides of bowl as needed. Transfer to large saucepan and set aside.

NOTES FROM THE TEST KITCHEN

MAKING A CUTOUT EDGE

1. Using small cookie cutters no larger than 1 inch wide, cut as many shapes as desired. Transfer to parchment paper–lined rimmed baking sheet, cover loosely with plastic wrap, and refrigerate for 30 minutes.

2. Brush edge of dough with water.

3. Attach some cutouts by pressing firmly into edge. Repeat to cover edge of dough, overlapping as desired. Bake remaining cutouts separately and place around perimeter of cooled pie.

7. Line chilled pie shell with double layer of aluminum foil, covering edges to prevent burning, and fill with pie weights. Bake on foil-lined rimmed baking sheet until edges are set and just beginning to turn golden, 25 to 30 minutes, rotating sheet halfway through baking. Remove foil and weights, rotate sheet, and continue to bake crust until golden brown and crisp, 10 to 15 minutes longer. Transfer to wire rack. (Crust must still be warm when filling is added.)

8. Meanwhile, add sugar to saucepan with squash mixture and cook over medium heat until thick, shiny, and reduced to 2½ cups, 10 to 15 minutes, stirring constantly. Return squash mixture to now-empty processor bowl; add cream, milk, eggs and yolks, and vanilla; and process until well combined and smooth, about 15 seconds. Transfer filling to warm crust. Reduce oven temperature to 300 degrees and bake until edges of pie are set but center jiggles slightly and registers 160 degrees, 25 to 35 minutes. Let pie cool completely on wire rack, about 4 hours. Serve.

CHAMPAGNE COCKTAILS

✔ WHY THIS RECIPE WORKS We crafted three festive sparkling wine cocktails ideal for entertaining: a classic Champagne cocktail, a Bellini, and a mimosa. For the Champagne cocktail, we poured Champagne over an Angostura bitters–soaked sugar cube and garnished the drink with a lemon twist. For the Bellini, we combined peach juice, peach schnapps, and sparkling wine. We fortified our mimosa with orange juice and orange liqueur.

Sparkling wine cocktails are one of the easiest ways to make a party feel festive. They're celebratory; they come together in a flash; and they don't require a stocked liquor cabinet, fancy barware, or even much mixing. And in many cases, you can put together a top-notch version on the cheap. Here I cover the sparkling wine basics, share how to mix three classic cocktails (Champagne cocktails, Bellinis, and mimosas), and provide helpful tips that apply to any bubbly cocktail.

Champagne, of course, is the gold standard of sparkling wine. It must be made in Champagne, France, using specific grapes and the region's traditional production method. But even the least expensive bottle of Champagne costs about $40. Great alternatives include prosecco ($8 to $30) and cava ($18 to $30), the second- and third-most-produced sparkling wines, respectively. Prosecco is made with an Italian grape using a different method that makes it less carbonated. It tends to have more residual sugar and a slightly lower acidity. Cava, a Spanish sparkler, is produced with grapes indigenous to Spain using the same method used to produce Champagne. It features similar levels of carbonation, acidity, and residual sugar.

Champagne is essential in a Champagne cocktail—and not just to make it true to its name. Made by pouring the wine over a sugar cube drenched in Angostura bitters and garnished with a twist of lemon zest, this cocktail evolves from the first sip to the last—and the flavors of the Champagne are primary until the very end. First, bursting bubbles aromatize lemon oils from the twist to make the initial sip bright and citrusy. Then the Champagne's flavors and aromas more fully take over, with whispers of the orange-and-spice-scented Angostura. Only in the final sips, when the sugar cube has fully dissolved to create a bitters-infused syrup at the bottom of the glass, does the Angostura supersede the Champagne. For the best experience, this cocktail's namesake ingredient is a must.

In virtually all other sparkling wine cocktails, it's fine to substitute a less expensive sparkling wine. When I poured an $8 prosecco into orange juice and Cointreau to make mimosas and compared them to a batch made with $45 Champagne, all tasters could tell the difference, but most found the cheaper bottle entirely acceptable since the juice and liqueur hid the nuances of the wine. Prosecco is the traditional choice for Bellinis, which are sweetened with peach juice and peach schnapps, and I wouldn't hesitate to use an inexpensive bottle to mix that drink either.

It's helpful to consult with a well-informed shopkeeper when selecting a sparkling wine, but to make your own educated guess, keep in mind that one of the biggest determining factors in the flavor profile is the grape varietal. Generally speaking, due to the grapes used to make each wine, Champagne is only slightly fruity, cava is a little fruitier, and prosecco is fruitier still. To select a quality sparkling wine similar to Champagne, look for the term "traditional method" or "crémant." Both indicate that the wine was made in the same manner as Champagne, so its flavor (and effervescence) will be comparable.

CHAMPAGNE COCKTAIL

Sparkling wine is best served at about 40 degrees. Cold suppresses sweetness, so wine will taste sweeter at warmer temperatures. Higher temperatures also make the wine lose its carbonation more quickly. This makes it initially fizzier and more aromatic, but the trade-off is that it becomes flat and loses its aroma faster. Wine poured into an unchilled flute shot from 38 to 48 degrees. But in a chilled flute, it rose only to 43 degrees. Be sure to chill the mixers, too.

Sparkling wine should be opened just before mixing cocktails. You can premix liqueurs and juices; just keep the mixers chilled in a vessel such as a pitcher. As guests arrive, simply pour the mixer into a flute glass, add the sparkling wine, and garnish. For the Champagne Cocktail, you can presoak sugar cubes up to 2 hours in advance or make our DIY Bitters Sugar Cubes.

—LAN LAM WITH LAWMAN JOHNSON, *Cook's Illustrated*

Champagne Cocktail

MAKES 1 COCKTAIL

We prefer Champagne here, but you can use another quality sparkling wine as long as it's brut or extra brut. Tilt the glass to a 45-degree angle and pour the wine down the side of the glass to minimize foaming. Use a channel knife to make the lemon twist. You can presoak the sugar cube up to 2 hours in advance or make our DIY Bitters Sugar Cubes (recipe follows).

- 1 sugar cube
- ¼ teaspoon Angostura bitters
- 5½ fluid ounces (½ cup plus 3 tablespoons) Champagne, chilled
- 1 lemon twist

Place sugar cube in small bowl. Add bitters to sugar cube. Transfer soaked sugar cube to chilled champagne flute. Add Champagne and garnish with lemon twist. Serve.

Bellini

MAKES 1 COCKTAIL

Either peach juice or nectar works well here. Tilt the glass to a 45-degree angle and pour the wine down the side of the glass to minimize foaming.

- 2½ fluid ounces (¼ cup plus 1 tablespoon) peach juice or nectar, chilled
- ¼ fluid ounce (1½ teaspoons) peach schnapps
- 3 fluid ounces (¼ cup plus 2 tablespoons) sparkling wine, chilled
- 1 thin slice peach (optional)

Add peach juice and peach schnapps to chilled champagne flute; stir with spoon to combine. Add wine. Using spoon, gently lift juice mixture from bottom to top of glass to combine. Garnish with peach slice, if using. Serve.

Mimosa

MAKES 1 COCKTAIL

Use strained fresh-squeezed orange juice here. We like Cointreau, but any orange liqueur will work. Tilt the glass to a 45-degree angle and pour the wine down the side of the glass to minimize foaming.

- 2½ fluid ounces (¼ cup plus 1 tablespoon) orange juice, strained and chilled
- ¼ fluid ounce (1½ teaspoons) orange liqueur
- 3 fluid ounces (¼ cup plus 2 tablespoons) sparkling wine, chilled
- 1 orange twist

Add orange juice and orange liqueur to chilled champagne flute; stir with spoon to combine. Add wine. Using spoon, gently lift juice mixture from bottom to top of glass to combine. Garnish with orange twist. Serve.

DIY Bitters Sugar Cubes

MAKES 64 CUBES

You can use any type of bitters you like here.

- ¾ cup sugar
- 2 tablespoons bitters

Stir sugar and bitters in bowl until well combined. Transfer mixture to large piece of parchment paper and press into 4-inch square. Use chef's knife to cut mixture into ½-inch cubes, being careful not to cut parchment. Transfer sugar square to rimmed baking sheet and let sit uncovered in cool, dry place for 24 hours. Sugar cubes can be stored in airtight container for up to 2 days.

NEW-FASHIONED GIN AND TONIC

✓ **WHY THIS RECIPE WORKS** The development of our Tonic Syrup caused a spark of creative cocktail inspiration: Was it possible to make a gin and tonic in the style of an old-fashioned, skipping the carbonation (and accompanying dilution) and presenting it instead as a stirred cocktail in a rocks glass? A bit of testing proved that not only was it possible, it was also extremely desirable. This cocktail has all the character of the original gin and tonic, but with a little more backbone and—dare we say—panache. If you think of gin and tonics as strictly summertime drinks, this concentrated version is your entry to serving them year-round. Following the traditional formula, we started with gin but then added tonic syrup only, rather than the customary carbonated tonic water. A few drops of old-fashioned aromatic bitters provided just the right amount of seasoning. We stirred it all together and then poured it over ice. The lime peel garnish was a nod toward a traditional gin and tonic feel and brought in the citrus finish that tasters were looking for.

I love a gin and tonic. It's as effortless to make as it is to drink: just gin, tonic water, and lime. As simple as it is, it's also complexly flavored: bittersweet with earthy, grassy, and citrusy notes. I also love an old-fashioned—it's potent, usually consisting of only whiskey, sugar, bitters, an orange twist, and a cocktail cherry. In this day and age, fusion cocktails abound, from the Bloody Maria, a Mexican-inspired Bloody Mary that swaps the vodka for tequila, to the boulevardier, which uses whiskey rather than gin for a riff on the Negroni. So what was stopping me from taking inspiration from two of my favorite cocktails and combining them into one? Nothing, except for a bit of creative mixology.

First, I'd have to decide which elements of each cocktail to include in my final drink—would I make a gin and tonic in the style of an old-fashioned, or vice versa? The answer came to me in the form of the Tonic Syrup recipe my colleague Nicole Konstantinakos developed for our *How to Cocktail* book. This syrup, which is occasionally used in conjunction with seltzer instead of tonic water in a gin and tonic, would be an easy way to craft a concentrated version of the drink. I could buy tonic syrup, sure, but I wanted a fully homemade drink. Nicole's syrup rivaled every store-bought version.

Before delving into the tonic syrup and other flavorings, I wanted to nail down the alcohol component—that is, which liquor (or liquors) to use and how much. Sticking with the gin and tonic flavor profile, I added none other than London Dry gin for its juniper-forward, crisp character. And to make sure that my drink was still in old-fashioned territory, I started with similar proportions: 2 ounces of the spirit per drink, which I'd boost with little more than a dash of tonic syrup and perhaps some other flavor enhancers.

Circling back to the tonic syrup, I found that 1½ teaspoons instilled plenty of bittersweet tonic flavor without overwhelming the drink. I stirred the mixture together with some ice—to sufficiently chill the drink and dilute it ever so slightly—and poured it over our Practically Clear Ice. (My colleague Joe Gitter spent weeks developing an easy at-home technique to get ice as close to clear as possible.) My reinvented gin and tonic was good, but it needed a bit more pizzazz. We often add bitters to elevate a cocktail, so why not try that here? I auditioned both old-fashioned aromatic bitters and citrus bitters; although I assumed that the latter would be a better match for the citrus-forward gin and tonic, my tasters actually favored the old-fashioned bitters for the subtle woodsiness and notes of warm spice that they contributed. Just ⅛ teaspoon heightened my drink to cocktail-menu status.

As a final nod to both the gin and tonic and the old-fashioned, I rubbed the rim of the glass with a strip of lime peel before tossing it into the glass. I present to you the New-Fashioned Gin and Tonic—a fusion drink for the ages.

—LAWMAN JOHNSON WITH NICOLE KONSTANTINAKOS AND JOE GITTER, *America's Test Kitchen Books*

New-Fashioned Gin and Tonic
MAKES 1 COCKTAIL

We prefer to use our homemade Tonic Syrup (recipe follows) here; however, store-bought tonic syrup will work. We like to strain the gin and tonic over Practically Clear Ice (recipe follows).

- **2 ounces London Dry gin**
- **1½ teaspoons Tonic Syrup (recipe follows)**
- **⅛ teaspoon old-fashioned aromatic bitters such as Angostura**
- **Strip of lime peel**

Add gin, tonic syrup, and bitters to mixing glass, then fill three-quarters full with ice. Stir until mixture is just combined and chilled, about 15 seconds. Strain cocktail into chilled old-fashioned glass half-filled with ice or containing 1 large ice cube. Pinch lime peel over drink and rub outer edge of glass with peel, then garnish with lime peel and serve.

Tonic Syrup

MAKES ABOUT 16 OUNCES

You can purchase cinchona bark chips online or in specialty spice shops; look for ¼-inch chips. You can purchase food-grade citric acid online or in grocery stores that sell canning supplies.

- 16 ounces water
- 2 tablespoons (½ ounce) cinchona bark chips
- 5 (3-inch) strips lemon zest plus ½ ounce juice
- 4 (2-inch) strips lime zest plus 1½ teaspoons juice
- 1 lemongrass stalk, trimmed to bottom 6 inches and chopped coarse
  Pinch table salt
- 1 cup sugar
- 2 tablespoons citric acid

1. Bring water, cinchona bark chips, lemon zest and juice, lime zest and juice, lemongrass, and salt to simmer in medium saucepan over medium-high heat. Reduce heat to low, cover, and cook, stirring occasionally, for 30 minutes.

2. Off heat, stir in sugar and citric acid until dissolved. Cover and let sit for at least 12 hours or up to 24 hours.

3. Set fine-mesh strainer over medium bowl and line with triple layer of cheesecloth. Strain syrup through prepared strainer, pressing on solids to extract as much syrup as possible; discard solids. (Tonic Syrup can be refrigerated in airtight container for up to 2 months. Shake gently before using.)

Practically Clear Ice

MAKES ABOUT 7 CUPS

We used silicone ice trays, but rubber ice trays also work. If you have larger trays, you may be able to fit only one in the baking dish.

- 6 cups distilled water

1. Fold 3 dish towels in half widthwise, then stack in 13 by 9-inch baking dish, allowing towels to overhang edges. Arrange two 6½ by 4½-inch silicone ice cube trays in center of prepared dish. Roll up additional towels and tuck into sides of dish as needed to ensure trays are packed snugly.

2. Bring water to boil in saucepan and let boil for 1 minute. Working in batches, carefully transfer water to 4-cup liquid measuring cup, then pour into trays. Let cool completely, about 30 minutes; you may have extra water. Place dish in freezer and let sit, uncovered, until ice is completely frozen, at least 8 hours.

CELERY GIMLET

WHY THIS RECIPE WORKS Celery flavoring a cocktail? Stay with us here. Muddled in a cocktail, celery adds refreshing and subtle grassy notes and a beautiful pale green color, creating a sophisticated and unique drink. We chose a classic gimlet—a bright and tart cocktail traditionally made with gin and lime cordial (sweetened lime juice)—in which to muddle celery, knowing that the vegetal flavors of the celery would complement the gin's botanical notes. We tested both celery stalks and leaves to see which would provide the most pronounced flavor, finding that muddled stalks gave the best fresh but delicate celery flavor, which paired beautifully with the zingy lime and the herbal notes of the gin. Originally used in the British navy as an appetizing way to prevent scurvy by giving sailors vitamin C–rich lime juice, gimlets are now frequently made with sweetened bottled lime cordial. We preferred fresh lime juice and simple syrup instead.

Celery certainly has its uses: It's an important ingredient in mirepoix, a crunchy element in many salads, and a popular snack with peanut butter or dip. But it's almost never the star of a dish. That wasn't always so. In the Victorian era, celery was considered a sophisticated and high-class food and commanded the price to prove it. It was often showcased as a centerpiece at fancy dinners and was brewed into tonics believed to have various curative effects. Whatever the reason for celery's fall from grace, I believe it still has the potential to inspire admiration rather than apathy. Perhaps a cocktail would be just the thing to once again show off celery's sophisticated side.

This idea first came to me while I was developing muddled cocktail recipes for *How to Cocktail*. I wanted to take the classic flavors of a gimlet (a simple cocktail typically made from nothing more than gin and lime cordial and believed to have been served to sailors in the British Royal Navy in the 19th century as a way to ward off scurvy) and amp them up by adding a muddled element. The botanical, piney flavor of gin (London Dry gin is the usual choice for a gimlet) is a perfect match for the sweet-sour cordial, so the trick would be to choose a muddled ingredient that would complement those notes.

When most people think of muddled drinks, they think of cocktails made using citrus such as lemon or lime or herbs such as basil and mint. These options make for many excellent drinks, but I wanted to get a bit more creative and explore more unusual possibilities. But before I could focus on the muddled part, I needed to settle on the basic formula for the gimlet. Instead of calling for lime cordial, a specialty ingredient that might require a separate trip to the liquor store to find, I decided to use a combination of fresh lime juice and simple syrup (a 1:1 ratio of sugar dissolved in water). This would also allow me to have better control over the sweet-sour balance of the drink. For one cocktail, I settled on ¾ ounce each of simple syrup and fresh lime juice. As for the alcohol, sticking with gin was a given; 2 ounces was just right.

Now for the muddling. Since I was going for something unconventional, I started my testing with options such as arugula, lemongrass, and makrut lime leaves. The citrusy, slightly floral flavor of the makrut lime leaves made for a nice cocktail, but I ended up dismissing them as a possibility because they can be hard to find; the same went for lemongrass. Arugula contributed an interesting peppery flavor, but I wasn't quite done experimenting. Casting about for more inspiration, it occurred to me to try celery. After all, many people enjoy celery-flavored soda, and I've heard of a few mixologists using celery leaves to make cocktails. Why not?

I tried muddling both celery leaves and celery stalks in separate tests to see if one had a better flavor. In a side-by-side taste test, I preferred the more celery-forward flavor produced by the muddled stalks, so I decided to use them moving forward. This had the advantage of making my ingredient list more accessible, since celery leaves can be hard to find at the store in sufficient quantities for making a cocktail. Just one small rib of celery was enough to contribute noticeable flavor to my cocktail, and a single celery leaf floated on top made a nice garnish.

Although understandably dubious at first, my tasters reacted with pleasant surprise after taking a sip of my concoction. Far from being out of place, the subtly bright, slightly vegetal celery flavor was a great complement to the floral, sweet, and sour notes of the gimlet, resulting in a drink with a distinctly sophisticated flavor profile.

While I might not construct a celery centerpiece for my next dinner party, I would certainly consider serving a batch of fresh and unquestionably refined celery gimlets. I think the Victorians would approve.

—CAMILA CHAPARRO, *America's Test Kitchen Books*

Celery Gimlet

MAKES 1 COCKTAIL

Our favorite cocktail shaker is the Tovolo Stainless Steel 4-in-1 Cocktail Shaker.

- **1 small celery rib, chopped, plus celery leaf for garnishing**
- **¾ ounce Simple Syrup (recipe follows)**
- **2 ounces London Dry gin**
- **¾ ounce lime juice**

Add celery and simple syrup to base of cocktail shaker and muddle until celery is broken down and all juice has been expressed, about 30 seconds. Add gin and lime juice, then fill shaker with ice. Shake mixture until fully combined and well chilled, about 30 seconds. Double-strain cocktail into chilled cocktail glass. Garnish with celery leaf and serve.

Simple Syrup

MAKES ABOUT 10 OUNCES

This syrup can be refrigerated for up to a month. Shake well before using.

- **¾ cup sugar**
- **5 ounces warm tap water**

Whisk sugar and warm water in bowl until sugar has dissolved. Let cool completely, about 10 minutes, before transferring to airtight container.

CELERY GIMLET

TEST KITCHEN RESOURCES

Not all products we tested are listed in these pages. Web subscribers can find complete listings and information on all products tested and reviewed at AmericasTestKitchen.com.

BEST KITCHEN QUICK TIPS

PUTTING LEFTOVER WINE TO USE

Amandine Weinrob of Oakland, Calif., likes to freeze leftover wine (any type will work) in ice cube trays. She then places the frozen cubes in a wine glass and pours in club soda or sparkling water to create a wine spritzer that develops as the cubes melt. Alternatively, she tops the frozen cubes with club soda, brandy, and chopped fresh fruit for a riff on sangria.

GRILL PREP KIT

Rather than gather paper towels, vegetable oil, and long tongs to grease the grates before every grilling session, Wayne Shirkson of Wilmington, Del., keeps a set of those items in a plastic tub at the ready. The kit is easy to transport out to the grill so that he always has just what he needs.

NONSTICK STEAMER BASKET

Sue Kelman of Waltham, Mass., prevents food from sticking to her bamboo steamer basket by lining it with a small coffee filter. The porous paper lets steam through and makes cleanup easy.

PORTABLE INGREDIENT STATION

Jeremy Doty of Phoenix, Ariz., stores frequently used ingredients—oil, salt, pepper, etc.—in an 8-inch square baking pan that he can easily transport as needed. The ingredients can sit conveniently next to his prep area, near the stove, or outside by the grill.

A WHIP-SMART WAY TO WASH MIXER BEATERS

To clean sticky batters, frostings, and doughs from her handheld mixer's beaters and her mixing bowl, Deborah Palmer of Carmichael, Calif., fills the dirty mixing bowl halfway with warm water, adds a drop of dish soap, lowers the attached beaters into the bowl, turns on the mixer—first to low speed and then up to medium—and beats for 1 minute. A quick rinse in the sink finishes the job.

ANOTHER WAY TO SKIN A MANGO

Rather than use a knife to remove mango skin (the exposed flesh can be slippery and difficult to handle), Rebecca Robin of Delray Beach, Fla., uses a thin-rimmed glass. After standing the fruit on its wider end and slicing lengthwise on either side of the pit, she grasps one mango half by its skin side with the narrow end pointing up and slides the rim of the glass between the mango flesh and skin, pressing against the heel of her hand and then upward against her palm. (If necessary, she sets the glass down to peel the uppermost portion of the fruit.) The flesh falls into the~glass in one piece.

FROZEN CHIPOTLE CHILE LOG

Michael Wirth of St. Louis, Mo., preserves leftover chipotle chile in adobo sauce by mincing it and transferring it to a 1-quart zipper-lock bag. He uses a bench scraper to push the minced chile to the bottom of the bag, rolls the bag around itself to press out the air, seals it, and freezes the minced chile in a log shape. He then cuts pieces off the frozen log as needed.

NEW USE FOR A PIZZA PEEL

Gerri Wilson of San Francisco, Calif., uses a thin metal pizza peel to transfer large baked goods such as cheesecakes, tarts, and cakes from a pan to a cake stand or serving platter. The large surface area of the peel ensures that the dessert stays intact during transport.

AN EASIER WAY TO CUT HARD SQUASH

A CLUE THAT BLACK SESAME SEEDS ARE TOASTED

Since black sesame seeds don't change color when toasted, it can be difficult to tell when they're ready. To make it easier, Steve Pitt of Rutherglen, Ontario, adds a few white sesame seeds to the skillet. When the white seeds have turned golden, he knows that the black seeds have also reached toasted perfection.

VACUUM-SEAL BAGGED SNACKS

Steve Kucinski of Worthington, Ohio, uses the sealing (not the vacuum) function on a vacuum sealer to close up bags of potato chips, pretzels, and even brown sugar between uses.

To halve a large winter squash, Laura Scheibel of Lee, N.H., runs a wide citrus zester/channel knife lengthwise along the tough skin. This creates a groove in which she can easily place her knife before applying pressure to split the squash.

REUSABLE COVER FOR COOKED STEAKS

Instead of wasting a sheet of aluminum foil to tent steaks as they rest after cooking, John Sturtz of Seoul, South Korea, uses a disposable aluminum pan. Like foil, the pan sits gently on top of the meat to help keep it warm, but it's reusable and easy to clean.

REUSING PARCHMENT PAPER

After using parchment paper to bake a batch of cookies or biscuits, Sheryl Ward of West Bend, Wis., finds that there's still plenty of life left in the parchment. She folds it up, puts it in a zipper-lock bag, and stores it in the freezer until she is ready to use it again. This keeps any oil residue on the paper from going rancid.

CAKE CARRIER TURNED POPCORN TOSSER

.After Hanna Engelhaupt of Heinrichsthal, Germany, makes homemade popcorn, she uses a cake carrier with a tight-fitting lid to toss the popped kernels with seasonings. After she's tossed the popcorn, she inverts the large lid of the carrier to use as a serving bowl.

DRY BAKEWARE IN THE OVEN

After completing a baking project, Sadie Stehlik of Marlborough, N.H., places washed baking sheets, wire racks, loaf pans, and muffin tins upside down in her still-warm oven to dry, saving space in her dish rack. To remind herself that the oven is occupied before turning it on again, she places a note on its door.

BEST KITCHEN QUICK TIPS

EASILY REMOVE VEGETABLES FROM AN ICE BATH

After vegetables are blanched, they must be dunked in ice water to halt their cooking. Michael DuBois of Monument Beach, Mass., sets a colander in the ice bath to easily remove the vegetables once they are cool.

RECYCLE SMALL BITS OF SPICES FOR SCENTED SUGAR

Inspired by vanilla sugar, Nancy Merritt of Severna Park, Md., adds nubs of whole spices such as nutmeg and cardamom to a small jar of sugar. The mixture can be used as a fragrant topping for baked goods or as a sweetener for tea.

REUSE PEPPER MILL TO GRIND SPICES

Anthony Rotolo of New York, N.Y., recycles peppercorn grinders with removable tops by using them to store and grind whole spices. After washing an empty grinder, he fills it with spices such as fennel seeds, coriander seeds, or cumin seeds.

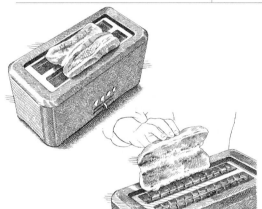

A NEW WAY TO TOAST SANDWICH ROLLS

When he wants to toast a large sandwich roll that won't fit in a traditional double-slotted toaster, John Goodman of Oak Park, Calif., slices the roll almost in half and opens it up. He then lays the roll on top of the toaster's dual heating elements and turns them on, being sure not to cover the slots entirely so that the toaster doesn't overheat. In a few minutes, he has a perfectly toasted roll.

WATER BALLOON ICE PACKS

Deborah Palmer of Carmichael, Calif., makes homemade ice packs by freezing water balloons; the size of the ice packs can be adjusted by filling the balloons with more or less water.

AN APPLE CORER FOR MELON POPS

Apple corers aren't just for apples. Jenny Bishop of Duluth, Minn., uses an apple corer to make "melon pops" by pushing the tool through the rind and pulling out plugs of the fruit. The rind functions as a handle for tidy eating.

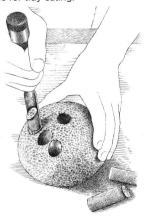

HOW TO STABILIZE CHIVES FOR SLICING

Slicing a bunch of chives can be a challenge since it's hard to hold the moist, slender stems in place. Penny Seavertson of Oskaloosa, Kan., wraps a narrow strip of dampened paper towel around the bunch to hold the stems together. This way, she can make quick, clean cuts into all the chives at once.

A SMART WAY TO GREASE A BAKING SHEET

The next time you need to grease a baking sheet, try this method from Jem Wilmer of Putney, Vt.: Drizzle oil onto the sheet, and then use the flat side of a bench scraper to spread it into an even layer. The tool's sharp edges make it easy to get the oil into the corners of the sheet, leaving it evenly greased from edge to edge.

AN EASIER WAY TO LABEL FOOD STORAGE CONTAINERS

In addition to using her washable wine-glass markers to distinguish guests' drinks at parties, Dawn Demeo of Groton, Mass., uses them to label glass or plastic storage containers. Writing directly on the containers is easier than using masking tape, and unlike the tape, which can be difficult to remove, the writing can be wiped right off with a wet cloth.

A VISUAL CUE FOR ROTATING BAKING SHEETS

When making cookies or sheet cakes that must be rotated halfway through their baking time, Valerie Lomus of Foxborough, Mass., attaches metal binder clips to the front corners of the baking sheets to help her track whether or not she's rotated them (for example, clips that start in the front right corner should move to the back left corner).

NEVER LOSE THE END OF PLASTIC WRAP AGAIN

Because plastic wrap clings to itself, it's easy to lose the cut edge of the roll after you tear a piece from the dispenser. Kerry Sloan of Philadelphia, Pa., came up with this nifty trick: Place a small piece of double-sided tape on the box, right behind the serrated cutter. The tape will automatically trap the edge of the plastic as you cut it.

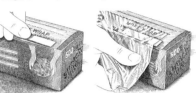

A NEW TOOL FOR OPENING JARS

Christina Kong of Woodside, Calif., uses a clean paint key (a tool for opening cans of paint) to release the vacuum seal on hard-to-open jar lids. She inserts the curled edge of the key under the lip of the lid and then twists slightly to release the seal.

FLATTENING OUT PARCHMENT PAPER

To smooth out curled-up sheets of parchment (or waxed) paper, Liz LeVan of San Antonio, Texas, rolls the sheets in the opposite direction around a rolling pin.

AN ORGANIZED APPROACH TO COOKING SOUS VIDE

Instead of clipping several bags of food around the sides of the pot or container when using his sous vide machine, Stuart Rogers of Toronto, Ontario, uses binder clips to attach them to an inexpensive wire file rack and then lowers the rack into the water. The rack keeps the bags submerged and separated, and the wires can easily be bent to accommodate thicker bags.

REMINDER TO SALT BREAD DOUGH

Some bread recipes call for letting the dough rest briefly before adding salt—a technique called autolyse. Doug Thomas of Minneapolis, Minn., pours the salt on top of the resting dough so that he doesn't forget to mix it into the dough later.

FREEZING AND STEMMING HEARTY HERBS

Susan Rickmers of Bloomsburg, Pa., has found that leftover bunches of hearty herbs such as thyme or rosemary not only hold up well when frozen but also are easy to prep. She freezes herb bunches in a zipper-lock bag, and when she needs some for a recipe, she simply rolls the bag between her hands so that the leaves fall off the stems.

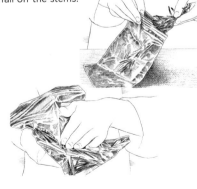

MAKING THE MOST OF FRESH HERBS

Fragrant, distinct, and abundant during warm months, these verdant sprigs have much more to offer than just a pop of freshness and color.

One of the fastest and most economical ways to boost the flavor of food is to add fresh herbs. That's long been the philosophy in cuisines around the world, particularly in Southeast Asia and the Middle East, where fresh herbs are an essential component at meals (often, whole sprigs are heaped onto platters and eaten like vegetables alongside richer dishes). Happily, there are more varieties than ever available at farmers' markets and grocery stores. All the more reason to work them into your daily cooking repertoire.

EIGHT HERBS YOU SHOULD BE COOKING WITH

We love the classic Simon and Garfunkel quartet (parsley, sage, rosemary, and thyme), but the herbs below are just as versatile and are worth snapping up if you come across them at the market or nursery.

1. CHERVIL

PROFILE: Grassy, anise-like sweetness

TRY IT IN: Egg and fish dishes

TIP: Combine chervil with arugula, lettuce, and endive to make classic mesclun mix.

2. GARLIC CHIVES

PROFILE: Garlicky, crisp, juicy

TRY IT IN: Stir-fries; as a substitute for scallions

TIP: Garlic chives are sometimes referred to as Chinese chives.

3. CURRY LEAVES

PROFILE: Lemony, cumin-y, menthol-y

TRY IT IN: Curries, potato and rice dishes

TIP: Curry leaves are unrelated to curry powder.

4. LAVENDER

PROFILE: Floral, perfumy

TRY IT IN: Syrups, custard, shortbread

TIP: Buy culinary, not ornamental, lavender, and use it sparingly.

5. LEMON VERBENA

PROFILE: Minty lemongrass, menthol-y

TRY IT IN: Infusions (drinks, syrups, jams, custards); salads (tender leaves only); with berries or stone fruit

TIP: Steeped in boiling water, it makes a fragrant tisane.

6. MAKRUT LIME LEAVES

PROFILE: Tangy, bright, floral

TRY IT IN: Thai curries and soups, cocktails and limeade, rice dishes, flavored salt

TIP: Use them as a fragrant garnish for proteins and vegetables by cutting out their tough spines and slicing the leaves very thin.

7. SHISO

PROFILE: Minty, citrusy, bitter, medicinal

TRY IT IN: Spring rolls, cold noodle salads, green salads (tear tough leaves), fried rice

TIP: Red shiso tastes more bitter than the green variety.

PREP SCHOOL

WASH; THEN SALAD-SPIN DRY
After rinsing delicate herbs, thoroughly dry them by spinning them in a paper towel–lined salad spinner. (Hearty herbs don't harbor much grit, but if they are dusty, you can give them a quick rinse.)

PACK LIGHTLY WHEN MEASURING
Press down slightly on herbs in the measuring cup to remove air pockets; do not pack them down firmly.

CHOP AND MINCE LIKE A PRO
Running your knife over a loose pile is inefficient. Here's a better way.

To chop: Gather leaves into tight pile and hold with your nonknife hand. Use rocking motion to slice thin. Turn sliced leaves 90 degrees and repeat.

To mince: Chop, then go over pile again by placing fingertips of your nonknife hand on top of knife spine and moving blade up and down with your knife hand while using knife tip as pivot.

8. SORREL

PROFILE: Juicy, lemony, tart

TRY IT IN: Creamy soups, salsa verde, salads; incorporated into a sauce; as a garnish for salmon or lamb

TIP: Like tender spinach and Swiss chard, sorrel shrinks way down when cooked, so start with an ample amount.

TWO BASIC CATEGORIES: HEARTY AND DELICATE

We classify most herbs as either hearty or delicate. These adjectives refer not only to their textural qualities (leaves that are sturdy and tough versus delicate and tender) but also to the strength or volatility of their flavor compounds; in general, volatile flavor compounds in hearty herbs are somewhat more heat-stable than those in delicate varieties. These categories also help clarify the best ways to prep, store, and cook most herbs.

HEARTY: Rosemary, thyme, oregano, sage, marjoram

DELICATE: Basil, parsley, cilantro, dill, mint, chives, tarragon

Fresh Herb Finishing Salts
MAKES ½ CUP

Flavored salts add crunch, mineral salinity, and concentrated flavor to meats and fish, popcorn, or even cocktails when used to rim a glass. Commercial versions are expensive, but making your own is easy and better preserves the flavor of the fresh herbs.

½   cup coarse or flake sea salt

Choose one of the following:

1½   cups finely chopped fresh basil
1   cup thinly sliced fresh chives
1   cup finely chopped fresh dill
1   cup finely chopped fresh tarragon
¼   cup finely chopped fresh makrut lime leaves

1. Line rimmed baking sheet with parchment paper. Combine salt and herb in large bowl. Pick up handful of salt mixture and rub between your hands to disperse herb throughout salt. Repeat until well combined, about 30 seconds. Transfer mixture to prepared sheet and spread into even layer.

2. Place sheet in 50- to 70-degree location away from direct sunlight. Let mixture sit until completely dry, 36 to 48 hours, raking mixture with fork every 12 hours to ensure herb dries evenly.

3. Rub mixture between your hands to break up any clumps of dried herb and evenly distribute herb throughout salt. Transfer to airtight container. (Herb salt can be stored at room temperature for up to 2 months.)

SAVVY STORAGE

Proper herb storage is all about controlling the leaves' exposure to moisture. Hearty herbs are adapted to survive in dry weather by taking in moisture through their leaves, so it's important to keep them dry. Delicate herbs take in and release a lot of water and therefore must be kept moist lest they wilt (but they should not touch liquid, which encourages rot).

FAVORITE STORAGE METHODS
When stored properly, many herbs will last at least a week.

Hearty: Store in original packaging or open zipper-lock bag; refrigerate.

Delicate: Wrap in slightly damp paper towels, place in open zipper-lock bag, and refrigerate.

A KEEPER WORTH KEEPING: COLE & MASON FRESH HERB KEEPER

This slim rectangular container kept herbs fresh longer than the others we tested. It also features adjustable height, which makes it easy to add and remove herbs; a vented lid, which staves off condensation; and dividers, which keep the contents tidy and organized.

USE SPRIGS FROM ROOT TO BLOSSOM

While some herbs don't have much use beyond their leaves, others (mostly delicate varieties) are edible up and down the sprig. Here's a breakdown of usable components besides leaves and their suggested applications.

ROOTS
Cilantro roots are aromatic, pungent, and citrusy. Cilantro stems with the roots attached are commonly found at Asian markets. The whole plant is increasingly available at conventional markets, too. Puree the roots into marinades and curry pastes; store unused roots in the freezer.

STEMS
Some herbs (such as cilantro, parsley, and basil) have delicate stems that can be minced or chopped with the leaves or pureed into sauces (such as pesto), curry pastes, or soups.

BLOSSOMS
In general, herb blossoms taste like their parent plants. Add them whole to salads or use them as an elegant garnish.

SEEDS
Some herbs (such as cilantro and dill) produce aromatic seeds that can be used whole, crushed, or ground.

NOT ALL HERBS CAN TAKE THE HEAT

Due to variability in the strength and volatility of their flavor compounds, hearty and delicate herbs behave differently when cooked. Here are general guidelines.

Hearty: Add early in cooking to ensure maximum flavor extraction.

Delicate: Use as a garnish or add for the last minute of cooking to preserve flavor and color.

BUYING AND PREPPING CHICKEN PARTS

For juicy, flavorful chicken, you need to be well informed before you even start to cook. Here's how to buy the right parts and prep them properly.

SHOPPING

LOOKING FOR A BARGAIN? BUY DRUMSTICKS

When we cooked bone-in chicken breasts, thighs, drumsticks, and wings and then stripped the meat from the bones to determine the price per edible ounce, we found that drumsticks were the cheapest and wings were the most expensive.

PART	PRICE PER POUND	PRICE PER EDIBLE OUNCE
Drumsticks	$1.69	$0.23
Thighs	$2.19	$0.29
Breasts	$3.29	$0.36
Wings	$2.49	$0.40

ALWAYS BUY AIR-CHILLED

Chicken with an "Air-Chilled" label has been cooled after slaughter by being hung from a conveyor belt that circulates around a cold room. Conversely, water-chilled chicken sits in a chlorinated bath, where it absorbs water that inflates cost. Air-chilled chicken is typically more tender, likely because the slower temperature drop gives enzymes in the meat more time to tenderize muscle tissue.

AVOID PACKAGED PARTS

The U.S. Department of Agriculture doesn't regulate the weight of chicken parts, so a package might contain pieces that vary dramatically in weight, which can make it hard to ensure that they cook at the same rate. In packages of split breasts and leg quarters, we found that the largest pieces could weigh twice as much as the smallest. Buy parts individually from the meat counter and select similar-size pieces.

DON'T FREEZE IN SUPERMARKET PACKAGING

We don't freeze chicken in its packaging (unless it is vacuum-sealed) because most packaging has air gaps that cause freezer burn. Instead, we wrap each chicken part in plastic wrap, place it in a zipper-lock freezer bag, press out the air, and freeze the parts in a single layer. And don't refreeze chicken: Its texture when cooked becomes significantly tougher.

DON'T BRINE WATER-CHILLED CHICKEN

We don't recommend buying water-chilled chicken, but if it's your only option, salt it, don't brine it. Chicken that absorbs water during processing can take up only so much of a brine. (The water it absorbs during processing drains off during cooking.) Salting water-chilled chicken delivers meat that retains just as much water as brined air-chilled chicken. For proper salt amounts and times, refer to the salting chart (below left).

SALTING VERSUS BRINING

Pretreating chicken with salt, whether dry or in a brine, helps it cook up juicy and well seasoned.

SALTING

Salting causes juices inside the meat to come to the surface. The salt dissolves in the exuded liquid, forming a brine that is eventually reabsorbed by the meat.

BENEFITS OVER BRINING: More convenient (no large container needed); does not add moisture to the exterior (meaning crispier skin)

CONS: Takes longer than brining

BRINING

Brining not only seasons meat but also promotes a change in its protein structure, reducing its overall toughness and creating moister meat.

BENEFITS OVER SALTING: Works faster; makes lean cuts juicier since it adds moisture

CONS: Can inhibit browning on skin or meat exterior; requires fitting a brining container in the refrigerator

	TIME	KOSHER SALT	METHOD
Boneless, Skinless Breasts	1 hour	¾ teaspoon per pound	Sprinkle salt evenly over both sides; cover loosely with plastic wrap and refrigerate.
Bone-In Chicken Pieces	At least 1 hour or up to 24	¾ teaspoon per pound	If chicken is skin-on, apply half of salt between skin and meat and half of salt on bone side. Refrigerate on wire rack set in rimmed baking sheet. (Wrap with plastic wrap if salting for longer than 12 hours.)

	TIME	COLD WATER	TABLE SALT
Boneless, Skinless Breasts (up to 6 breasts)	½ to 1 hour	1½ quarts	3 tablespoons
Bone-In Chicken Pieces (whole breasts, split breasts, whole legs, and/or drumsticks) (up to 4 pounds)	½ to 1 hour	2 quarts	½ cup

BREASTS

HOW TO BONE BREASTS

This method produces boneless, skin-on breasts, which aren't available at the supermarket.

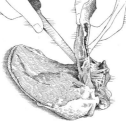

1. With breast skin side down, run tip of paring or boning knife between breastbone and meat, working from thick end toward tapered end.

2. Angling blade to follow rib cage, repeat cutting motion along breastbone to remove ribs and breastbone from meat.

3. Holding rib cage with 1 hand, locate wishbone in thick end of breast and cut along both sides with tip of knife to remove bones.

A NEW WAY TO CUT CUTLETS

Because a chicken breast is unevenly shaped and has a thick and a thin end, it can be tricky to turn into uniform cutlets. Our novel method makes the process foolproof: Cut each breast in half crosswise, and then cut the thicker piece in half horizontally. Place the pieces between two sheets of plastic wrap and gently pound them to ½-inch thickness.

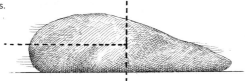

HOW TO TRIM BONELESS, SKINLESS BREASTS

Place breast with smooth, rounded side facing up. Use chef's knife to cut away any fat on sides, then trim any connective tissue from thick end. It's OK to leave white strip running along smooth side of breast; it won't be tough.

WHAT TO DO WITH THE TENDERLOIN

The tenderloin (also called a chicken tender) is the flap of meat that's loosely attached to the underside (or rib side) of a boneless, skinless breast. Unless you're making cutlets (in which case it will inevitably fall off during cooking), it's fine to leave it alone.

THIGHS

HOW TO BONE THIGHS

As with breasts, removing the bone from thighs yourself allows you to keep the rich, flavorful skin.

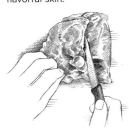

1. With thigh skin side down, locate bone. Using paring knife and using line of fat as guide, cut slit along length of bone to expose its top.

2. Using tip of knife, cut meat from both sides of bone with short slashing cuts.

3. Once most of bone is exposed, slide tip of knife under bone to completely remove it.

HOW TO TRIM THIGHS

With thigh skin side down (or skinned side for boneless, skinless thighs), check long side of thigh for cartilage and short side for fat pocket; trim with chef's knife. Flip thigh and trim any loose skin (or any fat from boneless, skinless thighs).

WINGS

HOW TO CUT UP WINGS

Separating wings into two pieces makes them easier to cook.

1. Using your fingertip, locate joint between wingtip and midsection. Place blade of chef's knife on joint, between bones, and, using palm of your nonknife hand, press down on blade to cut through skin and tendon.

2. Find joint between midsection and drumette and repeat process to cut through skin and joint. (Discard wingtip or save to use for stock.)

NO-FUSS PARTY APPETIZERS

Don't shortcut the cocktail hour just because you're preparing an elaborate meal. These easy bites will impress and still allow you to enjoy the party.

Goat Cheese Log with Hazelnut-Nigella Dukkah
SERVES 8 TO 10

CHEESE

- 6 ounces goat cheese
- 6 ounces cream cheese
- 1 small garlic clove, minced
- ½ teaspoon pepper

DUKKAH

- 1 teaspoon fennel seeds, toasted
- 1 teaspoon coriander seeds, toasted
- 1½ tablespoons raw sunflower seeds, toasted
- 1 tablespoon sesame seeds, toasted
- 1½ teaspoons nigella seeds
- 3 tablespoons hazelnuts, toasted, skinned, and chopped fine
- 1½ teaspoons paprika
- ½ teaspoon flake sea salt
- 2 tablespoons extra-virgin olive oil

1. FOR THE CHEESE: Process all ingredients in food processor until smooth, about 1 minute, scraping down sides of bowl as needed.

2. Place 18 by 11-inch sheet of plastic wrap on counter with long side parallel to counter edge. Transfer cheese mixture to center of plastic and shape into log with long side parallel to counter edge (log should be about 9 inches long). Fold plastic over log and roll up. Pinch plastic at ends of log and roll on counter to form tight cylinder. Tuck ends of plastic underneath log and freeze until completely firm, 1½ to 2 hours.

3. FOR THE DUKKAH: Grind fennel seeds and coriander seeds in spice grinder until finely ground, about 30 seconds. Add sunflower seeds, sesame seeds, and nigella seeds and pulse until coarsely ground, about 4 pulses; transfer to small bowl. Stir in hazelnuts, paprika, and salt. (Dukkah can be refrigerated for up to 3 months.)

4. Unwrap cheese log and let sit until outside is slightly tacky to touch, about 10 minutes. Spread dukkah into even layer on large plate and roll cheese log in dukkah to evenly coat, pressing gently to adhere. (Cheese log can be wrapped tightly in plastic and refrigerated for up to 2 days.) Transfer to serving platter and let sit at room temperature until softened, about 1 hour. Drizzle with oil and serve.

MAKE THE RIGHT AMOUNT
The volume and variety of items you make depend on what (if anything) will follow.

- Meal to follow in less than an hour: one to three appetizers; three to four pieces per person

- Meal to follow in more than an hour: one to three appetizers; four to six pieces per person

- No meal to follow: five to six appetizers; 10 to 12 pieces per person

Muhammara
SERVES 8 (MAKES ABOUT 2 CUPS)

- 1½ cups roasted red peppers, rinsed
- 1 cup walnuts, toasted
- ¼ cup crumbled plain wheat crackers
- 3 tablespoons pomegranate molasses
- 2 tablespoons extra-virgin olive oil
- ¾ teaspoon table salt
- ½ teaspoon ground cumin
- ⅛ teaspoon cayenne pepper, plus extra for seasoning
  Lemon juice
- 1 tablespoon minced fresh parsley (optional)

Pulse red peppers, walnuts, crackers, pomegranate molasses, oil, salt, cumin, and cayenne in food processor until smooth, about 10 pulses. Transfer to serving bowl, cover, and refrigerate for 15 minutes. (Dip can be refrigerated for up to 24 hours; let come to room temperature before serving.) Season with lemon juice, salt, and extra cayenne to taste, and sprinkle with parsley, if using. Serve with pita bread or crudités.

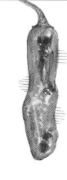

Blistered Shishito Peppers
SERVES 4 TO 6

- 2 tablespoons vegetable oil
- 8 ounces shishito peppers

Heat oil in 12-inch skillet over medium-high heat until just smoking. Add peppers and cook, without stirring, until skins are blistered, 3 to 5 minutes. Using tongs, flip peppers; continue to cook until blistered on second side, 3 to 5 minutes longer. Transfer to serving bowl, season with kosher salt to taste, and serve immediately.

HOW TO BUILD AN IMPRESSIVE CHEESE BOARD

You can't go wrong with cheese, but with some thoughtful preparation you can make a spectacular spread.

1. BUY A VARIETY For a mix of flavors and textures, choose one option from each profile: sharp and crumbly (like aged cheddar), soft and bright (like chèvre), firm and nutty (like Gruyère), tangy and funky (like blue), ripe and oozy (like Brie).

TIP: Plan on serving 2 to 3 ounces of cheese per person.

2. WARM IT UP Most cheeses are best at room temperature, so remove them from the refrigerator at least 1 hour before serving. Keep them wrapped until party time to prevent them from drying out.

TIP: You can quickly soften creamy cheese varieties such as Brie by placing them in a zipper-lock bag and letting them sit in 80-degree water.

3. CHOOSE NEUTRAL BREAD AND CRACKERS Mild-tasting baguette (sliced on the bias into wide, elegant pieces) and water crackers allow the cheese to shine.

TIP: Sliced bread stales quickly, so we brush the slices with extra-virgin olive oil, sprinkle them with salt, and toast them on a rimmed baking sheet in a 400-degree oven until they're golden brown.

Black Pepper Candied Bacon
SERVES 4 TO 6

¼ cup packed light brown sugar

1 teaspoon pepper

12 ounces center-cut bacon, halved crosswise

1. Adjust oven racks to upper-middle and lower-middle positions and heat oven to 350 degrees. Combine sugar and pepper in bowl. Arrange bacon on 2 aluminum foil–lined rimmed baking sheets and sprinkle with sugar mixture. Using your fingers, spread sugar mixture evenly over 1 side of slices so they are completely covered.

2. Bake until bacon is dark brown and sugar is bubbling, 20 to 25 minutes, switching and rotating sheets halfway through baking. Set wire rack over triple layer of paper towels. Remove sheets from oven as bacon finishes cooking and transfer bacon to prepared wire rack. Let cool for 5 minutes before serving.

Black Olive Tapenade
SERVES 6 (MAKES ABOUT 1½ CUPS)

⅓ cup pine nuts

1½ cups pitted kalamata olives

½ cup pitted salt-cured black olives

3 tablespoons capers, rinsed

2 teaspoons Dijon mustard

2 anchovy fillets, rinsed and patted dry

½ garlic clove, minced

¼ cup extra-virgin olive oil

1. Process pine nuts in food processor until reduced to paste, about 20 seconds. Scrape down sides of bowl and process until paste clings to sides and avoids blade, about 5 seconds. Repeat scraping and processing once (pine nuts should form mostly smooth, tahini-like paste).

2. Scrape down sides of bowl to redistribute paste, then add olives, capers, mustard, anchovies, and garlic. Pulse until finely chopped, about 15 pulses, scraping down sides of bowl halfway through pulsing. Transfer mixture to medium bowl and stir in oil until well combined.

3. Transfer to container, cover, and refrigerate for at least 18 hours or up to 2 weeks. Let come to room temperature and stir thoroughly before serving with baguette slices or crudités.

YOUR TOP BREAD QUESTIONS, ANSWERED

We answer your most common bread questions, from knowing when dough is properly risen to ensuring a boulangerie-quality crust.

HOW CAN I BE SURE THAT MY YEAST WILL WORK?

Yeast is a living organism, and its activity will decrease over time—even if the package is unopened. To check that your yeast is healthy, run the following test: In a small bowl, mix 1 teaspoon of yeast (active dry or instant) with ½ teaspoon of sugar and 1 tablespoon of room-temperature water. The mixture should look bubbly within 10 minutes; if it doesn't, it's time to buy a fresh supply of yeast.

HOW DO I FORM A PERFECTLY ROUND LOAF?

When shaping dough, it's important to stretch it so that the exterior forms a strong, taut "skin." This sets the loaf's structure and prevents gases from escaping at weak points, which would allow it to rise and bake unevenly. Professional bakers tuck and secure the ends underneath the dough ball while it's upright—a technique that takes lots of practice. Here's an easier way. (The method shown is for a symmetrical round loaf known as a boule. Traditionally, boules are transferred to linen-lined woven baskets known as bannetons or brotforms for the last rising step before baking.)

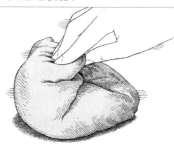

1. Place dough ball on lightly floured counter (or use flouring station; see tip below right) and gently pat into rough disk. Pull edges toward center in 4 or 5 places around circumference.

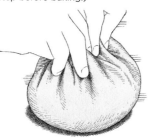

2. Gather and pinch corners of folds together to form sack shape; seal folds tightly to form tail.

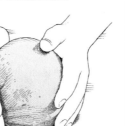

3. Turn dough on side so tail points toward your dominant hand.

4. Supporting dough with your nondominant hand, roll side of your other hand forward over tail, sealing seam tightly with side of your hand.

5. Roll ball over so tail and seam are underneath.

HOW CAN I TELL WHEN MY DOUGH HAS RISEN ENOUGH?

Recipes often call for letting dough rise until it's doubled in size, which can be hard to gauge when the dough is in a bowl. These tricks can help.

FOR THE FIRST RISE: Mark the Container

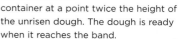

Place the dough in a clear, straight-sided container and stretch a rubber band around the container at a point twice the height of the unrisen dough. The dough is ready when it reaches the band.

FOR THE SECOND RISE: Poke the Dough

Press the dough gently with your knuckle or finger. If the dough springs back right away, that means the yeast is still actively fermenting and producing gases that help the loaf expand, so it needs more proofing. But if the dough springs back slowly and leaves a small indent, that indicates that the dough has expanded as much as it should before it goes into the oven, and it's ready to bake.

USE A FLOURING STATION

When shaping dough, it's important not to overdo it with the dusting flour. While you don't want the dough to stick and tear, you also don't want it to slide around freely; a little resistance between the dough and the work surface will help it develop a taut skin. Flouring the surface makes it too easy to overflour the dough, so we create a flouring station.

HERE'S HOW: Lightly flour area adjacent to work surface. Gently press unshaped dough into floured area once or twice to coat underside, then transfer to work surface and shape. Press dough lightly into floured area as needed to prevent sticking.

HOW CAN I TELL WHEN THE LOAF IS DONE?

Bake bread until it looks right: There is a wider window for doneness on the inside of a loaf than on the crust, so when you're baking bread, trust your eyes first and foremost. Feel free to use a thermometer for reassurance (we typically aim for 190 degrees for enriched breads and 205 degrees for lean breads), but if the bread is still pale, keep baking it, even if it's at or above the recommended temperature. And if it looks good, pull it from the oven, even if it is 5 to 10 degrees below temperature on the inside.

SIMILAR CRUMBS, VERY DIFFERENT CRUSTS
All three of these loaves reached the target temperature for the interior, but their crusts ranged from too pale to just right to almost burnt. The lesson? Pull bread from the oven when it looks done, not when your thermometer says it's done.

WHAT'S THE PURPOSE OF SLASHING THE DOUGH?

Making slashes through the dough's taut exterior creates designated weak spots in the surface that allow it to expand in the proper direction during baking, further guaranteeing a perfectly shaped loaf. When done well, slashes also allow you to embellish the crust with eye-catching designs. Most doughs can be slashed with a sharp paring knife or single-edge razor blade (bakeries often use a dedicated tool, called a lame, which we call for in our baguette recipe).

THREE BASIC SLASHING STYLES

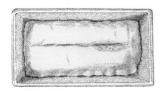

LONG SINGLE CUT: Make 1 cut lengthwise along top of loaf, starting and stopping ½ inch from ends.
USED FOR: Sandwich loaves

CROSS CUT: Make 2 slashes along top of loaf to form X.
USED FOR: Round loaves (boules)

TWO TIPS FOR SLASHING

• Act quickly and decisively; otherwise the tool will drag and create messy lines.

• Cut slashes between ¼ and ½ inch deep.

MULTIPLE SHORT CUTS: Make 3 (or more) evenly spaced diagonal cuts across width of loaf.
USED FOR: Torpedos, bâtards, and baguettes

HOW DO I MAKE THE CRUST REALLY CRISP?

The best way to ensure a crackly-crisp crust is to introduce steam. The steam's moisture converts the dough's exterior starches into a thin coating of gel that bakes into a glossy, crackly surface. Professional bakers use steam-injected ovens, but we found that you can mimic their effect in two ways.

1. BAKE IN A DUTCH OVEN: The lidded pot traps steam, which helps produce a shiny, crisp crust on single round loaves. We start the dough in an unheated pot in a cold oven; though it takes a little longer to bake than if you add the dough to a preheated pot in a hot oven, it works beautifully and it's easier.

2. POUR BOILING WATER ON LAVA ROCKS: Lava rocks, which are sold at hardware stores, offer abundant surface area that helps create steam. To use them: Adjust the oven rack to the lowest position (below the rack with the baking stone). Fill two aluminum pie plates with 1 quart of lava rocks each and place them on the rack below the stone before heating the oven. When you're ready to bake a loaf, pour ½ cup of boiling water into one of the plates of lava rocks and close the oven door for 1 minute to create an initial burst of steam. Then, working quickly, transfer the loaf to the oven and pour ½ cup of boiling water into the second plate of rocks.

CAN I REVIVE STALE BREAD?

Yes. The key is to heat stale bread to 140 degrees or higher, which temporarily reverses the retrogradation of its starch, making it soft again. But since the effect won't last, use revived bread immediately.

UNSLICED: If the bread is crusty, briefly pass it under a running faucet of cold water (for softer loaves, skip this step). Wrap the loaf tightly in aluminum foil, place it on the middle rack of a cold oven, and set the temperature to 300 degrees. After about 30 minutes (15 to 20 minutes for small or narrow loaves such as baguettes), remove the foil and return the loaf to the oven for about 5 more minutes to crisp up the crust.

SLICED: Bread slices can simply be toasted, though they don't need to get dry or even browned, just heated to 140 degrees or higher.

OUR MODERN GUIDE TO SPICES

Put aside the usual preground powders and commercial blends. It's time to get more out of your spice collection.

BROADEN YOUR SPICE PANTRY WITH THESE EIGHT ADDITIONS

As supermarket options continue to expand, so, too, should your spice collection. Here are a handful of our current favorites and a few ideas for how to use them.

ALEPPO PEPPER

WHAT IT IS: Crushed dried red Halaby chiles from Syria and Turkey

PROFILE: Complex, raisiny sweetness; moderate, slow-to-build heat

HOW TO USE: Add to marinade for kebabs; braise with greens; sprinkle over avocado toast

CARDAMOM (GREEN)

WHAT IT IS: Seed pods from *Elettaria cardamomum* plant in ginger family

PROFILE: Piney, floral; warm finish

HOW TO USE: Bake ground spice into cakes; sauté whole pods with onions for pilaf; braise crushed pods with lamb

FENNEL POLLEN

WHAT IT IS: Pollen harvested from wild fennel; traditional to Tuscan cooking

PROFILE: Honey-like, savory, delicately crunchy

HOW TO USE: Add to dipping oil; sprinkle over lemony pasta, creamy soups, pork dishes

GOCHUGARU

WHAT IT IS: Blend of crushed dried red Korean chiles that range in heat

PROFILE: Smoky-sweet, fruity, moderately spicy

HOW TO USE: Add to spice paste for kimchi; stir into chili oil; sprinkle over popcorn and caramelized onions

MUSTARD SEEDS

WHAT THEY ARE: Seeds from mustard plant; can be black, brown, or yellow, depending on varietal

PROFILE: Crisp, bright, mild, sweet (yellow); pungent, bitter, spicy (brown, black)

HOW TO USE: Add to chutneys, brine for pickles, rubs for roast pork/ham

SMOKED PAPRIKA (SWEET) (PIMENTÓN DULCE)

WHAT IT IS: Sweet red peppers dried over oak embers and then ground

PROFILE: Rich, woodsy smoke; fruity sweetness

HOW TO USE: Mix into chorizo; sprinkle over fried or mashed potatoes, hummus, eggs

SUMAC

WHAT IT IS: Ground dried berries of sumac bush; usually processed with salt

PROFILE: Lemony, earthy tang

HOW TO USE: Add to za'atar; sprinkle over fattoush or roasted root vegetables

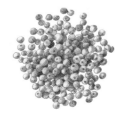

WHITE PEPPERCORNS

WHAT THEY ARE: Fermented, fully ripened black peppercorns with outer skins removed before drying

PROFILE: Floral and earthy, with a delicate heat

HOW TO USE: Add to hot-and-sour soup, dry rubs, stir-fries, gingerbread, flavorings for steamed fish

---

FOUR TIPS FOR BUYING AND STORING SPICES

Buy whole spices to grind as needed. Grinding releases the volatile compounds that give a spice its flavor and aroma.

Buy in small quantities and replace spices in a timely manner. Replace whole spices after two years and ground spices after one year.

Store ground spices in glass jars. Some spices contain high concentrations of oils that will soften and dissolve plastic.

Check freshness before use. Crumble a pinch of whole spice or dried powder between your fingers and smell. If it releases a lively aroma, it's still good.

THE FINEST GRINDER

A dedicated spice grinder such as our favorite, the Krups Coffee and Spice Grinder ($17.99), grinds whole spices to a fine, even grind and makes it easy to capitalize on the richer flavors and aromas of freshly ground spices.

CRACK IT FOR CRUNCH

When you want the crunch of cracked or coarsely ground spices for coating meat or sprinkling over finished dishes, here are two good ways to go about it.

MORTAR AND PESTLE

Use circular grinding motion, maintaining downward pressure at all times until spices are ground.

SKILLET/POT

On baking sheet, rock bottom edge of skillet over 2 tablespoons of whole spices until spices crack.

THREE WAYS TO TREAT YOUR SPICES

The way you treat a spice can impact its flavor in a dish.

BLOOMING alters a spice's flavor, bringing out deeper, more complex notes. Dissolving the aromatic compounds in fat allows them to spread evenly throughout the dish and binds them so that they don't readily evaporate during cooking.
Best for: Whole and ground spices

TOASTING in a dry skillet applies dry heat directly to spices. It brings their oils to the surface, resulting in bolder aroma; it also causes desirable chemical transformations in the aroma compounds. It's a method we reserve for whole spices, since toasting preground spices drives off too many flavor compounds.
Best for: Whole spices

LEAVING SPICES RAW preserves bright, clean top notes that get lost if you apply heat to them.
Best for: Whole and ground spices

DON'T BUY THESE BLENDS—MAKE THEM

A blend made from freshly ground spices will be more vibrant and aromatic than any you can buy. Some blends get added during cooking, while others can be sprinkled on at the last moment like garnishes.

Chili Powder

MAKES ABOUT ⅓ CUP

Mexican oregano is particularly robust, but any dried variety works.

- 2 ounces (7 to 8) dried New Mexican chiles, stemmed, seeded, and torn into ½-inch pieces (1½ cups)
- 1 teaspoon cumin seeds
- ½ teaspoon dried oregano, preferably Mexican
- 1 tablespoon paprika
- ½ teaspoon garlic powder
- ¼ teaspoon cayenne pepper

Working in batches, grind New Mexican chiles, cumin seeds, and oregano in spice grinder until finely ground, about 30 seconds. Stir in paprika, garlic powder, and cayenne.

HOW TO USE: Add to chili, rubs, barbecue sauce; sprinkle over Mexican street corn; rim a glass for a michelada

Sesame-Orange Spice Blend

MAKES ¼ CUP

This blend is inspired by shichimi togarashi, the Japanese seven-spice blend. Store the blend in an airtight container for up to one month.

- ¾ teaspoon grated orange zest
- 2 teaspoons sesame seeds
- 1½ teaspoons paprika
- 1 teaspoon pepper
- ¼ teaspoon garlic powder
- ¼ teaspoon ground ginger
- ⅛ teaspoon cayenne pepper

Place orange zest in small bowl and microwave, stirring every 20 seconds, until zest is dry and no longer clumping together, 1½ to 2½ minutes. Stir in sesame seeds, paprika, pepper, garlic powder, ginger, and cayenne.

HOW TO USE: Sprinkle over udon or soba noodles, rice, soft-cooked eggs, french fries, or grilled meats

Mild Curry Powder

MAKES ABOUT ⅓ CUP

We like Frontier Co-op Ground Turmeric.

- 2 tablespoons coriander seeds
- 1½ tablespoons cumin seeds
- 1 tablespoon yellow mustard seeds
- 1½ teaspoons black peppercorns
- 1½ tablespoons ground turmeric
- 1 teaspoon ground ginger
- ¼ teaspoon ground cinnamon

Grind coriander seeds, cumin seeds, mustard seeds, and peppercorns in spice grinder until finely ground, about 30 seconds; transfer to small bowl. Stir in turmeric, ginger, and cinnamon.

HOW TO USE: Add to curries, mulligatawny soup, or egg or chicken salad

Five-Spice Powder

MAKES ABOUT ¼ CUP

Store this blend in a glass container.

- 5 teaspoons fennel seeds
- 4 teaspoons white peppercorns or 8 teaspoons Sichuan peppercorns
- 1 tablespoon whole cloves
- 8 star anise pods
- 1 (3-inch) cinnamon stick, broken into pieces

Process fennel seeds, peppercorns, and cloves in spice grinder until finely ground, about 30 seconds; transfer to small bowl. Process star anise and cinnamon stick in now-empty grinder until finely ground, about 30 seconds; transfer to bowl with fennel mixture and stir to combine.

HOW TO USE: Rub on chicken breasts before searing; shake into whiskey sour; sauté with kale; use in mulled cider

15 WAYS TO BE A SCRAPPIER COOK

The more we cook, the more ways we discover to refresh and repurpose food and save money in the kitchen. Behold: our guide to culinary thrift.

1. REVIVE WILTED PRODUCE

LEAFY GREENS

(lettuce, spinach, arugula)

Soak greens in ice water for 30 minutes.

VEGETABLES WITH STALKS OR STEMS

(broccoli, asparagus, celery, scallions, parsley)

Trim stalks or stems on bias to expose more water-wicking capillaries. Stand produce in container filled with cold water for 1 hour.

2. REUSE CHARCOAL

You can replace up to half of the fresh coals called for in a recipe with partially spent ones that you filter from the ash.

TO PREPARE COALS: Immediately extinguish coals by cutting off air supply (dump coals into small metal trash can or container with lid and cover). Let cool. Place coals in chimney starter; shake and rap chimney starter over trash can to dislodge ash. Store coals until ready to use.

TO USE COALS: Place fresh coals in chimney starter first, then top with used coals.

3. STRETCH HOMEMADE STOCK

Rather than discard the solids after pressing out as much liquid as possible, "rinse" them once with ¼ cup of water per pound of meat/bones, strain the mixture, and then add the liquid to the stock. The "rinsing liquid" won't be as concentrated as the stock, but it's still surprisingly flavorful.

4. RECRISP STALE COOKIES, CRACKERS, AND CHIPS

Spread food in single layer on rimmed baking sheet (place larger cookies or graham crackers on wire rack set in baking sheet) and heat on middle rack of 225-degree oven until crisp (15 to 25 minutes), stirring (or flipping) halfway through heating.

5. SWAP OUT PARCHMENT PAPER FOR WAXED

Waxed paper can line a cookie tin, separate moist burger patties or steaks, cover foods in the microwave, prevent a rolling pin from sticking to dough, and wrap sandwiches or candy—and it's about a quarter of the cost of parchment. (Just don't bake with it; it's not designed to withstand high heat.)

6. LOVE YOUR LEFTOVERS

Unless you're reheating something that's liquid-based such as a soup or stew, avoid the microwave, which turns food steamy and soggy. But you can restore many foods—even pizza and skin-on poultry—to a fresh-tasting state by placing them on a rimmed baking sheet (proteins should be elevated on a wire rack to allow air circulation on all sides) and warming them in the oven.

7. BUY QUALITY ON THE CHEAP

Some of our favorite products are great bargains.

VANILLA EXTRACT: Baker's Imitation Vanilla Flavor ($0.12 per fl oz)

BLACK PEPPERCORNS: Tone's Whole Black Peppercorns ($1.14 per oz)

MAPLE SYRUP: Uncle Luke's Pure Maple Syrup, Grade A Dark Amber ($0.65 per fl oz)

CHEF'S KNIFE: Victorinox Swiss Army Fibrox Pro 8" Chef's Knife ($39.95)

PARING KNIFE: Victorinox Swiss Army Fibrox Pro 3¼" Spear Point Paring Knife ($9.47)

SERRATED KNIFE: Mercer Culinary Millennia 10" Wide Bread Knife ($22.10)

8. SIMMER SHRIMP SHELLS FOR STOCK

Simmer 4 ounces shrimp shells (harvested from 1½ pounds shrimp) in 1½ cups water for 5 minutes. (Shrimp flavor compounds are volatile, so a short simmer delivers the best results.) Use stock for seafood soups, stews, fideos, and risottos.

9. DECRYSTALLIZE HONEY— AND KEEP IT THAT WAY

Place honey jar in saucepan with 1 inch water and heat gently over low heat until honey is smooth.

To prevent recrystallization, stir in 2 teaspoons light corn syrup per 1 cup honey before transferring honey to clean jar. (By changing the overall blend of sugars present, corn syrup inhibits the formation of glucose crystals.)

10. COOK WITH LEFTOVER PICKLE BRINE

MAKE MORE PICKLES: Toss cucumber slices in colander with 1½ teaspoons table salt per 1 pound cucumbers. Let sit for 1 hour, then transfer to jar. Bring brine to boil; pour over cucumbers. Seal jar and refrigerate for at least 24 hours before eating. Pickles can be refrigerated for up to 2 weeks (don't reuse brine more than once).

REUSE THE BRINE FROM DILL PICKLES: Pour over warm potatoes before making potato salad.

PEPPERONCINI: Add a dash to Bloody Marys.

PICKLED JALAPEÑOS: Drizzle over steamed vegetables or grilled chicken or fish.

PEPPADEWS: Add to pan sauces.

NOTE: The vinegar in pickle brine is slightly diluted by water pulled from the vegetables, so don't substitute it one-for-one for vinegar or lemon juice. Some brines are very salty, so withhold any additional salt in the dish and season to taste at the end.

11. MAXIMIZE VEGETABLE YIELD

ASPARAGUS: You'll discard about 50 percent of thick spears by weight if you snap off the ends. To reduce the loss, trim 1 inch from the base and peel the lower half of each spear to remove the woody exterior.

BEET, RADISH, AND TURNIP GREENS: Sauté or braise as you would Swiss chard or mustard greens.

CABBAGE AND CAULIFLOWER CORES: Slice or chop the cores and cook them along with the leaves or florets in long-cooked dishes such as soups and stews.

CARROT TOPS: Finely chop them as a garnish or blend them into pesto with an equal amount of basil. Add the fibrous stems to stock for a light vegetal flavor.

LEEKS: To preserve about 15 percent more of the usable pale portion, cut leeks diagonally from the point where the leaves start to darken to the middle of the dark green portion. Peek inside to determine where light green turns dark. Cut diagonally again, preserving the light portion. Repeat twice to create a pointed shape with the pale leaves.

MUSHROOM STEMS: The stems of button, cremini, and portobello mushrooms are usable once you trim away the base. Avoid tougher, woodier stems such as shiitakes'.

12. SKIP WINE; USE VERMOUTH

When you need only a little wine for cooking and don't want to open a whole bottle, dry and red (sweet) vermouths make fine shelf-stable substitutes for up to ½ cup of white and red wine, respectively, since they keep for months in the refrigerator. Note that red vermouth is sweeter than red wine, but its flavor can be balanced in cooking with a few drops of lemon juice or red wine vinegar.

15. CUT BACK ON FOOD WRAPS

REPLACE PLASTIC WRAP: When covering dough rising in a bowl, use a pot lid, plate, or hotel shower cap. When covering food in the microwave, use a plate.

REUSE ALUMINUM FOIL, PARCHMENT PAPER, AND ZIPPER-LOCK BAGS: Unless they are ripped or really messy, these products can be wiped clean and reused multiple times.

13. BUY HIGH-YIELD, LOW-COST CHICKEN AND BROTH

PARTS: We cooked bone-in chicken breasts, thighs, drumsticks, and wings and then stripped the meat from the bones to determine the price per edible ounce. The most meat for your buck? Drumsticks, followed by thighs, breasts, and wings, respectively.

BROTH: Our Best Buy broth, Better Than Bouillon Chicken Base, costs as little as ⅓ of the price per fluid ounce of liquid broths. It also lasts for more than a year in the refrigerator.

14. RENDER FAT FROM MEAT SCRAPS FOR MORE FLAVORFUL COOKING

Don't toss the bits of fat and skin that you trim from roasts, stew meat, and whole birds; render their fat and use it as a more savory alternative to butter and oil for roasting potatoes, sautéing greens, frying eggs, and toasting rice for pilaf. (When heated, the fatty acids in unrefined animal fat oxidize to form new flavor compounds that make food taste more complex.) Store rendered fat in an airtight container in the freezer.

INTERNATIONAL YOGURTS

When Greek yogurt first became widely available in the United States around 2007, it caught on fast. These days, shoppers can choose from Bulgarian, Australian, and even Icelandic yogurts. How do these products compare to our longtime favorite Greek and American-style yogurts? To find out, panels of 21 America's Test Kitchen staffers sampled five styles of yogurt (a total of eight products): three Icelandic, two Bulgarian, one Australian, and our favorite Greek and traditional American-style yogurts for comparison. We tasted them in three blind tastings: plain; with homemade granola; and in tzatziki, a Mediterranean sauce flavored with cucumber, garlic, and dill. Nutritional information was obtained from the labels and is based on a 227-gram (about 1 cup) serving. An independent lab measured pH levels. The yogurt styles were too distinct to rank in a traditional best-to-worst format. Instead, we organized the winners of each category below by style (from thickest to thinnest).

RECOMMENDED · GREEK YOGURT

FAGE Total Classic Greek Yogurt
WINNER - GREEK

PRICE: $6.99 for 35.3 oz ($0.20 per oz)
PH: 4.24 FAT: 11 g SUGAR: 7 g PROTEIN: 20 g
STYLE: Greek
MADE IN: New York
INGREDIENTS: Grade A pasteurized milk and cream, live active yogurt cultures (*L. bulgaricus, S. thermophilus, L. acidophilus, Bifidus, L. casei*)
COMMENTS: Our favorite whole-milk Greek yogurt combines all the qualities we love about the style: It's "plush," "pillowy," and "buttery" in texture, and its "delicate" flavor is "acidic but not overly so." It was the "perfect backdrop" to the other ingredients in tzatziki and a good "neutral" base for granola.

RECOMMENDED · ICELANDIC YOGURT (SKYR)

GREEN MOUNTAIN CREAMERY Icelandic Style Yogurt
WINNER - ICELANDIC

PRICE: $4.99 for 24 oz ($0.21 per oz)
PH: 4.11 FAT: 8g SUGAR: 3 g PROTEIN: 24 g
STYLE: Skyr
MADE IN: Arizona
INGREDIENTS: Pasteurized whole milk. Contains the following live cultures: *S. thermophilus, L. delbrueckii subsp. bulgaricus, B. lactis, L. acidophilus, L. casei*
COMMENTS: Tasters loved that this skyr was "rich in flavor and body" and marveled that it didn't feel heavy despite being so thick. It had a "subtle yet distinct tanginess" and "plenty of flavor" without overwhelming the granola or the tzatziki.

RECOMMENDED · AUSTRALIAN YOGURT

WALLABY Organic Aussie Smooth Plain Whole Milk Yogurt
WINNER - AUSTRALIAN

PRICE: $5.99 for 32 oz ($0.19 per oz)
PH: 4.44 FAT: 8 g SUGAR: 10 g PROTEIN: 11 g
STYLE: Aussie
MADE IN: California
INGREDIENTS: Cultured pasteurized whole organic milk. Live and active cultures: *L. acidophilus, L. bulgaricus, S. thermophilus, Bifidus*
COMMENTS: This yogurt was significantly thinner than the Greek and Icelandic products but was thicker than the Bulgarian yogurt. This "very smooth and creamy" yogurt had more sugar than the Icelandic and Bulgarian styles. Some liked its "slight sweetness," while others wanted a bit more acidity.

RECOMMENDED · TRADITIONAL AMERICAN-STYLE YOGURT

BROWN COW Cream Top Plain Yogurt
WINNER - AMERICAN

PRICE: $3.99 for 32 oz ($0.12 per oz)
PH: 4.43 FAT: 9 g SUGAR: 13 g PROTEIN: 8 g
STYLE: Traditional whole-milk
MADE IN: New Hampshire
INGREDIENTS: Cultured pasteurized whole milk, pectin, 5 live active cultures: *S. thermophilus, L. bulgaricus, L. acidophilus, Bifidus*, and *L. paracasei*
COMMENTS: Our favorite traditional American-style whole-milk yogurt is a bit unlike others in this style: It's made without homogenizing the milk (an optional processing step that keeps the fat and milk from separating), so the cream forms a layer and rises to the top during fermentation. The flavor seemed "mild" or "neutral" at first and had "a mild dairy tang on the finish." It was on the sweet side, though, with the most sugar per serving of the products in our lineup. Many tasters described its fairly thin, loose consistency as "very familiar."

RECOMMENDED · BULGARIAN YOGURT

WHITE MOUNTAIN FOODS Whole Milk Bulgarian Yogurt
WINNER - BULGARIAN

PRICE: $8.99 for 32 oz ($0.28 per oz)
PH: 3.61 FAT: 8 g SUGAR: 5 g PROTEIN: 12 g
STYLE: Bulgarian
MADE IN: Texas
INGREDIENTS: Organic Grade A pasteurized whole milk and live cultures (*L. acidophilus, L. bulgaricus, S. thermophilus, B. bifidum*)
COMMENTS: If you're accustomed to ultrathick yogurt or sweet yogurt, this Bulgarian-style product may seem like "a different animal." It's unstrained and had a "looser, creamier texture." Some tasters thought it was "too thin," but others thought it "coated the granola nicely." Because we strained it before making tzatziki, the sauce had a "nice creamy texture." It was very tangy, and tzatziki made with it was "superflavorful."

FONTINA CHEESE

True fontina, which is in a class by itself, has been made in the northwest corner of Italy since at least the 13th century. This cheese, Fontina Val d'Aosta, has Denominazione di Origine Protetta (DOP) status, meaning that it must be made according to exact specifications. At your local supermarket, you're more likely to find cheeses labeled fontina, fontal, or fontinella. We rounded up seven cheeses labeled fontina, fontal, or fontinella, as well as an authentic Fontina Val d'Aosta, and tasted the cheeses plain and in baked breakfast strata. Nutrition information was obtained from product labels and manufacturers and was standardized for comparison using a serving size of 1 ounce (28 grams). An independent lab analyzed moisture levels. Information on the cheese origin, style, and cheese-making process was obtained from manufacturers. Prices were paid in Boston-area supermarkets and online. Scores were averaged, and the top six products are listed below in order of preference.

RECOMMENDED

MITICA Fontina Val d'Aosta

THE REAL DEAL: FONTINA VAL D'AOSTA

PRICE: $19.99 for 1 lb ($1.25 per oz)
AGED: 3 months
STYLE: Fontina Val d'Aosta
ORIGIN: Valle d'Aosta, Italy
SODIUM: 186 mg **MOISTURE:** 34.18%
INGREDIENTS: Raw cow's milk, rennet, salt, enzymes
COMMENTS: The nutty-sweet, funky, and earthy flavors of authentic Fontina Val d'Aosta appealed to tasters who love other complex cheeses such as Gruyère and Comté. In both applications, it was by far "the most flavorful." Many tasters liked that it "added dimension" to the strata. At room temperature, it was firm and dense but not crumbly. In strata, it melted beautifully.

BOAR'S HEAD Fontina Cheese

SUPERMARKET WINNER

PRICE: $8.49 for 9 oz ($0.94 per oz)
AGED: Proprietary
STYLE: Swedish
ORIGIN: United States
SODIUM: 170 mg **MOISTURE:** 40.38%
INGREDIENTS: Pasteurized milk, salt, cheese cultures, enzymes
COMMENTS: Our favorite fontina is Swedish-style, which is known for having a soft, creamy texture and a buttery, tangy flavor similar to that of gouda. Tasters found this cheese to be "really creamy and flavorful." Tasted plain, it was pleasantly soft. In strata, it melted completely and "blended in nicely with the other ingredients."

ZERTO Fontal

PRICE: $12.99 for 1 lb ($0.81 per oz)
AGED: About 5 weeks
STYLE: Fontal
ORIGIN: Belgium
SODIUM: 224 mg **MOISTURE:** 43.10%
INGREDIENTS: Pasteurized cow's milk, salt, rennet, starter cultures, lysozyme (from eggs)
COMMENTS: This soft, creamy fontal was similar to a Swedish-style fontina in texture and flavor. Our tasters thought that "it was a nice combination of creamy and tangy." In our plain tasting, it was one of the softest cheeses. That worked to its advantage in strata, where it melted completely and gave the strata "a luxurious texture."

RECOMMENDED *(continued)*

CARR VALLEY Fontina Cheese

PRICE: $9.99 for 1 lb ($0.62 per oz)
AGED: At least 3 weeks
STYLE: Swedish
ORIGIN: United States
SODIUM: 220 mg **MOISTURE:** 39.79%
INGREDIENTS: Pasteurized cow's milk, cheese cultures, salt, microbial rennet
COMMENTS: This Swedish-style fontina was very mild, with "a hint of nuttiness" and just a touch of tang. In both tastings, it reminded tasters a little of mozzarella—a pleasant spin on a very familiar flavor and texture. Tasters loved how "smooth and melty" it became in baked strata.

SARTORI Classic Fontina

PRICE: $4.19 for 5 oz ($0.84 per oz)
AGED: At least 2 months
STYLE: Italian
ORIGIN: United States
SODIUM: 170 mg **MOISTURE:** 34.77%
INGREDIENTS: Pasteurized milk, cheese cultures, salt, enzymes
COMMENTS: The "sharp," "distinctly sweet and nutty" flavor of this Italian-style fontina reminded many tasters of domestic Parmesan cheese. In both tastings, it also had a pronounced "tanginess." The sweetness and nuttiness of the cheese "enhanced the sweet flavor of the onion and egg in the strata." We liked the firm, relatively dry, almost crumbly texture when we sampled this cheese plain. But it didn't melt as smoothly or completely as our favorite fontina.

STELLA Fontinella

PRICE: $3.49 for 8 oz ($0.44 per oz)
AGED: 2 months
STYLE: Italian
ORIGIN: United States
SODIUM: 250 mg **MOISTURE:** 34.61%
INGREDIENTS: Fontinella cheese (pasteurized milk, cheese cultures, salt, enzymes)
COMMENTS: Because it was both "sweet" and "nutty" and had a firm texture, this cheese drew comparisons to Parmesan. Tasters found it especially "sharp" and "biting." Because it was harder and drier than many fontinas in our lineup, it didn't melt as well. Tasters liked the way the strata tasted but noted that "it could be more melty."

SUSHI RICE

Often sold in the United States as Calrose rice, this rice variety features short, squat grains and has a distinct stickiness when cooked. But sushi rice isn't used only in sushi—it's also a staple in many Asian and Asian American homes and is featured in dishes such as bibimbap, onigiri, and gimbap. We looked specifically for rice labeled sushi, Calrose, or Japanese-style and found eight nationally available products. Twenty-one America's Test Kitchen staffers sampled the rice two ways: rinsed and cooked in a rice cooker using standardized rice-to-water ratios and cooked on the stovetop according to package instructions. Ultimately, only the results from the rice cooker tasting were factored into our final rankings, since that test provided the most standardized comparison for tasters. All the rice we tasted was grown in California. We purchased all the products in Boston-area supermarkets, and the prices listed are what we paid. We used calipers to measure the length of 20 rice granules from multiple packages of each brand and averaged the results to get the length-to-width ratio of the grains. The products appear below in order of preference.

HIGHLY RECOMMENDED

LUNDBERG FAMILY FARMS
Organic California Sushi Rice
PRICE: $4.49 for 32 oz ($0.14 per oz)
LENGTH-TO-WIDTH RATIO: 1.6 to 1
COMMENTS: This rice was praised for its "small," "sticky" grains, which were the shortest of all the products we tried. Tasters thought that the "distinct," "bead-like" granules and "floral aroma" truly set this product apart. However, its rating bombed when we tried it prepared according to its package instructions: It was "wet," "watery," and "bland" from the double whammy of a 30-minute soak and a high proportion of water to rice. While we loved this "pleasant," "aromatic" rice when cooked in the rice cooker or according to our recipe, we don't recommend following the instructions on the package.

RECOMMENDED

SUSHI CHEF Premium Sushi Rice
PRICE: $4.19 for 20 oz ($0.21 per oz)
LENGTH-TO-WIDTH RATIO: 2.1 to 1
COMMENTS: While this product had longer granules than our winning rice, tasters still thought that it had "good cohesion without any gumminess." The grains were "distinct" and "slick," with a perfect amount of "chew." It also had "floral" notes and a slightly "earthy" "coconut" flavor that tasters found "subtle" and "pleasing."

BOTAN Calrose Rice
PRICE: $8.09 for 80 oz ($0.10 per oz)
LENGTH-TO-WIDTH RATIO: 2.2 to 1
COMMENTS: This rice had "longer," "thinner" grains than we expect in sushi rice, but tasters thought it cooked up "perfectly sticky" with a "good amount of chew." We didn't detect any interesting aromas in this rice; overall it was a bit "bland," but it would still make a good base for stir-fries.

GOLDEN STAR Calrose Rice
PRICE: $4.67 for 80 oz ($0.06 per oz)
LENGTH-TO-WIDTH RATIO: 2.2 to 1
COMMENTS: This rice had a "neutral," "clean" flavor with subtle "toasty," "buttery" afternotes. A few tasters thought that it "lacked the stickiness" we prize in this type of rice and instead had "firm," "distinct" grains. Though the texture was a bit "too al dente," most agreed it had a "balanced," "almost sweet" flavor.

RECOMMENDED (continued)

KYONG GI Medium Grain Rice
PRICE: $6.99 for 70.4 oz ($0.10 per oz)
LENGTH-TO-WIDTH RATIO: 2.2 to 1
COMMENTS: This Korean American rice had an "earthy" flavor and a slightly "fruity aftertaste." Most agreed that its "pleasant floral notes" added a unique aroma to the rice. The grains were "sticky" and "moist" and seemed "slightly longer" than other products.

NISHIKI Premium Medium Grain Rice
PRICE: $4.99 for 32 oz ($0.16 per oz)
LENGTH-TO-WIDTH RATIO: 2.1 to 1
COMMENTS: With some of the longest grains of the products we tried, this rice tricked a few tasters into thinking we had mixed long-grain rice into the lineup. While some tasters wanted shorter grains, many still liked this product's "moderate firmness" and "chew." A few tasters also noted that the rice was "bland" compared with other, more fragrant, products.

RICESELECT Sushi Rice
PRICE: $7.99 for 32 oz ($0.25 per oz)
LENGTH-TO-WIDTH RATIO: 1.7 to 1
COMMENTS: Though this product had some of the shortest grains in the lineup and tasters liked its "extra-short and round" granules, many thought that it had a slightly "chewy" texture. However, we liked its "roasty," "toasted" notes and "buttery" aftertaste, which reminded some tasters of "rice crackers." Overall, it was a "flavorful" rice but "a bit dry."

KOKUHO ROSE Japanese Style Rice
PRICE: $3.59 for 32 oz ($0.11 per oz)
LENGTH-TO-WIDTH RATIO: 2.1 to 1
COMMENTS: With a slightly "buttery" aftertaste that tasters enjoyed, this rice got full marks for flavor, but it fell a bit short on texture. Many noted that this product was somewhat "dry," with an al dente bite that was reminiscent of Arborio rice.

EXTRA-VIRGIN OLIVE OIL

A great extra-virgin olive oil tastes fresh, fruity, and lively, whether its flavor is mild and buttery or grassy and peppery. Recently, the manufacturer of our favorite supermarket extra-virgin olive oil changed the way it sources and produces its oil, so we went back to the drawing board, purchasing 11 nationally available top-selling extra-virgin olive oils, including four products labeled "robust," a recent addition to the category. Twenty-one America's Test Kitchen staff members tasted the products blind, in random order, first plain and then in two applications: in a simple vinaigrette on lettuce and drizzled over warm white beans. We also sent a set of the oils in unmarked, randomly numbered bottles to a group of expert olive oil tasters in California to get their opinions but did not include these opinions in our rankings. We purchased the oils in Boston-area supermarkets and online, and the prices listed are what we paid. Scores from the three in-house tastings were averaged, and the top seven products are listed below in order of preference.

RECOMMENDED

BERTOLLI Extra Virgin Olive Oil, Original, Rich Taste
CO-WINNER

PRICE: $6.99 for 16.9 oz ($0.41 per oz)
SOURCES: Italy, Portugal, Spain, and Tunisia (Depending on the time of year, this oil may also come from Greece, Australia, Chile, or Argentina.)
BOTTLED IN: Spain (plastic bottles), Italy (glass bottles)
HARVEST DATE ON BOTTLE: Yes
COMMENTS: Tied for first place, this oil was described as "very green, very grassy" and tasters said it brought a "nice balance and presence in the dressing," offering a "contrast of fruity, bitter oil with tangy vinegar." "This is one worth buying," one taster wrote. "The oil truly enhances beans and makes a simple dish feel special. It's flavorful immediately and finishes strong."

CALIFORNIA OLIVE RANCH Destination Series Everyday Extra Virgin Olive Oil
CO-WINNER

PRICE: $9.99 for 16.9 oz ($0.59 per oz)
SOURCES: California, Portugal, Chile, Argentina
BOTTLED IN: California
HARVEST DATE ON BOTTLE: Yes
COMMENTS: The reformulated international version of our previous supermarket favorite earned praise in vinaigrette for being "rich and fruity, so delicious," and "very olive-forward," with "good balance." "Tastes fresher and brighter" than other samples, one taster noted. Drizzled over beans, it was "superyummy. Now I get what this dish is supposed to be like: rich and complex and beyond either ingredient on its own."

FILIPPO BERIO Robusto Extra Virgin Olive Oil

PRICE: $6.99 for 16.9 oz ($0.41 per oz)
SOURCES: Greece, Italy, Portugal, Spain
BOTTLED IN: Italy
HARVEST DATE ON BOTTLE: No
COMMENTS: Drizzled on warm beans, this robust-style oil was "not overpowering but [had] distinctive flavor," and tasters called it "rich and buttery" and "bright and fresh." In the vinaigrette, tasters again called it "bright," with a pleasantly "bitter," "peppery" aftertaste. When tasted plain, it had "peppery, green punch."

RECOMMENDED (continued)

FILIPPO BERIO Extra Virgin Olive Oil

PRICE: $6.99 for 16.9 oz ($0.41 per oz)
SOURCES: Greece, Italy, Portugal, Spain, Tunisia
BOTTLED IN: Italy
HARVEST DATE ON BOTTLE: No
COMMENTS: While many tasters appreciated this oil's "smooth," "light," "soft and buttery" profile, some found its flavor a bit too "mild" and "muted," whether it was served over beans, in vinaigrette, or plain. Some complained of an aftertaste that was slightly too bitter.

CALIFORNIA OLIVE RANCH Destination Series Rich & Robust Extra Virgin Olive Oil

PRICE: $7.99 for 16.9 oz ($0.47 per oz)
SOURCES: California, Argentina, Chile, Portugal
BOTTLED IN: California
HARVEST DATE ON BOTTLE: Yes
COMMENTS: When tasted plain, this robust version of our co-winning oil was "grassy and then a bit too harsh" and very "bitter." Its scores improved when it was served over warm beans, where tasters said it had a "stronger flavor with a good taste, a bit peppery." In the vinaigrette, the oil was "pleasant but not outstanding."

COLAVITA Premium Selection Extra Virgin Olive Oil

PRICE: $11.49 for 17 oz ($0.68 per oz)
SOURCES: Italy, Greece, Spain, Portugal
BOTTLED IN: Italy
HARVEST DATE ON BOTTLE: No
COMMENTS: "Mild, buttery, neutral, not superdistinctive, but perfectly fine," this "gently peppery" oil was described as "middle of the road," "smooth," and "subtle," whether it was on beans or dressing a salad.

LUCINI ITALIA Premium Select Extra Virgin Olive Oil

PRICE: $22.79 for 16.9 oz ($1.35 per oz)
SOURCE: Italy
BOTTLED IN: Italy
HARVEST DATE ON BOTTLE: Yes
COMMENTS: Tasters found this pricier supermarket oil "quite bitter on the nose, very grassy, green, [and] more robust" than others in the lineup. With beans, the "green fruity oil complemented the beans nicely," and in salad dressing it was "balanced" and "pleasantly bitter." But those who prefer mild oils called it "a throat-burner."

KOSHER SALT

While we call for both table and kosher salt in our recipes, we generally prefer the larger, coarser grains of kosher salt for rubbing onto meat or sprinkling over foods. A handful of smaller companies and artisans manufacture kosher salt, but two major brands, Diamond Crystal and Morton, dominate the American market. Morton grains are considerably heavier, denser, and more uniform in shape and size than the hollow, pyramidal Diamond Crystal grains. One teaspoon of Morton kosher salt weighs 4.8 grams, while one teaspoon of Diamond Crystal kosher salt weighs just 2.8 grams, meaning that a given volume of Morton kosher salt will contain more salt than an equal volume of Diamond Crystal kosher salt. Diamond Crystal has long been the test kitchen's go-to kosher salt. We love it for the same reason that it's the preferred kosher salt of many food professionals: Diamond Crystal's soft, hollow crystals are easy to crush and sprinkle by hand. But since we also routinely call for measuring salt by volume when making a brine or a salt rub, we wondered if Diamond Crystal kosher salt really is the better choice. To find out, we conducted two blind tastings of the two kosher salts: plain and sprinkled on buttered bread. In both instances, tasters preferred the "delicate and fleeting crunch" of Diamond Crystal. In our second test, we set out to see if we could detect the same level of saltiness in two batches of chicken broth: one seasoned with 1 teaspoon of Morton and one seasoned with 1½ teaspoons of Diamond Crystal (identical amounts of the two salts by weight). Both salts dissolved well in the warm liquid, so there were no textural differences between the two broths, which tasted exactly the same. The products appear below in order of preference.

HIGHLY RECOMMENDED

DIAMOND CRYSTAL Kosher Salt
PRICE: $3.49 for 48 oz ($1.16 per lb)
SODIUM: 280 mg
SOURCE: Michigan
INGREDIENT: Salt
COMMENTS: Our favorite kosher salt for more than 25 years, these flakes have a "soft," "delicate" texture that's easy to crush between your fingers, so you can control the size of the salt crystals and distribute them evenly over food. Diamond Crystal kosher salt also dissolves rapidly. Because the flakes are hollow and irregularly shaped, 1 teaspoon of this salt contains fewer grains than 1 teaspoon of other brands and styles of salt. It contains no anticaking agents, but if any clumps form, just a gentle shake or stir is enough to break them up.

HIGHLY RECOMMENDED *(continued)*

MORTON Kosher Salt
PRICE: $3.59 for 48 oz ($1.20 per lb)
SODIUM: 480 mg
SOURCE: Canada
INGREDIENTS: Salt, yellow prussiate of soda (an anticaking agent)
COMMENTS: The bigger, harder, crunchier flakes of this major supermarket brand don't distribute as evenly or as consistently as flakes of Diamond Crystal. That said, we've still had good results with this salt in both sweet and savory applications. The trick is to make the proper measurement adjustments: When following a recipe developed with Diamond Crystal kosher salt, decrease the volume by 25 percent; when following a recipe that uses table salt, increase the volume by 50 percent.

TUNA PACKED IN OIL

In our desire to decode the teeming tuna aisle, we figured that there were just too many variables—the species of tuna, the packaging (can or jar), and the packing medium (oil or water), among others—to eliminate styles without tasting them all. So we narrowed our search to 16 products packed in oil, including both canned and jarred tunas and both albacore and yellowfin species, which are often labeled "white" and "light" tuna, respectively. Some were sold as "solid," others as "chunks," and yet others as "fillets." The oil they were packed in ranged from soybean oil to regular olive oil to extra-virgin olive oil. Some products specified that they were seasoned with sea salt, and a few included additives such as vegetable broth and pyrophosphates. (We eliminated pouched styles from this lineup after a pretasting showed that the soft pouch tends to smash and break up the big flakes and chunks we prefer for maximum versatility.) We removed them from their containers as carefully as we could to preserve their texture and served them plain in two blind tastings. The top seven products appear below in order of preference.

HIGHLY RECOMMENDED

TONNINO Tuna Fillets in Olive Oil
CO-WINNER

PRICE: $5.98 for 6.7 oz jar ($0.89 per oz)
INGREDIENTS: Tuna fish, olive oil (non hydrogenated), water, and sea salt
TUNA SPECIES: Yellowfin
COMMENTS: With "rich flavor," this "well-seasoned," "firm but tender," "meaty" yellowfin tuna won praise for its "clean," "bright" taste. Tasters appreciated that it was "moist," "slightly silky," and had "lovely large flakes." One taster said this tuna "feels like a major step above many others in this mix" and another said "I'd gladly eat this plain any day."

ORTIZ BONITO DEL NORTE Albacore White Tuna in Olive Oil
CO-WINNER

PRICE: $5.49 for 3.95 oz ($1.39 per oz)
INGREDIENTS: White tuna, olive oil, and salt
TUNA SPECIES: Albacore
COMMENTS: "Beautiful to look at" with "delicate layers," this "firm," "really well-seasoned" tuna—which a few tasters said was "almost too salty"—had a "wonderfully meaty and salty taste. A little bit of oil on the finish makes it sing." One taster remarked, "this is heads and tails (and fins?) above some others in this tasting."

RECOMMENDED

STARKIST Selects Solid Yellowfin Tuna in Extra Virgin Olive Oil

PRICE: $1.99 for 4.5 oz ($0.44 per oz)
INGREDIENTS: Fish (tuna), extra-virgin olive oil, sea salt
TUNA SPECIES: Yellowfin
COMMENTS: "This is one of the best samples I tasted. Not too salty or fishy," one taster raved. The "luxurious," "moist," "silky texture" and "fine flavor" made this tuna "rich and savory, tender, bright, lush. Yum." One taster remarked, "You can taste the buttery olive oil; the tuna is tender and flavorful."

RECOMMENDED (continued)

TONNINO Yellowfin Tuna Solid Pack in Olive Oil

PRICE: $3.69 for 4.94 oz ($0.75 per oz)
INGREDIENTS: Tuna fish, olive oil (non hydrogenated), water, and sea salt
TUNA SPECIES: Yellowfin
COMMENTS: Tasters described this yellowfin tuna as "oil-rich, salty, pleasingly tuna-forward," and "rich" in flavor, with a "rosy appearance" and a "firm" texture. But several also mentioned that it was "quite dry" and "tough," despite a "good overall taste."

WILD PLANET Albacore Solid Wild Tuna in Extra Virgin Olive Oil

PRICE: $4.49 for 5 oz ($0.90 per oz)
INGREDIENTS: Albacore tuna (Thunnus alalunga), organic extra-virgin olive oil, water, sea salt
TUNA SPECIES: Albacore
COMMENTS: "Well seasoned, bright, dense—but dry," one taster noted. With a "firm bite" to its texture, this white tuna was "easy to flake" and "meaty and rich," with "clean flavor" that "tasted like fish, but wasn't fishy." Still, many felt it could use a bit more moisture.

GENOVA Yellowfin Tuna in Extra Virgin Olive Oil with Sea Salt

PRICE: $2.99 for 5 oz ($0.60 per oz)
INGREDIENTS: Solid yellowfin tuna, extra-virgin olive oil, sea salt
TUNA SPECIES: Yellowfin
COMMENTS: A "lovely blend of tuna flavor and olive oil" with "salty, steaky," "meaty" texture, this tuna was "more moist than others" and had "fresh, strong flavor" that some tasters described as "juicy," "tangy," and "vibrant." Another taster noted that it "tastes strongly of olive oil" and was "briny, too."

STARKIST Solid White Albacore Tuna in Vegetable Oil

PRICE: $2.29 for 5 oz ($0.46 per oz)
INGREDIENTS: White tuna, soybean oil, water, vegetable broth, salt, pyrophosphate
TUNA SPECIES: Albacore
COMMENTS: "Very white and flaky" and "very soft," this "subtle" tuna was "moist, tender, and mild," though a few found it "moist to a fault" or "mushy." While some approved of the "not overpowering" flavor, calling it "classic" and "very pleasant," others found this tuna "neither here nor there."

SOUR CREAM

Sour cream isn't just a topping for potatoes; it's equally at home when dolloped on nachos, chili, latkes, and all sorts of soups. It's an essential base for dips, creating a texture that's creamy and the perfect consistency for scooping and adding a great tangy flavor. We also use it in some baking recipes to enhance moisture and richness. But which sour cream is best? To find out, we purchased four nationally available products and asked panels of 21 America's Test Kitchen staffers to sample them in three blind tastings: plain, in Sour Cream Drop Biscuits, and in Caramelized Onion Dip. Although we could ultimately recommend all the sour creams we tried, tasters generally preferred the products they perceived as milder; they liked milky sweetness with just a hint of tang. Tart sour creams received lower marks, especially when tasted plain. Ingredients were obtained from product packaging. The prices shown were paid in Boston-area supermarkets. Results from the tastings were averaged, and the products are listed below in order of preference.

RECOMMENDED

DAISY Sour Cream
PRICE: $2.79 for 16 oz ($0.17 per oz)
INGREDIENTS: Cultured cream
COMMENTS: The national best seller took the top spot overall, thanks to its "creamy texture" and "clean dairy flavor." Tasters said that dip made with it was "light and fluffy," and they appreciated the sour cream's mild tanginess, which allowed for "other flavors in the dip to come through." It also made for very "buttery" biscuits. While some tasters did say that it "could use more sour cream tang," most loved its "mild flavor."

HORIZON Organic Cultured Sour Cream
PRICE: $3.79 for 16 oz ($0.24 per oz)
INGREDIENTS: Cultured pasteurized organic cream, microbial enzymes
COMMENTS: This sour cream was a bit thinner than our top-ranked product, but tasters still described it as "tangy and smooth" when sampling it plain. Tasters praised its "nice acidity and balanced richness" in dip, and many thought it had a "nice kick of flavor" without being overpowering. Some said it made "the best-flavored biscuits," which were "assertively tangy."

RECOMMENDED (continued)

ORGANIC VALLEY Sour Cream
PRICE: $4.19 for 16 oz ($0.26 per oz)
INGREDIENTS: Organic cultured pasteurized nonfat milk, organic pasteurized cream, *acidophilus* and *bifudus* cultures, vegetarian enzyme
COMMENTS: Tasters were split on this sour cream's texture, which some described as "watery" and "loose." Many liked the "tart and tangy" dip made with this sour cream, but a few said it had a "barnyard funk taste" that was "almost cheesy." Biscuits made with it also had a cheese-like aftertaste.

BREAKSTONE'S All Natural Sour Cream
PRICE: $2.99 for 16 oz ($0.19 per oz)
INGREDIENTS: Cultured pasteurized Grade A milk and cream, enzymes
COMMENTS: When eaten plain, this product was a bit "too sour" and had a slightly "grainy texture." However, it fared better in dip, where its "tang balanced the sweet onions." Tasters also thought biscuits made with this product had a "nice buttery tang."

LARD

Lard had a tough time in the 20th century, but all along, a faithful few kept lard as a secret weapon for making extra-flaky, tender pie crusts and biscuits, Southern fried chicken, and Mexican foods such as tamales and carnitas. Lard is the traditional cooking fat of Thailand and parts of China, Italy, Poland, Hungary, and Mexico as well as Central and South America—not to mention the American South. We decided it was time to check out the lard market. We bought seven nationally available products and tasted them blind in biscuits, pie crust, and our recipe for Pork Carnitas. Twenty-one America's Test Kitchen staffers rated the results on flavor, texture, and overall appeal. Ingredients were obtained from product packaging and melting points and iodine values were provided by two independent laboratories. We purchased the products at Boston-area supermarkets and online and the prices shown are what we paid. The top six products are listed below in order of preference.

RECOMMENDED

U.S. DREAMS Lard
ARTISAN WINNER
PRICE: $11.99 for 1 lb ($0.75 per oz)
SOURCE: Online
INGREDIENTS: 100% pork lard
HYDROGENATED: No
IODINE VALUE: 55.5
MELTING POINT: 110° F
COMMENTS: Biscuits made with this nonhydrogenated, preservative-free lard made in Ohio came out "beautifully crisp and tender," with "clean, rich flavor." They were "lighter than others, crisp and perfect," with a "delicate crumb" that tasted "very neutral, almost buttery." Pie crust had "clean, buttery flavor" "devoid of any fatty funk," and a "very tender, flaky, and crisp" texture. In carnitas, this lard "made a substantial difference: moist, flavorful, and lovely."

TENDERFLAKE Lard
PRICE: $3.09 for 1 lb ($0.19 per oz)
SOURCE: Online
INGREDIENTS: Lard, BHA, BHT, citric acid
HYDROGENATED: No
IODINE VALUE: 60.7
MELTING POINT: 102.1° F
COMMENTS: This lard from Canada nearly tied for first place. Biscuits came out "notably rich, crisp, and tender—a beautiful specimen." Carnitas were "very tender," with a "perfect bite"; "rich and decadent." Tasters deemed this lard's pie crust "delicious; like butter" or "a Ritz Cracker" with "salty," "sweet," "nutty" notes and a "great flaky structure." One taster simply wrote: "Perfection."

JOHN MORRELL Snow Cap Lard
SUPERMARKET WINNER
BEST BUY
PRICE: $1.69 for 1 lb ($0.11 per oz)
SOURCE: Supermarket
INGREDIENTS: Partially Hydrogenated Lard, BHT and BHA added to help protect flavor
HYDROGENATED: Partially
IODINE VALUE: 62.5
MELTING POINT: 105° F
COMMENTS: With a "soft," "flaky," "moist" texture that "melts in your mouth," biscuits made with this widely available supermarket lard were a hit with tasters. Partial hydrogenation helped ensure the firmness of this fat, so pie crust came out "flaky" and "very, very tender." Its flavor was "neutral" and "mellow," leaving food "very tasty." Carnitas were full of "deep, rich pork flavor."

RECOMMENDED (continued)

ARMOUR Lard
PRICE: $3.99 for 1 lb ($0.25 per oz)
SOURCE: Supermarket
INGREDIENTS: Lard, BHA, propyl gallate and citric acid added to protect flavor
HYDROGENATED: Yes
IODINE VALUE: 58.5
MELTING POINT: 115° F
COMMENTS: Tasters enjoyed biscuits from this widely available supermarket lard, calling them "salty, clean, [and] savory," with a "crisp" exterior. Pie crust had "neutral" flavor, with "not much character" but "good flakiness" and was "definitely acceptable." Carnitas struck us as "rich, creamy, smooth, and meaty." One taster mused: "I've gotta say, carnitas made with lard are so good! Why did we ever make them with oil?"

GOYA Lard
PRICE: $2.28 for 1 lb ($0.14 per oz)
SOURCE: Supermarket
INGREDIENTS: Refined lard and hydrogenated lard, BHA, propyl gallate, and citric acid added to help protect flavor
HYDROGENATED: Partially
IODINE VALUE: 59.9
MELTING POINT: 116° F
COMMENTS: This supermarket lard gave biscuits "savory," "lightly porky taste." Pie crust was also "a bit on the pork-flavored side," though it was flaky. Carnitas made with this lard stood out: "Incredible almost-fried crispy exterior and meltingly tender, juicy, moist interior." "I want this, no tortillas, just straight up. Mmm, pork."

FATWORKS Pasture Raised Pork Lard
PRICE: $22.49 for 14 oz ($1.61 per oz)
SOURCE: Online
INGREDIENTS: Pasture raised pork fat, organic rosemary extract
HYDROGENATED: No
IODINE VALUE: 71.0
MELTING POINT: 98.3° F
COMMENTS: Tasters called this pricey artisan lard sold in glass jars "quite porky," "savory and lardy" in biscuits and pie crust, where it had a texture "like shortbread," with "more crumb than flake." It had the lowest melting point of the lards in our lineup; its label also says "premium cooking oil," and the fat appears semiliquid in the jar. In carnitas, it was "savory and incredibly satisfying," "with gamy, porky richness."

MILK CHOCOLATE

For years, artisanal dark chocolate bars have hogged all the glory. But who's to say milk chocolate bars can't be artisanal, too? With so many new products pushing the boundaries of milk chocolate, it was time to take another look. We went in search of milk chocolate bars that could be savored both by the piece and chopped up or melted as a cooking ingredient. We gathered 10 nationally available products and sampled them plain, with any distinguishing stamps, marks, or logos scraped off before tasting. To see if a higher or lower cacao percentage made a difference in cooking applications, we also sampled all the products in Milk Chocolate Pots de Crème and tried the highest- and lowest-cacao percentage products in Perfect Chocolate Chip Cookies and Chocolate-Chunk Oatmeal Cookies with Dried Cherries. However, the results of the pots de crème and cookie tastings were not factored into the final results because we primarily eat milk chocolate plain. Cacao percentages were obtained from packaging or provided by manufacturers. Ingredients and sugar amounts were taken from packaging, and sugar amounts were recalculated to a standard 40-gram serving. The top six products are listed below in order of preference.

RECOMMENDED

**ENDANGERED SPECIES CHOCOLATE
Smooth + Creamy Milk Chocolate**
PRICE: $3.49 for 3 oz bar ($1.16 per oz)
SUGAR: 14 g
INGREDIENTS: Milk chocolate (chocolate liquor, milk, sugar, cocoa butter, lactose, soy lecithin, vanilla)
CACAO PERCENTAGE: 48%
FIRST INGREDIENT: Chocolate liquor
COMMENTS: This nationally available chocolate from a once-small Oregon-based brand was "rich" and "intense," with "deep cocoa notes" and a "balanced" sweetness thanks to its high cacao percentage. Its texture was "smooth" and "snappy," and its "glossy texture" and "complex" flavor reminded some tasters of "artisan dark chocolate."

**SCHARFFEN BERGER Extra Rich
Milk Chocolate**
PRICE: $3.47 for 3 oz bar ($1.16 per oz)
SUGAR: 17 g
INGREDIENTS: Chocolate, sugar, milk, cocoa butter, nonfat milk, non-GMO soy lecithin, whole vanilla beans
CACAO PERCENTAGE: 41%
FIRST INGREDIENT: Chocolate
COMMENTS: Another chocolate with a relatively high cacao percentage, this product was "deeply cocoa" flavored, "on the border of milk and dark chocolate." It contains whole vanilla beans, and tasters picked up on "delicate" notes of "vanilla" and "coconut," which made this "a very well-rounded chocolate." Its texture was "silky" and "smooth," and it made perfectly thick pots de crème.

GODIVA Large 31% Milk Chocolate Bar
PRICE: $3.99 for 3.5 oz bar ($1.14 per oz)
SUGAR: 22 g
INGREDIENTS: Sugar, milk, cocoa butter, cocoa mass, natural flavoring, emulsifier (E322)
CACAO PERCENTAGE: 31%
FIRST INGREDIENT: Sugar
COMMENTS: Though this product had a lower cacao percentage than other highly ranked chocolates, many tasters thought its flavor was "rich" and "caramelly," not just uniformly sweet. Its texture was "smooth" and "slick." Overall, a "solid all-around milk chocolate."

RECOMMENDED *(continued)*

**HERSHEY'S Symphony Extra Large
Creamy Milk Chocolate Bar**
PRICE: $1.79 for 4.25 oz ($0.42 per oz)
SUGAR: 22 g
INGREDIENTS: Milk chocolate (sugar, milk, cocoa butter, chocolate, milk fat, soy lecithin, PGPR, emulsifier, vanillin, artificial flavor)
CACAO PERCENTAGE: Proprietary
FIRST INGREDIENT: Sugar
COMMENTS: Tasters thought this product was "sweet," "almost syrupy," with a "classic" milk chocolate creaminess and smooth texture. We picked up on "subtle vanilla notes," but otherwise its flavor was relatively "simple." The manufacturer wouldn't disclose the cacao percentage of its chocolate.

**LINDT Classic Recipe Milk Chocolate
Excellence Bar**
PRICE: $3.99 for 4 oz bar ($1.00 per oz)
SUGAR: 21 g
INGREDIENTS: Sugar, cocoa butter, milk, chocolate, skim milk, soy lecithin (emulsifier), barley malt powder, artificial flavor
CACAO PERCENTAGE: 31%
FIRST INGREDIENT: Sugar
COMMENTS: This chocolate was "soft" and "creamy," with a prominent "milkiness" and a slight "malted" taste from the addition of barley malt powder. Though tasters were split over the malted flavor, most agreed that this chocolate was "balanced," and "moderately sweet." It had a "classic" flavor.

CADBURY Dairy Milk Chocolate Bar
PRICE: $3.29 for 3.5 oz bar ($0.94 per oz)
SUGAR: 23 g
INGREDIENTS: Milk chocolate (sugar, milk, chocolate, cocoa butter, lactose, soy lecithin, PGPR, emulsifier, natural and artificial flavor)
CACAO PERCENTAGE: Proprietary
FIRST INGREDIENT: Sugar
COMMENTS: This product from a British brand is now being made and sold in the United States by the Hershey Company. It was "creamy," "sweet," and "ultramilky." The bars were thick enough to have "good snap," but still had a "tender," "melt-in-your-mouth" texture. Like other Hershey's products we tested, it has more sugar and milk than chocolate; many tasters found it "a bit one-note" or "a tad too sweet."

VERY DARK CHOCOLATE BARS

Darker chocolates—bars with 70-plus to 90-plus cacao percentages—are more popular than ever, thanks in large part to trendy low-carb, high fat diets such as the keto diet and consumers' desires to eat less sugar. Very dark chocolates—those with cacao percentages in the 90-plus range—not only contain less sugar per bar than lower-cacao-percentage darker chocolates, but they also offer a more nuanced and sometimes more complex chocolate flavor—making them an ideal choice for chocolate connoisseurs and health enthusiasts alike. We selected five nationally available bars ranging from 90 to 95 percent cacao and ate them plain, offering water and crackers as palate cleansers. While some tasters weren't initially thrilled about eating very dark chocolate, many were delighted to discover that some of these very dark bars, which contained only small amounts of sugar, were actually delicious. We also tasted a total of 22 bars in the 80- and 70-percent-cacao ranges. Chocolate bars were grouped into 90%, 80%, and 70% cacao categories, scores were averaged, and the top two products in each category are listed below in order of preference.

HIGHLY RECOMMENDED · 90% CACAO BARS

ALTER ECO 90% Deepest Dark Super Blackout Organic Chocolate Bar

WINNER · 90% CACAO BARS

PRICE: $2.99 for 2.65 oz ($1.13 per oz), plus shipping
FAT: 24.2 g **SUGAR:** 3.2 g **COCOA SOLIDS:** 11.8 g
BEAN ORIGIN: Ecuador and the Dominican Republic
INGREDIENTS: Organic cacao beans, organic cocoa butter, organic raw cane sugar, organic vanilla beans
COMMENTS: Our winning bar had a "good balance of bitter and sweet," with a "really nice, creamy texture" that was impressively "smooth." We also enjoyed the fruity undertones, with some tasters noting hints of berries, cherries, and peaches. As one taster put it, "What a beautiful chocolate!"

RECOMMENDED · 90% CACAO BARS

LINDT EXCELLENCE 90% Cocoa

PRICE: $3.29 for 3.5 oz ($0.94 per oz)
FAT: 22 g **SUGAR:** 3 g **COCOA SOLIDS:** 14 g
BEAN ORIGIN: Ghana, Ecuador, Madagascar, Papua New Guinea, and the Dominican Republic (company sources from all of these areas but would not confirm specific blend used for this bar)
INGREDIENTS: Chocolate, cocoa butter, cocoa powder processed with alkali, sugar, bourbon vanilla beans
COMMENTS: This chocolate was "surprisingly nice to eat" despite its mild sweetness, and we liked its "well-rounded chocolate flavor," which was "dark and cocoa-y" but "not bitter at all." It tasted "balanced," and we were fans of the smooth texture.

RECOMMENDED · 80% CACAO BARS

LINDT EXCELLENCE 85% Cocoa

WINNER · 80% CACAO BARS

PRICE: $3.49 for 3.5 oz ($1.00 per oz)
FAT: 18.7 g **SUGAR:** 5.3 g **COCOA SOLIDS:** 15.3 g
BEAN ORIGIN: Ghana, Ecuador, Madagascar, Papua New Guinea, and the Dominican Republic
INGREDIENTS: Chocolate, cocoa powder, cocoa butter, demerara sugar, bourbon vanilla beans
COMMENTS: Most tasters thought this bar had a great "silky" texture, with a "pleasant" flavor that was "quite mild in sweetness and bitterness." "It tastes like a dark and milk chocolate hybrid," said one taster, with others describing it as an overall "balanced" bar, flavor-wise, that was "easy to eat."

RECOMMENDED · 80% CACAO BARS (continued)

GREEN & BLACKS Organic 85% Cacao Dark Chocolate Bar

PRICE: $4.59 for 3.5 oz ($1.31 per oz)
FAT: 21 g **SUGAR:** 5 g **COCOA SOLIDS:** 13 g
BEAN ORIGIN: N/a (company did not respond)
INGREDIENTS: Organic chocolate, organic cocoa butter, organic cocoa, organic raw cane sugar, organic vanilla extract
COMMENTS: We liked this chocolate's "nice fruitiness" and "very smooth" texture, which tasters found "silky" and "creamy." Tasters enjoyed the flavor, too, saying "This is what I want out of dark chocolate," with its "bitter" but "nice cocoa flavor."

RECOMMENDED · 70% CACAO BARS

CHOCOLOVE Organic Dark 73% Chocolate Bar

WINNER · 70% CACAO BARS

PRICE: $3.55 for 3.2 oz ($1.11 per oz), plus shipping
FAT: 16 g **SUGAR:** 10.7 g **COCOA SOLIDS:** 13.2 g
BEAN ORIGIN: Africa and the Caribbean
INGREDIENTS: Fair trade certified organic cocoa liquor, fair trade certified organic cane sugar, fair trade certified organic cocoa butter, soy lecithin
COMMENTS: Our favorite 70-something bar offered "a good mix between bitter and sweet," with a "rich chocolate flavor" and "very smooth, creamy texture" that "melts perfectly." Some people picked up on fruity notes, such as berries and apricot, while others praised the "strong cacao" taste.

GODIVA 72% Dark Chocolate Bar

PRICE: $2.99 for 3.1 oz ($0.96 per oz)
FAT: 16 g **SUGAR:** 10.7 g **COCOA SOLIDS:** 12.8 g
BEAN ORIGIN: Africa, Central and South America, and parts of Asia
INGREDIENTS: Unsweetened chocolate processed with alkali, sugar, butter oil (milk), emulsifier (soy lecithin)
COMMENTS: This "gently sweet" bar didn't have a strong dark chocolate flavor, with one taster saying it lacked bitterness and "tasted like hot chocolate." Some tasters noted a coconut flavor, prompting the question, "Are there flavorings in here?" but overall we loved its "smooth texture," and found it a "proper snacking dark chocolate."

CORNMEAL

When the winner of our previous cornmeal tasting was discontinued, we decided it was time to re-examine our options. We chose five nationally available products, excluding cornbread and corn muffin mixes with added ingredients such as sugar and baking soda. When determining our lineup, we looked for fine-grind, yellow cornmeals because that is what we call for most often in our recipes. Twenty-one America's Test Kitchen staffers sampled each product (three labeled "fine" and two with no grind size listed on their labels) in Southern-Style Skillet Cornbread and, to see how the cornmeals performed when combined with flour, in Cornmeal Buttermilk Pancakes. Nutrition information and ingredients were taken from product labels or provided by company representatives, and are based on a 3-tablespoon serving size. We purchased the products either online or in Boston-area grocery stores, and the prices shown are what we paid. The products are listed below in order of preference.

RECOMMENDED

ANSON MILLS Antebellum Fine Yellow Cornmeal
PRICE: $5.95 for 12 oz ($0.50 per oz), plus shipping ($9.44 for four 12-ounce bags)
FAT: Not listed
INGREDIENTS: Organic John Haulk corn
DEGERMINATED: No
COMMENTS: Even though some people shudder at the word "moist," tasters commonly used it to describe the cornbread made with this cornmeal. It was soft and tender, with a smooth, cakey texture that "holds together nicely" and was "not too crumbly." Instead of being overpoweringly corn-forward, its flavor was more muted, with some tasters noting a "nice butter flavor."

GOYA Fine Yellow Corn Meal
PRICE: $1.99 for 24 oz ($0.08 per oz)
FAT: 0 g per serving
INGREDIENTS: Yellow corn meal enriched with iron, niacin, thiamin, riboflavin, folic acid
DEGERMINATED: No
COMMENTS: Our runner-up, another germ-in product, produced a really moist cornbread, with one taster saying it "melted in my mouth." Its texture was smooth, "more like a cake," and "holds together well" without crumbling. It had a somewhat muted, yet "pleasant" and "savory" flavor that we liked.

AUNT JEMIMA Yellow Corn Meal
PRICE: $11.00 for 80 oz ($0.14 per oz)
FAT: 0 g per serving
INGREDIENTS: Degerminated yellow corn meal, niacin, reduced iron, thiamin mononitrate, riboflavin, folic acid
DEGERMINATED: Yes
COMMENTS: This cornmeal was degerminated, which likely contributed to the relatively dry (but not too dry) crumb in the cornbread made from it. We liked the "nice medium texture" that was "not gritty but not as soft as others," as it was "just a bit crumbly" and "sturdy yet tender." It had a "buttery" flavor and mild corn taste that was discernible but not overwhelming.

RECOMMENDED (continued)

BOB'S RED MILL Fine Grind Cornmeal
PRICE: $2.59 for 24 oz ($0.11 per oz), plus shipping ($13.34 for two 24-oz bags)
FAT: 1.12 g per serving
INGREDIENTS: Whole grain corn
DEGERMINATED: No
COMMENTS: Even though the bag was labeled "fine grind," this meal looked a lot coarser than the rest. Tasters found its cornbread "grainy" and "rustic," with an "earthy" flavor. Some people liked the "large granules" and "nubbly texture," but one person lamented that the "flavor is pleasant, but it feels like I'm eating couscous."

QUAKER Yellow Corn Meal
PRICE: $2.69 for 24 oz ($0.11 per oz)
FAT: 0.5 g per serving
INGREDIENTS: Degerminated yellow corn meal, niacin, reduced iron, thiamin mononitrate, riboflavin, folic acid
DEGERMINATED: Yes
COMMENTS: Our lowest-ranked cornmeal was "dry," with a "crumbly" texture that one taster said "falls apart very easily"—which displeased a lot of tasters, though some liked the "nice gritty texture." This cornmeal also had a "prominent" corn flavor that, as one taster put it, "reminded me of a tortilla chip."

WHOLE DILL PICKLES

What do fried chicken, deli sandwiches, and backyard barbecue all have in common? They're good foods that are better when there's a crunchy, tangy pickle served on the side. We set out to find the best whole dill pickles, which are more substantial than spears or chips and ideal for either serving alongside a meal or enjoying as a snack. We purchased eight top-selling, nationally available products, one marketed as "garlic and dill," one labeled "kosher," and six labeled "kosher dill"—a style that originated in the kosher Jewish delis in New York City and now refers to any garlic-and-dill-flavored pickle. Seven products were vinegar pickles; we also included one lacto-fermented pickle. A panel of 21 America's Test Kitchen staffers sampled them plain—served chilled at a blind tasting—and rated their flavor, texture, and general appeal. The top seven products are listed below in order of preference.

RECOMMENDED

BOAR'S HEAD Kosher Dill Pickles
PRICE: $4.79 for 26 oz ($0.18 per oz)
STYLE: Vinegar
INGREDIENTS: Cucumbers, water, vinegar, carrots, salt, fresh dill, garlic, spices, 1/10 of 1% sodium benzoate (preservative), calcium chloride, natural flavors, EDTA (to preserve freshness), turmeric (for color)
REFRIGERATED: Yes
COMMENTS: These refrigerated pickles were perfectly crisp and "extra-crunchy." They also earned top marks for flavor: Due to the strong flavor of garlic and dill, tasters said these pickles "tasted almost homemade." A few slices of carrot, which do not affect flavor, are added to each jar.

MT. OLIVE Kosher Dills
PRICE: $5.19 for 46 oz ($0.11 per oz)
STYLE: Vinegar
INGREDIENTS: Cucumbers, water, vinegar, salt, calcium chloride, 0.1% sodium benzoate (preservative), natural flavors, polysorbate 80, and yellow 5
REFRIGERATED: No
COMMENTS: These shelf-stable pickles were crisp and crunchy enough for our tasters. They had "the right amount of tang" and tasted "very familiar," with a hint of garlic and dill and no strong spices.

DIETZ & WATSON Kosher Pickles
PRICE: $4.99 for 32 oz ($0.16 per oz)
STYLE: Vinegar
INGREDIENTS: Cucumbers, water, salt, vinegar, spices, garlic, dill, 1/10 of 1% sodium benzoate (preservative), turmeric, natural spices, flavorings
REFRIGERATED: Yes
COMMENTS: Tasters liked the texture of these "very firm and crunchy" refrigerated pickles. They also liked that they were "heavy on the garlic flavor" and "actually tasted of dill."

WOODSTOCK Organic Whole Kosher Dill Pickles
PRICE: $5.84 for 24 oz ($0.24 per oz)
STYLE: Vinegar
INGREDIENTS: Organic cucumbers, water, organic vinegar, salt, contains less than 2% of dehydrated organic garlic, calcium chloride, natural flavors, organic gum arabic, organic turmeric extract (color)
REFRIGERATED: No
COMMENTS: These shelf-stable pickles stayed crisp through the pasteurization process. The vinegar flavor was a little too strong. We preferred pickles that weren't quite so bracingly sour.

RECOMMENDED WITH RESERVATIONS

CLAUSSEN Kosher Dill Wholes
PRICE: $4.49 for 32 oz ($0.14 per oz)
STYLE: Vinegar
INGREDIENTS: Fresh cucumbers, water, distilled vinegar, salt, contains less than 2% of high fructose corn syrup, dried garlic, calcium chloride, sodium benzoate (to preserve flavor), spice, mustard seed, natural flavor, dried red peppers, polysorbate 80
REFRIGERATED: Yes
COMMENTS: We liked the "substantial crunch" of these pickles. Their flavor, which reminded tasters of anise, nutmeg, and even five-spice powder, was polarizing. A few tasters loved them, but the less heavily spiced pickles in our lineup had broader appeal.

VLASIC Kosher Dill Wholes
PRICE: $4.59 for 46 oz ($0.10 per oz)
STYLE: Vinegar
INGREDIENTS: Cucumbers, water, distilled vinegar, salt, calcium chloride, polysorbate 80, natural flavors, yellow 5
REFRIGERATED: No
COMMENTS: These shelf-stable pickles were "slightly less crisp" than our favorites but weren't too soft or soggy. In terms of flavor, there were "no surprises." Tasters liked their mild, briny flavor.

BUBBIE'S Kosher Dill Pickles
PRICE: $8.39 for 33 oz ($0.25 per oz)
STYLE: Lacto-fermented
INGREDIENTS: Cucumbers, water, salt, garlic, dill, spices, mustard seed, calcium chloride
REFRIGERATED: Yes
COMMENTS: The one naturally fermented pickle in our lineup had a little characteristic fizziness and great texture: crunchy, snappy, and satisfying. Most of the spice mix is proprietary, but the company shared that it includes whole black peppercorns, whole dill seeds, and crushed red chiles. Most of our tasters thought the pickles were "too heavy on the seasonings," but some did note that the pickles reminded them of good deli pickles.

COFFEE MAKERS UNDER $100

When we last tested coffee makers, we named a winner that makes exceptional coffee but costs almost $300. Meanwhile, less expensive coffee makers remain fixtures in many kitchens, so we wanted to know—do you really have to spend more than $100 to get a decent coffee maker? To find out, we tested nine coffee makers with stated capacities ranging from 8 to 14 cups. We got to know the coffee makers by brewing 12 ounces, 32 ounces, and a full pot of coffee in each, evaluating how easy the machines were to load, program, pour from, and clean. We held tastings of the coffee brewed in each machine and calculated the brewed coffees' extraction levels, a coffee industry term for how much of the ground coffee compounds end up in the final brew. The prices listed in this chart are based on shopping at online retailers and will vary. The top three coffee makers are listed below in order of preference. Note: Prices fluctuate constantly on Amazon; however, some readers pointed out the extremely large fluctuation of our favorite inexpensive coffee maker, the Bonavita 8 Cup One-Touch Coffee Maker. We purchased the Bonavita for around $94 at the time of testing, but we've seen price spikes up to around $150 for this model on Amazon. It's worth noting that we've also seen the price drop down regularly to under $100, so if you're interested in purchasing this model it may be worth waiting for a price drop.

HIGHLY RECOMMENDED	PERFORMANCE	TESTERS' COMMENTS

BONAVITA 8 Cup One-Touch Coffee Maker
PRICE: $149.99
CARAFE TYPE: Thermal
EXTRACTION LEVEL: 21.6%
TIME TO BREW 6 CUPS:
5 min, 56 sec
TIME TO BREW FULL POT:
6 min, 30 sec
BREWED COFFEE CAPACITY:
46 oz
BREWING TIME IN IDEAL TEMPERATURE RANGE: 71%
MODEL NUMBER: BV1900TS

FLAVOR ★★★
BREWING ★★★
CLEANUP ★★★
EASE OF USE ★★★

This coffee maker brewed hotter and faster than most other models, resulting in a smooth brew that tasters rated the most flavorful. Its thermal carafe kept brewed coffee hot for more than an hour, and pouring was tidy, with a responsive lever that stopped and started the stream of coffee. All of its parts were accessible and easy to clean, and the machine turned on with the push of a button and automatically turned off when it finished brewing. It had a smaller capacity than the other coffee makers we tested, but it could still brew enough to make about six 8-ounce cups of coffee. It wasn't programmable and was the most expensive model in our lineup; however, this was the only brewer in our lineup certified by the Specialty Coffee Association home brewer program as meeting all the standards for good coffee.

RECOMMENDED WITH RESERVATIONS

HAMILTON BEACH Programmable Coffee Maker
PRICE: $29.99
CARAFE TYPE: Glass
EXTRACTION LEVEL: 18.7%
TIME TO BREW 6 CUPS: 8 min, 50 sec
TIME TO BREW FULL POT: 13 min
BREWED COFFEE CAPACITY: 62 oz
BREWING TIME IN IDEAL TEMPERATURE RANGE: 3%
MODEL NUMBER: 46205

FLAVOR ★★½
BREWING ★★½
CLEANUP ★★★
EASE OF USE ★★

This coffee maker brewed decently extracted coffee that our tasters found mild and balanced. The water hovered just a few degrees under 195 through most of the brew cycle, producing better-extracted coffee than many of the coffee makers that hovered around 170 degrees for most of their brew cycles. It was relatively easy to fill, operate, and clean, but there was no indicator when the brew cycle was finished, and the pop-out door for the coffee filter wouldn't close unless the carafe was positioned just right. It is programmable, so you can have a fresh pot of coffee ready to drink in the morning without having to hit a switch.

NOT RECOMMENDED

BRAUN Brewsense Drip Coffee Maker, White
PRICE: $53.92
CARAFE TYPE: Glass
EXTRACTION LEVEL: 15.6%
TIME TO BREW 6 CUPS: 7 min
TIME TO BREW FULL POT: 13 min
BREWED COFFEE CAPACITY: 62 oz
BREWING TIME IN IDEAL TEMPERATURE RANGE: 0%
MODEL NUMBER: KF6050WH

FLAVOR ★
BREWING ★
CLEANUP ★★★
EASE OF USE ★★★

This coffee maker brewed full pots moderately well but was less consistent with half pots. Most tasters thought the resulting coffee from the half pots was "watery" and "bland." While the quality of the coffee this machine produced was inconsistent, especially with smaller batches, it was easy to load, program, and clean. We liked that it came with a reusable filter so that we didn't have to use paper filters (though you can, if you prefer).

TOASTER OVENS

The uses for a toaster oven go way beyond making toast. A good toaster oven functions as a small second oven, and can even take the place of your big oven. It can handle a 4-pound chicken or bake potatoes or a batch of cookies, and it heats faster, uses less energy, and is easy to clean. But which toaster oven is best? We selected 10 toaster ovens to put to the test. All but one of the toaster ovens had convection capability. We made toast and prepared our Best Baked Potatoes, Simple Broiled Asparagus, Weeknight Roast Chicken, slice-and-bake sugar cookies, tuna melts, and frozen pepperoni pizza in each model. We used thermocouples to track the accuracy of each oven when set to 350 degrees over 2 hours, and tested how well various baking pans and sheets fit in each oven. Finally, we evaluated the user-friendliness of each oven, noting how intuitive the ovens were to operate and how easy they were to clean. We also made 365 slices of toast in our winning oven to evaluate its durability over a year of simulated use. The prices listed in this chart are based on shopping at online retailers and will vary. Results from the tests were averaged, and the top four toaster ovens are listed below in order of preference.

HIGHLY RECOMMENDED	PERFORMANCE	TESTERS' COMMENTS

BREVILLE Smart Oven
PRICE: $269.95
EXTERIOR DIMENSIONS:
18.3 x 12.3 x 10.6 in
TYPE OF HEATING ELEMENT: Quartz
USABLE INTERIOR DIMENSIONS:
13.0 x 11.0 x 5.0 in
TOP RACK DISTANCE FROM
BROILER: 2 in
AVERAGE TEMPERATURE WHEN
SET TO 350 DEGREES: 352
MODEL NUMBER: BOV800XL

USER-FRIENDLINESS ★★★
BAKING ★★★
CLEANUP ★★★
ACCURACY ★★★
BROILING ★★★
ROASTING ★★★
TOASTING ★★★

Our previous winner once again aced all our tests. Its settings are intuitive and easy to use, and it's programmable, so you can set it to remember your preferences. Markers on the glass door helpfully instruct you to where to place the rack for each setting, and the interior of the oven has a nonstick coating for easy cleanup. Though it took longer than other products to toast, it was capable of making big batches of perfectly golden slices that were evenly browned from edge to edge.

DE'LONGHI LIVENZA Digital True Convection Oven
PRICE: $269.99
EXTERIOR DIMENSIONS:
18.6 x 12.0 x 11.7 in
TYPE OF HEATING ELEMENT: Nichrome
USABLE INTERIOR DIMENSIONS:
13.4 x 11.3 x 6.5 in
TOP RACK DISTANCE FROM
BROILER: 2.7 in
AVERAGE TEMPERATURE WHEN
SET TO 350 DEGREES: 343
MODEL NUMBER: EO 241250M

USER-FRIENDLINESS ★★★
BAKING ★★★
CLEANUP ★★★
ACCURACY ★★★
BROILING ★★½
ROASTING ★★★
TOASTING ★★★

A close second place, this toaster oven excelled at all our cooking tests, churning out evenly browned toast, tender potatoes, melty pizzas, and even a fully-roasted chicken with crispy skin. Its dials and digital display were a cinch to use, and its nonstick interior was extremely easy to clean. It broiled food quickly and efficiently since its top rack is located 2.7 inches from the broiler element; yet the rack was obscured by the handle so we couldn't see the food as it broiled—a minor inconvenience. Otherwise, this was an all-around great toaster oven.

RECOMMENDED

CUISINART Chef's Convection Toaster Oven
PRICE: $204.09
EXTERIOR DIMENSIONS: 19.8 x 13.2 x 11 in
TYPE OF HEATING ELEMENT: Quartz
USABLE INTERIOR DIMENSIONS:
14.0 x 12.2 x 3.25 in
TOP RACK DISTANCE FROM
BROILER: 2.4 in
AVERAGE TEMPERATURE WHEN
SET TO 350 DEGREES: 356
MODEL NUMBER: TOB-260N1

USER-FRIENDLINESS ★★
BAKING ★★★
CLEANUP ★★★
ACCURACY ★★★
BROILING ★★★
ROASTING ★★★
TOASTING ★★★

This toaster oven looked similar to the Breville with its large, backlit display; selector dial; roomy crumb tray; and enamel baking and broiling pans. We found it nearly as intuitive to use and extremely accurate—its temperature only varied an average of 6 degrees from our target temperature. Unsurprisingly, nearly everything we cooked in it came out flawless; potatoes were tender, chicken was beautifully roasted and juicy, cookies were evenly baked. Our only issue was the slightly complicated and confusing control panel, which had a big dial, digital screen, and half a dozen buttons.

CALPHALON Quartz Heat Countertop Oven
PRICE: $199.99
EXTERIOR DIMENSIONS: 18.5 x 12.0 x 11.4 in
TYPE OF HEATING ELEMENT: Quartz
USABLE INTERIOR DIMENSIONS:
13.5 x 10.5 x 4.5 in
TOP RACK DISTANCE FROM
BROILER: 3.75 in
AVERAGE TEMPERATURE WHEN
SET TO 350 DEGREES: 334
MODEL NUMBER: TSCLTRDG1

USER-FRIENDLINESS ★★★
BAKING ★★½
CLEANUP ★★★
ACCURACY ★★★
BROILING ★
ROASTING ★★★
TOASTING ★★★

There was a lot to like about this oven, from its easy-to-clean nonstick interior to its rubber seals that lock in heat. It made beautifully cooked chicken, golden toast, well-browned cookies, and melty pizza. Our one qualm was its rack positions. Unlike most ovens, which have at least three possible rack levels, this model had only two, and the highest one was 3.75 inches away from the broiler element. Unfortunately, this made the oven less effective at broiling; it took about 50 percent longer than other top-ranked ovens to melt cheese on tuna melts or to broil asparagus.

COOKWARE SETS

If you want to cook with confidence, quality cookware is essential. We usually insist that you buy cookware piece by piece so you pay for only what you need, but there have been some interesting developments since the last time we tested cookware sets, so we decided to take another look. We bought eight sets and compared the skillets, saucepans, sauté pans, and stockpots or Dutch ovens from each set. In the skillets, we browned beef for shepherd's pie and made steak with pan sauce. In the saucepans, we browned butter and made mashed potatoes. In the sauté pans, we made Swedish meatballs and sautéed kale. In the stockpots/Dutch ovens, we cooked angel hair pasta and made beef Burgundy. We rated the four pieces of cookware on their performance, ease of use, durability, and ease of cleanup. We also evaluated the full composition of pans in each set. The prices listed in this chart are based on shopping at online retailers and will vary. The top five cookware sets are listed below in order of preference.

HIGHLY RECOMMENDED | **PERFORMANCE** | **TESTERS' COMMENTS**

ALL-CLAD D3 Tri-Ply Bonded Cookware Set, 10 Piece
PRICE: $649.95
PIECES: 6 pans, 4 lids: 8 qt stockpot with lid (fully clad), 3 qt sauté pan with lid, 3 qt saucepan with lid, 2 qt saucepan with lid, 8 in fry pan, 10 in fry pan
MATERIALS: Fully-clad tri-ply stainless steel and aluminum
WHAT ELSE YOU MIGHT NEED: 12 in nonstick pan
MODEL NUMBER: 8400000962

EASE OF USE ★★★
PERFORMANCE ★★★
CLEANUP/ DURABILITY ★★★
COMPOSITION OF SET ★★★

These fully clad pans brown beautifully and feel balanced, the handles stay cool, and they're tough as nails. The set offers essential pieces in practical sizes that will last a lifetime. The set price is a bargain: The 8-quart stockpot alone usually retails for nearly $340.

RECOMMENDED

ALL-CLAD d3 Compact Collection 5-Piece Set
PRICE: $435.17
PIECES: 3 pans, 2 lids: 5 qt stockpot with lid, 3 qt saucepan with lid, 10.5 in skillet (lid from stockpot fits skillet)
MATERIALS: Fully-clad tri-ply stainless steel and aluminum
WHAT ELSE YOU MIGHT NEED: 12 in nonstick pan, Dutch oven or larger stockpot
MODEL NUMBER: ST40005

EASE OF USE ★★
PERFORMANCE ★★★
CLEANUP/ DURABILITY ★★★
COMPOSITION OF SET ★★

We love the compact, innovative design of this set: Its nesting cookware makes it easy to store. To nest, though, the skillet was wide (which we liked), but the so-called stockpot was stumpy and flat (it resembles a sauté pan); it was impossible to cook more than a pound of pasta in it, and even that was a challenge. If you're willing to work around this, it's a collection of sturdy, high-performance cookware.

POTLUCK Cookware Set
PRICE: $160.00 **BEST BUY**
PIECES: 4 pans, 3 lids: 8 qt stockpot with lid, 3 qt saucepan with lid, 1.5 qt saucepan with lid, 10 in skillet
MATERIALS: Fully-clad tri-ply stainless steel and aluminum
WHAT ELSE YOU MIGHT NEED: 12 in nonstick skillet
MODEL NUMBER: CKW-01

EASE OF USE ★★★
PERFORMANCE ★★★
CLEANUP/ DURABILITY ★
COMPOSITION OF SET ★★★

This set was a heartbreaker. It has well-designed, balanced pans with practical sizes and shapes and comfortable, cool handles at an outstanding price. Everything cooked beautifully. And then, on the last day of abuse testing, the skillet warped badly as we heated it to 500 degrees on an induction burner, leading us to worry about the set's durability. (A second copy of the pan did not warp when we heated it more gradually to 500 degrees, however.)

GREAT JONES Family Style Collection
PRICE: $395.00
PIECES: 5 pieces, 4 lids: 6¾ qt Dutch oven, 8 qt stockpot, 3 qt saucepan with lid, 3 qt deep sauté pan with lid, 9 in ceramic nonstick skillet
MATERIALS: Fully-clad tri-ply stainless steel and aluminum, enameled cast-iron Dutch oven, nonstick skillet
WHAT ELSE YOU MIGHT NEED: 12 in nonstick skillet
MODEL NUMBER: N/a

EASE OF USE ★★
PERFORMANCE ★★★
CLEANUP/ DURABILITY ★½
COMPOSITION OF SET ★★★

We loved that this set included mixed materials; the cast-iron Dutch oven made excellent stew and cleaned up easily, the fully clad metal stockpot worked well for pasta, and the nonstick pan was handy for eggs. We disliked the bent-metal-tube handles, which were uncomfortable and got hot. Cleaning the clad cookware was a pain; it became more stained than other pans, so it quickly looked worn-out.

MADE IN COOKWARE The Starter Kit
PRICE: $260.00
PIECES: 3 pans, 2 lids: 5 qt stockpot with lid, 2 qt saucepan with lid, 10 in frying pan
MATERIALS: Fully-clad 5-ply stainless steel and aluminum
WHAT ELSE YOU MIGHT NEED: 8 qt stockpot, 12 in nonstick skillet
MODEL NUMBER: KIT-5-STA-NA

EASE OF USE ★★
PERFORMANCE ★★★
CLEANUP/ DURABILITY ★★★
COMPOSITION OF SET ★★

Excellent browning and comfortable handles helped this cookware score well, but the dinky 5-quart stockpot, which was narrow and tall and just a bit bigger than our favorite large saucepan, was a big disadvantage when cooking pasta and stew. We could fit only 1 pound of pasta and had to stir furiously to keep it from sticking, and it took many more batches than usual to brown the beef for the stew. The frying pan's sides tapered down to a 7-inch cooking surface, which felt cramped.

WOKS

For years, we've tweaked conventional stir-fry recipes to achieve delicious results in a nonstick skillet rather than a wok, the traditional cooking vessel. Since American stove burners are flat, we aimed to get more contact with the heat source by using the broad cooking surface of a 12-inch skillet instead of the smaller bottom surface of a wok. Recently, we decided to question our assumptions and take another look at woks. We bought nine models, all measuring 14 inches from rim to rim, the size that our wok experts said is optimal for preparing anywhere from two to six servings. We picked woks with flat bottoms rather than traditional round bottoms. All were made of carbon steel, cast iron, or lightweight cast iron. In each wok, we stir-fried a wide range of ingredients and used a variety of techniques, including cooking in batches, steaming and crisping vegetables, handling piles of slippery noodles, and searing meat and seafood, noting how easy each wok was to use and clean. We found that a reliable wok was easier to use for stir-frying and can produce results at least as good as a nonstick skillet. The prices listed in this chart are based on shopping at online retailers and may vary. The top five woks are listed below in order of preference.

HIGHLY RECOMMENDED	PERFORMANCE	TESTERS' COMMENTS

TAYLOR AND NG Natural Nonstick Wok Set 12153 14" Carbon Steel
PRICE: $49.17
WEIGHT: 3 lb, 4.6 oz
MATERIALS: Preseasoned carbon steel, wood
FLAT COOKING SURFACE DIAMETER: 7 in
MODEL NUMBER: 12153

EASE OF USE ★★★
PERFORMANCE ★★★

This wok was the easiest and most comfortable to use. Its stay-cool wooden handles and light, balanced weight helped us maneuver and lift it. It offers the biggest flat cooking surface, and its thin, heat-responsive carbon-steel material helped us control temperatures. This was the only wok in the lineup to include a lid and the only carbon-steel wok that was preseasoned.

RECOMMENDED

WOK SHOP Carbon Steel Wok with Metal Side Handle, 14" flat-bottom
PRICE: $35.00
WEIGHT: 3 lb, 14.1 oz
MATERIALS: Carbon steel, wood (main handle)
FLAT COOKING SURFACE DIAMETER: 6 in
MODEL NUMBER: 0005

EASE OF USE ★★½
PERFORMANCE ★★★

This carbon-steel wok was responsive to heat, making it easy to control the temperature of the pan. We liked that its long, wooden main handle stayed cool, but some testers found that the handle's steep offset angle put their hands and arms in awkward positions. Combined with the fact that it's slightly heavier than our top-rated wok, it felt just a bit less maneuverable.

HELEN'S ASIAN KITCHEN Carbon Steel Wok, 14"
PRICE: $33.49
WEIGHT: 4 lb
MATERIALS: Carbon steel, bamboo
FLAT COOKING SURFACE DIAMETER: 6.25 in
MODEL NUMBER: 97004

EASE OF USE ★★
PERFORMANCE ★★★

While this wok cooked every dish well and was beautifully responsive to heat, it was slightly too heavy for many testers when it was full of food. We appreciated that the smooth, round bamboo handle stayed cool, but some testers felt that the handle was slightly too long to lift one-handed.

RECOMMENDED WITH RESERVATIONS

WOK SHOP Carbon Steel Pow Wok with Hollow Metal Handle, Made-USA, 14" flat bottom
PRICE: $35.00
WEIGHT: 2 lb, 15.4 oz
MATERIALS: Carbon steel
FLAT COOKING SURFACE DIAMETER: 6 in
MODEL NUMBER: 0010

EASE OF USE ★½
PERFORMANCE ★★★

This lightweight pan is designed to use its single, straight handle to flip food. Its hollow metal handle doesn't have time to get hot when restaurant chefs are stir-frying on high-powered stoves. But at home, with slower-moving recipes, the metal handle heats up, and that extra step of grabbing a pot holder made it less comfortable and efficient than our higher-rated woks. Its carbon-steel material transferred heat rapidly for excellent cooking results.

JOYCE CHEN 22-0060 Pro Chef Flat Bottom Wok Uncoated Carbon Steel, 14-inch
PRICE: $39.99
WEIGHT: 4 lb
MATERIALS: Carbon steel, plastic
FLAT COOKING SURFACE DIAMETER: 6.25 in
MODEL NUMBER: 22-0060

EASE OF USE ★½
PERFORMANCE ★★★

Food cooked well in this wok, which felt responsive to heat and easy to control, but its square plastic handles, set level with the rim of the wok, were a bit clunky to grab and didn't offer as much leverage as slightly angled handles on other models; combined with the wok's weight, it felt more difficult to maneuver than higher-rated woks. Water got trapped in the handles when we washed the wok, and trickled out later.

12-INCH NONSTICK SKILLETS

A good nonstick skillet is our go-to for all sorts of delicate and fast-cooking foods. We know what we like: a slick and durable coating, a wide cooking surface, and a comfortable handle. Several intriguing new models have hit the market recently, so we gathered a total of 10 nonstick skillets and put them through the wringer. We used them to make our Beef and Broccoli Stir-Fry, pepper and onion frittata, and pan-fried sole—recipes selected to test the pans' capacity, browning ability, and maneuverability. To zero in on the pans' nonstick coatings, we conducted a test that's standard in the cookware industry: cooking eggs in a dry skillet back-to-back, stopping either when they began to stick or when we had made 50 consecutive eggs. We did that at the beginning and end of testing so we could see if the coatings deteriorated with use. The prices listed in this chart are based on shopping at online retailers and will vary. The top five skillets are listed below in order of preference.

HIGHLY RECOMMENDED		PERFORMANCE	TESTERS' COMMENTS
OXO GOOD GRIPS Non-Stick Pro 12" Open Frypan PRICE: $59.93 WEIGHT: 2.40 lb OVENSAFE TO: 430°F COOKING SURFACE DIAMETER: 9¾ in INDUCTION-COMPATIBLE: No MODEL NUMBER: CW000960-003		CAPACITY ★★★ EASE OF USE ★★★ DURABILITY ★★½ NONSTICK ABILITY ★★★	The cooking surface was slick, both when new and after extensive use, and food never stuck. It's one of the lightest models we tested, so it was easy to lift and maneuver, but it was also sturdy and resisted denting. All of our testers liked its wide, comfortable handle. Like every other model, its surface became scratched when we used a knife as if to cut a frittata, but it otherwise held up well.
ALL-CLAD Stainless 12" Nonstick Fry Pan PRICE: $164.99 WEIGHT: 2.75 lb OVENSAFE TO: 500°F COOKING SURFACE DIAMETER: 9¼ in INDUCTION-COMPATIBLE: Yes MODEL NUMBER: 4112 NS R2		CAPACITY ★★★ EASE OF USE ★★½ DURABILITY ★★½ NONSTICK ABILITY ★★★	Our favorite induction-compatible nonstick skillet was just as slick and durable as our overall favorite, and we liked its generous cooking surface and gently sloped walls. It was noticeably heavier than our favorite, though very well balanced. The signature All-Clad handle, which is concave and a little sharp, offered a very secure grip but was uncomfortable to some testers. The pan became scratched during the frittata cutting test.

RECOMMENDED			
T-FAL Professional Non-Stick Fry Pan PRICE: $33.48 WEIGHT: 2.50 lb OVENSAFE TO: 400°F COOKING SURFACE DIAMETER: 9¾ in INDUCTION-COMPATIBLE: Yes MODEL NUMBER: H9090564		CAPACITY ★★★ EASE OF USE ★★ DURABILITY ★★½ NONSTICK ABILITY ★★★	This pan has a spacious and slippery surface. It's also very light, and the squishy handle is comfortable to hold. We have two criticisms: The cooking surface is slightly domed, so oil runs to the edges and fried eggs rarely turn out perfectly round, and it's too wide to fit a standard 12-inch lid.
MADE IN Stainless Steel Non Stick Frying Pan PRICE: $95.00 WEIGHT: 3.30 lb OVENSAFE TO: 500°F COOKING SURFACE DIAMETER: 9 in INDUCTION-COMPATIBLE: Yes MODEL NUMBER: N/a		CAPACITY ★★★ EASE OF USE ★★ DURABILITY ★★½ NONSTICK ABILITY ★★★	This skillet, from a relatively new direct-to-consumer company, impressed us throughout testing. As with other models, food never stuck to this pan's slick surface. The walls were tall enough for us to stir rapidly and shake food around without spilling. Although we liked the shape of the pan, some testers noted that when they tried to lift the pan when it was full of food, it felt unbalanced and much too heavy, as if the pan were being tugged out of their hands.
MISEN 12" Nonstick Skillet PRICE: $65.00 WEIGHT: 3.19 lb OVENSAFE TO: 450°F COOKING SURFACE DIAMETER: 9 in INDUCTION-COMPATIBLE: Yes MODEL NUMBER: N/a		CAPACITY ★★★ EASE OF USE ★★ DURABILITY ★★½ NONSTICK ABILITY ★★★	This pan, which is sold by a new direct-to-consumer company, did well in all of our recipe tests. Food never stuck, and the shape and slope of the walls kept food inside the skillet. It had a removable silicone sleeve covering most of its handle. Some test cooks liked it, but the sleeve was shorter than the handle and most testers noted that it interrupted their grips. This pan was also a little heavier than our favorites, and it felt unbalanced—most of that weight was in the business end of the pan.

8-INCH SQUARE BAKING PANS

Square baking pans are handy for making cakes and brownies, but that's not all. We also use them for recipes such as Chocolate Fudge, Honey Cornbread, and Nanaimo Bars. Because we call for them in so many of our recipes, we decided to find out which of the many pans on the market was the best. We purchased eight 8-inch square baking pans and used each to bake brownies made with our winning boxed brownie mix and yellow cake made with our Make-Ahead Yellow Cake Mix. After baking both the brownies and the yellow cakes, we used a paring knife to slice the desserts in the pans, cutting each into 16 squares. We repeated the cutting motion a total of five times for both brownies and cake. We washed each pan five times according to the manufacturer's instructions. We also made our Basic Brownies in our winning pan to see how it fared when lined with an aluminum foil sling, a method we frequently use in our baking recipes. The prices listed in this chart are based on shopping at online retailers and will vary. Results from the tests were averaged, and the top five baking pans are listed below in order of preference.

HIGHLY RECOMMENDED

FAT DADDIO'S ProSeries Square Cake Pan
PRICE: $13.48
MATERIAL: Anodized aluminum
CONSTRUCTION: Molded
DISHWASHER-SAFE: No
MODEL NUMBER: PSQ-882

PERFORMANCE
BAKED GOOD APPEARANCE ★★★
EASE OF CLEANUP ★★★
DURABILITY ★★½

TESTERS' COMMENTS
Our winner had it all: Straight sides, which produced attractive cakes with well-defined edges, and a ½-inch lip that made it easy to hold. It was the only metal model in the lineup that was molded, a construction technique that renders it seamless and therefore easy to clean (even though it is not dishwasher-safe). It lacked a nonstick coating, but baked goods released with ease when we greased and floured the pan. We did notice very faint scratches in the bottom of the pan after repeated passes with a paring knife.

RECOMMENDED

WILLIAMS SONOMA Goldtouch Nonstick Square Cake Pan, 8"
PRICE: $26.95
MATERIALS: Aluminized steel, Goldtouch ceramic-based coating
CONSTRUCTION: Folded
DISHWASHER-SAFE: Yes
MODEL NUMBER: 1983741

PERFORMANCE
BAKED GOOD APPEARANCE ★★★
EASE OF CLEANUP ★★½
DURABILITY ★★½

TESTERS' COMMENTS
Our previous winner still performed well, giving us beautiful cakes and brownies. It accumulated only light nicks after we sliced cake and brownies in it and was fairly easy to clean, but we noticed a few rust spots after inadvertently leaving it in the dishwasher for a couple of days. We checked the copies currently stocked in our kitchen and did not see any rust.

USA PAN 8 Inch Square Cake Pan
PRICE: $14.99
MATERIALS: Aluminized steel with silicone coating
CONSTRUCTION: Folded
DISHWASHER-SAFE: No
MODEL NUMBER: 1120BW

PERFORMANCE
BAKED GOOD APPEARANCE ★★★
EASE OF CLEANUP ★★½
DURABILITY ★★½

TESTERS' COMMENTS
This pan featured a ridged bottom and sides, which sometimes left faint marks on the finished baked goods, but it was nothing egregious. This model's straight sides produced square yellow cakes with clean edges, and though the pan showed minor scratches after the paring knife test, the marks weren't substantial. We also found a stray crumb stuck in one seam even after washing the pan, but overall this pan was easy to clean.

KITCHENAID Professional-Grade Nonstick Square Cake Pan, 8" x 8"
PRICE: $15.00
MATERIALS: Aluminized steel, multilayer nonstick coating
CONSTRUCTION: Folded
DISHWASHER-SAFE: Yes
MODEL NUMBER: KB2NSO08SQWT

PERFORMANCE
BAKED GOOD APPEARANCE ★★★
EASE OF CLEANUP ★★½
DURABILITY ★★½

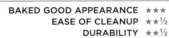

TESTERS' COMMENTS
Another model that turned out nicely browned baked goods, this pan had nearly 90-degree sides that made for cakes with straight sides. We did notice some faint scratching after cutting the brownies and cake in the pan. Food got caught in the pan's seams, so we had to pay close attention during cleanup.

RECOMMENDED WITH RESERVATIONS

STAUB Stoneware Square Baker, 8" x 8"
PRICE: $36.00
MATERIALS: Stoneware with glass porcelain enamel finish
CONSTRUCTION: Molded
DISHWASHER-SAFE: Yes
MODEL NUMBER: 7396010

PERFORMANCE
BAKED GOOD APPEARANCE ★½
EASE OF CLEANUP ★★★
DURABILITY ★★★

TESTERS' COMMENTS
This glazed ceramic stoneware model took longer to bake brownies and cake, but the baking times of both fell within acceptable ranges. The sides of our yellow cake were tapered, giving it a less polished appearance. We loved this model's handles, which were easy to grab whether greasing and flouring a pan or removing it from a hot oven. It remained scratch-free throughout testing, and its seamless interior was easy to clean.

BROILER-SAFE BAKING DISHES

A 13 by 9-inch baking dish is inexpensive, functional, and great for transporting goods. In the test kitchen, we put 13 by 9-inch baking dishes under the broiler when we want to crisp bread crumbs or brown the tops of a variety of dishes, but this direct-heat cooking method is too hot for our favorite glass baking dish as well as our winning 13 by 9-inch baking pan. We purchased seven broiler-safe baking dishes and used each to make a yellow cake, our Classic Macaroni and Cheese, and One-Pan Salmon with Rice, Broccoli, and Shiitake Mushrooms. After baking the cakes, we used a paring knife to slice the desserts in the dish, cutting them into 24 squares and checking for scratches. We used a metal spatula to portion and remove the other two foods from the dishes, also checking for scratches. We used oven mitts and dish towels when placing the dishes in and removing them from the oven. We also washed each dish five times according to manufacturer instructions (all were dishwasher-safe). The prices listed in this chart are based on shopping at online retailers and will vary. Scores were averaged, and the top five baking dishes are listed below in order of preference.

HIGHLY RECOMMENDED | PERFORMANCE | TESTERS' COMMENTS

MRS. ANDERSON'S BAKING Lasagna Pan with Handle (Rose)
PRICE: $50.99
WEIGHT: 5 lb, 2.6 oz
CAPACITY: 14.25 cups
DIMENSIONS: 12.5 x 8.63 x 2.63 in
HANDLE STYLE: Looped
DISHWASHER-SAFE: Yes
MODEL NUMBER: 98048RS

HANDLES ★★★
PERFORMANCE ★★★
CAPACITY ★★★

This dish had looped handles that were easy to grab, whether we were rotating the dish halfway through baking or removing it from the oven. We also thought it had the best capacity in the lineup at 14.25 cups—neither too generous nor too restrictive. Our winner accommodated all foods with ease and felt secure to grip even when full of hot, heavy food.

RECOMMENDED

STAUB 13x9 Rectangular Baking Dish, Dark Blue
PRICE: $49.99
WEIGHT: 5 lb, 11.4 oz
CAPACITY: 16.25 cups
DIMENSIONS: 13.25 x 9.5 x 2.94 in
HANDLE STYLE: Looped
DISHWASHER-SAFE: Yes
MODEL NUMBER: 40508-594

HANDLES ★★★
PERFORMANCE ★★★
CAPACITY ★★½

We liked this model's looped handles, which were secure to hold. The larger volume made for a slightly wider dish, which we generally found helpful; when we distributed broccoli and shiitake mushrooms alongside the salmon, it was easy because we had more surface area to work with—but it also meant that some rice showed through the vegetables even though the recipe says it shouldn't. We also liked that this 16.25-cup dish comfortably fit macaroni and cheese, allowing ample clearance at the top to keep bread crumbs contained.

BELLE CUISINE Rectangular Baking Dish 13.5 x 9.75
PRICE: $82.50
WEIGHT: 5 lb, 7.5 oz
CAPACITY: 16.25 cups
DIMENSIONS: 13.25 x 9.38 x 2.88 in
HANDLE STYLE: Looped
DISHWASHER-SAFE: Yes
MODEL NUMBER: 5571

HANDLES ★★★
PERFORMANCE ★★★
CAPACITY ★★½

Yellow cake looked lower and flatter in this dish than it did in the others, but when we cut into the cake for closer examination, we noted that slice thickness was perfectly fine. We did notice some rice peeking through the broccoli and shiitake mushrooms in the one-pan salmon (even though the recipe said the vegetables should cover the rice), but the finished dish was still aesthetically pleasing and the rice was not adversely affected. We also loved the looped handles.

HIC Lasagna Pan with Handles
PRICE: $54.99
WEIGHT: 4 lb, 6.6 oz
CAPACITY: 12.75 cups
DIMENSIONS: 12.63 x 8.75 x 2.25 in
HANDLE STYLE: Looped
DISHWASHER-SAFE: Yes
MODEL NUMBER: 98048

HANDLES ★★★
PERFORMANCE ★★★
CAPACITY ★★

We liked how easy our previous winner was to maneuver into and out of the oven thanks to its looped handles, but compared to other models with larger capacities, this one felt a little too small in some instances. The macaroni and cheese was even with the dish's sides, making it difficult to contain the bread-crumb topping, and we had less surface area to distribute vegetables when making the one-pan salmon.

RECOMMENDED WITH RESERVATIONS

LE CREUSET Heritage Covered Rectangular Casserole
PRICE: $109.95
WEIGHT: 5 lb, 2.6 oz
CAPACITY: 13 cups
DIMENSIONS: 11.63 x 7.63 x 2.5 in
HANDLE STYLE: Tabs
DISHWASHER-SAFE: Yes
MODEL NUMBER: PG07053A-33

HANDLES ★★
PERFORMANCE ★★★
CAPACITY ★★

Overall, this model did a good job of cooking everything. Its tab handles were somewhat easier to grip than other similarly designed handles, likely because this dish was on the smaller side, so it was easier to lift. But it was harder to get leverage on the small tab handles than on looped versions, and we found that because of the dish's small capacity, the salmon and vegetables were crowded (but ultimately cooked just fine) and the cake was more domed than others.

INEXPENSIVE STAND MIXERS

Stand mixers work wonders when you want to whip up baked goods such as layer cakes, cookies, meringues, or breads. But if you're only an occasional baker—or just don't have a lot of dough to spend on a stand mixer—do you really need a high-end model? We tested seven stand mixers, including our previous favorite inexpensive stand mixer. We focused on the key tasks of whipping, creaming, and kneading and rated them on ease of use and design. We used water to measure the actual capacity of the mixing bowls versus the manufacturers' stated capacity and weighed the mixers with bowls in place (but without attachments). We measured the distances between the bottoms of the bowls and each mixer's three attachments. The prices listed in this chart are based on shopping at online retailers and will vary. The top five mixers are listed below in order of preference.

HIGHLY RECOMMENDED	PERFORMANCE	TESTERS' COMMENTS
KITCHENAID KSM75WH Classic Plus Series 4.5-Quart Tilt-Head Stand Mixer PRICE: $207.99 SIZE: 4.5 qt WEIGHT: 21.8 lb ACTUAL CAPACITY: 3 qt DISTANCE FROM BOWL TO HOOK: 10 mm DISTANCE FROM BOWL TO WHISK: 6 mm DISTANCE FROM BOWL TO PADDLE: 5 mm MODEL NUMBER: KSM75WH	DESIGN ★★½ KNEADING ★★★ EASE OF USE ★★½ CREAMING ★★★ WHIPPING ★★★	Our previous favorite aced every test, whipping, creaming, and kneading quickly and thoroughly to give us fluffy whipped cream and meringue; light, tender cakes; and chewy, rustic breads. We did have a few design quibbles: We'd prefer a handled bowl (KitchenAid sells stainless-steel or glass bowls with handles separately). The tilt-head latch works fine, but it's slightly less convenient than buttons on other models, and we disliked that you could operate it with the head unlocked.

RECOMMENDED		
FARBERWARE 6 Speed 4.7-Quart Professional Stand Mixer PRICE: $99.99 SIZE: 4.7 qt WEIGHT: 14.7 lb ACTUAL CAPACITY: 3.5 qt DISTANCE FROM BOWL TO HOOK: 8 mm DISTANCE FROM BOWL TO WHISK: 3.8 mm DISTANCE FROM BOWL TO PADDLE: 3 mm MODEL NUMBER: SM3481RBG	DESIGN ★★ KNEADING ★★½ EASE OF USE ★★½ CREAMING ★★★ WHIPPING ★★★	With a tight gap between the attachments and the bowl, this mixer aced mixing and creaming, albeit with a high-pitched whine that was slightly unpleasant. When kneading, it stayed cool and steady, though it felt a little underpowered: We had to stop and mix some of the dry ingredients for our Bagel Bread by hand and raise the speed from medium to medium-high to help it along. The bowl locks in securely but lacks a handle. If you don't bake a lot of bread, this mixer is a really good option, especially given the price.
OSTER Planetary Stand Mixer PRICE: $199.99 SIZE: 4.5 qt WEIGHT: 12.75 lb ACTUAL CAPACITY: 3.3 qt DISTANCE FROM BOWL TO HOOK: 11.6 mm DISTANCE FROM BOWL TO WHISK: 6.5 mm DISTANCE FROM BOWL TO PADDLE: 6.3 mm MODEL NUMBER: FPSTSMPL1	DESIGN ★★★ KNEADING ★★½ EASE OF USE ★★½ CREAMING ★★½ WHIPPING ★★★	This compact, lightweight mixer is easy to lift, with simple controls. It was fine with lightweight food such as cream, egg whites, and cake batter but struggled a bit to incorporate ingredients in heavier cookie dough and ciabatta dough; we had to scrape the bowl more often. It kneaded without much rocking, but it was loud.

RECOMMENDED WITH RESERVATIONS		
BOSCH Compact Tilt-Head Stand Mixer PRICE: $159.00 SIZE: 4 qt WEIGHT: 6.4 lb ACTUAL CAPACITY: 3 qt DISTANCE FROM BOWL TO HOOK: 6.7 mm DISTANCE FROM BOWL TO WHISK: 2.5 mm DISTANCE FROM BOWL TO PADDLE: 5 mm MODEL NUMBER: MUM4405	DESIGN ★½ KNEADING ★★★ EASE OF USE ★½ CREAMING ★★½ WHIPPING ★★½	Tiny and feather-light, this unusual mixer works surprisingly well but slowly; we often found unmixed ingredients and had to run it longer. Its fussy design includes a built-in splash guard whose blue tint makes viewing the contents of the bowl difficult; its tiny opening was annoying, and the whole thing fell off more than once as the mixer rocked while kneading. That said, if you can't lift heavy items, this is a good option.
CUISINART SM-50R Stand Mixer PRICE: $154.25 SIZE: 5.5 qt WEIGHT: 16.65 lb ACTUAL CAPACITY: 3.6 qt DISTANCE FROM BOWL TO HOOK: 17.5 mm DISTANCE FROM BOWL TO WHISK: 6.5 mm DISTANCE FROM BOWL TO PADDLE: 10.4 mm MODEL NUMBER: SM-50R	DESIGN ★★★ KNEADING ★½ EASE OF USE ★★ CREAMING ★★ WHIPPING ★★½	This sturdy, attractive mixer was easy to operate, steady, and quiet but often struggled to whip egg whites and incorporate ingredients for cookie and ciabatta dough. We scraped the bowl often and tried higher speeds, hoping to improve results. While the whisk has two wires fairly close to the bowl, the rest of the wire loops are much shorter and farther from the bowl. With big gaps between attachments and the bowl, some ingredients stayed just out of reach, making for slow progress.

COUNTERTOP VACUUM SEALERS

Vacuum sealers can prevent the disappointment of freezing food only to find it covered in ice crystals a week later. A handheld vacuum sealer is fine for occasional use, but for those who do a lot of vacuum-sealing, we recommend investing in a countertop model because they're sturdier, easier to use, and more powerful. We tested seven countertop vacuum sealers to find the best product. With each model, we vacuum-sealed a wide variety of foods and stored them either in the freezer or in our pantry at room temperature. We monitored the tightness of the bags' seals and the quality of the food for several months. If manufacturers sold additional bags, we used those throughout testing. With other models, we used a set of generic bags sold by Nutri-Lock. We also performed a control test using oxygen-detecting tablets, using both generic and branded bags. We assessed the machines' power by measuring the amount of air each was able to extract from bags on average. The possible score range was from 0 percent, which is normal atmosphere, to 100 percent, which signifies that every single air molecule has been removed. The weight and dimensions of each machine were measured in-house. The prices listed in this chart are based on shopping at online retailers and will vary. The top four vacuum sealers are listed below in order of preference.

HIGHLY RECOMMENDED

	PERFORMANCE	TESTERS' COMMENTS

NESCO Deluxe Vacuum Sealer
PRICE: $90.02
WEIGHT: 6 lb 1 oz
DIMENSIONS: 15.75 x 7.75 x 4.75 in
VACUUM STRENGTH: 75.20%
COMPATIBLE WITH GENERIC BAGS: Yes
MODEL NUMBER: VS-12

HANDLING ★★★
PERFORMANCE ★★★
EASE OF USE ★★★

The simple, intuitive control panel; stellar performance; and moderate price of this midsize model made it ideal for most home cooks. The "gentle" setting and pulse mode both worked well when vacuum-sealing fragile foods such as strawberries. The handle locked the lid firmly into place with a reassuring click. A digital screen that tracked the machine's progress and built-in storage for a plastic roll were handy bonuses. Although the seal bar and gaskets are fairly high off the counter, two little tabs help keep the plastic bag in place while sealing.

VACMASTER PRO350 Professional Vacuum Sealer - 12" Seal Bar
PRICE: $399.00
WEIGHT: 19 lb 8 oz
DIMENSIONS: 15 x 13.75 x 6.25 in
VACUUM STRENGTH: 77.99%
COMPATIBLE WITH GENERIC BAGS: Yes, but company rep discouraged use
MODEL NUMBER: PRO350

HANDLING ★★½
PERFORMANCE ★★★
EASE OF USE ★★★

If you like tinkering with vacuum strength and seal times to find the optimal settings for your favorite foods, this heavy-duty machine might be for you. Most of our testers didn't need that level of customization—especially because it came at a premium price and footprint. But it was relatively easy to use and performed as well as our overall winner. It has built-in storage for a plastic roll and an integrated plastic cutter. The lid closed gently, which we liked, but it had to be held in place for the first few seconds of operation. It was also a little trickier to keep the bag in place because the platform was high and there were no tabs to keep the bag in place.

THE FOODSAVER FM2000 Vacuum Sealing System
PRICE: $71.03
WEIGHT: 3 lb 14¼ oz
DIMENSIONS: 16 x 5.75 x 4 in
VACUUM STRENGTH: 70.19%
COMPATIBLE WITH GENERIC BAGS: Yes, but company rep discouraged use
MODEL NUMBER: FM2000

HANDLING ★★★
PERFORMANCE ★★★
EASE OF USE ★★½

We loved the slim, compact design and sleek user interface on this vacuum sealer. When vacuum-sealing delicate or crunchy foods, we manually controlled the sealing process instead of letting the machine run automatically. A dial on the side of the machine moves the lid's latches through three positions—open, store, and operate—and required no physical force. We loved that the dial was clearly labeled and very easy to use. It didn't have a countdown screen like the two top scorers but was otherwise very easy to use. A removable tray inside the gaskets makes for easy cleaning.

RECOMMENDED

GOURMIA Vacuum Sealer
PRICE: $49.99
WEIGHT: 5 lb 4½ oz
DIMENSIONS: 15.75 x 8 x 3.5 in
VACUUM STRENGTH: 76.87%
COMPATIBLE WITH GENERIC BAGS: Yes
MODEL NUMBER: GVS455

HANDLING ★½
PERFORMANCE ★★★
EASE OF USE ★★½

The buttons and indicator lights were clearly labeled and easy to use, and it did a fine job of vacuum-sealing food. Unfortunately, handling was an issue. We had to press the lid very firmly to close it. First-time users couldn't figure it out and, once they understood what to do, they were surprised by the amount of force required to close the lid. Pressing the release buttons on the side of the machine opened the lid with a disturbingly sharp crunching noise. The gentle setting was a bit too gentle; it barely removed any air and we recommend using manual mode when sealing fragile items.

GRATERS

The shredding disk of a good food processor can make quick work of shredding a pile of vegetables or a block of cheese, but we like to keep a grater on hand for smaller shredding jobs or for those times when we don't want to drag out a big machine. It had been a while since we last tested these basic kitchen tools, and we wanted to know if our favorite still held up to the competition. So we bought eight products and put them to the test, using them to shred soft and hard cheeses, potatoes, and carrots. Two models were paddle-style graters, one model was two-sided, and the other five models were standard box graters. For testing, we focused on the large-holed side of the graters, since this is the side we use for shredding. In the end, we came up with two winners: a paddle-style grater, which allows for flexible positioning, easier cleanup, and a smaller footprint, and a box-style grater for those who prefer this style's greater security and shred containment. The prices listed in this chart are based on shopping at online retailers and will vary. The top four graters are listed below in order of preference.

HIGHLY RECOMMENDED	PERFORMANCE	TESTERS' COMMENTS
RÖSLE Coarse Grater `BEST PADDLE-STYLE GRATER` **PRICE:** $35.93 **HOLE TYPE:** Stamped **MATERIALS:** Stainless steel, rubber **HANDLE LENGTH:** 4.5 in **DISHWASHER-SAFE:** Yes, top rack only **CONSTRUCTION STYLE:** Paddle **GRATING SURFACE DIMENSIONS:** 6.5 x 3 in **TIME TO GRATE 1 LB POTATOES:** 1 min, 2 sec **MODEL NUMBER:** 95022	EASE OF USE ★★½ PERFORMANCE ★★★ 	With one of the largest, longest grating surfaces and ultrasharp teeth, our previous favorite effortlessly shredded foods of all sizes and textures, taking the least time to do so and generating virtually no waste. While testers wished this paddle-style grater's wire handle was a bit more comfortable to hold, its length made it easy to grip in a number of ways. Rubber-tipped feet kept the grater from slipping, and testers also loved how easy the grater was to clean and store.
CUISINART Box Grater `BEST BOX-STYLE GRATER` **PRICE:** $11.95 **HOLE TYPE:** Stamped **MATERIALS:** Stainless steel, plastic **HANDLE LENGTH:** 4.5 in **DISHWASHER-SAFE:** Yes **CONSTRUCTION STYLE:** Box **GRATING SURFACE DIMENSIONS:** 6.25 x 2.75 in **TIME TO GRATE 1 LB POTATOES:** 1 min, 17 sec **MODEL NUMBER:** CTG-00-BG	EASE OF USE ★★★ PERFORMANCE ★★½ 	This box grater had a large, long grating surface studded with stamped holes. Its teeth were just a hair less keen than those of our favorite paddle grater; nevertheless, it grated hard vegetables and soft cheese quickly and efficiently. Testers liked how stably this grater sat on the cutting board, thanks in part to the grippy plastic bumper around its base. And it had a large plastic handle that was comfortable to hold in different positions.

RECOMMENDED		
MICROPLANE Specialty Series 4-Sided Box Grater **PRICE:** $34.47 **HOLE TYPE:** Etched **MATERIALS:** Stainless steel, ABS plastic, polypropylene **HANDLE LENGTH:** 3 in **DISHWASHER-SAFE:** Yes **CONSTRUCTION STYLE:** Box **GRATING SURFACE DIMENSIONS:** 3.75 x 3.25 in **TIME TO GRATE 1 LB POTATOES:** 1 min, 38 sec **MODEL NUMBER:** 34006	EASE OF USE ★★ PERFORMANCE ★★½ 	With fairly sharp teeth on its etched holes, this box grater did a good job of shredding most foods; of the etched graters, it was the best at shredding mozzarella, though we still had to work harder to get the cheese through the holes and were left with a fair number of ungrated chunks. Its grating surface is a little smaller and shorter than we prefer and a little less rigid than those of graters with stamped holes, requiring more passes and more work to shred all the food. Its handle was small but otherwise easy to grip, and the rubber-tipped feet kept it stable on the cutting board.

RECOMMENDED WITH RESERVATIONS		
OXO GOOD GRIPS Etched Box Grater with Removable Zester **PRICE:** $29.95 **HOLE TYPE:** Etched **MATERIALS:** Stainless steel; TPE, ABS, and SAN plastics **HANDLE LENGTH:** 4 in **DISHWASHER-SAFE:** Yes, top rack only **CONSTRUCTION STYLE:** Box **GRATING SURFACE DIMENSIONS:** 4.5 x 2.75 in **TIME TO GRATE 1 LB POTATOES:** 1 min, 7 sec **MODEL NUMBER:** 11231700	EASE OF USE ★★ PERFORMANCE ★★ 	We loved this box grater's large, rubbery handle and stable, grippy base. And while the grating surface was a bit small, the ultrasharp teeth of its etched holes were great at shredding hard cheese and vegetables. But because those teeth were nearly flush with the thin, flexible grating surface, it was a real struggle to grate soft mozzarella—we had to get dangerously close to the teeth to control the block of cheese, and we ended up pushing it through the holes rather than shredding it, generating quite a few ungrated chunks in the process.

KITCHEN SPONGES

We expect a lot from the humble kitchen sponge. We use them to clean nonstick, traditional, and cast-iron skillets containing a variety of cooked-on foods; mixing bowls caked with sticky biscuit dough; stained carving boards; cheese-smeared box graters; dirty chef's knives; fragile wine glasses; small measuring spoons; and more. To identify the best sponge, we started by choosing eight widely available brands. Three of those brands offered multiple products, so we conducted an elimination round: scrubbing a cooked-on mix of onions and barbecue sauce from skillets and washing delicate wine glasses. Most products came in sets; one was sold individually. We used the sponges in our final lineup to clean a variety of tricky messes. We also sent three new copies of each sponge home with staffers for use in their kitchens. Dimensions, thickness, and water absorbency were measured in-house. Manufacturers provided information on product materials. The prices listed in this chart are based on shopping at online retailers and will vary. Scores were averaged, and the top five sponges are listed below in order of preference.

HIGHLY RECOMMENDED	PERFORMANCE	TESTERS' COMMENTS
O-CEDAR Scrunge **Multi-Use Scrubber Sponge** **PRICE:** $9.99 for pack of 6 ($1.67 per sponge) **MATERIALS:** Cellulose sponge with acrylic and polyurethane scrubbing surface **THICKNESS:** 1 in **DIMENSIONS:** 4.25 x 2.5 in **WATER ABSORBED:** 87.75 g **DISHWASHER-SAFE:** Yes **MODEL NUMBER:** N/a	COMFORT ★★★ VERSATILITY ★★★ CLEANING ABILITY ★★★ DURABILITY AND CLEANUP ★★★	This product looks like the classic blue sponge we've all used, but its plastic-based scrubbing side has ripples. These ripples added texture, which helped nudge off cooked-on food. This sponge was absorbent and durable, and it looked surprisingly clean at the end of testing. It was also our preferred size: thick enough to hold comfortably but small enough to maneuver in tight spaces.

RECOMMENDED		
TWIST Loofah Scrubber Sponge **PRICE:** $4.49 for pack of 2 ($2.25 per sponge) **MATERIALS:** Cellulose sponge with natural loofah scrubbing surface **THICKNESS:** 0.75 in **DIMENSIONS:** 4.5 x 2.75 in **WATER ABSORBED:** 88.88 g **DISHWASHER-SAFE:** Yes **MODEL NUMBER:** 278476	COMFORT ★★★ VERSATILITY ★★ CLEANING ABILITY ★★★ DURABILITY AND CLEANUP ★★½	Instead of a plastic-based abrasive, this sponge's loofah scrubber is made from a dried plant. The loofah fibers trapped some food in our tests, but we found that we could remove it with a little effort. The white cellulose portion of the sponge remained impressively clean and fluffy even after weeks of use. This product is a bit bulky but quite absorbent.
CASABELLA Sparkle Scrub Sponges **PRICE:** $3.99 for pack of 2 ($2.00 per sponge) **MATERIALS:** Polypropylene sponge surrounded by polyethylene terephthalate scrubbing material **THICKNESS:** 1.25 in **DIMENSIONS:** 4.25 x 3.25 in **WATER ABSORBED:** 64.91 g **DISHWASHER-SAFE:** Yes (top rack only) **MODEL NUMBER:** 8511305 	COMFORT ★★★ VERSATILITY ★★ CLEANING ABILITY ★★★ DURABILITY AND CLEANUP ★★½	Made of a foam core surrounded by many small sparkly plastic loops, this sponge was great for scrubbing; each of the loops acted like a mini scraper. One of the thickest and bulkiest in our lineup, this sponge was a tight squeeze for wine glasses but soft enough to compress for other small tasks. Although it trapped some food in its loops, we could remove it. The surface became discolored after we cleaned greasy skillets.
LYSOL Long Lasting **Non-Scratch Scrub Sponge** **PRICE:** $6.99 for pack of 6 ($1.17 per sponge) **MATERIALS:** Poly foam with nonscratch coating **THICKNESS:** 1 in **DIMENSIONS:** 4.25 x 2.5 in **WATER ABSORBED:** 46.48 g **DISHWASHER-SAFE:** Yes **MODEL NUMBER:** 2051878	COMFORT ★★★ VERSATILITY ★★½ CLEANING ABILITY ★★★ DURABILITY AND CLEANUP ★★	This sponge varies from a traditional double-sided sponge in two ways: Its base is foam, not cellulose, and the abrasive side has ridges. It cleaned tough messes effectively and was maneuverable. The foam became nicked during testing and had to be squeezed and rinsed repeatedly to get all the suds out. At the time of publication, this sponge was being rebranded as the Quickie Long Lasting Non-Scratch Scrub Sponge. The manufacturer told us there were no other changes being made to the sponge.
SCOTCH-BRITE Non-Scratch Scrub Sponge **PRICE:** $5.48 for pack of 6 ($0.91 per sponge) **MATERIALS:** Cellulose with scrubbing fibers and resin binder **THICKNESS:** 0.88 in **DIMENSIONS:** 4.5 x 2.75 in **WATER ABSORBED:** 86.5 g **DISHWASHER-SAFE:** Yes **MODEL NUMBER:** N/a	COMFORT ★★½ VERSATILITY ★★★ CLEANING ABILITY ★★★ DURABILITY AND CLEANUP ★★	We've all used this iconic blue sponge before, and it performed well enough until the sticky dough test. Its abrasive surface became dotted with little balls of dough that were nearly impossible to pick off, and when we did remove them, the sponge looked grubby. That said, it was absorbent and otherwise resisted stains. It's still a good sponge, but the scrubbing surfaces on the other sponges in our lineup were easier to rinse clean.

HONING RODS

We've all sat at holiday tables watching our host put on a show before carving the roast, slashing a knife back and forth against a honing rod. It sure looks impressive, but does it really sharpen a knife? To find out, we tested nine honing rods in a range of materials, sold as either honing or sharpening rods or steels. We used a glass cutting board to quickly dull the sharp edges of nine new chef's knives and then assigned one knife to each rod. We honed the knives, rating the rods on ease of use and performance and noting the condition of the knives at the end of testing. We also examined the blades and honing rods under a microscope. The prices listed in this chart are based on shopping at online retailers and will vary. The top five honing rods are listed below in order of preference.

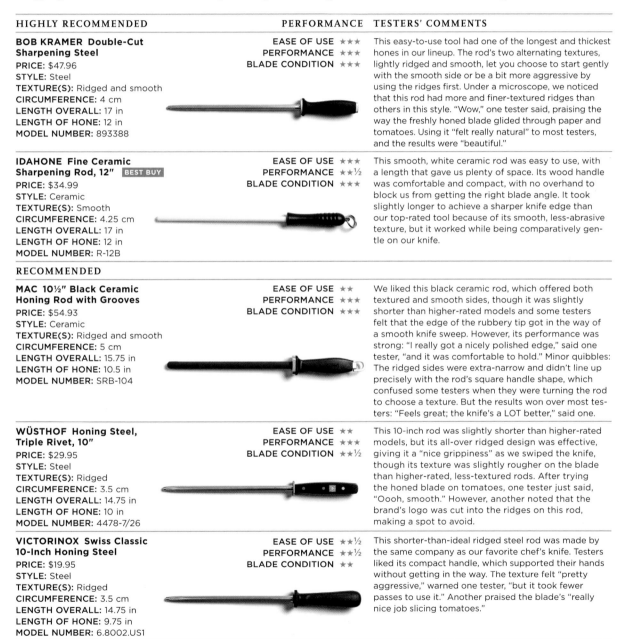

HIGHLY RECOMMENDED	PERFORMANCE	TESTERS' COMMENTS
BOB KRAMER Double-Cut Sharpening Steel PRICE: $47.96 STYLE: Steel TEXTURE(S): Ridged and smooth CIRCUMFERENCE: 4 cm LENGTH OVERALL: 17 in LENGTH OF HONE: 12 in MODEL NUMBER: 893388	EASE OF USE ★★★ PERFORMANCE ★★★ BLADE CONDITION ★★★	This easy-to-use tool had one of the longest and thickest hones in our lineup. The rod's two alternating textures, lightly ridged and smooth, let you choose to start gently with the smooth side or be a bit more aggressive by using the ridges first. Under a microscope, we noticed that this rod had more and finer-textured ridges than others in this style. "Wow," one tester said, praising the way the freshly honed blade glided through paper and tomatoes. Using it "felt really natural" to most testers, and the results were "beautiful."
IDAHONE Fine Ceramic Sharpening Rod, 12" `BEST BUY` PRICE: $34.99 STYLE: Ceramic TEXTURE(S): Smooth CIRCUMFERENCE: 4.25 cm LENGTH OVERALL: 17 in LENGTH OF HONE: 12 in MODEL NUMBER: R-12B	EASE OF USE ★★★ PERFORMANCE ★★½ BLADE CONDITION ★★★	This smooth, white ceramic rod was easy to use, with a length that gave us plenty of space. Its wood handle was comfortable and compact, with no overhand to block us from getting the right blade angle. It took slightly longer to achieve a sharper knife edge than our top-rated tool because of its smooth, less-abrasive texture, but it worked while being comparatively gentle on our knife.

RECOMMENDED		
MAC 10½" Black Ceramic Honing Rod with Grooves PRICE: $54.93 STYLE: Ceramic TEXTURE(S): Ridged and smooth CIRCUMFERENCE: 5 cm LENGTH OVERALL: 15.75 in LENGTH OF HONE: 10.5 in MODEL NUMBER: SRB-104	EASE OF USE ★★ PERFORMANCE ★★★ BLADE CONDITION ★★★	We liked this black ceramic rod, which offered both textured and smooth sides, though it was slightly shorter than higher-rated models and some testers felt that the edge of the rubbery tip got in the way of a smooth knife sweep. However, its performance was strong: "I really got a nicely polished edge," said one tester, "and it was comfortable to hold." Minor quibbles: The ridged sides were extra-narrow and didn't line up precisely with the rod's square handle shape, which confused some testers when they were turning the rod to choose a texture. But the results won over most testers: "Feels great; the knife's a LOT better," said one.
WÜSTHOF Honing Steel, Triple Rivet, 10" PRICE: $29.95 STYLE: Steel TEXTURE(S): Ridged CIRCUMFERENCE: 3.5 cm LENGTH OVERALL: 14.75 in LENGTH OF HONE: 10 in MODEL NUMBER: 4478-7/26	EASE OF USE ★★ PERFORMANCE ★★★ BLADE CONDITION ★★½	This 10-inch rod was slightly shorter than higher-rated models, but its all-over ridged design was effective, giving it a "nice grippiness" as we swiped the knife, though its texture was slightly rougher on the blade than higher-rated, less-textured rods. After trying the honed blade on tomatoes, one tester just said, "Oooh, smooth." However, another noted that the brand's logo was cut into the ridges on this rod, making a spot to avoid.
VICTORINOX Swiss Classic 10-Inch Honing Steel PRICE: $19.95 STYLE: Steel TEXTURE(S): Ridged CIRCUMFERENCE: 3.5 cm LENGTH OVERALL: 14.75 in LENGTH OF HONE: 9.75 in MODEL NUMBER: 6.8002.US1	EASE OF USE ★★½ PERFORMANCE ★★½ BLADE CONDITION ★★	This shorter-than-ideal ridged steel rod was made by the same company as our favorite chef's knife. Testers liked its compact handle, which supported their hands without getting in the way. The texture felt "pretty aggressive," warned one tester, "but it took fewer passes to use it." Another praised the blade's "really nice job slicing tomatoes."

NUTRITIONAL INFORMATION FOR OUR RECIPES

We calculate the nutritional values of our recipes per serving; if there is a range in the serving size, we used the highest number of servings to calculate the nutritional values. We entered all the ingredients, using weights for important ingredients such as meat, cheese, and most vegetables. We also used our preferred brands in these analyses. We did not include additional salt or pepper for food that's "seasoned to taste."

RECIPE	CALORIES	TOTAL FAT (G)	SAT FAT (G)	CHOL (MG)	SODIUM (MG)	CARBS (G)	FIBER (G)	SUGARS (G)	PROTEIN (G)
CHAPTER 1: SOUPS, SALADS, AND STARTERS									
Creamy White Bean Soup with Herb Oil and Crispy Capers	400	23	6	16	823	35	8	4	15
Tuscan Tomato and Bread Soup	306	16	3	4	845	33	5	12	10
French Onion Soup	589	30	15	67	1751	50	6	17	27
Mexican Street-Corn Chowder	420	23	4.5	25	930	46	7	14	20
Spring Pea Salad	180	13	2.5	0	480	12	3	5	5
Salade Lyonnaise	290	22	6	210	1030	3	1	1	14
Perfect Poached Eggs (per egg)	*73*	*5*	*1.5*	*186*	*126*	*0.5*	*0*	*0*	*6.5*
Harvest Bowl	400	24	6	25	790	40	6	20	7
Roasted Sweet Potatoes	*120*	*3.5*	*0*	*0*	*210*	*20*	*3*	*6*	*2*
Savory Seed Brittle (per 2 tablespoons)	*80*	*5*	*1*	*0*	*135*	*6*	*1*	*2*	*3*
Green Bean Salad with Cherry Tomatoes and Feta	152	11	3	8	194	11	4	6	4
Ultracreamy Hummus	217	12	1	0	287	23	7	4	8
Baharat-Spiced Beef Topping for Hummus	*90*	*7*	*1.5*	*15*	*160*	*1*	*0*	*0*	*5*
Spiced Walnut Topping for Hummus	*190*	*19*	*2.5*	*0*	*170*	*3*	*1*	*1*	*1*
Spinach-Artichoke Dip	305	28	10	49	438	5	2	1	9
Mediterranean Whipped Almond Dip	280	27	3	0	170	6	2	1	6
Seeded Crackers	*170*	*13*	*3.5*	*35*	*420*	*2*	*1*	*0*	*11*
Crunchy Kettle Potato Chips	170	13	1	0	200	14	1	0	2
Buttermilk and Chive Topping	*10*	*0*	*0*	*0*	*200*	*1*	*0*	*1*	*1*
Salt and Vinegar Topping	*0*	*0*	*0*	*0*	*190*	*0*	*0*	*0*	*0*
Smoky Barbecue Topping	*10*	*0*	*0*	*0*	*200*	*2*	*0*	*1*	*0*
Vietnamese Summer Rolls (Goi Cuon)	604	21	4	98	771	76	5	8	28
Vietnamese Dipping Sauce (Nuoc Cham)	*54*	*0*	*0*	*0*	*1770*	*13*	*0*	*11*	*1*
Fried Calamari	559	33	3	267	526	42	1	2	24
Quick Marinara Sauce	*93*	*7*	*1*	*0*	*185*	*8*	*2*	*5*	*2*
Spicy Mayonnaise	*402*	*45*	*7*	*23*	*520*	*0*	*0*	*0*	*0*
Mexican Shrimp Cocktail (Cóctel de Camarón)	166	6	1	119	832	15	3	8	15
CHAPTER 2: SIDE DISHES									
Skillet-Roasted Broccoli	203	18	1	0	388	9	4	2	4
Parmesan and Black Pepper Topping	*30*	*2*	*1*	*5*	*125*	*0*	*0*	*0*	*3*
Sesame and Orange Topping	*30*	*2.5*	*0*	*0*	*75*	*1*	*1*	*0*	*1*
Smoky Sunflower Seed Topping	*30*	*2*	*0*	*0*	*70*	*1*	*0*	*0*	*2*
Skillet-Roasted Carrots	132	7	1	0	409	16	5	8	2
Mustard Bread Crumbs and Chives	*45*	*2.5*	*0*	*0*	*100*	*4*	*0*	*0*	*1*
Smoky Spiced Almonds and Parsley	*45*	*4*	*0*	*0*	*75*	*1*	*1*	*0*	*1*
Spicy Maple Bread Crumbs	*45*	*2.5*	*0*	*0*	*80*	*5*	*0*	*2*	*0*
Braised Eggplant with Soy, Garlic, and Ginger	101	3	0	0	301	15	6	9	2

RECIPE	CALORIES	TOTAL FAT (G)	SAT FAT (G)	CHOL (MG)	SODIUM (MG)	CARBS (G)	FIBER (G)	SUGARS (G)	PROTEIN (G)
CHAPTER 2: SIDE DISHES *(continued)*									
Braised Eggplant with Paprika, Coriander, and Yogurt	*190*	*12*	*1*	*3*	*637*	*20*	*9*	*12*	*4*
Skillet-Braised Fennel	200	14	2	0	561	19	8	11	3
Roasted Butternut Squash with Apple	167	11	2	0	327	17	3	7	1
Asparagus Baked in Foil with Capers and Dill	108	8	5	20	406	8	4	4	4
Ultimate Extra-Crunchy Onion Rings	510	21	3	10	1320	66	2	11	12
Sweet Potato Crunch	383	12	7	31	566	64	7	20	5
Spanish Potatoes with Olive Oil and Wine (Patatas Panaderas)	277	12	2	0	562	36	5	3	4
Roasted Fingerling Potatoes with Mixed Herbs	272	11	1	0	304	41	6	2	5
Potato and Parmesan Tart	379	25	14	82	348	30	2	2	8
Cast Iron Potato Kugel	282	13	4	103	267	35	3	3	7
Louisiana-Style Cornbread Dressing	449	25	11	144	650	41	2	9	15
CHAPTER 3: PASTA, PIZZA, SANDWICHES, AND MORE									
Pastitsio	518	25	12	97	741	45	3	12	26
Creamy Spring Vegetable Linguine	390	8	3.5	20	680	59	1	3	17
Chilled Soba Noodle Salad with Cucumber, Snow Peas, and Radishes	217	6	1	0	622	34	2	2	8
Cast Iron Pan Pizza	672	38	15	69	759	56	4	4	27
Skillet Turkey Burgers	459	24	10	112	1051	26	1	3	34
Pickled Avocado	*98*	*7*	*1*	*0*	*262*	*7*	*3*	*3*	*1*
Double-Decker Drive-Thru Burgers	812	42	16	162	862	69	3	12	37
Classic Burger Sauce	*114*	*11*	*2*	*6*	*162*	*4*	*0*	*3*	*0*
Lamb Burgers with Halloumi and Beet Tzatziki	932	69	29	179	874	33	2	12	44
Pan Bagnat (Provençal Tuna Sandwich)	487	29	5	87	927	30	3	4	27
Hot Buttered Lobster Rolls	262	8	4	158	688	23	1	4	23
Cuban Sandwiches	1150	61	25	185	3300	89	1	2	57
Cuban Roast Pork with Mojo	*206*	*14*	*3*	*22*	*217*	*15*	*1*	*11*	*7*
Cuban Bread	*520*	*13*	*5*	*10*	*880*	*84*	*1*	*0*	*13*
Bacon, Lettuce, and Fried Green Tomato Sandwiches	1094	65	17	255	1188	93	5	11	32
Pupusas	491	26	14	65	578	45	4	0	22
Quick Salsa	*12*	*0*	*0*	*0*	*135*	*3*	*1*	*2*	*1*
Curtido	*154*	*0*	*0*	*0*	*1249*	*32*	*9*	*19*	*4*
Eggplant Pecorino	736	58	16	177	1069	39	13	18	22
Fresh Tomato Galette	442	31	17	101	532	31	3	4	12
Palak Dal (Spinach-Lentil Dal with Cumin and Mustard Seeds)	270	8	4	16	344	40	7	4	14
CHAPTER 4: MEAT									
Pan-Seared Strip Steaks	359	26	10	123	81	0	0	0	29
Sauce Verte	*153*	*14*	*2*	*1*	*120*	*6*	*2*	*1*	*2*
Garlic Steaks	837	74	25	198	642	3	1	0	40
Japanese Steakhouse Steak and Vegetables	625	48	21	142	953	14	3	6	36
Simple Hibachi-Style Fried Rice	*400*	*12*	*4*	*147*	*387*	*60*	*0*	*1*	*10*
Spicy Mayonnaise (Yum-Yum Sauce)	*157*	*17*	*3*	*13*	*224*	*1*	*0*	*0*	*0*
Sweet Ginger Sauce	*43*	*0*	*0*	*0*	*441*	*10*	*0*	*7*	*1*
White Mustard Sauce	*86*	*9*	*5*	*27*	*301*	*2*	*0*	*1*	*1*

RECIPE	CALORIES	TOTAL FAT (G)	SAT FAT (G)	CHOL (MG)	SODIUM (MG)	CARBS (G)	FIBER (G)	SUGARS (G)	PROTEIN (G)
CHAPTER 4: MEAT *(continued)*									
Roasted Beef Chuck Roast with Horseradish-Parsley Sauce	308	27	6	47	257	3	1	1	14
Shaking Beef (Bo Luc Lac)	344	24	9	96	835	8	1	4	24
Vietnamese Red Rice (Com Do)	*213*	*4*	*3*	*10*	*307*	*39*	*1*	*1*	*4*
Rice Pilaf with Beef and Carrots (Plov)	553	26	10	83	982	55	5	9	25
Green Chili with Pork (Chile Verde con Cerdo)	139	7	2	22	481	12	3	7	8
Spanish Grilled Pork Kebabs (Pinchos Morunos)	570	41	6	168	597	4	1	0	45
Spiral-Sliced Ham Glazed with Cider-Vinegar Caramel	360	10	3.5	100	2880	22	0	22	44
Lion's Head Meatballs (Shizi Tou)	573	35	13	145	1073	27	2	7	34
Goan Pork Vindaloo	346	22	6	80	102	11	2	4	25
Pork Cordon Bleu	801	56	15	245	890	26	2	2	47
Pork Stroganoff	789	37	15	189	1186	65	5	10	47
North Carolina Barbecue Pork with Eastern North Carolina–Style Barbecue Sauce	290	12	4	110	1550	8	0	6	33
North Carolina Barbecue Pork with Lexington-Style Barbecue Sauce	300	12	4	110	1560	10	0	7	33
Greek Meatballs	391	30	11	71	395	12	3	2	20
CHAPTER 5: POULTRY AND SEAFOOD									
Easy Grill-Roasted Whole Chicken	526	38	10	173	544	0	0	0	43
Chicken Schnitzel	1104	85	7	194	751	34	2	2	49
Apple-Fennel Rémoulade	*78*	*6*	*1*	*3*	*165*	*6*	*2*	*4*	*1*
Cucumber-Dill Salad	*45*	*2*	*1*	*2*	*239*	*5*	*1*	*2*	*2*
Japanese Fried Chicken Thighs (Karaage)	462	28	3	107	550	26	0	1	23
Grilled Boneless, Skinless Chicken Breasts	394	11	2	199	1184	9	0	9	62
Red Pepper–Almond Sauce	*124*	*10*	*1*	*0*	*190*	*6*	*3*	*3*	*3*
Grilled Jerk Chicken	921	66	16	255	1122	15	2	8	66
Chicken Provençal	592	41	10	196	487	16	2	3	36
Chicken Biryani	599	21	10	181	765	65	3	10	38
Soy Sauce Chicken Wings	578	39	10	252	1946	13	1	9	43
Chicken Croquettes with Lemon-Scallion Sauce	440	34	11	128	510	20	2	4	13
Cashew Chicken	596	32	5	125	1546	29	3	9	48
Whole Roast Ducks with Cherry Sauce	1378	125	42	241	960	24	1	21	37
Cod with Warm Beet and Arugula Salad	340	16	2.5	75	460	14	4	9	33
Oven-Steamed Fish with Scallions and Ginger	314	10	1	99	792	8	1	3	43
Butter-Basted Fish Fillets with Garlic and Thyme	416	26	12	145	599	3	1	0	42
Slow-Roasted Salmon with Chives and Lemon	227	18	3	36	184	3	0	2	14
CHAPTER 6: BREAKFAST, BRUNCH, AND BREADS									
Chocolate Brioche Buns	410	19	11	100	320	51	2	11	9
Stroud's Cinnamon Rolls	253	13	8	46	146	32	1	19	3
Crumpets	160	0.5	0	0	250	32	1	0	5
Yeasted Doughnuts	475	43	4	11	92	21	0	11	2
Chocolate Frosting	*120*	*3*	*1.5*	*0*	*15*	*25*	*0*	*23*	*1*
Raspberry Frosting	*80*	*0*	*0*	*0*	*15*	*21*	*1*	*19*	*0*
Jelly Doughnuts	*472*	*10*	*6*	*39*	*325*	*90*	*2*	*46*	*7*
Apple Cider Doughnuts	196	5	3	26	151	35	1	15	3
Italian Flatbreads (Piadine)	321	11	1	0	275	48	2	0	6

RECIPE	CALORIES	TOTAL FAT (G)	SAT FAT (G)	CHOL (MG)	SODIUM (MG)	CARBS (G)	FIBER (G)	SUGARS (G)	PROTEIN (G)
CHAPTER 6: BREAKFAST, BRUNCH, AND BREADS (continued)									
Brioche Hamburger Buns	295	14	8	64	223	35	1	4	7
Adjaruli Khachapuri	350	18	11	86	465	31	1	3	15
Sheet-Pan Hash Browns	294	14	2	0	401	40	5	2	5
Buckwheat Crepes	136	8	4	73	190	11	1	3	5
Buckwheat Crepes with Ham, Egg, and Cheese (Galettes Complètes)	420	29	15	320	900	12	1	3	28
Rye Crepes with Smoked Salmon, Crème Fraîche, and Pickled Shallots	580	36	20	220	1020	41	5	16	24
Whole-Wheat Crepes with Creamy Sautéed Mushrooms and Asparagus	500	33	19	195	700	37	4	11	18
Smoked Salmon Brunch Plates	470	39	11	230	800	10	3	6	22
Easy-Peel Hard-Cooked Eggs (per egg)	70	5	1.5	185	70	0	0	0	6
Congee (Chinese Rice Porridge)	134	4	0	1	205	21	0	1	3
Microwave-Fried Shallots	60	4	0	0	4	5	1	2	1
Stir-Fried Ground Pork Topping for Congee	112	9	3	27	104	1	0	0	7
CHAPTER 7: DESSERTS AND DRINKS									
Caramel-Espresso Yule Log	571	39	18	163	183	53	1	39	6
Chocolate Crumbles	160	9	5	15	50	21	0	10	2
Meringue Bracket-Style Mushrooms	45	0	0	0	25	11	0	11	1
Financiers (Almond–Browned Butter Cakes)	62	4	2	6	18	5	0	4	1
Chocolate Pavlova with Berries and Whipped Cream	400	22	14	55	55	50	5	39	5
Buttermilk-Vanilla Panna Cotta with Berries and Honey	282	23	14	84	177	17	0	17	4
Caramel-Coated Almonds	240	24	2	0	75	7	1	6	1
Peppery Strawberries	10	0	0	0	20	2	0	2	0
Apple Crumble	352	12	6	23	301	58	7	37	4
Pineapple Upside-Down Cake	555	19	12	94	373	91	2	68	5
Baci di Dama (Italian Hazelnut Cookies)	276	19	7	23	39	27	2	17	3
Chocolate Chip Cookie Ice Cream Sandwiches	354	20	12	70	237	42	1	31	4
Nanaimo Bars	230	15	9	20	75	24	1	20	2
Portuguese Egg Tarts	300	17	9	145	220	36	1	19	6
Fresh Plum-Ginger Pie with Whole-Wheat Lattice-Top Crust	559	31	19	100	378	69	5	36	7
Fresh Apricot, Vanilla, and Cardamom Pie with Rye Lattice-Top Crust	578	30	19	100	379	73	6	42	7
Chocolate Pecan Pie	840	61	28	179	396	69	4	47	9
Butternut Squash Pie with Browned Butter and Sage	550	36	22	190	480	50	2	24	7
Champagne Cocktail	162	0	0	0	9	12	2	6	1
Mimosa	195	0	0	0	6	29	3	22	2
Bellini	96	0	0	0	4	8	1	6	1
DIY Bitters Sugar Cubes	10	0	0	0	0	2	0	2	0
New-Fashioned Gin and Tonic	150	0	0	0	0	3	0	3	0
Tonic Syrup (per 1 oz)	50	0	0	0	10	13	0	13	0
Practically Clear Ice	0	0	0	0	0	0	0	0	0
Celery Gimlet	190	0	0	0	0	16	0	15	0
Simple Syrup (per 1 oz)	60	0	0	0	0	15	0	15	0

CONVERSIONS & EQUIVALENTS

Some say cooking is a science and an art. We would say that geography has a hand in it, too. Flour milled in the United Kingdom and elsewhere will feel and taste different from flour milled in the United States. So while we cannot promise that the loaf of bread you bake in Canada or England will taste the same as a loaf baked in the States, we can offer guidelines for converting weights and measures. We also recommend that you rely on your instincts when making our recipes. Refer to the visual cues provided. If the bread dough hasn't "come together in a ball" as described, you may need to add more flour—even if the recipe doesn't tell you so. You be the judge.

The recipes in this book were developed using standard U.S. measures following U.S. government guidelines. The charts below offer equivalents for U.S., metric, and imperial (U.K.) measures. All conversions are approximate and have been rounded up or down to the nearest whole number. For example:

1 teaspoon	=	4.929 milliliters, rounded up to 5 milliliters
1 ounce	=	28.349 grams, rounded down to 28 grams

VOLUME CONVERSIONS

U.S.	METRIC
1 teaspoon	5 milliliters
2 teaspoons	10 milliliters
1 tablespoon	15 milliliters
2 tablespoons	30 milliliters
¼ cup	59 milliliters
⅓ cup	79 milliliters
½ cup	118 milliliters
¾ cup	177 milliliters
1 cup	237 milliliters
1¼ cups	296 milliliters
1½ cups	355 milliliters
2 cups	473 milliliters
2½ cups	591 milliliters
3 cups	710 milliliters
4 cups (1 quart)	0.946 liters
1.06 quarts	1 liter
4 quarts (1 gallon)	3.8 liters

WEIGHT CONVERSIONS

OUNCES	GRAMS
½	14
¾	21
1	28
1½	43
2	57
2½	71
3	85
3½	99
4	113
4½	128
5	142
6	170
7	198
8	227
9	255
10	283
12	340
16 (1 pound)	454

CONVERSIONS FOR INGREDIENTS COMMONLY USED IN BAKING

Baking is an exacting science. Because measuring by weight is far more accurate than measuring by volume, and thus more likely to achieve reliable results, in our recipes we provide ounce measures in addition to cup measures for many ingredients. Refer to the chart below to convert these measures into grams.

INGREDIENT	OUNCES	GRAMS
Flour		
1 cup all-purpose flour*	5	142
1 cup cake flour	4	113
1 cup whole-wheat flour	5½	156
Sugar		
1 cup granulated (white) sugar	7	198
1 cup packed brown sugar (light or dark)	7	198
1 cup confectioners' sugar	4	113
Cocoa Powder		
1 cup cocoa powder	3	85
Butter†		
4 tablespoons (½ stick, or ¼ cup)	2	57
8 tablespoons (1 stick, or ½ cup)	4	113
16 tablespoons (2 sticks, or 1 cup)	8	227

* U.S. all-purpose flour, the most frequently used flour in this book, does not contain leaveners, as some European flours do. These leavened flours are called self-rising or self-raising. If you are using self-rising flour, take this into consideration before adding leavening to a recipe.

† In the United States, butter is sold both salted and unsalted. We generally recommend unsalted butter. If you are using salted butter, take this into consideration before adding salt to a recipe.

OVEN TEMPERATURES

FAHRENHEIT	CELSIUS	GAS MARK (imperial)
225	105	¼
250	120	½
275	135	1
300	150	2
325	165	3
350	180	4
375	190	5
400	200	6
425	220	7
450	230	8
475	245	9

CONVERTING TEMPERATURES FROM AN INSTANT-READ THERMOMETER

We include doneness temperatures in many of our recipes, such as those for poultry, meat, and bread. We recommend an instant-read thermometer for the job. Refer to the table above to convert Fahrenheit degrees to Celsius. Or, for temperatures not represented in the chart, use this simple formula:

Subtract 32 degrees from the Fahrenheit reading, and then divide the result by 1.8 to find the Celsius reading.

EXAMPLE:

"Roast chicken until thighs register 175 degrees."
To convert:

175° F – 32 = 143°
143° ÷ 1.8 = 79.44°C, rounded down to 79°C

INDEX

B

Baci de Dama (Italian Hazelnut Cookies), 234–36

Bacon

Black Pepper Candied, 273

Lettuce, and Fried Green Tomato Sandwiches, 95–97, 96

see also Pancetta

Baharat-Spiced Beef Topping for Hummus, 21

Bakeware

broiler-safe baking dishes, ratings of, 298

drying in oven, 265

greasing baking sheets, 266

rotating baking sheets in oven, 267

square baking pans, ratings of, 297

Barbecue Pork, North Carolina, *140*, 141–42

Bars, Nanaimo, 239–42, *240*

Bean(s)

Green, Salad with Cherry Tomatoes and Feta, 17–19, *18*

Ultracreamy Hummus, 20–22

White, Soup, Creamy

with Chorizo Oil and Garlicky Bread Crumbs, 4

with Herb Oil and Crispy Capers, 2–4, *3*

with Lemony Yogurt and Crispy Leeks, 5

with Quick-Pickled Celery, 5

Beef

and Carrots, Rice Pilaf with (Plov), 120–25, *121*

Chuck Roast, Roasted, with Horseradish-Parsley Sauce, 115–17, *116*

Double-Decker Drive-Thru Burgers, 82–83

Garlic Steaks, 110–13

Japanese Steakhouse Steak and Vegetables, *112*, 113–15

Pan-Seared Strip Steaks, 108–10, *109*

Pastitsio, 68–71, *69*

Shaking (Bo Luc Lac), 118–20

steaks, reusable cover for, 265

Topping, Baharat-Spiced, for Hummus, 21

Beet

greens, maximizing yield from, 279

Tzatziki and Halloumi, Lamb Burgers with, 83–86, *85*

Warm, and Arugula Salad, Cod with, 169–72, *171*

Bellini, 257

Berries

Buttermilk–Thai Basil Panna Cotta with Peppery Strawberries, 228

Berries *(cont.)*

and Honey, Buttermilk-Vanilla Panna Cotta with, 226–28, *229*

and Whipped Cream, Chocolate Pavlova with, 223–26, *224*

see also Raspberry(ies)

Biryani, Chicken, 160–61

Bitters Sugar Cubes, DIY, 257

Black Olive Tapenade, 273

Black Pepper Candied Bacon, 273

Blistered Shishito Peppers, 272

Blue Cheese and Potato Tart, 63

Bo Luc Lac (Shaking Beef), 118–20

Braised Eggplant with Paprika, Coriander, and Yogurt, 49

Braised Eggplant with Soy, Garlic, and Ginger, *46*, 47–49

Bread Crumbs

Garlicky, and Chorizo Oil, Creamy White Bean Soup with, 4

Mustard, and Chives for Carrots, 45

Spicy Maple, for Carrots, 45

Bread(s)

Adjaruli Khachapuri, 201–3, *202*

Brioche Dinner Rolls, *178*, 201

Brioche Hamburger Buns, 199–201

Brioche Sandwich Loaves, 201

Chocolate Brioche Buns, 180–83, *181*

Cornbread, 65

crackly-crisp crust for, 275

Crumpets, 186–88, *189*

Cuban, *93*, 94

Italian Flatbreads (Piadine), 196–99, *197*

questions and answers about, 274–75

rising dough, 274

salting dough, 267

sandwich rolls, toasting, 266

setting up flouring station for dough, 274

shaping dough, 274

slashing dough, 275

stale, reviving, 275

Stroud's Cinnamon Rolls, 183–85, *184*

tests for doneness, 275

and Tomato Soup, Tuscan, 5–7

Breakfast & brunch

Apple Cider Doughnuts, 195–96

Buckwheat Crepes, 206–7

M